917.76 Keating, William Hypolitus.
K -i   Narrative of an
        expedition to the source of
        St. Peter's River.

**OFFICIALLY WITHDRAWN
FROM THE
HENNEPIN COUNTY LIBRARY**

Please return on or before the date due. You are responsible for all materials borrowed on your card. All slips must remain in pocket. A charge will be made for any missing slips.

**HENNEPIN COUNTY LIBRARY
MINNESOTA 55435**

Bd.

NARRATIVE

OF

AN EXPEDITION

TO THE

SOURCE OF ST. PETER'S RIVER,

&c. &c. &c.

WANOTAN AND HIS SON

Published by G.B. Whittaker, London, 1825.

NARRATIVE

OF AN

EXPEDITION

TO THE

SOURCE OF ST. PETER'S RIVER,

LAKE WINNEPEEK,

LAKE OF THE WOODS, &c.

PERFORMED IN THE YEAR 1823,

BY ORDER OF THE HON. J. C. CALHOUN,
SECRETARY OF WAR,

UNDER THE COMMAND OF STEPHEN H. LONG, U.S.T.E.

COMPILED

FROM THE NOTES OF MAJOR LONG, Messrs. SAY, KEATING, & COLHOUN,

By WILLIAM H. KEATING, A.M. &c.

Professor of Mineralogy and Chemistry, as applied to the Arts, in the University of Pennsylvania ; Geologist and Historiographer to the Expedition.

IN ONE VOLUME

ROSS & HAINES, Inc.

Minneapolis, Minnesota

1959

LONDON:
PRINTED BY COX AND BAYLIS, GREAT QUEEN STREET.

TO

JAMES MONROE,

PRESIDENT OF THE UNITED STATES OF AMERICA,

THIS WORK,

CONTAINING THE RESULT OF OBSERVATIONS,

MADE ON AN EXPEDITION

UNDERTAKEN UNDER HIS ADMINISTRATION,

IS

VERY RESPECTFULLY INSCRIBED

BY

THE AUTHORS.

PREFACE.

In offering this work to the public, the compiler regrets that it has been delayed longer than was originally intended; the difficulties which he has encountered in the performance of a task for which he was entirely unprepared, afford him his only apologies. Inexperienced in the art of writing for the public, it is probable that he has fallen into many errors, which, with more time, he might have avoided; but works of the nature of this admit of little delay. Narratives of voyages of discoveries lose much of their interest if the publication be long deferred.

The principal object which the compiler had in view, was to unite the documents confided to him, so as to present a faithful description of the country over which the party travelled, and of the few adventures which interrupted the monotony of a journey through a wilderness.

It may be well to state, that the historical part of the narrative, together with the topographical and much of the descriptive matter, has been drawn from Major Long's notes. Mr. Colhoun's manuscripts, besides contributing to the same departments, and yielding the astronomical observations, have been very valuable in furnishing the greater part of the references to older writers. The comparisons between the observations made by our party and the assertions of former travellers, are almost entirely due to that gentleman. From Mr. Say's notes, all that relates to the zoology and botany of the country traversed has been obtained, as well as much of the matter relating to the Indians. This last department has been completed from the compiler's own notes, which have likewise furnished the geological observations. Besides which, the journals kept by each of the gentlemen have frequently completed the observations made by some other member of the party. It has been deemed unnecessary to state, in all cases, by whom the observations were made or recorded. This has, however, been done whenever the facts appeared sufficiently interesting to require that the names of the observers should be annexed to them.

As Major Long's report to the War Department presents a concise summary of the general features of the country visited by the party, it has been thought advisable to introduce it as a conclusion to the narrative. Having been ordered to the Ohio to make an experiment to improve its navigation, according to the provisions of a late act of congress, Major Long was absent from Philadelphia during the preparation of that part of the manuscript which follows the three first chapters of the first volume. This may account for some of the inaccuracies which the work will be found to contain: it is hoped that by his presence they would have been avoided.

The compiler has found it impossible, in the description of the scenery of the Mississippi, &c. to avoid the introduction of several words, which, although they are not sanctioned by the dictionaries, seem to be characteristic and essential in such descriptions: of this nature are the words—bluff, prairie, &c. The term creek, being used in different acceptations in England and America, has been avoided in all cases, though with some inconvenience. The word *run* will, it is believed, be found but once in the body of the work. Lest any false impression should be drawn from the introduction of the term *estuary*, it may be proper to state, that it has been inadvertently used in several cases to designate the outlets of streams where the tides do not reciprocate. In compiling from notes written by many persons under the disadvantages of fatigues, hardships, and privations, it is not easy, however it may be desirable, to avoid the use of all objectionable terms; for these and other inaccuracies which the work may contain, the compiler must plead in excuse the difficulties to which he has previously alluded.

The greater part of the Appendix will be found to have been prepared by Mr. Say. The loss which he experienced of the skins of many birds, quadrupeds, and fish, which he had collected, has prevented him from describing several new animals. It is believed, that if none of the shells collected had been lost, the amount of new species described would have been much greater. The plants preserved by Mr. Say were placed in the hands of Mr. Lewis D. Von Schweinitz, who kindly undertook to describe them: the result of his valuable observations will be found in the Appendix. With a view to give an idea of the climate of the country described, as well as to compare it with other places whose climate has been ascertained by older observations, the interesting tables prepared by Dr. Joseph Lovell, surgeon-general of the United States' army, have been introduced, with his general observations upon the same. They are compiled from the records kept at the various military posts. The climate of Philadelphia has been established by the results of the observations made by Mr. Reuben Haines, at his residence in German-town, six miles from Philadelphia; the great care which Mr. Haines bestows upon his observations, make them a fit term of comparison for all others. The introduction of these tables has superseded the necessity of recording the variations of temperature observed by our party—they were principally noted by Mr. Seymour.

It may be proper, however, to state that, valuable as are the results contained in the meteorological tables, they can only be considered as approximations, because an uniform method of making observations has not yet been adopted. Those who are conversant with thermometrical observations know what influence the situation in which the instrument is exposed, and the materials of which it is constructed, exercise upon the results which it indicates, and how guarded we ought to be in adopting comparisons made with different instruments, and placed in different situations. Of the influence of the materials, the party had an opportunity of convincing themselves, by placing two of Mr. Keating's thermometers in the same situation with that of the surgeon at Fort St. Anthony. The latter instrument consisted of a glass tube attached to a brass plate, on which the graduation was marked. One of Mr. Keating's was known to be a good instrument; it had been made in Paris, and had its graduation on a slip of paper enclosed in a glass tube: the other thermometer was a small pocket one, made by Mr. Fisher, of Philadelphia, and was provided with an ivory plate. The usual exposure of the surgeon's thermometer was to the south-west; the two others were placed near it. The results are indicated in the following table:

	Fisher's.	French.	Surgeon's.
July 4th, at noon	91°	89°	99° Fah.
Do. at 3 o'clock P.M.	96°	96°	106° do.
Do. at 8 do.	78°	78°	78° do.
July 8th, at 4 do.	119°	118°	128° do.

This proved that when exposed to the direct rays of the sun, or to their reflection by the parade-ground, the thermometer with the brass plate was uniformly ten degrees higher than that made entirely of glass, though at other times it stood at the same elevation. At the time these observations were made, the surgeon was absent.

At Fort St. Anthony, the thermometer was exposed to the south-west; at other posts we have seen it facing the east. Sometimes the instruments were protected from, at other times they were exposed to, the rays of the sun. There can be no doubt that some variations must arise from these causes; and we think it, therefore, desirable, in order to give the greatest value to the observations made at all the garrisons in the United States, that the surgeons should be **provided, at the public expense, with instruments of uniform and approved construction**; and that the observations should be made under circumstances as nearly similar as the great diversity in the situations of these posts will admit. Notwithstanding the variations produced by the causes to which we have alluded, we consider these tables as being very interesting, inasmuch as they afford the first comparative results upon the United States in general; embracing an immense extent of country, and including great diversities of climate.

We deem it but justice to state, that the observations which Messrs. Say and Keating made concerning the manners, &c. of the Indian tribes which they met, were greatly assisted by the valuable notes, furnished to them by the American Philosophical Society, and which where chiefly prepared by Peter S. du Ponceau, Esq., one of the Vice-Presidents of the Society; Professor Robert Walsh, Jun., one of the Secretaries; and by Dr. Samuel Brown, Professor of the Practice of Physic in the Transylvania University.

In conclusion, the compiler has much pleasure in acknowledging the great obligations under which he lies to George Ord, Esq., one of the Vice-Presidents of the Academy of Natural Sciences, and one of the Secretaries of the American Philosophical Society, for his assistance in the preparation of this work. Mr Ord's perusal of the greater part of the manuscript, previous to its being put to press, has preserved it from many of the inaccuracies which it would otherwise have contained.

W. H. K.

Note.—The undersigned begs leave to state, that Dr. Brown's name was inadvertently omitted in the Preface to the " Account of an Expedition from Pittsburgh to the Rocky Mountains." The gentlemen of that party were provided with the same notes, which were used on the second Expedition, and which were in both cases found very valuable.

THOMAS SAY.

Introduction

The major portion of this book was written by William Hypolitus Keating, a youth of 24, seated at a simple desk in a candle-lighted room in Philadelphia during the winter of 1823-24. He was paid $2 per day for writing it, and the United States government, which engaged him for the task, also paid the rent of the room, for fuel to heat it, candles to light it, and for the paper, ink and pens. The labor took about nine months.

As far as we know, Keating had not written a book previously, nor did he write another. Had he no other accomplishments to his credit, he deserves to be recorded in American history as one of our country's great young men. Of course he received recognition for contributions in other fields during his rather brief life but that is another story.

Commonly referred to as "Keating's Narrative" because of the prodigious labors he performed in the field and at the writing desk in order to make it possible, it is one of America's travel-exploration classics. Published in 1824, it undoubtedly attracted considerable attention in certain fields in its day, but since the travels it recounted did not point out a track to a gold field, did not result in annihilation of the travelers or cover a range as great as the Lewis and Clark expedition, it appears to have received somewhat scant attention from the public generally. There was therefore no second edition and the two volumes it comprised languished in government archives and in larger public and university and research libraries. There was an English edition, published in London in 1825.

It seems to have stimulated the interest of adventurers and big game hunters and geologists and naturalists, sending numbers of them along the route followed by Keating and his associates. It could excite into action only courageous and hardy men for it consisted of a frank and unadorned account of what any American might see, hear and experience if he made a trip from Philadelphia to the British Northwest by way of Columbus, Ohio; Fort Wayne, Ind.; Chicago; Fort Snelling and the Minnesota River and Red River of the North, returning via the Great Lakes. This was at the time largely hostile Indian country.

Young Keating left a mineralogy-chemistry professorship at the University of Pennsylvania to become geologist of the expedition. Maj. Stephen H. Long of the Army Topographical Engineers was in command as leader. Thomas Say, the naturalist; James E. Calhoun, nephew of the Secretary of War, serving as astronomer, and Samuel Seymour, the English engraver-painter were among others. Considering the potential danger, there also was an unbelievably small and feeble military escort. Keating and Say were chosen by Long to assume the additional duties of "literary journalists." Notebooks probably were kept by all of the party but it is apparent that young Keating jotted down the most copious notes and that he relied on them for much of what went into the book.

The party started out from Philadelphia on a rainy morning in April in light carriages known in those days as Dearborn wagons, later abandoned them for saddle-horses, subsequently employed canoes, skiffs, steamboats and stagecoaches, and returned to the starting point six months later, having traveled approximately 4,500 miles. This was a stupendous journey by the standards and conditions of those times and, considering the task assigned and the successful outcome, may well be termed epic.

Keating and his associates plagued their commanding officer by persistent requests that the party stop that they might leap out to examine pebbles, rock formations, flora, fauna and other natural phenomena, interview whites as well as Indians and study the hills, streams and land contours. Maj. Long occasionally was forced to restrain them in order to keep within his budget and the designated time limit.

Young Keating and his colleagues were in love with their chosen fields and their curiosity knew no bounds. They began their studies the first day out of Philadelphia with an examination of our country's first great highway, the National Road through Cumberland Gap, on the condition of which and its future needs they chose to make wise comments. Clearly cognizant of the curiosity the average American and the government itself had in anything and everything in this virtually undeveloped and mostly unknown region, they gathered up a fascinating potpourri of information in so many fields that it cannot fail to enthrall a great many readers for all time.

If our government ever received its money's worth from its servants, this was one of the times. The entire cost of conveying, feeding and supplying the undertaking, aside from the expense of the part-way military escort and preparation of the narrative for publication was less than $2,700.

It has occasionally been written that the expedition of 1823 had the purpose principally of determining and marking the 49th parallel at Pembina in what is now North Dakota, this being the point where the 49th and the Red River of the North intersect. That was only a small part of the assignment. A reader of the narrative will discover that there were fairly numerous purposes, having to do among other matters with international relations, commerce, the fur trade, Indian affairs, national expansion and even national defense.

As a result, the narrative became a colorful compendium of data and lore which ever since has been guide and instructor to the novice treading his way through the mazes of the history, legend and tradition associated with this part of the west, and by west in this instance is meant most of the area northwesterly of Philadelphia along the expedition route. The time was 41 years after the American Revolution, only eight years after the close of the War of 1812, and five years after the signing of the Convention of 1818 with Great Britain under which the 49th parallel became the international boundary between the two countries in North America.

Included in the territory examined by the Long Expedition was a once controversial segment of land looking much like a gigantic wedge of pie, lying between the Upper Mississippi and Missouri Rivers and between 49th parallel and the southern end of 20-mile long Lake Traverse on the western boundary of Minnesota. This was land with waters draining into Hudson Bay in the Arctic region, which since 1670 had been claimed by the British government-chartered, fur-trading giant, the Hudson's Bay Co. The area was not included in the Louisiana Purchase and it was not finally acquired by our country until five years before the expedition.

The orders handed Maj. Long were terse yet full. That he received additional oral instructions from the Secretary of War at a conference preceding the start is evident from a study of the official correspondence as well as in a cursory reading of the narrative. On the record, he was to "Make a general survey of the country in the route (and that meant from Philadelphia on), together with a topographical description, ascertain the latitude and longitude of all the remarkable points, examine and describe its productions, animal, vegetable and mineral, and inquire into the character, customs, etc., of the Indian tribes."

Off the record, he was to probe into persistent informal incursions into American territory, to map the terrain for defense, to ascertain transportation facilities, to probe the temper of the people beyond the order in the matter of aggressive military tendencies, and to ascertain agricultural and commercial possibilities. All these tasks were accomplished with distinction, and with such tact and assiduity that one might suspect the President and his cabinet might have been on the scene observing and unable to suggest any improvement of the technique and execution.

Everyone now living along the route traversed will find in the reading an enchanting disclosure of curious facts, attention-engaging personalities and strange happenings. Nothing was too unimportant to experience the neglect of the travelers. There was for instance, the interview at Newark, Ohio, with Capt. John Cleves Symes, the man who believed the earth was concave; the study of Indian earthworks and historic sites made famous during the Revolution and the French and Indian wars, and the charming colloquies with Wennebea, the Sauk dandy, in whose praise Keating penned what is probably one of the most noble tributes ever paid to an American Indian.

After listening to the youthful native, Keating wrote that his remarks "Breathe throughout a wisdom which would have done honor to the philosophers of old, and a morality of which no Christian need have blushed." Corruption of the Indians already was well along its course, however, but on the whole the expedition found them affable, generous and kind hosts. Keating devoted considerable space to a denunciation of a class of whites who were demoralizing the natives with liquor and knavery and expressed indignation and regret with the vigor and language of one far beyond his years. What has been written since by countless others has been but a repetition of his sentiments and words.

Perhaps one of the great contributions to ethnological research in those times was that of Keating and his fellows in their studies of the Algonquian and Siouan races, particularly the Chippewa and Sioux. The facts about these tribes in the Narrative are so comprehensive and detailed as to almost challenge the need for further study.

Of the buffalo and elk and their history from ancient times the book deals also in profuse detail, and it contains extensive fact and speculation concerned with the numerous earthworks of the natives found over most of the route. It considers the moral as well as the economic aspects of the fur trade, and delves into so many other subjects that to list them would be to compile a catalog. Many readers will learn what their home communities looked like many years ago.

It was as a geologist with remarkable understanding and vision for his years, however, that Keating distinguished himself most notably. In the face of prevailing opinion and a great body of opposition among scientific colleagues of the arm-chair school, he virtually spelled out a solution of the age-old mystery of rocks and soils out of place. Later Louis Agassiz and others were to shout out the fascinating story of the Ice Age, the effects of which Keating noted so carefully as he proceeded through our country's glacial lobe country. Keating noted also the fact that a great body of water, now referred to as ancient Lake Agassiz, once covered a large portion of the wedge-shaped triangle the party probed in what is now Minnesota, North Dakota and Manitoba.

"The whole of the country may be considered as an immense lake, interspersed with innumerable barren and rocky lands," he wrote in reference to conditions of long ago. Another remarkable statement by the youth, conceived as he studied the terrain on the lake bottom, now known as the fertile Red River Valley, was, "The traveler fancies himself in the center of a basin surrounded by an amphitheater of rising ground, at no great distance, but which constantly eludes his approach."

There was much that the explorers studied that was beyond their knowledge, of course, and Keating frankly confessed the party's ignorance in some fields, as for instance soil fertility and agricultural possibilities. "We are not qualified to speak," he commented as he expressed in tentative fashion the view that certain areas of the country were not suitable for cultivation. Nor did he and his colleagues envision what drainage of swamps and the breaking up of the grass-matted prairie sod would bring many years later. He did not conceive the role railroads would play in opening markets for the products of the soil.

One could easily believe that young Keating was a prodigy in his school days, and that in addition to majoring in mineralogy and chemistry he had received distinguished training in English, composition, natural science, philosophy, psychology and other subjects. That his mind was constantly in a ferment of curiosity and that he was constantly seeking the beyond-the-obvious meaning of what he observed is always apparent. His talent for expression was brilliant. Rarely had science and literature been so well combined.

It ought perhaps be pointed out that the year before he left on this odyssey he had suffered the embarrassment of disclosure that what he had identified as a new mineral which he named Jeffersonite actually was only a variety of pyroxene, a silicate. Certainly he retrieved himself in 1823 and in subsequent endeavors for this scientific faux pas.

James E. Calhoun, whose astronomical observations on the journey have not been challenged, contributed heavily to the historical research that is part of the Narrative, and Thomas Say, in addition to his assistance in the endless series of interviews, furnished the botanical and zoological commentary. Later he was to win fame for his volumes on American entomology. Seymour turned out the sketches for the book. His landscapes were adequate but his portraits showed his lack of skill in this field. Keating treated him with respect and charity in the Narrative but he is somewhat of an enigmatic figure in the story as he is in history.

The Long expedition was the first government endeavor of its kind which boasted scientists of such ability as Keating and Say. It was the second to be accompanied by an artist engaged for that purpose. (Seymour had accompanied Long on his expedition to the Rockies in 1819).

There was more than one similarity between this expedition and that of Lewis and Clark. Both were accompanied by a Negro. Both lost a member of the military escort, one by death, another by a mysterious desertion in the far north wilds. Leaders of both parties had difficulty with spelling, but in the case of the Narrative this will not be apparent to the reader because Keating had charge of the writing. He was meticulous enough to apologize for using such words as "prairie" and "bluff," words not mentioned in American dictionaries in those times.

At one point in the Narrative will be found a strange episode having to do with pine trees. It is probable that our occasionally impetuous travelers started a forest fire. Keating wrote about it with such naivete and innocence, however, that any forest-fire-conscious reader will need to be an incorrigible misanthrope not to overlook it.

Tribute should be paid finally to calm, pleasant and judicious Maj. Long, who so wisely and faithfully engineered the successful completion of the mission. Not even in the most trying crisis would he compromise his principles. Not a drop from the cask of whisky carried for medical purposes would he dole out to whining native beggars, no matter how threatening their attitudes. The entire expedition was run according to plan.

Still, this is chiefly Keating's Narrative, expressing mainly the young geologist's brilliant mind groping for and acquiring a great body of knowledge of western America for his country in the year 1823.

—Roy P. Johnson

Fargo, N. D.
Sept. 1, 1959

CONTENTS TO VOLUME I.

CHAP. I.
Page

Departure from Philadelphia.—Geology of the Alleghanies.—Cumberland Road.—Wheeling 1

CHAP. II.
Zanesville.—Salt and Iron Works.—Columbus.—Piqua. Indian Antiquities.—Ohio Canals.—Fort Wayne 28

CHAP. III.
Description of Fort Wayne and its Vicinity.—Fur Trade.— Potawatomis 75

CHAP. IV.
Carey Mission-house.—Lake Michigan Chicago 139

CHAP. V.
Rock River.—Menomones.—Geology of the Country West of Lake Michigan.—Prairie du Chien.—Sauks and Foxes 175

CHAP. VI.
Prairie du Chien.—Indian Remains.—Division of the Party. Mississippi.—Dacota Villages.—Fort St. Anthony. Falls.—River St. Peter........................ 242

CHAP. VII.
Geology of the Mississippi.—The Expedition ascends the St. Peter.—Character of the Country.—Arrival at Lake Travers...................................... 314

CHAP. VIII
Account of the Dacotas or Sioux Indians.—Their Divisions into Tribes.—Their Numbers, Language, Manners and Customs.—Notice of Wanotan, principal Chief of the Yanktoanan Tribe.—Description of the Columbia Fur Company's Establishment on Lake Travers 392

LIST OF PLATES.

VOL. I.

                                                                       Page

1. Wanotan and his Son, Frontispiece.

2. Map of the Country 1

3. Heads of Metea, &c. 84

4. View of the Maiden's Rock on Lake Pepin 292

5. Dacota and Chippewa Songs 456

VOL. II.

6. View of the Upper Falls of Winnepeek River 96

7. View of the Falls of Kakabikka 134

8. Shells, &c. two Plates .... Appendix.

BLACKMAN. WENNEBEA. MIETEA.
(Chippewa.) (Sauk.) (Potawatomi.)

Published by G. B. Whittaker, London, 1825.

Engraved by R. Vener.

THE MAIDEN'S ROCK ON THE MISSISSIPPI.

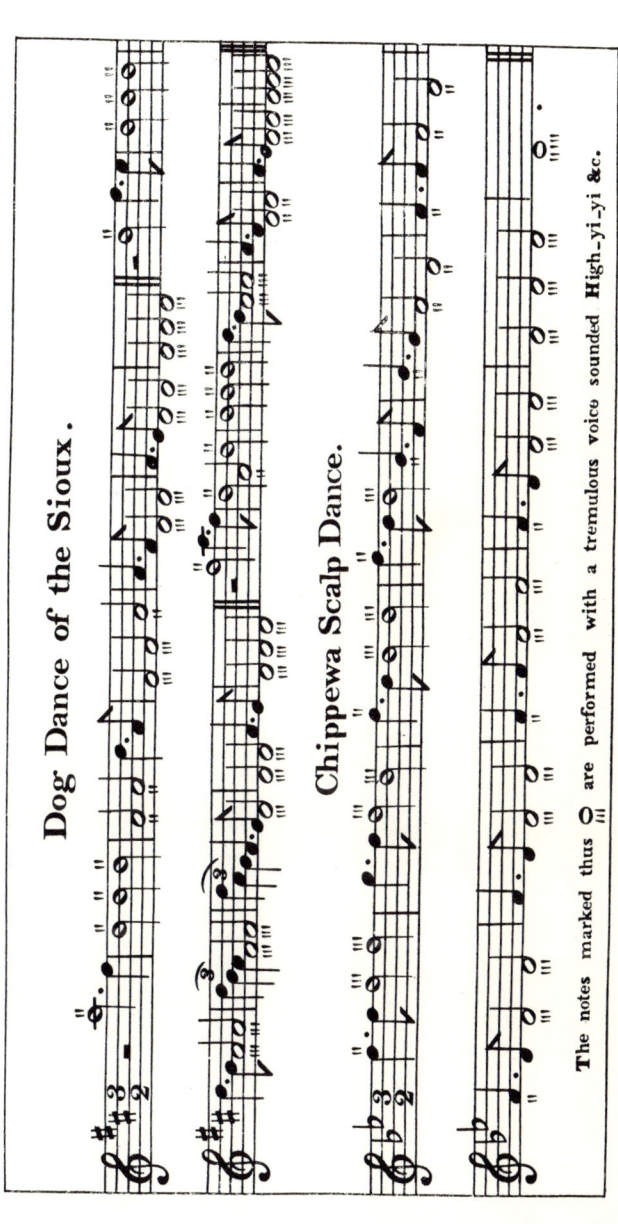

Designed by S. Seymour. UPPER FALLS OF WINNEPEEK RIVER. Engraved by R. Roser.

London, Pub.d by G.B. Whittaker, 1825.

FALLS OF KAKABIKKA.

Designed by S. Seymour. London, Pub.d by G.B.Whittaker, 1825. Engrav'd by R. Penner.

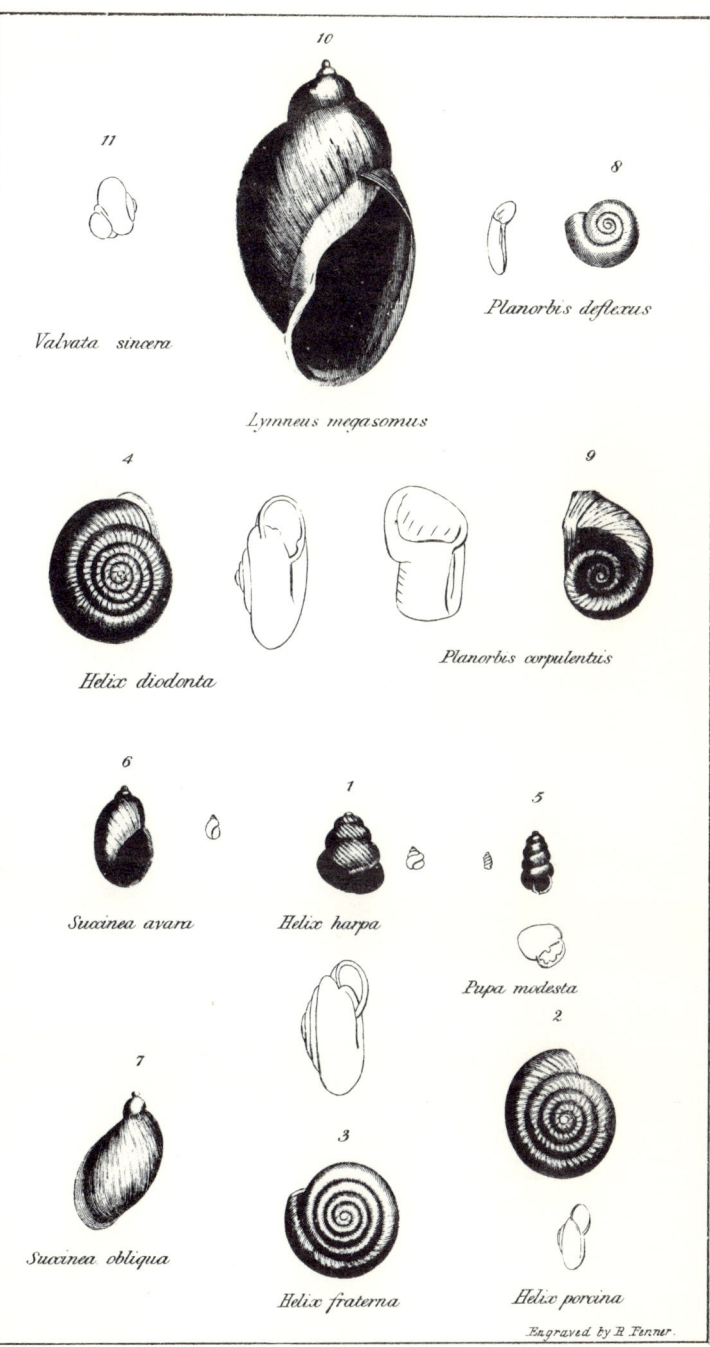

London, Published by G.B. Whittaker. April 1825.

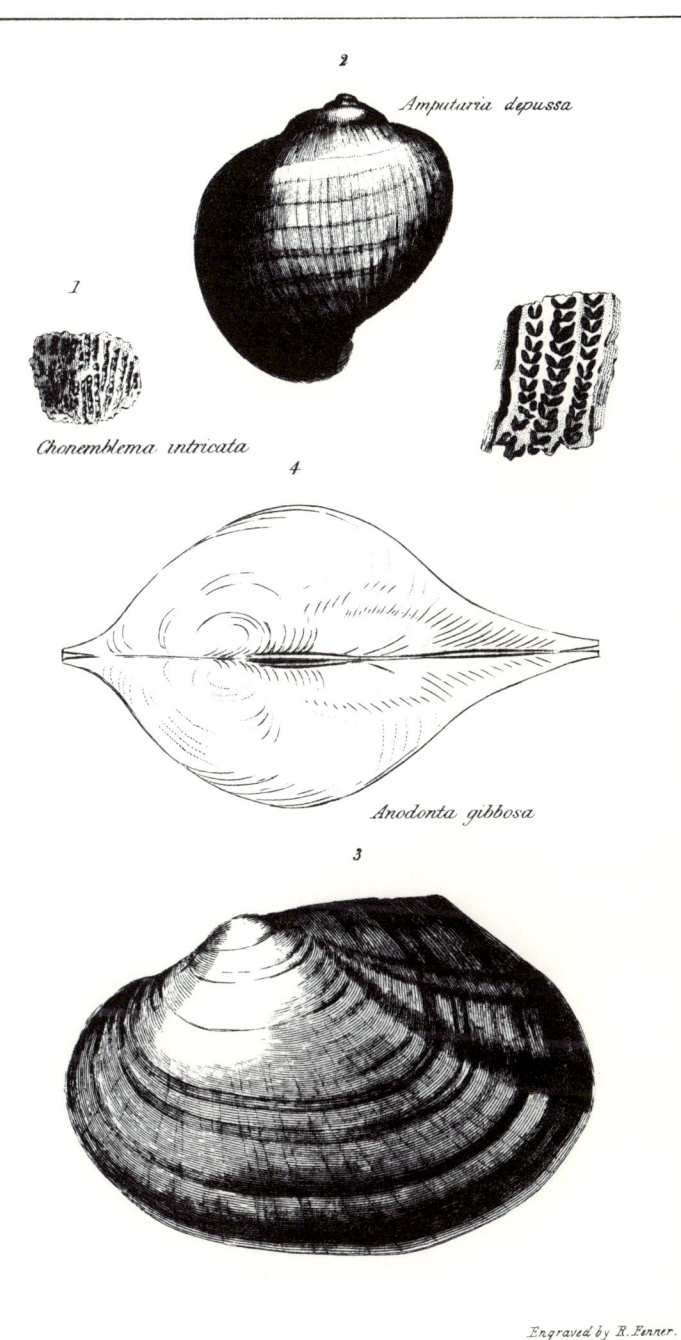

NARRATIVE OF AN EXPEDITION

TO THE

SOURCE OF ST. PETER'S RIVER,

&c. &c. &c.

CHAPTER I.

*Departure from Philadelphia.   Geology of the Alleghanies.
   Cumberland Road.   Wheeling.*

THE success which attended the expedition to the Rocky Mountains, and the important information which it imparted concerning the nature of the valley drained by the Missouri and its tributaries, of which nothing was known but what had been observed by Lewis and Clarke, induced the government of the United States to continue its endeavours to explore the unknown wilds within its limits. The first object which appeared to it deserving of investigation was the tract of country bounded by the Missouri, the Mississippi, and the Northern Boundary of the United States.

This triangular section includes about three hundred miles of longitude, and seven hundred of latitude. The late expedition, under the command of Governor Cass, had explored the southern shore of Lake Superior to the mouth of St. Louis river, and the water communication between Fond du Lac and the Mississippi, which river he ascended to the Upper Red Cedar or Cassina Lake, and then descended to the mouth of the Wisconsan. By this journey much light was thrown upon the history of the Upper Mississippi, which had been previously known only through the fascinating, but imperfect, and in many instances, fabulous accounts of old travellers, and through the hasty observations of the late General (then Lieut.) Pike, an officer whose zeal made him overlook difficulties which would have arrested a less hardy explorer, but who unfortunately was not provided with the means of making accurate observations.

All the later travellers who had visited the Upper Mississippi concurred in mentioning a river, discovered at the end of the 17th century, and known by the name of the St. Peter. This river, which empties itself into the Mississippi at a short distance below the Falls of St. Anthony, had not been visited by any traveller but Carver, whose account of it, published about the year 1778, contains many circumstances which might induce us to question the accuracy of his report.

The extent of the fur trade carried on by the British and American trading companies in that part of the country, the report of the easy communication between the head of the St. Peter and that of the Red River, whose waters running into Lake Winnepeek finally empty themselves into Hudson's Bay, and the various contradictory reports of the quality of the soil and the nature of the country on Red River, resulting from the conflicting interests of the two rival British companies, made it an object of interest to our government, to obtain correct information concerning the country which lies on the St. Peter and the Red River to the 49th parallel of north latitude, as well as to ascertain the nature of the country along our, as yet unsurveyed, northern boundary.

Accordingly, it was determined in the spring of 1823, by the Executive, " that an expedition be immediately fitted out for exploring the river St. Peter's and the country situated on the northern boundary of the United States, between the Red River of Hudson's Bay and Lake Superior."

The command of the expedition was entrusted to Major S. H. Long, and he received orders from the War Department, dated April 25, 1823, of which the following is an extract :—

" The route of the expedition will be as follows :— commencing at Philadelphia, thence proceeding to Wheeling in Virginia, thence to Chicago via Fort Wayne, thence to Fort Armstrong on Dubuque's Lead Mines, thence up the Mississippi to Fort St. Anthony, thence to the source of the St. Peter's River, thence to the point of intersection between Red River and the forty-ninth degree of north latitude, thence along the northern boundary of the United States to Lake Superior, and thence homeward by the Lakes.

" The object of the expedition is to make a general survey of the country on the route pointed out, together with a topographical description of the same, to ascertain the latitude and longitude of all the remarkable points, to examine and describe its productions, animal, vegetable, and mineral ; and to inquire into the character, customs, &c. of the Indian tribes inhabiting the same."*

* Reference was also made to the instructions which were issued by the War Department at the commencement of the Expedition to the Rocky Mountains, an extract of which is inserted in the Journal of that expedition.

The advanced state of the season admitting of no delay, the necessary preparations for the expedition were hastily made, and the party left Philadelphia on the 30th of April—consisting of STEPHEN H. LONG, Major United States' Topographical Engineers, commanding the Expedition—THOMAS SAY, Zoologist and Antiquary—WILLIAM H. KEATING, Mineralogist and Geologist—SAMUEL SEYMOUR, Landscape Painter and Designer. Messrs. SAY and KEATING were likewise appointed joint literary journalists to the expedition, and charged with the collecting of the requisite information concerning the names, numbers, manners, customs, &c. of the Indian tribes on the route.*

* Lieut. ANDREW TALCOTT of the United States' Topographical Engineers, had been appointed second in command of the expedition, and was to have assisted the commander in the astronomical and topographical department, but his services being required in another direction, JAMES EDWARD COLHOUN was appointed astronomer and assistant topographer, and leaving the City of Washington, proceeded to Columbus (Ohio), where he joined the party on the 20th of May.

DR. EDWIN JAMES, botanist, &c. to the Expedition to the Rocky Mountains, and Surgeon in the United States' army, had been appointed botanist, geologist, and physician to the expedition. In pursuance of which, orders were sent to him at Albany, where he then was, to join the party at Wheeling or Columbus, and as it was apprehended that he might have already left that place on his way to Bellefontaine on the Mississippi (to which post he had been previously ordered), letters were written with a view to stop him, but which unfortunately did not reach him in time, and when the party passed through Wheeling he was in Pittsburgh, where he remained until it was too late for him to overtake them. By this unfortunate circumstance the expedition was deprived of the services of this active officer. An apprehension that some unforeseen event might prevent Dr. James from joining the expedition, had induced the commanding officer to obtain a division of the services allotted to him, and the appointment of Mr. Keating to the geological department, while the botanical was reserved for Dr. James. It continued vacant during the expedition, a circumstance which was much

The party travelled in light carriages from Philadelphia to Wheeling, where they disposed of them and purchased horses in exchange. This part of the journey was performed in eleven days. The usual route through Lancaster, Columbia, York, and Gettysburgh, was travelled. Here they left the Pittsburgh turnpike-road and reached Hagerstown in Maryland by a cross road; from Hagerstown they continued along the Maryland turnpike-road to Cumberland, where it unites with the national road, upon which they travelled to Wheeling.

From Philadelphia to Wheeling, the Geologist has an opportunity of observing almost every formation, from the old primitive to the coal strata. On leaving Philadelphia, the primitive soon disappears, and is replaced by the transition limestone, which is of a blue colour, very much intermixed with quartz in veins running through the mass. There are also patches of white limestone which are observed in sundry places, and which, being of a highly crystalline character, might almost induce us to rank this limestone as primitive.

We find occasionally breaking through the limestone, hills composed of amphibolic rocks; this accident is more frequent as we approach the Brandywine. These hills are very readily discernible from the undulations of the limestone country, by the difference in their outward form, which in the limestone hills is mammillary, constituting low and rounded swells; while the amphibolic hills are steep, and covered with a wilder vegetation. Beyond Lancaster, the rocks assume a slaty appearance, which increased as we approached the Sus-

to be regretted. Mr. Say undertook however to collect such plants as might appear to him interesting, but with that diffidence with which a man will undertake a task with which he does not profess to be conversant.

quehannah. At Columbia we had an opportunity of observing the rock as it is laid bare in the bed of the river. It there appears to be the red sandstone, and is that mentioned by Mr. Maclure in his observations on the geology of the United States. It constitutes part of a red sandstone formation, which crosses through the states of New Jersey, Pennsylvania, Maryland, and Virginia. This formation extends in a general north-easterly direction. The rock appears to be nearly horizontally stratified, but from the slight inclination which it presents to the north, the strata are presumed to extend in a north-east and south-west direction.

The limestone and red sandstone, with its accompanying red slate, alternately appear on the west side of the Susquehannah. The limestone is generally found in the valleys, and the sandstone upon the acclivities of the hills, which are generally crowned with small patches of trap. This rock occurs, however, only upon the higher hills, where it seems to have protected the sandstone from decomposition.

On approaching Millerstown, the country assumes a more broken appearance; the limestone ceases, and the indications of crystallization are visible in the rocks. Millerstown (sometimes called Fairfield) is situated on the eastern side of, and at no great distance from that ridge which is generally called the *South* mountain, and which may be considered as the most eastern of the parallel ridges, which constitute the great chain of the Alleghany mountains, at least in the southern part of Pennsylvania. In the vicinity of this place, there are masses of a calcareous breccia, in every respect similar to that found on the Potomac, and which has acquired of late a well-merited celebrity, on account of its having been used for the beautiful columns which adorn the interior of the Capitol, in the City of Washington. This breccia, which is too well known to require description, consists of fragments of limestone of many kinds, differing in texture, colour, &c., all imbedded in a calcareous cement. Some of these fragments have a fine saccaroidal or subsaccaroidal grain, while others are compact. There are also fragments of white quartz intermixed with those of limestone. The breccia appears to form partial deposits in the coves or valley basins of that vicinity.

In the neighbourhood of this town there are numerous indications of the existence of large deposits of copper. The ores of this metal have been found in many places, and excavations were commenced as far back as the year 1798. Some of the ore obtained at this place was sent to England, where it is said to have been worked to advantage. An attempt was made last year to resume the operations, but with no great success. The want of a person qualified to determine as to the best spots at which to commence the excavations, may be considered as the principal obstacle existing at present to the success of these works. The ore hitherto extracted is not sufficiently rich to warrant works to any great extent, but some specimens which were analysed last year in Mr. Keating's laboratory in the University of Pennsylvania, yielded as much as thirty per cent. That the smelting of this ore could be made profitable, if a sufficiency of it were obtained, appears from the circumstance, that a ton of the ore which was sent to Centre county, to be reduced at one of the iron works, yielded about three hundred weight of metal.

The ore discovered in this vicinity varies, but is for the most part a mixture of the oxidule, (red oxide,) with the green carbonate, the hydrate, the copper pyrites, the sulphuret of copper, and grey copper ore. The whole of it appears very much intermixed with siliceous matter. These masses of copper ore are in a talcose slate—they are to be observed every where. Doubts exist as to the manner in which they lie; the sides of the excavations had sunk in so much, at the time the party passed through, that it was not in their power to determine that question: from the information which was received, it would appear probable, that the ore has been worked, in one place at least, on a vein running nearly east and west. The rock, as has been observed, is a talcose slate, which in some places appears to be penetrated with copper pyrites. These mines all lie in a hill known by the name of Jack's mountain; upon the top of which a porphyritic rock occurs. The crystals are of felspar; the cement is of a red colour, and appears to be compact felspar, *(petrosilex palaiopetre* of de Saussure;) besides the crystals of felspar, there are some of quartz and probably of mica. This porphyry appears principally upon the east side of the mountain towards the top—no indications of stratification were observable. The porphyry constitutes probably a subordinate formation in the talcose slate which reappears on the crest of the hill, and is there very abundantly studded with small crystals, which are presumed to be epidote. In descending on the west side of Jack's mountain, the blue limestone reappears, very distinctly stratified, the strata running north-east and south-west; it dips in most places about 80° to the south-east. The dip varies, however, being only in that described above as constituting the North mountain. The latter is a quartzose, the former an argillaceous slate; and the difference of dip is sufficient to distinguish them.

This clay-slate is formed of alternate layers of a very schistose mass and a more compact one. The layers vary in thickness, many of them, however, not exceeding a few inches. In the more compact layers there are indications of a globular structure consisting of concentric shales.

The slate is soon succeeded by a sandstone, which constitutes several of the mountains known by the local appellations of the Sideling-hill, Town-hill, &c. It is not possible to determine with precision the spot at which the sandstone of coal formations commences, indeed we think it probable that no such limit exists in nature. The process may have continued without any marked interruption from the time at which the transition formations were produced, until the coal and its accompanying strata had commenced to be formed. We observe, in most cases, that the slate and reddish sandstone occupy the base of the higher mountains, and constitute the whole of the lower ones; while the crest of the high hills is formed of a sandstone which in every respect resembles that of the coal formations. There seems likewise to be a difference in the organic remains contained in these rocks, for in the lower ones there are only vegetable inpressions, (chiefly stems,) while in the superior strata, shells belonging to the genus Terabratula or Productus, are very frequently met with.

We had an opportunity of ascertaining that the slate which occupies the whole valley of the Potomac, in this district, varies in its dip; sometimes inclining to the south-east, and at other times to the north-west. In one spot we observed the change in the dip produced by a very gentle undulation, without any disturbance or interruption of the stratification. Incumbent on this slate, is a limestone of a bluish colour, presenting signs of organic remains, and constituting Martin's Hill, which is one of the highest in the range. This limestone appears at first to be horizontally stratified, after which it assumes an inclined position, and on ascending becomes nearly vertical, while the top of the hill is crowned with large masses of limestone, quite free from stratification, and presenting only a very irregular division. Upon the summit of the mountain the limestone is cavernous, and contains many organic remains, among which the Terabratula and Productus are chiefly discernible. It is filled with veins of crystalline carbonate of lime, which in some places assumes regular forms.

From Cumberland to Wheeling the geology of the country is much simplified. The coal formation predominates without any interruption. It consists merely of alternating strata of slate-clay, sandstone, limestone, and coal. Of these the sandstone is the most abundant; it is generally fine-grained, composed principally of fragments of quartz connected by a siliceous cement. In some cases there is much mica, and at times a little felspar, so as to constitute in local formations a regenerated granite, not unlike that observable in the coal basin of St. Etienne in France; but these are rather mineralogical curiosities, and can scarcely be considered as forming a feature in the geology of this part of the route. The stratification is nearly horizontal, and is very distinct wherever the slate-clay is found;

but where this rock is deficient, the sandstone loses its stratified character, or at least ceases to present it in a distinct manner.

The sandstone frequently alternates with the slate-clay, and it is not uncommon to observe a real passage of the one into the other; in some cases, as in the neighbourhood of Cumberland, the slate-clay is very rare.

The limestone is compact, of a greyish or brownish colour, very argillaceous, emitting a strong argillaceous odour when breathed upon; it occurs in parallel stratification with the above mentioned rocks, and exists very abundantly all over the country, where it may be seen in many places alternating with the other strata; but we know of none where this can be so well observed as on the west bank of the Monongahela, in the neighbourhood of Brownsville, in those places where the road has been dug into the hill.

The coal has not yet been found to the eastward of Cumberland, but west of this town it occurs almost every where; it is found in beds which vary in thickness from an inch to several, sometimes ten, feet. It appears that these beds extend over the whole country, for the same may be traced for miles without any sensible alteration in its appearance. There are various beds at different levels and of different qualities, and it is from this circumstance, probably, that the coal of one neighbourhood is considered preferable to that of another, because they work upon beds at different levels; yet it may be also that in some cases they work upon one and the same bed, the quality of which may be improved or impaired from accidental circumstances. Small excavations are made in numberless places, so as to answer the wants of the consumers. It is generally obtained at the mouth of the pit for five dollars per hundred bushels, and is sometimes sold as low as four cents per bushel. In the town of Cumberland it usually sells for about ten dollars per hundred bushels.

The abundance of timber in that district, and the thinness of the population, have not yet rendered coal the exclusive fuel used, and it was not until we approached the vicinity of Wheeling that we found coal exclusively used in lime and brick kilns.

The most common disposition of the strata presents the sandstone as the lowest member of the formation; above it is the coal, which is itself covered by the slate, and the limestone covers the whole, and becomes itself a substratum for a superior bed of sandstone, &c.

The only substances of any importance which accompany these rocks, are iron pyrites, and probably the white pyrites. These minerals are so abundant through out the rocks, that they in many places produce a very rapid decomposition and destruction, that render them unfit for many uses of domestic economy; thus many of the beds of coal which would otherwise prove valuable, are so completely pervaded with pyrites that it is impossible to use them as fuel in private houses. This will probably ever prevent their being applied to metallurgical purposes. The pyrites not only penetrate the coal and its accompanying slate, but they extend even into the sandstone, to which they in many cases impart a tendency to decomposition, so great as to render it unfit for use as a building-stone. To the universal diffusion of this mineral we must attribute the circumstance that the country about Wheeling abounds in mineral springs, strongly charged with sulphates of iron and alumine. Indeed it is a matter of considerable surprise, that with such an abundance of vitriolic matter at hand, and with an inexhaustible store of coal in immediate contact with it, no attempt has yet been made to derive advantage from it, by converting it into green vitriol, alum, and sulphate of alumine. No doubt can be entertained of the facility with which this might be effected, and of the great advantage which would attend it. There is no place, we think, where chemical manufacturers of every kind could thrive to such advantage as at Wheeling. With coal mines even in the very heart of the town, with a constant and never-failing navigation, by means of which the products of its industry may be sent to a certain market, backed by a rich agricultural district to support the excess of its population, Wheeling seems destined to rise to a great affluence, becoming in a manner the emporium through which all the commerce between the east and west must pass.

We were much disappointed at not finding in the rocks as many organic impressions as we had expected; we could discover no shells in the rocks, though we have reason to believe that the limestone must in some places abound in them.

In the sandstone there are many vegetable impressions, apparently of palms. The vegetable matter has completely disappeared, leaving only an impression, which, although very distinct, was not sufficiently well characterised to allow a determination of its nature. This sandstone is of a greyish colour, middling-sized grain, and appears to be very micacious in some parts, while in others it consists of quartz nearly pure. The impressions are not very large, seldom more than ten or twelve inches long, and lie parallel to the stratification of the rock. At the hill over which the national road passes, in the immediate vicinity of Wheeling, the sandstone is about fifty or sixty feet in height, divided into layers of variable thickness: over this is a stratum of coal, eight feet thick. In this coal, as well as in the accompanying slate, there are many remains of vegetables converted into pure charcoal, and entirely free from bitumen. These, though numerous, are too imperfect to allow of determining the species to which they belong. This bed, as well as the other parallel ones, when not too much intermixed with pyrites, is worked by galleries running into the hill. The works are very carelessly carried on and the waste of coal is great. The propping is very rough and unsafe; frequent accidents occur from this circumstance. The ventilation is not understood, and many works have been abandoned from the foulness of the air, no attempt being made to correct it. No inconvenience has as yet been experienced from the inflammable gases; but the carbonic acid and the gaseous oxide of carbon are very abundant.

This bed of coal is separated from a superior one by a bed of slate-clay of about three feet in thickness, which from its unsoundness is always worked at the same time as the upper and lower beds of coal; although the upper coal be but six or eight inches thick and of a very inferior quality; but in this manner a safer roof is obtained for the excavation.

The limestone is considerably affected by the pyrites, and being in some places, as we were informed, magnesian, it gives rise to sulphate of magnesia, which might also probably be worked to advantage. The pyritous beds of limestone are only such as come into contact with the coal, the superior strata are said to be quite free from it.

The only circumstance worth mentioning concerning the coal mines is, that they have frequently been on fire, and that there are many indications of conflagrations at a remote period, probably caused by the spreading of the fires lighted at the surface by the Indians, to facilitate their hunting. From these conflagrations the slate is, in many places, observed to be quite altered in its appearance, so as to resemble porcelain jasper in its characters.

No iron ore has been found in this neighbourhood, and we looked in vain for indications of the argillaceous carbonate of iron, so usually to be met with in coal fields. We were informed that, at some distance from the town, large quantities of iron ore had been discovered, but which, from the characters ascribed to it, we were induced to believe were not the argillaceous carbonate, but the oxide and hydrate of iron.

Having thus presented in one connected view the various geological observations which were made on this part of the route, we return to notice the other interesting circumstances which attracted the attention of our party.

The route which we travelled is far more interesting to the general observer than that to Pittsburgh; the country along the Potomac offers many very fine views, among which none is more remarkable than that from Sideling-hill. The ranges of mountains, as they then present themselves, strike the traveller in the most favourable manner. The freshness of the vegetation is peculiarly grateful to the eye in the commencement of

May, and contrasts beautifully with the deep blue of the distant mountains. At times the road winds along the valley; and again it crosses the ridges, offering the greatest variety of scenery, and affording to the artist many views worthy of his pencil; for while the bottoms abound in rich and smiling prospects, the mountainous parts arrest the attention by their bold and gigantic features, and by the antique forests which cover them.

The season in which we commenced our journey was not very favourable to the proper display of vegetation: the frost had not yet disappeared in the mountainous districts, and the very heavy rains, which had fallen in great abundance this spring, had retarded all the products of the earth to an unusual degree; but the fine blossoms of the dogwood-tree (*Cornus florida*), which every where met the eye, amply compensated the want of other flowers.

Art has done little to add to the charms of the natural scenery, except in the construction of a road. The question of the propriety of opening, at the national expense, a communication between the Ohio and Potomac, had been so much the subject of discussion, as to make us desirous of observing the mode in which it had been executed, and the too favourable idea, which we are, perhaps, always led to form, of what carries with it a *national* character, together with an account of the immense expenditure incurred in the making of this road, had prepared us for a magnificent work. We were therefore somewhat disappointed at the state in which we found it, as it is very inferior in execution to the Maryland-road, which connects with it. There is in the whole of the national road but little to justify the high eulogiums which have been passed upon it. The immense expense, amounting to nearly two millions of dollars (Sp. D. 1,995,000), which has attended its construction, can only be accounted for by a reference to the difficulty of making a road across high and steep ridges, which perhaps had not been sufficiently explored, to ascertain the lowest levels and the most accessible points; and, as we think, to the injudicious manner in which the original contracts were given out. We were credibly informed, that in most cases the original undertakers did nothing themselves, but portioned out their contracts to a second set of contractors, and in some cases it happened that the third or fourth set alone performed the work, the other contractors sweeping away immense sums without any labour.* Had the route been properly divided into small lots, and these given only to such as were really qualified to execute the work, no doubt can exist that a considerable saving would have been obtained. The letting of it out into large sections had the disadvantage of making it an object of speculation, and of alarming many who would otherwise have offered themselves as contractors.

Another cause of the great expense which attended it, was the location of its western end in the valley of Wheeling creek, instead of carrying it over the high land. Some difference of opinion exists in the country as to the propriety of this selection. We were informed by many, that this location had been made, rather with a view to benefit private interests, than with a careful regard for the public good. Certain it is, that the number of bridges which were required in the route through the valley, added very considerably to the ex-

* One of these is said to have accumulated in this manner a fortune of one hundred and twenty thousand dollars.

pense of the road. There are no less than seventeen bridges over the main creek, within thirteen miles of this valley road. It is but justice to observe, that the bridges are, for the most part, substantial, well-built, and even elegant in their construction.* A circumstance which enhanced much the expense of the valley road, was the necessity of propping it in many places by a stone wall or parapet, amounting in the aggregate to at least one-fourth or one-third of the distance. The road has, however, along this route, the advantage of being carried almost on a dead level, and in other parts, where it crosses the mountains, it must be acknowledged that the ascents are better regulated than on any other road we have ever travelled. But a great defect which prevails throughout the whole route, and which we had not expected to meet with, is that of using stones of too large a diameter on the road. After all the improvements which have been, of late years, made in this important

---

* At the extremity of one of these bridges a monument has been erected, by a Mr. Shepherd, one of the principal contractors of this road. From an inscription on the monument, we learn that it was erected by "Moses and Lydia Shepherd, in honour of Mr. Speaker Clay, as a testimony of their gratitude to him, and of their high veneration for his public and private character." Mr. Clay is known to have advocated this undertaking, on the floor of congress, with much talent and zeal. There are, we believe, as yet, but few instances of monuments erected in our country by private individuals, to commemorate the public services of our statesmen, and we must regret that the taste which designed, and the hands which executed this monument, were not equal to the liberality which provided for it. We have seldom seen a more clumsy attempt at allegory, or a more unfortunate introduction of emblematical figures. The inscriptions are also equally deficient in taste, in grammatical construction, and in orthography. In order to improve its appearance, the stone, in itself a beautiful building material, has been covered with a wash or paint, which, having scaled off from some parts and remained upon others, contributes to give it a motley and uncouth appearance.

branch of engineering, and after the very just celebrity which the M'Adams' roads have obtained in England, we had hoped that the suggestions of this able engineer on this subject would have been more closely adhered to. Whatever may have been the defects or the mistakes which attended the location or execution, no doubt can exist as to the importance of the work itself, or as to the soundness of the policy which led to it. By the opening of it, the nation has gained a great deal; it has ascertained the practicability and the expediency of entering largely upon a system of internal improvements, the necessary consequence of which must be, to unite by closer bonds the distant parts of our vast country; and of all improvements, none can be more important, than such as tend to connect the waters of the Gulf of Mexico with those of the Atlantic. Immediately allied to this subject, is the possibility of making a water communication between the Ohio and Potomac. At a time when, by a broad and liberal policy, the executive of the United States has been authorized to apply to the consideration of this important object the united talents of the civil and military engineers of our country, and when a full and able report upon the practicability of this connexion may be expected from those most competent to decide upon it, we shall be excused from embodying here the imperfect information which a transient visit through the country has allowed us to collect.

We found some interest in that part of the route which lies near Smithfield, as being the scene of some of General Washington's earliest military operations. The ruins of Fort Necessity, constructed at that distressing season when the French troops, with their savage allies, extended themselves along the banks of the Ohio, and oppressed our frontier settlements, are still to be seen in what are called the Big Meadows, about fifty miles west of Cumberland. This fort was erected in the year 1754, and after having been defended with great valour, was surrendered in the campaign which preceded Braddock's defeat (Marshall's Life of Washington, vol. ii, p. 9), and the remains of it, still to be traced, show that the ditch was *inside* of the embankment, which comports better with Indian warfare.* The fort stands about a quarter of a mile to the south-west of the road, and it is difficult to trace its outline, but from the observations we made it would appear as if it had been triangular, and scarcely one hundred feet in length. It is said that when

* We are led to notice this fact more particularly, from the importance which Bishop Madison has attached to the circumstance of the ditch being inside of the ramparts in most, or perhaps in all the Indian remains, which are considered as fortifications. His opinion that these works were not of a military nature, appears to us very far from being proved. He quotes Livy and Polybius to show us, that, in Roman works, "the parapet or breastwork was formed of the earth dug out from the fosse and thrown up *on the side of the camp:*" and he further asks, "whether the military art does not require that the ditch should be *exterior.*" We do not consider this to be the question at issue. We have derived our notions of fortifications from the Romans, and we have continued to this day, probably with propriety, to place the ditch outside of the rampart; but this is no reason why works constructed by the Indians for military purposes, may not have had it otherwise. If we form our opinion of their notions of the military art from the traces still visible among the Indians, who, if they be not their lineal descendants, have at least succeeded to them in the inhabitance of that country (and it is more consistent to look to them than to the Romans in this case), we shall find that their usual practice is, when apprehensive of an attack from an enemy, to make a small excavation, by digging up a little earth, which they uniformly throw out in the direction from which they apprehend an attack, and then to descend into this hollow, where they find themselves sheltered from the missile weapons of their enemies. (Vide a letter on the supposed fortifications of the western country, from Bishop Madison of Virginia to Dr. Barton, Amer. Phil. Trans. vol. vi. i, p. 132.)

Washington first entered it his force amounted to six hundred men, but that having advanced on his march towards Fort Duquesne, he was abandoned by a considerable proportion of his men; and this circumstance, together with the information which he received, that the French were advancing against him with reinforcements, obliged him to abandon for the time his contemplated march, and to return to Fort Necessity, which he was engaged in repairing when the enemy made his appearance. The country in the vicinity was probably at that time destitute of timber, the growth upon it not being very large. A fine brook which flows near it, has retained the name of the unfortunate general, who, in the ensuing campaign, paid for his rashness by the loss of his life. Indeed, it is said, that the remains of General Braddock were interred within two miles of this fort, near the old road called Braddock's road, and at the spot where he died, during the retreat which closed this disastrous campaign.

In this vicinity there is a blowing spring, which is situated in an excavation on the side of a hill. The stream of air, which issues from a crack or crevice in the rock, is very considerable, and sufficiently powerful to extinguish a candle. By placing our ears near the crevice, we heard very distinctly the sound of water running under ground, probable upon a rocky and unequal bed; it runs out at a short distance lower down. This stream of air is doubtless produced by the same cause, which is made to operate in the construction of the water blasts, used in metallurgy. We had no means of collecting and examining the gas which escapes, but we had no reason to believe it other than atmospheric air.

This section of our route does not offer to the zoologist much subject of observation. The wild animals which formerly roved over this part of our country have been driven further west, or completely cut off by the advance of civilization, and the domestic animals which now occupy their place have nothing to characterize them. We cannot, however, omit noticing the extraordinary size and strength of the Pennsylvania waggon horse, which yields in these particulars to but few breeds. There are several appellations by which the different breeds of this useful animal are distinguished in Pennsylvania, such as the Conestoga, the Chester line, &c. but these are principally of a local import. The usual height of farm and waggon horses is about sixteen hands, or five feet four inches, measured according to the usual custom. We were credibly informed that horses, seventeen, seventeen and a half, and even eighteen hands high, are by no means rare. A few have been known to exceed that size; and we were told that one, the largest ever known in the country, had attained the gigantic size of nineteen hands, or six feet four inches. As a proof of the great strength which they sometimes attain, it is said that an experiment was once tried in the city of Lancaster, which resulted in a single horse's dragging around the court-house, on the bare pavements, without the intervention of wheels or rollers, two tons of bar iron, which had been bundled together for this experiment.

The town of Wheeling appears to be in a flourishing condition, and the increase in its population has been very great, since the completion of the national road. Business has taken a new direction; instead of centring as it formerly did in Pittsburgh, it now goes principally to Wheeling, which has the advantage of a much more permanent navigation all the year round. The population amounts at present to upwards of two thousand. The situation of the town is pleasant; the river here is about five hundred yards wide; and there is opposite to the town a large and beautiful island, nearly three quarters of a mile wide. The town is divided into the old and the new; the former is built upon a narrow bank, which extends between the river and the ridge of hills on the eastern shore; the new town is built a little below the old, on the river, and has a wider field to expand upon, owing to the junction of the lateral valley of Wheeling creek with that of the river. We regretted to find brick resorted to as a building material, not only in the construction of private houses, but even of churches and other public edifices, while a beautiful sandstone, admirably adapted to the purposes of architecture, and which might be obtained at a very low price, remains unwrought.

The weather was so unfavourable during the three days that we remained here, as to preclude the possibility of ascertaining by astronomical observations the latitude and longitude of this town.

In our walks along the banks of the river, which are covered with a vast deposite of alluvium, and which present, in this vicinity at least, no section of rocks, we were struck with the immense number of pebbles partaking of the nature of primitive rocks, which are strewed along the surface of the ground. They are not, it is true, of a large size, and their smooth and rounded surfaces attest that they have travelled far from their native sites. In examining our imperfect geological maps to endeavour to assign to them an origin, we feel at a loss to decide whence they may have been brought. We find no primitive formations nearer than those on the north side of our great lakes, which, from the aspect of the country, may be supposed to have given rise by their destruction to these extensive alluvia of primitive *débris*. Among these pebbles, chiefly of granite, gneiss, sienite, &c. we observed a rock formed of felspar, quartz, and handsome crystals of translucent garnets, which appear to be very abundantly disseminated throughout the rock.[*]

There is in Wheeling a glass-house, which we visited; the glass made here is very good; the sand which they use is brought down from the banks of the Alleghany, and appears to consist of silex nearly pure; the alkali added is principally unwashed ashes. We were somewhat surprised at hearing, that the clay used in the manufacture of their crucibles was brought from Germany, indeed we consider this very improbable, as a clay very well adapted to this purpose is found in many parts of the country. The atmosphere in the glass-house was extremely foul, owing to the sulphurous vapours disengaged from the coal.

The hills in the neighbourhood of the town are covered with masses of clay, sand, &c. which, as soon as they become penetrated with moisture, slide along the

[*] On the banks of the river there were but few shells, and these were referable principally to the Unio praelongus (Barnes), and to the Unio crassus, and Unio purpureus of Say. Among the land univalves, Mr. Say noticed the following shells, which had been previously described by him, *viz.* the Helix albolabris, Helix thyroidea, Helix alternata, Helix palliata, Helix profunda, Helix tridentata, Helix solitaria, Helix inornata. (Vide Nicholson's Cyclopœdia, Amer. Ed. and Journal of the Acad. Nat. Sci. of Philadelphia, vols. i. and ii.)

upper surface of the rocks, even where their inclination is but small. This feature is observable only on the northern slopes, the southern are much more abrupt. We were at first induced to attribute it to the effect of the winter frosts, but Colonel M'Ree, who has examined its appearance with care, attributes it principally to the action of moisture.

CHAPTER II.

Zanesville. Salt and Iron Works. Columbus. Piqua. Indian Antiquities. Ohio Canals. Fort Wayne.

HAVING spent three days in Wheeling, and changed our mode of conveyance, in order to accommodate ourselves to the state of the roads, rendered almost impassable for carriages by the unusual quantity of rain which had fallen this spring, we crossed the Ohio in a teamboat, propelled by two horses. The river is here divided into two branches by the aforementioned island, which is about three quarters of a mile wide; over the first branch of the river a team-boat plies constantly, and corresponds with a common ferry-boat on the other branch. The Ohio road is carried along the valley of a rivulet called Indian Wheeling, and is rendered extremely unpleasant to travel, by the frequent crossings of that brook. It was, however, so bad at that season of the year, that many preferred travelling up the bed of the creek to following the road. It has been observed by all travellers, that the Ohio runs in a valley, the average breadth of which does not exceed a mile and a half, the sides being lined by ranges of hills, which are generally termed the River Mountains; these vary considerably in height, generally ranging between three hundred and five hundred feet. After these are ascended, the country is rough, but the hills comparatively small. These are, however, very steep, probably owing to the nature of the stratification, which is horizontal throughout the country; for it is a fact, which general observation confirms, that those hills which are composed of rocks horizontally stratified, are generally steepest in their ascents, and present a tabular form at their summit. The coal formation of Wheeling is very extensive; the exact limits of this coal basin have not yet been traced with accuracy, but, as far as we are able to judge from the information obtained upon a country as yet but thinly settled, and in which the natural sciences have been little attended to, it would appear that it probably reaches as far to the north-east as Lawrenceville, in Tioga County, Pennsylvania, and perhaps may be considered as connected with that lately discovered in Tioga County (New York), near the head of Seneca Lake. The coal found in that place is, as we were informed, abundant, of an excellent quality, and well characterized as bituminous. The eastern limit may be taken to be formed by the main ridge of the Alleghany Mountains. Its western and southern limits we are not prepared to decide upon, but it is probable that its breadth bears but a small proportion to its length.

At Zanesville we had an opportunity to observe the geological features of the country to advantage. The bed of the Muskingum is deeply incased, and the stratification is laid bare for a considerable distance. It there presents the same features as in the vicinity of Wheeling, but the order of stratification and the character of the rocks are somewhat different.

A very fine break presents the following section: commencing at the lowest rocks, there is a sandstone of a tolerably coarse grain, filled with remains of vegetable substances converted into charcoal, in some cases partaking of a bituminous character, so that a gradual and invisible, but certain transition from the charcoal to coal manifestly takes place. These remains are, however, as far as we saw them, so much impaired, as to make it impossible to assign to them any particular place in fossil botany, though of their vegetable origin no doubt can exist. In remarking upon their position, we ascertained, that they generally lay in the direction of the stratification, very seldom intersecting it. Besides fragments of charcoal and coal, we found impressions of plants, some of which were tolerably well characterized. In one instance a *phyllolithos* (Martin) was collected in a very good state of preservation.

The sandstone in a few cases assumes a somewhat micaceous appearance, consequently a more slaty structure, and thence resembles that hereafter to be noticed. The rock immediately superincumbent is presumed to be a bed of clay-slate; though the junction being concealed, and the relative positions of the rock being only judged of by the general level of the country, it was not in our power to decide in a positive manner whether or not there were any other strata interposed between these two.

This clay-slate is very brittle, and easily divisible; on exposure to the atmosphere it very readily crumbles, and lays open to view concentric globules of argillaceous carbonate of iron, in every respect similar to those observed in other coal formations.

The iron ore is found in rounded or oval masses, somewhat flattened in the direction of the stratification; it appears to be quite abundant, and we doubt not, if made the object of exploration, would be found sufficiently so to justify the erection of iron works on a large scale.

some places about 30°, as may be very distinctly observed in the excavations made for cellars, &c. at Hagerstown.

This town is pleasantly situated in Washington county, Maryland, on the great turnpike road which leads from Baltimore to Cumberland. We saw here specimens of the white marble which occurs at Boonsborough, about ten miles south-east of Hagerstown. It is said to exist there in considerable quantities on the west side of the South mountain, not far from its foot. It was at first mistaken for gypsum by the people of the neighbourhood, and very abundantly applied to manure their lands, and it was only after its inefficacy had been demonstrated by experience, that its true nature was ascertained. This marble is of the finest white, with a subsaccaroidal grain, and may become of great use in buildings; it is, however, too fine-grained for statuary purposes. An analysis of it was made with a view to ascertain its purity; it was found to consist entirely of carbonate of lime, with little or no foreign admixture. It certainly belongs to the primitive formation, and corroborates the opinion we had formed at Millerstown, that the primitive rocks reappear to the west of the red sandstone formation; a circumstance not noticed in the geological observations of Mr. Maclure. It is probable, however, that the appearance of the primitive here is but partial, and confined to certain localities, where it rises through the incumbent strata of transition rocks. There is an extensive cave or grotto in the blue limestone, about seven miles to the east of Hagerstown, which has not yet been fully explored.

From Hagerstown to Cumberland the mountains are numerous, and the works which have been executed for the road have in many places laid the rock bare, so as to make its structure apparent. We there see a great variety in the nature of the rocks, all of which however are observed to belong to the transition or secondary; the former being observed near to Hagerstown, and passing gradually into the latter, which occur very distinctly in the vicinity of Cumberland. At first, the blue limestone, with a considerable, though varying, dip to the south-east, is seen gradually passing into a slaty rock, which finally predominates, and is a transition clay-slate, probably the *Grauwacken-shiefer* of German mineralogists. This however is found in parallel directions, alternating, as is believed, with this limestone, on a distance of several miles. After which, as we approach the North mountain, a sandstone of apparently very ancient formation, and which we feel inclined to refer to the red sandstone formation, occurs. It frequently acquires a reddish colour and, being in a great measure composed of quartz, assumes in some places the appearance of an *eisenkiesel*. Its stratification is very distinct, extending from north-east to south-west, and dipping to the northwest. This stratification is not visible on both sides of the mountain. The eastern slope being carried upon the crests of the strata, which are very brittle, a sort of soil is soon formed from the fragments of the rock, which entirely conceals it from view, but on the western slope it is very well marked. On the summit of the hill numberless fragments of trap rock are strewed in every direction. To the west of this ridge we again strike the clay-slate, which continues along the valley of the Potomac, being interrupted by the appearance of the blue limestone in the transverse valleys of the Big and Little Conolaway Creeks. This slate differs very much from

Resting upon the slate-clay, we observed a bed several feet in thickness, composed of a dark grey limestone very compact in texture, but presenting at the same time a slaty structure, and divisible in layers parallel to the stratification. This limestone is replete with organic remains, chiefly belonging to the Encrinite, Terebratula, Productus, &c. among which we also found a shell belonging to the genus Trochus or Turbo. These shells are very abundant in the rock; they are found, as far as we could judge, irregularly disseminated, and adhering so closely that it is impossible to separate them, or to divide the mass into specimens which shall exhibit their characters uninjured; but being for the most part formed of calcspar, they resist decomposition better than the compact limestone, in which they are imbedded, and from this circumstance the best specimens are found protruding from the weathered surfaces of the rock.

This bed offered great interest to the two naturalists of the expedition, to the one as zoologist, to the other as geologist. Mr. Say thought he beheld in it the confirmation of an opinion which he had long entertained, that, of all fossils, the Encrinus is that which resists decomposition best. Without pretending to dispute the correctness of the observation, as a general one, Mr. Keating thought the present instance did not confirm it, and that there were many spots where the bivalves (Terebratula and Productus) indicated a greater degree of hardness and solidity, by resisting the effects of the weather better than the Encrini. This we notice as being perhaps the only time that the two naturalists differed in their observations on the same fact, when coming under the notice of both.

Upon this limestone lay a bed of coal, of about two feet in thickness, and apparently of a very good quality. Some works of no great amount were undertaken here not long since, which are unattended to at present. We were told, however, that in other parts of the country this coal is worked to advantage. Coal is the usual fuel in the town, being worth from four to six cents per bushel.

It is covered by a bed of slaty rock, which in some cases assumes a decided appearance of slate-clay, and in other points runs into a micaceous sandstone, not unlike the micaceous parts of that noticed as the lowest stratum visible in this vicinity, and like the former it is filled with vegetable impressions of a very undecided character.

Over this slaty rock another bed of limestone occurs, the characters of which, resembling in every respect those of the stratum under the coal, require no further description. The superior bed, as well as the inferior one, is rich in impressions of Encrinites, Terebratula, Productus, &c. which shells retain their pearly lustre, and even in some cases their animal matter.

The limestone is covered with a fine vegetable mould, and affords a rich soil, not inferior to any of the limestone bottoms of Pennsylvania. We had no means of ascertaining what rocks lay below the first bed of sandstone observed in this break, but from what we could discover in the bed of the canal now digging in the neighbourhood of this town, we believe it to rest upon a sandstone, in every respect similar to that described in the first chapter, as existing in the neighbourhood of Wheeling, and we have every reason to believe that the same alteration of strata which exists there, would be found in like manner here, and that if shafts were sunk, inferior strata of coal might be reached.

Zanesville is a pleasant and flourishing town, situated at the junction of the Licking creek, and Muskingum, about ninety miles above the confluence of the Muskingum and Ohio. As a manufacturing town it possesses great advantages. A dam built across the two streams, a short distance above their junction, gives it a command of water power which is calculated to set in motion very extensive mills and manufactories. It was the observation of these natural advantages, that induced the late Mr. Zane * to fix upon it as a seat for a town, and the rapid growth of the place has raised it to a rank among the most thriving towns in the state of Ohio. A number of manufactories have already been established here, which appear to be conducted with spirit and enterprize; among these a manufactory of cut nails belonging to Mr. Reeves deserves notice. The iron for the manufactory is prepared by him from the pigs by the process of puddling and rolling. Glasshouses, in which both green and white glass are made, exist here; it is said that the clay from which they

---

* A few days before our arrival at Wheeling, Mr. Zane, the founder of Zanesville, died in that place. This man was extensively known as having been one of the first settlers in that state. He was one of those pioneers of civilization, of which the history of our western states presents us so many instances, men equally distinguished by a dauntless courage and unwearied perseverance, and by the success with which they resisted the aggressions of the aborigines, who frequently attempted, but in vain, to oppose those, whom they, perhaps very justly, considered as trespassers upon the soil which they had inherited from their fathers. Mr. Zane's character was highly respectable, and among the many anecdotes still current in Ohio, many of which attest his courage, there are none but such as are reputable to him as a man of feeling.

make their crucibles, and which is found at a short distance from the town, is excellent. Within four miles of Zanesville, on Licking creek, there is a furnace at which an hydrated oxide of iron is worked. The difference in the price between cast iron and pigs is so great as to enable them to convert the whole of their produce into hollow ware, which is readily disposed of at seventy dollars, while the pigs command only thirty dollars a ton. Bar iron, and that not of the best quality, is sold for one hundred and twenty-five dollars. The little iron, refined in this vicinity, is generally of an inferior character. The experiment of manufacturing the iron by rolling, as is done at Reeves' establishment, has not been attended with sufficient success to lead to a more general introduction of this process. We conversed with several intelligent iron masters on the subject, with a view to obtain accurate information on the advantages of this method over that of hammering, the result of which was, that the product obtained from rollers was not so uniformly good as that obtained by hammering, which, in the opinion of our informants, was owing rather to the defect of the workmen than of the process. The management of rollers is probably not well understood by them. We have taken occasion to record this information, because it appears to us that every thing that can throw a light upon the manufacture of iron is interesting. We consider the question of the propriety of using rollers as a highly important one, and as one not yet settled. We know that a strong prejudice exists in this country against the rolled iron, and that the results of experiments made in Pennsylvania are rather unfavourable; but we likewise know, that the process is very extensively carried on in England, where it has met with a decided preference in many instances; and the economy which attends it, must make it very desirable that it should prove successful. Experience shows that all innovations in the arts meet with objections; and the failure of those who attempt to repeat them without proper care or knowledge, is not unfrequently attributed to the imperfections of the process, instead of being charged to the inexperience of the operators.

It is a remarkable fact, that, with the admitted superiority of the British over American castings, no attempts have been made to work the same ore, and by means of the same fuel, which have proved so successful when used abroad. It is a truth, with which every person who feels an interest on this subject is conversant, that the clay ironstone is the principal ore used in England; that it is smelted by means of coke; that the products are extremely advantageous; that results equally favourable, if not more so, have been obtained in Silesia from the same ores; and that experiments which have been made on the same subject in France, have been attended with the happiest results. We may therefore wonder, that so much of this valuable ore is allowed to remain unwrought, in the midst of the very fuel which ought to be used to smelt it; and that a preference should be given to the hydrates and oxides of iron, worked with charcoal, very frequently to great disadvantage.

The furnace which we visited near Zanesville was built in 1809, and was, as we were told, the first erected in the state of Ohio; its inside is lined with fire-bricks, made of the clay which is used for crucibles in the glasshouse; and the proprietors informed us that it was their intention to make large bricks of the same materials for their hearths, as all the stones they had heretofore used had proved defective, and had obliged them to suspend their operations under a year's blast, at a time when the rest of the furnace was in a very sound state. This experiment, if successful, will be attended with great advantages to the country. The clay has been analyzed in Mr. Keating's laboratory in the University of Pennsylvania, and found to contain about seventy-two per cent. of silex, with alumine, little or no lime, and no metallic oxide.

The iron ore used here is a hydrated oxide, which yields in castings about thirty-three per cent. It smelts very readily of itself, requiring but a slight addition of about three per cent. of limestone. Among the great improvements which have been made at this place, is the connexion formed, by means of a canal with locks, between the upper and lower level of the Muskingum. The company who erected the dam were bound by their charter to keep a lock navigation in repair, and their improvements, which have removed all obstacles to the navigation, will doubtless prove very valuable, as they have afforded them a very extensive water-power. Salt was some time since obtained at Zanesville, and all along the Muskingum; but of late the works here have been abandoned, the springs being too weak. It appears that those below are very productive; it is calculated that one hundred gallons of water from these will generally yield about a bushel of salt, weighing fifty pounds; hence the water must contain upwards of six per cent. of salt. The establishments, as they are generally made in this country, contain twenty kettles of the capacity of ninety gallons each, costing together about seven hundred dollars; of these kettles or pans, fourteen are used for evaporating and six for crystallizing the salt. During the evaporation a sediment is formed, which is supposed by some to consist of loam and lime; no experiments have as yet been made to ascertain its nature. No use has ever been made of it; but it would doubtless prove very valuable in agriculture. The depth to which they bore varies much; it is generally about two hundred feet. In some cases the auger-holes, which are about three inches in diameter, have been sunk to seven hundred feet. The expense of course varies according to the depth, but the work is generally undertaken at from one dollar and fifty cents to two dollars per foot. In one instance, where the boring extended to upwards of one hundred feet, it was performed for seventy-five cents per foot. The whole capital required to put up salt-works in this neighbourhood is estimated at four thousand five hundred dollars; and when the work is prudently conducted, the business is considered very good; though the price of salt is at present very low.

It was in boring for coal, a few years since, that a deception was practised, which made considerable noise in the country, and produced much mischief in Zanesville and its vicinity. It appears well ascertained, at present, that the silver said to have been found in one of the auger-holes bored on the banks of the river, had been thrown in by some evil-minded persons. The pretended discovery induced many to speculate largely upon the mine, before the detection of the plot, whence they incurred great losses; this event occurred in the year 1819.

The banks of the river are strewed with vast numbers

of pebbles, much rolled, and evidently carried from a great distance. They consist principally of quartz, in some cases hyaline, in others partaking of the nature of jasper, agate, semiopal, &c.; fragments of granitic and amphibolic rocks are also to be met with here and there. Specimens of petrified Retipore and Favosites striata, Say, and of a new genus of the *Polypiers lamelliferes* of Lamarck,* were also observed on the shore. These petrifactions are siliceous and rolled, and bear the appearance of having been removed far from their original situation. Specimens of the Favosites striata are also common in this vicinity.

We observed near the bank of the river a considerable accumulation of common flint (quartz silex), which consisted of irregularly shaped blocks of silex, apparently nodules, which had been imbedded in a rock, in the manner in which the same substance lies in the chalk of the neighbourhood of Paris; its colour is black. Upon inquiry, we were informed that these blocks are gathered from the fields, where they are found loose and scattered; they do not carry with them the appearance of much attrition. They are used in the glass-houses in the preparation of fine white glass.

Among the features which strike the traveller, as he contemplates the scenery of Muskingum, none contribute more to give a character of originality to the landscape, than a rude bridge thrown across the river, in which the architect has contrived to connect three forks or arms, one of which reaches to the cape formed by the junction of the Muskingum and Licking creek, while the other two establish a connexion between the

* Appendix I. A.

opposite banks of the Muskingum, below the junction of the two streams. This presents an uncouth mass, contrasting well with the magnificence of the scenery. The bridge appears destitute of solidity, and will probably be soon replaced by a more elegant and permanent one. It is thus that the rude works of the first settlers in the west are disappearing gradually, and making way for the more improved structures of civilized life.

Having remained half a day in Zanesville, we continued our journey towards Columbus, which we reached on the 19th. The route between these two places offered us but little interest; to the mineralogist it presents none at all, being level, flat, and covered with an alluvium. We were informed that coal had been observed in many places, but in no instance of a quality to warrant its extraction; and that no where had it been worked beyond five miles west of the Muskingum. Our road, which led us through the valley of Licking creek, was very even. The rocks were always concealed from view, except in one or two places, where abrupt cliffs rose at too great a distance from the road to permit us to decide upon their nature; but their general aspect appeared to connect them with those observed in the vicinity of Zanesville.

Our attention was, however, soon directed in another channel. The country about the Muskingum appears to have been at a former period the seat of a very extensive aboriginal population. Every where do we observe, in this valley, remains of works which attest, at the same time, the number, the genius, and the perseverance of those departed nations. Their works have survived the lapse of ages; but the spirit which prompted them has disappeared. We wander over the face of the country; wherever we go, we mark the monuments which they have erected; we would interrogate them as to the authors of these mighty works, but no voice replies to ours, save that of the echo. The mind seeks in vain for some clew to assist it in unravelling the mystery. Was their industry stimulated by the desire of protecting themselves against the inroads of invaders, or were they themselves the trespassers? Did they migrate to this spot, and if so, whence came they? who were they? whither went they? and wherefore came they here? Their works have been torn open; they have been searched into, but all in vain. The mound is now levelled with the sod of the valley; the accumulated earth, which was perhaps collected from a distance into one immense mass to erect a monument deemed indestructible, over the remains of some western Pharaoh, is now scattered over the ground, that its concealed treasure may be brought to light. Every bone is accurately examined, every piece of metal or fragment of broken pottery is curiously studied, still no light has as yet been thrown upon the name and date of the once populous nation which formerly flourished on the banks of the numerous tributary streams of the Ohio.

Such were the reflexions suggested to us by our visit to the numerous mounds and Indian works which abound in this part of the country, the first of which we observed in the small village of Irville, situated eleven miles west of Zanesville. This mound was about fifteen feet in diameter, and four and a half in height; it appears to have had an elliptic basis. Our guide told us, that he was present when it was opened, and that there were a number of human bones, and among others a tolerably entire skeleton, which lay with its head to the north-west; the arms were thrown back over the head. Besides the bones, there were numerous spear and arrow points, and of the latter we picked up one on the spot. There was also a plate of copper of the length of the hand, and from five to six inches in width; it was rolled up at the sides, and had two holes near the centre; its weight, we were told, might have been about a quarter of a pound, but it was probably greater: for it must have been very thin, if, with these dimensions, it weighed so little. What could have been the use of it, except as an ornament, was not determined; indeed, the inhabitants of that part of the country are so much accustomed to dig up bones, and remains of the Aborigines, that they are very careless about observing or recording the objects found, and the circumstances under which they were discovered. We were told that pieces of copper, and even of *brass*, had been frequently collected. The copper may easily be accounted for, without a reference to a higher degree of civilization, or to an intercourse with nations more advanced in the arts. The existence of native copper, strewed upon the surface of the ground in many places, will easily account for the circumstance of its being used by the natives as an ornament, in the same manner as the Copper Indians of the north have been known, from the earliest days of their discovery by white men, to adorn their persons with it: but we cannot account for the discovery of ornaments of brass, unless we admit an intercourse with nations that had advanced in civilization. The existence, therefore, of fragments of this alloy in mounds, appears to us doubtful; for, if true, the Indians who constructed them must have been much more refined than we can suppose they were; or they must have had intercourse with civilized nations. The erection of these mounds, which appear to be in a great measure contemporary, was certainly much anterior to the discovery of this continent in the fifteenth century; and, therefore, it is not from Europeans that these pieces of brass were obtained, if, again we repeat it, they have been found in these works.

Besides this mound, there are many others in the immediate vicinity of Irville, some of which are of very great dimensions. We observed one, near the road, which had been but recently excavated at its summit; it was perhaps thirty-five or forty feet high. These mounds were for the most part overgrown with bushes; and from the scattered and irregular manner in which they lie, we could discover no order or plan in their relative positions; it does not appear that they were intended to be connected with any work of defence, but it is more probable that they were erected as mausoleums, and that the difference in their size was intended to convey an idea of difference in the relative importance of those whose bones they covered. We were informed that this valley and the neighbouring hills abound in excavations resembling wells; we met with none of these; they are said to be very numerous, and are generally attributed to the first French adventurers, who, being constantly intent upon the search after the precious metals, commenced digging wherever they observed a favourable indication. Not having seen any of these, we could not pretend to express an opinion upon their origin; but, from the number in which they are represented to be, as well as from their dimensions, they appear to us far exceeding the abilities of those to whom they are attributed, and to have required a much more numerous and permanent population than these adventurers are known to have brought over with them. We would, therefore, prefer the opinion which ascribes them to the same nations that erected the mounds, and who may have sunk these wells, either for purposes of self-defence, according to the usual mode of Indian warfare, or as habitations, in the manner known to be practised by some Indian tribes (vide Harmon's description of the *Carriers**), or finally, for some other cause as yet undiscovered. Their great depth, which is said at this time in many cases to exceed twenty feet, may be considered as an objection to the opinion which we have advanced. The supposition of Mr. Atwater, that these wells, which he states to be at least a thousand in number, were opened for the mere purpose of extracting rock crystal and hornstone, appears to us too refined; whatever may have been the advances of these nations in civilization, we have no reason to believe that they had carried them so far as to be induced to undertake immense mining operations, for the mere purpose of obtaining these articles. (Archæologia Americana, vol. i. p. 130.)

Newark is a pleasant little town, situated at the fork of Licking and Raccoon creeks, about twenty-five miles from Zanesville. Within a short distance of it are some very fine remains of Indian works, which we missed seeing, having been misinformed as to their real position; but we had less cause to regret this, as an excellent description of them has been published by Mr. Caleb Atwater. From his account of them, it would appear that these works must have covered several miles of country, and that they were perhaps connected with other works,

---

* Journal of a Voyage and Travels in the Interior of North America, by D. W. Harmon, Andover, 1820.

situated at a distance, by parallel walls extending over a space of thirty miles. Of the labour bestowed upon them, an idea can be formed from the circumstance, that among these works there " is a circular fort, containing about twenty-six acres, having a wall around it, formed by the ground which was thrown out of a deep ditch on the inner side of the wall; this wall is now from twenty-five to thirty feet in height." (Archæol. Am. i. 127.)

In the vicinity of Newark we observed an orchard every tree of which was propped, having, as we were told, suffered much from a violent south-westerly gale on Easter Sunday of this year. The fact would not have appeared to us worthy of notice, but for the observation that this gale of wind, which was felt very extensively throughout the country, was observed to have a different direction in different places; at Philadelphia it is known to have been from the north-east. It may be a question, whether these two gales were in any manner connected, and, if so, why they happened to proceed from different directions.

At Newark the party fell in with Captain John Cleves Symes, a man whose eccentric views on the nature of the globe have acquired for him, not only in America, but also in England, a temporary reputation. The partial insanity of this man is of a singular nature: it has caused him to pervert, to the support of an evidently absurd theory, all the facts, which, by close study, he has been enabled to collect from a vast number of authorities. He appears conversant with every work of travels, from Hearne's to Humboldt's; and there is not a fact to be found in these which he does not manage, with considerable ingenuity, to bring to the support of his favourite theory. Upon other subjects he talks sensibly, and as a well-informed man. In listening to his expositions of his views of the concavity of our globe, we felt that interest which is inevitably awakened by the aberrations of an unregulated mind, possessed probably of a capacity too great for the narrow sphere in which it was doomed to act; and which has consumed itself with the fire which, if properly applied, would doubtless have illumined some obscure point in the science which it so strongly affects. In another point of view, Captain Symes has a claim to our best sympathies for the gallantry with which he served his country during the war.

From Newark to Columbus the road passes through a moist and heavily-wooded country, well calculated for the growth of the beech tree, which was found here superior in size to any previously observed. This part of the route lying remote from any navigable streams, is almost destitute of population; and it was only when we came to the immediate vicinity of Columbus, that we again found ourselves in the midst of civilization.

The spot upon which the metropolis of Ohio now stands, presents a remarkable instance of those rapid changes which are so often to be met with in our western states. In 1812 only a single log cabin could be observed, where now a population of fifteen hundred inhabitants is seen enjoying all the comforts, and carrying on all the business of an old settlement. The situation of Columbus is, however, far from presenting advantages that can equal those of many other western settlements. Much difficulty and division appears to have prevailed in Ohio previous to the location of the seat of government; and this spot was probably selected by a sort of compromise, rather with a view to its central situation than from any great local advantage. It stands on the left bank of the Scioto, at about half a mile from Franklington, whose site on the right bank was thought too low and unhealthy.

The party were here joined by Mr. Colhoun, who had travelled from Washington city, by the national road, to Wheeling, and thence proceeded to Columbus, where he waited for the arrival of the expedition. Some further arrangements, required to accommodate ourselves to the country through which we had to travel, occasioned in this town a delay of one day, during which we experienced a remarkably heavy thunder-storm, which was accompanied by a wind apparently like a hurricane, its direction shifting at every moment; this produced much damage in the town, and among other things carried off both the gable ends of a house, the wind forcing a way for itself under the roof.

The banks of the Scioto are covered with pebbles, apparently from primitive formations; no rocks were visible in place, but the limestone used in the town, and which is filled with organic remains, is said to be found in the vicinity; it appears to be similar to that observed at Zanesville.

The wealth of Ohio has been so often the subject of discussion, that we felt an interest in ascertaining how far the reports circulated were correct. We found that, in fact, the produce yielded by agriculture so far exceeds all demands for it, that it has become a sort of dead stock in the hands of its owners. The price of grain has fallen so low, that the only mode of disposing of it consists in distilling it into whiskey, of which the price is twelve and a half cents per gallon, and when retailed in small quantities it sells at the rate of twenty-five cents per gallon. Such prices must of course be a check upon all industry, and at the same time productive of much mischief by offering a temptation to intoxication, which too many find it impossible to resist.

The weather had already set in very warm, the thermometer usually standing at noon at upwards of eighty degrees. Observations for latitude and longitude were commenced here, but were interrupted by the storm.

Wednesday, May 21st, the expedition left Columbus on its way to Piqua, situated on the Miami, about seventy miles west of Columbus, and likewise in the state of Ohio. The intermediate country is but thinly settled; the soil is black, and not very deep, seldom more than eight inches; it lies upon a bed of sand and pebbles, which are evidently the detritus of granitic rocks, similar to the large boulders observed every where throughout the country. No rocks to be met with in place. Although the country is very high, being probably, from the best measurements which have been made, at least three hundred and fifty feet above the surface of Lake Erie, and consequently upwards of nine hundred feet above the surface of the ocean, it is very wet, being swampy, with occasional open woods and soft marshy prairies, very unlike those that are described by travellers as existing to the westward, and which we afterwards met with on the St. Peter, &c. The whole of this part of our route led us irresistibly to the conclusion that we were travelling upon the bottom of some lake, whose waters had, at a comparatively modern period, broken their bounds and found their way to the ocean. It is true, that, in the present state of our geographical and geological knowledge of the valley drained by the Mississippi, it is impossible to assign any probable limits to this vast internal ocean; we know too little of the true direction of the different chains of mountains, which extend throughout this section of our country, or of their respective heights, to allow us to trace the limits of that powerful dam which formerly kept the whole of our western country under water; nor can we attempt to show in what places and from what causes the dam was forced: but the mere inspection of the high plains, which form the centre of the state of Ohio, must satisfy us, that they doubtless owe the characters which they now present to the recent sojourn of water. The country is covered with a very heavy growth of wood; many of the trees are upwards of five feet in diameter. These forests consist chiefly of oak, ash, elm, hickory, sugar-maple, black-walnut, beech, tulip, wild-cherry, &c. The cotton-wood tree and the garden-coral honeysuckle were first observed here in great abundance; the tulip, or *Liriodendron*, is the tree which attains the largest size. The soil, though good, is not of the first quality, and it is generally observed that the dark black soil, which predominates, is inferior in quality to a chocolate-coloured one which is occasionally met with. The average produce of the best crops of Indian corn amounts to about fifty bushels per acre; a good crop of wheat yields about thirty bushels. The increase of population in this district is far from being as rapid as it promised to be; the want of a market, the unhealthiness of all the marshy lands,* and the constant impulse to an emigration further to the west, have prevented many settlements being

---

* Besides the ague and intermittent fevers, we were informed that a very fatal disease had prevailed during the last summer; it is well known to the west under the name of the sick stomach, or milk sickness, and is supposed to be produced by drinking milk, which has become unwholesome from some cause or other; many persons died of it last year.

made, remote from the streams. Wild and unimproved land may be had, in most places, at two dollars per acre, and there is still some public land, belonging to the United States, which may be purchased at one dollar and a quarter per acre. The surface of the country presents some slight undulations. The only stream of any consequence which we met between the Scioto and the Miami, was Mad River, a tributary of the latter. The name which it bears was given to it on account of the wildness of its scenery, and of the agitation of its waters, resulting from the roughness of its bed. This is one of the most romantic streams which the western country presents. Instead of the wide, and frequently dry bed, in which the other streams run with a slow and lazy pace, Mad River descends in many parts of its course through a narrow and contracted channel, with the rapidity of a torrent. Notwithstanding the uncultivated and uninhabited state of the country, we saw but little game; this consisted of a few deer and wild turkeys, which, however, kept so far from our course as to prevent our firing at any.

The town of Urbanna is small, but neatly laid out. We met here with a family of emigrants lately removed from New Jersey, for the purpose of raising the Palma Christi, and manufacturing from it castor oil, which they propose sending to the eastern cities, by the way of New Orleans; they have already planted twelve acres of it, and, from the experiments which have been made, anticipate much success in this culture.

We stopped for a day at Piqua, a small town situated on the west bank of the Miami river, and on a spot which appears to have been the seat of a numerous Indian population. The river is navigable for keel boats, a few miles above the town, during half the year. The town is built in a semicircular bend of the river, so that its streets, which are rectilinear, and parallel to the chord of the arc, are terminated at both ends by the water. The spot is one of the most advantageous in the country for a large population; the situation is very fine for defence against aggressors; and we find that, with their accustomed discrimination, the Indians had made this one of their principal seats. The remains of their works are very interesting, and being, we believe, as yet undescribed, we surveyed them with such means as were at our disposal. They consist for the most part of circular parapets, the elevation of which varies at present from three to five or six feet, but which bear evident marks of having been at one time much higher; many of them are found in the neighbourhood of the town, and several of them in the town itself. The plough passes every year over some parts of these works, and will probably continue to unite its levelling influence, with that of time, to obliterate the last remains of a people, who, judging from the monuments which it has left behind, must have been far more advanced in civilization than the Indians who were found there a century or two ago; and of whom a few may still be seen occasionally roving about the spot, where their fathers met in council.

We observed one elliptic and five circular works, two of which are on the east bank of the river, the others are on the west. The ground appears, in all cases, to have been taken from the inside, which forms a ditch in the interior; its depth cannot of course be ascertained at present, as it is in great measure filled up, but it must have been considerable. The area, within the ditch, probably retained the level of the surrounding country. The parapet may have been from three to four feet wide, but from slow decay it appears much wider. The first which we visited (A.)* is situated at about a quarter of a mile to the south-west of the town, and half a mile westward of the river; it appears to have been the most important of all, and forms, as it were, the centre round which the others were disposed. Its form is circular; its diameter is about one hundred and fifty feet: it has a gateway from eight to ten feet wide, which faces the river. Immediately connected, and in close contact with it, to the south-south-east, there is a small circular work (*a*), the parapet of which is considerably higher; its diameter is about forty-three feet; it has no gateway or opening whatsoever. It has generally been considered as intended for a look-out post; but this opinion appears incorrect, from the circumstance that it is not raised high enough for this purpose; that its size is much greater than what would be required for a mere post of observation ; and finally, that its construction essentially differs from that which is recorded by Mr. Atwater and other observers, as belonging to such posts of observation. There is nothing to support this opinion but its situation, which is in the most elevated part of the plain. We, however, think it more probable that it was considered as a strong hold, which should be resorted to in the last extremity. This opinion accounts for all the characters which we observe about it. Its situation, near the main fort at the centre of the works ; its smaller dimensions, which, while they would admit a considerable force, would permit it to be defended more easily than the extensive works with which it is connected : the height and thickness of its parapet confirm this belief. The circumstance of there

* See the annexed plan.

being no gateway is an additional proof for us, that it was intended to be used like the citadel of a modern fortress, as the last spot in which the remnants of a defeated army might be concentrated in order to make a decisive stand against their aggressors.

Proceeding in a direction south sixty-five degrees east from the first work, at a distance of about seven hundred and sixty feet, we find another fortification (B.), which, like the former, is partly situated in a ploughed field, but which passes also over a by-road. In this old work, the white man has built his barns, stables, &c., and appears anxious to hurry on the destruction of what would, if uninjured by him, have resisted the assaults of time. The parapet of this fort is not quite so elevated as that of the former; its dimensions are larger, being about two hundred and twenty-five feet in diameter; it has a gateway fronting that in the first fort, and similar to it. If any covered way ever existed by which these two works were connected, it has disappeared, no trace of it being at present visible.

Taking again the first fort (A.) as a centre, and proceeding from it in a course north eighty-five degrees east, we find another circular enclosure (C.), distant seven hundred and fifty feet from the first, and about five hundred and forty feet in a northerly course from the second; its parapets are higher than those of the other two; its diameter is about one hundred and fifty feet; it is provided with a gateway fronting that of the first fort. Between the second and third forts (B. and C.), and near the bank of the river, there are remains of a waterway (W.), formerly connected, as we suppose, with the third fort; these remains consist of a ditch dug down to the edge of the river; the earth from the same having been thrown up principally on the south side, or that which fronts down the river; the breadth between the two parapets is much wider near the water than at a distance from it, so that it may have been used either for the purpose of offering a safe passage down to the river, or as a sort of harbour, in which canoes might be drawn up; or perhaps, as is most probable, it was intended to serve both purposes. This water-way resembles, in some respects, that found near Marietta, but its dimensions are smaller. The remains of this work are at present very inconsiderable, and are fast wasting away, as the road which runs along the bank of the river intersects it, and, in the making of it, the parapet has been levelled and the ditch filled up; this is much to be regretted, as this work, if it could be seen in its perfect state, would perhaps discover the motive which led to the erection of these fortifications, the attacks against which they were intended to provide, and the means by which the resistance was to be effected. But the largest of the works on the western bank still remains to be noticed. This work (D.) is of an elliptical form, and of great eccentricity; its conjugate and transverse diameters measuring eighty-three and two hundred and ninety-five feet; it is situated six hundred feet in a direction north forty degrees east from the first fort, its transverse axis extends nearly east and west; we observed no gateways. This work is almost effaced; its parapet does not rise quite a foot above the ground.

We crossed the river in a canoe, and landed at the foot of a very steep hill, about one hundred feet high. On the top of this hill, remains of a fort (E.) in a very good state of preservation, are to be seen; it lies in a direction north sixty degrees east from the first fort which we visited, and is one hundred and twenty-three feet in diameter; it is placed in a very commanding position, on the brow of the hill which has unfortunately been partially washed away, and has carried down with it about one-third part of the works. There is at present but one gateway visible, which is on the east side, and is about six or eight feet wide. This part of the works is one of the most interesting, it having as yet received no injury from the hands of man. It is covered with trees of a very large size. Upon the top of the parapet we found the trunk of a tree, which had evidently grown long after the rampart had been constructed, and probably long after it had ceased to be the theatre of bloodshed and of assault. The interior part of the trunk was very much decayed; but we counted two hundred and fifty concentric layers in what appeared to be less than the outer half: whence we concluded that this tree was certainly upwards of five hundred years old at the time it was cut down. These works all bear the impress of a very remote antiquity; in some cases, trees of a very large size are seen growing upon the trunks of still larger trees. We have, as we conceive, no data to enable us to refer them to any definite date; but we are well warranted, from all their characters, in assigning to them an antiquity of upwards of one thousand years.

At about fifty rods to the north-north-west of the last-mentioned work there is another, which is circular, and of a much larger size. It has two gateways, one fronting east, and the other west. We did not see this last, but we are indebted to some of the inhabitants of Piqua for a description of it.

About these forts there are, as might be expected, many Indian arrow-heads, and other remains to be found;

those which we saw present however nothing peculiar. We observed both the war and the peace arrow-head, or that which is used in hunting, and which is distinguished from the war arrow-head by the absence of the acute shoulder, with which the war-arrow is always provided, in order to cause it to remain in the wound, from which it cannot be extricated without much danger and pain to the patient: whereas that used in hunting is such as can be withdrawn without difficulty. For the same reason, while the latter is attached to the arrow very firmly, the war head adheres to it but imperfectly: so that after it has entered into the body, if the arrow be withdrawn, the head remains buried in the flesh. Among other things found near these fortifications was a piece of broken pottery, which was considered as of Indian manufacture; but on examining it closely, we immediately recognized it to be a fragment of a small earthen crucible, and from its appearance we believe it to be of French manufacture, as it resembles more the French than the German crucible. Taking this into consideration, and bearing in mind that the first French settlers in this country were constantly looking out for ores of gold, silver, &c., we entertain no doubt that this, instead of being of Indian manufacture, is a fragment of a crucible probably imported from France, and used in some docimastic experiment.

We had an opportunity the ensuing day, on our way to Fort St. Mary, to see the remains of an old Indian work, which consists of stones apparently resulting from the destruction of a stone wall which is supposed to have been erected by the same nation. It is situated about three miles west of Piqua, on a bluff, elevated about thirty feet above the level of the valley of the river. The wall, which is considered by some as having been erected for purposes of defence, stood near the brink of the hill, facing to the south-east. It has been completely thrown down, but its limits may be very distinctly traced by the stones which lie on the ground, forming an ellipsis, whose axes are respectively fifteen hundred and nine hundred feet.* This work is stated, upon the authority of Col. Johnston, to enclose an area of seventeen acres. The longest axis extends in an east and west line; the distance of the nearest point of the ellipsis to the river was estimated to be about seven hundred yards. At its south-eastern part, it is supported by a circular earthen fort, similar to those previously described, and measuring about thirty-six yards in diameter. The stones of which the wall was built are all rolled, mostly granitic; few of them are calcareous: they are in every respect similar to those we find scattered over the country, and especially on the banks of the river. At present they form a loose pavement, about six feet wide round the ellipsis. The figure of the ellipsis deviates in some cases from a strict regularity, probably to accommodate itself to the surface of the country as it then was. In sundry parts, and more especially towards the west side, are many gateways or interruptions in the walls, which are generally from six to eight feet wide. Behind these, and within the area of the ellipsis, we find a number of stones, heaped up in the form of mounds, which are supposed

* This, as well as the measures given for the preceding works, must be taken as approximate. When the distance was small, it was determined by means of a measuring tape; when long, by pacing the ground; the measure of the pace having been first determined by experiment. The courses or directions are correct, having been taken with a compass.

to be the remains of small works, thrown up for the defence of the gateway, and so situated that one munnd will protect two gateways. Although the general opinion seems to be favourable to the idea, that this stone wall was erected as a fortification, we by no means consider this as proved. All the stones which are found there, if arranged so as to form the highest possible wall, would probably not rise above from four and a half to five feet; but, in order to afford the wall any degree of solidity, it would be necessary to give it such a breadth as would probably reduce its height to less than three feet. On the part of those who do not consider this as the remains of a military work, it may be argued, that we have no proof of these stones having ever formed a wall; that they may have been gathered for the purpose of forming the elliptical pavement which they now present. That this may have been constructed from motives which we cannot at present conceive is no proof that such motives may not have existed; further it may be said, that, admitting these stones to be the remains of a wall, it is not probable that it was made for military purposes, as a work of this kind would certainly not have been erected for the protection of a small force, and as a large number of persons collected in it would have been quite unprotected against arrows and other missile weapons. That the situation, though a commanding one, appears quite untenable for want of water, which can only be procured by descending the hill towards the river, in which case the party venturing out would be exposed to be cut off by the enemy. A spring was, it is true, observed within the elliptic enclosure; but the small quantity of water which it affords at present, renders it improbable that it should have been at any time sufficient for the consumption of so large a force as would have been required in the defence of so extensive a work. The number of gateways, it may be said, likewise excludes the possibility of its being intended as a work of defence; for they are very numerous, and sometimes within four or five feet of each other. The unevenness of the ground, part of the wall being along the sides of the hill, and much lower than the rest, may be urged as another strong objection to its being considered as a military work. If it should not have been intended for the purposes of war, what was the intention of those who erected it? Its extent, the labour which it required in order to accomplish it, its form and situation, in fine, all its characters would then concur in leading to the belief that it must have been a religious monument; probably forming an arena where their sacred festivals, their games, their ceremonies could be conveniently carried on. The number of the gates, the heaps of stones which lie near them, all tend to prove that no other origin can be safely ascribed to it. It was suggested that this may perhaps be the remains of a pound, similar to those made by the Indians to this day, for the purpose of entrapping buffalos and other wild animals. But this opinion is likewise excluded by the little resistance which a wall of such small dimensions, formed by the union of uncemented stones but loosely piled together, would have presented to the powerful efforts of the wild animals which it would have been intended to enclose. Its situation, on an uneven ground, likewise excludes this hypothesis from any claim to plausibility.

The stones used vary much in size, from that of a

walnut to the largest which a man may carry. Doubts may exist whether this wall was raised upon an earthen parapet; if there was one of this kind, it has certainly disappeared almost entirely, yet in a few places the elevation formed by the stones appeared greater than might have been expected from the quantity of materials which were observed. It is, therefore, not impossible that, in some places at least, the wall may have been supported by an earthen parapet. The motive for which these stones were collected will probably ever remain a secret; and we must be contented with surmises, all of which are unsatisfactory, because all are founded upon hypothetical manners, which we ascribe to the authors of these works. When we observe a circular rampart with a fosse, a gateway, and a traverse inside of the gateway, we discover a similarity to our modern fortifications, and we immediately consider that this may have been erected for the same purpose; without inquiring into the foundation which we have for assigning to them the same system of fortification which we have adopted. In examining into the character of man, whether civilized or savage, we are, it is true, struck with the powerful influence which two of the most opposite passions, a warlike and religious spirit, will exercise over him; and to one or both of these we may attribute his most astonishing actions, whether good or bad. The experience of every nation proves, that almost all religious faiths have led to the undertaking of vast works. Without recurring to the Egyptian and Indian antiquities, we find in the splendid remains of Greece and Rome, in the colossal and magnificent Gothic cathedrals of the middle ages, and even in the more recent edifices of modern times, that religion has at all periods been the principal motive which induced men to exert their genius, and expend their labour in construction. Judging, by the same test, of the nations long since extinct, which at one time covered the banks of our western streams, we should not be surprised if the remains of their finest works bear the character of having been undertaken, partly at least, with religious views.

On the road from Piqua to this stone wall we passed a very large mound, which had been partially cut down in order to make room for the road. This mound has, as we believe, never been opened. In this vicinity, and near the bank of the river, is the residence of Colonel John Johnston, the Indian agent, a man whom we should judge to be of estimable feelings as, unlike most of the settlers in this new country, he has respected the remains of these Indian works, and has not suffered the ploughshare to pass through them. Colonel Johnston observes, that he does not know that any Indian works have been found due north of Miami county (Ohio), though they occur to the south and south-west as far as the Floridas. (Western Gazetteer, p. 290.) About half a mile to the south of the town at Piqua, there is an old Indian cemetery; it is situated upon a level piece of ground, elevated about twenty feet above high water mark, and in a romantic spot intersected by a small brook. The surface of this place is formed by limestone rocks, lying bare and deposited in horizontal strata. Upon these rocks it appears that the corpses were placed, and that they were covered with slabs of stone, some of which were tolerably large; over these a thin soil has been formed, in the lapse of ages, and this supports a scanty herbage.

Upon reaching the spot, we found that most of these mounds had been broken open, for the purpose of burning into lime the fragments of stone which composed them, and of avoiding thereby the trouble of working into the solid rock. We opened several, but in all cases we found the bones very much injured; indeed, all of them were more or less broken except one, which was evidently a toe bone. They had become very much altered, and were yellow and cellular. We took specimens with us to examine them chemically, with a view to ascertain what changes they had undergone; but they were lost with part of our collections. The objects which seemed to resist decomposition most effectually, were teeth. Of these we found, however, but few, not more than half a dozen; two of them were milk teeth, the rest had belonged to adults; they were rather of a small size, and worn out almost to the root. The bones all lay scattered and without order; they were fragments of the cranium, the arms, shoulders, &c., which almost crumbled under the pressure of the fingers. The only objects that we noticed with them, were the two incisor teeth of a ground squirrel, which were probably of fortuitous deposition.

The rocks in the neighbourhood of Piqua are uniformly composed of a white limestone, of a compact texture, but containing many cavities filled by crystallized carbonate of lime. It is filled with organic impressions, among which Mr. Say determined the Flustra (expanded and branched), the Terebratula, the Caryophillæa, and probably several others. A rolled specimen, which is supposed not to belong to this formation, contained a tolerably good impression of *Favosites striata*, S.

We also found here a specimen of primitive limestone with mica; but it was evidently rolled, and bore no resemblance to the rocks which occur in place in this vicinity. At Piqua the rocks are all very well stratified, the strata being nearly horizontal. This limestone is found to yield, by burning, a lime of a tolerably good quality It is stated that salt springs have been discovered in various places near Piqua, but we met with none.

There is a very considerable rapid in the Miami at this place, which has induced a company to cut a canal for the accommodation of the ascending navigation. This improvement is now completed, and affords them a fine water-power, with a fall of nine feet. This, together with the fertility of the adjoining country, which is represented as formed of a very rich prime soil, of a chocolate colour, will doubtless soon lead to the erection of extensive grist mills at this place; the capital of the company not being adequate to the undertaking, the mills which they have established are by no means suitable to the power of which they can dispose. The Miami is fordable here at almost all seasons of the year, but there is a very good bridge over the river. The name of the town is derived from that of one of the principal tribes of the Shawanese Indians, who formerly roved through this part of the country, spreading themselves as far as the Pickawa Plains, situated about seventy-five miles to the south-east. This tribe is now nearly extinct: the few remaining descendants of it have united themselves with the Miamis, and are settled in the vicinity of Fort Wayne.

After spending a very interesting day in Piqua, in the examination of its antiquities, we left this place with a feeling of gratitude for the kind attentions shewn to our party by the inhabitants of the town, and particularly by the Register of the Land-office, Major Oliver, late of the Army, whose acquaintance with the country made him a very interesting companion in our investigation of the antiquities of the vicinity.

The country through which we travelled lies near the head waters of Loramie creek, one of the tributaries of the Miami. We entered this day upon what may be termed the table land, that divides the waters of the Lakes from those of the Gulf of Mexico, and continued on it, or in its immediate vicinity, until we reached Prairie du Chien on the Mississippi. As we shall have frequent opportunities of recurring to the singular feature which this country presents, in the interlockage, almost every where apparent, between the head streams of two mighty rivers whose waters fall into the ocean at a distance of upwards of two thousand miles, we need not enter at present into many particulars. It will suffice to state, that after leaving the tributaries of the Miami, we came, in less than two hours' ride, to the rivers which send their waters to the Gulf of St. Lawrence. The intermediate country is wet and marshy; there is no appearance of a ridge, properly speaking; it is an elevated flat *plateau*, the nature of which is marshy.

This remarkable feature in the topography of the state of Ohio has not escaped the attention of its inhabitants. We find that the possibility of establishing a connexion between the rivers that discharge themselves into the lakes, and the tributaries of the Ohio, has long since been asserted by the statesmen of the west. The only point which remained unsettled was, what direction should be given to the proposed works, and which of the many routes suggested was preferable? On this point it cannot be doubted that the prerequisite information had not been obtained, and consequently that no decisive answer could be given; in the absence of authentic calculations, prepossessions founded on local interest were, perhaps, allowed to exercise too great sway. To avoid these evils, and with a view of doing justice to the whole state, the legislature of Ohio, by a very liberal policy, appointed a board of commissioners to examine the whole country, make accurate surveys of the various routes which had been suggested, ascertain, by guaging or otherwise, the quantity of water on each route; and finally *locate* lines of canals upon such routes as appeared to them practicable. They were directed to submit the result of their operations to the legislature, who would then be enabled to decide upon the merits of the respective routes.

These duties were too extensive and too arduous to admit of their being executed in one season; and the commissioners have been arrested in many of their surveys by the unhealthiness of the country through which they were obliged to carry on their operations. We have taken pains to acquire information on this interesting subject, and we are inclined to consider that which we have received as correct, because it was obtained from persons conversant with it, and particularly from M. T. Williams, Esq., of Cincinnati, one of the acting commissioners, with whom we had the pleasure of travelling for a few days; and who, in the many conversations which we had with him, has shown himself master of the subject. We have likewise drawn part of our information from the able report made on the 21st January, 1824, by the canal commissioners to the general assembly of Ohio, for copies of which we are indebted to Mr. Williams.

From this report it appears that the routes proposed may be reduced to four, viz;—

The first route would be to connect the waters of the Grand river of Lake Erie with the Ohio, at the mouth of the Big Beaver creek. This route, being very close to the Pennsylvania line, and in some parts east of it cannot be eligible by the state of Ohio, if any other practicable route can be found. From the surveys made by Judge Geddes, or under his direction, it would appear that this summit, which is known by the name of the Mahoning summit level, is elevated three hundred and forty-two feet above Lake Erie, and two hundred and fourteen feet above the Ohio at the mouth of Big Beaver creek.* This canal would therefore require upwards of five hundred and fifty feet of lockage. The question whether or not a sufficiency of water can be obtained on this route is still undecided.

The second route contemplates connecting the Muskingum with the lake, which may be done either by the Tuscarawas and the Cuhayoga creeks, or by the Killbuck and Black rivers; a third division of this route

---

* We have here adopted the measurements given by the canal commissioners in their report, though we are afraid that a mistake may have escaped their notice; the height of this summit level was stated by a gentleman whom we met at Columbus to be three hundred and twenty-four feet, which appears more correct, for by a comparison of the difference of level between Lake Erie and the mouth of the Muskingum, the fall of the Ohio from the town of Beaver in Pennsylvania to Marietta, would be one hundred and fifty-two feet, if we adopt the calculations of the commissioners; whereas, upon the other data it would be but thirty-six feet, which is much more probable.

purposes ascending the Killbuck, continuing along the summit level in an easterly direction to the Cuyahoga and descending that stream to the lake. These three plans may be considered as parts of one general route the preference of any one being a question, which it will only be important to decide, after the propriety of adopting the Muskingum route shall have been decided in the affirmative. The summit level between the Killbuck and Black River, is elevated three hundred and thirty-seven feet above Lake Erie and three hundred and sixty-one above the Ohio at Marietta. It would therefore require near seven hundred feet of lockage. The level between the Cuyahoga and Tuscarawas has been found to be four hundred and four feet above Lake Erie and four hundred and twenty-eight above Marietta. The locks would therefore exceed eight hundred and thirty feet; this section of the Muskingum route. though longer, and crossing a higher summit than that up the Killbuck, would probably be preferred, as being more easily supplied with water.

The third route for the canal is that which would connect the Scioto and Sandusky rivers. These streams, passing nearly in a north and south line through the centre of the state, seem at first sight to be the most eligible for the canal if it be practicable to execute it in this direction. Doubts had been entertained concerning the quantity of water which might be obtained on this summit, but as Judge Geddes and Mr. Forrer had ascertained that most of the head waters of the Great Miami river might be brought upon the summit level of this route, generally designated in Ohio as the Tyamochte level, hopes were entertained that it would prove practicable. This level is elevated about three hundred and fifty-four feet above the lake, and four hundred and fifty-five above the mouth of the Scioto, whence it will require about eight hundred and ten feet of lockage. Upon a further survey of the country, and guaging the streams, the commissioners have however come to the final conclusion, that the supply of water on this route would probably be insufficient to overcome the losses by leakage, evaporation, &c.; and that it would leave no supply of water for the expenditure in the passage of boats through the locks. In their calculations they have assumed as a basis the loss of water by leakage, evaporation, &c. on the New-York canals, which has there proved much greater than had been anticipated, as it amounts to an average of one hundred cubic feet per minute, for every mile of canal route. This amount was reduced by proper allowances for the difference in the nature of the country through which it was contemplated that the canal would pass; but, even with these allowances, they have been led to believe, that " the upper levels on the Sandusky and Scioto route, could not be supplied with the necessary quantity of water in dry seasons, by either of the methods proposed and considered; and the board after deliberating on the subject, from the facts and views laid before them by the acting commissioners, came to the conclusion that a further expenditure of time or money in *locating* a canal line on the Sandusky or Scioto route would be inexpedient, unless some other method should be devised, or some other source of supply discovered." It has therefore become, to say the least, " *extremely* doubtful whether a canal on the Sandusky and Scioto route can ever be made."

The fourth route which has been suggested, and which is termed the western route, has for its object to unite the waters of the Great Miami and Maumee rivers, by means of Loramie creek and the Auglaize river. The summit level in this case will be elevated three hundred and eighty-nine feet above Lake Erie, and five hundred and forty above the Ohio near Cincinnati; occasioning therefore a lockage of about nine hundred and thirty feet. This route appears to be the best supplied with water; it would pass through a section of country inferior to none in America, in the fertility of its soil, or the amount of surplus productions which it is capable of sending to market; it would become a source of immediate and extensive profit, by the quantity of water which it would bring to the termination of the canal at Cincinnati, affording power for extensive and valuable hydraulic works, which are there much needed. The commissioners appear to be of opinion that the bed of the river ought not to be pursued, but that a thorough cut ought to be made. The summit level would be in the vicinity of Fort Loramie. This canal would probably be about two hundred and fifty miles long. The supply of water would be amply sufficient even for locks of the size of those on the New-York canal. Allowing the expense to be the same as in New-York, this canal would probably cost about three millions of dollars; but the experience which has been acquired in the construction of that work, warrants us in believing that a similar undertaking may hereafter be performed at a more economical rate. However this may be, no doubt can exist as to the benefits which Ohio would reap from this canal.

From all that has been stated, it appears that the last of these routes is that which offers at present the most decided advantages, but the plan which the commissioners have in contemplation, and which, if practicable, will we doubt not, at their suggestion, be undertaken by the state of Ohio, is one that would prove as beneficial to that state as it would be honourable to it. This plan would be to make a canal which would unite with the lake as near the north-east angle as nature will permit, and passing through the great vallies of the Muskingum, the Scioto and the Miami, in a south-westwardly direction enter the river Ohio near the south-west corner of the state. The commissioners appear to be aware of the difficulties they will have to encounter; but the data they have already collected on this subject, are favourable to the execution of the scheme, and if, they should be equally successful during the summer of 1824, in establishing the complete connexion, they will have the honour of having suggested a course, which, if it be not adopted at present, will be so at a future time; for, after the undisputed benefits which canals have afforded wherever they have been made, it is impossible to doubt that, with the great natural advantages, which she possesses, Ohio will be among the first to enrol herself among the patrons of an extensive system of internal improvement.

After crossing Loramie creek two or three times, we reached St. Mary's river, which unites at Fort Wayne with the St. Joseph to form the Maumee. The historical recollections which connect themselves with the section of country through which we travelled, compensate the little interest which it offers to the naturalist. To him nothing can be more annoying than to pass over a marshy, swampy country, where no rocks appear *in situ*, and where but few boulders are met with; where the animals are few in number, and apparently afraid to risk themselves in spots in which their speed would avail them but little. It is true, that the pursuits of the botanist might have been carried on successfully, in a situation where an abundant growth of plants would probably have offered him objects worthy of his notice; and this would have compensated the rest of the party for the apparently uninteresting character of the country; for, in an expedition of the nature of ours, the success of each individual in his peculiar pursuit becomes a source of gratification to all. Being, however, unaccompanied by a botanist, we found in this part of Ohio nothing to interest us but the resollection of the busy scenes of war which had, at a former time, been enacted in this district. As the principal field upon which all the military operations of Generals St. Clair, Wayne, and Harrison, were conducted, there is much cause to dwell with pleasure upon the spot. A vast difference exists, however, between the theatre of Indian warfare and that of the military undertakings of civilized nations. The descriptions of the spots, upon which the latter occur, are so much more accurate that they never can be mistaken; while of the former we seldom know the exact seat. Even the history of the defensive works which were erected, soon loses part of its interest by the destruction of the works themselves. We read of the deeds done in the neighbourhood of Fort Loramie by the French, or of the Miami villages by St. Clair, but, if we travel over the ground, we find but few traces of these deeds. At Fort St. Mary, which was one of General Harrison's principal dépôts in 1813 and 1814, we see but the remains of a half-ruined blockhouse, and of a very miserable hut surrounded by pickets, which are fast falling to decay. A few years more and the remains of these works will be sought for by the traveller as unsuccessfully as we now search for the spots upon which St. Clair fought and Wayne conquered. A young growth of trees is rising, which, if not levelled by the axe of the forester, will soon conceal the last traces of the clearing made by Wayne for the advance of his army, which was pointed out to us as Wayne's road.

The party arrived in the afternoon of the 24th of May at Fort St. Mary, just in time to avoid a heavy rain. A solitary log-house marks the spot where a little village formerly throve, under the protection of the French fort, erected at this place. It stands on St. Mary's river, at a distance of fifty-eight miles by land from Fort Wayne; the distance by water is probably about one hundred and thirty-eight miles. The river is navigable, during half the year, for large boats, carrying from one to two hundred barrels; during the rest of the year, in dry seasons, there is scarcely water enough in it to float a canoe, and its course is very much impeded by drift wood. A little limestone of a very inferior quality has been found on the river bank, below the fort. From Piqua to St. Mary the soil is only of second quality, being in many places too wet and swampy for grain. The weather had become very hot; at noon, Fahrenheit's thermometer stood in the shade at eighty-eight degrees. Our party began to suffer much from the inconvenience of mosquitoes and other insects. The entertainment which we received along the road was observed to become more and more rough, and to denote our speedy approach to the last limits of civilization. The cotton-wood tree became much larger as we advanced, Mr. Say noticed the Papilia thoas and ajax in great number.

On leaving, on the 25th May, the miserable hut which had afforded us a shelter during the storm, our route led us along the banks of the St. Mary, which we followed down to its confluence with the St. Joseph, occasionally coming in sight of the river and keeping off from it, at times, according as its course was a straight or devious one: we travelled for twelve miles over the swampy country through which this river flows, after which we came on a beautiful dry prairie, known by the name of Shane's prairie, and at eighteen miles from Fort St. Mary we crossed the river at a settlement called Shanesville; both the prairie and settlement (which consists of but one family), owe their appellation to an interpreter, who is a half-breed Indian, his father was a Canadian, his mother an Ottawa.* He was employed as an interpreter and spy by General Harrison, during his western campaigns, and is considered as having acquitted himself of his duties faithfully; on the conclusion of the war he was rewarded by the grant of half a section (three hundred and twenty acres) of land, which he has divided into town lots; he resides within a short distance of Shanesville on part of his grant. The soil being considered of the best quality, and the situation on the river an advantageous one, he has already sold some parts of it. No man is better known in this part of the country than Shane; his influence among the Indians is great, and he enjoys a high degree of popularity with the white settlers, founded upon the uniformly good character which he maintained during the war, and upon the unbounded confidence reposed in him by General Harrison. He was

---

* ŏ't-t'ǡ-wȧ'. Whenever an Indian word occurs for the first time, its orthography and pronunciation will be indicated by using Walker's key. The sign (') prefixed to a vowel indicates that it is short, while the sign (‛) shows it to be long, the unaccented vowels have the usual quantity.

absent from home at the time we passed there, but we afterwards met with him at Fort Wayne.

The late heavy rains had so much swollen the St. Mary that it was impossible to ford it. We passed it in a canoe—our horses swam across. Fourteen miles of bad roads, leading however through a country remarkable for the excellence of its soil, and for its fine luxuriant growth of white and black oak, beech, hickory, shellbark, &c. brought us to a new settlement, where, notwithstanding the badness of the accommodations, we were happy to find a hospitable reception. Near to this house we passed the state line, which divides Ohio from Indiana.

In the state of Ohio we met with no Indians. Their numbers appear to be diminishing very rapidly. We were informed that they do not exceed two thousand, consisting principally of Ottawas, Miamis, Senecas, Wyandots, &c. This neighbourhood abounds, as we were informed, in wolves, deer, and raccoons; bears are few, and the panther is seldom seen; we met with no wild animal whatever, on this part of our route. The distance from this to Fort Wayne is twenty-four miles, without a settlement; the country is so wet that we scarcely saw an acre of land upon which a settlement could be made. We travelled for a couple of miles with our horses wading through water, sometimes to the girth. Having found a small patch of esculent-grass (which from its colour, is known here by the name of blue-grass), we attempted to stop and pasture our horses, but this we found impossible on account of the immense swarms of mosquitoes (*Culex*) and horseflies (*Tabanus*), which tormented both horses and riders in a manner that excluded all possibility of rest.

At a distance of about nine miles from Fort Wayne we observed a large ash which had been blown down, the tree had been divided in part of its length, and a small trough had been excavated in it, in which an Indian child had been deposited, and the upper segment of the tree replaced to cover the corpse, and the whole secured by a neat little frame. This rude grave had been torn open, doubtless by some white man, to rob it of the trifles with which the tenderness of an Indian parent supplies its offspring when about to travel to the land of spirits. The deceased must have been an infant, for the trough was not more than twelve inches long. We were informed that among the Potawatomis, this is a frequent, though not an universal mode of disposing of their dead. These solid coffins or rude sarcophagi are often suspended in trees.

We arrived at Fort Wayne at an early hour in the afternoon of the 26th of May. The distance from Wheeling to Columbus is one hundred and forty miles, which we travelled in six days; that from Columbus to Fort Wayne amounts to one hundred and fifty-eight miles, which we performed in the same time, making an average of twenty-five miles per day.

CHAPTER III.

Description of Fort Wayne and its vicinity. Fur Trade. Potawatomis.

At Fort Wayne we made a stay of three days, during which our time was usefully and agreeably employed in acquiring some information concerning the manners and institutions of the Indian tribes which inhabit its vicinity. To a person visiting the Indian country for the first time, this place offers many characteristic and singular features. The town or village is small; it has grown under the shelter of the fort, and contains a mixed and apparently very worthless population. The inhabitants are chiefly of Canadian origin, all more or less imbued with Indian blood. Not being previously aware of the diversity in the character of the inhabitants, the sudden change from an American to a French population, has a surprising, and to say the least, an unpleasant effect; for the first twenty-four hours, the traveller fancies himself in a real Babel. The confusion of languages, owing to the diversity of Indian tribes which generally collect near a fort, is not removed by an intercourse with their half-savage interpreters. The business of a town of this kind differs so materially from that carried on in our cities, that it is almost impossible to fancy ourselves still within the same territorial limits ; but the disgust which we entertain at the degraded condition in which the white man, the descendant of the European, appears, is perhaps the strongest sensation which we experience ;

it absorbs all others. To see a being in whom, from his complexion and features, we should expect to find the same feelings which swell in the bosom of every refined man, throwing off his civilized habits to assume the garb of a savage, has something which partakes of the ridiculous as well as of the disgusting. The awkward and constrained appearance of those Frenchmen who had exchanged their usual dress for the breech-cloth and blanket, was as risible as that of the Indian who assumes the tight body coat of the white men. The feelings which we experienced while beholding a little Canadian stooping down to pack up and weigh the hides which an Indian had brought for sale, while the latter stood in an erect and commanding posture, were of a mixed and certainly not of a favourable nature. At each unusual motion made by the white man, his dress, which he had not properly secured, was disturbed, and while engaged in restoring it to his proper place, he was the butt of the jokes and gibes of a number of squaws and Indian boys, who seemed already to be aware of the vast difference which exists between them and the Canadian fur-dealer. The village is exclusively supported by the fur-trade, and will probably continue to thrive as long as the Indians remain in any number in this vicinity. It has, however, declined from year to year, owing to the gradual diminution of the Indian population. The traders seldom leave the town, but they have a number of Canadians in their service, known by the appellation of *Engagés*, who accompany the Indians during their summer hunts, supply them with goods in small quantities, and keep an eye upon them, so that they shall not defraud their employers by selling to others the produce of their hunts. The furs brought here consist, principally, of deer and raccoon skins; bear, otter, and beaver, have become very rare. The skins, when brought by the Indians, are loosely tied or rolled; they are separated, folded, and made into packs three feet long and eighteen inches wide, which are exposed to a heavy pressure under a wedge press. These packs generally contain from forty to fifty deer skins, and about two hundred raccoon skins. Bear skins, being rare, are not put up in packs, but are used to cover the other furs. The prices of skins vary every season, according to their quality and abundance. In 1823, the skins were worth at Fort Wayne—

For Deer (bucks)	Sp. D. 1 25
(does)	1 00
Raccoon	50
Bear	3 00 to 5 00

The quantity of furs annually made up at this post is, as we are informed by a competent and disinterested judge, about two hundred packs, the average value of which may be fifty dollars each, making an aggregate of ten thousand dollars. But this value is rather a nominal than a real one, as the furs are paid for to the Indians at the prices just quoted, in goods which are passed off to them at a price at least double the amount of prime cost and expense of transportation. So that to the dealer the real expense attending the purchase of furs does not amount to one-half of their nominal value. They are usually sent down the Maumee to Lake Erie, and thence to Detroit, where they are for the most part purchased by the American Fur Company. At the time when we visited Fort Wayne, the number of Indians there was considerable. This is one of the stations at which the Potawatomis, Miamis, &c. receive their annuities. The late Indian agent, Mr. Hays, was on the point of leaving the post, previous to which he was desirous of paying them an annuity, but this being the time of the year when they attend to their farming avocations, the chiefs had used their influence to keep their people from going to the fort. This delay prevented the immediate distribution of the annuity, and offered to the most idle and worthless of the tribes an inducement and an excuse for frequenting the town.

Fort Wayne, as it now stands, was erected in 1814, on the site of the old fort, the situation of which had been selected by General Wayne after his victory over the Indians. It is a square palisade, protected at two of its angles by block houses, calculated to be defended by artillery. The fort is considered as a good specimen of stockade fortification, which answers very well as a defence in Indian warfare. An improvement which it possesses, and which these works do not all present, is that of giving to the roofs of the barracks and other buildings enclosed by the palisade an inclination in one direction only, and this towards the area of the work; the advantage of which is to afford to the besieged a protection against their assailants, when forced to ascend the roofs, in order to put out fires occasioned by arrows conveying combustibles to the tops of houses, as is frequently practised by the Indians. The fort lies on the east side of St. Mary's river, immediately opposite to its junction with the St. Joseph. On the other side of the Maumee we were shown the spot rendered conspicuous by the defeat of General Harmer's army in 1791. This might, we think, more correctly be called Harden's defeat, as by the account of it furnished both by Marshall and Ramsay, it appears that the detachment that was cut up was commanded by Colonel Harden.* Indeed, the whole of the country about the upper part of the Grand Miami and Maumee (generally called in the history of that war the Miami and Miami of the lake,) is interesting, as being the theatre of the war which raged from 1791 to 1794, when a stop was put to it by the great victory achieved by by General Wayne over the confederated Indian nations, on the 20th of August of that year. This may be considered as one of the most memorable events in our history, since the close of the war of the revolution, as it was obtained in front of a British fort which had been erected at the Maumee rapids evidently for the protection of the Indians.

General Wayne's victory was soon followed by the treaty of Greenville, concluded by him in the succeeding year; a treaty " by which the expensive and destructive war which had long desolated that frontier, was ended in a manner perfectly agreeable to the United States."

The situation of Fort Wayne was considered at the time of that treaty, as a favourable one to keep the Indians in check, and prevent the recurrence of the hostile measures which terminated in that treaty. It was one of the most advanced posts of the *cordon* which was drawn along the western limits of Ohio for the protection of the frontiers. It must be admitted that its position is a very judicious one for a work of this kind, although it would be very improper in a war with an enemy possessed of artillery, as it is commanded by several eminences in the vicinity. During the late

* Marshall's Life of Washington, vol. iii. p. 302.

war, it was besieged for some time by the Indians, and a few men were killed on both sides. The garrison having made resistance, the Indians cut a log into the form of a field-piece, painted it black, and placed it on one of the heights within gunshot of the fort; they then summoned the garrison to surrender. Although aware that all resistance against artillery would be vain, the officer in command refused to comply with the summons. The Indians, finding their *ruse de guerre* to be unsuccessful, raised the siege.

No garrison is at present kept up at this place, and it is probable that even in the case of a future war, this post, like many others formerly considered of great importance, will be so surrounded with a white population, as to render any military force in its vicinity unnecessary. The works offer now a comfortable and suitable residence to the gentlemen attached to the Indian department. The removal of the garrison, and the decrease of the fur trade, will probably effect for a while the growth of the settlement. But it will eventually resume the importance to which it is entitled from its advantageous situation; as a central point at which three respectable streams connect, it must become the seat of an extensive trade. The St. Mary being navigable during part of the year for one hundred and thirty miles, the St. Joseph for fifty miles, and the Maumee offering during the spring, to boats carrying three hundred barrels, a free navigation along the whole of its course to Lake Erie, (one hundred and sixty miles,) a considerable quantity of produce will necessarily pass at Wayne. The prosperity of the town will be increased by the arrangements made by the government of the United States for the sale of the public land in the vicinity. At the time we passed through, we were informed that all the land about the village, and even that upon which it stands, was public property, but that orders had been issued to sell the whole, with the exception of about thirty acres near the fort, which were reserved for the use of the Indian agency. This accounted for the mean appearance of the houses, which are of log, rudely put up, the roofs being made of clap boards kept down by logs. No person felt inclined to lay out money in building on property which could not be sold. The point of land upon which the town stands appears to be sandy, and of an inferior quality, but we were told that a very excellent soil prevailed in the vicinity. It was expected that the property would sell well, and it was thought that the quarter section, (160 acres,) upon which the town is situated, would yield at public sale ten thousand dollars. We were somewhat surprised to find that the inhabitants of the town expressed no dissatisfaction at the prospect of the sale of a property upon which they had been residing, free of rent, for so many years, and that not the least question was raised as to the justice or propriety of a measure, by which they were about to be dispossessed of the small improvements which had been made by their fathers and themselves. But the population of Wayne partakes in this respect of the indifference and carelessness that characterize the two races from the admixture of which they have sprung. A circumstance which will add considerably to the future prosperity of Wayne, is its being at the commencement of the short portage of eight miles which separates the Maumee from the Wabash. An extensive trade has already been carried on through this route, and as it offers the most direct communication between the head of Lake Erie and the northern parts of Indiana, it will doubtless daily increase in importance.

In the vicinity of Fort Wayne, on the west bank of the river, we were shown a small tree growing on the spot where "Little Turtle" was buried. This was one of the most celebrated Indian chiefs ever known to white men. His character is well remembered by the old residents among the Indians, and from the accounts which have been given of him, we find but few names on record in the history of Indian chiefs that can be compared to his. His character will contrast advantageously with those of King Philip Pontiac, and Tecumseh. The influence which he appears to have possessed over the Indians was unbounded. Under these circumstances, it is to be regretted that all the facts connected with his life and character, have not been collected with care. He is the same whom Volney describes as having met with in Philadelphia in the year 1798. From the abstract furnished us by this able traveller of the conversations which he had with Little Turtle and with his interpreter, Captain Wells, we are led to form a very high opinion of the sound philosophy, and excellent judgment possessed by this chief. Of his military talents we can entertain no doubt, since it is well ascertained that to him is chiefly to be ascribed the success which the Indians met with during the years 1791 and 1792. Like King Philip, Tecumseh, &c. he is said to have entertained at one time the hope of forming an extensive coalition among the Indians, with a view to retrieve the soil of which they had been so unjustly deprived; but meeting with difficulties, which he probably foresaw would be invincible, he, with more foresight than either of those chiefs, soon discovered that the day for such measures had long since passed away, and that the only advisable course, which remained for his nation to adopt, would be to make peace with the invaders, and endeavour to improve by their superior information. In this manner he succeeded in rescuing them from that destruction, to which King Philip and Tecumseh were hurrying on their brethren, at the time that they themselves became victims to the wars which they had been instrumental in producing. Doubtless his great spirit flattered itself with the hope that, by an advancement in the arts of civilized life, his brethren would regain that importance which they seemed to be on the point of losing for ever. He had predicted the awful consequences of the approach of white men, "No wonder," said he, "the whites drive us every year further and further before them, from the sea to the Mississippi. They spread like oil on a blanket; and we melt like snow before the sun. If things do not greatly change, the red men will disappear very shortly." How well-founded this apprehension has proved, and how rapidly the prediction has been verified, let the experience of every traveller to the west attest.

Little Turtle died in the year 1804 or 1805, and his death at that time is very much to be regretted, as the attachment which he had contracted for the American nation had become so great, that it is presumed he would have used his influence, which was very great, to prevent the Indians of that vicinity from joining the British during the late war; and no doubt can be entertained that a peaceful policy, if supported by a man of his weight, would have prevailed.

The naturalists to the expedition being aware that few or no skulls of Indians exist in the collections of our Atlantic cities, were desirous of procuring some, and among others they would have been pleased to obtain that of this celebrated chief. It would, in their opinion, have been interesting to observe, whether the examination of this head would have afforded any support to the new, and as yet uncertain, science of Phrenology. The principal traits which have been collected of the character of Little Turtle might have been compared with the developments of the brain, and this comparison would perhaps have led to some interesting results. They were likewise in hopes, that by disinterring it they might have rescued, (for a while at least) from final decay, the head of one of the greatest men who, to our knowledge, have adorned the character of the American aborigines. But upon consulting with the gentlemen of the Indian department, they found that the memory of Little Turtle was so much revered by his nation, and the visits of Indians to the grave of departed friends were so frequent, that such an attempt could not pass unnoticed, and that this apparent sacrilege would doubtless irritate them, and might lead to unpleasant consequences. The hope of obtaining this head was therefore abandoned.

The expedition was as kindly treated as they could have wished, by the gentlemen attached to the Indian department at this place. General Tipton, (the present Indian agent,) and Mr. Hays, (the late agent,) afforded them all the facilities in their power; and to Mr. Kerchevel, the sub-agent, they are under great obligations for the information which his long experience of the Indians, and his acquaintance with their language enabled him to communicate. In order to afford to the party an opportunity of obtaining the best information, General Tipton sent for one of the principal chiefs in that vicinity, with whom they conversed for two days.

The name of this man is Metea,* (which signifies in the Potawatomi language, *Kiss me.)* He was represented to us as being the greatest chief of the nation; we had, however, an opportunity of ascertaining afterwards, that he is not the principal chief, but that he has, by his talents as a warrior and his eloquence as an orator, obtained considerable influence in the councils of his nation. He may be considered as a partisan, who, by his military achievements, has secured to himself the command of an independent tribe. He resides on the St. Joseph, about nine miles above Fort Wayne, at an Indian village called Muskwawasepeotan,† *(town of the old red wood creek.)* Being a chief of distinction, he came accompanied by his brother; as his rank required that he should be assisted by some one to light his pipe, and perform such other duties as always devolve upon attendants. Metea appears to be a man of about forty or forty-five years of age; he is a full-blooded Potawatomi; his stature is about six feet; he has a forbidding aspect, by no means deficient in dignity; his features are strongly marked, and expressive of a haughty and tyrannical disposition; his complexion is dark; like most of the Potawatomis whom we met with, he is characterized by a low, aquiline, and well-shaped nose; his eyes are small, elongated, and black; they are not set widely apart; his forehead is low and receding; the facial angle amounts to about 80°. His hair is black, and indicates a slight tendency to curl; his cheek bones are remarkably high and prominent, even for those of an Indian; they are not, however, angular, but present very dis-

* Mĕ-t'ĕ-ă'. † Mŭs-kwă-w'ă-s'ĕ-p'ĕ-ŏ'-t'ăn.

tinctly the rounded appearance which distinguishes the aboriginal American from the Asiatic. His mouth is large, the upper lip prominent; there is something unpleasant in his looks, owing to his opening one of his eyes wider than the other, and to a scar which he has upon the wing of his nostril. On first inspection, his countenance would be considered as expressive of defiance and impetuous daring, but upon closer scrutiny, it is found rather to announce obstinate constancy of purpose, and sullen fortitude. We behold in him all the characteristics of the Indian warrior to perfection. If ever an expression of pity or of the kinder affections belonged to his countenance, it has been driven away by the scenes of bloodshed and cruelty through which he has passed. His dress was old and somewhat dirty, but appeared to have been arranged upon his person with no small degree of care; it consisted of leather leggings buttoned on the outside, a breech-cloth of blue broadcloth, and a short checked shirt over it; the whole was covered with a blanket, which was secured round his waist by a belt, and hung not ungracefully from his shoulders, generally concealing his right arm, which is rendered useless and somewhat withered, from a wound received during the late war, when he attacked with a small party of Indians, the force that was advancing to the relief of Fort Wayne. His face was carefully painted with vermillion round his left eye. Four feathers, coloured without taste, hung behind him secured to a string, which was tied to a lock of his hair. In our second interview with him, he wore a red and white feather in his head, that was covered with other ornaments equally deficient in taste. Mr. Seymour took a likeness of him, which was considered a very striking one, by all who knew Metea. (Plate III.)

The chief was accompanied by his brother, who is much younger and resembles him, but whose features indicate a more amiable and interesting disposition. We observed, that during the interview, the latter treated Metea with much respect, always preparing and lighting his pipe, and never joining in the conversation, unless when addressed by the chief. On entering the room where the gentlemen of the party were, Metea shook hands with the agent, but took no notice of the rest of the company, until General Tipton had explained to him, through his interpreter, the nature of the expedition; the objects of his great father, the President, in sending it among the Indians; and the information which would be expected from him; he informed him likewise that his time and trouble would be suitably rewarded. The chief then arose from his seat, shook hands with all who were present, told them that he would very willingly reply to all their questions, but that according to usage, he was bound to repeat to his nation all the questions that would be asked, and the replies which he would make; that there were certain points, however, on which he could give no information, without having first obtained the formal consent of his community: that on those subjects he would remain silent, while to all others he would reply with cheerfulness, and that after they should have concluded their inquiries, he would likewise ask them some questions, upon points which he thought concerned his nation, and to which he trusted they would in like manner reply. He then resumed his seat, and answered with much intelligence, and with a remarkable degree of patience, all the questions which were asked of him.

The Potawatomis, whose name, as sounded by them-

themselves, is Potawatome,* (in their language, "we are making fire,") appear to be connected not only by language, but also by their manners, customs, and opinions, with the numerous nations of Algonquin origin. The languages of all these nations bear evident marks of a common origin, and in some cases appear only to be dialects of the same tongue; and although diversities of dress and of dialect distinguish them, their customs and usages are evidently, for the most part, the same. Their traditions as to their origin are very uncertain. They believe that the first meeting between them and the Miamis occurred at a time not very remote.

The Potawatomis resided on the banks of Lake Michigan. Of their first meeting with the Miamis, the following tradition appears to be fresh in the recollection of all. It is said that a Miami, having wandered out from his cabin, met three Indians whose language was unintelligible to him; by signs and motions he invited them to follow him to his cabin, where they were hospitably entertained, and where they remained until dark. During the night, two of the strange Indians stole from the hut, while their comrade and host were asleep; they took a few embers from the cabin, and placing these near the door of the hut, they made a fire, which being afterwards seen by the Miami and his remaining guest, was understood to imply a council fire in token of peace between the two nations. From this circumstance the Miami called them in his language Wahonaha,† or the makers, which being translated into the other language, produced the term by which this nation has ever since been distinguished.‡ All the Indians of this part of the

* Pŏ-tă-w'ă-tŏ'-mè.   † W'ă-h'ŏ-nă-hă.

‡ This tradition, together with a considerable part of the circumstances

country recognise their alliance with the Delaware Indians, whom they seem to consider as their forefathers, applying to them in councils the appellation of " Grandfathers," and recognising their right of interfering and of deciding in last resort in all their national concerns. This right extends, however, only so far as to make their approbation necessary to the adoption of any important measure. Should it be withheld, the matter is again referred to the nations, for consideration in their separate councils; and should they persevere in the measure, it would bring on a separation of the alliance, and the nation refusing to submit to the decision of their grandfathers, would be considered as strangers. No such instance is, however, recorded, and it is a remarkable trait in the character of all Indian institutions, as far as we observed, that the principle of the binding influence of the will of the majority is unknown. In all their decisions, unanimity must be obtained, and very seldom fails to be procured. Firmness of purpose and an invincible perseverance in all plans against national enemies, seem with them to be united to a great spirit of conciliation among themselves, and to an indifference as to the final result of any measure which they advocate in their councils. The success of a measure depends altogether upon the personal influence of the man who brings it forward. If he be one whom they deem wise in his generation, or if he be supposed to be gifted with supernatural talents, they will yield to his suggestions without

which we shall embody in the following pages, was obtained from the Agent's Interpreter, Mr. Joseph Barron, a man whose long residence among the Indians, extensive acquaintance with their character, together with his unimpeachable veracity, confer much value upon all the information obtained from him.

opposition; if, on the contrary, he be possessed of but little weight, he meets with no support, and his good sense probably induces him to relinquish his scheme.

When the Miamis first met with the Potawatomis, they applied to them the title of younger brothers; but this was afterwards changed, and their seniority acknowledged, from the circumstance that they resided further to the west; as those nations which reside to the west of others are deemed more ancient. This was settled in a council of the two nations, held some time after their first meeting; the Potawatomis being at present acknowledged and styled elder brothers, and the Miamis younger brothers: but the council fire is always held with the Miamis. By some it is mentioned, that they have no recollection of the Potawatomis having ever assisted at any council fire but one, which was held on the St. Joseph, (of Lake Michigan?) and at which the Chippewas, Potawatomis, and Ottowas were present.*

Their notions of religion appear to be of the most simple kind; they believe in the existence of an only God, whom they term Kashamaneto,* or Great Spirit. Kasha means great, and Maneto an irresistible almighty being. The epithet of Kasha is never applied to any other word, but as connected with the Supreme Being. It would be highly indecorous to apply it to a

* This statement is taken from a valuable manuscript of observations concerning the Indians, communicated to the party by Dr. Thomas P. Hall, Surgeon U. S. A. Dr. Hall was stationed at Chicago at the time we visited that post. His opportunities of obtaining information were such, as to render his notes valuable, and they are particularly so in the medical parts, from which we have made many extracts. As the observations, which he made, relate principally to the Potawatomis, it has been thought proper to connect them with those made at Fort Wayne.

† Kå-sh'à-må-nè-t'ò.

house, a horse, or any other visible object. Yet it is, in a few instances, applied to a good man, in order to give more force to the expression, by connecting his good qualities with those which they ascribe to the Great Spirit. They recognise also an Evil Spirit, whom they call Matchamaneto* (from matcha, which signifies bad). This unfavourable epithet is not restricted in its application, but is extended to all unpleasant or disagreeable objects. They consider themselves as indebted to the Good Spirit for the warm winds from the south, while the Evil one sends the cold winds and storms of the north. The Matchamaneto resides in the cold regions of the north, where the sun never shines. The Kashamaneto, on the contrary, dwells at the "midday-sun's place." Their worship appears to be principally addressed to the Evil Spirit, whom they think it expedient to propitiate; the good one needing no prayers, for his natural goodness will always induce him to assist and protect man without being reminded of it by his petitions; neither do they believe that their prayers to the Evil Spirit can in any manner displease the Good. In certain cases, however, as when afflicted with disease, or when impelled to it in a dream, they will offer a sacrifice of living animals to the Kashamaneto. This is generally done at the suggestion of one of the chiefs or leaders, who calls all the warriors together, explains to them his views, and appoints one of them to go in search of a buck, to another he commits the killing of a raccoon, to a third he allots some other animal to be killed; and when they have been successful in their respective hunts, they meet and fasten the first buck which they kill, upon a high pole, and leave it in this

* Mât-ch'à-má-nè-t'ô.

situation, so that it may serve as a sacrifice to the Great Spirit. Any other animal would answer as well as a buck. Upon the remainder of the chace they feast. After having boiled the animal, they partake of it in the name of the Great Spirit. The object of these sacrifices is to obtain luck in their pursuits, whether of hunting or fighting; these feasts are generally accompanied with prayers, dancing, singing, &c. The only period when they have regular sacrifices is during the winter and spring of the year, at which time many of the warriors give feasts; each selects the time that suits him best, and invites such guests as he thinks proper. Having assembled them all, he rises, takes a sort of tambourine formed by fastening a piece of skin or parchment upon a frame, he beats upon this and addresses himself to the divinity, accompanying his invocation by many violent gestures. They have no set form of prayer; when he has concluded, he resumes his seat, hands over the tambourine to another, who proceeds in the same manner. They have regular songs, which they sing together on such occasions. No other music is ever used but that of the tambourine.*

Among the Potawatomis polygamy is not only allowed but even encouraged; a man has two or more wives, sometimes four, according to his skill and success as a hunter. The number of wives which an Indian keeps, is equal to that which he can support and maintain; he,

* Among the Shawanese there is a solemn festival called the green corn dance, which resembles the offering of the first fruits as enjoined to the Israelites. This practice is said to exist among the Creeks, Cherokees, and other southern tribes, but is unknown to the Potawatomis and other nations, which live in the neighbourhood of the Shawanese. It is said, that among the latter, however ripe an individual's corn may be, h will not pluck it until after the celebration of the festival.

therefore, that has many, is respected as being a better or more favoured hunter than he that has but one wife. Dr. Hall observes that polygamy exists in the proportion of twenty-five per cent., that some men have three, four, or five wives, and one man was known to have eight. They appear to be very attentive to the proper education to be given to children, in order to impart to them those qualities both of the mind and body, which shall enable them to endure fatigue and privation, and to obtain an influence, either in the councils of the nation, or during their military operations. When questioned on this subject, Metea replied, that while he was yet very young, his father began to instruct him, and incessantly, day after day, and night after night, taught him the traditions, the laws and ceremonies of his nation. "This he did," said Metea, "that I might one day benefit my country with my counsel." The education of boys generally commences at ten or twelve years of age; they accustom them early to the endurance of cold, by making them bathe every morning in winter. They likewise encourage them to habituate themselves to the privation of food. In this manner, children are observed to acquire, more readily, the qualifications which it is desirable for an Indian to possess. Parents use no compulsory means to reduce their children to obedience, but they generally succeed in obtaining a powerful influence over them, by acting upon their fears; they tell them that if they do not behave themselves as they are bid, they will irritate the Great Spirit, who will deprive them of all luck as hunters, and as warriors. This, together with the constant and never ceasing importance, which the children observe, that their parents attribute to luck in all their pursuits, is found to have the desired effect upon the minds of young persons, fired with the ambition of becoming distinguished, at some future day, by their skill and success. Their fasts are marked by the ceremony of smearing their faces, hands, &c. with charcoal. To effect this, they take a piece of wood of the length of the finger, and suspend it to their necks, they char one end of it, and rub themselves with the coal every morning, keeping it on until after sunset. No person, whose face is blackened, dare eat or drink any thing during that time; whatever may be the cravings of his appetite, he must restrict them until the evening arrives, when he may wash off his black paint, and indulge, moderately, in the use of food. The next morning he repeats the ceremony of blackening his face, and continues it from day to day, until the whole of his piece of wood be consumed, which generally takes place in the course of from ten to twelve days.

After this term, they either suspend their mortifications, or continue them according as the exigencies of the case seem to require. From the information which was communicated by the interpreter and others, it does not appear that, in any one instance, have the Indians ever been known to break their fasts, whatever may have been the temptation to which they were exposed; so powerful, indeed, is their superstitious dread of that ill luck, which would attach to a transgression of their rules, that even children have been, in vain, tempted to take food when at the houses of traders, and beyond the control of their parents; in all cases they have declined it; neither does it appear that, during those seasons of mortification, they indulge after sunset, in any unreasonable gratification of their appetite; in this respect, therefore, they prove themselves more consistent than the Mahometans, who are said, while their Ramadam or lent lasts, to make up by the debaucheries in which they indulge in the night time, for the painful restrictions imposed upon them during the day, by the precepts of their prophet. The same apprehensions which will prevent an Indian, whether man or boy, from tasting food, while covered with this coating of charcoal, will not allow him to shorten the term of his penance by consuming the piece of wood too hastily. If he does not use it sparingly he is certain that the charm or virtue with which he invests it, will be dispelled. In addition to these mortifications, the Indian attempts to impress upon his offspring a permanent and unshaken belief in the existence of a Great Spirit, ruler of the universe, whose attributes are kindness to men, and a desire of relieving them from all their afflictions: the necessity of doing all that may be grateful to him is often recurred to, in those exhortations by which every Indian parent instructs his sons, both morning and evening. It does not appear that the same care is extended to the religious principles of females. We never heard of their joining in fasts or mortifications; they are not allowed to take a part in the public sacrifices, and as they have no concern in the noble occupations of war or the chace, it probably matters but little whether or not they are agreeable in the sight of the Great Spirit. The only inducement which they have to pray is, that they may continue to hold a place in the affections of their husbands; but the men, being quite indifferent upon this point, would deem it unworthy of their superior rank in the creation, to bestow a thought upon the subject.

These Indians are represented as displaying, among

the men of their own tribe, many of the virtues which have long been considered as peculiar to man in a state of civilization. Children incapacitated from labour or exertion, by accident or deformity, are carefully attended to, and seldom allowed to suffer, from a privation of any of the comforts which the rest of the tribe enjoy. It is considered disgraceful in a man, to inflict any injury upon a helpless or unprotected person. It is said that, in a few instances, children born deformed have been destroyed by their mothers; but these instances are rare and, whenever discovered, uniformly bring them into disrepute, and are not unfrequently punished by some of the near relations. Independent of these cases, which are but rare, a few instances of infanticide, by single women, in order to conceal intrigue, have been heard of; but they are always treated with abhorrence. In like manner, when going out on hunting excursions, elderly parents have been known to be abandoned or exposed to a certain death; but these were likewise rare cases, which may be considered as always carrying with them a severe punishment, by the utter contempt and detestation in which those who committed them were held. When questioned upon this point, Metea denied that it had ever happened; "as they have taken pains to raise us when we were young," said he, "it is but fair that we should return this care to them in their old age." Instances have, however, occurred even among the Potawatomis; one of which took place on the Milwacke, when a decrepit old woman, who had no horse to remove her from that place, was burned by them. In painful and violent diseases, Indians are sometimes killed at their own request, and afterwards burned to prevent contagion or the disease falling upon another. Their attention to old persons, and their respect towards them, may be considered as virtues in which they pride themselves most, and which they exercise most frequently. To ideots they likewise generally extend a kind and humane treatment. By their relations, ideots are always treated with tenderness; but the idle and foolish, who are not connected with them, though they never abuse, will sometimes ridicule them; in this respect, imitating the treatment to which they are so inhumanly, yet so frequently exposed, from the unthinking, even among civilized nations. There are some persons among them who think that ideots are possessed of more intellect than they make show of, and who believe them to be endued with much intelligence; but by none are they held in the light of sorcerers. The same opinion is likewise entertained of insane persons, who are supposed by some to hold converse with the Deity; this opinion is not, however, universally adopted. Care is taken, in the physical education of the Potawatomi, from his earliest age, that his body should be straight and well-formed; no attempt, however, is made to change the shape of the head: the observations which have been made on this subject by various travellers, apply only to certain nations, one of which is designated by the term of *Flat-heads*, and it is highly incorrect to consider them as general. The shape of the head is one of the features which assist most in the discrimination of the various tribes. It is at least as easy, for a person well acquainted with the Indians, to distinguish between the different nations, as it is among white men to observe differences between the various races that inhabit Europe; to an Indian this is even easier, as his long habits of scrutiny have made him quick at noticing differences which would escape the attention of less practised observers. "We know every tribe at first sight," said Little Turtle, " the shape, colour, legs, knees, and feet, are all to us certain marks of distinction."

If, in the intercourse of the Potawatomi with men of his own tribe, we observe many of the virtues and finer feelings which adorn mankind in all situations; we have, unfortunately, cause to regret, that in his conduct towards other nations, he appears under very disadvantageous colours. To a stranger, if he be not an enemy, it is true, that he will extend the most unrestricted hospitality: his principles, as well as his habits of life, prevent his greeting him, or joining him in conversation; but all that the most liberal spirit can do, to secure to him a friendly and fraternal reception, is cordially done. In all his actions, words, and motions, the stranger must, however, take heed lest he reveal himself to be an enemy; for in that case, not the bread that they have been breaking together, nor the tobacco of which they have both smoked, nor the sacred laws of hospitality, could protect the guest from the vengeance which the Potawatomi considers as enjoined upon him by the paramount obligation of destroying his enemy, or that of his nation, wherever he may meet with him. Their feeling of hatred and resentment against all nations with which they are at war, has led them to deeds, from the recital of which we shrink with disgust. Among these there is none more horrible, and on the subject of which so much difference of opinion has existed, as that of cannibalism, as ascribed to them by numerous travellers. We find it asserted, in plain terms, by some of the oldest writers upon America.* But it has been brought into question by many, who, having never visited the Indians, have been influenced by a laudable incredulity, springing doubtless from a justifiable wish to close their eyes and ears against evidence which bears so hardly upon human nature. With these feelings the gentlemen of the expedition first heard the reports of the anthropophagi of the Potawatomi, and yielded but

---

* The fact which we advance here of the cannibalism of the Potawatomis, is not new, as regards the North American Indians, though some travellers may have asserted it not to exist among them.

"I think," says Hennepin, "that the Neros and Maximinians of old never invented greater cruelties to test the patience of martyrs, than the torments to which the Iroquois expose their enemies. And when we saw that their children were cutting slices of flesh from the slave whom their parents had murdered with the most unheard of cruelties, and that these young anthropophagi were eating the flesh of this man in our own presence, we withdrew from the hut of the chief, and we would eat with them no longer, and we retraced our steps through forests to Niagara river."—Page 40, and again, in page 304.

" In this confusion it was not difficult for the Iroquois, united with the Miamis, to carry away about eight hundred slaves, both women and young men. These anthropophagi ate immediately several old men of the Illinoies nation, and burned a few others who had not strength enough to follow them to the country of the Iroquois, more than four hundred leagues distant." He however makes an exception in favour of the Nadiousioux, (Sioux?) whom he asserts, "not to be so inhuman, and not to partake of human flesh." (Page 68. Description de la Louisianne, &c. &c. par le R. P. Louis Hennepin, &c. Paris. 1683. 12mo.)

Even Adair, who may be considered as the great sceptic on this subject, in the same page in which he rejects the charge as a false one, states that he could not learn " that they had eaten human flesh, only the heart of the enemy, which they all do sympathetically, (blood for blood,) in order to inspire them with courage." * * * * " To eat the heart of an enemy will, in their opinion, like eating other things before mentioned, communicate and give greater heart against the enemy," &c. Page 135. History of the American Indians, by James Adair, Esq. London, 1774. 4to.

an unwilling ear to every thing that could induce a belief in the existence of this disgusting trait in the character of the north-west Indians. Truth compels them however to assert, that the reports which they have received on this subject were so frequent, so circumstantial, and derived from such respectable sources, that any concealment of it, or any apparent incredulity on their part, would be a dereliction of duty. Even the most incredulous of the party, or those disposed to entertain the most favourable opinion of the Indians, were at last compelled to acknowledge that all doubt on the subject had been removed from their minds. They have been asked, whether they had ever been present at such a feast? and they have heard it asserted by respectable persons, that nothing but the autoptical observation of the travellers, could induce them to place any credit in this imputed cannibalism; to this it may be replied, that, travelling as they did, at a time when the Indians were comparatively in a state of peace, when few and but accidental hostilities had occurred among them, and these always at a distance from the route which they pursued; it could not be expected that they should have been themselves eye-witnesses to these infamous orgies. But if it can be adduced in support of their assertion, that the fact has been acknowledged by the Indians themselves, by those that had perpetrated the deed, that it has been uniformly admitted by the interpreters and traders who have long resided among them, who are connected to them by the intermixtures, who are themselves partly Indians, and who declare that they have been present at the time it took place; if the names of the individuals who became victims to it, can be mentioned; if the additional circumstance of its having been observed at several thousand of miles distance, but among those Indians who are known to be of the same nation, and who speak dialects of the same language, be taken into consideration; if these facts should be corroborated by names expressive of this custom, given to certain places by the Indians themselves, and if all these should be found to concur with the observations recorded in the histories of the first travellers in America (who, whatever may have been their errors, must be considered as having adhered more closely to truth than is generally supposed); then, with all this circumstantial evidence strongly and uniformly bearing on one side of the question, is it possible for the most sceptical to refuse his belief to this fact, whatever may be the horror which attends it? We are far however from asserting, that this practice has prevailed universally among the Indians; the evidences on the subject of the cannibalism of the Dacota or Sioux Indians (Naudowessies of Carver) are too few and too suspicious; they are refuted by too many contradictory facts to permit us to place any confidence in them; but the case is otherwise with the Chippewas, the Miamis, the Potawatomis, and all the other Indian nations, which are known to be of Algonquin origin.

The motives which impel them to cannibalism are various: in some cases it is produced by a famine over the country, and of this we shall be able to cite a number of well attested instances, some of which carry with them very horrible features, when we treat of the Chippewa tribes, west of Lake Superior. Another, and a more frequent cause, is the desire of venting their rage upon a defeated enemy, or a belief that, by so doing, they acquire a charm that will make them irresistible. It is a common superstition with them, that he that tastes of the body of a brave man acquires a part of his valour, and that if he can eat of his heart, which by them is considered as the seat of all courage, the share of bravery which he derives from it is still greater. It matters not whether the foe be a white man or an Indian; provided he be an enemy, it is all that is required. Mr. Barron has seen the Potawatomis, with the hands and limbs both of white men and Cherokees, which they were about to devour.

It is well attested, that one of the officers attached to General Harmer's command was taken prisoner by the Miamis previously to the defeat of the whole army, and tortured by them in the most cruel and unrelenting manner for three days, on the west bank of the Maumee. The Indians declared that he had behaved with a remarkable degree of fortitude. Pieces of flesh were cut off from his body, roasted, and eaten by them in the presence of the agonized victim. No exclamation or groan could be drawn from the intrepid prisoner, until a squaw thrust a burning brand into his privates, when he was heard to exclaim, " Oh my God!" A young Indian warrior then declared that the prisoner, having proved himself a brave man, should no longer be kept in agony, and put a period to his sufferings by despatching him with his tomahawk.

One of the best attested instances, is that of Captain Wells who was killed after the capture of Chicago in 1812. This man, who had been a long time among the Indians, having been taken prisoner by them at the age of thirteen, had acquired a great reputation for courage; and his name is still mentioned as that of the bravest white man with whom they ever met. He had almost become one of their number, and had united himself to a descendant of Little Turtle. At the commencement of hostilities between Britain and the United States, he sided with his own countrymen, while the Indians of this vicinity all passed into the British service. When the fort was afterwards besieged by the united Indians, Captain Wells was there, having arrived just two days before with the orders from General Hull for the evacuation of the post. Wells was killed after the action, his body was divided, and his heart was shared, as being the most certain spell for courage, and part of it was sent to the various tribes in alliance with the Potawatomis, while they themselves feasted upon the rest.

Among some tribes, cannibalism is universal, but it appears that among the Potawatomis it is generally restricted to a society or fraternity, whose privilege and duty it is, on all occasions, to eat of the enemy's flesh; at least one individual must be eaten. The flesh is sometimes dried and taken to the village. Not only are the members of this fraternity endued with great virtues, but it is said they can impart them, by means of spells, to any individual whom they wish to favour. No warrior can be elected into the association, except by the unanimous consent of its members. In such a case, the candidate for this distinction, which is held in great esteem, makes a fine present to the society. We shall have an opportunity of recurring on some future occasion to this subject, and we shall be enabled to prove the participation in this nefarious practice, of many Indian tribes collected together on a memorable occasion, at the siege of Fort Meigs, in 1813. We do not wish to be considered as asserting that human flesh is usually, or as a matter of preference, eaten by these

Indians, or by any others with whom we may have met; but that it has been eaten on many occasions under the most aggravating circumstances, and without the least shadow of necessity, we consider as fully established.

Of their first origin, their ideas appear to be very confused. They all consider the earth as their mother, and some of them are impressed with the belief that they formerly resided under ground, and that they rose out from it. On this subject Mr. Keating held a conversation of more than an hour with Richarville, one of the principal chiefs of the Miamis, who gave him a long but confused account of the division which exists among the Miamis, into two tribes, one of which considers itself as having risen from the waters, and the other from the centre of the earth. Those of Neptunian origin, made their way as is believed, to the surface, by climbing up trees, &c. The man who gave this account is a half-breed Miami, his father having been a Frenchman; he speaks very good French. At the time we saw him, he was dressed like a trader, and from his appearance, manners and language, we should never have suspected him to be any other than a Canadian fur-dealer. He is said, however, to possess considerable influence with his tribe. He sometimes assumes the Indian costume, with the exception of the blanket, for which he always substitutes a *capote*. In the conversation which we had with him, we had reason to consider him as well entitled to the reputation which he has acquired, of being one of the most artful and deceitful of his nation. He declined meeting the party in conference, stating that the other chiefs of his tribe were absent, and that the circumstance of his holding a conference with white men might expose him to suspicion, which would the more readily attach to him on account of his being himself but a half-breed. This reason was too plausible to allow of our objecting to it: and we regretted that we could not put to the test the sincerity of his offer to answer all our questions, in a few days, when the other men of his nation should have arrived. The gentleman of the party who conversed with him, observed that he had never met with a man whose manners evinced so much cunning and subtilty as those of this chief. Affecting not to understand questions to which he did not choose to reply, and involving all his answers in obscurity, he imparted no information concerning the points upon which he was questioned, except, in the instance already alluded to, of the division of the Miamis into two tribes, whose origins are supposed to be so different. This might be considered as very interesting, if any confidence could be placed in such a man as Richarville. Of his craft and worthlessness an idea can be formed from the circumstance that, when negotiating on the part of the Miamis a treaty with the commissioners at Chicago, he made it an indispensable condition that a tract of nine sections of land should be secured to him in fee simple, while the rest of his nation are merely joint-tenants on their lands, and destitute of the privilege of disposing of the same, except with the consent of the Government of the United States. It must be regretted, that this mode of obtaining the assent of chiefs to a treaty, by private presents, grants, &c. should ever have been allowed. It was, we believe, first introduced by the French, whose object was, by these pretended treaties, to which the chiefs of the nations were bribed to give their consent, to obtain a colour of right which the French government could afterwards maintain against European nations. This practice has existed so long, and is so universal, that it would, perhaps, be difficult to make a treaty with the Indians, if presents or grants were withheld from the chiefs; but in order to put to the test the correctness of the principle, we need but look to the feelings which would be excited if an European power, while discussing the terms of a treaty with our government, were to offer or to consent to give any private presents to the negotiators on the part of our country. Richarville retains his attachment to the British government, and although residing upon our territory, and sharing in the annuity paid by the United States to the Miamis, he still holds a commission in the British service, and his name still appears on the half-pay or pension list of Great Britain.

Metea told us that the Potawatomis thought that they had always existed in the neighbourhood of Lake Michigan: that the first man and woman had been made by the Great Spirit. God sowed the seed and the men sprung up. When called upon to explain what he meant by this, he gave to understand that he had used the language in a figurative point of view, and as a parable. Their tradition at first mentioned but one original couple, the parents of the red people, from whom they believed themselves to have descended. But when they became acquainted with the different races of men, they supposed a couple of white, and another of black, had likewise been created by the Great Spirit, and that these had given rise to the white and black people whom they had since seen, but Richarville had not troubled himself much with thinking on this subject. Soon after the white men came among them, they were told that, far to the setting sun, there was a race of people whose features and complexion resembled theirs. This had led them to think and discuss this matter frequently among themselves; they had often inquired from other nations whence they came, but they found strong reasons to adhere to their old traditions, that the land on which they now resided was that upon which the Great Spirit had first placed them. Metea has always been of the opinion that there is but one God, who is a Supreme Being, but that he made a Spirit or God to be under him, whose special duty it is to take charge of the Indians. This he thought to be the common opinion of all Indians whom he knew. This inferior Deity stood to the Supreme Being in the same relation that the red man stands to the white. The existence of a Bad Spirit is considered as proved by the circumstance of there being bad men, for a Good Spirit could not have made any thing that was evil.

When questioned as to his opinion of a future life, and the immortality of the soul, he unhesitatingly replied that he had heard the white men talk of those things, but that he had no belief whatever in them. He thought that after the death both body and spirit decayed and disappeared; nor would he at all acknowledge a belief in the doctrine, which he had heard asserted by the interpreter to be generally entertained by the Indians, that the spirits of the departed returned after death to the Master of Life. In replying to this question, he made use of a strong expression, " as a dog dies, so man dies—the dog rots after death, so does man decay after he has ceased to live." Being asked if it was true that they placed provisions near the dead, both at the time of death and afterwards, and if true, wherefore this was done—if both spirit and body decayed together? He replied that this custom really prevailed, but he knew of no other foundation for it, than a dream of one of their ancestors, that a departed friend had appeared to him, and told him he was hungry, which induced him to take provisions to the grave of that man—he knew of no other cause for it. We felt some anxiety to obtain a more satisfactory answer from Metea on this point, as we knew that, at the funeral of a nephew of his, he had once expressed himself thus in the presence of Mrs. Hackley,* who repeated it to Major Lonk. "His spirit has fled upon a long journey, and you must give him provisions that he may feed upon during his journey." Although all our attempts at obtaining a different answer from Metea proved abortive, we incline to the opinion that the doctrine of the immortality of the soul and of a future state of reward and punishment, is generally entertained by them, and that it probably existed previous to their intercourse with white men. Our opinion does not merely rest upon the general prevalence of this belief among all those who have made the least advance above the lowest state of barbarism, but upon the uniform opinion on this subject, expressed to us by those who were most conversant with Indian manners, and who had enjoyed the best opportunities of becoming acquainted with them. From Mr. Barron we heard that they generally admitted the existence of a future life;

---

* Mrs. Hackley is the daughter of the late Captain Wells, by a Miami-squaw, who was either the daughter or adopted child of Little Turtle. Having received her education among white men, she unites to the manners of civilized life, many of the interesting peculiarities which distinguish mankind in its primitive state.

of which however, they entertained very confused ideas, believing for the most part that the spirits of those who had lived a good life, went to a country where they could pursue without fatigue their favourite occupation of hunting, where animals would be plenty and fat. Not so with the spirits of the bad; theirs would be a country barren and nearly destitute of animals, where the chase would become a painful and unprofitable occupation. At any rate, they hold that their existence is at the disposal of the Great Master of Life. Many, however, when asked whither their spirits went after death, carelessly replied that they knew not what became of them, they saw them not leaving the body. One of the strongest facts in corroboration of their entertaining a belief in futurity and the immortality of the soul or spirit, is, that they all believe in ghosts or phantoms. "Once," said Mr. Barron, " on approaching in the night a village of Ottawas, I found all the inhabitants in confusion: they were all busily engaged in raising noises of the loudest and most inharmonious kind. Upon inquiry, I found that a battle had been lately fought between the Ottawas and the Kickapoos, and that the object of all this noise was to prevent the ghosts of the departed combatants from entering the village."

It is impossible, in seeing them at present, not to feel convinced that the time for correct information has passed away; they have imbibed from the missionaries so many notions which certainly did not belong to them originally, and the crafty policy of their chiefs to counteract the effect of their intercourse with white men has raised so many idle and false traditions, that it is difficult to distinguish the genuine from the false doctrines attributed to these nations in their original state. Of the many interesting customs which, according to their traditions, were formerly prevalent, the dereliction of none is more to be regretted than of that which accompanied their marriage ceremony. This has now nearly disappeared from among them. Their intermarriages with other nations have become so frequent, and the demoralizing tendency of their intercourse with the traders has been so great, that it has led them to neglect practices which were recommended to them by a venerable antiquity.

The form of courtship which existed formerly, is stated to have been as follows; when a young man had conceived an attachment for a female, or that he wished to make her his wife, he gave the first intimation of his design, by throwing a deer into the lodge belonging to the girl's parent. This he would repeat for several days, from ten to fifteen; after which, the father usually asked him what object he had in doing so, and whether it was to obtain his daughter. The young man having replied in the affirmative, the relations of the girl would, if they approved of the connexion, prepare a dress for the youth, which they would take to his house, and there the damsel's father would invest him with it. He would then take him home with him and introduce him to the bride; there the lover remained for the space of ten or twelve days until his friends had prepared the presents they intended for his wife's family, and had taken them to their house. It was usual for the young couple to dwell with the wife's parents for the term of a year, during which time the husband was, as it were, a servant in the family, giving to his father-in-law all the produce of his hunting. At the expiration of this term, he was at liberty to remove his wife to his own house, and treat her as he pleased. The opinion which is entertained by the Missouri Indians, and by all those who reside along the banks of the Mississippi, that it would be the height of indecorum in a man to speak, or even to look upon his son-in-law, does not exist at present, and is believed never to have prevailed among the Potawatomis. The power of the husband over his wife was unlimited; he might even put her to death if he chose, and she had lost all claim to the sympathy and protection of her own relations. They never would resent any treatment which she had been made to endure.

There was no fixed time for marrying; girls were sometimes betrothed at a very early age, long before maturity. The presents which it was customary to make, were of the most valuable kind, and consisted of horses, venison, guns, &c. In some instances it happened that the parties were mutually attached, and that they contracted a secret engagement, marrying without the consent of their parents. But these breaches of ceremony were usually made up, by the interchange of presents between the parents on both sides, who then confirmed the marriage.

It was usual for them, when an Indian married one of several sisters, to consider him as wedded to all; and it became incumbent upon him to take them all as wives. The marrying of a brother's widow was not interdicted, but was always looked upon as a very improper connexion. The union of persons related by blood was likewise disliked, and discouraged. An incestuous connexion was at all times considered as highly criminal, but no punishment was attached to it. Instances of it are not, however, as rare as might be expected. Among the Potawatomis we heard of several. We were told at Chicago of two cases, which were accompanied by circumstances of an aggravated nature. A Potawatami of the name of Wagakenagon* died a short time since, aged about fifty; he had married his mother-in-law, previously to which he had been connected with two of his daughters. He denied the connexion with his elder daughter, who, however, acknowledged that he had seduced her, by promising to teach her a spell by which she would be enabled to destroy her enemies, by writing their names on sand. A few months afterwards, he was detected in an intercourse with his second daughter, whom he had likewise seduced. Both the women openly confessed their guilt, but with very little appearance of shame. This did not prevent their marrying subsequently. After these abominable transactions, he married their grandmother, who was the mother of his first wife. Another man belonging to the same nation, and who had become a chief by the death of his brother, is known to have had intercourse with a woman that was the mother of his first wife. He afterwards deserted both, and took a third wife. The two other women, both mother and daughter, were subsequently married; this man's name was Ozanotap† (*Yellow-head*). But all these connexions are held in utter abhorrence by the nation at large, and those who contract them are considered as base and worthless members of the community.

The circumstances which attend funerals are likewise worthy of notice. They have, it is true, but few cere-

---

* Wá-gá-ké-ná-gón.   † Ozán-ó-táp.

monies at the time of the removal of the corpse; but the manner in which this duty is performed deserves mention. The greatest pains are taken that all should be transacted in the most decorous manner; the spot selected is always as dry as the circumstances of the place will admit of. The body of the deceased is clothed in his best garments, and, if the relations can afford it, new clothes are obtained for this purpose. His moccassins, rifle, knife, money, silver ornaments, in fine, the whole of his property is placed near him: the corpse is laid with its face turned to the east. A small quantity of food is placed near the head. The funeral is generally attended by all the relations, who express their grief by weeping; but yells, dances, &c. are not customary on such occasions. The deceased is buried in an erect, seated or inclined posture, according to the wishes and directions which he may have given previous to his death, for these are always most implicitly obeyed. The graves in which they are buried are generally from four to five feet in depth. If the deceased had, previous to his death, expressed a wish to be deposited in a tree, this is attended to; otherwise the corpse is always interred. When the corpse is to be deposited in a tree, it is first sewed up in a blanket, and this is suspended from the branches. The friends of the deceased visit it frequently, until they observe that the body is decaying; they then shake hands with it, and bid it a last farewell; but even after this they return yearly to visit the spot where it is deposited, and they uniformly leave some food near it. At the time of the funeral, they frequently light a fire near the head of the grave, and upon this they prepare their feast, throwing a part of the food on the grave for the use of their friend. If they have whiskey, they likewise sprinkle some on the ground; but of this they are sparing, doubtless from the belief that the living require it much more than the dead. An invocation is then made to the deceased, who is entreated to speed his course direct to the Great Prairie, without casting his eyes back; for they hold, that if, on his way to the land of Spirits, he were to look behind him, it would bring ill luck upon some one of his relations, to whom it would be a signal that his company was required by his departed friend. It is usual to mark the grave with a post, on which are inscribed in hieroglyphics the deeds of the deceased, whether in the way of hunting or of fighting. It is not uncommon for the survivors to adopt a male or female child as a substitute for their lost relative. When they bury a corpse in a trough hollowed out of a tree, they prefer one of ash wood, as they observe that it is less easily penetrated by water.

We are informed, that they profess to have been well acquainted with the art of making maple sugar previous to their intercourse with white men. Our interpreter states that having once expressed his doubts on the subject in the presence of José Renard, a Kickapoo chief, the latter answered him immediately, with a smile, " can it be that thou art so simple as to ask me such a question, seeing that the Master of Life has imparted to us an instinct which enables us to substitute stone hatchets and knives for those made of steel by the whites; wherefore should we not have known as well as they how to manufacture sugar? He has made us all, that we should enjoy life; he has placed before us all the requisites for the support of existence, food, water, fire, trees, &c.; wherefore then should he have withheld from us the art of excavating the trees in order to make troughs of them, of placing the sap in these, of heating the stones and throwing them into the sap so as to cause it to boil, and by this means reducing it into sugar." In this short reply of the Kickapoo, we have a brief sketch of the rude process practised by the Indians in the preparation of the maple sugar. Previously to this they had learned the art of making and using pottery, but had abandoned it for the purpose, as Metea told us, of using wooden troughs, and hot stones; perhaps because their pottery did not stand fire well. The evaporation resulting from the action of the hot stones, produced a crystallization of sugar in the trough. Their process was a tedious and imperfect one, which probably required much time before it could be improved; to use the language of Nacoma, a Delaware, " Brother, there is a great difference between the white man and the Indian; we believe that we are not endued with the same natural advantages which you possess, since we discover those things alone which nature places before us; we derive advantage from such tools and implements as she has provided for us, only so far as they appear to us useful, but without any attempt to inquire into their nature; you, on the contrary, have received from the Master of Life, the disposition to erect to yourselves a system of education that enables you to treasure up the knowledge which you may have acquired, to endeavour to prosecute your discoveries, to make new applications of them, and to dive into those things with which you are unacquainted." We shall have an opportunity of comparing these ideas of the Delaware chief with the reflections made by a Sauk Indian, who attended the expedition as a guide, and we shall be confirmed in the belief that, with all their apparent contempt for white men, the Indians are frequently obliged to acknowledge the superiority of the civilized man, which however they improperly consider as the cause, and not as the effect of civilization.

The use of salt previous to the arrival of the Europeans is likewise claimed by the Indians. They trace the origin of their acquaintance with this valuable condiment, to the observation of the preference given by elks to the water from salt licks; having tasted it, they liked it, and took some to boil their vegetables with, and having found it palatable, they boiled down the water in the manner that they had done the sap, and thus obtained salt. It is not improbable, that the sediments of white salt, which are frequently observed during dry seasons, in the vicinity of salt springs, may have taught them that it was by evaporation that the substance could be separated from the water which holds it in solution; for although the Indians were totally igorant of the nature and causes of evaporation, they had noticed the process, and were aware that it could result as well from the action of fire as from that of the sun.

Prior to their intercourse with white men, it appears that these Indians were not acquainted with any intoxicating liquors; if we except a decotion of a plant resembling the whortleberry, which was used by the Chippewas in cases of sickness only; it produced vertigo. As this fact was ascertained by Dr. Hall at Chicago, where the Chippewas and Potawatomis frequently meet, it is not improbable that the latter were also acquainted with it, but it was never used except in cases of sickness. To the Europeans they are therefore indebted for all the evils which have attended too free a use of spirituous liquors.

The Potawatomis are not divided into tribes designated by the name of animals, as is reported to be the case with the Missouri Indians, but they are distinguished merely from their local habitations. Those that live on the St. Joseph form a small tribe, in every respect similar to those residing near Chicago, or near Lake Michigan. Although not divided into regular tribes, they have a sort of family distinction, kept up by means of signs resembling those of heraldry. These signs are, by them, called Totem;* they are taken from an animal or from some part of it, but by no means imply a supposed relationship with that animal, as has been incorrectly stated. It is merely a distinguishing mark or badge, which appears to belong to every member of a family, whether male or female. The latter retain it even after matrimony, and do not assume that of their husbands. It does not appear that this implies the least obligation of the Indian, to the animal from which it is taken. He may kill it or eat it. The *totem* appears to answer no other purpose than that of distinguishing families; it does not imply any degree of nobility or inequality of rank among them. It is the same custom, which is improperly attributed by Carver to the Dacota or Sioux Indians (Naudowessie).

Independently of the name which he bears, and of the *totem* or badge of family to which he lays claim, an Indian has frequently a kind spirit to watch over him and assist him. This tutelar saint is, of course, held in high veneration, and nothing is done that could in the least offend him. The mode in which each Indian becomes acquainted with the name or nature of this ministering spirit, is by dreams, in which he fancies that the Master of Life reveals himself to him in his

* Tŏ-t'ĕm.

sleep, under the form of some tangible object in creation, generally of an animal; under this shape the Great Spirit holds converse with him, and the Indian ever after supposes that this is the form in which he may expect to see the Great Spirit appear to him. To this animal, whom he considers as a medium of communication between him and the Master of Life, he addresses his prayers and states his wants; he consults it in all his difficulties, and not unfrequently conceives that he has derived relief from it. Of course, he abstains from eating of the animal, and would rather starve than sacrilegiously feed upon his idol. But he holds the animal as a friend to himself alone. He knows that others have different spirits, and hence does not think himself bound to protect that animal against his companions, because he knows that there is no virtue in the animal for any one but himself. Sometimes, instead of the whole animal, it is only in some part of it that the charm resides, and in this case he will feel no hesitation in eating of all the other parts of the beast.

In their conversation, the Indians frequently display considerable humour. Their attempts at wit are numerous and often successful; but their wit, as well as the general tenour of their conversation, is obscene: in proof of this, we might, if it were necessary, mention several instances; but they have been so frequently noticed by the travellers who have preceded us, that we feel ourselves excused from doing it. As an instance of an attempt at what they consider as wit, the following was related to us: an Indian called for milk; when they were about to give him some, he pointed to a whiskey bottle, and observed that it was the milk of that black cow that he wanted. Such an observation is sure to draw peals of laughter from all about them, which encourages them to proceed. But, perhaps, the most remarkable trait in their conversation is, that they feel none of that delicacy or restraint, which, among civilized nations, has proscribed many words from general use. With them every idea which enters into their head, or every word which they think of, is uttered without any respect for the company present. With this apparent obscenity in their conversation, the Indians are very guarded in their actions, and their manners indicate a considerable degree of native modesty. In this they generally excel the white men who live with them; and it is a fact, well attested by the experience of all who have spent any time among them, that they are seldom or never observed in an obscene or indecorous attitude.

Metea was asked, whether he had ever heard of any tradition accounting for the formation of those artificial mounds, which are found scattered over the whole country; when he immediately replied, that they had been constructed by the Indians as fortifications, before white men had come among them. "After men had been made," said he, " they scattered themselves over the surface of the earth, and lost all knowledge of each other. When they afterwards met, it was with fear and caution; they were engaged in wars, during which they erected these works, which served for defence, until treaties and alliances were made between them." He had always heard this origin ascribed to them, and had known three of them which are supposed to have been made by his nation. One is at the fork of the Kankakee and the Des Plaines rivers, a second on the Ohio, which, from his description, was supposed to be at the mouth of the Muskingum; he visited it, but could not describe the spot very accurately; and a third, which he had also seen, he states to be on the head waters of the St. Joseph of Lake Michigan. This latter is about forty miles north-west of Fort Wayne, and five or six miles distant from an Indian village called Mangokwa, on a small stream which empties itself into the St. Joseph; it is a round hill about as large as Fort Wayne. Major Long, who saw those on the St. Joseph and at the mouth of the Kankakee, on a former visit to this country, considers them as natural, and not artificial elevations. One of the Miami chiefs, whom the traders have named Legros, once told Baron that he had heard that his father had fought with his tribe in one of the forts at Piqua; that the fort had been erected by the Indians against the French, and that his father had been killed during one of the assaults made upon it by the French.

The chieftainship is hereditary among the Potawatomis. If a chief should be destitute of male heirs, sons or nephews, he assembles the warriors of his tribe, and appoints one of them as his successor. Should he die without leaving any male heir, and without having adopted any, then the warriors convene and appoint one of their number to succeed to the vacant dignity; "for a nation cannot exist," says Metea, "without a leader." In their councils no regular debate takes place. The first man who is nominated as chief, generally unites all votes; it is evident that much must depend upon the influence of him who nominates a candidate. It is, however, usual to ascertain the wish of the people beforehand, and for this reason they are always consulted.

In like manner, if a man be desirous of leading a war-party, he mentions it to others, secures their assistance, and then publicly announces his intention in the village, when such as please follow him. Previous to his departure, he performs his religious ceremonies, and prepares what is termed his " medicine" or spell, by which he hopes to insure success. If the chief of the village be opposed to the scheme, he undertakes to prevent it, by influencing their superstitious fears. To this effect he counteracts, as they suppose, the spells prepared by the warrior, by walking round him in a circle, and then resuming his place. This they so firmly believe to vitiate the medicine, that it immediately puts a stop to the expedition. The power of the chief appears to rest exclusively upon his personal influence. He can use no coercive measures to obtain what he wishes, or prevent what he dislikes. Although the Indians have notions of right and wrong, they have no means of rewarding the former and redressing the latter; the chief cannot punish a man for any offence whatsoever. If the crime committed be flagrant, the party that deems himself injured may seek for redress in a forcible manner, but there is no mode of obtaining it by fair and legal means. In some cases, however, a breach of faith may be punished; if, for instance, a chief wishes to undertake a military operation, he convenes his warriors, and states his views; should they agree to it, they declare their assent by presenting him with a string of wampum, which is kept as an evidence of their acquiescence. Should any one of those who have agreed to go afterwards break his promise, he is liable to be punished by forfeiture of part of his property, or by expulsion from the village. A string of wampum is sometimes sent from one village to another, with a piece of tobacco attached to it as a proof of the faith of the messenger. It has often been stated, that the Indians in no instance whatever punished their children. This is not correct as a general rule. Mr. Colhoun was informed, that the Potawatomis sometimes enjoin upon their children, as a punishment, the use of the charcoal and its accompanying fast. He also observes, that the circumstance of chastisement being inflicted by some Indians, is confirmed by Joutel's statement, that the Illinois and Cadoquias punished their children by throwing water in their faces; and by Jones's observations, that the Shawanese had the same practice, and likewise threw them into brooks.* The power of the chief is exercised only so long as he behaves himself in a manner agreeable to the wishes of his warriors, for though the dignity be an hereditary one, it is not uncommon for them to depose their chiefs. The principal prerogative of the chief is to conduct all military operations. When once war is declared, he cannot conclude peace without the consent of his warriors. The duty of dividing the annuity paid to them by the United States' Government, likewise devolves upon the chief. Formerly the partition was made by him in the manner that he thought best, but some cases of malversation have led to a different method. The money is paid to the principal chief of the nation; who calls his people round him, places them in a circle, and then throws a dollar to each all round, continuing this operation until the whole of the money is disposed of. In this

* Vide "Journal Historique du dernier Voyage de M. de la Salle, par Joutel." Paris, 1714, p. 283 and 342, and "Journal of two visits to some nations of Indians west of Ohio river, in 1772 and 1773, by the Rev. D. Jones."

division the father of a family receives an equal share for every individual in his household, whether male or female, child or adult. The annuities paid to the Miamis amount to eighteen thousand dollars. The last census, taken a few years' since, made their numbers eleven hundred and seventy-two, of whom three hundred were warriors. An accurate amount of the Potawatomi population could not be obtained here; it has been variously stated; we heard it rated at ten thousand, which is probably far beyond the true number. Those who receive their annuities at Fort Wayne, are not numerous, and the census of Indians in the state of Illinois does not admit of more than twelve hundred Potawatomis. The payment of their annuities on the United States' territory is very much to be regretted; they ought to be paid to them on the Indian reservations, where, by a humane law, no spirituous liquors can be sold. If some means were taken of holding a sort of fair for cattle and implements of agriculture, at the time that the annuity is paid, they might, perhaps, be induced to apply to the purchase of useful objects the money which is at present wasted in procuring spirits. Under the present system, the moment an Indian receives his annuity, he immediately converts it into whiskey; the deplorable effects of which upon their system are too well known to require that we should dwell upon them; but we may be permitted to add the testimony of what came under our own inspection to the great mass of information which has already transpired on this subject. During the three days that we stayed at Fort Wayne, we saw two Indians tomahawked. The first case happened the night of our arrival; this man was very severely cut in the head by some unknown person. It was supposed that it was by one of the French *engagés*. At the time this occurred, they were all concerned in a drunken frolic. The next day, on visiting the fort, we met at the gate a few Indians, one of whom was in a state of intoxication; and we were informed by a boy, that he had threatened to shoot his wife. A few moments after, while we were engaged in conversation with the Indian Agent, word was brought to him, that the Indian had drawn his knife and severely wounded her in the forehead. It appeared the only provocation she had given him was the attempting to draw him away from the town, and induce him to return to his village. In both these cases the loss of blood was very considerable, and such that it was believed none but Indians could have survived it; but they are so inured to pain and privations of every kind, that it cannot be doubted that they recover from wounds which, to other men, would prove fatal. The excellent surgical assistance which they receive in all cases of wounds and bruises, may also be considered as one of the causes which tend to restore them to health. These assaults are, however, so common here, that no one appears surprised at them; they are considered as an every-day occurrence. Generally, an Indian will, after he has recovered from his drunken frolic, express great regret for the fatal effects which have attended it. This is peculiarly the case where he is at a distance from the white population, and where intoxication has not become with him an habitual or daily vice; otherwise the frequent repetition of these bloody frays renders him callous to their consequences. As an instance, we were told, that some time since, when the Baptist Missionary Society were allowed to occupy Fort Wayne as one of their stations, an Indian brought to the fort the corpse of his brother, and asked the Rev. Mr. M'Coy, who superintended the establishment, to provide for the funeral. On inquiry, Mr. M'Coy found that the deceased had been murdered, a short time before, by the very Indian who had brought him in. When questioned as to the cause of his brother's death, the murderer carelessly raised the cloathing from the breast of the deceased, and exhibited five or six wounds which he had inflicted with a knife, nor could any emotion of compunction be observed in his unyielding countenance. These evils may all be traced to the unfortunate circumstance, that the prohibition to sell spirituous liquors to the Indians extends only to their territory. If congress were to include in this prohibition all lands belonging to the United States, the evil could be partly, if not wholly remedied. The inducement to smuggle liquor and sell it clandestinely might be sufficiently great to prevent the mischief from being completely removed, but it would certainly render it rare. Perhaps, also, if the agents were required to pay them their annuities in the Indian reservation, and at a time when an opportunity would be given them of laying out their money in the purchase of cattle, implements of agriculture, and other useful or innocent articles, while the introduction of spirituous liquors would be closely guarded against, the great evil of intoxication would be rendered still more rare. Whatever measures congress may choose to adopt to civilize the Indians, it is not difficult to foresee that they will ever prove unsuccessful unless a check be immediately put to the sale of ardent liquors among them. The law that prohibits the sale of it within their territory having proved insufficient, a more general system of restriction must be adopted.

Experience has likewise proved, that the term *sale* was not sufficiently comprehensive. The giving of spirits ought to be subjected to the same regulation; for it has been observed on the Missouri, as well as on the Mississippi, and probably every where throughout the Indian country, that, if prohibited from selling it, the traders will give it to the Indians as an inducement to trade with them, taking care that the price of the liquor be included in that of the tobacco or other articles sold to them at the time.

All Indians concur in considering intoxication as improper, and as the source of every evil. Among crimes, those that are held to be most atrocious, are murder, theft, and the violation of the advice and directions of their parents. Many, however, are said to be " foolish," and not sensible of crime. Rape is considered as visited by the anger of the Great Spirit, and is never practised but upon females in a state of intoxication. In the treatment of their wives, they are often severe and brutal; if they should prove lazy, or be deemed so by their unrelenting husbands, or if careless of their children, they are not unfrequently beaten with clubs. Among women no crime is considered so flagrant as infidelity to their husbands; this is punished with blows, and sometimes with cutting off the nose, or other mutilations. Seldom do the Potawatomis punish it with death, and it is very rare that they vent their resentment against the paramour. The barbarous punishment noticed by Mr. Say, in the account of the manners of the Otos, Omawhaws, and other Missouri Indians, which he described under the name of the Round in the Prairie (*tour de la prairie* of the Canadians), is not known among the Potawatomis.

The Indians are liable to more distempers than might at first be expected from their mode of living. Croup is one of the most common diseases; in some seasons, most of their cases are fatal, while in others all the patients recover. No medicine is applied in this disease, except the maple sap, or sugar dissolved in hot water. Adults find relief from vomiting. Sore throat appears, also, to be one of their most frequent complaints, especially in the morning; but it soon passes off. They are often bitten by rattlesnakes; the wound is cured among the Potawatomis by poultices of the Seneca snake-root, draughts of violet tea, and *Eupatorium perfoliatum :* they have other remedies, which they keep secret. The venom of the snake is considered greater at some periods of the moon than at others; in the month of August it is most so. These Indians entertain a high degree of veneration for the rattlesnake, not that they consider it in the light of a spirit, as has frequently but incorrectly been asserted, but because they are grateful to it for the timely warning which it has often given them of the approach of an enemy. They therefore seldom kill it, unless when a young man fancies that he requires a rattle, in which case he will have no hesitation in killing a snake; which act he, however, always accompanies by certain forms. He introduces it by many apologies to the animal, informing it that he wants the rattle as an ornament for his person, and by no means to make fun of it, and in testimony of his amity to the species, leaves a piece of tobacco near the carcass. The fang of the snake is held to be a charm against rheumatism and other internal pains; the mode of applying it consists in scratching the affected part with it until it bleeds. In their rude midwifery, they use the rattle to assist in parturition; it is then administered internally; it is not, however, used as an emmenagogue. Leprosy is known among them, and has been observed under some of its most horrible features. In a case, known to Dr. Hall, the patient required some one to be constantly scraping his body and limbs with a knife. A double handful of furfuraceous matter was daily discharged; he died in the course of six months; his feet had turned as black as gunpowder.

Fevers are common among the Potawatomis, and are either bilious, intermittent, remittent, or continued; they afflict most those who follow the game to the interior of the country; while those who reside along the shores of the lake enjoy much better health. The Indians observe that the easterly winds are the most wholesome, the southerly produce dullness and laziness, the north wind is too cold, and that from the west is very uncomfortable. Hæpatitis is not common; when it occurs, it is relieved by repeated vomiting until the bile is completely evacuated; if the bile be not discharged, the white of the eye turns yellow, and continues so until death ensues. Hydrocephalus and dropsy are, it seems, unknown to them. Small-pox is frequent, but is always introduced by white men; it does, not, however, commit any great depredation. At one time it raged among them, and proved disastrous and incurable. Its evil effects were suspended by the introduction of the practice of inoculation and vaccination, which Little Turtle made known to them. Having never known the small-pox to be violent but once, they have not entertained that opinion of its return at periodical times, which is said to be held by other nations. Dr. Hall's offer to vaccinate them was accepted by many, and declined by others.

Metea told us that vaccination had been abandoned only for want of the virus; he expressed a great wish to obtain some, and said if he had it, he would use his influence to disseminate it.

Syphilis was, according to Metea, known to the Indians in its mildest form prior to the arrival of white men among them. It is considered as having increased in virulence and frequency, since the promiscuous intercourse of white men and squaws which is not interrupted, according to the uniform practice of Indians, during the period of the catamenia. When the disease is in its mild state, they cure it very readily by timely application to their medicine men; the principal remedies are decoctions of the red root and the prairie willow root, as also of sassafras. In such cases they drink very plentifully. These remedies are not applied to the disease in its worst forms: we heard that they had remedies, which, even in these cases, were considered as certain, but of which we could not ascertain the nature. In all such diseases, they apply to their regular doctors, who are said to charge very extravagant fees. These men combine the use of spells with that of herbs, and are held in very great esteem. Their materia medica consists of astringents, cathartics, emetics, mucilages, and sudorifics. Among the emetics most in use, we heard of pills made from the product of the evaporation of a decoction of the horse-chesnut boiled down to a viscous state. One of their sudorifics is said to consist in the application of a poultice of maize, boiled as for food, which is spread over the body of the sick person, who first extended on a board or skin. The maize employed in this application is afterwards used as food. The berry of the prickly ash is used by them as a warming medicine for inward complaints. They have no vesicatories but fire and hot water, which are applied for sore joints and rheumatism. Phlebotomy is performed with a small knife or with a thin lamina of flint attached to a stick in the manner of a fleam, and stuck into the flesh in the same way. For a pain in the head they bleed in the bend of the arm, or above it; for one in the side below the bend; and if the pain be in the back they bleed on the right or left ankle, according as it inclines to the right or left side. Bleeding is never resorted to in fevers.

Calculous symptoms are accurately described, but the disease and its causes are unknown to them. The process of parturition is generally easy, the woman being on her knees; it is sometimes assisted by bending the body over a cord, the ends of which are attached to the top of the cabin; the funis is regularly tied and cut. The operation of turning is unknown; no manual assistance is resorted to, even in cases of wrong presentation; and many instances have occurred in which the fœtus became putrid before it was expelled. They have professed midwives, who are paid for their attendance; these are principally old women. Men are never allowed to assist at the delivery of a woman. A general opinion has prevailed that all Indian women bathed in cold water immediately after parturition. This is however extremely incorrect; the practice exists among the Sioux or Dacotas, and among many other nations, but we very much question whether any nation of Algonquin origin practises it. The Potawatomi women are very careful not to expose themselves to cold after child-birth, and do not bathe for ten days unless the weather be very warm. The placenta not being always expelled naturally, they have recourse to a strong medicinal draught; it is stated, that if it should remain for several days, the husband takes his wife upon his shoulders, and carries her about for some time; the motion is said to assist in its expulsion. Mothers always nurse their children, and continue to suckle them for a great length of time, in some instances for three, four, or more years, if no subsequent pregnancy occur; in one case a mother was observed suckling a child twelve years of age. When the mother's milk fails, the child is fed with an extract of sweet maize in boiling water, and medicines are administered to renew the secretion. Metea had never heard of a total failure of a woman's milk while nursing her child: during a temporary interruption of it they sometimes commit children to the care of a friend who acts as nurse; but this practice is disapproved of. Parturition is seldom fatal: when it proves so, it is attributed to ignorance or carelessness on the part of the midwife; in women of indolent habits it is said to be painful, in the active it is much less laborious.— Sterility is very common, but does not expose women to contempt, though it is frequently the cause of their being cast off by their husbands. The period of gestation varies from eight to nine months, and is seldom attended with sickness or nausea. Menstruation commonly commences at the age of fourteen, and continues until fifty, and in some cases sixty years; it is not uncommon to see a woman with grey hair, whose catamenia has not ceased. Many women become disabled from child-bearing by accidents during their first gestation, although still very young. Menstruation is often irregular with them; when too abundant, they have remedies which are represented as very successful, but which Metea declined indicating, as it was not usual for them to talk of these things except when called upon professionally, and with a fee. In a suppression of the menses they seldom apply any remedy; as they are apprehensive that this might be productive of sterility, which is by all Indian women considered as the greatest curse that can be entailed upon them. During the period of the catamenia, women are not allowed to associate with the rest of the nation; they are completely laid aside, and are not permitted to touch any article of furniture or food which the men have occasion to use. If the Indians be stationary at the time, the women are placed outside of the camp; if on a march, they are not allowed to follow the trail, but must take a different path and keep at a distance from the main body. This practice, which appears to prevail wherever man retains his primitive simplicity and purity of manners, has been very unphilosophically considered by Adair and other theoretic writers as a strong confirmation of the descent of the aborigines of America from the ten lost tribes of Israel. But as Charlevoix observes, " one must have good eyes, or rather a very lively imagination, to perceive in them all that some travellers have pretended to discover."* The late Mr. Samuel Prince, of Boston, who resided three or four years in Owhyhee, assured Mr. Colhoun that the natives of that island are equally scrupulous with regard to the catamenia, and that during its continuance the women are secluded in houses without the villages. This custom of Owhyhee has not, we think, been noticed by any traveller that we have met with.

* Charlevoix's Journal Historique, Letter 23d.

It has been often asserted that it was a common practice with Indian women to destroy the fœtus. This may be correct as respects certain nations, but it ought by no means to be considered as applicable to all; and we know it to be incorrect as respects the Potawatomis. All travellers concur in representing them as very proud of the number of their children. Where the mild and humane provisions of the Christian faith do not prevail, children form almost the only link which binds man to woman for life. It is the only obstacle to that constant repudiation of wives which occurred previously to the Christian dispensation; hence, independently of the moral turpitude of the deed, it would be the height of impolicy in a woman to impair the strongest claim which she has upon her husband's affections; but besides these considerations, the Potawatomi woman is prevented from attempting to destroy the fœtus, from the fear which she entertains that abortion would be followed by the death of the parent.

Askabunkese, one of the most celebrated physicians among the Potawatomis, being asked whether chlorosis was known to them, said that he did not know it; the women were too modest to inform the men, and would knock him down with a stick if he were to inquire of them.

Among the Potawatomis, the practice of medicine is considered quite distinct from that of jugglery. Both are in great repute, but it appears that there is no interference. The man of medicine has, it is true, recourse to spells and incantations to add to the virtue of the plants which he uses; but this is totally unconnected with the avocations of the sorcerer and juggler, whose object is amusement, and who are resorted to for the recovery of lost articles, or to answer questions about persons and things at a distance, for which they sometimes are paid by the more ignorant; but they are soon detected in their clumsy arts. The sorcerers are treated with much respect, being held in great awe. They generally perform their tricks in the twilight, or during the night. Prophets formerly existed in great number, and were much revered; but the failure which attended the predictions made by the great prophet of the Shawanese, the brother of Tecumseh, has opened their eyes on this subject and satisfied them that he, as well perhaps as the others who had enjoyed reputation among them, was merely a tool in the hands of a designing chief, to deceive the Indians into measures which he wished to effect.

The Potawatomis have a number of war songs, formed for the most part of one or two ideas, expressed in short and forcible sentences, which they repeat over and over, in a low humming kind of tune, which to our ears appeared very monotonous; they have no love songs, the business of singing being always connected with warlike avocations. We took down the words of one of their songs as follows: —

Yŏ-wă kwă-tă-mă-nŏĭ mĕ-chĕ-mŏ-kŏ-măn.
What do I hear behind me? the Americans
nŏ-tŏ-tă-wă-nĕ-kă pĕ-tĕ-kă-wă,
are entering our village. Prepare yourselves to fight.
Kă-nă-mĕ-tă-sĕ wĕ-tă-sĕ nĕ-pŏ-wăn.
We must die. Victory or death.

The translation of two others is annexed with a view to give an idea of the purport of their songs. " When I march against mine enemies, the earth trembles under my feet;" this is sung with considerable force by a warrior; the others joining in chorus, to the words ya, wa, often repeated, and concluded with a general whoop.

Another, which is very short, consists merely in the repetition of the words, "The head of the enemy is cut off, and falls at my feet;" with the exclamation ha-ha-ha, frequently repeated.

Singing is always attended by the dance, and if possible, by intoxication, in which case it becomes incoherent and unintelligible. The only musical instruments which they use are the drum, rattle, and a kind of flageolet. They have various kinds of dances known by the name of the war dance, medicine dance, Manito, or spirit dance, wabano, metawee, mewicine, and beggar's dance. Their games are numerous and diversified; they resemble many of those known to civilized men; such as gymnastic exercise, battledore, pitching the bar, ball, &c. tennis and cup-ball, for which they use the spur of the deer with a string attached to it. They are fond of games of chance, particularly cards, which they have received from traders, &c.

The Potawatomis are for the most part well proportioned, about five feet eight inches in height, possessed of much muscular strength in the arm, but rather weak in the back, with a strong neck, and endowed with considerable agility. Their voice is feeble and low, but when excited very shrill; their teeth are sound and clean, but not remarkable for regularity. In persons of feeble habits, or of a scrophulous tendency, the teeth are found to decay much faster than in others. Dentition is said to be a painful process among Indian children, a circumstance which we had not expected. Their complexion is very much darkened by exposure to the sun and wind, while those parts which are kept covered, are observed to retain their native brightness. Children are red when new-born; after a few years they assume the yellow colour. Their sight is quick and penetrating, but blindness is frequent from the intense application of the eye in still hunting, and from exposure to the alternate, and, in some cases, united action of the sun and snow; doubtless, also, on account of the constant smoke in their huts. Their hearing is usually good when young; but is often affected in old age, probably by the effect of cold, or the usually disordered state of their stomach. Their olfactory nerves are said to be inferior in acuteness to those of the white man; which is singular, considering the extent of the sense of smelling among wild animals. We should have believed that man in his primitive state would be possessed of a more acute sense of smelling than when civilized; the facts stated on this subject of the Caraibs being able to trace men through the woods by the scent, like hounds, and of their distinguishing " the track of an Englishman, or a negro, from that of a Frenchman or a Spaniard, by the sense of smelling," if true, would be a strong confirmation of this doctrine.* It is said that the Arabs cannot bear the smell of a city.

Their endurance of cold is great. Their powers of digestion are strong, but exposed to severe trials. The quantity of food which an Indian will take when he has it in abundance, is surprising, and if considered in connexion with what is related by Captain Parry of the appetite of the Esquimaux, would lead us to believe that this is not peculiar to any nation of Indians, but that it belongs to man in general in his wild state. We find that it extends also to the half-breeds who live among

* Archæologia Americana, vol. I. p. 426.

them. The observations made at a later period of the expedition, upon the quantity of buffalo meat consumed by every man of the party, confirm this. The usual allowance of fresh buffalo meat to the guides and boatmen of the fur trading companies is not less than eight pounds per day; and it is probable, that during the short time the party were among the buffalo, the ration of each of the gentlemen averaged about four pounds. This is not to be attributed to any want of nutritive power in the flesh of the buffalo, but to the great facility that attends the digestion of this food, and to the irregular habits which even the most civilized men readily acquire as soon as they find themselves beyond the pale of society. Certain it is, that if well provided with food, and not engaged in hunting, the Potawatomi will eat from ten to twenty times a day. Frequent exposure to privation of food has, however, accustomed him to endure the want of it with more fortitude, and perhaps with less real inconvenience, than the white man. There is also probably a moral support which the red man receives from the recollection, that, however frequent, and however long have been the intervals during which he was deprived of all subsistence, they have always terminated in time to secure him from absolute famine; he, therefore, always retains the hope of being soon restored to abundance. The white man, less accustomed to these privations, considers himself as lost the very first time that he misses his usual allowance, and is thus deprived of the great accession of physical strength which proceeds from moral courage. Notwithstanding their great fortitude, the men of this nation are sometimes liable to unaccountable depression of spirits, which seldom, however, leads them to commit suicide; we heard of two instances only, one of which was in a fit of intoxication, and the other to get rid of a scolding wife.

This account of the Potawatomis might have been lengthened out by adding many circumstances which were related to us concerning their manners and opinions; but having given the most important, we shall refrain from noticing the remainder, except in a few instances, when treating of other Indian tribes; in which case they may assist in a comparison between the different nations.

CHAPTER IV.

Carey mission-house. Lake Michigan. Chicago.

THE only person worthy of note, whom the party met at Fort Wayne, besides those already alluded to, was Captain Riley, the same gentleman who has interested the world by an account of his sufferings in Africa. He has formed a settlement on St. Mary's river, fourteen miles above Fort Wayne, which he has called Willshire, in honour of the British consul who redeemed him from captivity. The spot which he has selected is said to be the only one that affords a water-power within fifty miles of Fort Wayne; from which circumstance it will probably increase in importance. The party made arrangements to cross the wilderness, of upwards of two hundred miles, which separates this place from Chicago; they fortunately met here the express sent from the latter place for letters, and detained him as a guide. His name was Bemis, and we have great pleasure in stating, that of all the United States' soldiers who, at various times, accompanied the expedition in the capacity of escort or guide, none behaved himself so much to their satisfaction as this man. On the 29th of May, the party left Fort Wayne; the cavalcade consisted of seven persons, including the soldier, and a black servant, called Andrew Allison: there were in addition two horses loaded with provisions. The first day the party travelled but twenty miles, and encamped on the bank of a small stream known by the name of Blue-grass; this is the last of the tributaries to the Mississippi which are met with in Indiana; all the streams which we crossed during the ensuing five or six days empty their waters into Lake Michigan. The country to the west of Fort Wayne is much more promising than that which lies east of it. Though wet, and in some places swampy, it is much less so than that through which we had previously travelled. The soil is thin, but of good quality; prairies are occasionally met with. The forests consist of white oak, shellbark, aspen, &c. The weather, which was cloudy in the morning and showery in the afternoon, cleared up towards sunset, and our first night's exposure was attended with no evil consequences. The meadow on which we halted, was covered with a fine short grass, which afforded us a soft couch, while it secured to our horses plentiful and palatable food. The streams we crossed this day were inconsiderable; the first, known by the name of Eel river, is one of the head branches of the Wabash: it was considerably swollen at that time; we forded it with some difficulty, and met on the west bank a party of traders, who had been encamped there some time with a large quantity of furs, which they durst not trust across the stream in its present state of elevation. They were nearly destitute of provisions, and we supplied them with one day's rations. A ride of thirty miles took us the next day to a fine river called the Elkheart, which it had been our intention to ford before night. Upon reaching its banks we found it so much swollen as to preclude the possibility of crossing it, unless a raft could be made; but as this would have detained us too long, we preferred attempting to make our way down the left bank of the stream. We were led to take this course from the circumstance, that the usual path crosses back to the left or southern bank, about twenty miles below the first crossing. The country travelled over this day, consisted of low flat ridges, the summits of which presented extensive levels interspersed with many small lakes and lagoons. These ridges are not more than ten or fifteen feet in height, their sides are so steep as to make them sometimes difficult of ascent for horses. The country is almost destitute of timber, until within a few miles of the Elkheart, when we entered the river bottom, in which we found a noble forest of oak, black and white walnut, wild cherry, beech, poplar, ash, bass or linden, white and sugar maple, &c. the soil upon which it grows appearing to be of the very best quality, but somewhat wet. Among the plants observed upon the prairie land, Mr. Say noticed a lupin with blue flowers, in full bloom and in great abundance; a fine cypripedium, and the wild flax, which grew in great plenty. Some of the small lakes or ponds are surrounded exclusively with a thick growth of white cedars, none of which are seen elsewhere, or intermixed with any of the forest trees on the more elevated ground. One of the most curious characters of the prairie, was the number of conical depressions in the earth, resembling the sink holes in the neighbourhood of St. Louis; they are from eight to ten or more feet in depth, and from twenty to thirty in diameter. They remind the geologist of numerous funnel-formed holes which are observable in gypsum formations, and particularly in the muriatiferous gypsum of the vicinity of Bex in Switzerland, Moutiers in Savoy, &c. No rocks appear *in situ* any where along these prairies, but they are covered with granitic boulders, bearing evident marks of attrition. The soil is likewise thickly studded with water-worn pebbles, and is therefore far inferior in quality to that over which we passed the preceding day. The grass of these prairies is generally short and dry.

One of the greatest inconveniences we encountered at this stage of our journey, and which was felt still more sensibly when travelling on the prairies west of the Mississippi, was the great range of the thermometer. We noticed this day that at sunrise it stood at 38° (of Fahrenheit's scale), while at noon it had risen to 72°. So great a variation of temperature is productive of very heavy dews, to which we were frequently exposed, as we often neglected pitching our tents at night. When rising in the morning, we found our clothes as wet as if they had been drenched in water. Whether the usual elevation of these prairies prevents the dew from being attended with the sickliness which generally prevails in the vicinity of rivers, or whether the mode of living which men adopt when crossing the prairies, protects them against the noxious influence of the dew, we know not; but it is remarkable that none of the party suffered from it. In no instance were any of us affected with either cold or rheumatic pains; and if in one or two cases symptoms of fever prevailed, it was at a time when we had left the prairies.

A few Potawatomi Indians were met this day on their way to Fort Wayne. The trail which we followed was struck by that which leads to one of their villages, about fifteen miles distant. The weather was hazy throughout the day; in the evening light clouds were observed. A gentle breeze from the north-west prevailed during the day. Our horses had been fastened, to prevent their rambling into the woods; meeting with but a scanty supply of grass in the neighbourhood of the river, a spot which was overgrown with bushes, and which offered them no other food but the bark of trees, many of them broke the bark ligaments with which they were secured, and strayed to a considerable distance from the camp; these ligaments are called, in the language of the travellers to the west, "hobbles." The pursuit after the horses in the morning occasioned a great loss of time, which was however increased on discovering that the black boy (Andrew) had not returned with them, having unfortunately lost his way in the woods. Our search after him having proved vain, we wrote directions for him to pursue our track, affixed them to a tree, and were on the point of leaving the camp, when fortunately he made his appearance. It is probable, as we afterwards found out, that he would have perished in the woods had he not come in just at that moment; for it would have been impossible for him to trace the party in the thick forest through which our course led us: neither would it have been prudent for us to have remained any longer there, as our horses gave evident signs of their having been on short allowance since noon of the preceding day. Andrew's return to the camp enabled us then to attend to what appeared to be the most important object, which was to seek for a place where the horses might pasture to advantage. We therefore resolved upon following as short a course as we could to the prairie land, endeavouring at the same time to keep near enough to the river to reach the second crossing before night. In this attempt we met with great difficulties, from the closeness of the forest and the swampy nature of the ground. The horses laboured much to get through, and when we stopped at noon to pasture them on a small patch of grass, we found that our progress during four hours had been but about six miles. We had met with a bold and hitherto undescribed stream, about twenty yards wide, which empties itself into the Elkheart about three miles below the usual crossing, and which we have designated in our map as the south-west branch of that river. From the rapidity and depth of this branch we anticipated the same difficulties which we had encountered the evening before; but on continuing along the bank, for some time, we observed a large tree that had fallen across, and that afforded a safe and commodious bridge for ourselves and baggage, while our horses swam over. The afternoon of that day was consumed in passing through swamps, in which our horses were frequently in danger of being lost. At one place three of the horses, with their riders, were near being severely hurt, by the fruitless efforts of the former to get over a bad hole. We were happy to get through without any more serious injury than that of being smeared with dirt from head to foot, and with the loss merely of a few spurs that stuck to the bottom of the pool. After one of the most trying days that any of us ever recollected having undergone, we encamped, at sunset, in a place so low that we could scarcely get a spot dry enough to spread our blankets; and before we had partaken of our evening meal, the mosquitoes arose in such numbers around us, that we were deprived of all rest for the night. We had likewise the mortification of finding that our horses were almost as badly off for grass this evening as the last. The distance travelled this day did not exceed twenty miles. Our course had been entirely directed by the compass, and was nearly west. An Indian trail which we observed in a direction north 40° west, was followed for a while, with the hope that it would take us to an Indian village, but it only led us back to the Elkheart, which we found as deep and as rapid as at our last encampment. We observed here the remains o a frail canoe, which, for a moment, we thought might assist us in crossing the river; but the weakness of this little vessel, soon convinced us of the impossibility of trusting to it; it was made of the bark of the linden or elm, procured by cutting through to the wood transversely, first at the foot of the tree, and then again about twelve feet above this. A longitudinal cut, uniting these two, allowed the bark to be shelled off in a single piece. It had then been reversed, so that the inner surface, while on the tree, formed the outside of the boat; the whole was finished by causing the middle part to bulge out, by means of sticks placed athwart, while each end was pressed in, and rendered watertight. This path having misled us, we retraced our steps until we ascended a bank, about twenty-five feet high, which runs parallel with the river, and we continued along the edge of this through thick woods of elm, prickly ash, red haw, spice wood, papaw in flower, &c. Our situation during the night was a very uncomfortable one, and little calculated to please those of the party, who were, for the first time, engaged on an exploring expedition. To be placed in the midst of a dense forest, surrounded by bogs, from which our horses had been extricated with great difficulty, uncertain as to the possibility of reaching, by this route, the spot at which we wished to arrive, tormented by insects, our horses faint for want of food, and all this at the commencement of our journey through the woods, was rather a discouraging situation. Anxious to escape from these difficulties, we resumed our journey on Sunday, the 1st of June, at as early an hour as we could, and were engaged for about five hours, in difficulties still greater than those of the preceding day. The thickness of the forest having obliged us to dismount and lead our horses, we waded, knee deep, in the mire, and met with a new obstacle in the necessity of making frequent halts, to replace on the horses the baggage which was thrown off, during the many leaps which they had to take over the fallen trees. After a while we reached a high and dry prairie, partly covered with young aspen bushes, rising to the height of from eight to ten feet, and so thick that it was almost impossible to keep the whole of the party in sight; this reminded Major Long of some of the difficulties he had experienced in travelling through the cane brakes of Arkansaw. On halting at noon, we discovered the Elkheart at no great distance, and from the account of our guides, concluded that we had got through our difficulties. To the younger travellers it was a source of much gratification, to find that the fatigues of that morning had exceeded all that their more experienced companions had ever met with, as it was to them a sure warrant that they had not overrated their powers in undertaking the journey. At our noontime's encampment, we found the angelica plant, and the wild-pea-vine. We soon struck a trail, and, about three miles below, came to the lower crossing of the river; it was still so high that it would have been impossible to pass, but we experienced great pleasure in ascertaining that we had again fallen into the usual track from Wayne to Chicago. We observed here, for the first time, the *equisetum* growing in abundance. In the afternoon we travelled with ease and comfort over a prairie country interspersed with occasional spots of woodland. One of these prairies which was about five miles wide and one and a half long, was as level as possible, and as far as the eye could observe, it resembled a smooth unruffled sheet of water. The scene was enlivened, and the solitude interrupted by the quick flight of the deer which we disturbed while feeding, and which darted across our path with a rapidity that baffles description. About sunset we arrived at a romantic stream called Devil's river, and here we encamped upon as beautiful a spot as the most fastidious could have wished for; we pitched our tent for the first time, and while partaking of a comfortable meal, in the open air, spent a more pleasant evening than perhaps we could ever have expected to enjoy in such a solitude. There was a still sublimity in the scene, which we have in vain looked for on many an occasion. The dreariness of our last encampment contrasted so strongly with the calmness of the present, that it powerfully reminded us of that constant mutability in the situation of man, which perhaps finds its parallel only in the unceasing changes which his ideas and his feelings undergo.

The next day we proceeded along the southern bank of the Elkheart, and observed its junction with the St. Joseph. This last mentioned stream is known by the appellation of St. Joseph of *Lake Michigan*, in contradistinction to the river of the same name which empties itself into Lake Erie, and which we saw at Fort Wayne. The St. Joseph of Michigan is a fine stream, deeply incased; it is about one hundred yards wide, and being at that time very full, was both deep and rapid; it was the finest stream we had met with since we left the Muskingum, or perhaps the Ohio. A beautiful prairie with a fine rich soil, offered to the party an easy mode of travelling, and the occasional glimpses which they caught of the St. Joseph and its adjoining forests, afforded them a series of varied and ever beautiful prospects, which were rendered more picturesque by the ruins of Strawberry, Rum, and St. Joseph's villages, formerly the residence of Indians, or of the first French settlers. It was curious to trace the difference in the remains of the habitations of the red and white man in the midst of this distant solitude. While the untenanted cabin of the Indian presented in its neighbourhood but the remains of an old cornfield overgrown with weeds; the rude hut of the Frenchman was surrounded with vines, and with the remains of his former gardening exertions. The asparagus, the pea-vine, and the woodbine, still grow about it, as though in defiance of the revolutions which have dispersed those who planted them here. The very names of the villages mark the difference between their former tenants; those of the Indians were designated by the name of the fruit which grew abundantly on the spot, or of the object which they coveted most: while the French missionary had placed his village under the patronage of the tutelar saint in whom he reposed his utmost confidence. Near to these we found two traders settled in the vicinity of Indian lands, or, as is believed by many, upon the reservation itself; where they probably carry on a lucrative trade, if, as we were informed by one of them, a skin, valued at one dollar, was obtained for five gunflints, which had cost him a cent a piece. This is, however, the least evil; our objections to this trade would be much lighter, if the Indians were liable to be defrauded only of their dues; but great as is this injustice, it bears no comparison to the evils growing out of the constant temptation of liquor to which they are exposed, and which, as is too well known, it is impossible for them to resist. It is really shocking to observe the manner in which, notwithstanding the laws of the land, the dictates of sound reason, and morality, and the active efforts of the United States' agents, the traders persist in their practice of offering liquor to the Indians, the effect of which is to demoralize and to destroy them.

There is in this neighbourhood an establishment, which, by the philanthropic views that have led to its formation, and by the boundless charity with which it is administered, compensates in a manner the insult offered to the laws of God and man by the traders. The reports which we had received of the flattering success which had attended the efforts of the Baptist missionaries on the St. Joseph, induced us to deviate a little from our route to visit their interesting establishment. The Carey mission-house, so designated in honour of the late Mr. Carey, the indefatigable apostle of India, is situated within about a mile of the river, and twenty-five miles (by land) above its mouth. The ground upon which it is erected is the site of an ancient and extensive Potawatomis village, now no longer in existence. The establishment was created by the Baptist Missionary Society in Washington, and is under the superintendance of the Rev. Mr. M'Coy, a man, whom, from all the reports we heard of him, we should consider as very eminently qualified for the important trust committed to him. We regretted that at the time we passed at the Carey mission-house, this gentleman was absent on business connected with the establishment of another missionary settlement on the Grand river of Michigan; but we saw his wife, who received us in a very hospitable manner, and gave us every opportunity of becoming acquainted with the circumstances of the school. The spot upon which the houses are built, and the agricultural pursuits carried on, was covered with a very dense forest seven months before the time when we visited it, but by the great activity of the superintendant, he has succeeded in the course of this short time in building six good log houses, four of which are connected, and afford a comfortable residence to the inmates of the establishment; a fifth is used as a school-room, and the sixth forms a commodious blacksmith's shop. In addition to this, they have cleared about fifty acres of land, which are nearly all inclosed by a substantial fence; forty acres have already been ploughed and planted with maize, and every step has been taken to place the establishment upon an independent footing. The school consists of from forty to sixty children, of which fifteen are females. They are either children of Indians, or half-breed descendants of French and Indian parents; there being about an equal number of each. It is contemplated that the school will soon be increased to one hundred. The plan adopted appears to be a very judicious one; to instruct them in the arts of civilized life, to teach them the benefits which they may derive from them, without attempting to confuse their heads by ideas of religion, the value of which it is in their present state, impossible for them to appreciate. It is only after they shall have been familiarized with the blessings attendant upon civilization, that they may be induced to turn, with effect, their attention to the sublime principles of that dispensation to which we are indebted for all those comforts. To attempt to christianize them before they have been civilized, would be to expect of them a maturity of reasoning far beyond that of which experience teaches us that they are possessed. In his present state of wildness and ignorance, it is impossible for the Indian to appreciate the vast difference which exists between his heathen superstitions and the pure morality of the gospel. Could we entertain a doubt of what must strike every reflecting man as true, we need but open the books of the Catholic missionaries, whose zeal first induced them to visit the trackless wastes of America, to ascend her as yet unknown rivers, and to risk every hazard and surmount every obstacle, conveying the glad tidings of the gospel, and baptising in the name of the Lord. What say they of their success, they were heard with patient attention, for such is the practice of the Indian, but what root did their words strike in the minds of their pupils? Father Hennepin, one of the most celebrated of these missionaries, has accounted for their ill success in the true way. " There are," says he, " several obstacles to the conversion of the Indians, but in most cases the chief difficulty arises from the indifference which they manifest for every thing. If we instruct them in the creation of the world, and in the mysteries of the Christian religion, they say that we are right, and they generally applaud what we tell them. They would hold it to be a great breach of manners to intimate the least doubt as to the truth of all that we teach them, but having heard and praised all that we had to say, they pretend that we ought to show the same deference for the tales which they relate to us; and when we tell them that all they have advanced is false, their reply is, that as they have acquiesced in all that we have stated, it is foolish on our part to interrupt them and deny the truth of which they assert." " All that thou hast taught us," say they, " respecting the belief of thy country is doubtless true as respects thy people, but it is otherwise with us who belong to a different nation, and who dwell upon lands which are on this side of the great lake." It is this indifference in all matters of faith, this belief that their doctrines were as good as those of the missionaries, that may be considered as the true source of the failure of all attempts to christianize them. But after their ideas shall have been expanded by a proper acquaintance with the arts of civilized life, then they cannot fail fully to appreciate the superiority of our faith over theirs.

The plan adopted in the school, purposes to unite a practical with an intellectual education; the boys are instructed in the English language, in reading, writing, and arithmetic, they are made to attend to the usual occupations of a farm, and to perform every operation connected with it, such as plowing, planting, harrowing, &c.; in these pursuits they appear to take great delight; the system being well regulated, they find time for every thing, not only for study and labour, but also for innocent recreation, in which they are encouraged to indulge; and the hours allotted to recreation may perhaps be viewed as productive of results fully as important as those accruing from more serious pursuits. In visiting Indian villages, we observed that the children seldom played together in the manner in which those of the white men unite for recreation. The pursuits of the Indian boy are of a solitary nature, he imitates the chase, practises shooting at a mark in order to acquire a sure aim, prepares his arrows, &c., but seldom appears to enjoy that community of pleasures from which a taste for society would necessarily spring. By inducing the boys of the Mission-house to play together, they will soon discover how many of the comforts and pleasures of life arise from the communion of souls; and they will be led to form attachments which will attend them through life, and which may induce them after they have left the peaceful abode of the missionary, to continue in the course which has already been to them the fruitful source of so much delight. The females receive in the school the same instruction which is given to the boys, and are in addition to this, taught spinning, weaving, and sewing, both plain and ornamental; they were just beginning to embroider, an occupation which may by some, be considered as unsuitable to the situation which they are destined to hold in life, but which appears to us very judiciously used as a reward and stimulus; it encourages their taste and natural talent for imitation, which is very great; and by teaching them that occupation may be connected with amusement, it may prevent their relapsing into that idleness which has been justly termed the source of all evils. They are likewise made to attend to the pursuits of the dairy, such as the milking of cows, churning of milk, &c. The establishment is intended to be opened for children from seven to fourteen years old, but they very properly receive them at a much earlier age, and even where a great desire of learning was manifested, older persons have been admitted. All appear to be very happy, and to make as rapid a progress as white children of the same age would make; their principal excellence rests in works of imitation; they write astonishingly well, and many display great natural talent for drawing. The institution receives the countenance of the most respectable among the Indians; there are in the school two of the grandchildren of Topaneba*, the great hereditary chief of the Potawatomis, who has his residence upon this river. The Indians visit the establishment occasionally, appear pleased with it, and show their favour to it by presents of sugar, venison, &c., which they often make to the family of the missionary. Some of the parents of the half-breed scholars pay for their children's board, and contribute in this manner to the support of the establishment; which, being sanctioned by the War Department, receives annually one thousand dollars from the United States, for the support of a teacher and blacksmith, according to the conditions of the treaty concluded at Chicago in 1821, by Governor Cass and Mr. Sibley, commissioners on the part of the United States. By this treaty about four or five millions of acres of land were relinquished by the Potawatomis. It was one of the conditions of the purchase, that a small tract of the Indian reservation should be conveyed in fee simple to the Baptist missionaries, for the purpose of forming a school and agricultural establishment. It is said that the Indians themselves selected this spot as being the site of their old village; this must have been very populous, as the remains of corn-hills, which are very distinctly visible at this time, are said to extend over a thousand acres. The village was finally abandoned about fifty years ago, but there are a few of the oldest of the nation who still recollect the site of their respective

* Tŏ-pă-nĕ-bă.

huts; they are said frequently to visit the establishment, and to trace with deep feeling a spot which is endeared to them by " the memory of past joys, pleasing and mournful to the soul."

The Carey Mission-house has been very liberally supported by the charitable contributions raised throughout the western states. The family have a flock of one hundred sheep, collected in Tennessee, Kentucky, and Ohio, and are daily expecting two hundred head of cattle from the same states. These contributions, together with the produce of their farm, will, it is thought, prevent them from being exposed to suffer as much from scarcity of provisions as they have already done. When we visited them, they were on short allowance, owing to the loss of a load of wheat which had been sent from Fort Wayne in a waggon a short time before we left that place, and which had been embarked in pirogues at the upper crossing of the Elkheart; by the accidental upsetting of the pirogues the whole of the cargo was lost.

We were told that the family had been deprived of the use of milk, during the whole winter, from the circumstance of their cows feeding upon a kind of wild onion which grows in the prairies. It may be well to state, that notwithstanding the great objection which the Indians generally have to the use of milk, the children in the school have become quite fond of it. In order to give a greater extension to their establishment, they contemplate engaging Shane as an interpreter and assistant; from what we saw of this man while at Fort Wayne, we were not led to form so high an opinion of him as we had entertained from reports received on St. Mary's river.

No rock appears in place near the establishment, and we met with none on our way from Devil's river, except in one place where we observed, in a ravine, a calcareous formation evidently of the latest date, and which probably still continues to increase—it was filled with vegetables, some of which were unaltered, while others appeared to have undergone a partial decomposition.

Having engaged an Indian to lead us back from Mr. M'Coy's to the Chicago trace, we resumed our journey on the 3d of June. Our guide's hoary head would have satisfied even Humboldt himself, that his assertion " that the hair of Indians never becomes gray," was too general.* We have met with many instances, and the circumstance is so natural that we should not have mentioned it, but for the importance attached to the slightest observation of a traveller so accurate as Humboldt generally is. After travelling about ten miles through a prairie, we parted from our guide, who considered himself amply rewarded with about half a pound of gunpowder. We then entered upon what is termed, the Fourteen Mile Prairie, which, for the first seven miles, presented an extensive plain, uninterrupted by the least elevation, and undiversified by the prospect of a single tree. We had occasion to observe, on a former occasion, that the route which we travelled carried us along the height of land that separates the waters tributary to the Mississippi from those which empty into the lakes; and we had an opportunity of seeing this confirmed, in this place, by the fact that a communication between those waters had been effected, during wet seasons, through the Fourteen Mile Prairie. It appears that a very deep swamp,

* Polit. Ess. on the Kingdom of New Spain, (Lond. 1811,) vol. i. p. 150.

which we avoided by our visit to the mission station, establishes a connection between two streams, one of which empties its waters into the Kankakee, while those of the other run to the St Joseph. This has afforded, and still continues to afford every year, an easy communication for canoes and small boats. An intercourse has likewise existed, in wet seasons, across the prairie, east of the trader's establishment which we passed on the preceding day. At noon we rested our horses in the vicinity of the remains of an Indian village, named the Grand Quoit, and we observed a few Indian lodges scattered along the edge of the forest which encloses this prairie. On discovering our party on the prairie, the tenants of the lodges immediately rode out of the woods, advanced towards us, and opened a conversation with our guides. Their intercourse with white men, and the consequent departure from their original customs, were observable in the circumstance of their commencing the conversation, and in their minute inquiries respecting our object and intentions in visiting the country. They are said to experience a great scarcity of food, which we can readily believe from the total absence of any kind of game which we had observed upon the route. An Indian who rode up near us, while we were partaking of our dinner, stopped, and appeared to long after food; but called for none. We offered him some, which he very thankfully accepted, and seemed to eat with great voraciousness.

Our party was this day overtaken by an express, who brought letters from Wayne, to Major Long; one of them was from Dr. James, stating that he had been waiting in Pittsburg for the party. From the contents of his letter, we concluded that the hopes, which had been hitherto entertained, of his being able to effect a junction with us, were vain. These were the last letters received from our friends, until we found some on our return at the Sault de St. Marie.

At about forty-three miles from the Carey station, the trail, which we followed, struck the shores of Lake Michigan; this was a source of great gratification to us; as the last twelve miles of our road had been very dangerous, on account of the numerous deep holes formed in it; to these may be added the many superficial roots that projected from the beech trees, in every direction, and that exposed the horses to frequent stumbling. The forest was almost exclusively composed of the finest growth of beech; on some of the higher grounds we found, in great plenty, the partridge or fox-berry, (Gaultheria procumbens,) with its aromatic red fruit, in a state of perfect maturity; it was accompanied by the whortleberry in full blossom. We saw this day the first white pine, and in some places this tree was very abundant. We had been following for some time the valley of a small stream, called by the French, *Rivière du Chemin*, (Trail River,) but on approaching near to its mouth, our path winded to the south, and we found ourselves at the base of a sand-hill of about twenty feet in height; the fog which arose behind it, and the coolness of the air warned us of our approach to the lake; and on turning along the base of the hill, we discovered ourselves to be on the beach of Lake Michigan. The scenery changes here most suddenly; instead of the low, level and uniformly green prairies, through which we had been travelling for some time past, or of the beech swamp which had offered us such difficulties during the last four hours of our ride, we found ourselves transported, as it were, to the shores of an ocean. We were near to the southern extremity of the lake; the view, towards the north, was boundless; the eye meeting nothing but the vast expanse of water, which spread like a sea, its surface at that time as calm and unruffled as though it were a sheet of ice. Towards the south, the prospect was limited to a few hundred yards, being suddenly cut off by a range of low sand-hills, which arose to a height varying from twenty to forty feet; in some instances rising perhaps to upwards of one hundred feet. When we first approached the lake, it was covered with a mist, which soon vanished, and the bright sun, reflected upon the sand and water, produced a glare of light quite fatiguing to the eye. Our progress was in a south-westwardly direction, along the beach, which reminded us of that of the Atlantic on the coast of New Jersey. The sand-hills are undulating and crowned at their summits with a scrubby growth of white pine and furze; while the brow, which faces the lake, is quite bare. In the rear of the hills, but invisible from the beach, spreads a level country supporting a scattering growth of white pine, oak, beech, hophorn-beam, (Ostrya virginica,) &c. East and west of us, a continuous narrow beach, curved gradually towards the north, and bounded by the lake and the hills, was all that the eye could observe. At our evening's encampment of the 4th of June, we were at the southernmost extremity of the lake, and could distinctly observe that its south-eastern corner is the arc of a greater circle than the south-western. The beach is strewed with fragments of rocks, evidently primitive, and probably derived from the decomposition of the same masses, which, by their destruction, have given rise to the immense deposite of sand and pebbles that forms the bottom of the lake. These fragments, which are all rolled, vary much in size; the largest we observed weighed, perhaps, twenty or thirty tons. They consist of granite, mica and clay-slates, hornblende, &c. The hills appear to have been produced by the constant accumulation of sand, blown from the beach by the strong north-westerly winds which prevail during the winter season—the sand is loose and uncemented. In a few places traces of lignite and peat are to be met with; doubtless resulting from the decomposition of the partial vegetation which grew upon these hills, and which was successively destroyed and buried under the sand; perhaps, also, from some of the drift-wood which is often carried ashore by the waves.

The lake appears to abound in fish, judging from the quantity that we saw gliding along the surface of the water; upon the beach there were many that lay dead, and that, in some places, rendered the air quite fetid. These belonged chiefly to the pike, the salmon-trout, &c. We cannot learn that there is any great variety in the fish found in this lake. The streams passed this day, during our ride along the beach, were inconsiderable; the first is termed the *Rivière des Bois*, probably from the quantity of drift-wood observed near it; the English appellation for it is Stick river; the second which we met, was the Big Calamick, (Kenomokonk* of the Indians,) where the party dispersed, during the evening, each to attend to his own avocations. Major Long and Mr. Colhoun commenced observations for latitude, which they found difficult to complete on account of the fog which spread over the lake. Hunting and fishing parties were sent out, but which returned without having met with any success.

The colour of the streams which we passed indicates

* Kĕ-nŏ-mŏ-kŏnk.

their origin in a swamp; and the great excess of water in this fen during some seasons, together with the loose nature of the sandy bar which divides it from the lake, causes it frequently to force the dam, and open to itself a new passage into the lake. There are, near to this place, two streams, one of which, named Pine river, was opened last year; the other, termed New river, was formed a short time before. We crossed both these streams, as well as the little Calamick, and finding that the travelling on the beach had become very uncomfortable, owing to a heavy fog, and a strong lake wind which announced an approaching storm, we crossed the sand-hills, and travelled on the prairie; in this manner we were well sheltered from the wind. Our path led us over the scene of the bloody massacre perpetrated in 1812, when the garrison of Chicago was entirely destroyed by the Indians (principally Potawatomis), after they had abandoned the fort, and in violation of the pledge given to them by the Indians. No traces are now to be seen of the massacre; the bones, which are said to have remained for a long while bleaching upon the prairie, were at last gathered up and buried, by order of Captain Bradley, who had the command of the new fort, built on the ruins of the old one; but no one could point out to us the spot where they had been deposited. While resting at noon, on the bank of New river, we observed how difficult it is to judge correctly of objects on the prairie; and, at the same time, how great is the similarity between the prairie wolf and the dogs owned by the Indians. While seated at dinner, we were told that one of the soldiers had discovered a wolf, and was about to fire upon it. The whole party saw the animal, and remained convinced that it was a wolf, until one of the men observed an Indian hut in the distance, and suggested that it might be a dog belonging to the tenant of the hut, which information induced the soldier to desist from shooting; a few moments afterwards an Indian made his appearance on the prairie, and called the animal to him. This Indian was remarkable for the length of his beard, which, contrary to their usual custom, he had allowed to grow to the length of one inch and a half; his dress was indicative of the same slovenly disposition. We were obliged to commit to his charge one of the horses; this was the only one that had travelled the whole distance from Philadelphia; but he had become unable to proceed, having been affected for some time past with the distemper; and, notwithstanding all the care that was taken of him, he had become so faint that, even without any load, we found it impossible to make him keep up with the rest of the horses. The Indian undertook to take care of him for a few days, and then lead him to the fort, which promise he faithfully performed.

In the afternoon of the fifth of June, we reached Fort Dearborn (Chicago), having been engaged eight days in travelling a distance of two hundred and sixteen miles, making an average, of twenty-seven miles per day. Our estimate of the distance exceeds the usual allowance by sixteen miles, on account of the circuitous route which we took to avoid crossing the Elkheart. At Fort Dearborn we stopped for a few days, with a view to examine the country and make further preparations for the journey to the Mississippi.

In taking a retrospective view of the nature of the country travelled over, we find that from Fort Wayne to twenty miles west of Devil river, it presents as it were two distinct surfaces. The first, or lower one, is a level moist prairie, covered with luxuriant herbage; the second, or upper one, is abruptly elevated twenty-five or thirty feet above the prairie land, and consists of a succession of flat ridges, uniform in height, but of unequal breadth, that are frequently disconnected by narrow straits of prairie land; from this circumstance the lower level presents a continuous surface, while the upper one is broken into distinct ridges insulated in the midst of the prairie. The soil of the ridges is poor and gravelly, covered with a thin growth of shrubby oaks; it appears to have been occasioned by what has been termed an ancient alluvial formation (probably similar to those extensive deposits which are said to constitute the great plains that are observed in South America); this formation having been afterwards divided by valleys of a still later origin, has produced a lower level that is filled with a newer alluvium probably resulting from the action of causes which still continue to operate—as we had an opportunity of remarking in the prairie, east of the trading house which we visited previous to our arrival at the Carey station. To these ridges succeeds a broken country, consisting of insulated hills of a soil still inferior, but having more trees. Among the oaks that grow here we observed, for the first time, the hickory interspersed.

Fort Dearborn is situated in the State of Illinois, on the south bank, and near to the mouth of Chicago river; the boundary line between this state and that of Indiana strikes the western shore of Lake Michigan ten miles north of its southernmost extremity, and then continues along the shore of the lake until it reaches the forty-second and a half degree of north lattitude, along which it extends to the Mississippi. The post at Chicago was abandoned a few months after the party visited it. Its establishment had been found necessary to intimidate the hostile and still very powerful tribes of Indians that inhabit this part of the country; but the rapid extension of the white population to the west, the establishment along the Mississippi of a chain of military posts which encloses them, and at the same time convinces them of the vigilance of the government, and of the inevitable destruction which they would bring upon themselves by the most trifling act of hostility on their part, have, it is thought, rendered the continuance of a military force at this place unnecessary. An Indian agent remains there, in order to keep up amicable relations with them, and to attend to their wants, which are daily becoming greater, owing to the increasing scarcity of game in the country.

We were much disappointed at the appearance of Chicago and its vicinity. We found in it nothing to justify the great eulogium lavished upon this place by a late traveller, who observes that "it is the most fertile and beautiful that can be imagined." "As a farming country," says he, "it unites the fertile soil of the finest lowland prairies with an elevation which exempts it from the influence of stagnant waters, and a summer climate of delightful serenity."* The best comment upon this description of the climate and soil is the fact that, with the most active vigilance on the part of the officers, it was impossible for the garrison, consisting of from seventy to ninety men, to subsist upon the grain raised in the country, although much of their time was devoted to agricultural pursuits. The difficulties which the agriculturist meets

* Schoolcraft's Narrative Journal of Travels (Albany, 1820), page 384.

with here are numerous; they arise from the shallowness of the soil, from its humidity, and from its exposure to the cold and damp winds which blow from the lake with great force during most part of the year. The grain is frequently destroyed by swarms of insects. There are also a number of destructive birds of which it was impossible for the garrison to avoid the baneful influence, except by keeping, as was practised at Fort Dearborn, a party of soldiers constantly engaged in shooting at the crows and blackbirds that committed depredations upon the corn planted by them. But, even with all these exertions the maize seldom has time to ripen, owing to the shortness and coldness of the season. The provisions for the garrison were, for the most part, conveyed from Mackinaw in a schooner, and sometimes they were brought from St. Louis, a distance of three hundred and eighty-six miles up the Illinois and Des Plaines rivers.

The appearance of the country near Chicago offers but few features upon which the eye of the traveller can dwell with pleasure. There is too much uniformity in the scenery; the extensive water prospect is a waste uncheckered by islands, unenlivened by the spreading canvass, and the fatiguing monotony of which is increased by the equally undiversified prospect of the land scenery, which affords no relief to the sight, as it consists merely of a plain, in which but few patches of thin and scrubby woods are observed scattered here and there.

The village presents no cheering prospect, as, notwithstanding its antiquity, it consists of but few huts, inhabited by a miserable race of men, scarcely equal to the Indians from whom they are descended. Their log or bark-houses are low, filthy and disgusting, displaying not the least trace of comfort. Chicago is, perhaps, one of the oldest settlements in the Indian country; its name, derived from the Potawatomi language, signifies either a skunk, or wild, onion; and each of these significations has been occasionally given for it. A fort is said to have formerly existed there. Mention is made of the place as having been visited in 1671 by Perrot, who found " Chicagou" to be the residence of a powerful chief of the Miamis. The number of trails centering all at this spot, and their apparent antiquity, indicate that this was probably for a long while the site of a large Indian village. As a place of business, it offers no inducement to the settler; for the whole annual amount of the trade on the lake did not exceed the cargo of five or six schooners, even at the time when the garrison received its supplies from Mackinaw. It is not impossible that at some distant day, when the banks of the Illinois shall have been covered with a dense population, and when the low prairies which extend between that river and Fort Wayne, shall have acquired a population proportionate to the produce which they can yield, that Chicago may become one of the points in the direct line of communication between the northern lakes and the Mississippi; but even the intercourse which will be carried on through this communication, will, we think, at all times be a limited one; the dangers attending the navigation of the lake, and the scarcity of harbours along the shore, must ever prove a serious obstacle to the increase of the commercial importance of Chicago. The extent of the sand banks which are formed on the eastern and southern shore, by the prevailing north and north-westerly winds, will likewise prevent any important works from being undertaken to improve the post of Chicago.

The south fork of Chicago river takes its rise, about six miles from the fort, in a swamp which communicates also with the Des Plaines, one of the head branches of the Illinois. Having been informed that this route was frequently travelled by traders, and that it had been used by one of the officers of the garrison, who returned with provisions from St. Louis a few days before our arrival at the fort, we determined to ascend the Chicago river in order to observe this interesting division of waters. We accordingly left the fort on the 7th of June, in a boat, which, after having ascended the river about four miles, we exchanged for a narrow pirogue that drew less water; the stream we were ascending was very narrow, rapid, and crooked, presenting a great fall; it continued so for about three miles, when we reached a sort of swamp designated by the Canadian voyagers under the name of *le petit lac*. Our course through this swamp, which extended for three miles, was very much impeded by the high grass, weeds, &c. through which our pirogue passed with difficulty. Observing that our progress through the fen was very slow, and the day being considerably advanced, we landed on the north bank, and continued our course along the edge of the swamp for about three miles, until we reached the place where the old portage road meets the current, which was here very distinct towards the south. We were delighted at beholding for the first time, a feature so interesting in itself, but which we had afterwards an opportunity of observing frequently on the route, *viz.*: the division of waters starting from the same source, and running in two different directions, so as to become the feeders of streams that discharge themselves into the ocean at immense distances apart. Although at the time we visited it, there was scarcely water enough to permit our pirogue to pass, we could not doubt, that in the spring of the year the route must be a very eligible one. Lieut. Hopson, who accompanied us to the Des Plaines, told us that he had travelled it with ease, in a boat loaded with lead and flour. The distance from the fort to the intersection of the Portage road and Des Plaines, is supposed to be about twelve or thirteen miles; the elevation of the feeding lake above Chicago river was estimated at five or six feet; and, it is probable, that the descent to the Des Plaines is less considerable. The Portage road is about eleven miles long; the usual distance travelled by land seldom however exceeds from four to nine miles; in very dry seasons it has been said to amount to thirty miles, as the portage then extends to Mount Juliet, near the confluence of the Kankakee. When we consider the facts above stated, we are irresistibly led to the conclusion, that an elevation of the lakes of a few feet (not exceeding ten or twelve), above their present level, would cause them to discharge their waters, partly at least, into the Gulf of Mexico; that such a discharge has at one time existed, every one conversant with the nature of the country must admit; and it is equally apparent that an expenditure, trifling in comparison to the importance of the object, would again render Lake Michigan a tributary of the Mexican gulf. Impressed with the importance of this object, the legislature of Illinois has already caused some observations

SOURCE OF ST. PETER'S RIVER. 169

to be made upon the possibility of establishing this communication; the commissioners appointed to that effect, visited Chicago after we left it, and we know not what results they obtained, as their report has not reached us; but we have been informed that they had considered the elevation of the *petit lac* above Chicago to be somewhat greater than we had estimated it. It is the opinion of those best acquainted with the nature of the country, that the easiest communication would be between the Little Calamick and some point of the Des Plaines, probably below the Portage road; between these two points there is, in wet seasons, we understand, a water communication of ten or twelve miles. Of the practicability of the work, and of the sufficiency of a supply of water no doubt can exist. The only difficulty will, we apprehend, be in keeping the communication open after it is once made, as the soil is swampy, and probably will require particular care to oppose the return of the soft mud into the excavations.

In the immediate vicinity of Chicago, a secondary limestone is found, disposed in horizontal strata; it contains many organic remains. This limestone appears to us to be very similar in its geological as well as mineralogical aspect, to that observed above the coal formation on the Miami; but no superposition being visible, it is impossible for us to determine at present its relative age; we, however, incline to the opinion, that it is one of the late secondary limestones. We have to regret that the specimens which were obtained of the same have been lost, and that we are deprived of the opportunity of comparing them with those collected in other parts of our route. This limestone, which lies exposed to view in some places, is for the most part covered with an alluvial deposit consisting of the detritus of primitive rocks. Upon the shore of Lake Michigan, specimens of native copper have likewise been occasionally picked up. We have in our possession, owing to the liberality of Dr. Hall, a specimen which is part of a mass, weighing two pounds, found by the express from Chicago to Greenbay; it was picked up on the lake shore, about five miles south of the Milwacke, a stream which empties into the lake, about eighty-five miles north of Chicago; the spot at which it was found is known by the name of the Soapbanks, and is stated by Mr. Schoolcraft to consist of a bed of white clay; Dr. Hall was led to visit the spot in hopes of finding more copper, but met with none. We have dwelt upon this fact merely from the great importance which has been attached to every locality of native copper, by those who are induced to believe that, where a specimen exists, a mine ought to be looked for. In reading the relations of travellers on the subject, we become satisfied of the incorrectness of this conclusion; wherever the copper has been found, it has always been in detached masses, generally of a small weight, and appearing evidently out of place. We must not therefore expect to find veins in their vicinity; if the existence of copper in the west deserves all that importance which it has received, a circumstance which we very much question in the present state of the country, it is not upon the study of the localities of these fragments of native copper that we are to waste our time and means. The main object must be to ascertain whence they came; and this can only be determined by an examination of the nature of the valleys, of the extent and abundance of the alluvial deposite in which they are found, and of the original primitive formations, from the partial destruction of which these extensive deposits of alluvium, and the large boulders which accompany them, have received their origin. But these are considerations which we shall not broach at present, as they will find their place more naturally, at a later period of this work.

Although the quantity of game in this part of the country is diminishing very rapidly, and although it is barely sufficient for the support of the Indians, still there is enough, and particularly of the smaller kind, to offer occupation to the amateur sportsman. There are many different kinds of aquatic birds, which feed upon the wild rice (Zizania aquatica), and other plants that thrive in the swamps which cover the country. Mr. Say observed, among others, the mallard (Anas boschas), shoveller-duck (A. clypeata), blue winged teal (A. discors), common merganser (Mergus serrator), common coot (Fulica americana), stellate heron or Indian hen (Ardea minor), &c. &c. In the lake there is also a great quantity of fish, but none appears to be of a very superior quality; the white fish (Coregonus albus, Lesueur), which is the greatest delicacy found in the lakes, is not caught at Chicago, but sometimes twenty or thirty miles north of it.

Observations for latitude and longitude, were made here by Mr. Colhoun, from which the situation of this place was found to be in latitude 41° 59′ 53″ N.—longitude 86° 47′ 15″ W.—Magnetic variation 6° 12′ East.*

During our short residence at Chicago, we were, by

---

* See Appendix II. The longitude cannot be depended upon with cirtainty, as there was some doubt as to the *error* of the watch.

the favour of Dr. Wolcott, the Indian agent, furnished with much information concerning the Indians of this vicinity, through his interpreter, Alexander Robinson, a half-breed Chippewa, who informed us that the Indians who frequent this part of the country are very much intermixed, belonging principally to the Potawatomis, Ottawas, and Chippewas, (ochepewag,*) from which circumstance a great admixture of the three languages prevails here. The vicinity of the Miamis has also, in his opinion, tended to adulterate the language of the Potawatomis in the neighbourhood of Fort Wayne; and it is believed that this language is spoken in the greatest purity, only along the banks of the St. Joseph of Lake Michigan. Robinson did not suppose the Potawatomis to exceed two thousand five hundred souls; but it is probable that their number must be greater, especially as they are united with the Kickapoos, whose population amounts to six hundred in the State of Illinois. According to his observations, the Potawatomis believe that they came from the vicinity of the Sault de St. Marie, where they presume that they were created. A singular belief, which they entertain, is, that the souls of the departed have, on their way to the great prairie, to cross a large stream, over which a log is placed as a bridge; but that this is in such constant agitation, that none but the spirits of good men can pass over it in safety, while those of the bad slip from the log into the water, and are

* (ò-ch'-ê-pê'-w'àg) We have in the course of this work conformed with the general usage in the spelling of this word, dropping the final *y* used by many authors; but from the above method of spelling it, according to its pronunciation, it will be readily observed that the usual orthography can give no idea of the true Indian pronunciation of this word. The final letter ought to be pronounced in a manner intermediate between the *g* and *k*.

never after heard of. This information they pretend to have had revealed to them by one of their ancestors, who, being dead, travelled to the edge of the stream, but not liking to venture on the log, determined to return to the land of the living, which purpose he effected, having been seen once more among his friends, two days after his reputed death. He informed them of what he had observed, and further told them, that while on the verge of the stream, he had heard the sounds of the drum, to the beat of which the blessed were dancing on the opposite prairie. This story they firmly believe.

With a view to collect as much information as possible on the subject of Indian antiquities, we inquired of Robinson whether any traditions on this subject, were current among the Indians. He observed, that their ancient fortifications were a frequent subject of conversation; and especially those in the nature of excavations made in the ground. He had heard of one, made by the Kickapoos and Fox Indians, on the Sangamo river, a stream running into the Illinois. This fortification is distinguished by the name of Etnataek.* It is known to have served as an intrenchment to the Kickapoos and Foxes, who were met there and defeated by the Potawatomis, the Ottowas, and the Chippewas. No date was assigned to this transaction. We understand that the Etnataek was near the Kickapoo village on the Sangamo.

The hunting grounds of the Potawatomis appear to be bounded on the north by the St. Joseph (which on the east side of Lake Michigan separates them from the Ottowas) and the Milwacke, which on the west side of the lake, divides them from the Menomones. They

* (ĕ'tn'ăt'ăĕ'k.)

spread to the south along the Illinois river about two hundred miles; to the west their grounds extend as far as Rock river, and the Mequin or Spoon river of the Illinois: to the east they probably seldom pass beyond the Wabash.

CHAPTER V.

Rock river. Menomones. Geology of the country west of Lake Michigan. Prairie du Chien. Sauks and Foxes.

HAVING spent a few days in Chicago, the party left that post on Wednesday, June 11th. By the instructions received from the War Department, Major Long had the option of striking the Mississippi at Fort Armstrong, or at Dubuque's lead mines, and then ascending that river to Prairie du Chien. It appeared to him, however, that if the direct route to Prairie du Chien, across the prairies, was practicable, it would save several days; but upon inquiry no person could be found who had ever travelled through the prairies in that direction; and although from the description of the country, the route was supposed to be very practicable, yet from the impossibility of procuring a guide, it would have been relinquished, had not an old French engagé, of the name of Le Sellier, undertaken to direct the party. This man, who had lived for upwards of thirty years with the Indians, had taken a wife among the Winnebagoes, and settled on the head waters of Rock river; knowing the country as far as that stream, he presumed that he could find his way thence to Fort Crawford, situated on the Mississippi near the junction of the Wisconsan. Under his guidance the party proceeded on the first day of their journey, in a general direction nearly west, for about seventeen miles. The first stream passed, on that day, was the Chicago river, which we crossed about half a mile above the fort, and immediately above the first fork (or Gary river); the party next came to the River Des Plaines, which is one of the head branches of the Illinois; it receives its name from a variety of maple, which by the Canadians is named *Plaine*. In Potawatomi the river is termed Sheshikmaoshike Sepe* (which signifies *flumen arboris quæ mingit*). This appellation is derived from the great quantity of sap which flows from this tree in the spring. We crossed the Des Plaines about four miles above the Portage road; it was forty yards wide, and so deep that part of our baggage was wet while fording it, but fortunately none materially injured. The length of the Des Plaines from this ford to its source is about fifteen miles, that to its confluence with the Kankakee about forty miles.

We encamped on the east bank of a small stream, about eight yards wide, designated by the Indians under the name of Otokakenog,† which means the *uncovered breast*. The voyagers call it De Page river, from a Frenchman of that name, who died and was buried on the banks of this stream. The De Page enters the Des Plaines about half a mile above its junction with the Kankakee. From Chicago to the place where we forded the Des Plaines, the country presents a low, flat, and swampy prairie, very thickly covered with high grass, aquatic plants, and among others with the wild rice. The latter occurs principally in the places which are still under water; its blades floating on the surface of the fluid like those of the young domestic plant. The

---

* Shè-shîk-mâ-ò-shî-ke Sè-pè.   † ò-tò-kâ-kè-nóg,

whole of this tract of country is overflowed during the spring, and canoes pass in every direction across the prairie. Near the fording of the Des Plaines there is a Potawatomi village, some of the inhabitants of which came to converse with us, while we were encamped at noon during a thunder storm. The birds we saw to-day consisted of prairie hens or grous (Tetrao cupido), reed-birds (Emberiza oryzivora, Wilson), sand-hill cranes (Grus caandensis), curlews, &c. Many badger holes were observed; we saw at the garrison one of these animals, that had been reared in the fort, and whose playful inoffensive manners, had made him a general favourite.

A ride of about eighteen miles brought us to the banks of Fox river, which is a fine stream about one hundred and thirty yards wide, the scenery of which is varied by several islands scattered through its channel. The country, which consisted of prairie land, became handsomely wooded in the neighbourhood of the river; a couple of Indian lodges seen in the distance, gave an appearance of inhabitance to the spot. These we found to belong to the Menomone,* or wild rice eaters, a nation that appears to be fast decreasing in numbers. The reports concerning the Menomone nations are so various, and we observed so few of them on the route, that we had not an opportunity of forming an opinion upon the disputed point of the Algonquin origin. It is said that few, if any, white men have ever been able to learn their language; and we have been assured by the late Indian agent at Greenbay (Major John Biddle), that he had found it difficult to obtain an inter-

* M'è-nŏ-m'ŏ-n'è.

preter capable of conversing with them in their own language. A considerable intercourse has, however, existed between them and white men; but it is said to be principally in the Algonquin languages, the prevailing medium of intercourse being the Chippewa, Ottawa, and Potawatomi languages, or as in most cases a mixture of these three dialects. The few Menomones whom we met with were of a light colour, resembling much that of the light Mulattoes in our Atlantic states, probably nearer the colour of individuals resulting from an admixture of five-eighths European with three-eighths of African blood. It is said that this light colour which distinguishes the Menomones from other Indians, results from a general admixture of European blood. But we have been assured, that even when of pure Indian extraction, they are of a lighter colour than their neighbours, and are therefore often called the White Indians. Whether they be descendants of the Algonquins, or of a different race of men, is a question of much importance, and which, perhaps, may yet be resolved by those, whose opportunities of obtaining information on that subject are greater than ours were. If they be sprung from a different race of men, it may still be questioned whether they settled here previously or subsequently to the Algonquin tribes. Charlevoix says that they were not populous in his time. "This is to be regretted," he adds, " for they are very fine men, and the best shaped of all Canada; they are even taller than the Pouteouatamis. I am assured that they have the same origin, and nearly the same language as the Noquets and Saulteurs, (Leapers;)* *but they add, that they have also a particular language, which they keep to themselves.*"† The Meno-

---

* Chippewas. † Journal Historique, Letter 19th.

mones at present reside principally on the west shore of Lake Michigan north of the Milwacke, in the vicinity of Greenbay, and on the head waters of Fox river, (of Greenbay,) of Menomone river, &c. Their personal appearance is very favourable, and indicative of more neatness, and of a greater taste for ornament, than that of any other of our north-western Indians. Their mode of preparing belts, garters, sheaths for knives, moccasins, &c. and of ornamenting them with beads, and with the coloured quills of porcupines, evinces much taste, and this of the best kind. It does not appear that with them the mere combination of many gaudy colours constitutes beauty; but this is made to depend more upon the proper union of the three colours, white, red, and blue united, to form symmetric and varied designs.

The Fox river, which we crossed, must not be mistaken for the same which runs north-eastwardly into Greenbay of Lake Michigan. Its course is in a different direction, being nearly south-west; it falls into the Illinois about fifteen or twenty miles below the confluence of the Des Plaines and Kankakee.

The Fox river of the Illinois is called by the Indians Pishtako.* It is the same which is mentioned by Charlevoix under the name of Pisticoui, and which flows, as he says, through the country of the Mascoutins. At present it is claimed, at least in this part, by the Potawatomis and Kickapoos, who are incorporated together; the Menomones are allowed to remain there, on account of their being connected by intermarriages. The river has a fine gravelly bottom, and was very easily forded. On the west side we reached a beautiful but

* Pĭsh-t'ă-kŏ.

small prairie, situated on a high bank, which approaches within two hundred and fifty yards of the edge of the water; and upon this prairie we discovered a number of mounds, which appeared to have been arranged with a certain degree of regularity. Of these mounds we counted twenty-seven; they vary from one to four feet and a half in height, and from fifteen to twenty-five in length; their breadth is not proportional to their length, as it seldom exceeds from six to eight feet. They are placed at unequal distances, which average about twenty yards; they are chiefly upon the brow of the hill, but some of them stand at a greater distance back. Their form appears to have been originally oval; and the slight depression in the ground, observed sometimes on both sides of a mound, seems to indicate, that it has been raised by means of the earth collected in its immediate vicinity. We remained ignorant of the causes which may have given rise to their construction, or of the circumstances under which they were executed. Of their artificial nature, no doubt could be entertained. They may probably have been ancient dirt lodges, similar to the ruins observed by Mr. Say, during the expedition to the Rocky mountains, and which were known to be the remains of lodges that had existed within the memory of some of the Indians then living. It does not appear that the Indians, who reside near the Fox river, have any recollection or tradition on this subject. Our guide informed us, that they believed, upon the authority of the missionaries, that these mounds were of antediluvian origin, and probably erected as places of retreat for their families in time of war.

Proceeding two miles further, through a thinly wooded country, we crossed a brook four yards wide; and six miles further of fine rolling prairie, interspersed with light woods, brought us to our encampment of the 12th of June. As we stopped upon the encamping ground, a night-hawk flew away and abandoned two eggs, which she appeared to have deposited on the ground, without preparing any kind of nest; they were of a dull white colour, thickly spotted over with dirty brown blotches. A heavy shower, accompanied by thunder and lightning, made the weather very comfortable. But a high wind, which arose during the night, rendered travelling very unpleasant in the morning. At about twenty-eight miles in a general westerly course from the Pishtako, we came to a beautiful winding stream, called the Kishwake,* Cottonwood. It is about twelve yards wide, and is a tributary of Rock river. About one mile and a half below the place where we forded this stream, we saw a small Indian village, designated by the name of Wakesa,† (little bend,) from its situation at one of the bends of the Kishwake. It consisted of four lodges, the population of which was computed to amount to at least sixty persons, as there were many crowded into one lodge; the village is chiefly inhabited by Menomones, with a few Potawatomis who have intermarried with them. We stopped at the lodge of the chief, whose name is Kakakesha‡ (Crow). He, together with many of his people, was engaged in his corn-fields; on seeing the strangers, they gave the dog-whoop, and collected at the house at which we had stopped. They were all tall and muscular men, well built, and better looking than the Potawatomis generally are; their countenance was agreeable, and denoted none of that severity about the mouth which

---

* Kîsh-w'ă-kè.   † Wă-kĕ'să.   ‡ K'ă-k'ă-kĕ'-sh'ă.

Volney ascribes to those whom he saw. The chief is a very old man and quite bald; at the time he approached us he had a child-board on his back, in which he carried his little grandson. Although advanced in years, Kakakesha had none of the decrepitude of old age; there was much dignity in his manner, The women were all very ugly, and the children looked like little imps, in whose countenance, and apparently deformed bodies, we could scarcely discover the embryo of men so tall and elegant as those who stood before us. Most of their youth had gone out on a hunting excursion. The men whom we saw were almost naked, having no other garment than the breech-cloth, but as we drew near them they gathered up their blankets; the women had a sort of short gown and a blanket; the children ran about naked, with no other appendage than a belt round their loins. It is curious to observe that all Indians, whether old or young, wear a belt, even when they have nothing to attach to it; and the children, who seldom assume the breech-cloth until they attain the age of puberty, have all a belt tied round them, as soon as they can run about. The house, which we visited, was about twenty feet long by fifteen wide, and full twelve feet high at its centre. Seen from a distance, it resembled a log-house; but on approaching we discovered it to be formed of bark, secured to a frame made of poles, and covered with the same material. It had the appearance of being very comfortable. The fire was made in the middle of the house; two sides of the interior were occupied with a frame, three feet high and four or five feet wide, which was covered with blankets, skins, &c. and on these the inmates sleep and eat; upon these we were invited to sit down. There is no sign of partition, or of any thing that can serve as a skreen to separate or divide one part of the family from another. A woman who was sick, lay in the lodge exposed to view, until the child, which was taken from the chief's back, and which was her's, was handed over naked to her. Whether from this circumstance, or to avoid the curious glances of some of our party, who appeared to be watching the sick woman's motions, we know not, but a blanket was soon suspended in order to conceal the patient from view.

The disposition of these Indians was friendly. The object of the expedition was explained to them, to which they made no reply, but the chief directed his squaw, who was a very fleshy women, to give us some maple sugar in return for the tobacco we had presented him; he expressed his regret at having no fresh meat to give us; but added, that if his hunters returned that evening with meat, he would send some to our camp. We were a little shocked at their familiar disposition, which we at first mistook for intentional impudence; they all collected round us, took our guns, and began to examine them with care, appeared to be highly pleased with the double-barrelled guns of some of the gentlemen of our party; one of them even drew Mr. Say's hunting knife from the sheath, and after having examined it, returned it; he then took Mr. Say's hat, which was a white beaver one, and after having also examined this with care, tried it on his own head. All this, however, appeared to proceed rather from childish curiosity than from any intention to give offence. After some time, they began to beg for bacon, which soon compelled us to leave them.

In order to avoid all further importunity, we travelled ten miles before night, and encamped on a fine piece of level ground, which was watered by a small stream that discharged itself three miles below into the Kishwake. The thermometer was observed, at six o'clock, P. M., to be at eighty-two degrees in the shade, but no inconvenience was felt from the heat, owing to a fine westerly breeze which prevailed during the day.

On the 14th of July, the party reached Rock river, which is the most important tributary of the Mississippi, between the Illinois and the Wisconsan. Rock river is termed, in the languages derived from the Algonquin, Sinsepe,* and in the Winnebago Weroshanagra,† both which names have the same signification as the English term. It forms the division between the hunting grounds claimed by the Potawatomis, on the eastern side, and those of the Sauks, Foxes, and Winnebagoes on the west. At the place where we crossed the river it was about one hundred and twenty yards wide; and its depth was such that it could not be forded at that time, though we were informed that it is customary for horses loaded with furs, to cross it without difficulty. We were ferried over in a small canoe, sent for us from an Indian village in the vicinity. We crossed Rock river just above the mouth of the Kishwake, the same stream which we had passed the day before, but which, from its great increase, we scarcely recognised, when we saw it three miles above its mouth, where we were again obliged to cross it. Opposite to the mouth of the Kishwake there is a large island in Rock river. At the lower crossing of the Kishwake, we passed through an Indian village, designated by the name of the river, and which is inhabited by a mixed race of Potawatomis, Chippewas, Ottawas, Menomones, &c.

* Sin-sè-pè. † Wè-róshâ-nâ-grâ.

The chief, who belongs to the first of these nations, was away at the time we were there, and in his absence we saw no person who could converse with us. A lad, who was in the village, and who, as we were told, was the son of the late chief, when spoken to, made no answer, but seemed to be very stupid; although the other Indians did not appear destitute of intelligence, yet not one of them could converse with us. This, indeed, is one of the characteristics of Indians. The business of receiving and replying to speeches belongs to the chief, it is one of his proudest prerogatives, and it is one in which he chiefly endeavours to excel; while the other Indians, seeming to consider it as no concern of theirs, pay no attention to it, and are always at a loss when spoken to by those whom they are accustomed to treat with respect or with regard; but with the traders, whom they ridicule, and for whom they openly profess the most manifest contempt, they will join in conversation very freely and familiarly. After having crossed Rock river, we stopped to dine on the high bank which confines it on the west side, and were not a little amused at the apparent delight with which the little Indian boy, who had brought the canoe to us from Kishwake village up Rock river, ate the bread and bacon which we gave him; it really seemed as though it were the most delicate food that he had ever tasted.

The valley of Rock river is about half a mile wide at this place; it is utterly destitute of rocks, differing, in this respect, very much from the characters observed higher up, and which have entitled it to the name that it now bears. We could not, however, ascertain whether the rocks were there in place, or merely boulders. We had, in the course of the morning, observed a spot where the limestone appeared *in situ;* this was, in every respect, similar to that found near Chicago. The boulders and pebbles which, from Chicago to Fox river, had not appeared to be as numerous as in some other parts of the route, were, after we had seen the limestone in the morning, found to increase rapidly in number, though not perhaps in size. From his former observations upon the country, Major Long thought we were approaching what has been considered the lead formation of the west, and this was confirmed by the assertion of our guide, that much lead had been found on some of the tributaries of Rock river, where it is worked by the Indians, in small quantities for their own use. This induced us to make a careful examination of the country, with a view to ascertain whether any lead ore occurred upon our route, and if it did, under what circumstances. We met with none; but from all the characters observed in the country, we hesitate not in considering its surface to be covered by an ancient alluvium, the alluvium of mountains of the Wernerian school; and in which, of course, if any lead should be found, it must be out of its original site. This alluvium consists principally of a bed of loose and uncemented pebbles, varying in size from the smallest grain to the dimensions of an apple, and interspersed with boulders, which are frequently of very large dimensions: but these do not appear to be so frequent here, whether it be because they are buried in, and concealed by the pebbles, or because they were not deposited here, we had no means of determining. The alluvium appears to consist chiefly of the detritus of primitive rocks, such as fragments of quartz, granite, sienite, &c. but as far as we could observe, without any trace of a metalliferous mineral. There are also many fragments of limestone, interspersed throughout the mass. Under the alluvium, the limestone observed in the morning probably extends to a great distance. From the observations which we have been able to make, we believe it to be the same limestone formation, which extends from Piqua to Fort St. Mary, and which is seen near Fort Wayne, Chicago, and Rock river. Whether it be the same as that observed further east, or in what relation it stands to it, we are not desirous of deciding positively, but we believe it to be at least as modern as that found above the coal formations of Wheeling and Zanesville, and perhaps more so. We have spoken of the supposed lead formations of Rock river; not having visited Dubuque's lead mines, or those in the state of Missouri, it would be impossible for us to express a decided opinion upon their nature; but from all that we have heard on the subject, as well as from what has been written upon these lead mines, we can scarcely hesitate in considering the ore as being equally out of place there. Whether the original sites, from which it has been detached, are still to be found in the vicinity, is a point which those alone who have seen the country are competent to decide, if indeed, the question can, in the present state of science, be resolved; the authors who have written upon this subject have, as it appears to us, left the question open; for while they assert that the lead is found in clay, they appear to us desirous to convey, at all times, the impression that it is in place, as we are informed that it " is found in detached pieces and solid masses. *in veins and beds* in red clay, and accompanied by sulphurate (sulphate?) of barytes, calcareous spar, blende, iron pyrites, and quartz."* Now, that all the indications mentioned by those who have seen the mines, justify a belief that the lead is not in its original site, we consider as satisfactorily proved. That the lead ore as well as the accompanying minerals, must be out of place, is equally apparent, from the circumstance, that while the clay is said to repose upon the limestone, the ore is not stated to have ever been worked in this rock. We are told, that " the greatest proportion of lead ore is, however, found imbedded in, and accompanied by the sulphate of barytes resting in a thick stratum of marly clay, bottomed on limestone rock. The rock is invariably struck at a depth of from fifteen to twenty feet, and puts a stop to the progress of the miner in a common way. To go further it is necessary to drill or blast, and this creates an expense which the generality of diggers are unwilling to incur, if not unable to support."† Again, we find " in digging down from fifteen to twenty feet, the rock is generally struck : and as the signs of ore generally give out on coming to the rock, many of the pits are carried no further."‡ Finally, in his visit to Dubuque's lead mines, performed in the year 1820, Mr. Schoolcraft observed, that the ore " had been chiefly *explored in alluvial soil;*" though he at the same time states, that " it generally occurs in beds or veins."§ From the specimens which we have seen, as well as from all that we have heard and read, we cannot hesitate in asserting it as our opinion, that no lead has as yet been discovered on the Merrimeg or Mississippi in a metalliferous lime-

---

* View of the Leads Mines of Missouri. New York, 1819. p. 67.
† Idid, p. 69. ‡ Ibid, p. 108.
§ Schoolcraft's Narrative Journal of Travels, &c. p. 344.

stone;* but that, wherever it has been found, it has always been in an alluvium, and never in regular veins or beds, nor even in masses, which might be considered as coeval, with the substances in which they are imbedded.

On both banks of the Kishwake, not far from its mouth, there are many mounds in every respect similar to those met with on Fox river, but scattered along the bank without any apparent order. Mr. Say counted upwards of thirty of these mounds. It is probable that they were formerly the cemeteries of a large Indian population which resided on the banks of the Kishwake, and which had perhaps its principal village at the beautiful confluence of this stream with Rock river.

In travelling over a prairie country, the party were often obliged to lengthen or shorten their day's journey, in order to accommodate themselves to the scarcity of water and wood. The afternoon of the 14th of June we encamped at three o'clock, as the distance to the next camping ground would have led us too far into the evening. The afternoon was employed in taking observations for longitude, and in making such repairs and alterations in our travelling equipage as had become necessary. Our horses' backs had been chafed by the saddle, notwithstanding all the care taken to keep them in a sound state, which was dictated not only by huma-

---

* By metalliferous limestone, we allude to that in which the lead-mines of Cumberland and Derbyshire in England, of Vearin in Belgium, &c. are found. This limestone is by most geologists considered older than the coal, and probably in many instances connected with transition formations; according to Conybeare and Philips, it is placed under the name of mountain limestone, between the old red sandstone formation, and the coal measures. (Vide Geology of England and Wales, London, 1822, part 1. plate, fig. 3.)

nity, but also by a provident attention to our own interest; for very little experience is required to satisfy a traveller that much of his comfort and expedition, on such a journey as ours, depends upon the circumstance of his horse's back not being galled, as it otherwise torments and tires the animal before he has performed much work. For the information of other travellers, we may mention, that after having tried many applications, we have found none that succeeded so well as white lead moistened with milk, as long as this could be procured; after we had left the settlements, sweet oil was used as a substitute for milk; whenever the application was made in the early stage of the wound we have found it to be very effectual. It is likewise a convenient one to carry on an expedition, as a couple of ounces of white lead sufficed for the whole of our party during more than a month.

The succeeding morning the weather was very fair, and the party continued its course over fine undulating prairies, expanded in every direction, so as to appear in some cases unbounded by woods. The only defect which we observed in the country between Chicago and the Mississippi, is the scarcity of wood, which is more seriously felt on the west side of Rock river, than to the east of it. This will perhaps be the principal difficulty in settling the country; otherwise the land is good, not hilly, sufficiently watered, and would, we doubt not, prove productive if well worked. Limestone is frequently to be met with, even west of Rock river; in other places the soil lies upon pebbles of white hornstone; the boulders are not sufficiently abundant to prove injurious to agriculture. We observed as a distinction between those seen within the two last days, and those met with east of Rock river, that the former contain principally hornblende instead of mica in their composition, while the boulders near Lake Michigan were chiefly granitic. The rock, which has given rise to the hornblendic boulders, is one of a peculiar and interesting nature; it differs from sienite by the presence of quartz, from granite by the substitution of hornblende for mica. This rock has not received much attention from European authors; it does not appear to occupy a very important rank in the geology of Europe, while, on the contrary, it is very abundant in North America. Those who are conversant with the mineralogy of New Jersey, know that it constitutes most of the primitive rocks which are found in West Jersey, and which have been described either as granite or sienite; however extensive that deposit may be, it bears no comparison to the extensive formation of this rock, which we shall have occasion hereafter to describe, and from which the fragments, which constitute the boulders found in Illinois, Indiana, Ohio, &c. have, as we believe, been detached.

After travelling eighteen miles, we reached a small stream, designated by the name of Pektannons,* a diminutive of Pektannon,† a neighbouring stream into which it discharges itself a few miles below. The meaning of this last in the Sauk language is *muddy*, and it is re-

---

* Pĕk-tăn-nŏns.

† Pĕktănnŏn. As we have had frequent opportunities of observing a nasal termination in Indian words, belonging both to the Sauk, Dacota, and other languages, we have adopted the sign (n) to designate this sound, which is equivalent to the nasal termination of the French language, thus in the word Pektannon, the last syllable is pronounced by the Indians, exactly as the word *non* is by the French.

markable that the same name has been applied to the Missouri by the Sauks. Our guide informed us that it was very common for the Sauks to form a diminutive of a word, by the addition of a hissing sound at the end, as in the abovementioned instance. Observing that Le Sellier seemed to have gone beyond the limits of the country with which he was acquainted, Major Long thought it would be desirable to endeavour to procure an Indian, as a guide to Prairie du Chien; and as we were in the vicinity of an Indian village, Le Sellier was sent a-head, to request one of the men to accompany us. The village to which he went was situated on the main stream, about three miles from the place where we had halted for dinner on the Pektannons; it consisted of seven permanent and three temporary lodges, inhabited principally by Sauks, Foxes, Winnebagoes, Menomones, and Potawatomis. Their chief is a Sauk; he was absent, but we saw his elder brother, whom we engaged to accompany us to Prairie du Chien. His name was Wanébea Namoeta* (spinning top), the chief's name was Wabetejee† (white cedar). We visited the inside of their bark lodges, which were very comfortable; the number of men appeared to us much greater than that of women in the village. Being aware of our approach, from the information received through Le Sellier, they had manifested their friendly disposition by hoisting flags, or white rags, all around their village, and, among others, three white flags hung from the head and arms of a large cross, rudely cut out, which marked the grave of some departed white man. Their behaviour was less familiar than that of the Indians whom we had last

* W͏ȧnē̇ʹbʹeȧ Nȧmȯʹētȧ. † W͏ȧbĕʹtēʹjʹee.

met with; but as they evinced the same curiosity to examine our arms, we were led to ascribe their greater reserve, to the admonition given that morning to the Frenchman, that the familiar manner with which he behaved towards them, must be discontinued in our presence, as to that we ascribed their forwardness. The men of this village were distinguished from those observed in other places, by their unusually dark and expressive eyes, the playful smile of their mouth, and their well-formed nose. We found them very short of provisions; they offered us, however, a bowlful of maize, which was very acceptable, as our bread-corn had been consumed. One of the party observed in the lodge a large basket, full of acorns, intended no doubt for food. We proceeded that afternoon a few miles further, and encamped on a beautiful spot near the Pektannon; it was on the verge of a fine wood. The adjoining prairie afforded our horses the finest pasture that could be wished for; an attempt to fish was made, but it proved unsuccessful. It does not seem that these rivers abound in fish, and the Indians place no dependence upon the produce of the fishery for their support. While encamped this evening, we were visited by several Indians, who came from the village, and who behaved themselves in a very becoming manner. In order to compare the language of the Winnebagoes, as spoken here, with that contained in the vocabulary obtained by Major Long in the year 1817, and which is recorded in the " Account of an Expedition to the Rocky Mountains," (vol. 2, p. lxxxvi.), we read to one of these Indians, who was a Winnebago, the words as published in the vocabulary, with a view to ascertain whether or not he understood them; the attempt was rather a difficult one, as he had to convey the meaning of the Winnebago term in the Sauk language to Le Sellier, who translated it into French to one of the party by whom it was reduced into English. The result of this threefold translation was, however, that he recognised, without hesitation, about one-third of the words; the meaning of the remainder, which he did not readily understand, being conveyed to him through the Sauk language, he repeated about one-half of them with a slight variation, frequently no other than the addition of a termination in *ra*, which appeared to be a sort of dialect. Some of the words he seemed not to recognise at all, even after their supposed meaning had been explained to him through the interpreter.

Major Long, whose health had been somewhat impaired for a few days previous, was so severely affected, on the 15th, with fever and sick stomach, that we began to apprehend that his indisposition would prove a serious one, but the timely application of medical assistance fortunately relieved him.

Wennebea, of whom we have preserved a very good likeness, taken by Mr. Seymour (plate III. middle figure), is a young and good looking Indian, whose face denotes more cheerfulness than is generally observed in the countenance of man in the savage life. He seems to be of a lively, cheerful disposition, judging from the laughter which frequently animated his conversation with Le Sellier; to us he was always uniformly polite and obliging. His dress consisted, as usual with the Indians of this country, of a blanket thrown over his shoulders, and reaching to his ankles; a breech-cloth of blue broad-cloth; buckskin *leggings* and moccassins of the same material. The leggings are very similar to a Chinese garment that supplies the place of pantaloons; they reach up to the hips, covering the whole limb, and are secured to thongs tied to a leather belt around the waist. Garters, generally very much ornamented with porcupine quills, beads, and other fanciful articles, support the leggings immediately below the knee. His pipe was stuck into the plaited hair which he wore on the crown of his head. He was provided with a gun, of the kind distinguished by the name of Mackinaw gun, with a spare ramrod, shot-pouch, &c. Wennebea rode a little bay-mare, with a long untrimmed tail; she was so small that his legs appeared almost to sweep the ground as he travelled over the prairie; but the little animal was a fiery one, probably about four years old; her growth had doubtless been stunted by too early an application to labour. We could not help, frequently, expressing our admiration at the graceful and easy manner in which this man rode across the plain, occasionally allowing his blanket to drop upon his horse's back, and displaying the stout and symmetric shoulders and chest, which generally characterize man when in a state of nature, and unimpaired by the effeminating habits and vices of civilized life. We scarcely recognised our guide a few days afterwards, when we saw him with a calico shirt, which he had borrowed from Le Sellier and which concealed his well-formed limbs; on inquiring into the cause of this addition to his usual costume, we were told, that the sun being very hot on the prairie, he had accepted the offer to protect his shoulders, against its influence, by means of a shirt. This proves how ready these Indians are to abandon their natural manners, and to assume the artificial ones of civilized man. Wennebea wore this garment at first with an apparent air of ostentation, which confirmed us in our opinion, that the Indian is no wiser than the white man in this respect, often priding himself upon the acquisition of a garment, which detracts from, rather than adds to, his personal appearance. He seemed to be well acquainted with the country, and followed no track across the prairie; but his course was directed by landmarks, such as hills, woods, &c. He appeared to guide himself, likewise, by the situation of the sun in the heavens; but we were satisfied, on more than one occasion, of the inaccuracy of those who suppose that an Indian has an infallible method of discovering, at all times, the direction in which he wishes to travel, and that he never can be lost. His habits of observation enable him, it is true, to discover signs, which would probably escape the attention of the less experienced white man. Thus, if the sun be obscured, his keen eye will sometimes detect, from habit, its place in the heavens; at other times, it is said that he can, by close inspection, discover very faint shadows, which would elude the observation of a less practised eye. When these characters fail, he may, in a forest, point with certainty to the north, from the circumstance, that the moss grows more abundantly upon that side of a tree than upon the others. But if left on a prairie, at a distance from trees, when the heavens are deeply clouded, or during the prevalence of a dense fog, the Indian, as well as the white man, will often be unable to direct himself properly. We frequently observed during the march, that he skreened his eyes with his hands, and seemed to study very attentively the distant points of woods and the surrounding prairie, whether to make sure of the proper route, or to discover signs of game or enemies, we know not.

Wennebea led us in a general north-westerly direction, at first through thin woods, which gradually disappeared, their place being supplied by an extensive and apparently boundless prairie, which occupied us a whole day in crossing it. The woods consisted of small oaks without undergrowth; the prairie, upon which we were travelling, was undulated, and extended itself along the base of the dividing ridge between the streams tributary to the Mississippi and those which fall into Rock river. This ridge stretched on our left, in a direction nearly parallel to our general course; it appeared to be in some places from one hundred to one hundred and fifty feet high, and from six to eight miles distant. Soon after we entered the prairie, a deer crossed our route about two miles ahead of us: Wennebea started in pursuit, but returned in the course of an hour, after a fruitless and fatiguing chace. He brought back, however, a curlew (Numenius longirostris), a bird of which we occasionally roused a pair or two. We frequently observed the majestic sand-hill crane (Grus Canadensis), striding across the prairie. This animal, if taken young, can, it is said, be domesticated with ease. Two or three of them were kept last season at Chicago, being allowed to pass freely before the sentinels; but they never failed to return to their nests. We also saw on the prairie the fine swallow-tailed Hawk (Falco [Milvus] furcatus), flying over us. Our guide showed us a spot where an action had been fought, about sixty or seventy years ago, between the Sauks and the Peoras; the former were successful and lost but one man, while they killed ten of the enemy. This took place on an elevated hill, commanding an extensive view of the prairie, and crowned with a forest in which the engagement is said to have taken place.

The country becomes interspersed with hills, which contribute to vary the scenery; among others which were very distinct, we observed two, rising close along side of each other, forming two twin peaks insulated in the midst of the prairie; the distance between the two being about one mile and a quarter in an east and west direction; they are visible for upwards of thirty miles, and constitute one of the best landmarks we have ever seen. They are called in the Sauk language Enneshoteno* (which signifies the two mountains being composed of ennes,† two, and oteno,‡ hills). Our guide informed us that the hill marked on the maps as the Smoky-hill (*Montagne qui bouccane* of the French), lay a long day's march (about thirty miles) in a northeasterly course from our noon encampment of the 16th. This hill has received from the Indians the appellation of Muchowakunin,§ Smoky mountain, from the circumstance of its summit being generally enveloped with a cloud or fog, and, as we are told, not from any tradition of smoke having ever issued from it. To the left a point of highland is in sight, which is said to be at the mouth of the Moschaoko,‖ (always full), a stream that falls into the Mississippi. In the evening we encamped on the left bank of the Wassemon,¶ a beautiful tributary of the Pektannon; it is called after an Indian chief of that name, who resided on its banks; it means, in the Sauk language, *lightning*. On the banks of this stream

---

* ĕ′n-n'ĕ-sh'ŏ-tĕ²′-n'ŏ.   † ĕ′n-n'ĕs.   ‡ ŏ-tĕ²′-n'ŏ.
§ Mŭ-ch'ŏ-w'ă-kŭ′-n'ĭn.   ‖ Mŏschăŏkŏ.   ¶ Wăssĕmŏn.

we observed the limestone in place, forming cliffs of about fifty feet in height; the rock is in very distinct horizontal stratification; its structure is in many parts crystalline, or perhaps it may more properly be called gravelly and sandy; it contains many cells or cavities, some of which are filled with crystallizations of carbonate of lime; much white hornstone appears disseminated throughout the mass. The hornstone is sometimes seen to constitute small oeds or layers from one to three or four inches in thickness, which are continued for several feet in length; frequently also appearing under the form of flattened irregular nodules, lying in an almost continuous line for a considerable distance, and with their long or flattened side parallel to the stratification; resembling in this respect the disposition of the clay-iron stone in the slaty strata that accompany the bituminous coal. Organic remains are by no means uncommon, though they are not found as abundantly as in some other spots of our route; they consist of Terebratulites, Encrinites, and a Madreporite, (Linné); the true nature of the last of these could not be ascertained without a comparison of characters, which we were unable to make on the spot, and which the loss of all the specimens collected between Fort Wayne and Fort St. Anthony has prevented Mr. Say from making since; the rock is of a greyish-yellow colour, with a loose structure. We are aware that some of the characters which we have given of this rock might lead to the opinion that it resembles the mountain or carboniferous limestone of Messrs. Conybeare and Phillips; and consequently that it is the same as the metalliferous limestone of other geologists; but we should consider this opinion as a very hasty, not to say an incorrect one. Although its cavernous nature, its indications of crystallization, and its organic remains, present an apparent correspondence with those of that limestone, as described by the Rev. W. D. Conybeare, in the excellent " Outlines of the Geology of England and Wales," (Part I. p. 353.) we incline to the opinion that this rock is of a much later formation; we believe it to be connected with a limestone which was subsequently observed on the Mississippi, between Prairie du Chien and St. Anthony, and in which we observed an *oolite* and a pulverulent limestone similar to the calcareous ashes described by Mr. Freiesleben in his elaborate account of the formations of Thuringen. If we compare the characters of this rock with those of the limestone observed by Mr. Freiesleben, and described by him under the name of *zechstein* and *rauchwacke*, we shall be surprised at the great similarity in their appearance. The " *zechstein* is a compact, hard and tough limestone of an ash-grey colour, passing into blackish-grey, distinctly stratified, without however presenting any slaty appearance, or at least much less so than the inferior beds; it contains specks and some veins of calcareous spar and gypsum; also crystals of quartz, &c.; it likewise offers sometimes specks of galena. It generally presents but few petrifactions, Corallites and Millepores, as well as several species of Trebratulites; Ammonites, &c. have been found in it."

" Above this compact limestone another stratum of calcareous rock is found which is known in the country under the name of *rauchwacke* (smoky wacke); it is a limestone probably intermixed with silex, of a dark-grey, sometimes blackish colour, with a somewhat scaly fracture, occasionally fine-grained, sometimes though seldom oolitic, hard, tough, and filled with pores or cavities; this last feature is characteristic; it may be observed even in those parts of the stratum which appear most compact; the cavities are angular, long, and narrow (as in a cracked clay); the interior of the cavities is lined with small crystals of calcspar, these cavities are sometimes large, being several yards in length and breadth, &c."

He afterwards proceeds to describe the ashes or pulverulent substance found near it. This, from its great similarity to the residue of the combustion of wood, is designated in Germany by the name of *asche* (ashes). These characters when taken into connection, appear to us to correspond so well with those observed on the Wassemon, on the Mississippi, and throughout the country between Rock river and Prairie du Chien, that we feel strongly induced to consider the limestone of this country as analogous to that observed by Mr. Freiesleben. This limestone is by some European continential geologists referred to the *Lias* of English geologists; but we would rather refer it with Messrs. Conybeare and Phillips to the newer magnesian or conglomerate limestone of England; to this, we think it has the strongest analogy. It is probably connected, as we have already intimated, with the limestone situated above the coal fields of Wheeling and Zanesville; it extends over those parts of Ohio and Indiana, where salt has been found; it is observed cellular, cavernous, &c. on the banks of the Wassemon; it is connected with real calcareous ashes on the Mississippi. The presence of the oolite which was observed here in a single spot, does not militate against the position which we have taken, as we find it stated by Conybeare and Phillips (page 302), on the authority of Mr. Wynch, that the magnesian limestone is occasionally oolitic. It presents in many of its points the characters of the *rauchwacke*, and especially the cellular or cavernous structure; it is seldom found very abundantly strewed with organic remains; its colour is the pale buff passing to the ash-grey. In fine, the more attentively we examine it, the more closely do we find it to connect itself with the formations of Thuringen, and with those which cover so extensive a part of England, and more particularly with that observed in Yorkshire by Professor Buckland; offering thus, as it appears to us, a beautiful confirmation of the analogy established between the various kinds of this limestone, observed in divers parts of Europe. There is an experiment which would, as we conceive, place the matter beyond a doubt; this would be an analysis of the limestone with a view to ascertain the quantity of magnesia which it contains, and we regret much that the loss of our specimens has deprived us of the opportunity of making this analysis. But we think the case sufficiently strong to justify us in considering this as the formation corresponding to the magnesian limestone of England, and the *rauchwacke* and *zechstein* of Thuringen.*

In offering those remarks to geologists, we have not overlooked the very correct observation of one whose experience adds value to the advice which he gives to

* The reader is referred to the Outlines of the Geology of England and Wales, by the Rev. W. D. Conybeare and Wm. Phillips, &c. London, 1822, p. 300, et seq. Traité de Géognosie, par J. F. D'Aubuisson de Voisons, Paris, 1819, vol. ii. p. 336, 337, 343, 353. J. C. Freiesleben's Geognostiche Arbeiten, (Beytrag zur kentniss des kupferschiefer-gelirges).

naturalists; indeed we have found the truth of Mr. D'Aubuisson's remark fully exemplified here. " Let us further observe," says he, " that the influence of localities becomes more sensible as we draw near to modern epochas, and we shall be convinced of the difficulty of drawing certain conclusions as to the identity of two calcareous formations somewhat distant." If with this remark before us, we are thought to have ventured too much in supposing a connection between the formations of England and Germany, and those west of the Alleghanies let it be remembered that we only offer this as a suggestion to the future investigator of our western limestone, in order that he may turn his attention to the subject with more favourable opportunities of observation than those afforded us by a transient visit to the country. We shall have occasion to mention some further facts which we consider as adding strength to the opinion which we have advanced. But there is another question which naturally arises; if, as Mr. Freiesleben has described it the *zechstien* presents specks of galena or sulphuret of lead; if, as Mr. Conybeare states, the galena is seen " occurring in strings in the magnesian limestone of Nottingham and Durham; if it has been occasionally found in the conglomerate beds associated with this formation, particularly near Mendip-hills, in England; if it contains veins of sulphate of barytes at the Huddleston quarry near Sherburn, between Ferrybridge and York; if it is traversed by veins of sulphate of barytes near Nottingham, at Bramham Moor, &c. may it not then be asked, whether these considerations do not render it probable that the great lead deposit of the west is in this limestone? and is it not likely that all that has been worked in an alluvium has been detached from this formation? These are questions upon which, in the present state of our acquaintance with the western limestone, we must profess ourselves unable to give a decided opinion; but, from various circumstances which we need not dwell upon, we should incline to consider the lead ore as probably existing in an older limestone which we think lies under this; and which may be connected with the mountain or carboniferous limestone of Messrs. Conybeare and Phillips, the metalliferous limestone of other geologists.

The country becomes more undulated as we draw nearer to the Mississippi; the ridges are low but somewhat steep, owing to the horizontal stratification of the rocks; one of the sides very frequently discovers the composition of the hills by a steep break. At other times the country presents the waved appearance of a somewhat ruffled ocean; it is covered with a short dry grass, the vegetation generally appearing inferior to that of the alluvial country through which we had previously passed. This waved appearance seems to have been caused by the production of valleys subsequently formed, and extending from north-east to south-west, all dipping to the latter point; these are said to continue almost in a straight line to the Mississippi. Our object being to strike that river at a point further north, our course which approached to a north-west direction, obliged us to cross all these ridges and valleys nearly at right angles. No granitic blocks were to be seen; this is accounted for by the fact that we were no longer upon the alluvial formation, but upon the magnesian limestone which rises to a greater height, constituting the dividing ridge between the Mississippi, Rock river, and the Wisconsan, and perhaps connecting itself with what have been termed the Wisconsan hills.

The features which we observed from the Wassemon to the Wisconsan are extremely interesting. At a distance of a few miles north-west of the former stream, the vegetation presented a sudden and striking change, announcing a corresponding one in the geological character of the country. We ascended a rough, steep, and hilly ground, which was covered with heavy timber, and with a very thick underwood, consisting principally of young oak and aspen. This thick brush-wood continued for about two miles, when we struck the bank of a small stream, remarkable for the beauty of its scenery, which differed from any that we had hitherto met with. The brook runs in a deep and narrow glen, the sides of which are very steep, and in some places vertical; they are covered at their summit with a dense vegetation, which extends over the edge of the rock, and imparts a character of austerity and of gloom to this secluded valley, which finds not its parallel in any that we recollect having ever seen. The dark colour which the water receives from the deep shadows cast by the high steep bank and its overhanging vegetation, forms a pleasing relief to the glare, so uniformly fatiguing, of the unsheltered prairie. This spot conveyed so much relief to the eye and to the mind, that the party could not repress their delight on beholding it. The geologist who connects a change in the nature of the subjacent rock, with a diversity in the character of the country, or of its vegetation, would naturally find an explanation for the new features which the country assumes by observing that the high banks of this glen are formed of sandstone rocks, the nature of which we had an opportunity of studying with attention during a great part of our journey of the 18th of June. We observed that the sandstone is distinctly superposed to the limestone; that it constitutes upon it hills, which vary from thirty to one hundred feet and upwards; these hills are divided by valleys, in the bottom of which the limestone reappears in place. The sides of the hills are steep, and but few indications of stratifications are observable, except where the valley is partly excavated in the limestone itself; in which case the lower part of the hill is less steep, but presents a distinct stratification. The line of superposition of the sandstone over the limestone, may also be traced with considerable accuracy by the examination of the vegetation. Whenever the latter rock prevails, the surface is even and smooth, or modified by gentle swells, covered with a thick and long grass, and forming an uniform fine green meadow-like country, while the sandstone invariably imparts to the surface an asperity which is as distinct as the vigorous growth of trees with which it is covered, and as its abundant undergrowth, which denotes a strong and productive soil, having a tendency to bear heavy forests.

The rock is a white sandstone, formed of fragments of fine transparent and colourless quartz, united by a cement, which, in some parts, appears to be ferruginous, while in others it is colourless, and probably of a calcareous nature. In some parts the cement is quite invisible, and would almost lead to the belief that the union of the grains was the result of crystallization. This sandstone appears in fragments or tatters, and constitutes the remains of a formation, which probably covered the whole of the limestone, at least in this part of the country. That it is above the limestone, no doubt can exist, in our minds, as we saw the immediate superposition. It sometimes appears, it is true, to sink below the level of that rock; and this led us at first to apprehend that there might be an alternation of strata, but a careful examination of all these spots has left no doubt in our minds, that in these cases the sandstone is deposited in coves or valleys formed in the limestone previous to the deposition of the sandstone; these cases are, however, not common, and we may safely state, as a general rule, that not only the sandstone is relatively above the limestone, but that it is even, in almost all cases, at a greater absolute elevation; and the spot, at which we first met with it, west of the Wassemon, was considerably elevated above the usual level of the limestone; for, wherever the sandstone has retained its position, it has protected the limestone against decomposition, and hence, in such places, the latter rock still continues to rise to a higher level than where it is laid bare, and exposed to the destructive influence of atmospherical agents. We also observed very distinctly, that while the valleys, formed in the limestone at a time anterior to the deposition of the sandstone, were few, those produced subsequently were numerous, as was indicated by the great roughness and unevenness of the sandstone country, and by the many undulations in the uncovered limestone which we have already had occasion to mention. From the observations made on the 18th, it was thought very probable that all the hills observed at a distance on the 17th, were formed of this sandstone; and from some characters which had appeared, at the time, to present an anomaly, it was inferred that the Enneshoteno or twin mountains, near which we had passed that day, without stopping, were probably also remains of the general sandstone formation which extended over the whole country. No organic remains were observed in the sandstone, or in the limestone which is beneath it; but no doubt can exist that they may contain some, and that the limestone probably contains many.

Proceeding towards the Wisconsan, the country presents an alternation of rolling and undulated prairie, interspersed with hills composed of either one or the other of these rocks. The sandstone is found in most places to be covered with thin flattened fragments of a stone, differing in its nature and texture from the character of the other rocks, whether of limestone or sandstone. These fragments are generally observed to vary from three to twelve inches in length, from two to eight in breadth, and from one quarter to one inch in thickness; they present appearances of having been weathered, but not of having been rolled; they are very abundant, and we could account for them in no other way than by admitting that they were the remains, probably the harder parts of a stratum that had at one time covered the sandstone, but that had disappeared almost entirely, leaving only these fragments to attest its former existence and situation. On examining these fragments with care, we found them to be very uniform in their characters; their composition is in great measure calcareous, but from their greater hardness we consider it as partly siliceous; they are replete with organic remains; these are principally referrible to the Productus, Terebratula, &c. We saw none but what belonged to bivalves. The existence of these fragments was observed upon many elevations, over a considerable extent of country, while in the vallies no trace of them could be seen. Generalizing the observations made during the three last days of our journey previous to our arrival on the Mississippi, we are led to admit that there are, or rather that there were formerly, two distinct formations of limestone in this country, and that they were separated by a thick stratum of sandstone; of these two limestone formations, the older one, which we have already described with minuteness, we have been induced to consider as coeval with, or analogous to, the magnesian limestone of England. The superior formation is distinguished by the circumstance of its containing harder fragments or nodules of limestone, which alone remain to establish the fact of its former existence; that it contained no hornstone or flinty quartz, as observed in the former, we are led to believe, because had they existed they must necessarily have resisted decomposition as well or better than the calcareous nodules which are now found alone. The much greater abundance of shells in these nodules, and the total absence of the Madreporites appear to us to be very characteristic distinctions between these and the subjacent limestone, though, perhaps, too much weight ought not to be assigned to the absence of the Madreporites, as these from their loose and more porous texture may have been unable to resist the decomposing causes which appear to have affected this formation. In some places a limestone bed was observed upon the sandstone, but these depositions were so partial, and, in all cases, the ground was so much overgrown with bushes, that we were unable to examine their characters with any degree of minuteness. This striking difference, however, we observed, and we are led to consider it as constant, that the inferior limestone, whenever it appears exposed, is covered with small scales or fragments of the hornstone nodules whose existence has already been alluded to, while none of the flat, calcareous fragments, abounding in shells, are found upon it; whereas these were uniformly observed to the exclusion of the scales of hornstone upon the surface of the calcareous stratum that is over the sandstone. If contrary to the opinion which we have been led to adopt, the limestone be supposed to constitute but one formation, whether above or below the sandstone; then will we ask, whence come these flattened fragments, observed upon the sandstone? If from the remains of a more solid stratum in the limestone itself, why, let us again ask, are not these likewise observed upon the inferior limestone itself? Why is not the hornstone, which appears to characterize the lower limestone, also observed upon the sandstone? We might further ask, if the limestone above and below the sandstone bed be the same, ought we not to find signs of calcareous beds subordinate to the sandstone, and should we not have a right to expect an interposition of limestone in the immense bed of sandstone which, as we have previously stated, is often one hundred feet in thickness? Yet this we never observed to be the case.

If an alternation of sandstone and limestone strata belonging to the same formation were indicated by the characters previously alluded to, should we not be entitled to expect that the fragments and detritus of both should be found together? Yet in the valleys of the sandstone country, and particularly in the beautiful and romantic one which rested upon the limestone, and was enclosed by sandstone hills, we observed no fragments of the former rock, and but a few large blocks of sandstone which had evidently fallen of late from the sides of the valley. While travelling on the hills we observed that they were covered, in certain parts, with a thin stratum of fine sand, resulting from a slight decomposition of the rock, as is observable in all sandstones of a loose texture.

From what has been previously observed on the comparative age of the limestone of the Wassemon with the formations of Europe, we readily discover that this sandstone cannot be older than the variegated sandstone (Bunt sandstein) of Werner, and we have reason to consider it as an analogous formation. This of course corresponds with the new red sandstone or red marl of English geologists. In this formation in England the red marl certainly predominates; we are not, however, to be surprised, if in America we should find the marl almost deficient, and the sandstone in its place; for it cannot be expected that the same uniformity, which exists between the primitive or general formations of the old and new continent, will be observed between the secondary or partial formations; if we can trace a general resemblance, we have perhaps gone further than we were justified in expecting. With the variegated sandstones of Germany this formation presents a great analogy, and perhaps its most remarkable difference, though undoubtedly a very trifling one in reality, is in the colour, which is seldom red, though it occasionally becomes so. This, among many other instances, proves the great desideratum that geologists should agree upon names more intelligible and less arbitrary than those which have been usually adopted; if the formations of Europe and America are to be compared, (and the daily progress of science proves that even those of Asia and Africa will soon be sufficiently investigated to enable us to take them into consideration,) we ought to have better names than those derived from the most fugitive of all characters, that of colour.

The limestone formation, the existence of which above the sandstone we think we have been enabled to establish, appears to us from its mineralogical as well as its geological characters, to connect itself with the Lias of England, and more particularly with that variety so well known in France and Germany under the name of *Calcaire coquillier* (muschel kalk of Werner), which constitutes, as is well known, the upper bed of what was formerly termed the Jura limestone; and which is inferior to the great oolitic series of England, of which it forms, as it were, the foundation. This oolitic series must not be considered as including the oolites which have been occasionally observed in the Jura limestone of the French, the *zechstein* of the Germans, and the magnesian limestone of England. In all these instances the oolite forms but a partial, and probably an accidental deposit in a limestone, which is certainly inferior to the variegated (*Bunt*) sandstone, or new red sandstone formation. We have in this account of the western limestones studiously avoided, until this time, introducing the terms of Alpine and Jura limestones, and comparing them together, as it appears to us well established, that the greatest confusion has prevailed from the indiscriminate application of these words. The truth of this will be acknowledged by those who recollect, that by some geologists, the two names have been used to indicate the same limestone (at least in certain cases), while some have removed almost all the Alpine limestone into the transition formations, and others have extended the Jura limestone to make it include the *muschel kalk* of Germany, which we have good grounds for considering as coeval with the

Lias of England. It will, doubtless, be observed by those who have made a particular study of the limestone formations to which we have alluded, that there are some apparent contradictions in our statement. That for instance, the *asche* and the oolite observed on the Mississippi cannot be considered as connected together, and with the cavernous limestone of the Wassemon, without bringing together limestones, which in Europe at least, are found of very different ages, unless we adopt the opinion that this oolite is subordinate to the magnesian limestone. This we are disposed to do, as we have no reason to believe that the formations of the Mississippi are superior to those of the Wassemon, or that they are separated by the new red sandstone formation; if we could venture to express an opinion, where much doubt really exists, we would say that the oolite was of the same age as the *asche*, or pulverulent limestone, and that it probably constitutes merely an accidental modification of the magnesian limestone similar to that observed " at Hartlepool, on the coast of Northumberland, where a stratum of hard white oolite exists, the grains composing it being about the size of a mustard seed," and similar to the oolitic varieties which Mr. Freiesleben observed sometimes, though seldom, in the *rauchwacke*.

If in the rude and unsatisfactory sketch which we have presented of these formations, we have thrown any light upon a doubtful and obscure point, we doubt not we shall be excused by the experienced geologist, for the apparent contradictions which we may have revealed. Our object has been to state the facts as they came under our notice, and without any intention to establish a connexion between the formations of Europe, and those which we have described. If the facts militate against observations made abroad, we must regret it; but we have only stated them as they have appeared to us. Our opinion remains, however, unchanged, that whenever these observations shall be repeated under more favourable circumstances, the difficulties will vanish, and the analogy between the formations of Europe and ours, will appear still greater; a due allowance being of course made for those differences which result from the local circumstances that may have influenced these partial deposits.

Those geologists, who have been called upon to make observations in a wild and uncultivated country, where the rocks are frequently concealed by a luxuriant vegetation, where the industry of man has not penetrated by means of quarries, wells, &c. into the bowels of the earth, and where no facilities exist to roam at large in search of breaks, will, we think, appreciate the difficulties which we have had to encounter in the examination of this section of the country; difficulties which have been increased by the loss of our specimens, whence we have been obliged to depend exclusively upon the descriptions recorded in our notes at the time, without being allowed an opportunity of comparing the characters of the rocks with those observed on former occasions.

Observations were made by Mr. Colhoun for the purpose of ascertaining the longitude of our encampment on the Wassemon, which he determined to be 90° 4′ 45″ West. The latitude was also obtained by observations made at midnight, and was found to be 42° 30′ 10″ North. We remarked with pleasure the surprise and delight expressed in Wennebea's face, during these observations. His astonishment at the characters of the mercury, used for an artificial horizon, showed that he had never seen any thing like it; his delight was strongly marked every time he placed his finger upon the bright and dense mercury, and observed the fluid, receding from his touch, and receiving an impression as though it had been water; yet, as he observed, not possessed of the property of wetting his finger like the latter fluid. He was shown the construction of the sextant, and very soon learnt the use of it. As soon as he saw the double image of the moon, he raised his two fingers in token of what he had seen. To one disposed to indulge in the sublime views of Plato, on the immortality of the soul (Cic. de Senec. cap. 21), it would have appeared as if there floated in Wennebea's mind, at that time, an indistinct recollection of what had once been familiar to him. His mind seemed to have received a deep impression from the contemplation of the heavens, but it still remains questionable with us, whether his feeling were produced by the wonderful grandeur of the planets, which he had beheld, and by the associations with which he connected them, or by the ingenuity of white men, who, with a sort of talisman, had brought, within the sphere of his vision, objects which were previously unknown to him, and imparted to him thereby, as it were, a new sense. It seemed as if his mind was overflowing, and he very willingly answered the questions which were put to him, concerning his ideas of the objects he had been beholding. He believed the sun to be the residence of a male Deity, who looks placidly upon the earth, and who being propitious to man, exposes to his view the wild beasts and serpents which cross his path. He thought, that immediately after death the soul quits its mortal residence, and journies towards the setting sun, where, if its life had been spent in a manner agreeable to the Deity, it finds no difficulty in stepping over the agitated log which stretches across the gulf. It then becomes an eternal inhabitant of the "Village of the Dead," situated in a prairie, that abounds in all the pleasures which the simple imagination of the Indian can covet. The moon, on the contrary, he held to be inhabited by an adverse female Deity, whose delight is to cross man in all his pursuits. If, during their sleep, this Deity should present herself to them in their dreams, the Indians consider it as enjoined upon them by duty, to become *cinædi*; they ever after assume the female garb. It is not impossible that this may have been the source of the numerous stories of hermaphrodites, related by all the old writers on America.

Wennebea thought that the Great Spirit had a human form, was white, and wore a hat. It is remarkable that this personification of the Supreme Being under a different appearance from their own, is not peculiar to the Sauks; the Mexicans and Muypuscas represented him as white, and wearing a beard; the Santees, according to Lawson, held the belief that he was white. "They made answer," says he, "that they had been conversing with the White Man above (meaning God Almighty)*." It would be curious to inquire whether there was any connexion between this white complexion attributed to the Deity, and the prophecies which are said to have prevailed among some of the Virginia tribes, as well as at Quizquiz near the Mississippi, of the coming of white men among them.†

* A New Voyage to Carolina, by John Lawson. London, 1709, p. 20.
† Purchas's Pilgrimage, p. 843. Narrative of Dé Soto's Invasion of Florida, written by a gentleman of Elvas, and translated by Hackluyt. London, 1609, p. 90.

These reported prophecies, existing previous to the discovery of this continent (concerning the arrival of white men), are represented by the early writers as very common; whether they really existed in the country, or were artfully circulated by the invaders, may be a matter of doubt. Montezuma, in a speech to his subjects, in the presence of Cortez, is said to have alluded to this subject. An old writer, John de Laet, reports, on the authority of the Spaniards, the same belief to have been prevalent in the island of Cozumel, on the coast of Yucatan. This author enters into many particulars on this subject, which we are disposed to consider as altogether of his own invention.*

On the 17th of June our route was diversified by hills and valleys. The Smoky mountain to the east, and Dubuque's to the west, formed distinct objects of vision, while the long ridge, covered with forests, which extended to the left, indicated the course of the "Great river," as the Mississippi has been emphatically called in the Algonquin languages.

A badger was this day discovered by the dogs in the prairie, and after they had brought it to bay, the Indian killed it with his tomahawk; it was cooked for dinner, and those who ate of it, found it very good. This was near a small stream, called by the Indians Mekabea Sepe,† or Small-pox river; it is the *Rivière de la Fièvre*, which is said to enter the Mississippi opposite to Dubuque's mines.

On the morning of the 18th the sun shone indistinctly through a mist, which offered us the singular phenome-

---

* Joannis de Laet, Americæ utriusque Descriptio. Lugd. Bat. 1633, lib. 5, cap. 27, or p. 273.

† Mè-k'à-bè-'à Sèpè.

non of a beautiful Iris without rain. We encamped that afternoon at an early hour, on a small stream which is a tributary of the Wisconsan and, as we supposed, at a distance of about twelve miles from the place where we intended to cross that river.

The next morning, after a fatiguing ride over a rough and hilly country, we reached the banks of the Wisconsan: as we could not ford it we prepared a light raft, and sent Bemis across to obtain boats at Fort Crawford. From the account of our guides, we thought we were opposite to a point in the river, known by the name of the *Petit cap au Gres* (little sandstone bluff), situated about six miles above the confluence of the Wisconsan and Mississippi; but we afterwards found that we were nine miles higher than our guides had reported us to be. The place where we encamped, until means of transportation across the river could be procured, was in a wood at the foot of a high and steep bank; it was almost the only dry place in the vicinity, the river bank above and below it being swampy. The river was about a third of a mile wide, and the current very rapid.

About sunset we observed two boats advancing up the river, in one of which Colonel Morgan, the commanding officer at Fort Crawford, had come up with Lieutenant Scott to meet our party. This polite attention on the part of the Colonel, gave us a foretaste of the hospitable reception which we met with during our stay in his quarters.

Although it was late, yet as the weather was fine, the party effected a crossing of the Wisconsan, and having relieved their horses of all unnecessary baggage, the gentlemen proceeded under Colonel Morgan's guidance towards the Fort. It was eight o'clock when they left the Wisconsan, and about eleven when they reached the Mississippi. This ride, at a late hour, was one of a most romantic character; the evening was fair and still; not a breath of wind interrupted the calmness of the scenery; the moon shone in her full, and threw a pale light over the trackless course which we travelled. Our way lay across a beautiful country, where steep and romantic crags contrasted pleasantly with widely extended prairies, which, seen by the uncertain light of the moon, appeared to spread around like a sheet of water. Our party was sufficiently numerous to form a long line, which assumed a more imposing character from the dark and lengthened shadows which each cast behind him. All seemed to have their spirits excited by the sublimity of the scene. Even the Indian, whose occupations must have accustomed him to such excursions, appeared to have received an accession of spirits, and the loud whoops which he occasionally gave, as he attained the summit of a hill, enlivened the ride. Our course was a winding one along the glens which divide the bluffs; and whenever we rode in the direction of the moon's rays, the vivid flashes of light, reflected by our military accoutrements, contributed to impart to the whole a character entirely new to many of the gentlemen of the expedition. It was impossible to be a sharer in this splendid prospect, without joining in the enthusiasm to which it naturally gave rise: and however much disposed the mind may be at such an hour, and in such a solitude, to recall, with deep feeling, the image of abodes endeared by the presence of far distant friends, it would have been impossible for any one of us to wish himself at that moment on any other spot, but in the deep and narrow valleys, or on the smooth prairies, which have imparted to this portion of the scenery of the Mississippi, a character of sublimity and beauty, which we should perhaps vainly seek for on any other point of the long extended course of the "Father of Rivers."

At Prairie du Chien we sojourned for five days; the object of this delay was to obtain the escort which was to accompany the party up the St. Peter. While Major Long's attention was engaged in superintending these preparations, the gentlemen attended to their respective departments. The distance from Chicago to Prairie du Chien, by the route which the party travelled, is two hundred and twenty-eight miles, which, having been performed in nine days, gave an average of twenty-five miles per day. No person had ever gone through this route in a direct line before we did, which is surprising, when we consider the extent and antiquity of the trade carried on in this part of the country, and the facilities which the route affords. On no part of our journey have we travelled with more comfort to ourselves, the soil being dry and firm, well watered and sufficiently interspersed with woods to afford us a constant supply of this article for fuel; the grass is generally fine, so that our horses fared well; the country only became rough as we approached the Wisconsan. This river, like the Ohio, seems to unite with the Mississippi in a hilly country; the hills rise to the height of from one hundred and fifty to two hundred feet; their sides are abrupt, and their soil is but indifferent. The Wisconsan has been, for a long time past, the usual communication between the lakes and the Mississippi. About one hundred and eighty miles above the mouth of the Wisconsan, this river comes so near to the Fox river of Greenbay, that a portage of two thousand five hundred yards, across a low and level prairie which is occasionally overflowed, establishes a connection between the two streams. From the portage down to the mouth of Fox river in the Greenbay of Lake Michigan, the distance is computed at from one hundred and fifty to one hundred and eighty miles. The Wisconsan river, which takes its rise near the hills of the same name, extends at least one hundred and fifty miles above the portage. It is represented as having, throughout its course, a rapid current, and but a shallow channel, from which circumstances the ascent is difficult and troublesome. Fox river is formed by the union of two branches, one of which rises at a short distance from the portage road; its course, which is at first westwardly, soon takes a general easterly direction, but the river is at all times very crooked; it falls into Greenbay near Fort Howard.

The country through which these rivers pass, is inhabited by the Menomones, Winnebagoes Sauks, and Foxes, but principally by the two first mentioned nations; the Menomones being chiefly found near the mouth of Fox river, and the Winnebagoes near the portage road, and in the vicinity of the lake which bears their name. The latter are considered as being of distinct origin from the Algonquin tribes; their language is said to present much greater difficulties. It abounds in harsh and guttural sounds, and in the letter *r*, which does not appear to be common in the Algonquin languages. We have already had occasion to advert to the termination in *ra*, added to many of the words by the Winnebago whom we saw on the Pektannon. It is difficult to obtain correct information concerning their manners and characters, as a strong prejudice appears to prevail against them. They are considered unfriendly to white men, and this, instead of being viewed in the light of a favourable trait in their character, as indicative of a high spirit, which can resent injustice and oppression, and which will not crouch before the aggressor, have been the occasion of much ill-will towards them; they have been, probably without cause, charged with many offences which they did not commit. If we can place any dependence upon the character given to them by Carver, we should consider them as no worse than other Indians; indeed his acquaintance with them appears to have left a favourable impression upon his mind. Their appellation in their own language, is believed to be Otchagras; whence the term Winnebago has been derived we have not been able to ascertain, not having met with it in any author prior to Carver. By the French they were called *Puants* or Stinkers, which name is attributed by Charlevoix, to their feeding principally upon fish. " I judge," says he, " it was there (on the borders of the lake) that living on fish, which they got in the lake in great plenty, they gave them the name of *Puants,* because all along the shore where their cabins are built, one saw nothing but stinking fish which infected the air."

In a manuscript narrative of a journey from Bellefontaine on the Missouri to the falls of St. Anthony, and to the Wisconsan portage, performed in 1817, by Major Long, we have observed the following account of their mode of conveying information by a sort of hieroglyphic writing.

" When we stopped," says Major Long, " to dine, White Thunder (the Winnebago chief that accompanied me) suspecting that the rest of his party were in the neighbourhood, requested a piece of paper, pen and ink, to communicate to them the intelligence of his having come up with me. He then seated himself and drew three rude figures, which at my request he explained to me. The first represented my boat with a mast and flag, with three benches of oars and a helmsman; to show that we were Americans, our heads were represented by a rude cross, indicating that we wore hats. The representation of himself was a rude figure of a bear over a kind of cypher representing a hunting ground. The second figure was designed to show that his wife was with him; the device was a boat with a squaw seated in it; over her head lines were drawn in a zigzag direction, indicating that she was the wife of White Thunder. The third was a boat with a bear sitting at the helm, showing that an Indian of that name had been seen on his way up the river, and had given intelligence where the party were. This paper he set up at the mouth of Kickapoo creek, up which the party had gone on a hunting trip."*

While at Prairie du Chien, we endeavoured to obtain from Wennebea as much information as we could concerning his nation; and this, together with the notices collected from him and Le Sellier during the journey, constitutes the basis of the following account of the manners of the Sauks. As they are evidently of Algonquin origin, and therefore connected with the Potawatomis, we have only retained such parts of the information as had not been mentioned before, or in which a difference was observed between the two nations.

The Sauks call themselves in their own language

---

* Major Long's MS. Journal of a voyage, &c. 1817, No. 1, folio 27.

Sakewe.* They are a brave, warlike, and as far as we could learn, a generous people. The great reduction in their numbers arose from their hostility to the French and their allies, and also to the wars which they formerly waged against the Indians on the Missouri and Mississippi, such as the Pawnees, the Omawhaws, the Sioux, the Iowas, &c. Owing to the rapid advance of the white population, and the increasing influence of our government over them, they are becoming more peaceable, and from this circumstance their numbers are probably on the increase. Their historical recollections do not extend far back; but they have been told that about sixty years since, when the French occupied the country, one of the Sauk chiefs by the name of Menetomet,† found himself surrounded with about sixty of his nation by a party of French and Indians, belonging to other tribes, amounting altogether to two thousand. Menetomet then addressed his men, bidding them not to fear, for he had been favoured with a vision from the Great Spirit that informed him that if they all fought bravely, not one of them should perish. Encouraged by this assertion, they fought with such desperation as to break the ranks of their assailants, and escape without the loss of a single man. They were afterwards led by their chiefs towards the *Butte de Mort* on Fox river, and were on the point of being cut off by their enemies, when a peace was effected by the intervention of a French officer. Wennebea informed us that his grandfather was in this party; had it been cut off the nation would, as he thinks, have been totally annihilated: for these composed the whole force of the Sauks. Their

* Sâ-kè-w'è.   † Mè-nè-tò-mêt.

numbers have since considerably increased, as, according to his estimate, the nation now consists of upwards of a thousand warriors; in this number are included all the active able-bodied, and middle-aged part of the nation. This great accession to their numbers results, principally, from their system of adopting their prisoners of war. The real number of warriors of pure Sauk extraction, does not, in his opinion, exceed two hundred. The Fox nation, which appears to be very closely united with the Sauk, was at that time likewise much reduced: it is stated that, at one time, there were but three lodges of Fox Indians left: these reports are probably in some respects exaggerated. The system of adoption seems to be carried to a great extent, and the duties which it involves are of a peculiar character; it seems to have in a great measure stifled all patriotism and attachment to their kin. It is true, that men, reputed good among them, ought not to wander from tribe to tribe, nor from village to village: neither is it prudent for them to do so; for, in case of hostilities breaking out, the new comers would always be the first sacrificed. If a man should marry in a different nation from his own, he continues to live with his wife's nation as long as they remain at peace; but should a war be declared, he must leave his wife and return to his tribe. This does not, however, apply to one who has been made prisoner: if a captive be adopted as one of the nation of his captors, he must forsake all his former ties; he settles in the nation that adopts him, forfeits all allegiance to his native tribe, and contracts new obligations. It is his duty, in case of hostilities, to side with his new friends against his old ones; it becomes even proper for him to do all in his power to promote the views of his adopted

VOL. I.   Q

nation, by killing as many of their enemies as he can; he may even (and it is his duty to do it) kill his own father, and, as our guide added, " nay even his grandfather." In so doing he is not thought to violate any of the obligations of nature, for his adoption has altogether cancelled his former bonds. The expression of Wennebea, "nay even his grandfather," cannot surprise those who have visited the Sauks, or studied to make themselves acquainted with their peculiarities; as one of their most striking precepts is, that the more distant, in the ascending line, a parent is, the more is he entitled to respect and affection; hence the killing of a grandfather would, under common circumstances, be considered as far more atrocious than the murder of a father.

To this high opinion of the duties incumbent upon adopted citizens, and to the general humanity which induces them to spare the lives of their prisoners, we may safely attribute the great accession of numbers which their nation has acquired within the last century. The Sauks have not always resided where they are at present found. Their recollection is that they formerly lived upon Saganaw Bay of Lake Huron, and that about fifty years since they removed, by the way of Greenbay, from the lake shore to their present abode. They seem to consider the name of their nation to be connected with that of Saganaw Bay, and probably derived from it. They have no account of any former migration, but entertain the opinion that the Great Spirit created them in that vicinity.

With a view to ascertain what were their ideas of moral excellence, we asked Wennebea what, in their opinion, constituted a good man. He immediately replied, that in order to be entitled to this appellation, an Indian ought to be mild in his manners, affable to all, and particularly so to his squaw. His hospitality ought to be boundless; his cabin, as well as all that he can procure, should be at the disposal of any one who visits him. Should he receive presents, he ought to divide them among the young men of his tribe, reserving no share for himself. But what he chiefly considered as characteristic of a good man, was to be mild and not quarrelsome when intoxicated. A good man should keep as many wives as he can support, for this will enable him to extend his hospitality more freely than if he have but one wife. Being asked whether by this he meant that an Indian should offer his squaw to strangers, as is practised by the Missouri nations, he replied that no man of any feeling could do such a thing; he thought there was no man so base as to be guilty of this. Adultery is strictly prohibited; so also is an indiscriminate intercourse of sexes. No good man would encourage it, or partake in it; for men were not made like dogs for promiscuous intercourse; but there are some women, whose passions are not controlled by reason, and these will always find men disposed to share in their shame: no good man would, however, do so. Neither would a virtuous man always put away his wife for adultery; he ought to admonish and reprove her. Should she continue in her evil practices, then he will be justifiable in discarding, or punishing her. There are among the Sauks some men so base that they will throw off their male garments, assume those of females, and perform all the drudgery allotted to the latter sex, becoming real *cinædi*. They are always held in contempt, though by some they are pitied, as labouring under an unfortunate destiny which they cannot avoid, being supposed to be impelled to this course by a vision from the female spirit that resides in the moon. Upon the subject of intoxication, Wennebea spoke with much feeling and philosophy. "Intoxication," said he, " is a bad thing; the Indian has been seduced to it by the white man: when our forefathers were first offered liquor they declined it; for they had seen its evil effects upon white men. At last two old men were bribed to taste it; they liked it and took more; they were then affected by it, their language became more voluble; they were merry in their wine. Pleased with the experiment they repeated it, and induced two others to join them; thus did the evil spread gradually. To drink a little is not improper, but to drink to intoxication is not right; our ancestors have forbidden us to do it. You white men can take a little and refrain from more, while the red man follows but the impulse of his feelings; if he takes a little, he requires more, and will have it if he can get at it in any way. You encourage us in this practice; your agents, your traders, instead of withholding it, offer it to us, make us take it, and when we have had a little we lose all control over ourselves. We had no intoxicating draughts before the white man came among us, and we were better men; this has been the ruin of us; all our broils and our quarrels spring from intoxication; some of our women take to liquor; they lose all shame, and become common." It is melancholy to think of the truth contained in these words; not only do our traders, in violation of all law, sell or give liquor to the Indians, but even the agents frequently give them some when they visit the forts, either to keep up a sort of popularity among them, or to rid themselves of their importunities, thus encouraging this fatal propensity, instead of checking it altogether. In this respect the Jesuits were wiser, if not more humane, than our countrymen, since they are reported by 'Grangula, an Iroquois chief, " to stave all the barrels of brandy that are brought to our cantons, lest the people, getting drunk, should knock them in the head."*

It is the duty of a good Indian to offer, on many occasions, sacrifices to the Master of Life; he ought to give feasts frequently, and expose the skins of white deer upon trees, as an offering to the Great Spirit. In such cases, he never partakes of the entertaiment himself; but his friends eat it all up, with the exception of a small part which is thrown into the fire. The business of men consists in hunting, fighting, building their lodges, digging their canoes, taking care of their horses, making wooden spoons, &c.; while it is the duty of women to hew wood, to carry water, to plant and raise corn, to take care of their families, and, in the absence of the men, they must attend to their horses, build their lodges, &c. Man's chief and best occupation is hunting; he will never fight unless aggrieved by his enemies, in which case it becomes his duty to resent the injury. A good hunter is held in high esteem, and will obtain as many wives as he chooses, because they know that he can support them; but the good warrior is esteemed the first man in the nation.

A woman, in order to deserve the appellation of good, ought to be endued with most of the qualities which constitute virtue among civilized females. To be obe-

---

* "Lahontan's new Voyages to North America, done into English. London, 1703." Vol. i., p. 40.

dient and affectionate to her husband is her first duty. Kind to all her children, partial to none; affable and courteous to all men, avoiding, however, the appearance of familiarity with any. Her chastity should be inviolate, even at the risk of death; she ought to be industrious, in order that her husband may be wealthy, and able to extend his hospitality widely. When asked what were the qualifications which were most sought after in the selection of a wife, and if beauty had any influence, Wennebea replied, that they cared but little for a handsome wife, their object being to get a good one, who could attend to all their work, and behave herself as became a good woman. "We are not absolutely regardless of beauty," said he, "but we think it a trifling advantage compared with goodness, and therefore pay but little attention to it; some young men are foolish and attend to it, but these are few, and they soon learn to take good wives, without minding their charms." Being asked what constituted female beauty, he laughed and said, a light complexion, large hazel eyes, a well-formed nose, red lips, and a figure rather small and well proportioned: they seem to have a dislike to very fat women. When questioned as to other points of beauty, he seemed not to have made a study of them; their faces, he said, might be more or less handsome, but in other respects women were all the same. Feeling a little encouraged, he continued in a strain so obscene, as even to put to the blush our old interpreter, Le Sellier; which, with a Canadian trader, might be supposed not to be an easy thing.

It was impossible not to observe in the general tenour of Wennebea's conversation that he admitted a superiority on the part of white men over Indians, at least in foresight, judgment, and capacity, to acquire information. Wennebea thought that when the Master of Life made the white man, he gave him the power to improve in knowledge and the arts; he taught him how to manufacture all the articles that he wanted, such as cloth, guns, &c. To the red man he gave nothing but his bow and his dog; intending him therefore for no other occupation than that of hunting. This appeared to be a favourite idea with Wennebea; he frequently dwelt upon this partition of the good things of the earth, in which the poor Indian had received but his bow and his faithful dog. It was not alluded to in the spirit of complaint or as a hardship, but merely in support of a deep conviction on his part, that, while the white man was made capable of improvement in the arts, the red man was predestined to remain stationary, and live by hunting, for which alone he had received, from the All-ruling Spirit, natural advantages. We related to him the belief entertained by other Indians, who justify their hunting life by saying that, in the origin, God divided all animals equally between the red and the white man; and that while the latter took great care of his share, the former merely wrapped his up, loosely, in his blanket, and having left it for a while, he found, on his return, that all the animals belonging to him had escaped into the woods: it was therefore to recover his lost property that he had addicted himself to hunting. Wennebea observed that he had never heard of this belief before; but he thought, if it were true, it was a wise decree of the Master of Life, for, he added, if the Indian had not suffered his share to escape into the woods, he would have destroyed and wasted it in a short time, and been ever after left to starve, as he wants the provident care of the white man; but as it is at present, the Indian can only use his property gradually, and according as his wants require it.

Wennebea declined entering upon any particulars relating to their belief in an after life, being apprehensive that any conversation on that subject would disturb the quiet of his departed relations. According to Le Sellier, he makes a difference between the *soul* and the *spirit;* the former being probably, in his opinion, nothing else but the principle of vitality; its seat is in the heart; all animals are gifted with souls, as they are endowed with vitality. He believes that the soul alone goes to the other world; the body decays after death. We observed in him, and in all the Indians whom we met with, that they entertained not the least belief of the resurrection of the body, as has been asserted of them by some authors; while they generally appeared to be convinced of the immortality of the soul or spirit, and of an after existence.

The Indians are particular in their demonstrations of grief for departed friends. These consist in darkening their faces with charcoal, fasting, abstaining from the use of vermilion and other ornaments in dress, &c. They also make incisions in their arms, legs, and other parts of the body; these are not made for the purposes of mortification, or to create a pain, which shall, by dividing their attention, efface the recollection of their loss, but entirely from a belief that their grief is internal, and that the only way of dispelling it is to give it a vent through which to escape. Their outward signs of grief are not merely of a temporary kind; they are more lasting than among those who consider themselves as higher in the scale of refinement than the red man. Wennebea observed that he had abstained, for the last fifteen years, from the use of vermilion on account of the loss of a valued friend, and he meant to persist in this practice for ten years, longer; the deceased was no relation, merely a friend. Public opinion requires of them some mourning for departed relations; but the Indian graduates his expressions of grief according to the value in which he held the deceased, not according to the mere relation in which nature or accident placed him in life: for his friend he entertains a feeling deep, warm, and unalterable. Their friendship is seldom divided between two objects: hence they have not those bands of brothers which are stated by Lewis and Clarke to exist among some of the tribes they visited, but the adoption of a brother is very common with them; it is always founded upon sincere friendship, and in the exposed and wandering life of the Indian, opportunities are not wanting to display the extent of this feeling. An Indian will willingly endanger his own life to save that of his adopted brother; and should one of the two be killed, there is no duty more strongly enjoined upon the survivor, or which he more willingly discharges, even at the risk of much personal danger, than that of avenging his friend's death.

Against the charge of cannibalism, Wennebea defended his nation with considerable zeal. This practice, he admitted, existed among the Winnebagoes, Chippewas, Dacotas, and other Indians; but he denied its ever occurring among the Sauks, except in a few instances, in which persons that were very lean and thin, would eat a small piece of the human heart, together with other medicines, in order to fatten themselves. When asked whether this must not be considered as offensive to the

Deity, he replied that he knew not; he had never held converse with the Great Spirit; he had heard other men say that they had enjoyed visions, and conversation of this kind, but, for his part, he never credited them.

Suicide is, according to Wennebea, common among the Sauks, more so with women than men. Grief and jealousy appear to be the predisposing causes with women, and envy, at the power or consequence of others, is the motive which impels men to this deed. Our guide, whose simple system of ethics agrees better with that of the white man than is generally admitted, considers suicide as an improper act; it does not appear to him to accord with the wishes of the Great Spirit; he that gave us life, says Wennebea, has alone the power of taking it way.

Music seemed to have a powerful effect upon him, and particularly martial music; he expressed himself in enthusiastic terms on the subject; while at Fort Crawford he seemed delighted with the *réveille*. The bugle was his favourite instrument. When asked why he preferred it, his answer was, that its notes were so fine, he fancied they must reach the ear of the Great Spirit himself: whenever the sound of the bugle was heard, his attention was immediately directed to it; his eyes sparkled, and his language became more animated.

The principal disease of the Sauks is one, the nature of which we could not well ascertain from his description of it: it is different from dysentery (being at all times unattended by bloody discharges), neither is it the hemorrhoids or hernia. It appears to be a mortification of the intestinal canal or duct, which is brought on by the use of green corn, unripe fruits and vegetables, &c.: it is more common among men than women. If timely remedies be not applied, it proves fatal in the course of four days; the disease is unaccompanied by pain. He declined mentioning the remedies which have been successfully applied, as he entertains the common superstition on this subject.

Intermittents appear to be very prevalent. The small-pox has been known at different periods; our guide, who is about thirty-five years of age, recollects two periods, but does not know at what interval of time they happened; it is thought that it will shortly recur among them. Of parturition and gestation, his account agreed with that obtained at Chicago; being asked how long the pains of labour endured among women, he said they varied, sometimes four days, at other times two days or less, and in some cases scarcely long enough to give a man time to smoke a pipe.

We shall close this protracted account of Wennebea's information, with an anecdote which appears to us to connect itself with a point of some interest in our history; it was related to us spontaneously by Wennebea, and having been written down in his own words, shows the train of ideas of which he was susceptible.

" You know," said he, " that we always carry medicine bags about us, and that in these we place the highest confidence; that we take them when we go to war; that we administer of their contents to our relations when sick, &c. The great veneration in which we hold them, arises from our deeming them indispensable to obtain success against our enemies. They have been transmitted to us by our forefathers, who received them at the hands of the Great Master of Life himself. We never venture upon a warlike undertaking unless, by their means, our chiefs should have previously had visions advising them to do so. When we are near to our enemies, they impart to us the faculty of beholding in the heavens great fires passing from one cloud to another. If these fires be numerous, long-continued and extensive, it is a sure sign to us that in the part of the heavens where we behold them, there are enemies; that they are powerful and numerous, and that we must avoid them. If, on the contrary, they be few, faint, and not frequent, then it is a token that our enemies are weak, and that we may attack them with a certainty of success. These are not visions, but realities; we do not dream that we see these fires, but we actually behold them in the heavens; for this reason do we value our medicine bags so highly, that we would not part with them while life endures. True, some of us did at one time, at the instigation of the Shawanese prophet (Tecumseh's brother), throw them away, but this proved to us the source of many heavy calamities, it brought on the death of all who parted with their bags. To this cause do we attribute the great mortality which we experienced during the late war against the Americans. He (the Shawanese prophet) came to us, and by artifice induced us to throw away our medicine, a circumstance which we have since had cause to regret. His artifice was this; he convened all our chiefs, and told them that he had been favoured with an interview with the Great Spirit, who had imparted to him extensive powers; that he could recall the dead to life, and perform many such astonishing deeds; that he could restore youth to the aged, &c. that the medicine in our bags, which had been good in its time, had lost its efficacy; that it had become vitiated through age: he added that, if we would throw away our medicines, he would perform in our presence, the miracles which he had spoken of, and that, if we followed him, he would ensure us a victory over our enemies. Induced by these promises and flattering expectations, many of our chiefs cast away their bags, a circumstance much to be regretted. It is true, that some who were then assembled challenged the Prophet to work the miracles which he had announced. There, said they, are the bodies of many who have been killed in battle; restore them to life, as thou sayest that thou canst do. But he evaded their challenge by saying to them, I cannot achieve these wonders for you, unless you previously comply with my request to throw away your medicine bags; such of you as shall do so will, on your return, find your children or your friends, that have long since been dead, restored to life. Many were satisfied and did as he bid them; but not one of them ever returned to his home, to see if his promises were fulfilled; for they all fell in battle, on account, as we have always believed, of their having parted with their medicine bags. I," added Wennebea, " spoke to him plainly ; I told him he wished to impose upon us; that our bags had not lost their virtue ; that still in the hour of need we applied to them, and generally with success; that we kept them in our villages, and that when our friends were sick, we applied to them for relief; and that if we were not successful in all cases, at least we were so in most instances. But he was very angry at me, and his brother Tecumseh, who was near to us, laid his hand upon me and offered to strike me, which he would have done had he not been prevented."

Thus spoke Wennebea Namoeta, a Sauk Indian of the

tribe of Pacohamoa* (which signifies *Trout*); his brother had succeeded to the dignity of chief, although he was younger, being considered a man of more talent; and so Wennebea himself admitted him to be. We regretted that we did not meet with this chief, we should have liked to see what his abilities are; he may be a better warrior or a more impressive orator, but we question much whether he surpasses our guide in genuine philosophy. We have with regret shortened the communication of the observations made by this interesting man; we should have wished to give them entire. They breathe throughout a wisdom which would have done honour to the philosophers of old, and a morality of which no Christian need have blushed. Indeed they speak strongly in favour of the doctrine, that wisdom and morality are the spontaneous growth of the human heart, the seeds of which have been implanted by the Great Creator himself; that civilization does not produce them; that the real benefit which results from it is, that, in some instances, it may curb the passions which would otherwise impede their growth. The Indian appears to us to possess ideas of virtue and morality, which are fully as valuable as those that are supposed by some philosophers to be the exclusive appanage of civilization. True, they are, perhaps, but too frequently checked in their growth by the uncontrolled sway which his evil propensities exercise over him; propensities which, as we believe, have been unfortunately increased, by an indiscriminate intercourse with the most worthless of white men, who, to serve their own selfish ends, have not been ashamed to stimulate the Indian to deeds

* På-cò-hå-mò-å.

which his own good sense would have prevented him from perpetrating.

On the route from Chicago to Fort Crawford we saw but one deer, at which, however, we had no opportunity of shooting. We likewise observed but a single wolf, which was of the kind called Prairie wolf. If to these we add the badger, which was killed on the 17th of June, we shall have the list of the only quadrupeds seen upon upwards of two hundred miles of prairie land. The extreme scarcity of game in a country so remote from a white population as this is, must be striking to every observer; and it becomes the more so, if we take into consideration the abundance of fine grass which grows upon it. We know of no other manner of accounting for this scarcity, than by attributing it to the pacific state of the Indian tribes that own these hunting grounds. Being free from all apprehensions of enemies, they hunt without reserve, and destroy the game more rapidly than it can be reproduced. They appear, since their intercourse with white men, to have lost the sagacious foresight which previously distinguished them. It was usual with them, formerly, to avoid killing the deer during the rutting season; the does that were with young were in like manner always spared, except in cases of urgency; and the young fawns were not wantonly destroyed: but at present, the Indian seems to consider himself as a stranger in the land which his fathers held as their own; he sees his property daily exposed to the encroachments of white men, and therefore hunts down indiscriminately every animal that he meets with; being doubtful whether he will be permitted to reap, the ensuing year, the fruits of his foresight during the present, and fearing lest he may not be suffered to hunt, undisturbed, upon his property for another season. To this cause, and to the increase in their numbers produced by a long continued peace, we must attribute the scarcity of game at present observed. The population must, however, soon cease to increase if they do not betake themselves to agricultural pursuits, as the rapid diminution in the quantity of game will eventually deprive them of the means of subsistence. We are not to wonder that an Indian population, apparently so small as that which we know to exist here, should be comparatively large for the country to which it is restricted in its hunts, if we bear in mind the observations of Little Turtle on the subject, " You whites contrive to collect upon a small space a sure and plentiful supply of food. A white man gathers from a field, a few times bigger than his room, bread enough for a whole year. If he adds to this a small field of grass, he maintains beasts, which give him all the meat and clothes he wants, and all the rest of his time he may do what he pleases; while *we* must have a great deal of ground to live upon. A deer will serve us but a couple of days, and a single deer must have a great deal of ground to put him in good condition. If we kill two or three hundred a year, 'tis the same as to eat all the wood and grass of the land they live on, and that is a great deal."*

Among the birds observed, Mr. Say has recorded a single Red-headed Woodpecker,† together with the Ferruginous Thrush,‡ Towhee Bunting,§ Song Spar-

---

* Volney, ut supra, p. 384.
† Picus erythrocephalus.
‡ Turdus rufus.
§ Emberiza erythropthalma.

row,* Chipping Sparrow,† Bartram's Sandpiper,‡ Raven,§ Reedbird, and a Crow ‖ which was first heard near the Wisconsan.

In the vegetable kingdom, the same gentleman observed that the Gerardria was found, about the 15th, with its petals nearly of full length, but that afterwards they were found much shorter. A beautiful specimen of Cassida was likewise seen: its elytra were of a fine green colour, tinged with golden; and the exterior margins were pale.

* Fringilla melodia.   † Fringula socialis.
‡ Tringa Bartramia.   § Corvus corax.
‖ Corvus corone.

CHAPTER VI.

Prairie du Chien. Indian remains. Division of the party. Mississippi. Dacota villages. Fort St. Anthony. Falls. River St. Peter.

OUR arrival at Prairie du Chien, at a late hour in the evening of the 19th of June, prevented us from obtaining a sight of the Mississippi; but early the next morning we hastened to take a view of this important river, which, from its extent, the number and size of its tributaries, the importance of the country which it drains, will bear a comparison with any known stream of the old or new continent. It is one of those grand natural objects, the sight of which forms an era in one's life.

To have been the first civilized man who viewed the mighty Mississippi, was, as we conceive, by no means an undesirable distinction. And, however difficult it may be, at this distant epoch, to ascertain who that man may have been, the inquiry is not the less interesting or useful in the history of human discoveries. So far as our reading extends at present, injustice is done to Alvar Nuñez Cabeza de Vaca. He traversed North America from Espiritu Santo (Tampa) Bay, to New Galicia, between the years 1528 and 1537, and consequently must have seen this river, having crossed it, above or at its mouth; though in his " Naufragios " he has given neither name nor description by which it can be identified: his curiosity was repressed by extreme suffering, and the little hope he entertained of again seeing his country. Hernando de Soto arrived at its banks below the Arkansaw in 1541, and found it there called " Chucagua ;" his body was thrown into it the next year, near the mouth of Red river. If we mistake not, two vessels under the command of Wood, an Englishman, entered its mouth about 1636.* Father Marquette and the Sieur Joliet, to whom the discovery has been generally attributed, did not see the Mississippi before 1673. They entered from the Wisconsan and descended to the Arkansaw. Coxe, whose object is to prove that the English discoveries on the Mississippi intervened between those of the Spaniards and the French, tells us,† that, among the savages, for about half its course, it was called Meschacebe, afterwards Chucagua, Sassagoula, and Malabanchia. It is said that at Guachoya (probably an old place on the Mississippi above Red river), it was called " Tamaliseu, in the country of Nilco, Tapatu ; and in Coça, Mico ; in the port or mouth, Ri."‡ The French first called it Colbert, then St. Louis river. The Spaniards had previously called it Rio Grande, Spirito Santo.

At Prairie du Chien, the breadth of the river is estimated at one-half of a mile, including a long and narrow island. Its current, though rapid compared with

---

* We have endeavoured, but in vain, to find our authority for this statement; but it has entirely escaped our recollection. This is not, however, the same Colonel Wood of Virginia, whom Coxe mentions as having discovered several branches of the great rivers Ohio and Meschacebe.—(Coxe's Carolana, p. 120.)

† Description of the English province of Carolana, by Daniel Coxe, London, 1741, p. 4.

‡ Narrative of de Soto's Invasion, ut supra, p. 122.

that of many other streams, is gentle when contrasted with that of the same river lower down; it is only when it has been swollen by the Missouri and the Ohio, that it acquires the extreme rapidity which characterises it. The village of Prairie du Chien is situated four or five miles above the mouth of the Wisconsan, on a beautiful prairie, which extends along the eastern bank of the river for about ten miles in length, and which is limited to the east by a range of steep hills, rising to a height of about four hundred and thirty-five feet, and running parallel with the course of the river, at a distance of about a mile and a half; on the western bank, the bluffs, which rise to the same elevation, are washed at their base by the river. Pike's mountain, which is on the west bank, immediately opposite to the mouth of the Wisconsan, is about five hundred and fifty feet high. "It has received its name from having been recommended by the late General Pike, in his journal, as a position well calculated for the construction of a military post to command the Mississippi and Wisconsan. The hill has no particular limits in regard to its extent, being merely a part of the river bluffs which stretch along the margin of the river on the west, for several miles, and retain pretty nearly the same elevation above the water. The side fronting upon the river is so abrupt, as to render the summit completely inaccessible, even to a pedestrian, except in a very few places, where he may ascend by taking hold of the bushes and rocks that cover the slope. In general the acclivity is made up of precipices, arranged one above another, some of which are one hundred and one hundred and fifty feet high. From the top we had a fine view of the two rivers, which mingled their waters at the foot of this majestic hill."* The Prairie has retained its old French appellation, derived from an Indian who formerly resided there, and was called the Dog. The village consists, exclusive of stores, of about twenty dwelling houses, chiefly old, and many of them in a state of decay; its population may amount to one hundred and fifty souls. It is not in as thriving a situation as it formerly was. Carver tells us, that when he visited it, in 1766, it was " a large town containing about three hundred families; the houses," he adds, " are well built after the Indian manner, and pleasantly situated on a very rich soil, from which they raise every necessary of life in great abundance. This town is the great mart where all the adjacent tribes, and even those who inhabit the most remote branches of the Mississippi, annually assemble about the latter end of May, bringing with them their furs to dispose of to the traders."† " I should have remarked," says the same author, " that whatever Indians happen to meet at La Prairie *le* Chien, the great mart to which all who inhabit the adjacent country resort, though the nations to which they belong are at war with each other, yet they are obliged to restrain their enmity, and to forbear all hostile acts during their stay there. This regulation has long been established among them for their mutual convenience; as, without it, no trade could be carried on."‡

The fort, which is one of the rudest and least comfortable that we have seen, is situated about one hundred and fifty yards from the river. Its site is low and unpleasant, as a slough extends to the south of it. The river

---

* Major Long's MS. 1817, No. 1. p. 37.
† Carver's Travels, Philadelphia, 1796, p. 31.   ‡ Idem, p. 62.

bank is here so low and flat, that, by a swell which took place in the Mississippi, the summer before we visited it, the water rose upon the prairie, and entered the parade, which it covered to the depth of three or four feet; it penetrated into all the officers' and soldiers' quarters, so as to render it necessary for the garrison to remove from the fort, and encamp upon the neighbouring heights, where they spent about a month. The waters having subsided, at the end of that time, they returned to their quarters: the old men about the village say that such an inundation may be expected every seven years. The village also suffered much from the inundation; though the ground being somewhat higher, the injury done to it was not so great. The fort was originally erected for the protection of the white population at the village: as a military post, its situation is by no means a judicious one, for it commands neither the Mississippi nor Wisconsan; but, as the necessity which led to its construction is daily becoming less urgent, this position will doubtless soon be abandoned. One of the block-houses of the fort is situated upon a large mound, which appears to be artificial. This mound is so large, that it supported the whole of the work at this place, previous to the capture of the fort by the British and Indians during the late war. It has been excavated; but we have not heard that any bones, or other remains, were found in it.

This is by no means the only mound found in the vicinity of the Prairie. There are very numerous remains of Indian works on the Wisconsan, near the *Petit Cap au Grés;* Messrs. Say, Keating, and Seymour, went to examine them. They found the bluffs which border upon the Wisconsan, about four miles above its mouth, covered with mounds, parapets, &c. but no plan or system could be observed among them, neither could they trace any such thing as a regular enclosure. Among these works, they saw an embankment, about eighty-five yards long, divided towards its middle by a sort of gateway, about four yards wide; this parapet was elevated from three to four feet; it stood very near to the edge of the bluff, as did also almost all the other embankments which they saw. From this circumstance, they were led to consider them as raised for the protection of a party placed there, either for the defence of the bluff, or to command the passage of the river. For either of these objects, it must be acknowledged that the selection of the position would be very advantageous. No connexion whatever was observed between the parapets and the mounds, except in one case, where a parapet was cut off by a sort of gateway or sally-port, and a mound was placed in front of it, as it were, to command the gateway; but instead of being inside, in the manner of a traverse, it was outside, and could have served no other purpose, that they could think of, but to allow some of the party to proceed a few steps in advance of the works, and reconnoitre the enemy; though it must be acknowledged, that the enemy might, under cover of this mound, have approached, perhaps, without being perceived, or at least with the advantage of a breast-work. In one instance the works or parapets seemed to form a cross, of which three parts could be distinctly traced; but these were short: this was upon a projecting point of the highland. The mounds, which the party observed, were scattered without any apparent symmetry, over the whole of the ridge of highland, which borders upon the river. They were very numerous, and generally from six to eight feet high, and from eight to twelve in diameter. In one case a number of these, amounting perhaps to twelve or fifteen, were seen all arranged in one line, parallel to the edge of the bluff, but at some distance from it.

These are not the only works in this vicinity; it appears that the mounds and parapets extend not only along the Wisconsan, but upon the bluffs which run parallel to the Mississippi and limit the Prairie to the east. From the description which Mr. Say and his companions gave to Major Long, of what they had seen, it appeared that these could not have been the same as those he observed in 1817. According to his MS. Journal of 1817, (No. 2, fol. 22,) "the remains of ancient works, constructed probably for military purposes, were found more numerous and of greater extent, on the highlands, just above the mouth of the Wisconsan, than any of which a description has been made public, or that have as yet been discovered in the western country. There the parapets and mounds were found connected in one series of works; whenever there was an angle in the principal lines, a mound of the largest size was erected at the angle; the parapets were terminated by mounds at each extremity, and also at the gateways; no ditch was observed on either side of the parapet. In many places the lines were composed of parapets and mounds in conjunction, the mounds being arranged along the parapets at their usual distance from each other, and operating as flank defences to the lines.

"The remains were observed in the interior of the country in a direction towards Kickapoo creek; they were situated for the most part on the ridges, but a few also in the valleys. Those on the ridges had the appearance of having been intended to resist an attack on both sides, being for the most part a single parapet of considerable extent, crossed at right angles by traverses, at the distance of twenty or thirty yards from each other; and having no ditch upon either side. Those in the valleys appeared to have been constructed, to command the passage of the particular valleys in which they were situated. We saw no works which exhibited signs of having been complete enclosures, but the whole were in detached parts, &c."

The following account of the nature of the country, back of the prairie, extending towards Kickapoo creek, (a tributary of the Wisconsan, which empties itself on the north bank about twenty miles above its mouth,) is extracted from the same MS.

" The country is divided into numerous hills, or rather ridges, of various shapes and dimensions, but generally of an equal altitude, by valleys and ravines, some of which have fine streams of spring-water running through them. The hills are generally elevated from three hundred to four or five hundred feet above the vallies; they are handsomely rounded upon their top, but abrupt and precipitous on their sides, and almost inaccessible, except through the numerous ravines by which they are cut. The valleys are many of them broad, and appear well adapted to tillage and pasture; the highlands are also well calculated for the raising of grain. The country is generally prairie land, but the hills and valleys are in some places covered with a scattering growth of fine timber, consisting of white, red, and post oak, hickory, white walnut,* sugar tree, maple, white and blue ash, American box, &c."

* Juglans cinerea.

It is probable that Prairie du Chien was formerly the seat of a large Indian population. The beauty of the country, its favourable characters for hunting, its delightful situation on the banks of the river, must have made it a pleasant abode for Indians; it is doubtful, or at least we have not been able to ascertain, to what nation belonged the family of the Dog Indians, whose name it bears. This family has become extinct; the traditions concerning the fate of its members are very indistinct; it is said that a large party of Indians came down the Wisconsan from Greenbay, and after having massacred nearly the whole of them, returned again to the Bay; that a few of the Dogs, who had succeeded in making their escape to the woods, returned after their enemies had evacuated the prairie, and reestablished themselves in their former residence; and that these were the Indians found at that place by the first French settlers.

This spot, like many of those early settled, has been graced with traditions, which, if they contribute but little to the history of our north-west Indians, adorn at least with the charm of romance and fable some of its most beautiful scenery. Among these, that which is related of one of the caverns on the banks of Kickapoo creek, appears to us to deserve notice. It is said that, in one of the niches or recesses formed by the precipice, there is a gigantic mass of stone presenting the appearance of a human figure. It is so sheltered, by the over-hanging rocks, and by the sides of the recess in which it stands, as to assume a dark and gloomy character. They relate, on this subject, that long since, a battle was fought on the banks of the Mississippi between the inhabitants of the prairie and their enemies; in which conflict the latter were victorious, and succeeded in killing a great number of the former; that an inhabitant of the prairie, who was a very good woman, having received several wounds during the engagement, effected her escape and withdrew to the hills, where she was near perishing with hunger; that while wandering along the banks of this stream, a kind spirit took pity of her, and converted her into this monument to which he, moreover, imparted the power of suddenly killing any Indian that approached near it. This power was exercised until the spirit, tired of the havoc which he had committed, ceased to display his vengeance any longer. Although the natives may therefore, at present, approach the statue with impunity still they hold it in fear and veneration, and none passes it without paying it the homage of a sacrifice of tobacco, &c.

There are at present but few Indians in the immediate vicinity of the fort, and none can give an account of the works which are so abundantly scattered over the country. They say that the only means by which they can account for them is to suppose that the country was probably inhabited, at a period anterior to the most remote traditions, by a race of white men, similar to those of European origin, and that they were cut off by their forefathers. This supposition is grounded upon the circumstance of their having found human bones buried in the earth at a much greater depth than that at which they are accustomed to inter their dead; and in graves which differ from theirs, inasmuch as they are unaccompanied by instruments of any kind, whereas they never omit depositing the arms, &c. with the corpse of the deceased. It is also said that tomahawks of *brass* (?) and other implements differing from those in common use among the present Indians, have likewise been found under the surface of the ground. The fortifications appear to them likewise to be a proof of the correctness of their opinion, as none of the Indians are in the habit of constructing works of a similar character, and as indeed they are unacquainted with the utility of them.

"Mr. Brisbois, who has been for a long time a resident of Prairie du Chien, informed me that he saw the skeletons of eight persons, that were found, in digging a cellar near his house, lying side by side. They were of a gigantic size, measuring about eight feet from head to foot. He added that he took a leg bone of one of them and placed it by the side of his own leg, in order to compare the length of the two; the bone of the skeleton extended six inches above his knee. None of these bones could be preserved as they crumbled to dust soon after they were exposed to the atmosphere."*

We saw a number of Indian graves on the prairie, but as they were modern they offered nothing peculiar. They resemble the graves of white men, but the sod over them is covered with boards or bark, secured to stakes driven into the ground, so as to form a sort of roof over the grave; at the head, poles were erected for the purpose of supporting flags; a few tatters of one of these still waved over the grave. An upright post was also fixed near the head, and upon this the deeds of the deceased, whether in the way of hunting or fighting, were inscribed with red or black paint. The graves were placed upon mounds in the prairie, this situation having doubtless been selected as being the highest and least likely to be overflowed.

From a series of observations, taken at this place, it

* Major Long's MS. No. 2, folio 25.

results, that Fort Crawford is situated in latitude 43° 3″ 31″ north, and longitude 90° 52′ 30″ west. The magnetic variation amounts here to 8° 48′ 52″ east.

Previous to leaving the prairie, Major Long provided for the safe return of Bemis to his garrison, by placing him under the protection of Mr. Rolette, a gentleman of the American Fur Company, who was on the point of travelling to Greenbay by the Wisconsan and Fox rivers. Between the forts at the Bay and Chicago a regular intercourse existed at that time by means of an express sent, at stated times, with despatches. We have had great pleasure in ascertaining that this man, whose conduct had entitled him to the most unqualified praise, returned to his regiment without accident.

Our party was here reinforced by an escort, consisting of a corporal and nine men, under the command of first Lieutenant Martin Scott, of the 5th regt. United States' Infantry, who was selected to command the guard. Major Long secured the services of a half-breed interpreter, by name Augustin Roque. The object in taking this man, was to afford to the gentlemen, charged with the collecting of the Indian information, an opportunity of acquiring from him an insight into the manners and customs of the Dacota Indians, previous to the party's travelling through their country. They were, however, very much disappointed in the character of this man, who enjoys, in the country, a much higher reputation for intelligence and observation, than they were led to ascribe to him, and as the information which he contributed was but trifling, it has been thought proper to embody it with that resulting from personal observations, and from conversations with the interpreters who subsequently accompanied the expedition. With a view to proceed, with as much speed as possible to Fort St. Anthony, where the last preparations were to be made, Major Long divided the party here, and travelled by land with Mr. Colhoun; while the other gentlemen ascended the Mississippi in a boat. The land party was accompanied by George Bunker (a soldier), John Wade (a boy of the garrison, who acted as Sioux interpreter), and Andrew (the black boy). Tommo, a Dacota (Sioux) Indian, acted as guide to the party; he was a tall, gaunt Indian, probably about fifty years old. After having crossed the river in the boat, the two parties separated; and Major Long continued his journey on horseback, along the right bank of the Mississippi.

The route from Prairie du Chien to Fort St. Anthony was attended with greater difficulties than had been anticipated. It was extremely rough and hilly; there being no beaten track, the party were frequently led to the edge of a precipice, and compelled to retrace their steps and seek a more gradual descent. These difficulties arose from their travelling, for the most part, at a distance from the river, with a view to shorten the road; the highlands, which they had attempted to keep, were frequently cut by transverse valleys, opened by streams, tributary to the Mississippi. In the crossing of these streams, much difficulty was experienced from the swampy nature of the ground, in which the horses were frequently mired. The distance at which they travelled from the Mississippi seldom exceeded five or six miles. The guide said it would be difficult to travel at a greater distance, although it might shorten the route, because the country was too thickly wooded, and water very scarce; this last circumstance can only be accounted for upon the supposition, that the water escapes through the numerous sinks observed in the ground. The forest, traversed by the party, consisted principally of oak, basswood, ash, elm, white walnut, sugar tree, maple, birch, aspen, with a thick undergrowth of hazel, hickory, &c. In the bottoms the wild rice, horsetail, may-apple, &c. were found. The eye is charmed by the abundance of wild roses which are strewed over the country, and the palate is not less delighted with the excellence of the strawberry, which is remarkable for its fine fragrance, and which was, just at that time, in a state of perfect maturity. A small Indian village, of five lodges, was passed on the 26th; it is situated on a stream, supposed to be the upper Iowa. Judging from the number of women and children which the party saw, the population must be dense; there were but two or three men in the village; the rest were probably hunting, especially as a large herd of Elk were seen in the morning by the boys of the party, while in search of the horses, that had strayed during the night time to a distance of eight miles from the camp. The whole population of the village seemed to have no other culture than about two acres of maize, which was planted without order in hills, and which had at that time risen but about eight inches above the ground.

At the encampment of the 27th, observations were taken at three o'clock, A. M. (of the 28th), by which the latitude of this place was determined to be 43° 47′ 57″ north. About one mile north of this, the party crossed a river, called in the Dacota language, Hoka* (*Root*),

* Hô-kå.

which is supposed to be the Rivière Longue* or Rivière Morte of Lahontan, and the Mitschaoywa of Coxe ;† this is the same stream which Coxe afterwards calls Meschaouay.‡ But it is impossible to read the Baron Lahontan's account of this river, without being convinced that the greater part, if not the whole, of it is a deception. By his own account he must have ascended it upwards of one hundred and eighty leagues; have met on its banks three distinct nations, the Eokoros, the Essanapes, and the Gnacsitares, the names of which are not recorded by any later traveller; have seen a population considerably greater than that which could have existed there: in a word, his description bears such evident marks of fiction, that we can credit no part of it.

Major Long's party passed on the the 28th down a valley, bounded on both sides by high bluffs and precipices; their ride was a picturesque one; the green sward of the ravine contrasted richly with the greyish hue of the lime and sandstone bluffs, which rose like high walls on either side of them. At last the valley widened, and they found themselves almost instantaneously in sight of the majestic Mississippi, in whose broadly extended valley nature displayed herself with gigantic features. The river, one of the largest in the world, rolling its waters with an undiminished rapidity, in a bed checkered with islands, was a spectacle, which, however often observed, always filled the mind with

* Lahontan, ut supra, Let. 16. vol. i., p. 112.

† Description of the English province of Carolana, by the Spaniards called Florida, and by the French la Louisiane; by Daniel Coxe, Esq. London, 1741, p. 19.

‡ Idem, ibid. p, 63.

awe and with delight. It was impossible to behold the great devastation in the earth's surface, whether considered as caused by the Mississippi or as pre-existing to it, without being induced to look back to the causes which may have produced this phenomenon. But here man finds himself baffled in every attempt to dive into the abyss of past times; he may contemplate the scenery, but cannot unravel the mysteries of its creation. Deep strata of sandstone and limestone are disclosed; they have preserved, as yet, the elevation of the hills undiminished, but have not protected their sides from waste. "When we entered on the prairie, towards the close of the day," says Mr. Colhoun, from whose notes this description is chiefly extracted, " a landscape was presented, that combined grander beauties than any I ever beheld; far as the eye could follow, were traced two gigantic walls of the most regular outline, formed, as it were, by successive faces of pyramids. Between them, extended a level verdant prairie, the scene of the Python flexures of the Mississippi. My sensations were prolonged by the reflection that I had before me one of the noblest rivers in the world; they were enhanced when I saw the evidences of a grand catastrophe. Majestic as is the Mississippi, there was a time when it swept along, a stream, more than one hundred-fold its present volume."

Whatever might be the reveries in which the party were indulging, they were soon recalled to the dull realities of travelling, by the howling and barking of a band of dogs, that announced their approach to an Indian village, consisting of twenty fixed lodges and cabins. It is controlled by Wapasha,* an Indian chief

* Wå-på-shå.

of considerable distinction. In his language (Dacota), his name signifies *the red leaf.* A number of young men, fantastically decorated with many and variously coloured feathers, and their faces as oddly painted, advanced to greet the party. One of them, the son of the chief, was remarkable for the gaudiness and display of his dress, which, from its showy appearance, imparted to him a character of foppishness. In his hair he wore two or three soldiers' plumes; his moccasins of stained buck-skin were tastefully puckered at the toes, and his breech-cloth was quite tawdry. The chief is about fifty years of age, but appears older; his prominent features are good, and indicative of great acuteness and of a prying disposition; his stature is low; he has long been one of the most influential of the Dacota Indians; more perhaps from his talents in the counsel than his achievements in the field. He is represented as being a wise and prudent man, a forcible and impressive orator. His disposition to the Americans has generally been a friendly one, and his course of policy is well spoken of. The Major's party having no other interpreter than Wade, who proved less serviceable than had been expected, could hold but a short conversation with him, and therefore proceeded on their journey, and encamped two miles above the village. Near this place a number of mounds were seen, arranged in nearly a right line along the margin of the river: they were of inconsiderable height, but covered a large surface. Indian remains were observed, in great plenty, for the ensuing two days, extending along the banks of the Mississippi, and especially near the shores of Lake Pepin, along which the land party travelled on the 30th. These mounds and remains attest, of course, the former existence of a very dense population along the lake. It must have been a stationary one, for these works could not have been executed in a short space of time. We are, likewise, led to believe that they were erected by the same nation that constructed the fortifications described by Carver as existing on the bank of the Mississippi, a little below Lake Pepin. The latitude of the encampment, near the lower extremity of the lake, was found, by observations made on the evening of the 29th of June, to be 44° 18′ 37″ north.

Having travelled twenty-two miles along its western shore, Major Long arrived on the evening of the 30th at an Indian village, which is under the direction of Shakea *(the man that paints himself red)*; the village has retained the appellation of Redwing (*aile rouge*), by which this chief was formerly distinguished. The provisions of the party being almost consumed, and the boat having been seen the preceding day at a short distance below the land party, Major Long thought it more prudent to wait here the arrival of the other division, in order to get a fresh supply of provisions. About ten o'clock, on the morning of the first of July, the boat appeared in sight of the village, and signals having been made, the gentlemen landed. The whole party being again united, the chief invited them to his lodge, with a view to have a formal conversation with them.

Shakea is one of the most distinguished of the present leaders of the Dacotas. It does not appear, however, that he is entitled by birth to rank as a chief; but the influence, which he possesses, is founded altogether upon his great military attainments; it is said that he has never been defeated, although he has shared in more actions than almost any other Indian. The respect with which he is treated, which far exceeds that usually paid to a partisan chief, has induced him to assume an importance and a formality, seldom to be met with among the Indians of the present day. As a compliment to the party, the United States' flag was hoisted over his cabin, and a deputation of some of his warriors waited at our encampment to invite us to his lodge. We were received in due ceremony; the chief and his son, Tatunkamane* (the walking buffalo), were seated next to the entrance. We took our stations near them, on the same bed-frame, while his warriors seated themselves on the frame opposite to us: as soon as we entered, the chief and his son rose, and shook hands with each of us. The calumet of peace was placed in the centre of the cabin; the bowl resting on the ground, and the stem supported in an inclined position by a forked stick, planted in the ground for the purpose. The chief then rose, shook hands with the party a second time, raised the pipe from the ground, and holding the bowl towards himself with the stem elevated, he commenced a speech, which was delivered with much vehemence; the purport of it was an acknowledgment of satisfaction, at seeing a party sent by his Great Father (the President), and a general expression of good-will and respect towards the American Government; he also inquired as to the nature of the expedition and its object. Very often, during his speech, the commencement of a sentence was in the concluding terms of the preceding one; the warriors, at each sentence, testified their approbation of his sentiments, in deep-toned responses, sounding like the syllables *ah-hah*, pronounced strongly, and in a nasal and

* Tâtŭnkâmânê.

guttural manner. Major Long stated, in reply, the nature and object of the expedition, the views of the Government in sending it among the Indians, the friendly disposition of the President towards all his red children, &c. With all this the chief appeared well pleased, as also with the presents of tobacco, powder, shot, &c. which were given to him; but he stated that his warriors had been much distressed of late, by the loss of numerous friends and relatives, on which account their faces were painted black, that they had not a single drop of spirits to comfort them in their afflictions, and " hoped that their Father would give them some of their Great Father's milk, to gladden their hearts." But they were informed that the expedition was totally unprovided with this article, as it was their Great Father's wish, that the Indians should not receive from white men liquor, the effect of which was to drive away their senses, make them quarrelsome and sick. Shakea assented to the truth of this, and acknowledged that the use of liquor was very injurious to them; but seemed, however, to regret that he could not make himself merry on the occasion of the glad tidings which he had received from his Great Father. Both he and his son made speeches, which were not remarkable for the beauty or originality of the ideas; these, may, however, have lost their force through our interpreter's inelegant and unanimated translation. But the gestures, which accompanied the words of the orator, were more remarkable for force than for grace or significance. A young Indian who acted as pipe-bearer to the chief (an office of dignity), then lighted the pipe, passed it round to all, commencing with Major Long, proceeding with our party, and concluding with the warriors and interpreter. The pipe-bearer supported the bowl, while each person present drew two or three whiffs. He then smoked of it himself, and, drawing out the stem, presented it to Major Long in token of respect. The bowl, which he kept, was of the red stone found on the St. Peter; the stem was of wood, and made in the usual manner of the Dacota pipe : its length is about three feet, it is flattened, being about two inches wide, and three-eighths of an inch thick : it tapers a little towards the upper extremity; a hole is perforated through it with a hot iron; the pipe stem is painted with a blue clay, which, by long exposure to the air, assumes a green colour; the upper extremity, to about one-third of its length, is ornamented with porcupine quills variously dyed, so as to present beautiful designs : it is also adorned with the small feathers of birds, pigeons, &c. and with the hair of the deer, stained red. Some of these pipes are very elegant, and require a great deal of time in their preparation; they are made by the females. The chief distinction between the Dacota and Chippewa pipe is, that the latter is cylindrical and about an inch in diameter; while the former is, as as we have just mentioned, flattened. Both nations use bowls of the same stone, which is generally red, sometimes however black; they are often curiously carved, &c.

The conversation concluded with another general shaking of the hand. The frequency of this ceremony, during the interview which we had with the Redwing chief, who is considered as pertinaciously adhering to all their old customs, led us to inquire whether the practice of shaking hands originally existed among the Indians, or if it was not introduced among them by Europeans. An acquaintance with many nations has proved, that the modes of salutation varied according to the diversity which exists in their manners, languages, &c. It would, therefore, be singular, that the same practice, which prevails among us, and which we received from our British ancestors, had existed among the Indians, whose neighbours we have, in the course of ages, become. With a view to clear this point, we have collected a number of authorities, relating exclusively to the North American Indians, from which we have been led to believe, that the practice of shaking hands was acquired by their intercourse with white men.

We find that among many Indians a different mode of salutation formerly prevailed. Probably one of the most usual methods for an Indian to welcome a stranger, was to pat his own breast, arms, and legs, and then those of the stranger. We are told that the Indians on the Canada coast received Jacques Cartier by " feeling him and rubbing his arms and breast with their hands, according to their custom of caressing."* And again, a chief " desired the captain to give him his arms that he might kiss and touch them, as is their practice of welcoming in the said land."† The practice of rubbing down the limbs of the stranger was, probably, first introduced for the purpose of relieving him from his fatigue, at least we infer it from the words of Father Hennepin, who says, " At the entry of the Captain's Cabin, who had adopted me, one of the Barbarians, who seemed to be very old, presented me with a great Pipe to smoak, and weeping over me all the while with abundance of Tears, rubbed both my Arms and my Head. This was

---

* Lescarbot, Histoire de la Nouvelle France, à Paris, 1618, p. 254.
† Idem, ibid, p. 302.

to shew how concerned he was to see me so harassed and fatigued: and indeed I had often need enough of two Men to support me when I was up, or raise me when I was down. There was a Bear-Skin before the Fire, upon which the youngest Boy of the Cabin caused me to lie down, and then with the Grease of Wild Cats anointed my Thighs, Legs, and Soles of my Feet."* This treatment was among the Dacotas.

Alvar Nuñez also observes, that the rubbing of the body was a mode of salutation with many nations west of, and probably about, the mouth of the Mississippi, and indeed at a great distance inland. In the account of the first expedition to Virginia in 1584, the narrator expresses himself thus: Granganimeo, an Indian on the coast of what was then called Virginia, made " all signes of joy and welcome, striking on his head, and his breast, and afterwards on ours, to shewe that we were all one."† When they reached the north end of the island of Roanoak, they were entertained by Granganimeo's wife, in a house that had five rooms; their feet were washed in warm water.‡ The practice of washing the feet is also mentioned by Joutel, in his account of De la Salle's Expedition; and the Chevalier de Tonti says, " the chiefs of the nation came towards us; we were conducted through a double file of armed young men, to very neat cabins; the remainder of our entertainment was as grotesque as it was wild; women of a

* A New Discovery of a Vast Country in America, by L. Hennepin. London, 1698, p. 210.

† Account of a " Voyage of Captains Amadas and Barlow to part of the country now called Virginia" (in Hackluyt's Collection). London, 1589, p. 729.

‡ Idem, ibid, p. 731.

dark complexion, but very well formed and half naked, washed our feet in wooden troughs."* Different practices prevailed among other nations. The Clamcoets near the Bay of St. Bernard, sometimes saluted a stranger by rubbing his breast and arms with their hands, sometimes by blowing into his ear;† while the Cenis, who reside on their northern limit, had a different usage. Twelve old men, with the right hand raised to the head, ran up with loud cries and embraced the French.‡ In Carolina the practice of scratching the shoulder probably prevailed. " At noon," says Lawson, " we stay'd and refresh'd ourselves at a Cabin, where we met with one of their War-Captains, a Man of Great Esteem among them. At his Departure from the Cabin, the Man of the House scratch'd this War-Captain on the Shoulder, which is look'd upon as a very great Compliment among them;"§ and again, " They are free from all manner of Compliments, except Shaking of Hands, and Scratching on the Shoulder, which two are the greatest Marks of Sincerity and Friendship, that can be shew'd one to another."‖ Of the Esquimaux we find the following related, in the account of Davis's first voyage in 1585 : " At length one of them, poynting up to the Sunne with his hande, would presently strike his brest so hard that we might

---

* Relations de la Louisianne et du fleuve Mississippi. Amsterdam, 1720, being Vol. 5, of a " Recueil de Voyages," &c.

† Journal historique du dernier Voyage de M. de la Salle, par Joutel. Paris, 1713, p. 74, 84.

‡ Idem, ibid, p. 220.

§ A new Voyage to Carolina, by John Lawson, Gent. London, 1709, p. 42.

‖ Idem, ibid, p. 201.

here the blowe."* When John Ellis imitated their action the Esquimaux approached with confidence. In a tribe of Esquimaux discovered by Captain Ross, the practice of pulling noses is said to exist. " Sacheuse called to us to pull our noses, as he had discovered this to be the mode of friendly salutation with them."† This was in latitude 75° 55' N. and longitude 65° 32' W.

The practice of shaking hands is, however, related of several Indians; Du Pratz states it to exist among the Natchez in particular, and Indian nations generally, referring however to those on the Mississippi.‡ Miantonimo, a Narraganset chief, after a conference with the Governor, gave him his hand for the absent magistrates;§ but this was subsequent to 1637. The habit of embracing or kissing is alluded to more frequently. At Hochelega, now Montreal, the French were welcomed by the women, who kissed their faces.|| In the fourth voyage made to Virginia, in 1587, it is said that the Indians of the island of Croatoan (on the coast of North Carolina) " threwe away their bowes and arrowes, and some of them came unto us, embracing and entertaining us friendly."¶ So also of the Esquimaux in Davis's second voyage, in 1586; " they came running to mee and the rest, and embraced us with many signs of hartie welcome."** Wherever the Spanish

* Hackluyt's Collection, p. 778.
† Ross' Voyage, London, 1819, p. 86.
‡ Histoire de la Louisianne, par Du Pratz, à Paris, 1758. Tome 2, p. 237.
§ Hubbard's Narrative of Indian Wars, Brattleborough, 1814, p. 54.
|| Lescarbot, ut supra, p. 327.
¶ Hackluyt's Collection, ut supra, p. 767.
** Idem, ibid, p. 781.

authors are consulted, we find that, in addition to the ceremony of embracing generally, they mention the kissing of hands and prostrating themselves; thus, although it is stated, that the chief Muscoço welcomed Juan Ortiz, who fled to him for protection by embracing him and kissing his face,* yet we find, that when the same chief went to the Spanish camp, he kissed De Soto's hands.† The Cacique of Casqui (on the Mississippi) is also stated to have prostrated himself before De Soto.‡ Garcilaso de la Vega, mentions as a mode of salutation, prostration and kissing of the hands; but these were probably to superiors, and in token of veneration. The following practice, observed at Kecoughtan (near Chesapeake Bay), is a curious one, but whether used as a mode of salutation or not, we are unable to tell. " Landing at Kecoughtan, the Savages entertained them (the voyagers) with a doleful noyse, laying their faces to the ground and scratching the earth with their nayles."§

From the instances which we have cited, and we might have adduced many more, we are led to believe that, wherever the practice of shaking hands has been observed, it had probably been received from the English; for the only three instances which we have mentioned are those from Hubbard, Du Pratz, and Lawson. The first of these authors states it of the New England Indians; the second is comparatively a modern writer, his book having been published as late as 1758; and Lawson's authority, though generally very good, is

* La Florida del Inca, en Madrid, 1722, p. 28.
† Idem, ibid, p. 33.
‡ Narrative of De Soto's Invasion, written by a gentleman of Elvas, and translated by Hackluyt. London, 1609, p. 96.
§ Purchas' his Pilgrimage, London, 1614, p. 768.

less decisive in this instance, because being himself an Englishman, he might be more ready to ascribe this practice to the Indians than any other, and because he speaks of Indians who had already some acquaintance with the English; besides, we find that he describes twice the practice of scratching the shoulder, as a mark of great respect, from which circumstance we are led to believe, that this was the original practice of the Carolina Indians. The practice of kissing hands and of prostration, being only mentioned by Spanish writers, was probably the consequence of an intercourse with Spaniards. That of embracing appears more general, but it is also restricted chiefly to French authors, or to those who treat of Indians that had been in habits of intercourse with the French. One exception presents itself, however, to our recollection; it is in the first reception of Captain Lewis by the Shoshonees. "The three men leaped from their horses, came up to Captain Lewis, and embraced him with great cordiality, putting their left arm over his right shoulder and clasping his back, applying at the same time their left cheek to his, and frequently vociferating ah-hie! ah-hie! ' I am much pleased, I am much rejoiced.' The whole body of warriors now came forward, and our men received the caresses, and no small share of the grease and paint of their new friends."[*] Notwithstanding this instance, we consider the practice of embracing as not original with the Indians in general, but probably in most cases derived from the French. Indeed, we have ourselves heard the Indians ridicule the frequent kissing which

---

[*] History of the Expedition under the command of Captains Lewis and Clarke. Philadelphia. 1814. vol. i, p. 363.

they observed among the Canadians, and consider it as unworthy of men.

The Redwing chief is, at present, far advanced in years, but he is still respected on account of his former distinguished achievements. When Major Taliaferro, the Indian agent, visited him, not long since, with Morgan, the principal war chief of the Sauks, the latter told Tatunkamane to his face, when shaking hands with him, that he considered him as a very unimportant personage, and that he only took him by the hand out of respect to his father, who had been, to them, so brave and active an enemy. The Sauks will long remember the injury this chief did them. Some of the warriors whom we saw in the chief's cabin were very fine looking men. One of them, whose face was covered over with charcoal, bore so strong a resemblance to the portraits of Napoleon, that all our party were struck with it. It was rather to Bonaparte as first consul, than as emperor, that the resemblance was great, for he had not the corpulence which the ex-emperor had acquired; not only his features, but even the conformation of his head, shared in the general resemblance. We could not learn that he was a distinguished man in the nation.

Among the many Indians whom we saw at the village, one of those, who frequented our company most, was an old man, by the name of Wazekota* (Shooter from the pine-top), who was an intolerable beggar. He professed much friendship for us, was very fond of showing his knowledge of our language by the frequent repetition of the English monosyllable of Indian John in the Spy. This, together with a few of the most common expres-

* Wă-zè-kŏ-tá.

sions, such as how d'ye do, good by, &c. completed his whole stock of English words. This man's name bears a striking analogy to that of the principal chief of the Issati or Nadouessis, whom Hennepin met on the Mississippi, and whom he calls " Ouasicoudé (that is to say, the Pierc'd Pine").* He accompanied Major Long on part of his journey in 1817, but scarcely recollected the circumstance, being at present very old. These Indians were much pleased with the sight of our travelling map; they displayed great intelligence on the occasion, understanding it immediately; tracing several rivers with their fingers; mentioning their names; pointing to the portages, &c. Wazekota laid his finger upon the Falls of St. Anthony, which he called Hahawotepa.† They appeared quite surprised to find that so large a district of country could be represented on so small a compass, and at the same time be so distinct. The magnetic needle and the mercury likewise attracted their notice; they expressed much surprise on observing that iron floated upon this fluid with the same buoyancy that cork would upon water. They considered all these things as mysterious.

Three Menomone Indians were here on a visit, having just returned from the St. Peter, where they had been hunting. It is supposed that sixty or seventy warriors of their nation will unite with Redwing's band, although the principal of the three, a fine looking stout man, thought proper to apologize for this band, saying to us, that the Sioux were hogs and beggars, destitute of food, and ignorant of the duties of hospitality; but that when

---

* Father Hennepin's Works, ut supra. London, 1698, p. 217, and Relations de la Louisianne, &c. p. 292.

† Hăhăwŏtĕpă.

we should arrive among the Chippewas, we should be received as strangers should be; subsequent experience has by no means satisfied us of the superiority of the Chippewas over the Dacotas. The complexion of these Menomones was lighter than that of any Indians we saw on the journey; one of them spoke French; the principal one had abundance of wampum about his neck, together with a necklace of cowries (Cypræa moneta). We afterwards learned from the Indian agent at St. Anthony, that this is an eminent war leader, and that, when his party unites with Redwing's, he will be recognized as the principal war chief. This Menomone told us, that the tumuli observed behind the village were artificial, and ancient cemeteries. Tommo, and the Sioux, whom we consulted on the subject, all considered them as natural elevations. As they do not bury their dead, but dispose of them on scaffolds, they seem to be unacquainted with the ancient practice of interring.

After a very interesting visit to this village, the gentlemen again separated. Major Long's party, having been provided with a portion of the boat's provisions, which were becoming scanty, continued their journey by land that afternoon, and reached Fort St. Anthony the next evening without meeting with any accident. The route from the Indian village was off from the river, it was rolling, less hilly than had been previously travelled; the tumuli increased in number, exceeding in abundance any that the party had ever seen before; at times upwards of one hundred of them were in view. A stream about thirteen yards wide, which they crossed a short time after leaving the village, is called by the Indians Eamozindata*

* èámózíndátá

(High rock), from a white pyramidal rock which rises to a considerable height near this stream, a few miles above the place where they crossed it. Being aware of its existence, and knowing that it would not lengthen the journey much, they were anxious to pass near it; but, whether from superstitious motives or not, Tommo seemed unwilling to guide them in that direction. This man was not one of the pleasantest that the party could have had to accompany them; although he was selected as one of the best in the vicinity of Prairie du Chien, he was not agreeable. He was a listless, indifferent kind of man; an incessant smoker; his pipe, which was connected with his tomahawk, was in constant use; it was made in the form of a shingling hatchet. The part which corresponded with the hammer was hollowed out for the bowl, and the handle was perforated so as to serve as the stem of the pipe: he adverted to the pipe as the Indian's only solace in hunger. This man had a curious specific when unwell; it was to climb a tree, cut the top so that it would bend, and then let himself drop down from it to the ground.

The first boulders which had been seen from Rock river were observed by Mr. Colhoun, at about seven miles from Fort St. Anthony; they consisted of granite. A very great change in the country above Lake Pepin was visible; the bluffs were not so high, they were more frequently interrupted, and gave a new character to the scenery of the river. The distance by land from Prairie du Chien to the St. Peter is two hundred and eleven miles; it was travelled in eight days, hence at an average of twenty-six and a half miles per day. This may be considered as the first section of our journey; the whole distance from the Philadelphia to this place, was near thirteen hundred miles, which were travelled in sixty four days, stoppages included. This affords an average of twenty miles per day.

Having followed Major Long's division from the Prairie to this place, we shall take a hasty glance at the observations made by the other division, during their progress up the river.

This division consisted of Messrs. Say, Keating, and Seymour, with Roque (the interpreter). The boat was manned by the corporal and eight soldiers, under the command of Lieutenant Scott. They were provided with an eight-oar barge with a sail, or rather their *tent-fly*, which was used as a substitute for one. After parting with Major Long, on the west bank of the river, the barge proceeded up the Mississippi, but had not been long on its course before symptoms of misconduct broke out among the men; and Mr. Scott then discovered that, while the whole party were conversing with Major Long, on the river bank, the men had broached the keg of liquor, and helped themselves to its contents so bountifully as to be soon affected by it. As soon as they were heated by the exercise of rowing, the effects of the whiskey became but too evident. They lost all respect for their officer, and but for the firm stand which he took upon the occasion, a mutiny would inevitably have broken out; but, having called for his pistols and loaded them in their presence, he assured them that the first man who attempted a mutiny must do it at the risk of his life; the crew being, however, too much affected by the liquor to be able to stem the strong current of the Mississippi, the boat was ordered to the shore, and the party lay by for a few hours.

In the evening the men being a little sobered, they resumed their journey, and encamped at night above the Painted Rock river, on the west bank of the Mississippi. The distance travelled that day did not exceed nine miles. The bluffs, which appear to be limestone (but we were at too great a distance to determine the fact with certainty), continue on both sides of the river, and rise to a considerable height. In one place the rock is very steep, and apparently inaccessible: the difficulty of the undertaking was, probably, the motive which induced the Indians to attempt to climb it; and, having succeeded, they wished to perpetuate the recollection of their success, by painting upon it, with red colours, a few grotesque figures. It is said that, when these are effaced by time, or washed away by the rain, they are soon replaced by other sketches, left there by the Indians, who are constantly passing up and down the river. The Painted Rock, like every frail attempt to distinguish, by artificial means, those things which nature, in her wild designing, has clothed with an uniform garb, seizes more powerfully upon the imagination of the trading voyager on our western streams, than the finest natural features of their splendid scenery; it has become, therefore, as it were, a landmark which assists the traveller in tracing his progress through these desert regions. The weather was fair and warm; the wind slight but adverse, so that the sail was not hoisted. This first day's voyage on the Mississippi was delightful to those who had never been on that river before; the magnificence of the scenery is such; its characters differ so widely from those of the landscapes which we are accustomed to behold in our tame regions; its features are so bold, so wild, so majestic, that they impart new sensations to the mind:

the very rapidity of the stream, although it opposes our ascent, delights us; it conveys such an idea of the extensive volume of water which this river ceaselessly rolls towards the ocean. The immense number of islands which it imbosoms, also contributes to the variety of the scenery, by presenting it constantly under a new aspect.

On the 26th of June the wind was fair, and, starting early, the party proceeded up with considerable speed; the country and its scenery presenting pretty nearly the same characters as on the preceding day. In the course of the morning, they saw the appearance of a cavern in the rocks, and landed to explore it, but found it to be merely a small excavation of no account; this, however, gave Mr. Keating an opportunity of observing that the bluff consisted of limestone, which, in the upper parts, became very loose, and assumed the characters of the *asche*, as mentioned in the preceding chapter. Fragments of a beautiful oolite were observed below it; they were loose and angular, some of them of a large size. No doubt could exist that they were in the immediate vicinity of their original sites, but the nenessity of taking advantage of the fair wind, did not permit a search after the rock itself. On the left bank of the river, a small stream was observed to put in; at its mouth two Menomone lodges were situated; but they were closed, the inhabitants having, doubtless, gone on their summer-hunts. At some distance beyond this they passed, on the right bank, the mouth of the Iawa, a river celebrated in Indian warfare as the scene of a bloody rencounter between the Sioux and Sauks. At forty-five miles from Fort Crawford there is a Winnebago village of a few huts; it was surrounded by handsome corn-fields. At the mouth of Bad-Axe river, a little beyond this, the party exchanged a few words with two Menomone Indians who were descending in a canoe. Two remarkable capes or points were observed on the right bank of the Mississippi, below Iawa river; the lower one is designated by the name of Cape *Puant*, because, at a time when the Sioux and Winnebagoes (*Puants*) were about to commence hostilities, a party of the latter set out on an expedition to invade the territory of the Sioux, and take them by surprise; but these, being informed of the design, collected a superior force, and lay in ambush near this place, expecting the arrival of their enemies. As soon as the Winnebagoes had landed, the Sioux sallied from their hiding places, pressed upon them as they lay collected in a small recess between the two capes, drove them into the river, and massacred the whole party. Garlic cape, just above this, strikes the voyager by the singularity of its appearance. In shape it represents a cone, cut by a vertical plane passing through its apex and base; its height is about four hundred feet. The peculiarity of its appearance has made it a celebrated landmark on the Mississippi. Mr. Seymour, whose pencil was frequently engaged in sketching the beautiful features of the Mississippi, took a hasty view of this, as the boat passed near it. The valley is, in this part, almost entirely filled by the river which laves the base of the bluffs on both sides. The river spreads, in some places, to the width of three or four miles; its channel being very much interrupted by numberless islands, which render the navigation difficult. The bluffs are generally from four hundred to five hundred feet high, intersected with numerous ravines, and exhibiting signs of being the commencement of a hilly and broken inland country.

One of the soldiers was this day very sick of *mania a potu*. At times he was perfectly insane, probably from having suddenly given up the use of strong liquor, in which he had previously indulged himself very freely. He continued sick during the rest of the voyage up the Mississippi. It was a horrid sight, in a small boat, not more than thirty feet long, in which the party were much cramped for want of room, to behold a man affected with occasional fits of raving, and these of the most distressing kind: he made frequent attempts to throw himself overboard, which at last induced Mr. Scott to have him secured to the mast: he was very loquacious in his insanity, replying as he thought to the voice of his officers at Prairie du Chien, whom he fancied he heard calling him; at times he became ironical, bursting into a wild and convulsive laughter, then launching out into profane and abusive language; in fine, exhibiting all the workings of a disordered imagination. At one of the encampments, he broke his bonds and wandered near a swamp; men were sent after him, who were out a long time before they overtook him: he was, for a while, given up for lost, and it was by the most fortunate chance that he was at last discovered, by one of the men, wading through a swamp; had he proceeded much further he must have perished in this fen. Mr. Say having administered to him the proper remedies, he gradually recovered, but finding it agreeable to abstain from work, feigned sickness, and his insanity was observed apparently increasing while the other symptoms indicated a general improvement in his health; suspecting that he was *playing the old soldier*, Mr. Say prescribed the use of an oar as a sudorific, by which he soon recovered the use of his lost senses.

The party had encamped for the night on a prairie, between Raccoon and Bad-Axe rivers, but the mosquitoes, which had hitherto proved very tormenting, becoming still more so, they determined, at eleven o'clock at night, to resume their journey. If a sleepless night was to be spent, it was better to pass it in the boat, in the middle of the stream, where, at least, they would be relieved from the torment of the mosquitoes. The breeze, which was favourable, allowed the barge to proceed with considerable rapidity for three hours, when the wind increased into a gale, which rendered the navigation dangerous. After having attempted, for a time, to continue to proceed, in despite of the violence of the storm, they were obliged at last to draw near the shore. A very heavy rain fell for several hours, to which they remained exposed in the boat, having no protection but that afforded them by their blankets. Notwithstanding the comfortless situation in which they found themselves, there was an irresistible interest in the scene. A storm is, at all times, one of the most splendid phenomena in nature; but when experienced in the gloomy forests of the Mississippi, in the midst of a solitude, with no companions but a few fellow-sufferers, standing in a shivering attitude in a small boat, it receives an additional interest; every flash of lightning displays a scene which the painter would wish to fix upon the canvass. The loud peals of thunder resound more forcibly when reverberated by the rocky bluffs, which border upon the river, and they contrast sublimely with the low but uninterrupted muttering of the rolling waters. About sunrise the storm ceased, the weather cleared up, the party resumed their journey, and continued it until breakfast time, when they were gratified to stop and make a fire to dry their clothes and repair the damge occasioned by the storm. While at their encampment of the preceding evening, the attention of the party was suddenly roused by the faint and indistinct sounds of a human voice, singing at a distance. It was soon evident that the words were English, and the air a familiar one to all the party; after a while the noise of a paddle was distinctly heard, and by hailing they brought to the shore a canoe that was gliding down the river, with two discharged soldiers from Fort St. Anthony. The country which borders upon the river abounds in rattlesnakes, the party killed several during their journey to Lake Pepin, above which, it has been said, that they are never seen. In examining the head of this serpent, Mr. Say's thumb was punctured by several of the small acute teeth, while it pressed upon the roof of the mouth; and on laying open the vesicle of poison, a portion of the fluid flowed under the thumb, and found its way into one of the punctures, and although the quantity must have been very small, it gave rise to much pain and numbness in the part; it however soon subsided, producing but little swelling.

The travelling on the 27th was not very rapid, owing to a head wind, but no time having been spent on shore, the party reached the Prairie de la Crosse in time to encamp there; this has been incorrectly called the Cross (*crux*) prairie. The name of this spot is derived from a game very much in favour among the Indians; it is played with a ball, and is probably not very unlike some of the games of the white men. This prairie being very level and fine, is admirably well calculated for this purpose; and was formerly much frequented by the Indians. There were a few remains of Indian encampments upon it, of one of which the party took possession, for the purpose of sheltering themselves during the night. Within a few yards of their encampment they discovered several graves, over which flags were hanging, indicating that the deceased had been men of some consequence. The party proceeded, early the next morning, and passed the mouth of Black river, one of the most important tributaries of the Mississippi; it is much resorted to for the purpose of obtaining timber, as the forests, which grow upon its banks, are much finer than those on the Mississippi. Not only does it supply the Fort at Prairie du Chien, but even, as we are informed, much of the " pine timber used at St. Louis is cut here."* The voyagers have remarked that the number of islands, in this part of the Mississippi is so great, that there are but few spots where both banks of the river can be seen at the same time; this is, however, the case, at a short distance above the mouth, of Black river; and one mile above this place the bluffs on both sides of the river, approach within eight hundred yards of each other. The wind being ahead, and strong, the progress of the boat was slow. On the evening of the 28th, the party reached the spot which has been described, by all travellers, as a great natural curiosity, though, in fact, it presents nothing extraordinary. It is termed by the voyagers, the *Montagne qui trempe dans l'eau.* This, which we understand to be but the translation of the Indian name for it, means " the mountain that soaks in the water." It is a rocky island corresponding with the adjoining bluffs, and separated from the left bank of the river by a narrow

---

* Major Long's MS. 1817, No. 2, folio 4.

sluice. This insulated portion of highland appears, when seen from a distance, to stand in the middle of the stream, and its base is washed by the water; but on approaching towards it, it is found to be very near the east bank of the river; and as well as the party could judge from the opposite bank, along which they were coasting, there was at that time, but little or no water between the " mountain" and the left bank. Pike has, in his journal, stated its height at about two hundred feet; from a trigonometrical admeasurement of it, made in 1817, Major Long estimates its elevation at five hundred feet; although his instruments did not allow him to take his measurements with the greatest accuracy, yet this must be very near the true height; since the island is as elevated as the adjoining bluffs, which are among the highest that are to be seen above the Wisconsan.

Mr. Schoolcraft has been led into error, in his account of it, when he represents the island, on which it stands, as being four or five miles in circumference. Mr. Scott, who travelled down the Mississippi a week after we ascended it, measured it, and found it to be only a mile in circumference. Neither can we agree with the same author when he states that it " divides the river into two equal halves, and gives an immense width to the river."* Perhaps the most remarkable feature about this mountain is that " it is the third island of the Mississippi from the gulph of Mexico to this place that has a rocky foundation similar to that of the neighbouring bluffs, and that rises nearly to the same height as these."† The other islands in this river are merely

* Narrative Journal of Travels, &c. by H. R. Schoolcraft, p. 335.
† Major Long's MS. No. 2, folio 5.

formed by the alluvion collected by the stream, and are chiefly sandy; many of them are covered with a fine vegetation.

Early on the 29th, the boat reached Wapasha's village; the gentlemen landed, and were disappointed on being informed that they had missed of seeing Major Long's party by about an hour. Being anxious to become better acquainted with an Indian, who is held in such high esteem among the powerful and extensive nation of the Dacotas, as Wapsha is, they gave the old chief an invitation to enter into their boat, which he readily accepted, but declined accompanying them up to Fort St. Anthony, as his band had heard, that morning, of the approach of their enemies, the Chippewas, on the river of the same name; he had sent out some of his warriors to scout, and thought it incumbent on him to remain and watch over his band; but as our party was ascending in the direction in which his warriors had gone, he said he would proceed with us that far. The gentlemen were interested by the apparent calmness with which he spoke of the approach of his enemies. No consternation prevailed in the village; the men were, it is true, all painted, as for war, and a number of them were absent; but the old chief was lying down with the greatest unconcern; his preparations for departure were, however, soon made, and he accompanied the party in the boat; his son-in-law and another Indian paddling his canoe in the rear. Wapasha spoke of the advantages of the arts and agriculture; of his wish to see them introduced; he expressed his desire to accept the invitation, given him by the Indian agent, to accompany him to the seat of government, as he was anxious to see how every thing was managed among the white men. One of the objects of which he spoke with the greatest rapture was the steam-boat, which had ascended the river in the spring, and which he considered as a wonderful invention. We were told that when this boat had come up, he was taken on board, and the machine was exhibited to him; he appeared to take great interest in the explanations of it, which were given to him. During Major Long's visit to Wapasha's village in 1817, he witnessed part of a very interesting ceremony known by the name of the bear dance. " It is usual to perform it when a young man is anxious to bring himself into notice; and it is considered as a sort of initiation into the state of manhood. On the ground, where it was performed, there was a pole supporting a kind of flag, made of a fawn's skin dressed with the hair on; upon the flesh side of it, were drawn certain figures indicative of the dream which the candidate had enjoyed; for none can go through this ceremony, who has not been favoured with dreams. To the flag a pipe was suspended as a sacrifice; two arrows were stuck up at the foot of the pole; and painted feathers, &c. were strewed upon the ground near it. These articles appertained to the religious rites, which accompany the ceremony, and which consist in bewailing and self mortifications; the object of these is that the Great Spirit may be induced to pity them and assist them in the undertaking. At two or three hundred yards from the flag there is an excavation which they call the bear's hole, and which is prepared for the occasion; it is about two feet in depth, and has two ditches, each one foot deep, leading across it at right angles. The candidate places himself in this hole to be hunted by the rest of the young men, all of whom, on this occasion, are dressed in their best attire, and painted in their neatest style. The hunters approach the hole, in the direction of one of the ditches, and discharge their guns, which were previously loaded with blank cartridges, at the youth who acts the part of the bear; whereupon he leaps from his den, having a hoop in each hand, aed a wooden lance; the hoops serving as forefeet to aid him in characterising his part, and his lance to defend him from his assailants. Thus accoutred, he dances round the plain, exhibiting various feats of activity, while the other Indians pursue him and endeavour to trap him, as he attempts to return to his den; to effect which, he is permitted to use, with impunity, any violence that he pleases against his assailants, even to taking the life of any of them. This part of the ceremony is performed three times, that the bear may escape from his den and return to it again, through three of the avenues communicating with it. On being hunted from the fourth, or last avenue, the bear must make his escape through all his pursuers, if possible, and fly to the woods, where he is to remain through the day. This, however, is seldom or never accomplished, as all the young men exert themselves to the utmost, in order to trap him. When caught, he must retire to a lodge prepared in the field for his reception; there he is to be secluded from all society during the day, except that of one of his particular friends, whom he is allowed to take with him, as an attendant. There he smokes and performs various other rites which superstition has led the Indian to consider as sacred; after this ceremony is ended, the youth is considered as qualified to act any part, as an efficient member of the community. The Indian who has had the good fortune to catch the bear and overcome him, when endeavouring to make his escape to the woods, is considered a candidate for preferment, and is, on the first suitable occasion, appointed a leader of a small war party, in order that he may have a further opportunity of testing his powers, and of performing some essential service in behalf of his nation. It is accordingly expected that he will kill some of their enemies, and return with their scalps."*

Wapasha informed the gentlemen in the boat, that the Chippewa Indians had been very troublesome, frequently descending the river that bears their name, and cutting off small parties of the Dacotas that were hunting. He spoke also of the advantages of having a mill built at the rapids of Chippewa river, as had been promised to them by the American government; finally, after a few hours' conversation, he left the boat, and crossed over in his canoe to the spot where his outposts were supposed to be. The party encamped that evening on a sandbar in the Mississippi, opposite to the mouth of Buffalo river. The next morning, a head wind detained the boat a long while, but it afterwards shifted, and the party ascended so rapidly, that early in the afternoon they found themselves within a few miles of the lower extremity of Lake Pepin; they were very desirous of visiting the fortifications described by Carver as being on the Mississippi, " some miles below Lake Pepin." Mr. Schoolcraft states, upon the authority of a Mr. Hart, a trader, that they are on the west bank of the river, a circumstance not mentioned by Carver. We spoke with the oldest traders in the country; with those who had been all their lifetime in the habit of encamping in that vicinity,

* Major Long's MS. 1817, No. 2, folio 6.

but met with none who had ever seen them or heard of them. Mr. Rolette, a partner in the American Fur Company, mentioned that he supposed the most probable place was at a well-known spot on the river, called the "Grand Encampment," situated a few miles south of Lake Pepin. This gentleman, who had encamped there very frequently, had, however, never observed any thing like fortifications. On drawing near to the bank at this place, a regular elevation of the ground, parallel to the water's edge, struck us as an artificial embankment; but on landing, and inspecting it, the gentlemen of the party unanimously agreed, that there was here no appearance of ancient works, but that the features observed were natural. The next question was, whether this was the place visited and described by Carver, and whether he had seen artificial works, or mistaken for them the natural peculiarities of the surface; upon this point there was a difference of opinion. Messrs. Say and Scott thought that the description of the locality, given by Carver, was sufficient to identify it with this spot, and that as it was impossible that they should not have observed fortifications covering near a mile of ground, upon a prairie that is not more than two and a half miles wide, it was probable that this traveller had mistaken a natural for an artificial embankment. Agreeing in the fact that there were no artificial works here, Mr. Keating considered this as proof that the Grand Encampment was not the spot alluded to by Carver; for, although the general description agrees with that given by the traveller, yet the same might be said of many other spots; the minuteness of the description which Carver gives of these remains, precludes, as he thought, the opinion that he had mistaken a natural embankment.

Although no gentleman of the party would be willing to ascribe to Carver a scrupulous adherence to truth, (personal observation having convinced them all of the many misrepresentations contained in his work), yet the description of these mounds appeared to one of them entitled to more credit, because, as it is believed to be the first which was given by any traveller in America, it cannot be supposed to have been copied from others; because the authority of Mr. Hart's testimony seems to be on that side of the question, as well as that of General Pike, who probably saw the spot mentioned by Carver, as we find in his journal this observation: " Stopt at a prairie on the right bank descending, about nine miles below Lake Pepin; went out to view some hills, which had the appearance of the old fortifications spoken of, but I will speak more fully of them hereafter."* Whether these were similar to those which he describes as having seen on the Prairie de la Crosse,† we have not been able to ascertain. But the strongest argument in favour of the existence of the fortifications described by Carver, is the circumstance of the many mounds and remains observed by Major Long and Mr. Colhoun, between Wapasha's village and the St. Peter, many of which were seen near the southern extremity of Lake Pepin. Although it does not appear that they met with any parapets, yet as these were found near the Wisconsan, in connection with the mounds, there is reason to believe that they may likewise have been erected in this vicinity. Taking all these facts into consideration, Mr. Keating was led to the conclusion, that Carver had really seen

* An account of Expeditions to the Source of the Mississippi, &c. by Major Z. M. Pike, Philadelphia, 1810, p. 98.
† Idem, p. 18.

the works which he has described, but that they probably were not at the Grand Encampment.* The party landed at another place above this, which appeared to correspond with the description of the locality, but their search here was likewise unsuccessful. At a late hour in the afternoon they reached the southern extremity of Lake Pepin, and proceeded until sunset, when the weather appearing stormy, they encamped upon a sandy point that projects about six miles above its southern extremity. They had not been there many hours before a high northerly wind began to blow, which proved the propriety of their encamping there; for the navigation of this lake is represented as very dangerous whenever the wind blows fresh. *Le lac est petit, mais il est malin*, was the reply of the interpreter to a question as to the propriety of continuing our course during the night. The next morning the weather was fair and calm, we resumed our journey through the lake, with great ease, until we came within about three miles of its upper extremity, when the wind increased; we were soon satisfied, by our own observation, that the slightest breath of wind will produce a heavy swell upon this lake. From this circumstance, it is usual with the voyagers on the river, to cross it, if possible, at night; experience having satisfied them that it is generally calmer then than during the day. The lake is about twenty-one miles long, and its breadth, which varies from one to three miles, may be averaged at about two and a half. Towards its southern extremity the valley widens considerably, from the circumstance that Chippe-

---

* Vide Three Years' Travels through the Interior Parts of North America, &c. by Captain Jonathan Carver, Philadelphia, 1796, p. 35.

wa river unites with the Mississippi at this place. That river is about five hundred yards wide at its mouth, and is navigable at all seasons of the year, by pirogues, for fifty miles; and in time of freshes they can proceed much farther up. Lake Pepin, in most places, fills nearly the whole of the valley between the contiguous bluffs. In two spots, however, a handsome piece of meadow land is observed, which will offer great inducements for the establishment of farms. The general direction of the lake is from west-north-west to east-south-east. The scenery along its shores constrasts strongly with that of the river. Instead of the rapid current of the Mississippi winding round numberless islands, some of which present well-wooded surfaces, while others are mere sand-bars; the lake presents a smooth and sluggish expanse of water, uncheckered by a single island, and whose surface, at the time we first observed it, towards the close of the day, was unruffled; nothing limited the view but the extent of the lake itself; the majestic bluffs which enclose it extend in a more regular manner, and with a more uniform elevation than those along the river. When seen from the top of one of these eminences, the country is found very different from that in the vicinity of the mountain island passed on the 28th of June, for it is rather rolling than hilly; and the quantity of timber upon it is comparatively small, especially to the west, where it assumes the general characters of an elevated prairie land. About half way up the lake, its eastern bank rises to a height of near four hundred and fifty feet, of which the first one hundred and fifty are formed by a perpendicular bluff, and the lower three hundred constitute a very abrupt and precipitous slope, which extends from the base of the bluff to the edge of the water.

This forms a point, projecting into the lake, and bounded by two small basins, each of which is the estuary of a brook that falls into the lake at this place. The wildness of the scenery is such, that even the voyager who has gazed with delight upon the high bluffs of the Mississippi, is struck with uncommon interest on beholding this spot. There is in it what we meet with on no other point of the far-stretching valley of the Mississippi, a high projecting point, a precipitous crag resting upon a steep bank, whose base is washed by a wide expanse of water, the calmness of which contrasts with the savage features of the landscape; but this spot receives an additional interest from the melancholy tale which is connected with it, and which casts a deep gloom over its brightest features. Cold and callous must be the heart of the voyager who can contemplate unmoved and uninterested the huge cliffs that enclose this lake, for

"Wild as the accents of lovers' farewell
Are the hearts which they bear, and the tales which they tell."

"There was a time," our guide said, as we passed near the base of the rock, "when this spot, which you now admire for its untenanted beauties, was the scene of one of the most melancholy transactions that has ever occurred among the Indians. There was in the village of Keoxa, in the tribe of Wapasha, during the time that his father lived and ruled over them, a young Indian female, whose name was Winona, which signifies 'the first-born.' She had conceived an attachment for a young hunter, who reciprocated it; they had frequently met, and agreed to an union, in which all their hopes centred; but, on applying to her family, the hunter was surprised to find himself denied; and his claims superseded by those of a warrior of distinction, who had sued for her. The warrior was a general favourite with the nation; he had acquired a name by the services which he had rendered to his village when attacked by the Chippewas; yet, notwithstanding all the ardour with which he pressed his suit, and the countenance which he received from her parents and brothers, Winona persisted in preferring the hunter. To the usual commendations of her friends in favour of the warrior, she replied, that she had made choice of a man, who being a professed hunter, would spend his life with her, and secure to her comfort and subsistence; while the warrior would be constantly absent, intent upon martial exploits. Winona's expostulations were, however, of no avail, and her parents, having succeeded in driving away her lover, began to use harsh measures in order to compel her to unite with the man of their choice. To all her intreaties, that she should not be forced into an union so repugnant to her feelings, but rather be allowed to live a single life, they turned a deaf ear. Winona had at all times enjoyed a greater share in the affections of her family, and she had been indulged more than is usual with females among Indians. Being a favourite with her brothers, they expressed a wish that her consent to this union should be obtained by persuasive means, rather than that she should be compelled to it against her inclination. With a view to remove some of her objections, they took means to provide for her future maintenance, and presented to the warrior all that in their simple mode of living an Indian might covet. About that time a party was formed to ascend from the village to Lake Pepin, in order to lay in a store of the blue clay which is found upon its banks, and which is used by the Indians as a pigment. Winona and her friends were of the company. It was on the very day that they visited the lake that her brothers offered their presents to the warrior. Encouraged by these, he again addressed her, but with the same ill success. Vexed at what they deemed an unjustifiable obstinacy on her part, her parents remonstrated in strong language, and even used threats to compel her into obedience. "Well," said Winona, " you will drive me to despair; I said I loved him not, I could not live with him; I wished to remain a maiden, but you would not. You say you love me, that you are my father, my brothers, my relations: yet you have driven from me the only man with whom I wished to be united; you have compelled him to withdraw from the village; alone he now ranges through the forest, with no one to assist him, none to spread his blanket, none to build his lodge, none to wait on him; yet was he the man of my choice. Is this your love? But even it appears that this is not enough, you would have me do more; you would have me rejoice in his absence; you wish me to unite with another man, with one whom I do not love, with whom I never can be happy. Since this is your love, let it be so; but soon you will have neither daughter, nor sister, nor relation, to torment with your false professions of affection." As she uttered these words she withdrew, and her parents, heedless of her complaints, resolved that that very day Winona should be united to the warrior. While all were engaged in busy preparations for the festival, she wound her way slowly to the top of the hill. When she had reached the summit, she called out with a loud voice to her friends below; she upbraided them for their cruelty to herself and her lover: " you," said she, " were not satisfied with opposing my union with the man whom I had chosen, you endeavoured, by deceitful words, to make me faithless to him; but when you found me resolved upon remaining single, you dared to threaten me; you knew me not, if you thought that I could be terrified into obedience, you shall soon see how well I can defeat your designs." She then commenced to sing her dirge; the light wind which blew at the time wafted the words towards the spot where her friends were; they immediately rushed, some towards the summit of the hill to stop her, others to the foot of the precipice to receive her in their arms, while all, with tears in their eyes, entreated her to desist from her fatal purpose; her father promised that no compulsive measures should be resorted to. But she was resolved, and as she concluded the words of her song, she threw herself from the precipice, and fell a lifeless corpse near her distressed friends. " Thus," added our guide, " has this spot acquired a melancholy celebrity; it is still called the Maiden's rock, and no Indian passes near it without involuntarily casting his eye towards the giddy height, to contemplate the place, whence this unfortunate girl fell, a victim to the cruelty of her relentless parents."

In the annals of civilized life, the sad tale of Winona's adventures has been but too often realized; and the evidences of the powerful influence of feeling over women are too well known, to produce any sensation of surprise at their recurrence. But it is seldom that the wild inhabitant of the forest is admitted to possess the same depth of feeling. Judging of both sexes from the instances which have been related of the apathy, assumed or real, of the Indian warrior, too many are induced to believe, that the uncivilized condition of the savage deprives him of, or stifles in him, all passion;

but this is not the case. The fate of Winona has many parallels, which are not all equally well known. There were, in the circumstances of this case, several conditions which tended to impart to it a peculiar interest; the maid was one who had been a favourite in her tribe; the warrior, whom her parents had selected, was one of note; her untimely end was a public one—many were witnesses to it: it was impressive in the highest degree; the romantic situation of the spot, which may be thought to have had some influence over the mind of a young and enthusiastic female, who found herself at that time "perplexed in the extreme," must have had a corresponding effect upon those who witnessed it. Wazecota, who was there at that time, though very young, appeared to have received an indelible impression from it; and when relating it to Major Long, in 1817, the feelings and sensations of his youth seemed to be restored; he lost the garrulity of age, but spoke in a manner which showed, that even the breast of the Indian warrior is not proof against the finest feelings of our nature. Had Winona, instead of taking the fatal leap, put an end to her existence in the midst of a forest, by suspending herself to a tree, as is generally practised by those Indian women whom distress impels to suicide, her fate would still have been unknown to us; a few of her friends might have wept over her untimely lot, but the traveller would have passed over the spot where she had ended her woes, without having his sympathies awakened, as they now are, by the recital of this terrible catastrophe. While the circumstances of this tale were related to us, Mr. Seymour was engaged in sketching this interesting spot. We have introduced his view of it here, as it gives a correct idea of the scenery of the upper part of the Mississippi, which has never, we think, been accurately represented. We regretted that it was not possible to reduce, to the proper size, a fanciful delineation of the tragic event which we have related. Mr. Seymour painted one of this kind, in which the landscape was represented with the most faithful accuracy, but which he animated and enlivened by the introduction of a numerous party of Indians, in whom the characteristics of the Dacotas where strikingly delineated. The unfortunate Winona was represented at the time when she was singing her dirge, and the various groups of Indians below indicated the corresponding effect upon the minds of the spectators.

The first European that ever reached this lake was Father Hennepin, who saw it in the month of April, 1680, and who gives the following description of it: "About thirty leagues above Black river we found the Lake of Tears, which we named so, because the savages, who took us, as it will be hereafter related, consulted in this place what they should do with their prisoners; and those who were for murthering us, cryed all the night upon us, to oblige, by their tears, their companions to consent to our death. This Lake is formed by the Meschasipi, and may be seven leagues long and five broad. Its waters are almost standing, the stream being hardly perceptible in the middle." We have not been able to discover the origin of the name which the lake now bears; it is evidently a French name. While ascending the lake, we observed floating upon the surface a large fish which had been wounded with a harpoon or lance; we caught it, and found it to be a Paddle-fish.* This fish is distinguished by a protuberance or rostrum,

* Platirostra Edentula (Lesueur). Vide Appendix I. B.

which extends from the nose about fourteen inches, and which, from its resemblance to the form of a paddle, has obtained for it the common appellation of paddle-fish. The Mississippi unites with the upper extremity of the lake by three channels, which are separated by islands. Upon one of these we landed, and found the passenger-pigeons to be very numerous, so that in a few minutes a number of them were killed. We likewise saw here a rattlesnake, which disproves the assertion of some authors that this animal is not found above Lake Pepin. It is probable, however, that they are scarce above this place, as this was the last one seen by our expedition. Mr. Schoolcraft states, that Governor Cass' expedition likewise met with it above Lake Pepin, and he even observes, that it exists as high on the Mississippi as the Falls of St. Anthony. One of the guides, Joseph Reinville, whom we shall have occasion to mention hereafter, informed Mr. Colhoun that he had killed them on Big Stone Lake, which is near the head of the St. Peter.

About four miles above the lake is the site of Redwing's village, at the mouth of Cannon river. Immediately below the village there is a singular hill, which, from its form, which is supposed to resemble a barn, has been called the Grange; it is about three quarters of a mile long, and four hundred feet high. Its acclivity on the east or river side is very abrupt, on the west or prairie side it is quite vertical; it stands insulated from the rest of the highlands. Immediately upon the highest point of the Grange, Major Long, who ascended it in 1817, observed an artificial mound, whose elevation above its base was about five feet.

Having left the Redwing village early in the afternoon of July 1st, the party continued to ascend the river; the current had again become very strong; they proceeded that evening to a place below the St. Croix river ; this stream enters the Mississippi on its left bank ; at its mouth it is about one hundred yards wide, but immediately above it expands to a breadth of from three-fourths to two miles, and forms what is called the St. Croix Lake. Pike, in his journal, describes the Mississippi, for a considerable distance below the St. Croix, as of a reddish appearance in shoal water, but black as ink in deep.* The red colour is owing to the sand seen at the bottom, which is of that hue; the dark colour is no more than what is common to deep water that is moderately limpid.

On the 2d of July we passed what is termed the narrowest place on the Mississippi, below the Falls of St. Anthony; the river is here free from islands, and not more than one hundred or one hundred and twenty yards broad. Pike† states that his men rowed across in forty strokes of the oar : but Major Long found, in 1817, that his " boat crossed it, from a dead start, in sixteen strokes."‡ A great change in the scenery of the river is perceptible ; instead of running between two parallel walls of considerable altitude, the river there passes through a rolling prairie country, where the eye is greeted with the view of extensive undulated plains, instead of being astonished by the sight of a wild and gigantic scenery. At the St. Croix the bluffs seldom rise to two hundred feet above the water level. The valley, through which the river runs, is more uniform in its breadth, but the river is crooked and its channel impeded by sandbars ;

* Pike, ut supra, p. 24. † Idem, ibid
‡ Major Long's MS., 117, folio 12.

and the current rapid, so that the progress of the boat was slow. The party landed, for a few minutes, to examine a stone which is held in high veneration by the Indians; on account of the red pigment with which it is bedawbed, it is generally called the painted stone. They remarked that this was the first boulder of primitive rock which they had seen to the west of Rock river, and this place corresponds well with that at which these boulders were first observed by Mr. Colhoun while travelling by land. It is a fragment of sienite, which is about four and a half feet in diameter. It is not surprising that the Indians should have viewed this rock with some curiosity, and deemed it wonderful, considering that its characters differ so materially from those of the rocks which are found in the neighbourhood. A man who lives in a country where the highest hills are wholly formed of sandstone and secondary limestone, will necessarily be struck with the peculiar characters of the first specimen of granite that comes under his notice, and it is not to be wondered at, that one who "sees God in all things," should have made of such a stone an object of worship. The Indians frequently offer presents to the Great Spirit near this stone; among the offerings of their superstition, the party found the feather of an eagle, two roots of the "Pomme de Prairie" (Psoralea esculenta, Nutta¹), painted with vermilion; a willow branch, whose stem was painted red, had been stuck into the ground on one side, &c. The gentlemen broke off a fragment of this idol, to add to the mineralogical collections, taking care, however, not to leave any chips, the sight of which would wound the feelings of the devotee, by convincing him that the object of his worship had been violated. The party landed at a short distance above, to visit the cemetery of an Indian village, then in sight. The cemetery is on the banks of the river, but elevated above the water's level; it exhibits several scaffolds, supporting coffins of the rudest form; sometimes a trunk (purchased from a trader), at other times a blanket, or a roll of bark, conceals the body of the deceased. There were, also, several graves, in which are probably deposited the bones, after all the softer parts have been resolved into their elements by long exposure to the atmosphere. Returning to the boat, the party ascended and passed an Indian village, consisting of ten or twelve huts, situated at a handsome turn on the river, about ten miles below the mouth of the St. Peter; the village is generally known by the name of the *Petit Corbeau*, or Little Raven, which was the appellation of the father and grandfather of the present chief. He is called Chetanwakoamane* (the good sparrow hunter). The Indians designate this band by the name of Kapoja,† which implies that they are deemed lighter and more active than the rest of the nation. As the village was abandoned for the season, we proceeded without stopping. The houses which we saw here were differently constructed from those which we had previously observed. They are formed by upright flattened posts, implanted in the ground, without any interval, except here and there some small loopholes for defence; these posts support the roof, which presents a surface of bark. Before and behind each hut there is a scaffold, used for the purpose of drying maize, pumpkins, &c. The present chief is a good warrior, an artful, cunning man, remarkable among the Indians for his wit, and, as is

* Chĕ-tăn-wă-kŏ-ă-mă-nė.   † K'ăpŏ'jă.

said, for his courtesy to white men, endeavouring, as far as he can, in his intercourse with the latter, to imitate their manners.

Above this village, there is a cave which is much visited by voyagers; we stopped to examine it, although it presents, in fact, but little to admire; it is formed in the sandstone, and is, of course, destitute of those beautiful appearances which characterize the caverns in calcareous rock. It is the same which is described by Mr. Schoolcraft, whose name, as well as those of several of Governor Cass' party, we found carved on the rock. In his account of it, Mr. Schoolcraft states it to be the cavern that was visited by Carver, but adds that "it appears to have undergone a considerable alteration since that period." It appears from Major Long's MS. of 1817, that there are two caves, both of which he visited: the lower one was Carver's; it was in 1817 very much reduced in size from the dimensions given by Carver; the opening into it was then so low, that the only way of entering it was by creeping in a prostrate position. Our interpreter, who had accompanied Major Long, as a guide, told us that it was now closed up; it was probably near the cemetery which we have mentioned. The cavern which we visited, and which Mr. Schoolcraft describes, is situated five miles above; it was discovered in 1811, and is called the Fountain cave; there is a beautiful stream running through it, whose temperature, as observed by Major Long on the 16th of July, was 46° (F.) and by Mr. Schoolcraft, on the 2d of August, 47°. The temperature of the atmosphere, the day that Major Long made his observation, was 89°. From these results, as well as from several others which we obtained, we have been led to adopt about 46° as the average temperature of springs in this latitude, and in this district of country.

At a late hour in the night of the 2d of July the boat entered the St. Peter, and proceeded up the river opposite to the fort; but it being too late to approach the works, the gentlemen spent the night on the south bank of the river, preferring to lie out in the open air, rather than to share with a Frenchman and his Indian family the shelter of a hovel. The distance, by water, had always been estimated at about ninety leagues, or two hundred and seventy miles. In Mr. Schoolcraft's journal it is estimated at two hundred and sixty-five miles. It was measured on the ice in February 1822, by Sergeant Heckle, of the garrison, who reduced the distance to two hundred and twelve miles; his measurement was made by means of a perambulator of his own invention; he is said to have made allowance for the crooked channel followed by voyagers; from the time which we consumed in ascending, making a due allowance for the speed of the opposing current, we should have estimated the distance at two hundred and twenty miles. The time required for this journey varies from eight to twenty and twenty-five days, according to the wind; for it is impossible to row against the current with a strong head-wind. Our boat made the trip in seven days and a half, which was considered the shortest that had been known of at the fort. In 1817, Major Long ascended in eight days to the falls, which are nine miles higher; Pike was eighteen days in reaching the same spot. Mr. Scott, who returned to Prairie du Chien the next day after his arrival at the fort, reascended the river, completing his voyage to and from the

Prairie in nine days and a half, a speed hitherto unknown. The average passage down the river is three days; it has been performed in forty-eight hours.

The streams that enter the Mississippi between the Wisconsan and the St. Peter are numerous, but for the most part unimportant. Those which alone deserve to be mentioned are, on the west side, the Cannon, Root, and Iawa rivers; on the east side, the St. Croix, Chippewa, and Black rivers. Of these the St. Croix and Chippewa rise near some of the streams tributary to Lake Superior. It was the Chippewa river that Carver ascended after having visited the Falls of St. Anthony, and thence descending one of the neighbouring streams, probably the Montreal river, reached Lake Superior. The St. Croix rises near the head waters of the Bois Brulé, which also falls into the Lake; there is a portage of two miles between these streams. This is one of the routes upon which most trade has been carried on. Lake St. Croix extends thirty miles, beyond which the river continues navigable for about twenty miles, when its navigation is said to be obstructed by a rapid; but above this, the stream is a very pleasant one to travel, and sufficiently deep for loaded canoes.

Game seems to be disappearing very rapidly from the face of the country. Buffaloes, of the largest size, were formerly found here; a few were still to be seen in 1817, on the river that bears their name, and that discharges itself into the Mississippi below Lake Pepin; but since the establishment of the garrison at Fort St. Anthony they have all been destroyed or have removed further west. The party that travelled in the boats, saw abundance of pigeons, but, with the exception of these, no other kind of game; the only animal observed besides these was the rattlesnake (Crotalus horridus), of which they killed four or five.

The land party, although provided with an excellent hunter, killed but a few pigeons; some of them saw a large herd of elks. Game will be judged to be very scarce where two parties, travelling by land and by water, can kill but two or three dozen of birds upon a distance of upwards of two hundred miles.

The river abounds in turtles (Testudo [Trionyx] ferox, Linn., and T. [Emys] geographica, Lesueur*), at least judging from the great number of eggs which our men picked up in the sand; it appears that the animal deposits her eggs on the sand-islands, which abound in the river, generally at a distance from the water, she covers them up with sand, and abandons them; the heat of the sun supplies the place of incubation. The men collected them in great number, and appeared to be very fond of them.

The mineralogical observations were unfortunately prevented by the circumstances under which the party travelled. Hastening towards the St. Peter, and apprehensive lest a delay on shore might deprive them of the advantage of a fair wind, they landed near the bluffs but seldom, and never for any length of time. Their usual stoppages were on sandbars, and even there but for a short time; they frequently travelled late at night, and sometimes even the whole night. Under these circumstances, the only feature that could be observed was, that the country was formed of limestone and sandstone; that the former was, in one instance at least, oolitic and pulverulent; that the sandstone was white, loosely ag-

---

* Journal Acad. of Nat. Sciences, vol. i. p. 86, pl. 5.

gregated, and horizontally stratified, but its connexion with the limestone was never determined; the sandstone prevails above Lake Pepin, the limestone below it; and probably to this we may attribute the difference observed in the characters of the stream and its banks after we had passed the lake. The sand appears to be chiefly formed by the detritus of the sandstone; it not unfrequently contains cornelians, agates, jaspers, &c., which present characters analogous to those observed on the Rhine below Oberstein, and in Scotland, where they are distinguished by the name of Scotch pebbles. They bear evident marks of having been washed away from a secondary trap formation. We shall have occasion to observe, at a future period, that a formation of this kind was traversed by the expedition. In one or two instances, while examining the sand with the microscope, a white transparent topaz was extracted from it; it is probable that, had more time been taken on land, many would have been found. Although much rubbed, still the form of the prism of the topaz, with its dihedral summit, could be well made out.

The party in the boat experienced much fatigue during this portion of the journey, from the want of rest at night, and the cramped situation in which they were in the boat; but a stay of a few days at Fort St. Anthony refreshed them, and prepared them to resume their journey.

Fort St. Anthony is situated on the high bluff which rises on the right bank of the Mississippi, and the left of the St. Peter, at the confluence of the two streams. Although this spot had been visited and described by Pike in 1806, and subsequently by Major Long in 1817, who, in his report to the War Department, recommended the establishment of a permanent post at this place, it was not until the summer of 1819, that military works were commenced here. Col. Leavenworth, with part of the fifth regiment, arrived here in August, 1819, and all that has been done here was subsequent to this period. The fort is in the form of a hexagon, surrounded by a stone wall; it stands on an elevated position which commands both rivers. The height of the half-moon battery, which fronts the river, is one hundred and five feet above the level of the Mississippi. It is not, however, secure from attacks from all quarters, as a position within ordinary cannon shot of it rises to a greater elevation; but, as long as we have to oppose a savage foe alone, no danger can be apprehended from this. If a resistance against a civilized enemy, provided with artillery, were required, possession might be taken of the other position, which would command the country to a considerable distance, and protect the present fort, which is in the best situation for a control of the two rivers.

The garrison consists of five companies of the 5th infantry, under the command of Col. Snelling. The great activity which has been displayed by the officers and men, has already imparted to this place, situated as it is at an immense distance from civilization, many of the comforts of life. The quarters are well built, and comfortable: those of the commanding officers are even elegant, and suitable for the principal military post to the north-west. There were, at the time we visited it, about two hundred and ten acres of land under cultivation, of which one hundred were in wheat, sixty in maize, fifteen in oats, fourteen in potatoes, and twenty in gardens, which supply the table of the officers and men with an abundant supply of wholesome vegetables.

On the 6th of July we walked to the falls of St. Anthony, which are situated nine miles, (along the course of the river, seven by land) above the fort. The first glimpse which we caught of the fall was productive of diappointment, because it yielded but a partial view, but this was amply redeemed by the prospect which we obtained of it when the whole fall opened itself before us. We then discovered that nothing could be more picturesque than this cascade. We had been told that it appeared like a mere mill-dam, and we were apprehensive lest a fall of sixteen feet would lose all its beauty when extended upon a breadth of several hundred yards: but we soon observed that this was by no means the case. The irregular outline of the fall, by dividing its breadth, gives a more impressive character. An island, stretching in the river both above and below the fall, separates it into two unequal parts, the eastern being two hundred and thirty yards wide, and the western three hundred and ten. The island itself is about one hundred yards wide. From the nature of the rock, which breaks into angular, and apparently rhomboidal fragments of a huge size, this fall is subdivided into small cascades, which adhere to each other, so as to form a sheet of water, unrent, but composed of an alternation of retiring and salient angles, and presenting a great variety of shapes and shades; each of these forms in itself a perfect cascade, but when taken together in one comprehensive view, they assume a beauty of which we could have scarcely deemed them susceptible. We have seen many falls, but few which present a wilder and more picturesque aspect than those of St. Anthony. The vegetation which grows around them is of a corresponding character. The thick growth upon the island, imparts to it a gloomy aspect, contrasting pleasingly with the bright surface of the watery sheet which reflects the sun in many differently coloured hues. The force of the current above the fall is very great; but, as we were told that it could be forded, we determined to attempt to cross immediately above the fall. The place at which we forded was within a few yards of the edge of the rock; and as we passed we could not repress a feeling of apprehension at the danger which we were incurring. The water never, it is true, rose above two feet and a half, but the rock upon which we were treading was very smooth, and the force of the current such, that we were frequently exposed to slip; while at the same time we were convinced, that if we made but a single false step, we must inevitably perish, as it would have been impossible to regain a foothold had it once been lost. We crossed over to the island, and having gone round it to the eastern part of the fall, Messrs. Say and Colhoun forded over from this to the left bank of the river; in this they experienced even greater difficulty than before, as the water was deeper and its current more impetuous. Mr. Keating attempted it, but found himself unable to accomplish it, being at the time considerably debilitated by a fever, which he had had for the two or three preceding days; finding himself alone upon the island, and being apprehensive that his companions would not return in that direction, but would cross below the fall, he determined to regain the western bank; in this he met with great difficulty. Twice he attempted to cross, but before he had reached the middle of the stream, finding his strength failing, he was compelled to return to the island; at last, the recollection that he would not recover it by a longer stay there, and the conviction that the waters

x 2

of the stream would probably continue to roll on undiminished to the end of time, induced him to make a final effort to reach the shore, in which he succeeded. Some time after, Messrs. Say and Colhoun were seen returning with difficulty, and one of the stoutest of the soldiers went over and assisted them; their strength was nearly exhausted at the time they reached the bank. However fatiguing this excursion may have been, it was very gratifying, as it afforded them a fine view of the fall under all its aspects. None of the party had seen a water-fall for some time past, and to this may probably be attributed the great pleasure which they derived from it; for it bears no comparison to many which they subsequently met with. Concerning the height of the fall, and breadth of the river at this place, much incorrect information has been published. Hennepin, who was the first European that visited it, states it to be fifty or sixty feet high. It was this traveller that gave it the name which it now bears, in honour of St. Anthony of Padua, whom he had taken for the protector of his discovery. He says of it, that it "indeed of itself is terrible, and hath something very astonishing." This height is, by Carver, reduced to about thirty feet; his strictures upon Hennepin, whom he taxes with exaggeration, might with great propriety be retorted upon himself, and we feel strongly inclined to say of him, as he said of his predecessor, "the good father, I fear, too often had no other foundation for his accounts than report, or at least a slight inspection." Pike, who is more correct than any traveller, whose steps we have followed, states the perpendicular fall at sixteen and a half feet;* Major Long measured it in

---

* Pike, ut supra, App. to Part I. p. 51.

1817 with a plumb line, from the table rock from which the water was falling, and found it to be the same. Mr. Colhoun measured it while we were there, with a rough water-level, and made it about fifteen feet. The difference of a foot is trifling, and depends upon the place where the measurement was made; but we cannot account for the statement made by Mr. Schoolcraft, that the river has a perpendicular pitch of forty feet, and this so late as fourteen years after Pike's measurement. The same author states the breadth of the river, near the brink of the fall, to be two hundred and twenty-seven yards, while Pike found it to be six hundred and twenty-seven yards, which agrees tolerably well with a measurement made on the ice. Messrs. Say and Colhoun obtained an approximate admeasurement of five hundred and ninety-four yards; this resulted from a trigonometrical calculation, the angles having been measured with a compass that was small and not nicely graduated, and the base line having been obtained under unfavourable circumstances. Below the fall, the river contracts to about two hundred yards; there is a considerable rapid both above and below; a portage of two hundred and sixty poles in length is usually made here; the whole fall, or difference of level between the place of disembarking and reloading, is stated by Pike to be fifty-eight feet, which is probably very near the truth; the whole fall to the foot of the rapids, which extend several miles down the river, may be estimated as not far short of one hundred feet.

Two mills have been erected for the use of the garrison, and a sergeant's guard is kept here at all times. On our return from the island, we recruited our strength by a copious and palatable meal, prepared for us by the old sergeant; whether from the exercise of the day, or from its intrinsic merit, we know not, but the black bass (Chicla œnea, Lesueur),* of which we partook, appeared to us excellent.

The vegetation consists of oak, hickory, walnut, pine, birch, linden, cotton-wood, &c.

This beautiful spot in the Mississippi is not without a tale to hallow its scenery, and heighten the interest which, of itself, it is calculated to produce. To Wazekota, the old Indian, whom we saw at Shakea's, we are indebted for the narration of the following transaction, to which his mother was an eye-witness. An Indian of the Dacota nation had united himself early in life to a youthful female, whose name was Ampota Sapa, which signifies *the dark day;* with her he lived happily for several years, apparently enjoying every comfort which the savage life can afford. Their union had been blessed with two children, on whom both parents doated with that depth of feeling which is unknown to such as have other treasures beside those that spring from nature. The man had acquired a reputation as a hunter, which drew round him many families, who were happy to place themselves under his protection, and avail themselves of such part of his chase as he needed not for the maintenance of his family. Desirous of strengthening their interest with him, some of them invited him to form a connexion with their family, observing, at the same time, that a man of his talent and importance required more than one woman to wait upon the numerous guests whom his reputation would induce to visit

---

* Journal Acad. Nat. Sci. vol. ii. p. 214, plate.

his lodge. They assured him that he would soon be acknowledged as a chief, and that, in this case, a second wife was indispensable. Fired with the ambition of obtaining high honours, he resolved to increase his importance by an union with the daughter of an influential man of his tribe. He had accordingly taken a second wife without having ever mentioned the subject to his former companion. Being desirous to introduce his bride into his lodge in the manner which should be least offensive to the mother of his children, for whom he still retained much regard, he introduced the subject in these words: "You know," said he, "that I love no woman so fondly as I doat upon you. With regret, have I seen you of late subjected to toils, which must be oppressive to you, and from which I would gladly relieve you, yet I know no other way of doing so than by associating to you in the household duties one, who shall relieve you from the trouble of entertaining the numerous guests, whom my growing importance in the nation collects around me. I have, therefore, resolved upon taking another wife, but she shall always be subject to your control, as she will always rank in my affections second to you." With the utmost anxiety, and the deepest concern, did his companion listen to this unexpected proposal. She expostulated in the kindest terms, entreated him with all the arguments which undisguised love and the purest conjugal affection could suggest. She replied to all the objections which his duplicity led him to raise. Desirous of winning her from her opposition, the Indian still concealed the secret of his union with another, while she redoubled all her care to convince him that she was equal to the task imposed upon her. When he again spoke on the subject, she pleaded all the endearments of their pas life; she spoke of his former fondness for her, of his regard for her happiness, and that of their mutual offspring; she bade him beware of the consequence of this fatal purpose of his. Finding her bent upon withholding her consent to his plan, he informed her that all opposition on her part was unnecessary, as he had already selected another partner; and that if she could not see his new wife as a friend, she must receive her as a necessary incumbrance, for he had resolved that she should be an inmate in his house. Distressed at this information, she watched her opportunity, stole away from the cabin with her infants, and fled to a distance where her father was. With him she remained until a party of Indians, with whom he lived, went up the Mississippi on a winter-hunt. In the spring as they were returning with their canoes loaded with peltries, they encamped near the falls. In the morning as they left it she lingered near the spot, then launched her light canoe, entered into it with her children, and paddled down the stream singing her death-song; too late did her friends perceive it: their attempts to prevent her from proceeding were of no avail; she was heard to sing, in a doleful voice, the past pleasures which she had enjoyed, while she was the undivided object of her husband's affection; finally, her voice was drowned in the sound of the cataract, the current carried down her frail bark with an inconceivable rapidity; it came to the edge of the precipice, was seen for a moment enveloped with spray, but never after was a trace of the canoe or its passengers seen. Yet it is stated by the Indians that often in the morning a voice has been heard to sing a doleful ditty along the edge of the fall, and that it ever dwells upon the inconstancy of her husband. Nay, some assert that her spirit has been seen wandering near the spot with her children wrapped to her bosom. Such are the tales or traditions which the Indians treasure up, and which they relate to the voyager, forcing a tear from the eyes of the most relentless.

CHAPTER VII.

Geology of the Mississippi. The Expedition ascends the St. Peter. Character of the Country. Arrival at Lake Travers.

THE country about the fort contains several other waterfalls, which are represented as worthy of being seen. One of them, which is but two miles and a half from the garrison, and on the road to St. Anthony's, is very interesting. It is known by the name of Brown's Fall, and is remarkable for the soft beauties which it presents. Essentially different from St. Anthony's, it appears as if all its native wildness had been removed by the hand of art. A small, but beautiful stream, about five yards wide, flows gently until it reaches the verge of a rock, from which it is precipitated to a depth of forty-three feet, presenting a beautiful parabolic sheet, which drops without the least deviation from the regular curve, and meets with no interruption from neighbouring rock, or other impediments, until it has reached its lower level, when it resumes its course without any other difference, than that produced by the white foam which floats upon its surface. The spray, which this cascade emits, is very considerable, and when the rays of the sun shine upon it, produces a beautiful Iris: upon the surrounding vegetation the effect of this spray is distinct; it vivifies all the plants, imparts to them an intense green colour, and gives rise to a stouter growth than is observed upon the surrounding country. On the neighbouring rock the effect is as characteristic, though of a destructive nature; the spray striking against the rock, which is of a loose structure, has undermined it in a curved manner, so as to produce an excavation, similar in form to a Saxon arch, between the surface of the rock and the sheet of water; under this large arch we passed with no other inconvenience than that which arose from the spray. There is nothing sublime or awfully impressive in this cascade, but it has every feature that is required to constitute beauty; it is such a fall as the hand of opulence daily attempts to produce in the midst of those gardens upon which treasures have been lavished for the purpose of imitating nature; with this difference, however, that these natural falls possess an easy grace, destitute of the stiffness which generally distinguishes the works of man from those of nature. The stream that exhibits this cascade falls into the Mississippi about two miles above the fort; it issues from a lake situated a few miles above. A body of water, which is not represented upon any map that we know of, has been discovered in this vicinity within a few years, and has received the name of Lake Calhoun, in honour of the Secretary at War. Its dimensions are small. Another lake of a much larger size is said to have been discovered about thirty or forty miles to the north-west of the fort. Its size, which is variously stated, is by some supposed to be equal to that of Lake Champlain, which, however, from the nature of the country, and the knowledge which we have of the course of the rivers, appears scarcely possible.

An object, which had appeared to us worthy of inquiry long before we visited the Indian country, was to ascertain whether the natives, who are accurate observers of every natural occurrence, had any tradition or recollection of having witnessed the fall of meteoric stones. Since the fact of the fall of these heavy bodies from the atmosphere has been proved to the satisfaction of the most sceptical, numerous observations, recorded by ancient historians, have been collected to prove that the occurrence is much more frequent than one would at first be led to expect. On being informed of the existence of a painted stone, which was held in great veneration by the Indians of the Mississippi, we entertained a hope that it might prove of this nature; we experienced, therefore, no slight degree of disappointment in finding it to be merely a boulder of sienite. We have, as we think, in our intercourse with the Indians, been able to trace an indistinct notion on the subject of meteorites. The following belief, which is common to several nations, but which principally prevails among the Sioux, appears to bear upon this point. They state, that whenever a tree is affected by lightning, a stone of a black or brown colour may be found at its foot; it is said to be very heavy, and to have been, in some cases, picked up while hot: several of our guides stated that they had seen them, and had owned some of them. These stones are held in some esteem, as being uncommon, but no supernatural or mysterious property is attached to them. We think it probable, from the respectable sources from which we received this report, that the Indians may have mistaken the phenomena which attend the fall of these aerolites for the effects of lightning, and having, in a few instances, observed these stones and picked them up while still hot, been led to consider them as the usual attendants upon lightning. There seems to be reason to believe that an aerolite fell a few years since at St. Anthony; but all attempts to find it proved fruitless.* We

---

* Colonel Snelling has kindly communicated to one of the party, the circumstances

have, with a view to obtain further information on the subject, examined every stone which we observed as having been held in veneration by the Indians, but in no case have we been able to detect any meteoric appearance in them.

cumstances observed on that occasion; and we have his permission to insert the annexed letter on the subject.

"*Fort St. Anthony, July 8th*, 1823.

" Sir, On the evening of September 20th, 1822, while crossing the parade of this post, from the store to my own quarters, I was startled by a brilliant light in the atmosphere, and looking up, saw a meteor passing in a direction nearly from north-west to south-east, and, as well as I could judge, at an angle of about fifty degrees with the horizon; it appeared of uncommon magnitude, and passed so near me that I distinctly heard its sound, which resembled that of a signal rocket; in its descent, my view of it was intercepted by the Commissary's store, but I heard it strike the ground, when it sounded like a spent shell, though much louder. I went immediately to the sentinel at the corner of the store, and asked him if he had seen any thing extraordinary; he replied that a large *ball of fire* had passed very near him, and struck in the public garden which borders the river St. Peter; he appeared much agitated; after requesting him to mark the spot where it fell, I proceeded to the other sentinels, whose accounts, as far as their stations allowed them to judge, agreed with his. The next morning I went early to the spot where the meteoric stone was supposed to have fallen, but could not find it; the ground is alluvial and much broken into holes or hollows. I continued my search until the breakfast hour; but my ordinary avocations called off my attention, and I did not look for it again, which I have since regretted, as I think it might have been found by going to a greater depth in search of it. The evening was uncommonly fine, and the concurring testimony of all the persons who saw it, with my own observation, I presume will be sufficient evidence that it was no illusion.

" I have communicated this incident, as the question whether meteoric stones do or do not fall from the atmosphere, has recently excited much interest, and it may be deemed in some measure of importance in support of the affirmative proposition.

" Respectfully, I am, Sir, your obedient servant,
' Wm. H. Keating, Esq. " J. SNELLING, *Col. U. S. Army.*

"Extracts from Dr. Purcell's meteorological register, September 20, 1822. Thermometer at 7 A. M. 54°; at 2 P. M. 70°; at 9 P. M. 56°. Wind N. W. weather clear—light fresh wind."

A singular appearance was observed in the heavens, between three and four o'clock on the morning of the 9th of July. The night had been stormy, much rain had fallen, and frequent flashes of lightning had been observed, but at that time the heavens presented to the north a vivid sheet of light of a yellowish hue, and brighter than the most intense lightning we recollect witnessing. Although the light was constant, it was not a steady one; frequent coruscations were observed; they were rather of the nature of the beams, than of the arches described by Captain Franklin.* The light which it produced was such, that the reflection of it from the parade ground awoke us, though our windows opened to the south-west. The effect was the same as if the whole row of barracks had been on fire. This light continued without interruption for about fifteen minutes; during the first five minutes, the rain fell with an impetuosity which we do not recollect to have ever seen surpassed. It might be truly said to fall in torrents: loud peals of thunder were occasionally heard. After the phenomena had continued about a quarter of an hour, the light vanished, and sunk into the dark gray usually observable of a misty morning before sunrise. The atmosphere appeared to be very highly charged with electric fluid, but we were unfortunately not prepared to observe the influence of this Aurora upon the magnet, &c. The heat had been great the day before; the wind was high all night, and from the south-south-west.

The bluff, upon which the fort is built, offers a good opportunity of observing the geological structure of

* Narrative of a Journey to the Polar Sea, by John Franklin, Captain R. N. London, 1823.

the country. It consists of several strata, all disposed in parallel and horizontal superposition. On the surface of the ground, blocks of limestone are found, which appear to be the remains of a stratum that has, in a great measure, disappeared; these are, in most cases, of a compact and earthy texture, destitute of any organic remains, exhibiting occasional specks of a crystalline nature which are observed to be calcareous; as, notwithstanding their small volume, they present a distinct rhomboidal cleavage. The first stratum which is observed is about eight feet thick; it is formed of limestone, and presents a very distinct slaty structure. The texture of the rock is compact, its fracture splintery and uneven: organic remains abound in it. These are, as far as we saw, exclusively Producti; they lie in the rock as thick as possible; a small vacant space is generally observed between the inner and the outer casts of the shell. This is however generally filled up with a crystallization of calcareous spar; the form of the crystals cannot be made out on account of their extreme tenuity. The colour of this limestone, as well as of the loose blocks found upon it, is a light grayish yellow. This stratum rests upon another calcareous bed, which differs from the preceding, in the total absence of organic remains, and in its colour, which is of a light blue. Its structure is more compact, so is its fracture; its horizontal stratification is distinct, but the stratum being thicker, it is better adapted for being employed in building. It produces, in fact, an excellent stone, which admits of being hewn, and which is the chief material used in the construction of the fort; this bed is from fifteen to twenty feet thick. When examined with the microscope, the rock presents very general signs of crystallization; its texture becomes subsaccaroidal, and veins of calcspar, of an inconsiderable thickness, traverse it in every direction. There are also cavities in which crystals of carbonate of lime (the *cuboide?* of Haüy) are distinctly seen. In this bed the workmen state that they find substances resembling their catfish (Silurus, Linn), and which they consider as petrifactions of the same; we saw nothing of the kind; neither could they discover any at the time we were there. We at first, however, thought they had probably observed icthyolites, but a subsequent and more minute description of the objects observed by the workmen, satisfied both the naturalists, that they were probably not organic remains, but mere accidents of fracture, or *lusus naturæ*. Independent of the building-stone which it yields, this bed is likewise valuable, as producing the best lime of any found in the vicinity. Immediately under this bed of limestone, in parallel stratification, we observed the sandstone which constitutes the principal mass of the bluff, being about sixty feet in thickness. It is a very friable stone, and in some cases the grains, of which it is formed, are so loosely united, that it appears almost like sand. Every fragment, if examined with care, seems to be a regular crystal; and we incline much to the opinion, that this sandstone must have been formed by a chemical precipitation, and not by mere mechanical deposition. The process of its formation may have been a very rapid one, such as is obtained in the manufacture of fine salt, and to this may be attributed the circumstance of its loose texture. The grain is very fine; its colour is white, sometimes a little yellowish, in which case, it resembles in texture, colour, &c. the finer varieties of Muscovado sugar. The loose texture of the rock is probably the cause of its presenting but few indications of stratification. The rock, which we have just described, rests upon a slaty limestone, which has a striped aspect; the stripes or zones are curved. This limestone appears to be very argillaceous, and is a little softer than the preceding; its structure is quite earthy; it effervesces strongly in nitric acid; its colour is a light yellow: the thickness of this bed is about ten feet. Below this another stratum of limestone is found, which imbeds small black pebbles of quartz, and assumes, therefore, in a slight degree, the characters of a pudding stone or conglomerate. Its grain is more crystalline than that of the preceding stratum. It is filled with small cavities, probably the result of a contraction during the consolidation of the mass. Its colour varies from a bluish to a yellowish grey. This stratum is about seven feet thick. It rises but four feet above the level of the water, and the only rock visible under it, is another variety of limestone which differs from the preceding, inasmuch as its grain is much finer and its texture more earthy. It is only visible for four feet; the bed of the river appears to be excavated, near the fort, in this stratum of limestone. Neither of these limestone formations under the sandstone contain any traces of organic remains. If we consider the three inferior beds of limestone, as being modifications of the same formation, as we doubtless ought to do, then we shall find this bluff to be composed of three different formations; a superior one of limestone, with abundant impressions of shells in one of its beds; an intermediate one of sandstone; and an inferior calcareous formation, without any organic remains. The latter certainly bears some resemblance to the limestone found on the Wassemon, though we are unwilling to pronounce upon their identity.

The river runs upon a bed of sandy alluvium, resulting from the destruction of the bluffs, but in many places the rock is laid bare. These observations upon the geology of the bluff upon which the fort is erected, correspond with those made at the Falls of St. Anthony, with this exception, that, at the latter place, our observations are limited to the three superior strata, *viz.* the slaty limestone with organic remains, the blue limestone destitute of these, and the sandstone with a loose texture. The falls are occasioned by the fissures which occur in the superior limestone, and which allow the water to penetrate through this bed to the sandstone, which, being of a loose texture, is soon washed away; in this manner thick plates of limestone are left unsupported, and soon fall by their own gravity. This process is constantly causing the fall to recede towards its source. What length of time has been required to bring the falls to their present situation, it is not in the power of man to ascertain; but we may well see that it must have been immense. The difference of level between the head of the fall, and the level of the river at the fort, being, as we have stated, estimated at about one hundred feet, and the strata running in a horizontal position, we can readily account for the additional strata observed under the sandstone at the fort, and which are concealed at the falls.

It would remain for us, in order to complete this view of the geology of the falls, to inquire whether the limestone observed at the falls, corresponds with that superior to the sandstone south of the Wisconsan, and if that, found near the level of the river at the fort, be analogous to that observed under the sandstone, between the Wisconsan and the Wassemon. We shall not affect a degree of certainty which we do not possess, but we may be permitted to advance an opinion that the sandstone is probably of analogous formation, and that, therefore, the strata of limestone, which we found at the falls, correspond with that stratum of whose existence, at a former period, between the Wassemon and the Wisconsan, we think we have evident proofs. We have in our possession, specimens taken in both places, filled with apparently the same organic remains, and exhibiting characters in the rock which correspond as well as could be expected from pieces, collected at three hundred miles distance from each other. We must regret that the circumstances under which we ascended the Mississippi have not enabled us to offer a more conclusive opinion upon this point, or upon the identity or difference between the limestone inferior to the standstone at the fort and that observed previous to our arrival at Prairie du Chien.

To one, fond of the pleasures of hunting and fishing, a residence at Fort St. Anthony would offer an opportunity of enjoying these occupations. Catfish has been caught at the falls weighing one hundred and forty-two pounds. Among the birds, observed by Mr. Say, were the Woodcock,* the House Wren,† the Flecker,‡ the Hairy Woodpecker,§ the Towhee bunting, &c. &c.

The soldiers, that had accompanied us from Fort Crawford, having proved unequal to the fatigues of the

---

* Scolopax minor. Gmelihn.   † Certhia familiaris, Linn.
‡ Picus auratus, Linn.   § Picus villosus, Linn.

journey, and the term of enlistment of some of them having almost expired, Col. Snelling ordered them back to their garrison, and furnished us with a guard consisting of a serjeant, two corporals, and eighteen soldiers, selected from his command. Lieut. Scott was appointed to conduct the detachment to Prairie du Chien, and return with all convenient speed, and Lieut St. Clair Denny, of the 5th Infantry, received the command of the new guard, until Mr. Scott should overtake the expedition; after which he had the option of continuing with the party, or returning to Fort St. Anthony.

Provided with this new and more efficient escort, the party left Fort St. Anthony late in the afternoon of the 9th of July. They had exchanged their interpreter for another, Joseph Renville, a half-breed of the Dacota nation, who undertook to act both as interpreter and guide. The very able manner in which he performed these duties; the valuable information which he communicated concerning this nation of Indians, and the universal satisfaction which he gave to every member of the expedition, requires that something should be stated of this man, whose influence among the Sioux appears to be very great.

Joseph Renville is the son of a French trader on the Mississippi, probably the same mentioned by Pike. His mother being a Sioux resident at the village of the Petit Corbeaux, he was brought up among the Indians, and deprived of all education excepting such as his powerful mind enabled him to acquire, during his intercourse with white traders; it was, therefore, rather an education of observation than of study. We have met with few men that appeared to us to be gifted with a more inquiring and discerning mind, or with more force and penetration than Renville. His mother being connected with an influential family among the Indians, he was early brought into notice by them; his object appears to have been, from his first entrance upon the pursuits of life, to acquire an ascendancy over his countrymen. This, he knew, could only be obtained by the most daring and persevering course of conduct; and, accordingly, we have it from respectable authority, that he never desisted from any of his pretensions, and that whatever he had undertaken, he never failed to achieve. As a trader, he was considered active, intelligent, and faithful to his employers; his usefulness depending, in a great measure, upon the influence which he possessed over the Indians. When, at the commencement of the late war, the British government determined to use the Indians as auxiliaries, Col. Dickson, to whom the chief direction of this force had been entrusted, selected Renville as the man upon whom he could place most dependence: to him, therefore, was the command of the Sioux given, with the rank, pay, and emoluments of a captain in the British army. In this new situation he distinguished himself, not only as an active, but as a humane officer; to him the Americans, are, we doubt not, indebted for the comparatively few injuries done by the Sioux; he repressed their depredations, and prevented them from sharing in those bloody and disgusting transactions which disgraced the conduct of the Chippewas, the Potawatomis, Miamis, Ottowas, &c.

After the war, he retired to the British provinces, retaining the half-pay of a captain in the line; he then entered the service of the Hudson's Bay Company, for whom he traded several years at the head of Red river. Being dissatisfied with their employ, he left them, and finding it impossible to retain his pension as a British officer, unless he continued to reside in the British territory, he voluntarily relinquished it, and returned to his old trading post towards the sources of Red river. This being within the territory of the United States, he, with several of the former agents and clerks of the British traders, established a new company under the name of the Columbia Fur Company. Of this Renville may be considered as being the principal prop, as it is to his extensive acquaintance with the Indian character that they are indebted for the success which has hitherto attended their efforts.

Renville's character has not been exempt from the obloquy which always attends those who take decisive and independent measures. It has been thought, that having been born on the Mississippi, and, therefore, within the actual limits of the United States, he ought not to have joined the British during the late war. In extenuation, it ought to be remembered, that he was of Canadian origin; that all the French traders have uniformly considered themselves as British subjects; and that the trade upon the upper Mississippi was entirely in their hands. His separation, or, as it has been termed, his desertion from the Hudson Bay Company's service, has always been objected to; but we believe there were grounds of complaint on both sides, and having heard him commended by those who were interested on neither side of the question, we are unwilling to believe that any blame attaches to him in this transaction. We found him uniformly faithful, intelligent, and as veracious as any interpreter we ever had in our company.

Mr. Joseph Snelling, son of the Colonel, volunteered to accompany the expedition as an assistant guide and interpreter, for which situation he had qualified himself by a winter's residence among the Indians; his services were accepted. Thus reinforced, the party, amounting in the aggregate to thirty-three persons, took leave of the officers of the garrison by whom they had been kindly received, by none more so, than by Colonel Snelling and Lieutenant Nathan Clark, who hospitably entertained the party during their stay at the fort. In order to examine both the river and the adjacent country, the party was divided; Major Long ascended in a boat with Messrs. Keating, Seymour, and Renville. A corporal, twelve soldiers, and the black boy accompanied them. The men were divided into four canoes, in which the bulk of the stores and provisions was embarked.*

The land party consisted of Messrs. Say, Colhoun, and Lieutenant Denny, with a sergeant, a corporal, seven soldiers, and a boy, Louis Pellais, hired as a Chippewa interpreter. It was determined that the two divisions should, as far as practicable, keep company together, and encamp every night, if possible, at the same place.

At the point where we embarked, which may be considered as the mouth of the St. Peter, this stream is about ninety yards wide; it lies in latitude 44° 53′ 49″ north, longitude 93° 8′ 7″ west. The magnetic variation

---

* An Italian gentleman, whom we found at Fort St. Anthony, asked, and obtained leave to travel with the expedition: he continued with them until the 7th of August. This is the gentleman who has lately published an account of his discoveries on the Mississippi; we have read it.

amounts to 10° 28' 40" east. These result from a series of observations made by Mr. Colhoun during our stay there. The river is called in the Dacota language Watapan Menesota,* which means "the river of turbid water." The term Watapan, which in that language signifies river, is always prefixed to the name of the stream; thus the Mississippi is called Watapan Tancha, (the *body of rivers*, because all the other streams are considered as branches or limbs, this being the trunk), the Missouri is termed the Watapan Mene Shoska,† "the river of thick water." In the Potawatomi, Sauk, and other languages of Algonquin origin, the substantive follows the adjective, as Mese Sepe,‡ Pektannon Sepe, &c.

The name given to the St. Peter is derived from its turbid appearance, which distinguishes it from the Mississippi, whose waters are very clear at the confluence. It has been erroneously stated by some authors to signify clear water. The Indians make a great difference, however, between the terms *sota* and *shósha;* one of which means turbid, and the other muddy. At the mouth of the St. Peter there is an island of considerable extent, separated from the main land by a slough of the Mississippi, into which the St. Peter discharges itself. The Mississippi is here, exclusive of the island, about 250 yards wide. In ascending it, particularly in low water, boats pass through this slough, as it affords a greater depth than the main branch on the east side of the island. It was probably, as Carver suggests, this island, which being thickly wooded

---

* Wătăpăn Mĕn'ĕsótă.   † Shósh'ă.   ‡ Mĕsĕ Sĕpĕ.

and lying immediately opposite to the mouth, concealed the St. Peter from Hennepin's observation. No notice of this river is to be found in any of the authors anterior to the end of the 17th century. Indeed, it is only by close research that we have been enabled to trace the discovery of this river so far back. Charlevoix states,* that le Sueur was sent by M. d'Iberville to make an establishment in the Sioux country, and to take possession of a copper mine that he had there discovered (*que le Sueur y avait découverte*); he ascended the St. Peter forty leagues to " la Rivière Verte," which comes in on the left.† Though only the last of September, the ice prevented him from ascending that river more than a league. He thererefore built a fort, and spent the winter at that spot; in April, 1702,‡ he went up the Rivière Verte to the mine, which was only three quarters of a league above his winter establishment. In twenty-two days they got out more than thirty thousand pounds of ore (*de matière*), of which four thousand pounds were selected and sent to France. The mine was at the foot of a mountain ten leagues long, that seemed to be composed of the same substance. After removing a black burnt crust, as hard as rock, the copper could be scraped with a knife. Several reasons, but particularly the want of pecuniary means, prevented le Sueur from following up the discovery. This account corresponds in part with that contained in a very interesting manuscript belonging to the American Philosophical Society, and which appears to have been written with considerable

* Charlevoix, Histoire de la nouvelle France, à Paris, 1744, tome 4, p. 165 and 166.
† As he ascended, right bank ?
‡ This ought probably to be 1701.

care and accuracy. We find it therein stated, that the said " le Sueur arrived at the mouth of the Mississippi with M. d'Iberville in December, 1699; that he brought over with him thirty workmen. He had been," says the author of the MS. " a famous traveller from Canada, and was sent by M. L'Huillier, a principal contractor (*fermier général*) under government, in order to form an establishment near the source of the Mississippi. The object of this enterprize was to obtain from that place, an ore of green earth which that gentleman had discovered; the following was the origin of this undertaking, in 1695: M. le Sueur, by order of the Count de Frontenac, Governor General of Canada, caused a fort to be erected on an island on the Mississippi, upwards of two hundred miles above the Illinois; in order to keep up peaceful relations between the Sioux and Chippewa nations, which reside on the shores of a lake upwards of five hundred leagues in circumference, which lake lies one hundred leagues east of the river; the Sioux reside upon the upper Mississippi. In the same year, according to his orders, he descended to Montreal, with a chief of the Chippewa, named Chingouabé, and a Sioux, called Tioscaté, who was the first of his nation that ever was in Canada; and as they expected to draw from his country many articles valuable in trade, the Count de Frontenac, the Chevalier de la Cailliere, and de Champigny, received him very amicably. Two days after their arrival, they presented to the Count de Frontenac, in a public assembly, as many arrows as there were Sioux villages, and they informed him that all those villages entreated him to receive them among his children, as he had done to all the other nations which they named one after the other, which favour was granted to them. M. le Sueur was to have reascended the "Mississippi" as early as 1696, with that Sioux chief who had only come down upon an express promise that he should be taken back to his country; but the latter fell sick in Montreal, and died after thirty-three days disease. M. le Sueur finding himself thus released from his pledge to return into the Sioux country, where he had discovered mines of lead, copper, and earth, both blue and green, resolved upon going over to France, and asking leave of the court to open those mines; a permission to this effect was granted to him in 1697. About the latter end of June, in the same year, he embarked at la Rochelle for Canada: as he was crossing Newfoundland banks he was captured by a British fleet of sixteen ships, and by them taken to Portsmouth; but peace having been soon after concluded, he returned to Paris to obtain a new commission, as he had thrown his overboard, lest the English should become acquainted with his scheme. The French court directed a new commission to be issued to him in 1698. He then went over to Canada, where he met with various obstacles which compelled him to return to Europe. During this interval of time, part of the men whom he had left in charge of the forts which he had erected in 1695, being without intelligence from him, abandoned them, and proceeded down to Montreal."*

* " Journal historique concernant l'établissement des Français à la Louisianne, tiré des mémoires de Messrs. d'Iberville & de Bienville commandans pour le Roi au dit pays, et sur les découvertes et recherches de M. Bénard de la Harpe, nommé au commandement de la Baye St. Bernard; par M. Bénard de la Harpe," MS. This is stated to be a copy of the original, which was, in the year 1805, in the possession of Dr. Sibley, as appears

Thus it appears from this manuscript, that le Sueur's discoveries of blue earth were made in 1695, but that all further operations were interrupted until 1700; we find in the same manuscript, under the date of the 10th of February, 1702, that le Sueur arrived at the mouth of the Mississippi that day with two thousand cwt. (quintax), of blue and green earth. An extract from a narrative of his voyage is then given from the time that he left the Island of Tamarois (12th July), unto the 13th December, 1700. From this extract, which is fraught with interest, as it is the first account we can find, in which St. Peter's river is mentioned, we gather that he reached the mouth of the Missouri on the 13th of July, 1700, and the mouth of the Wisconsan on the 1st of September; and that, on the 14th, he passed Chippewa river, on one of the branches of which, he had, during his first visit to the country, found a piece of copper weighing sixty pounds. He next entered Lake Pepin, which is designated by that name in the manuscript, although Hennepin had, in 1680, called it the Lake of Tears, and notwithstanding the appellation of Lac de Bon Secours, which Charlevoix applies to it.

from a note annexed to it, certifying it to be a true copy, and dated Natchitoches, October, 29th, 1805. From the manuscript it appears that M. de la Harpe was on the lower Mississippi in the early part of the 18th century, and that he continued there until the commencement of the year 1723. His appointment to the command of St. Bernard's Bay, was made in the year 1721. He appears to have proceeded to it at that time; but owing to the weakness of his garrison, he found himself unable to continue his post there. His journal throws considerable light upon the history of the discoveries of the French on the lower Mississippi, and is closed with a memoir upon the importance of the colony of Louisiana, and upon the situation of that colony in 1724; together with some observations upon the best passage to the Western Ocean, and upon the origin of the Indians of America.

On the 16th he passed the St. Croix, so called from the name of a Frenchman, who was wrecked at its mouth. Finally, on the 19th of September, he left the Mississippi, and entered the St. Peter's river, which comes in from the west bank. By the first of October, he had ascended this river forty-four and a quarter leagues, when he entered the Blue river, the name of which is derived from the blue earth found on its banks. At the mouth of this river he made an establishment, situated, as la Harpe states, in latitude 44° 13' north. He met with nine Sioux, who informed him that this river had its course through the lands of the Sioux of the west, the *Ayavois* (*Iawas*), and the Otoetata, who lived further back. We infer that these were the same streams which he had ascended in 1695, from the circumstance that they are mentioned as well known, and not as recently discovered; and more especially from the observation of la Harpe, that the eastern Sioux having complained of the situation of the fort, which they would have wished to see at the confluence of the St. Peter and Mississippi, M. le Sueur endeavoured to reconcile them to it. " He had foreseen," says la Harpe, " that an establishment on the Blue river would not be agreeable to the eastern Sioux, who are the rulers of all the other Sioux, and of the other nations which we have mentioned, because they were the first with whom the French traded, and whom they provided with guns; nevertheless, as this undertaking had not been commenced with the sole view of trading for beavers, but in order to become thoroughly acquainted with the quality of the various mines *which he had previously discovered there*, he replied to the natives that he was sorry that he had not been made sooner acquainted with their wishes, &c. but that the advanced state of the season prevented his returning to the mouth of the river." No mention is made, in this narrative, of the stream being obstructed with ice, a circumstance, which, had it really occurred, would, we think, have been recorded by de la Harpe, who appears to have been a careful and a curious observer, and who undoubtedly saw le Sueur's original narrative. On the 14th of October the works were completed and were named Fort L'Huillier.

On the 26th, M. le Sueur went to the mine with three canoes, which he loaded with green and blue earth; it was taken from the mountains near which are very abundant mines of copper, of which an essay was made in Paris by M. L'Huillier, in the year 1696. This is the last historical fact of any interest contained in the extract from le Sueur's journal. M. de la Harpe observes, " la suite des mémoires de Monsieur le Sueur n'a point paru," which would seem to imply that the former part had been published; yet we find no notice taken of this traveller's memoirs in any of the catalogues of works on America, to which we have had access. It is not mentioned in the "Bibliothecæ Americanæ Primordia," published by a member of the Society for the propagation of the Gospel in foreign parts, London, 1713; nor in the " Bibliotheca Americana, or Chronological Catalogue of curious Books in print or manuscript on the subject of North and South America," in London, 1789; nor in the " Catalogue of Mr. Warden's Books on America, Paris, 1820," from which circumstance we are induced to doubt whether it was ever made public. We even find no account of de la Harpe's manuscript, whence we suppose that it has not yet been brought into notice.

The river St. Peter is found traced on some of the old maps of Louisiana; for instance, on that which accompanies the *Recueil de Voyages*, published in Amsterdam in 1720, upon which Fort L'Huillier is marked. Upon this map a coal mine is also designated, as existing about ten leagues up the St. Peter. If this be not purely ideal, it must have resulted from mistaking lignite for that mineral, as this is not a coal country.

Coxe, whose general accuracy entitles him to considerable praise, and who appears to have taken great pains to collect information on the subject of the discoveries made in Louisiana, has, by a strange oversight, left out St. Peter's river, and introduced on his map, the Rivière Longue, the Lake of Thoyago, and all the fables of Lahontan, in whom he seems to place much confidence. This is the more remarkable, as the Carolana, published in 1741, was twenty years later than the Amsterdam Recueil. The St. Peter is mentioned in an incidental manner by Charlevoix in his Journal Historique, but he attempts no description of it.* We have sought in vain for the origin of the name; we can find no notice of it; it appears to us at present not unlikely, that the name may have been given by le Sueur, in 1795, in honour of M. St. Pierre de Repantigni, to whom Lahontan incidentally alludes, as being in Canada in the year 1789.† This person may have accompanied le Sueur on his expedition. It has been, we know not upon what authority, suggested that the French

---

* Ut supra, pages 110, 295, and 296.   † Lahontan, vol. i., p. 136.

name of this river, St. Pierre, was a corruption of the Sans pierres (without stones), said to have been given to it, because no stones occur along its bank for a considerable distance from its mouth. It is very strange, that notwithstanding the great importance which seems to have been attached in France to le Sueur's discoveries, so little should have been said by other authors, concerning this explorer and the regions which he discovered.

Carver is the only traveller who states that he visited this river, merely from motives of curiosity; but a close perusal of his book, has satisfied us that he professes too much. He asserts that he "proceeded upon the river about two hundred miles, to the country of the Naudowessies of the plains, which lies a little above the forks formed by the Verd and Red Marble rivers." He states that he resided five months among the Naudowessies, and that he acquired their language perfectly. We are inclined to doubt this; we believe that he ascended the Mississippi to the Falls of St. Anthony, that he saw the St. Peter, and that he may even perhaps have entered it; but had he resided five months in the country, and become acquainted with their language, it is not probable that he would have uniformly applied to them the term of Naudowessies, and omitted calling them the Dacóta Indians, as they style themselves. It is probable that Carver derived his name from the source from which the other travellers received that of Nadiousioux, from which Sioux has been derived by abbreviation. This is the term applied by the Chippewas to the Iroquois; it signifies *stranger* properly speaking, but with them is synonymous with enemy. The term Dacota, by which the Sioux call themselves, signifies in their language the *united or allied,* because the whole nation consists of several allied tribes. In his account of the river St. Peter, Carver attributes to it a breadth of nearly one hundred yards for two hundred miles; whereas at the distance of one hundred and thirty miles it was but seventy yards wide, and was found to be rapidly diminishing in size. He also ascribes to it " a great depth," which is not the case at any distance above its mouth.

We saw no branch of the river coming in from the north but a few small tributaries not entitled to notice; Carver's river, which had been inserted on most of the maps made since the publication of his book, has therefore been omitted on that which accompanies this work. It is scarcely possible that if Carver had ascended the St. Peter two hundred miles, he would have reported, without contradicting them, the exaggerated accounts of the great extent of this river, or attributed to it a rise near the Shining (Rocky) Mountains; but besides these inaccuracies, some of which may perhaps be partly accounted for by his having seen the river at a time when it was unusually high, and when a mere brook may have been so much swollen as to be mistaken for a small branch of the river, yet we cannot place any confidence in him, on account of the many misrepresentations contained in his work. Almost all that he relates as peculiar to the Naudowessies, is found to apply to the Sauks, or some other nation of Algonquin origin. Thus on reading to Renville, Dickson (the son of the late Col. Dickson), and to several other of the half-Indian interpreters whom we saw on the St. Peter, that part of chapter 12th of his work, in which he relates that " the Naudowessies have a singular method of celebrating their marriages, which seems to bear no resemblance to those made use of by any other nations that he passed through," these men all exclaimed that it was fabulous, that such a practice had never prevailed among any of the Daçotas, though they believed it to be in use with some of the Algonquin tribes. The practice of having a *totem* or family distinction, exists, as we have already stated, among the Sauks, &c., but it is quite unknown to the Sioux, to whom it is attributed by this writer. It is, we believe, clearly proved at present, that the land, which he claimed by virtue of a grant from the Indians, was never conveyed to him by them. Attempts were made in 1817, by two of his grandsons, to have the claim recognized by some of the Indians now living ; they ascended the river at the same time that Major Long did, but were not successful. An instrument, purporting to be the original treaty, was afterwards sent to Canada, and placed in Renville's hands by those who had an interest in the claim : he was requested to show it and explain its nature to the Indians, and to endeavour to obtain a confirmation of it from them ; but, as he informed us, he could find no individual among them who had the least recollection or tradition of this conveyance, or even of the names which are purported to have been affixed to the deed; the Indians have no hesitation in asserting, that there never were among them any Dacota chiefs of the name. When chapter 5th of Carver's work was read to Renville and the other men, they denied the truth of its contents ; but immediately recollected the designs of a snake and a tortoise, which were affixed to the treaty, no doubt to make it tally with the account of their family distinctions contained in that chapter of his travels. His vocabulary appears certainly to have been taken from the Dacota language: it may have been obtained from the Indians along the banks of the Mississippi, but was more probably copied from some former traveller; for a reference to old works will prove that Carver derived much of his information from them, though no credit is given to their authors for it. A comparison of his account of the manners of the Indians with that given by Lahontan, shows that he was familiar with that author. His statement of the division of the year by the Indians into twelve moons, with the addition, at the end of the thirtieth, of what they term the lost moon, &c., is extracted, and in some places copied, almost verbatim, from Lahontan's; his account of the qualifications of men is undoubtedly drawn from the same author; and a comparison of chapter 12th of Carver's Description of the Indians, with Lahontan's " Account of the Amours and Marriages of the Savages," will show too close a coincidence to consider it as merely accidental. Yet no reference is made by Carver to the work of his predecessor. We have introduced these observations upon the work of Carver, because as he was the only traveller that published an account of the St. Peter, he has been frequently quoted as an authority. We might have enlarged the list of errors, whether wilful or unintentional, into which this author has fallen, but we have said enough to show that his statements cannot be relied upon as correct.

Major Long's party ascended the river five and a half miles, and stopped for a few moments at a village called Oanoska* (which signifies the great avenue or stretch),

* Oānōskā.

situated on the right bank; they then proceeded about one mile higher up, where they lay by in a deserted cabin on the left bank. The cabin having been carefully closed in order to secure it against injury from wild animals, they took down the skins which hung at the door, and made themselves comfortable in it. While at supper, they received a visit from an old squaw, who came from the village below, to see what they were doing. The lodge, as she informed them, was her's, but as the men had all gone out hunting, she had removed down to live with her daughter. Having observed a fire near her cabin, she was apprehensive that some injury would be done to it; they however satisfied her that their intentions were friendly; and Renville informed the gentlemen that no offence could be taken at their intrusion in the house, as they were travelling in an official capacity; but that if other Indians, or voyagers that were not known, had taken that liberty, it would have been held highly improper. There was something gratifying, and yet melancholy, in the recollection that we had thus for awhile bid adieu to civilization, and that before us we had nothing but a wide and untravelled land, where no white men resided, except such as had forsworn their country and the friends of their youth; who, either out of aversion for society, or for the sake of lucre, had withdrawn from its social circle, to dwell in the midst of the uncivilized tenants of the forest. It was while indulging in these reflections, by the light of a few embers, that we received this unexpected visit from the owner of the lodge. Her wrinkled brow, her decrepid mien, her slovenly appearance, gave her a somewhat terrifying aspect, as seen by the uncertain light that played upon her haggard features; her shrill voice contributed also to heighten the awfulness of this untimely visitor: but our interpreter having explained to us the object of her visit, we had leisure to observe her companions, who were two of her grand-daughters: these were as handsome and as good-looking as Indian females can probably be; they were young, about fifteen or sixteen; their complexion was so light that we could scarcely credit the assertion of our guide that they were full-blooded Indians; their features were regular; the large dark eye which distinguished the elder would have been deemed beautiful any where; their forms, which were good, were perhaps taller than those which we usually found among Indian women. But what added most to their charms, was the gay, good-humoured appearance which brightened their eye and animated their features. While the old hag was muttering her discontent, they were smiling, and, as she extended her bony hand to receive the present offered her, the damsels burst out into a laughter which displayed a beautiful set of teeth. Their observations upon our party seemed to afford them as much gratification as we derived from the examination of theirs, and the merriment which it occasioned them was displayed in the most unreserved manner. After a visit of about half an hour, they all withdrew, leaving us to the undisturbed occupancy of the lodge. This visit offered us food for conversation until we retired to enjoy, what had been for the last two months the object of our anxious anticipations, a night's rest upon the secluded banks of the St. Peter. We this day met Major Taliaferro going down the river in a canoe. In order to afford us an opportunity of studying the manners of the

Indians in council, he had kindly undertaken to ascend to the village of the Sisiton band of the Sioux, for the purpose of holding a council with them in our presence, and with this view had left the fort that morning; but having been informed on the river that they had all dispersed on their summer-hunts, he returned the same evening.*

The next day we travelled about thirty-five miles : at six miles from the night's camp, we passed the small village of Tetankatane; all the men were absent on their hunts. We proceeded up the river, and, at a distance of about twenty miles, Mr. Say was spoken to on shore. Instructions were sent through him to the land party, to meet Major Long, at a village two miles higher, in order to take advantage of the canoes, for the transportation of the baggage across the river, as the right bank becomes here better for travelling than the left. The flotilla reached this village about twelve o'clock, and waited five hours, during which the land party did not join them; men were sent out in various directions and guns fired, but no answer being returned, we concluded that they had proceeded higher up the river. We re-embarked and ascended ten miles to a small wood, where we encamped for the night. The village, at which we had expected to meet the other party, is called Taoapa;† it consists of fifteen large bark lodges, in good order; they were arranged along the river. Some of them were large enough to hold from thirty to fifty persons,

---

* Swarms of an insect of the Linnean genus Ephemera, were observed by the party along the banks of the river. It has been described by Mr. Say under the name of Baëtis bilineata, S (Appendix I. Entomology). The surface of the river was in many places absolutely covered with the remains of these insects, who, having gone through their short-lived existence, fell upon the water and were carried down the stream.

† Thóåpå.

accommodated as the Indians usually are in their lodges. The ground near it is neatly laid out, and some fine corn-fields were observed in the vicinity. There were scaffolds annexed to the houses, for the purpose of drying maize, &c.; upon these we were told that the Indians sleep during very hot nights.

The banks of the river had thus far been low, and covered with a fine rich vegetation; the trees attained a large size near the river, but they did not extend far into the interior of the country. Near Fort St. Anthony there is a fine piece of bottom, exposed to occasional inundations. The line of bluffs, which borders upon the Mississippi; does not extend far from that stream, but gradually sinks in height, until it finally disappears near the village of Oanoska. The soil along the river is of the best quality. After ascending about thirty miles, the bluffs reappear, and rise to an average height of seventy-five feet on the left bank. In the bottoms, the elm forms the principal growth of the country, and thrives. In the rear of the village of Taoapa a swamp extends, and divides it from the bluffs. The grass grows in some places to the height of six feet, as was principally observed east of the village, by some of the party who undertook to walk down to the place where Mr. Say had been spoken to. We saw about the village no stones of any kind; but, on the right bank, Major Long observed a number of fragments of primitive rock, and also some secondary limestone, which appeared to him to be *in situ*. There were some scaffolds, upon which several corpses were placed. In the midst of the corn-fields a dog was found suspended, his head decorated with feathers, and with horse-hair stained red; it was probably a sacrifice for the protection of the corn-fields, during the absence of the Indians. On the right bank, Major Long observed numerous ancient tumuli or artificial mounds, some of which were of a large size; they occupy a considerable extent of the prairie upon which they are situated. In one part they formed a line of about half a mile, in a direction parallel with the river, from which they were distant about three hundred yards. The mounds were erected at a distance of from twelve to fifteen yards asunder, and when observed from one end of the line, presented the appearance of a ridge or parapet.

Proceeding early the next morning, the land party was found encamped six miles above the village, on a fine piece of rising ground, which the voyagers have called the Little Prairie. They had not been able to reach the village from the inexperience of their guide, who had kept them in the rear of the swamp. The river was observed to widen much at places; it was here about seventy yards broad; its current, which had always been inconsiderable, compared with that of the Mississippi, increased as we advanced. The cause of this is, that the great volume of water, which the Mississippi rolls down, backs up the waters of most of its tributary streams, and produces a real pond at their mouth. This is no doubt the cause of the lake formed by the St. Croix, &c.

Our flotilla assisted the land party in crossing the river, after which we again separated; and the boat having ascended a few miles, came to rapids formed by two bars of sandstone, which extend across the river, producing a fall of about four feet within twenty yards. The water in the river, at the time we ascended, was of an average height, remarkable neither for its abundance nor scarcity; and at this stage we found at the falls just water enough to float our boats and canoes, with the baggage and stores in them, the crew and passengers walking alongside, and dragging them up the rapid. A shoal below had likewise required that our canoes should be lightened. Another rapid, about half a mile above, proved more difficult to pass. There being a sufficient depth of water, we ascended in the boat and canoes: one of the latter missed the channel, which is narrow, and in which there is a rapid current; the canoe drifted down against the rock, and fears were entertained that it would be lost; but with considerable labour, and after about half an hour's detention, it was at last brought up safe. The aggregate fall of the two rapids is seven feet. At a short distance above this we stopped for an hour; this gave us an opportunity of observing the nature of the country. The stream is there incased by a vertical bank, about ten or twelve feet high, the base of which is washed by the river. Ascending this bank, we find a level valley, which is about a quarter of a mile wide; this is limited by a steep and rugged bank, of about twenty feet in height. Having ascended this bank, a beautiful prairie, apparently very extensive, displayed itself to our view. The steep bank, which exposes the disposition of the rock, shows it to be a sandstone formation in a horizontal stratification, and of a fine crystalline grain, the colour varying from white to yellow: this sandstone is, in every respect, similar to that found at Fort St. Anthony. Six miles above the rapids there is a small Indian settlement, called Weakaote.* It was deserted, but consisted of two lodges and the ruins of a third, near which there were two scaffolds. On these scaffolds, which are from eight to ten

* Wèakàotè.

feet high, corpses were deposited in a box made from part of a broken canoe. Some hair was suspended, which we at first mistook for a scalp; but our guide informed us that these were locks of hair torn from their heads by the relations, to testify their grief. In the centre, between the four posts which supported the scaffold, a stake was planted in the ground: it was about six feet high, and bore an imitation of human figures, five of which had a design of a petticoat, indicating them to be females; the rest, amounting to seven, were naked, and were intended for male figures. Of the latter, four were headless, showing that they had been slain; the three other male figures were unmutilated, but held a staff in their hand, which, as our guide informed us, designated that they were slaves. The post, which is an usual accompaniment to the scaffold that supports a warrior's remains does not represent the achievements of the deceased, but those of the warriors that assembled near his remains danced the dance of the post, and related their martial exploits. A number of small bones of animals were observed in the vicinity, which were probably left there after a feast celebrated in honour of the dead. The boxes in which the corpses were placed are so short, that a man could not lie in them extended at full length, but in a country where boxes and boards are scarce, this is overlooked. After the corpses have remained a certain time exposed, they are taken down and interred. Our guide (Renville) related to us, that he had been a witness to an interesting, though painful circumstance, that occurred here. An Indian who resided on the Mississippi, hearing that his son had died at this spot, came up in a canoe to take charge of the remains, and convey them down the river to his place of abode; but on his arrival, he found that the corpse had already made such progress towards decomposition, as to render it impossible for it to be removed. He then undertook, with a few friends, to clean off the bones; all the flesh was scraped off and thrown into the stream, the bones were carefully collected into his canoe, and subsequently carried down to his residence.

The two parties having exchanged a few words at this place, continued their journey. The boats proceeded but three miles beyond this, to an encamping ground. The navigation had been an easy one except at the rapids. In a few places, however, snags were seen, which partly impeded the main channel. The next day they were found more numerous, as were also the sandbars, which sometimes rendered the navigation of the river troublesome. The skiff which had been obtained for Major Long and the gentlemen's use, as more pleasant than a canoe, was found very inconvenient, being leaky and slow of motion, so that we gladly embraced the opportunity of exchanging her for a fine canoe, belonging to a trader whom we met returning to Fort St. Anthony. The forests, which had principally consisted of cotton-wood, birch, &c. were observed to become more luxuriant, and to be replaced by a heavy growth of oak and elm. The soil appeared excellent and deep, the roots extending sometimes three feet under ground. The sandbars and small islands are covered with groves of willow. A few hills, composed principally of loose sand, were observed during the journey of the 12th; one of which, distant about half a mile east from the encampment, was estimated at about one hundred and fifty feet in height. The latitude of the camp, on the evening of the 12th of July, was observed to be 44° 33' 59" N.

which shows that the general direction of the river thus far is south of west. We reached the extremity of the forest the next morning, and found on the prairie a small party of Indians encamped. We were told that the principal of these was the old chief who formerly resided at Weakaote. He has thirty or forty warriors under his command, who intend to remove from their old residence to this spot, as the other place is considered unhealthy; by white men it is called Fever Sandbar.

Notwithstanding these circumstances, the St. Peter is generally deemed very healthy, and in despite of the unfavourable name applied to the sandbar, it is said to be free from intermittent fevers. Our party continued all in health except one of the soldiers, who had a few chills and fits of fever, which were soon checked. It was supposed that he had brought the seeds of it from the Mississippi.

Prairie land was again observed to border upon the river, the number of islands increased, and the navigation became extremely tedious. At one of the landing places, we observed a block of granite of about eighty pounds' weight; it was painted red and covered with a grass fillet, in which were placed twists of tobacco offered up in sacrifice. Feathers were stuck in the ground all round the stone.

In the afternoon, one of the canoes was unfortunately upset; the men who were in it regained the shore with some difficulty, but much of the cargo was lost or damaged. Among the articles lost, the most important was a keg of tobacco, which was intended for presents to the Indians, and a considerable part of our ammunition, which getting wet, became either totally unfit for use, or very much damaged. We had scarcely repaired, as much as lay in our power, the bad effects of this accident, when we observed the heavens overcast with dark clouds, portending an approaching storm. We immediately landed, with a view to shelter our stores and our persons against the rain. About seven in the evening, the storm broke out with more violence than usually happens in our climates. The precautions which we had taken proved of but little or no avail; the stores, which had been carefully packed up in a canoe, and covered up as well as our means permitted, were much damaged by the water, which half filled the canoe. Among them was our biscuit, coffee, sugar, &c. The tent had been pitched in as favourable a spot, with respect to the trees, as the ground would admit of, but not sufficiently so as to render it either safe or comfortable. Several trees, in the vicinity of the tent, were struck with lightning, and the wind blew with such force that the crash of falling timber was frequently heard during the night. The rain continued to pour down with great abundance until morning, when we were pleased to observe the sun rise fair, and afford us a chance of drying our baggage and stores. That spot being inconvenient for the purpose, we proceeded a few miles higher up to an old wintering camp of the traders; we remained there several hours, our canoes being occupied in transporting the baggage of the land party to the left bank of the river. The St. Peter is here fordable for horses. During our stay at this place, Major Long found that the combined effects of the two calamities, experienced within the last twenty-four hours, had required a change in our mode of travelling. The navigation of the river had been very slow, since we had advanced but about one hundred and thirty miles in six days; and it threatened to become still more tedious on account of the increasing shallowness of the water. Our provisions were not sufficient to support so large a party; and the country being destitute of animals, afforded us no supply. The only game killed, from the time that the party left the fort, were two ducks. Our guide further informed us, that if we continued to ascend the St. Peter in canoes, we should lose much precious time, arrive on Red River after the buffalo had left it, and find it, probably, impossible to reach the head of Lake Superior before the winter season had commenced; in which case, we should be compelled to winter somewhere west of the lakes. As this comported neither with Major Long's wishes, nor with the instructions which he had received from the War Department, it induced him to relinquish the plan of ascending in canoes, and to send back nine soldiers, retaining but twelve men as a guard, which in the present dispersed state of the Indians promised sufficient protection. By proceeding all in one party on land, much time would necessarily be saved, and the bends of the river need not be followed. Although this plan did not afford us as good a prospect of becoming acquainted with the nature of the country as the mode we had heretofore followed, yet, in the present state of our affairs, it was judged to be the only one that could be adopted with prudence; and as this modification in our manner of travelling required a corresponding change in the arrangement of our baggage, we proceeded a few miles higher up, to a fine prairie, where we found good pasture for our horses. The spot upon which we encamped has received the name of the Crescent, from a beautiful bend which the river makes at this place. The two parties having united here, a day was spent with drying the baggage, and separating the damaged provisions from those that were still fit for use. The acetous fermentation having commenced in our biscuit, such parts of it as were not too much injured were roasted over the fire.

As this was the highest spot on the St. Peter which we reached in canoes, it may be well to recapitulate the general characters of this stream, as we observed it from its mouth to the Crescent, a distance of one hundred and thirty miles by water.

The breadth of the river varies from sixty to eighty yards, but averages about seventy; its depth is such that it cannot be forded for about forty-five miles from its mouth. At Fort St. Anthony, the St. Peter is said to be about sixteen feet deep. The depth diminished rapidly as we proceeded up the river, and, in some places, our canoes had barely water enough to float them; yet the river was not considered very low at that season. In times of floods it can be ascended much higher, without inconvenience, by loaded canoes. The current, which is almost imperceptible at Fort St. Anthony, increases, and in some places is quite rapid; during the three last days it was found to average about one mile and a half an hour. The bed of the river is chiefly sand, arising from the destruction of the sandstone in which it is excavated. The banks usually rise to about twelve or fifteen feet, and are chiefly, if not altogether, composed of sandstone. On the last day, we saw a bluff that rises to sixty or eighty feet; it consists of white sandstone, and is called the white rock; limestone is, however, found in the country in various places. The granitic boulders, which appear to be quite deficient in the lower part of the river, are found tolerably abundant after passing the village of Taoapa. In some cases they assume a very large size; one of them was of an elliptical form; it was twelve yards in periphery, and five feet high; it is evidently out of place, and forms a conspicuous object in the prairie. The designs made upon it by the Indians, consisting of thick lines divided by intermediate dots, prove that it was with them an object of veneration. There are likewise amphibolic boulders scattered over the country. The bed of the river presents but few islands below the rapids, but above these it is chequered with numerous small sandy islands, which change the direction of the channel, and contribute to the rapidity of the current. The largest of these islands does not exceed three hundred yards in length, and thirty in breadth. The river is a very meandering one; so much so that the canoes were seldom steered for five minutes at a time in the same direction. The courses of the river varied from south-west to north-east, and in some cases even were south-east. The situation of Camp Crescent was estimated, by Mr. Colhoun, from observations taken under unfavourable circumstances, to be about latitude 44° 21′ 27″ north, longitude 94° 15′ west; so that, during our progress up the St. Peter, we had made but 65′ of westing, and 32′ 22″ of southing. The river receives in this extent no tributary of any importance; a few small rivulets, not exceeding ten or twelve in number, enter it occasionally from the right or left bank. Those only which deserved any mention are, Elk, which enters from the right bank, about twenty miles above the fort, and the small rivulet which comes in from the left bank about forty miles above the fort, and which is probably the same as Carver's river; at about twenty-five miles below the Crescent a shallow stream, six yards wide, enters from the left bank.

In our description of the observations recorded by the party in the canoes, we have included those made upon the nature of the river, &c. by the land party, and it may suffice to mention that the difficulties which they experienced were very great, owing to the nature of the country over which they travelled. At times it was so marshy, that they could not proceed without much danger to themselves and their horses; and, in one or two instances, the ground was so soft that they were obliged to construct causeways or bridges, to enable their horses to pass over it. The forests which they traversed consisted chiefly of maple, white walnut, hickory, oak, elm, ash, linden (Tilia Americana), interspersed with grape-vines, &c. The absence of the black walnut on the St. Peter, and near Fort St. Anthony, was particularly observed. The rosin plant was not seen after leaving Prairie du Chien. The yellow raspberry was abundant in many places, and ripe at the time the party passed through the forests. The course of the party was generally in the valley of the St. Peter, not far from, and frequently in sight of, the river, which offered them some fine water-scenery, presenting, however, a great degree of sameness; its principal defect is the want of objects to animate the scenes; no buffalo ranging across the prairie, no deer starting through the forests, no birds interrupting the solemn stillness which uniformly reigns over the country, the St. Peter rolls in silence its waters to the Mississippi. Where game is scarce, the Indian of course finds no inducement to hunt, and hence the party frequently travelled for whole days, without seeing a living object of any kind. This appeared, however, to be the track of Indians going out on their hunts, and accordingly traces were occasionally observed upon trees. In such places the trees were generally barked to a proper height: in one instance, four adjoining trees bore the representation of an Indian with wings, painted with red earth; a number of transverse lines were also drawn across the tree: this design was intended to convey the information that the Redwing chief had passed in that direction with a party, the strength of which was designated by the number of transverse streaks. From the numerous tumuli observed along the river, we were confirmed in the belief that this scarcity of game has not always prevailed in this part of the country, but that this stream was once inhabited by as extensive a population as can be supported by game alone, in the most favoured regions.

On the 15th of July the party, reduced in number to twenty-four, left the Crescent. They were provided with twenty-one horses, two of which were disabled. Nine were allotted to the officers and gentlemen of the party; the remaining ten being required as pack-horses to convey the provisions and baggage, the soldiers were all obliged to walk; which, however, as the country was fine prairie, and the day's march short, was not considered a very hard duty. We proceeded across some fine rolling prairies, in a course south of west, for about nine miles, when we saw the remains of Indian habitations; they were deserted. Upon · a scaffold, raised eighteen feet above the ground, and situated upon an elevated part of the prairie, the putrefying carcass of an Indian lay exposed to view. It had not been enclosed in a box, but merely shrouded in a blanket, which the wind and atmospheric influence had reduced to tatters. Fifteen horizontal black marks, drawn across one of the posts that supported the scaffold, designated, as we were informed by Renville, that so many scalps had been offered in sacrifice to the deceased, by those who danced at the funeral.

Our guides told us, that the mouth of the Terre Bleue river is about six leagues to the south-east of this spot. This is the principal tributary of the St. Peter, and is said to furnish about two-thirds as much water as the main branch of the river which retains the name of St. Peter. It enters from the right bank, and rises in the "Coteau des Prairies," a highland that stretches in a northerly direction between the Missouri and the St. Peter, and of which we shall have occasion to speak hereafter. By the Dacotas it is called Makatọ Osa* Watapa, which signifies "the river where blue earth is gathered." We never were nearer to this river than at this place, and we regretted that circumstances prevented our visiting it in order to acquire some knowledge of its character. We were unsuccessful in our attempts to obtain some of the blue earth from the Indians, an object which appeared to us of some importance, in order to determine its composition by analysis. It is evident that this is the same thing that was worked by Le Sueur at the close of the 17th century, for a copper ore. From its colour, we are inclined to consider it as more probably a phosphate of iron; but we have had no means of ascertaining its nature. Our guides informed us, that had we proceeded in our canoes, it would have required two days to reach the mouth of the Blue Earth river, on

* Măkătŏ Osă.

account of the great bend which the river makes at the Crescent, but by the route which we pursued we avoided the bend. It has been stated, that the locality of this blue earth, as well as that of the red stone used for pipes, were considered as neutral grounds, where the different nations of Indians could meet and collect these substances without apprehension of being attacked; but we have not heard this report confirmed. The mouth of the Blue Earth river is the chief residence of a tribe of the Dacotas, who call themselves the Miakechakesa,* and who are generally known by the traders by the name of Sisitons. They are a warlike and powerful band, and at that time were considered as unfriendly to the Americans on account of the government's having arrested, and sent to St. Louis for trial, one of their tribe who had killed a white man. It was chiefly from them that hostilities had been apprehended, and the force which we had taken at Fort St. Anthony was intended to protect the party against an attack from them; but, in order to evince a friendly disposition on the part of our government, Major Taliaferro had intended to hold a council with them at the same time. The news of their being dispersed on their summer hunts was the principal reason which induced Major Long to desist from his intention of visiting the mouth of the Terre Bleue, and which determined him to order back part of our escort.

In the evening, the party encamped on the bank of a small pool, which forms one of a group of ponds dignified with the appellation of the Swan Lakes, on account of the abundance of these birds said to exist in their

* Miåkčchåké's'ă.

neighbourhood. The Indian name is Manha tanka ota-menda,* which signifies the lake of the many large birds Observations were made by Mr. Colhoun to determine the longitude of this place; although taken at a time when the sun was very low, they served to correct the observations made at the Crescent. These lakes are more properly marshes, the quantity of water in them varying according to the seasons. We had passed several of them during the day; in one of these marshes our pack horses were several times exposed to much difficulty; and the mule that carried the biscuit having stumbled, part of our provisions were wet and damaged. Proceeding the next day on our course, we struck the St. Peter about noon, and found its current very rapid, but its size reduced to nearly one-half of that which it presented at the Crescent. This confirmed the report of our guides, that the Terre Bleue almost equals the St. Peter in the quantity of its waters. We had been able to trace the course of the river during the morning, by the line of woods which skirts it, and by the bluffs which border upon its right bank, rising to a height of from sixty to eighty feet; on the left bank the bluffs are neither so high nor so abrupt. The country, however, almost every where discovers its horizontal stratification by the steep acclivities which it forms, even in the prairies; presenting rather the appearance of *steppes* than of the rounded swells which generally characterize prairie land. At a small distance from our course we observed horizontal ledges of rock, which we were inclined to consider as the limestone that lies on the sandstone. Animals of every kind still continued

Månhå tånkå otåmendå.

very scarce. A garter-snake was killed near Swan Lake, upon which our guides took occasion to inform us, that the rattlesnake had sometimes been found near these lakes, but never to the north of them; this appearing to be their northernmost limit in this direction. The botany of the country was diversified by the reappearance of the Gerardria, a plant which had not been seen since we left Chicago. Near Swan Lake two elevations were observed, which appeared to be artificial tumuli. Some depressions were also seen, and these were by Renville called forts, but by whom they were scooped out, if indeed they be artificial, he could not inform us.

We crossed the St. Peter at noon, immediately above a ripple; our horses sank to their girths in the water. One mile further, we passed a small stream about fifteen yards wide, and eighteen inches deep, having a white sandy bottom; it is designated by the name of the *Rivière aux Liards* (Cottonwood),* from the abundance of this tree on its banks; by the Indians it is called Warhoju Watapa.† A bloody fray is stated to have occurred at the junction of the Aux Liards and St. Peter; it arose between two tribes of Sioux, who met there with traders. The latter having furnished them with liquor, the Indians drank to intoxication, quarrelled among themselves, and killed seven of their number. In travelling through an Indian country, many places are pointed out that have acquired a similar melancholy celebrity, and that tend to confirm the traveller in the conviction, of the heavy responsibility which attaches to those who have introduced, and still persist in carrying liquor among the Indians.

* Populus angulata. † Wárhóju.

Our journey during the afternoon was continued along the valley of the St. Peter, which was observed to be from one to one and a half mile wide. The adjacent prairie is elevated about eighty feet above the level of the river. A feature which struck us was the abundance of fragments of primitive rocks which were strewed in this valley: they were for the most part deeply imbedded in the ground, and bore but few traces of attrition; their bulk was very large. For a while we doubted whether we were not treading upon the crest of a formation of primitive rocks, which pierced through the superincumbent formations: but a close observation evinced such a confusion and diversity in the nature of the primitive blocks, as well as such signs of friction, as satisfied us that these were out of place; still they appeared to warrant the geologist in his prediction, that the party was approaching to a primitive formation, and that certainly the valley of the St. Peter had been one of the channels through which the primitive boulders had been removed from their original site. This assertion was fully substantiated, two days afterwards, by the discovery of the primitive rocks *in situ*. A very considerable swell between the river and the right bank of the valley, was supposed to be formed by the primitive rocks rising to a greater level than usual. If it be occasioned by an accumulation of fragments and boulders, as the nature of its surface might lead to believe, it is a very interesting feature in the valley.

We passed soon after two Indian lodges, in one of which was the chief Wamendetanka (War Eagle), generally known by the name of the Black Dog. He rules over the small village of Oanoska, situated near the mouth of the St. Peter. He is not a man of note, neither is he acknowledged as an independent chief, but being the head of an extensive family, he separated from his tribe some years ago; he leads about forty warriors. We stopped but a short time at his lodge, to exchange a few words with him; we admired much the appearance of his sons and daughters, who are tall, graceful, and well-formed. He is about fifty years of age, and has much dignity in his appearance.

The journey of the 18th of July, being across the prairie, offered but little interest. The monotony of a prairie country always impresses the traveller with a melancholy, which the sight of water, woods, &c. cannot fail to remove. During that day we enjoyed no view of the river, and the great scarcity of springs, and wood for cooking, made the travelling uncomfortable; to these we must add a temperature of about 94°, exhibited by the thermometer when in the shade, and protected against all radiation of heat. But the greatest annoyance which we had to encounter, were the mosquetoes, which arose in such swarms, as to prove a more serious evil than can be imagined by those who have not experienced it. We never were tormented at any period of our journey more than when travelling in the vicinity of the St. Peter. The mosquetoes generally rose, all of a sudden, about the setting of the sun. Their appearance was so instantaneous, that we had no time to prepare ourselves against them; whenever we had the good fortune to encamp previous to their sallying from their hiding places, our great object was to complete our evening meal before they commenced their attack, for this we found ourselves unable to resist; and we have not unfrequently been so much annoyed by these insects, as to be obliged to relinquish an unfinished supper, or to throw away a cup of tea, which we could not enjoy, while stung on all sides by countless numbers of mosquetoes. When a high wind reduced their numbers, we found some relief from remaining in a dense cloud of smoke; but even this proved of no avail, when, from the calmness or heat of the atmosphere, their numbers were undiminished. In such cases, our only alternative was to endure their stings, or to smother under the weight of a blanket in which we wrapped ourselves up, covering our faces, hands, &c. To protect our feet and legs, we were obliged to lie with our boots on. The annoyance continued until some time after sunrise, when the increasing heat of the day drove them back into their recesses. The sleepless nights which we frequently passed, when exposed to this torment, rendered this part of our journey the most fatiguing. Our horses fared even worse, for they were exposed, like us, during the night, to the sting of the mosquetoe, and during the day the big horse-fly proved equally noxious.

The soil of the prairies is not uniform in quality: in some instances it was remarkably fine, and of an intense black colour; the grass, consequently, grew to a considerable size, was luxuriant, and of a rich green hue. In other parts the soil is sandy, greyish, and appears to be of an inferior quality; its produce then presents a similar inferiority; the blades of grass are scattered, short, of a yellowish and sickly aspect. The earth appears dry, and scorched with the heat of the sun.

The party had frequent opportunities of remarking the difficulty which exists, to determine with accuracy the nature or size of objects seen at a distance. Sand-hill cranes, seen on the prairie, were by some of the company mistaken for elks.

Among the birds observed on the prairie, besides the sandhill crane, are the reed-bird, black-bird,* yellow-headed black-bird,† the black breasted tern;‡ the last of which was very abundant. Mr. Say shot the female of the Mergus cucullatus, and a blue-winged teal. Among the reptiles, besides the common garter-snake,§ there was one with lateral red spots.‖ A coluber, like the melanoleucus, but spotted, and similar to that found on the Missouri, was killed on these prairies. In several of the marshes, the huts of the muskrat were found very abundant. The herbarium was enriched by the addition of a beautiful specimen of the Lilium Philadelphicum, which was still seen flowering, though it had nearly ceased to bloom. Another great ornament of the prairies is the Lilium Superbum. The Gerardria was still occasionally seen. This plant is, as we were informed, considered by the Indians to be a specific against the bite of the rattlesnake; the root is scraped and the scrapings applied to the wound; it is said that, if used upon a recent wound, a single application will suffice. The boulders, which are so common in the valley of the St. Peter, are but seldom seen on the praries.

After proceeding another half day on the prairie, the party found itself on the banks of the Chanshayape¶ watapa, or the stream of the "tree painted red." This is a beautiful rivulet, which was about eight yards wide where we crossed it. It runs in a wide and romantic valley. The bluffs which rise on both sides, are formed of a fine white sandstone. We stopped for a few

---

* Oriolus, [Zanthornus, Cuvier,] phœniceus.
† Oriolus, [Zanthornus, Cuvier,] icterocephalus.   ‡ Sterna.
§ Coluber ordinatus.   ‖ Coluber parietalis.
¶ Chănshăyăpĕ.

moments on the edge of the bank, previous to descending into the valley, to enjoy the beautiful and refreshing scenery which offered itself to our view, and which formed a pleasing contrast with the burned and blasted appearance of the prairie. The junction of the valley of the St. Peter with that of its tributary, about two miles below the place where we stood, occasioned an expansion of both valleys at that spot. The beautiful and diversified vegetation, springing luxuriantly on the banks of both streams, the rapid current of the waters rushing to one common point, formed a landscape, which, at that time, appeared to us as smiling and as beautiful as any we had ever beheld. But it is probable that much of its charms arose from the contrast which it presented with the wearisome views of the boundless prairies: perhaps, also, we found ourselves in better spirits to enjoy the scenery, from perceiving, near these banks, the first trace of the buffalo, whence we drew prospects of a speedy change in our fare, together with hopes of soon sharing in the sports of an active and interesting chase. Though narrow, the Redwood, whose course is a long one, has its sources in the Coteau des Prairies. Red pipestone is said to exist on its banks, at three days' journey from its source.

At the spot where these two valleys unite, a very interesting fragment of rock was observed; it was evidently out of place; its mass was enormous; it was of an irregular hemispherical form, about forty or fifty feet in circumference; it had been cleft, as we thought, by lightning. The rock was blackened, and a few bushes and trees near it bore signs of having been on fire. The conflagration does not appear to have spread to a distance; and, from its situation, the fire could scarcely have been made by a traveller. We searched in vain, during the short time that we stopped near it, for traces of fusion upon the rock. This mass is granitic, and presents very distinctly the appearance of a formation in concentric shales. Rocks were observed at some distance which, from their white colour, were presumed to be sandstone. Above the junction of the rivulet with the St. Peter, a rapid occurs in the river, called Patterson's rapid. We were at too great a distance to see it, but it is not very considerable. We were, from observations made higher up on the river, induced to consider the rocks which occasion it, as primitive.

On the evening of the 18th of July, we encamped on the banks of the river. When descending into the valley from the prairie, with a view to select a suitable spot for our evening's camp, our attention was suddenly called to the new features which it displayed. High rocks of a rugged aspect arose in an insulated manner in the midst of the widened valley, through which the St. Peter winds its way. We spent the rest of the afternoon in examining them, and experienced no little satisfaction in finding them to be primitive rocks *in situ.*

The pleasure we experienced sprang not from the mere associations of home, connected with the view of a primitive formation which we had not seen since the first five days of our journey; but it resulted also, in a great measure, from the certainty that we had at last arrived at what we had long been looking for in vain. We had traced those scattered boulders, which lay insulated in the prairies, from the banks of the Muskingum to this place; we had seen them gradually increasing in size and number, and presenting fewer signs of attrition as we advanced further on our journey. Two days before, their number, size, and features, had induced the geologist of the party to predict our speedy approach to the primitive formations, and it was a pleasing confirmation of his opinions to find these rocks really *in situ,* within thirty miles, in a straight line, of the place where he had made this assertion. The character of these rocks was examined with care, and found very curious. It seemed as if four simple minerals, quartz, felspar, mica, and amphibole, had united here to produce almost all the varieties of combination which can arise from the association of two or more of these minerals; and these combinations were in such immediate contact, that the same fragment might, as we viewed one or the other end of it, be referred to different rocks; while, in some places, granite was seen perfectly well characterized, varying from the fine to the coarse-grained; in others, a gneiss, mica slate, greisen (quartz and mica), compact felspar (Weisstein of Werner), sienite, greenstone, and the sienite with addition of quartz, forming the amphibolic granite of D'Aubuisson, were equally well characterized. The only rock composed by the union of two of these principles which we did not observe, but which may perhaps exist there, is the graphic granite (Pegmatite, Haüy). These rocks are not very extensive; the circumference of the largest probably does not exceed one quarter of a mile; they rise to about thirty-five feet above the level of the water. Their form is irregular; their aspect rugged and barren compared with the fertile bottom of the valley; their general colour is of a dark gray; they appear to be the summit or crest of primitive rocks which lie beneath this valley, and which protrude at this place through the superior strata. As the adjoining prairies are elevated about fifty feet above the level of the river, these primitive rocks are observable only in the valley; they doubtless constituted at one time a continuous ridge, but have been divided into insulated masses by the corroding action of the stream, whose very circuitous bed winds between them. They extend upon a distance of about six miles in the direction of the valley. After having examined almost every one of these masses, we feel unwilling to decide with certainty, which of the primitive combinations predominates; for the passage of the one into the other is more constant and more sudden than in any other primitive formation that has ever come under our notice. Indeed, we know of none with which to compare it, except it be that which we observed at a subsequent period of the expedition, between Lake Winnepeek and the Lake of the Woods; but even there the features were somewhat different, for they were on a larger scale. The passages which we there observed, were sometimes to be traced only upon large masses; whereas on the St. Peter, it would have been difficult to break off a fragment of a cubic foot in size presenting an uniform character of composition. It is, however, probable, as far as our observations extended, that granite is the predominating rock. These masses bear very evident signs of a crystalline origin, but the process must have been a confused one. Tourmaline is found disseminated throughout the rock, yet in no great abundance. In one or two spots where the mass assumed a more slaty appearance than in other places, a faint tendency to a stratification, directed from north-north-east to south-south-west, with a dip towards the south, was observed. Viewing the insulated masses from the prairie, they appeared to be directed in a transverse line through the valley, and in a north-easterly course, so that this may be the remains of a dike which existed across the valley, but which was finally broken. This observation was, however, a partial one, and it would be improper to attach much weight to it. When calling the attention of our guide to the difference between these rocks and those observed below, he appeared to have been aware of it himself, and stated that rocks similar to these extended down the valley, to about four miles below Redwood rivulet; it was partly from this circumstance that we inferred that Patterson's rapids were probably formed by a bar of these rocks rising across the bed of the river. This appeared to us to be the more probable from the circumstance that a rapid, known by the name of the Little Falls, occurs just above the place of our encampment of the 18th, and that it is occasioned by a ledge of granitic rocks, over which the river passes at this place. In the examination of this spot two points appeared to us chiefly to deserve our attention, in order to avoid all source of error; the first was to ascertain that the rocks were really *in situ;* the second, that they were primitive and crystalline, not conglomerated or regenerated rocks, such as are sometimes observed. But upon these two points we think that not the least doubt can be entertained. The immense mass of these insulated rocks, the uniform height to which they attain, the uniform direction in which they lie, prove them to be in place; while an attentive inspection of their nature shows them to be really crystalline. There is a gradual though rapid passage of the granite into the sienite, which proves them to be of contemporaneous formation, and which precludes the idea that the rock is formed by the union of fragments of granite, sienite, &c. cemented together.

The discovery of this granitic formation here appeared to us the more interesting, as its small extent might easily have prevented us from observing it, had not chance brought us to the river at this place; for if we had been travelling on the prairie, within half a mile of the edge of the bank, the greater height of the bluff would have concealed these rocky islands from our view. We feel, therefore, unable to decide, whether they do not recur at some of the other bends of the river, which we avoided; yet, from the character of the stream itself, we doubt it; for we find that as soon as these rocks protrude into the valley, they occasion rapids and falls in the river, while otherwise its course is smooth. Had we not seen the " Little rapids," which we passed on the 11th, we might have been induced to consider them as resulting from the appearance of the primitive rocks at the surface, but having examined with care the sandstone rocks, by which they are produced, and having ascertained that no other rapids are found in the St. Peter, between these and the Patterson falls, we are induced to believe that this is the only place where the granite may be seen *in situ*. In attempting to connect this primitive formation with those observed elsewhere, we find that it lies in a direction about west-south-west, at a distance probably not exceeding eighty miles, of the " granitic and hornblende rocks," which Mr. Schoolcraft states as having seen " occasionally rising in rugged peaks and beds," on the Mississippi.*
We feel, however, disposed to consider all this section

---

* Schoolcraft's Narrative, ut supra, p. 288.

of our country as reposing on this granite, and we entertain but little doubt of its identity with the sienitic granite observed at a later period of our journey, and which we first struck near Fort Alexander, at the mouth of Winnepeek river.

The latitude of our encampment on the banks of the St. Peter, that evening, was determined by observations to be 44° 41′ 26″ north. The variation of the compass at this place was 12° 21′ 20″ east.

From the interesting features which the valley displayed at this spot, the geologist felt desirous that the party should ascend along the banks of the river, with a view to examine these granitic masses, should they recur; but this was deemed impracticable, on account of the length of time which would be consumed in following the bends of the river. The reports which we had previously received of the abundance of game, had not been confirmed; we had, on the contrary, found none at all, and our stores were wasting away too fast to permit any delay. It was then proposed to divide the party, and, while the main body proceeded with the necessary expedition towards the trading establishments at the head of the river, to allow the geologist, with one or two companions, to continue his route in the valley. But this Major Long did not deem prudent, for in the present dissatisfied disposition of the Sisitons, the division of the party must necessarily expose it to be cut off by them, should they fall in with it. The regret which this occasioned was, however, dissipated, on observing that the primitive rocks did not continue long in the valley; for having been allowed to travel along the banks of the river for half a day, Mr. Keating saw the last of them, at about four miles above the little falls; and he was assured by his guide that they did not recur for a considerable distance. We had, nevertheless, an opportunity of seeing from a distance, in the bed of the river, a rocky island, which appeared to us to bear the character of the primitive rocks near Patterson's rapids. Our guides insisted that it was a sandstone. We have generally found them to be such accurate observers of natural objects, that we wished to visit the rock, and see how far their reports could be depended upon; but that would have required several hours,—a waste of time which it was thought the object did not warrant. In the evening we again observed the primitive rocks in the valley, and encamped upon one of these knolls; it was composed of a rock partaking alternately of the characters of mica slate and gneis, which appeared stratified nearly east and west, the strata being almost vertical. This knoll was so small, that we could not presume, from the direction of its strata, to draw conclusions as to that of the rock in general.

The occurrence of these primitive knobs disturbs the current of the river, and renders the navigation difficult and hazardous. Five miles below the encampment of the 19th, there is a place where the boats and their loads are carried for the distance of a mile; from which circumstance the place is called the Grand Portage. By this portage the canoes avoid thirteen rapids; these, with twenty-six other rapids, constitute all the obstructions to the navigation of the river, from its source to its mouth. In a good stage of the waters, there are, however, but two portages, of which this is one. Among the tributaries passed on that day, only one deserves to be mentioned; it is called the Pejehata Zeze*Watapan,

* Pèjèhâtâ Zèzè.

the yellow medicine. It is about the same size as the Redwood, and rises, in like manner, at the base of the Côteau des Prairies. Nearly opposite to it a small stream falls in; the Indians call it the Chataba* *(that hatches sparrow-hawks),* the traders term it *L'Eau de Vie.* On our map we have retained the term Epervier, which, being in use among some of the traders, and intelligible both to French and English travellers, appears likely to prevail.

While riding across the prairie that day, we were met by two Indians, who ran towards us with great speed. They proved very friendly in their disposition, and informed us, that on the preceding day they had killed a buffalo bull in that vicinity, and that the Indians on Lake Travers had already killed many, the buffalo being unusually abundant that season. This news was the more gratifying to the party, as they had been for the last few days on short allowance. Having informed the Indians of the spot where we proposed to encamp, they came to it in the evening with their families, and pitched their tents near ours; they then offered us a feast, which we of course accepted, and at which we partook of the buffalo meat, that had been cut into long and thin slices, about one-eighth of an inch thick, eight inches wide, and eighteen long. These had been jerked in the sun, and were subsequently boiled without salt, and served out to us in wooden dishes. It was tough and tasteless, and disappointed those gentlemen of the party who had never eaten of the buffalo meat, and who had heard it highly extolled; this disappointment arose, however, from the circumstance of its being jerked, instead of fresh meat. What remained of the feast was, according

* Châtâbâ.

to the Indian usage, our property, and we therefore had it conveyed to our tents. The feast was ushered in with the usual ceremonies of shaking hands, smoking, &c.

The St. Peter dwindles into a very small stream, probably not more than fifteen or twenty yards wide in any part, above Patterson's rapids. It is fordable every where. The valley presents a fine rich soil, rather swampy in places, and covered with high grass and wild rice; it is often woody. Wherever the primitive rocks are found, they are bare. The trees consist principally of cotton wood and ash. In the prairies Mr. Say found the spotted frog (Rana halecina of Kalm and Daudin), figured by Catesby. It was very plentiful near the marshes. The young whip-poor-will was found at that time nearly strong enough to fly The mosquetoes increased in abundance and virulence as we advanced.

A short day's journey brought the party to the *Lac qui parle,* which is an expansion of the river about seven and a half miles long, and from one quarter to three quarters of a mile wide. The name of this lake is a translation of the Indian appellation Menda e a,* but whence it has received it we know not. We have not been able to discover or to hear of any remarkable echo in its vicinity, which might have given rise to it. It is not, we believe, an uncommon name for Indians, and we know of at least one river that has a somewhat analogous appellation; it is the *Riviere qui appelle,* a tributary of the Assiniboin, and whose Indian name has merely been translated by the traders. Previous to reaching Lac qui parle, we passed two small tributaries of the St. Peter, on the right bank; one of which is called by the traders Beaver, by the Indians Watapan intapa,† which "signifies the river at the head," as they

* Měndă è ă.   † Intăpă.

consider the lake to be the head of the St. Peter. Six miles above our encampment of the 19th, a larger stream, called by some Chippewa river, but by the Dacotas Mea Wahkan* Watapan, the River of the Spirit Banks, falls in from the left side. The Mea Wahkan is said to take its rise near the head waters of Red river, with which it interlocks. On Beaver rivulet, the bank, which was high and steep, was found to consist of loose white sand. Near this bank there were seven or eight artificial tumuli, all placed on a straight line except one, which was in advance of the others. On the two largest, which were five feet high, and thirty feet in diameter at the base, recent graves, of a kind now much used by the Indians, were observed. In these the corpse is deposited in a very shallow excavation, or more frequently upon the surface of the ground, and stakes are placed over it, forming a sort of a roof. These stakes are very necessary to protect the remains of the dead against the rapacity of wolves, who, if they were merely interred, would dig them up. In this case, notwithstanding the great strength of the stakes, the grave had been broken open, and its contents scattered over the ground. The wolves appear to be very abundant in these prairies. We have frequently heard them barking in the night, and occasionally seen them. Two young wolves were seen near Beaver rivulet, and easily caught by the soldiers, to whom a reward was offered if they would carry them alive to Mackinaw; but they both made their escape during the night. In the dull monotony of a journey across the prairie, destitute of interest, and uninterrupted by any incident, the capture of these wolves created such a sensation in the party as will not be

* Meá Wáhkán.

readily conceived by those who have not experienced how eagerly man seizes the first opportunity of being relieved from his own thoughts, when he has been left to the uninterrupted exercise of them for a certain length of time.

We spent half a day in the vicinity of Lac qui parle; our tents were pitched on an eminence near the lower extremity of the lake, commanding an extensive prospect, adorned with this beautiful sheet of water. The country, as we advanced, evidently became more elevated, but no hills of any magnitude were visible except the bluffs of the rivers and rivulets. The elevation to which they attain frequently equals, and sometimes exceeds, one hundred feet. The precipices, to which these bluffs give rise, are the boundaries of extensive and undulated plains, destitute of woods; trees are only seen skirting the banks of the water-courses. Above the lake the bluffs diminish in height; those along the valley of the St. Peter not exceeding forty feet; in some cases they disappear, and gentle slopes blend gradually the prairie and the valley of the river. At the upper end of the lake, the St. Peter has lost all its characters; it is a rivulet of from twenty to thirty feet wide; its bed is very much obstructed with high grass and wild rice; its waters are almost stagnant. Five leagues above this, a brook from the right bank joins with the St. Peter; this is called the Hra Wahkan,* or Spirit Mountain, from the name of a hill near which it rises. The primitive rocks are again seen in place, scattered here and there across the valley; one of these was remarkable for the beauty of its felspar, which is very lamellar; it has an easy cleavage, and is inter-

* Hrå Wåhkån.

mixed with quartz, giving it almost the appearance of a graphic granite. As we advanced, the rocks assumed a more decided character, and were found to be principally either a common or a sienitic granite. Besides those in place, vast numbers of fragments of primitive rocks, presenting little or no alteration, lie scattered in every direction, and attest that this has been the seat of a great destruction. An Indian family was met near the banks of the river, who stated that they had descended it in order to ascertain the prospect of the ensuing harvest of wild rice, and informed us that it was very promising; the grain, they thought, would be ripe in the middle of August; the weather was, in fact, very favourable to its growth, the temperature having kept up for the last few days at nearly 90°. We were likewise informed by them that an inroad had been made by the lower Sisitons upon the lands of the Sauks on the Des Moines river, and that, not meeting with their enemies, they had attacked the Iawas, killed a number, and taken many prisoners.

It is interesting, as we proceed, to find that the same devotional spirit which we observed below still exists. Many rocks are used as consecrated spots, at which the Indian pauses to offer a sacrifice to the ruling spirits. A very large block, covered with circles, crescents, and crosses, designed with red paint, was considered sacred to the heavenly bodies, and these marks were held to be designations of the sun, moon, and stars. The party was likewise occasionally gladdened with a view of fresh tracks of the buffalo.

On the 22d we reached another, and the last, expansion of the river. It is also improperly called a lake;

by the Indians it is termed Eatakeka,* which has been interpreted " Lac des grosses Roches," Big Stone Lake. Our view to the west was this day bounded by an extensive ridge or swell in the prairies, known by the name of the " Côteau des Prairies." It is distant from our course about twenty or thirty miles; its height above the level of the St. Peter is probably not short of one thousand feet. According to the best information which we have obtained, this ridge commences about the 49th parallel of north latitude, and between the 98th and 99th degrees of west longitude from Greenwich. It proceeds in a direction nearly south-south-east, passes east of the group of small lakes called Devil Lake, divides the tributaries of the St. Peter from those of the Missouri, and extends southerly as far as the head of the Blue Earth, where it gradually widens and sinks to the level of the surrounding country.

A second ridge, or Côteau des Prairies, is said to run in a direction nearly parallel to that which we have just described. It commences at the southern bend of Mouse river, near the 48th parallel of latitude, and proceeds in a course nearly south-east for about eighty miles, when it turns to the west of south, and continues probably beyond the 44th, where it likewise sinks and disappears. In the valley between these two ridges, the Rivière de Jacques, or James River, runs and empties itself into the Missouri about the 43d degree of latitude. Thus the Côteau des Prairies may probably be considered as changing the course of the Missouri, above the Mandan villages, from an easterly to a southerly direction, and as keeping it in that direction for nearly three

* E'âtâkèkâ.

hundred miles, when the river reassumes a course east of south, which it keeps until it unites with the Mississippi. It is to the vicinity of the Côteau to the St. Peter on the one side, and of the Mississippi on the other, that we are to attribute the small size of the tributaries of the St. Peter. In fact, they are mere brooks conveying the waters on the east side of the ridge; but, probably, about the spring of the year, they are much swollen by the thawing of the snow and ice upon the ridge; it is in this manner that we may account for the water-marks found along the bluffs which inclose their comparatively large valleys.

Its distance from our course prevented us from visiting the Côteau, which we should otherwise have done. It was intended that Mr. Keating should examine this remarkable feature in the country, in order to ascertain what its geological characters are; but as we were generally informed that no rocks are seen at its surface, that it presents an uniformly smooth prairie-like appearance, the ascent being gradual and easy on both sides, and as it would have taken three days to go to its summit and return, this excursion was not made.

The Côteau des Prairies may truly be considered as the dividing ridge between the tributaries of the Mississippi and those of the Missouri. It is probably formed by the elevation of the granitic or other primitive rocks above the usual level of the prairies. These may have been covered in a mantled-formed manner by the secondary and alluvial rocks, so as to be entirely concealed from view, and to be made to assume the general features of prairie land. We cannot, however, resist the belief, that a geologist who would follow it in its whole course from the Assiniboin to the Blue Earth, would be rewarded by the discovery of the granitic formations, if not along the whole of its crest, at least in some of the ravines which head near it, and in which perhaps a superposition of secondary rocks might be observed.

After having left the Big Stone Lake, we crossed a brook which retains the name of the St. Peter, but which cannot be considered as part of that river; the St. Peter may, in fact, be said to commence in Big Stone Lake, and this to be but a small tributary from the Côteau des Prairies; it was less than seven yards wide. This stream soon leaves the main valley and turns to the west, where a lateral trench in the prairie, known by the name of a " Coulée," gives it a passage. Had we visited the Côteau, we should have ascended this *Coulée*, to trace the stream to its source. It divides itself, as we are informed, into two branches; one of which runs in a direction west by south for about twelve miles. The source of the northern and larger branch is in Polecat Lake, about twice that distance, and bearing, from the point at which it leaves the main valley, about west by north. The length of the stream, following all its windings, is about forty or fifty miles. Polecat Lake, whose dimensions are one and a half mile in length by half a mile in breadth, is frequently dry, and the stream often conveys but little water to the Big Stone Lake.

By the route which we travelled, the distance from the mouth of the St. Peter to the head of Big Stone Lake is three hundred and twenty-five miles, of which we ascended one hundred and thirty by water. We entertain no doubt that the distance, in a direct line by land, would fall short of two hundred and thirty miles; and that the whole length of the river, including all its bends, does not exceed five hundred miles. The traders, whose estimates almost always exceed the truth, do not ascribe to it a length of more than six hundred miles. How different these observations are from the opinions formerly entertained of this stream, may be judged from the assertion of Breckenridge, that it is a thousand miles long. Other authors allow it twelve hundred miles. Carver states it, on the authority of the Indians, to take its rise in the same neighbourhood as, and within the space of a mile of, the source of the Missouri; he adds that the northern branch rises from a number of lakes near the Shining Mountains. But we can place no dependence upon the information which he gives from second-hand, when we find it blended with such fictions as are contained in the following extract: "The river St. Pierre, which runs through the territory of the Naudowessies, flows through a most delightful country, abounding with all the necessaries of life, that grow spontaneously, and with a little cultivation it might be made to produce even the luxuries of life. Wild rice grows here in great abundance, and every part is filled with trees, bending under their loads of fruits, such as plums, grapes, and apples. The meadows are covered with hops and many sorts of vegetables, while the ground is stored with useful roots, with angelica, spikenard, and ground-nuts as large as hens' eggs." We were not so fortunate as to meet with those apples, plums, and other good things, which grew spontaneously sixty years since in the country.

The St. Peter, in our opinion, probably never can be made a commodious stream; for although it flows over gradations, and not upon a slant, yet, as these gradations are accumulated into the upper third of the distance between Big Stone Lake and the mouth of the river, the expense of rendering it navigable, by damming and locking, would far exceed the importance of the object. The plan would doubtless be found very practicable, but the scarcity of water during the greater part of the year would render these works unavailing. From considerations upon which it is unnecessary to dwell, and the accuracy of which might be disputed, though they appear to us to lead to correct results, we have estimated the fall in the river, or difference of level between the Lac qui parle and the mouth of the river, at about fifty or sixty feet. According to this estimate, the average fall does not exceed two or three inches per mile.

The river having taken a bend to the west, we continued our route in what appeared to have been an old water-course, and, within three miles of the Big Stone Lake, found ourselves on the banks of Lake Travers, which discharges its waters by means of Swan or Sioux river into the Red river of Lake Winnepeek, whose waters, as is well known, flow toward Hudson's Bay. The space between Lakes Travers and Big Stone is but very little elevated above the level of both these lakes; and the water has been known, in times of flood, to rise and cover the intermediate ground, so as to unite the two lakes. In fact, both these bodies of water are in the same valley; and it is within the recollection of some persons, now in the country, that a boat once floated from Lake Travers into the St. Peter. Thus, therefore this spot offers us one of those interesting phenomena, which we have already alluded to, but which are no where perhaps so apparent as they are in this place. Here we behold the waters of two mighty streams, one of which empties itself into Hudson's Bay at the 57th parallel of north latitude, and the other into the Gulf of

Mexico, in latitude 29°, rising in the same valley within three miles of each other, and even in some cases offering a direct natural navigation from one into the other We seek in vain for those dividing ridges which topographers and hydrographers are wont to represent upon their maps in all such cases; and we find a strong confirmation of that just observation of a modern traveller, that "it is a false application of the principles of hydrography, when geographers attempt to determine the chains of mountains in countries, of which they suppose they know the course of rivers. They suppose that two great basins of water can only be separated by great elevations, or that a considerable river can only change its direction where a group of mountains opposes its course; they forget, that frequently, either on account of the nature of the rocks, or on account of the inclination of the strata, the most elevated levels give rise to no river, while the sources of the most considerable rivers are distant from the high chains of mountains."*

The country which extends between the forty-fifth and forty-eighth parallels of latitude, and between the ninety-third and ninety-seventh of longitude, presents perhaps an example of the interlockage of the sources of rivers, which few, if any other spots on the surface of the earth, can equal. Here no high ridge extends to divide the sources of three of the largest streams that are known. The mighty Mississippi, and many of its tributaries, run from the same lakes or swamps, which supply the waters of Nelson's river and of the St. Lawrence. This limited tract of country includes the head of the Sioux river, and

* Introduction to "Humboldt's Political Essay of the Kingdom of New Spain, translated by John Black. London, 1811," page lxxxvi.

Red fork of Red river, of the grand fork of Rainy Lake river, of the St. Louis river, of Lake Superior, of Rum river, the Mississippi proper, the Riviere de Corbeau, and the St. Peter. The Indian and the trader constantly pass in their canoes from one to another of these rivulets, and without meeting with half the difficulties which they experience lower down upon the same streams, when swelled to the size of mighty rivers, for in fact the whole of that country is an immense swamp. Carver, who states this important feature of the country, destroys all the value of this information, by placing in the same district the sources of the Oregan, or Great River of the West.

In tracing the general aspect of the country, of its ridges and streams, we have omitted the little incidents which attended our progress from Lac qui parle to Lake Travers; and although the trifling adventures which attend a travelling party lose all their importance when compared to the constant and invariable features of the natural scenery, yet, as this part of our route was more diversified by incident than any that had preceded it, we may be permitted to dwell upon it for a moment. While travelling over the prairie which borders upon that part of the St. Peter that connects Lac qui parle with Big Stone Lake, our attention was roused by the sight of what appeared to be buffaloes chased across the prairie. They, however, soon proved to be Indians; their number, at first limited to two, gradually increased to near one hundred; they were seen rising from every part of the prairie, and after those in the advance had reconnoitred us, and made signals that we were friends, by discharging their guns, they all came running towards us, and in a few minutes we found ourselves surrounded by a numerous band. They had at first been apprehensive that we might be enemies, and this was the cause of the different manœuvres which they had made previous to discharging their guns. The effect of these guns, fired upon the prairie in every direction, and by each, as soon as he had acquired the requisite degree of certainty that the strangers were friends, was really very beautiful. As they approached we had an opportunity of observing that these Indians were good-looking and straight; none were large, nor were any remarkable for the symmetry of their forms. They were, for the greater part, destitute of clothing, except the breech-cloth, which most of them wore. A few, however, and these adults, had divested themselves of this almost indispensable article of dress. We were indeed surprised to see some old men among them quite naked, and no notice appeared to be taken of it by the others. Some of them, and particularly the young men, were dressed with care and ostentation; they wore looking-glasses suspended to their garments. Others had papers of pins, purchased from the traders as ornaments. We observed that one, who appeared to be a man of some note among them, had a live sparrow-hawk on his head, by way of distinction; this man wore also a buffalo robe, on which eight bear tracks were painted. Some of them were mounted on horseback, and were constantly drumming upon the sides of their horses with their heels, being destitute both of whip and spur. Many of them came and shook hands with us, while the rest were riding all round us in different directions. They belonged, as we were told, to the Wahkpatoan,* one of

* Wåhkpåtóån.

the tribes of the Dacotas. Their chief being absent, the principal man among them told us that they had thirty lodges of their people at the lower end of the lake, and invited us to visit them, which invitation was accepted. These Indians demonstrated the greatest friendship and satisfaction at seeing us. As we rode towards their lodges, we were met by a large party of squaws and children, who formed a very motley group. These squaws had no ornament, nor did they seem to value themselves upon their personal appearance. We observed that both they and the men had very handsome small feet and hands. The moccassins, which they usually wear, prevent their feet from spreading, as is the case with those who walk unrestrained by any kind of shoe. From the use of these, as probably also from the habit of walking with caution, their feet retained a beautiful arched form. The dress of the women consisted of a long wrapper, with short sleeves, of dark calico; this covered them from the shoulders to the waist; a piece of blue broadcloth wound two or three times round the waist, and its ends tucked in, extended to the knee. They also wore leggings of blue or scarlet cloth. Their forms were rather clumsy; their waists not very delicate; they exhibited a great breadth of hips. Their motions were not graceful, and their walk reminded one of the party of the praise in the song of the modern Greek, as recorded by Dodwell, " My love walks about like a goose."

The village, to which they directed us, consisted of thirty skin lodges, situated on a fine meadow on the bank of the lake. Their permanent residence, or at least that which they have occupied as such for the last five years, is on a rocky island (Big Island), in the lake nearly opposite to, and within a quarter of a mile of, their present encampment. Upon the island they cultivate their corn-fields, secure against the aggressions of their enemies. They had been lately engaged [in buffalo hunting, apparently with much success. The principal man led us to his lodge, wherein a number of the influential men were admitted, the women being excluded; but we observed that they, with the children, went about the lodge, peeping through all the crevices, and not unfrequently raising the skins to observe our motions. They soon brought in a couple of large wooden dishes, filled with pounded buffalo meat boiled, and covered with the marrow of the same animal; of this we partook with great delight; it was the first time that several of the party had tasted the fresh buffalo meat; and it was the first meal made by any of us upon fresh meat, since we had left Fort St. Anthony. During the entertainment, Major Long made known to them the objects of the expedition, at which they appeared very much gratified. As we rose to depart, we were informed that another feast was preparing for us in one of the adjoining tents, of which we were invited to partake. We were too familiar with Indian manners, not to know that the excuse of having just eaten a very hearty meal would not be considered as sufficient among them; and so we readily resigned ourselves to the necessity of again testifying our friendly disposition, by doing honour to their meal. In order to save time, we had it brought into the same lodge. It consisted of a white root, somewhat similar in appearance to a small turnip; it is called, by the Dacotas tepsin,* by the French the " Pomme blanche or Navet de Prairie."† It was boiled down into a sort of mush or hominy, and was

* Têpsìn.   † Psoralea Esculenta, Nuttall

very much relished by most of the party; had it been seasoned with salt or sugar, it would have been considered delicious. This was held, even by the guides, to be a great treat. As we were rising from this second meal, we were informed that a third one was preparing for us; we begged to decline it, having a considerable distance to travel that afternoon; but we were informed that this would be a great disappointment to him who had prepared the feast, as in order to outdo all others he had killed a dog, which is considered not only as the greatest delicacy, but also as a sacred animal, of which they eat only on great occasions. In order to meet his wishes we deferred our journey for an hour, but the repast not being then prepared, we were compelled to leave the village, to the great and manifest mortification of our third host, and to the no small disappointment of most of our party, who were desirous of tasting the sacred animal. In order to make a return for the civilities which we had received at the hands of the Indians, we informed them that if they would dispatch a messenger with us, we should send them, from a neighbouring trader's house, some tobacco, all ours having been lost on the river. They gladly accepted the proposal, and sent two lads with us for it. In the afternoon, we reached a house belonging to the American Fur Company; it is situated about half way up the lake. Mr. Moore, the superintendent, showed us every attention, and supplied us with as many of the articles which we required, as he could dispose of. In the vicinity of Mr. Moore's house we saw lamb's quarter,* which was more than seven feet high. This plant was, at that time, almost too old for use, but until then it had proved a

* Chenopodium album.

very valuable addition, at our meals, to the extremely small ration of biscuit, which, at that time, was reduced to about one ounce per day for each man. At Mr. Moore's we ate of a very good fish, called the buffalo fish. We had met, on the bluff which commands his house, two Indian lodges, in one of which was Tantanka Wechacheta* (the buffalo man), an Indian who claims the command of the Wahkpatoans. We had declined his invitation to stay at his lodge in the afternoon, being desirous of reaching Mr. Moore's house as early as possible, but we promised to return about sunset, and he accordingly made all due preparations to receive us. The chief, and his principal men were in waiting. We entered the skin lodge, and were seated on fine buffalo robes, spread all round; on the fire, which was in the centre of the lodge, two large iron kettles, filled with the choicest pieces of buffalo, were placed. When the chief took his seat, he had near him a large pouch or bag, decorated with but little taste, although he seemed to have gathered up all that he could collect in the way of ornament. Among other things we observed an old and dirty comb. He had, since our first visit, bedaubed his face with white clay. Tatanka Wechacheta is a young man, slender, but well formed, rather tall, with a wide mouth, large eyes, which, when we saw him, had an unusual expression of fierceness, from being remarkably bloodshot; otherwise we should judge that his appearance would be prepossessing. Among the many Dacotas with whom we have met, few present any remarkable expression of cunning, still less those dreadful looks which distinguished the Potawatomi partizan

* Tåtånkå Wĕchåchĕtå.

Metea. Their faces are faithful indices to the equanimity of their souls; yet the action of the muscles and the bones of the face are not concealed, as they often are in the white man, by a load of flesh. This, together with his deep sunk eye, renders the Indian capable, on great provocation, of assuming and exhibiting the most terrific passion. On the right of the chief sat one who is held in high veneration by his tribe, being the greatest medicine or magic man among them. His cures are considered as miraculous; they are wrought by spells as well as by herbs, with which he is considered to be very conversant. In his countenance it was not difficult to discover a mixed expression of knavery and hypocrisy. Soon after our arrival at the lodge, an Indian entered it, whom it required but little skill in physiognomy, to mark out immediately as a stranger; his complexion was, at least, one shade darker than that of the Dacotas; his features differed materially; his face was rounder and shorter; his mouth was wider; his eyes had more of the European than native American character; he appeared to be very old; his locks were hoary; his face bore perhaps the character of an old Frenchman, more than of any other nation. We were informed that he was an Assiniboin, who had been made a prisoner many years since. He seemed to be kindly treated, though a sort of butt for the jokes of the Dacotas, whether men, women, or children. After the customary preliminaries of shaking of hands, smoking the pipe of peace, &c. we proceeded to the feast, which we found excellent. The buffalo meat had been selected with care, the fat and lean judiciously portioned out, the whole boiled to a proper degree, and, in fine, though our appetites were not stimulated by a long fast, this repast appeared to us one of the best of which we had ever partaken. Our hosts were gratified and flattered at the quantity which we ate; the residue of the feast was sent to our soldiers. In this, and every other instance, where we have been invited to a feast by the Indians, we observed that they never eat with their guests.

Tatanka Wechacheta is the nephew of a man of considerable distinction among the Wahkpatoan Dacotas. Since the death of his uncle, which took place lately, he has attempted to be considered as his successor; but the former was never duly acknowledged as chief, this title residing in Nunpakea, a man of considerable bravery, who, by the influence of his family and of his talents, acquired that dignity, in preference to his first cousins, on the death of their father.

Our host boasted of the many flags and medals which his uncle had obtained from our government, and which were then in his possession; these, and the influence of his great magician, may probably secure to him the dignity to which he aspires, if he has talent enough to uphold it. After the feast was over, our host rose, shook hands with all the gentlemen of our party, then resumed his seat, and delivered a speech, which, at the time, appeared to us very pertinent and interesting. It was delivered with apparent feeling, but not without some hesitation; his gestures were vehement and unmeaning. Having expressed to Renville our satisfaction at the speech, he immediately observed that it expressed too much adulation, and too much whining; had Tatanka Wechacheta been the chief that he professed himself to be, his tone would have been more imposing, and his style more dignified and decisive. We have preserved the following very imperfect sketch of this speech:—

"Brothers, The subject, upon which I am to address you, is grievous to me; and this grief is the motive which has thus far prevented me from speaking to you. Since the lamented death of my revered uncle, who died last year, I have been called upon to succeed to him, but as I am not endued with experience to know how to direct myself, I shall follow the advice which I have received from him, and therefore I rejoice at seeing you, and I am gratified by your visit.

"I regret that my followers are now all absent. This is not the season when we, the Indians, are together; this is our hunting season. In the autumn, we collect in our villages to meet the traders. Had you seen us thus collected, you would have found me at the head of a large and powerful band of men, at present I am alone; still I am pleased to see you.

"Brothers, There are two roads which we the Dacotas usually travel; my uncle trod both these paths. The first led him to the British, far towards the rising sun. From them he received both kindness and honour; they made him many presents, among which were flags and medals. The other road led him to the Americans at St. Louis; this road he subsequently travelled. From them he, in like manner, received flags and medals. These he has bequeathed all to me.

"I should have unfurled my flags at your approach, but I am unacquainted with the customs of your nation, and I am new in the duties of my rank. I am ignorant how to act; but I am desirous of following the advice of my dying uncle, who bade me remain at peace with the Americans, and always consider them as my friends; and as such I hold you.

"My Friends, I am poor and very destitute; not so

was my uncle. But I have as yet followed neither of the roads which he travelled. Since I have been called upon to rule over my people, I have dwelt among them, and have not been able to visit St. Louis, in order to obtain presents of powder and tobacco.

"I have already told you that my followers are absent. They are hunting to the north; I have left with them my flags; I know not whither you are going; but I presume you may meet with them. They will exhibit to you my flags; and you will know them, for they are those of your nation. I shall send them word of your intention to travel that way, and bid them, if they see you, treat you with becoming respect, assist you, supply you with provisions, and with whatever else you may require.

"My Friends, I am poor, and could not do much; but I have prepared this little feast; you have partaken of it, and it has gratified me. I am young and inexperienced in speaking, but I have done my best. Again, I thank you for your flattering visit."

CHAPTER VIII.

Account of the Dacotas or Sioux Indians. Their divisions into tribes. Their numbers, language, manners, and customs. Notice of Wanatan, principal chief of the Yanktoanan tribe. Description of the Columbia Fur Company's establishment on Lake Travers.

WE have collected together all the information which we have obtained on the subject of the Dacotas. It results, either from our own observations, or from conversations with those able to communicate facts, either at Prairie du Chien, Fort St. Anthony, or Lake Travers. He who has contributed most to it is Renville; we are aware that all the information which he has given us cannot be depended upon. He was uneducated, not free from prejudices, not entirely exempt from the superstitions of his mother's countrymen. His opportunities of improvement, but more especially his inquiring mind, had made him sceptical upon many points; still upon some he appeared credulous: we believe it not impossible, that he may sometimes have attempted to give information which he did not possess, or to exaggerate truths into fictions. We, at the time, carefully recorded all that he told us, and have since made use of such parts only as appeared to us correct, endeavouring to omit all that may have sprung from ignorance, credulity, or a taste for the marvellous.

The Dacotas are a large and powerful nation of Indians, distinct in their manners, language, habits, and opinions, from the Chippewas, Sauks, Foxes, and Naheawak or Killisteno, as well as from all nations of the Algonquin stock. They are likewise unlike the Pawnees and the Minnetarees or Gros Ventres. They inhabit a large tract of country which may be comprised within the following limits:—From Prairie du Chien on the Mississippi by a curved line extending east of north, and made to include all the eastern tributaries of the Mississippi, to the first branch of Chippewa river; the head waters of that stream being claimed by the Chippewa Indians; thence by a line running west of north to the head of Spirit Lake; thence by a westerly line to the Rivière de Corbeau; thence up that river to its head near Otter-tail Lake; thence by a westerly line to Red River, and down that river to Pembina; thence by a south-westerly line to the east bank of the Missouri near the Mandan villages; thence down the Missouri* to a point probably not far from Soldier's River; thence by a line running east of north to Prairie du Chien. This tract includes about seven degrees of latitude, viz. from the 42° to the 49°, and nine of longitude, viz. from 90° 30′ to 99° 30′. These boundaries, as well as all the subsequent facts which we shall state, do not apply to the Assiniboins, a revolted band of the Dacotas, who separated from them a long time ago, and who reside to the north of the 49th degree of latitude. We will have occasion to recur to them hereafter.

This immense extent of country is inhabited by a nation calling themselves, in their internal relations, the Dacota,† which means the allied, but who, in their external relations style themselves the Ochente Shakoan,‡

---

* According to Lewis and Clarke, they hunt on both banks of the Missouri and its tributaries, from the 43d to the 47th degree of latitude. (vol. 1. p. 61.)

† Dăcŏtă.   ‡ Ochĕntĕ Shăkŏăn.

which signifies the nation of seven (council) fires. This refers to the following division which formerly prevailed among them, *viz.*

1. Mende Wahkan toan, or people of the Spirit Lake.
2. Wahkpa toan, or people of the Leaves.
3. Sisi toan, or Mia Keckakesa.
4. Yank toan an, or Fern leaves.
5. Yank toan, or descended from the Fern leaves.
6. Ti toan, or Braggers.
7. Wahkpako toan, or the people that shoot at leaves.

These form two great divisions, which have been distinguished by the traders into the names of Gens du Lac, and Gens du Large. Those that resided about Spirit Lake, and who are now principally found along the banks of the Mississppi; and those that rove in the prairies; these may be considered as including all the six last tribes.

All the Dacotas speak the same language; yet some distinctions of the nature of dialects appear to prevail in some words, as spoken by the roving or by the stationary Indians. From the circumstance of these differences being trifling, we are led to believe, that the seven tribes were originally one, and that the name of Dacota, or allied, must not be considered as implying an union or amalgamation of different nations. We hope that we shall not be accused of indulging in a fanciful comparison, when we observe that we see, in the use of this word by them, the same meaning as it has with us; probably they sprung from one common root, divided into tribes according to their local distribution upon the surface of the country, and then, speaking the same language, and having the same enemies, they found it convenient to unite in one confederacy for their mutual safety. We do not, however, profess to have a sufficient acquaintance with their language, or with philology in general, to decide the question. Perhaps one skilled in this science could discover in their language a combination of several originally distinct tongues. If such ever existed, all recollection of it has been effaced among them.

To ascertain the number of any Indian tribe has always been considered one of the greatest desiderata, but at the same time one of very difficult attainment. The numbers of this nation have been variously stated by different travellers. We have had no opportunity of forming any opinion of our own on this subject; but they have been represented to us by all who knew them as extremely numerous. We have already stated, in another place, that we had seen lodges large enough to hold fifty inhabitants. We have likewise to observe, that they chiefly subsist upon the buffalo, an animal which exists in herds* of tens of thousands on the prairies between the Missouri and Mississippi, and which, within a few years past, was extremely abundant east of the Mississippi; from this it may be argued, that the means of subsistence far exceed the consumption of a much larger population than has ever been ascribed to the Dacotas. It must likewise be remembered, that it is a characteristic of the Indian never to destroy more than he can consume; in this, differing much from the white hunter, who will frequently kill a buffalo for its tongue or its marrow bones, leaving the rest of the animal as a

* The term *band*, as applied to a herd of buffalo, has almost become technical, being the only one in use in the west. It is derived from the French term *bande*.

prey to the wolves. In the destruction of the buffalo, the white man cannot even plead the inducements of trade, since a great many are killed whose hides are never turned to use. With these observations we will offer a census of the population of the Dacotas, as furnished to us by Renville, remarking, however, that it is usually considered as exaggerated.

Names of villages or parties of Dacotas.	No. of lodges.	Warriors.	Souls.
Gens du lac, or Mendewahkantoan.			
1. Keoxa (Wapasha's, &c.)	40	70	400
2. Eanbosandata (Red Wing's)	10	25	100
3. Kapoja (Petit Corbeau's)	30	70	300
4. Oanoska (Black Dog's)	30	40	200
5. Tetankatane	10	30	150
6. Taoapa	30	60	300
7. Weakaote	10	10	50
Gens du large, or roving Dacotas.			
8. Miakechakesa (or Sisitons)	130	260	1000
9. Wahkpakota	100	200	800
10. Wahkpatoan	120	240	900
11. Kahra (a band of the Sisitons)	160	450	1500
12. Yanktoanan	460	1300	5200
13. Yanktoan	200	500	2000
14. Tetoans	900	3600	14,400
Adding for stragglers	100	200	800
	2330	7055	28,100
Strength of the Hoha or Assiniboins	3000	7000	28,000
Total force of the Dacotas (before their division)	5330	14,055	56,100

SOURCE OF ST. PETER'S RIVER. 397

Previous to their division the Assiniboins belonged to the Yanktoanan tribe.

The above estimate falls somewhat short of that which Renville made some time before, when he was in the service of the Hudson's Bay Company. He then visited all the Dacota villages, camps, &c. and by a close calculation estimated the number of warriors, exclusive of the Assiniboins, at 7,600. This band, having always been estimated at very nearly the same number as all the other Dacotas, will give an aggregate (according to these data), of 15,000 warriors. Admitting the proportion of one-fourth the nation able to bear arms, which is probably very near the truth, it would give as a total 60,000 souls; who would occupy about 6000 lodges. In counting the lodges we allude to the skin tents which contain from eight to ten individuals, young and old; for the permanent cabins on the Mississippi contain from three to ten families each, and it is said that one cabin, has, in some cases, furnished from fifteen to twenty warriors.

As almost every traveller, who has visited the Dacotas, has given a different enumeration of their divisions; some reckoning but seven, while others admit as many as twenty-one tribes; it may be well to observe that this distribution into fifteen parties is merely introduced with a view to facilitate a better acquaintance with the nation. We believe that there are but seven tribes among the Dacotas, as their name of Ochente Shakoan implies; the divisions which we have admitted in the Mende Wahkantoan, are probably not very important, and we know that similar ones exist among the several tribes of roving Dacotas; we have no doubt that the Tetoans are divided into many parties, such as the Tetons of the Burnt wood, the Tetons Okandandas, Tetons Mennakenozzo, Tetons Saone, &c. as enumerated by Lewis and Clarke. If we have not made use of any of these divisions in most of the other tribes, it is because we could not obtain them so accurately, and also because they are less important : a hunter, who has no fixed residence, will willingly pass from one party of Indians to another, belonging to the same tribe as he does, and this he will be ready to do at any time ; but he who has his lodge, his cornfields, &c. is much more inclined to attach himself to the village in which he lives; and, accordingly, we find that the residences of the Dacotas, on the Mississippi, &c. are still, for the most part, kept up in the same places, where Carver saw them in 1766.

The population of the Dacotas varies, according to the different travellers. Carver estimates the Naudowessies of the plains, (independent of those of Spirit lake), at upwards of two thousand; but as he includes in these the Shiennes and Omawhaws, who, at present at least, form distinct nations, it is evident that we can draw no conclusion from his statement. Lewis and Clarke establish their numbers at about two thousand five hundred and fifty warriors, which upon the data of one warrior to four souls, admits a population of about ten thousand; but this is undoubtedly far under the truth. Pike states their population at twenty-one thousand six hundred and seventy-five, including three thousand eight hundred and thirty-five warriors. We believe the aggregate which he gives is nearly correct, but that he allows too few warriors. Among such Indians as have partially acquired habits of civilized life, the proportion of one warrior in five souls may be very nearly true; but among the roving bands, which constitute the majority of the Dacotas, we would not admit the ratio to be less than one to four; for the number of children and old men is proportionally much smaller. Youths are, at a very early age, counted as warriors; probably every male, above the age of sixteen, may, in reality, be enumerated as such.*

From these observations we are led to admit, that the population of the Sioux nation cannot be under twenty-five thousand souls, and that it includes at least six thousand warriors.

The following synopsis of the usual residence of the Dacotas, and of the actual state of the villages or parties above alluded to, may be of use as a term of comparison for future travellers.

1. KEOXA.—Their chief is Wapasha; they have two villages on the Mississippi, (one on Iawa river, the other near Lake Pepin); they hunt on both banks of the Mississippi, near Chippewa river and its tributaries. The chief holds his situation by hereditary tenure; his father was a great warrior; the present chief is a wise man, addicted to agriculture. Keoxa signifies "relationship overlooked," because they unite or have connexion between nearer relations than the other Dacotas; first cousins, uncles, and nieces, and even brothers and sisters intermarry.

2. EANBOSANDATA means "vertical rock," from a rock on Cannon River. Their chief is Shakea, who has

* Vide Carver, ut supra, p. 50—Lewis and Clarke, vol. i, p. 60.—Pike, appendix to Part I, p. 66.

always been considered as dependent upon Wapasha; he rose to his station by military talents. They have two small villages, one on the Mississippi, the other on Cannon river; they hunt on the head waters of that stream.

3. KAPOJA means "light;" they are supposed to be more active than the other Dacotas. Their present chief is a very distinguished man, and belongs to one of the oldest families of chiefs among the Dacotas, he being the fourth of his family in direct line. At a meeting of many Indian nations, which took place at Lake Travers about four or five years ago, there were present, besides some men from all the tribes of Dacotas, many from the Assiniboins, Mandans, Minnetarees, Iawas, and other nations, who all addressed him by the name of "Father," acknowledging thereby, not only his superiority over all the other Dacota chiefs, but even that of the Dacota nation over theirs. At this meeting they exchanged and renewed pledges of friendship, &c. The festivities which lasted about a fortnight, consisted of dances, songs, and repasts; the principal feast was celebrated on the 25th of June. Buffaloes were then very abundant in the country, and a great number were killed. The chief to whom the flattering distinction of *Father* was thus applied, is the same that is generally called Petit Corbeau by the traders, Chetanwakoamane by the Dacotas.* Renville interpreted for this Indian at the time when he visited the Drummonds island, in 1815. He reproached the British government for the situation in

---

* This chief formed one of the deputation who visited the City of Washington, in July, 1824.

which they left the Indians. When told by Colonel M'Coy, the Indian agent for the British, that he acted in compliance with one of the stipulations in the treaty with the United States, the chief replied, that the British government had deceived them; they were at peace with the Americans in 1812; but they had been excited to acts of hostility; at the time that he spoke, they were at war with the United States, having been instigated to it by the British, who then deserted them. He could not believe that it was on account of their stipulations; he summoned them to fulfil their promises, or he must charge them with fraud and cowardice. When he was invited to settle in Canada, and assured of support and maintenance for himself and his band, he indignantly replied, that he required none of their support; he would fight, and himself obtain peace for his nation, and they would support themselves upon their own lands. The Kapoja Indians have but one village, which is on the Mississippi, below the St. Peter; they hunt on the St. Croix river.

4. OANOSKA signifies great avenue. Wamendetanka, (War Eagle,) their chief, was formerly a dependant on Petit Corbeau. He has but one village on the St. Peter; he hunts on the Mississippi, above the Falls of St. Anthony.

5. TETANKATANE, (Old Village.) This is the oldest village of the Dacotas. At the time when Wapasha's father ruled over the nation, there were four hundred lodges there. Wapasha formerly lived in that village, but having removed from it with the greater part of his warriors, a few preferred remaining there, and chose one of their number as a leader. His son, Takopepe-

shene,*(Dauntless,) now rules over them. He is considered a dependant of the next following chief; he has but one village on the St. Peter, three miles above its mouth; he hunts on this river and the Mississippi.

6. Taoapa. The chief of this party is called Shakpa,† which means six. He inherited his station, and is a distinguished man, ranking in the nation third only to Wapasha and Petit Corbeau. He has but one village: it is situated on the St. Peter, between which river and the Mississippi he hunts.

7. Weakaote. A small band which is dependant upon the preceding.

8. Meakechakesa derives its name from a point in the river which has been cut off and forms an island. Their chief is called Wahkanto, or "blue spirit;" he rules by right of his family. His tribe has no fixed villages, no mud or bar cabins like all the preceding tribes; they reside all the year round in skin lodges, which they shift from place to place. Their chief rendezvous is on the Blue Earth river; they hunt upon that stream in winter; during the summer season they pursue the buffalo as far as the Missouri.

9. Wahkpakota, or the "shooters at leaves," which they mistake for deer. Their last leader was Shakeska, (White Nails,) who died in 1822. This tribe has a very bad name, being considered to be a lawless set of men. Shakeska rose to his station by his military talents. They have a regular hereditary chief, Wiahuga, (the Raven,) who is acknowledged as such by the Indian agent, but who, disgusted by their misbehaviour, withdrew from them and resides at Wapasha's. This

---

* Tăkŏpĕpĕshĕnĕ.   † Shăkpă.

measure would have been disapproved of in ordinary cases, but, owing to the bad name which they have, he is considered as justifiable in deserting his tribe. They have no fixed villages; they inhabit skin lodges, and rove near the head of Cannon and Blue Earth rivers. Their hunting grounds are in that vicinity and westward of it.

10. WAHKPATOAN means " the people beyond those that shoot at leaves," because they live higher up on the river. Nunpakea (twice flying) is the name of their chief. One of the deeds by which he has acquired respect as a warrior, was achieved at the age of twenty. He was, with a party of Dacotas, on the lands of the Chippewas, and was encamped on the edge of a lake; an island opposite to his camp was occupied by a considerable party of Chippewas; in the middle of the night, he swam over alone to the island, killed one of the enemies, scalped him, and returned unobserved to his friends with the scalp of his enemy. This tribe hunts near Ottertail Lake, one of the sources of Red river.

11. KAHRA, (Wild Rice.) These Indians dwell in very large and fine skin lodges. The skins are well prepared and handsomely painted. They have no permanent residence, but frequently visit Lake Travers. Their hunting grounds are on Red river. They follow Tatankanaje, (the Standing Buffalo,) who is a chief by hereditary right, and who has acquired distinction as a warrior.

12. YANKTOANAN, (the Fern Leaves.) This is one of the most important tribes, as its population amounts to one-fifth that of the whole nation. They have no fixed residence, but dwell in fine skin lodges, well dressed and decorated. Their hunting grounds are very extensive,

spreading from Red river to the Missouri. They frequent, for purposes of trade, Lake Travers, Big Stone Lake, and the Shienne river. Their principal chief is Wanotan, (the Charger,) of whom we shall speak hereafter.

13. YANKTOAN, (descended from the Fern leaves,) are in every respect similar, and probably separated from the last mentioned. Their leader, Tatanka Yuteshene* (he who eats no buffalo), is distinguished both as an hereditary chief and as a warrior. They frequent the Missouri, and generally traffic with the traders upon that river. Their hunting grounds are east of, and adjoining to, the Missouri.

14. TETOANS, (Braggers.) According to Renville, this tribe includes one-half of the Dacotas, and it is probably here that his calculations are most likely to be erroneous. They reside in skin lodges, and are constantly roving between the St. Peter and the Missouri. They trade on both rivers, and are held to be very hostile to white men; they are great boasters, and hence their name. They are not considered braver than the other tribes. Their chief, Chantapeta†, (Heart of Fire,) is a very powerful warrior.

We may add of the Assiniboins, whom the Dacotas call the Hoha, (revolted,) that they formerly belonged to the tribe of the Yanktoanan. They boast of having upwards of 3000 skin lodges, of which Renville once saw three hundred pitched in one place. Their grounds are north of Pembina, towards the Assiniboin river, and west of Lake Winepeek. They are at war with the Blackfeet Indians, and are said to send war parties every

---

* Tàtànkà Yùtèshènè.   † Chàntàpètà.

year as far as the Rocky Mountains. They have been fighting the Dacotas ever since their separation; but there seems to be at present a mutual tendency to a reunion. Their present chief rose by his military achievements; his name is Minayoka (Knife-bearer).

The cause of the separation of the Assiniboins from their former friends is variously related. The following has appeared to us to be the prevalent tradition on this subject. It is said that, about fifty years* ago, a quarrel arose between two influential families of the Yanktoanans, at the time that they were hunting in the vicinity of Lake Travers. A young man, belonging to one of these families, seduced the wife of one of the warriors of the other family, and conveyed her to his camp. The injured husband pursued them, and, in his attempt to rescue his wife, was himself slain. His father and two brothers, accompanied by two of his uncles, went to the seducer's camp, with a view to obtain the corpse of their deceased relation. On their way to the camp, they met with a party of the friends of the murderer; a quarrel ensued, and three out of the five perished, without having succeeded in killing one of their opponents. The distressed parent survived this conflict, and, swearing that he would avenge his losses, he betook himself to a camp of his friends, stated his wrongs, and obtained a party of sixty warriors who marched out with him. They proposed to the aggressor's friends to compromise the matter, by delivering over two of their party to the parent, so that he might offer them as propitiatory victims to the spirits of his four departed kinsmen. This

* The separation probably occurred at a much earlier period. Dates are soon forgotten by Indians. Hennepin mentions a nation of the Assinipoils, who probably are the same. Charlevoix calls them Assiniboils.

offer having been rejected, a battle was fought, in which the seducer lost twenty of his party; his opponents lost but five. It would be needless to go through the long list of engagements fought, or to relate how each party, as often as it was vanquished, swore revenge against its enemies, and recruited itself among its friends. Suffice it to say, that the breach widened; the nation was divided; a long and bloody civil war ensued; the aggressor and his friends withdrew to the north, ceased to pay any allegiance to the confederacy, and formed a new nation, to which the term Hòha, which means revolted, was applied by the Sioux. The Chippewas, who call the Dacota nation Boines, distinguished the insurgents by the term of Assini Boines, which, according to some interpreters, means revolted Boines, but which, by the greater number, is supposed to be derived from the Chippewa word Assin, which signifies stone. Ever since this band has been known under the name of Assiniboin, or of Stone Indians. Whence the Chippewa derived this last appellation, we know not; but we believe we have been told, that it was from the frequent use of stones, as a weapon of defence by the Hohas. Henry describes the instrument and the manner of using it.

The Dacotas have no tradition of having ever emigrated, from any other place, to the spot upon which they now reside; they believe that they were created by the Supreme Being on the lands which they at present occupy. Of the origin of white men they have no idea, having never reflected upon the subject; they have preserved a faint tradition of their first meeting with a white man, but who this was, and when it took place, they are unable to tell. They believe that he was a Frenchman, and that he was first discovered by a party of Mende Wahkantoan; as soon as the Dacotas saw him they were much surprised at his dress and complexion; they took him prisoner, secured him, and brought him to their camp. He had in his hand a gun. By means of signs they asked him the use of that instrument; he pointed out to them that with it he could take away the life of any object he pleased; they then placed a man before him, challenging him to the proof of what he had advanced; upon his refusal to do it, they placed a dog before him, which he immediately shot and killed. Terrified at the report of the gun, they all ran off, considering him as the spirit of the thunder; as he remained there, they returned to him, called him by the name of Thunder, and held him in great awe and veneration.

Their first discovery by white men is referred by Charlevoix* to the year 1660, when he states that they were met by two Frenchmen proceeding west from Lake Superior. Father Hennepin's visit to the Falls of St. Anthony did not take place till upwards of twenty years after this. Previous to Charlevoix's writings, the Dacotas had been referred to a Chinese origin. This idea is supported by Carver, but upon such weak analogies of language as must surprise us, when advanced by one who certainly was not destitute of judgment and observation. Pike ascribes to them a Tartarean origin, on the ground of " their guttural pronunciation, their high cheek bones, their visages and distinct manners, together with their own traditions, supported by the testimony of neighbouring nations."

The Dacotas have a very simple system of religion. They believe in the existence of a Supreme Being, and

---

Hist. de la Nouv. France, tom. 2. p. 98.

of a number of subordinate ones, whose powers, privileges, and attributes vary much. The Supreme Being is by them called Wahkan Tanka, or Great Spirit. They worship him, considering him as the Creator of all things that exist, and as the Ruler and Disposer of the Universe; they hold him to be the source of all good, and the cause of no evil whatever. The next spirit in respect to power, is the Wahkan Shecha, or evil spirit; his influence is far less extensive than that of the Wahkan Tanka, and it is exclusively exerted in the performance of evil. He is co-eternal with the former, incapable of doing any good, the promoter of all wars, strifes, &c. Although partially under the control of the Great Spirit, yet it is not in the power of the latter entirely to check him. Their third divinity is the Thunder, for which they have the greatest awe. They fix its residence to the west, and some believe it to dwell upon the summit of the Rocky Mountains. It is almost unnecessary to add, that all thunder storms in that section of the country proceed from the west. To each of these spirits they extend their worship. It has been incorrectly stated of the Dacotas that they do not worship the Supreme Being, thinking it unnecessary to supplicate an all-bountiful power. On the contrary, they offer sacrifices to the Great Spirit, in gratitude for favours received. In sacrificing to the evil spirit, their object is to propitiate him, to induce him to avert his anger from them, or to extend to them his support in war. But it is the Thunder which is considered as the main agent in warlike operations, and to it do they chiefly apply for victory. Sacrifices to these three powers are offered nearly in the same manner. They begin by elevating a pipe towards the spirit. He who gives or ordains the sacrifice, after having addressed the being to whom it is offered, takes up the calumet, and raises the stem upwards towards the sky, if it be intended for the good spirit; if for the evil deity, he points the stem towards the south; if for the thunder, the pipe is directed to the west. When it is intended that the object sacrificed shall remain exposed to the atmosphere, it is fastened upon a stake, which is elevated or inclined in like manner. Human sacrifices are not known to have ever been resorted to, except in one instance about forty years ago. The Sioux had destroyed several Chippewa lodges, and taken a few women and children. Wamendetanka's father, who was a partizan warrior, expressed his belief that the sacrifice of a child would ensure him good luck. Accordingly he offered one to the evil spirit to obtain success in war. The child was fixed upon a pole, which was inclined towards the south; the death of the victim was procured by tying a rope round its neck. In addition to these three principal deities, the Dacotas acknowledge many subordinate ones; a female spirit, for instance, resides in the sun, a male inhabits the moon; both these are connected; they are considered as benevolent beings. No particular doctrine prevails as to the nature of the stars. The sacrifices of the Dacotas are accompanied with prayers, but not with dances. If one of the nation should observe any object elevated by another on a pole, as a sacrifice to a spirit, and he be at that time in need of the same, he will not hesitate to take it, substituting some tobacco or other offering in its place. This is, however, practised only with the offerings to the inferior spirits; for no Dacota would dare to remove that consecrated to the Supreme Being.

The ideas of the Dacotas, respecting a future state, differ but little from those of other Indians; and we may receive them with less diffidence, as they have had but little intercourse with missionaries, whether Catholic or otherwise; still, in some of their credences, as related to us, it was impossible not to discover a few of the doctrines of Christianity, which had probably crept in unnoticed by them. The Dacotas admit that there are in man two distinct essences, to which they respectively apply the terms of Wanare* and Wahkan,† which our interpreters translate by soul and spirit. They believe that after death the souls go to the Wanare Tebe, or dwelling-place of the souls: that, in order to reach it, they have to pass over a rock, the edge of which is as sharp as that of a knife; those who fall off go to the region of the evil spirit, where they are kept constantly chopping wood, carrying water, &c. being frequently flogged by their relentless master.

Those, on the contrary, that have passed safe over the rock, have a long journey to travel; and as they proceed they observe the camping places of the souls that have preceded them; at these spots fires are ready made for their accommodation; finally, they reach the habitation of the Wahkan Tanka, or Great Spirit. There they find many villages of the dead; they meet with some spirits there, who point out to them the way to the residence of their friends and relations, with whom they are reunited. Their life is an easy and a blissful one, they hunt the buffalo, plant corn, &c. It is believed, that when children are on the point of death, their departed relations return from the land of souls in order to convey

* Wănărĕ. † Wăhkăn.

them thither. Women are liable to go to either of the places, but all are entitled to a situation in the land of the blessed, except such as have violated their chastity, committed infanticide or suicide.

Their system of Ethics is as simple. Men are held to go to the residence of the Great Spirit if they be good and peaceable, or if they die by the hand of their enemy. If they perish in a broil with their own countrymen, their souls are doomed to the residence of the Evil Spirit. Suicide is with them attended with the same penalty as with women, but it is of very rare occurrence. Women are, in their opinion, bound at all times, whether single or married, to be chaste. If an unmarried female prove otherwise, she usually endeavours to conceal her shame by procuring abortion; this is held to be highly criminal; but it is the cause and not the act of abortion which is censured; for married females frequently obtain miscarriages with the knowledge and consent of their husbands, and to this no objection is made. Widows that prove with child, seldom resort to the same means, but they endeavour to conceal the birth of their offspring; and this is considered as equally criminal. Suicide is very common among the Dacota women; they are impelled to it by extreme sorrow and affliction; but it is held dishonourable. As most women inflict it upon themselves by hanging, they are said to go to the regions of the wicked, dragging after them the tree to which they were suspended. This fact has already been recorded by Bradbury, who adds, that they are doomed for ever to drag this tree, and that for this reason they always suspend themselves to as small a tree as can possibly sustain their weight.

The Dacotas repel the charge of cannibalism with

great horror; they assert that they have never been guilty of it, but charge their neighbours with the crime. Renville states, as a circumstance for which he is willing to vouch, that he was present at the siege of Fort Meigs, in the year 1813. The fort was besieged by general Proctor, at the head of the British army, attended by a corps of about three thousand Indians, consisting of Dacotas, Patawatomis, Miamis, Ottowas, Wolves, Hurons, Winnebagoes, Shawanese, Sauks, Foxes, Menomonies, &c. They had all shared in the battle except the Dacotas, who had not yet engaged against the Americans, and who were then on their way to Quebec. While Renville was seated, one afternoon, with Wapasha and Chetanwakoamane, a deputation came to invite them to meet the other Indians, the object of the meeting not being stated; the two chiefs complied with the request. Shortly after, Frazier, (an interpreter,) came and informed Renville that the Indians were engaged in eating an American, and invited him to walk over to the place. He went thither, and found the human flesh cut up, and portioned out into dishes, one for each nation of Indians. In every dish, in addition to the flesh, there was corn. At that moment they called upon the bravest man in each nation, to come and take a portion of the heart and head; one warrior from each nation was allowed a fragment of this choice morsel. In the group of Indians present, there was a brave Dacota, the nephew of Chetanwakoamane, known by the name of the "Grand Chasseur." They invited him to step forward and take his share, and among others a Winnebago addressed him, and told him that they had collected their friends to partake of a meal prepared with the flesh of one of that nation that had done them so much injury. Before the

Sioux warrior had time to reply, his uncle arose and bade his nephew rise and depart thence; he then addressed himself to the Indians: "My friends," said he, "we came here, not to eat Americans, but to wage war against them; that will suffice for us; and could we even do that if left to our own forces? we are poor and destitute, while they possess the means of supplying themselves with all that they require; we ought not therefore to do such things." His comrade, Wapasha, added, "We thought that you, who live near to white men, were wiser and more refined than we are who live at a distance; but it must indeed be otherwise if you do such deeds." They then rose and departed. Renville is positive that he could not have been deceived, for it was the head, heart, both hands and feet of a man that he saw in the dishes; and he saw some of the warriors partaking of them. The British officers were in their camp, and not aware of the transactions that were going on among the Indians. When informed of them they expressed great dissatisfaction. Col. Dickson, having sent for the Winnebago who had first set this thing on foot, asked him what could impel him to such horrid deeds, when he coolly replied, that it was better for him to do as he did, than to behave as the Americans had done, who had burnt his house, killed his wife and daughter, and mutilated their corpses. Col. Dickson then bade him depart, and never again appear in his presence. Gen. Proctor gave him the same directions. It appears that the victim of this feast, whose name we could not ascertain, was a prisoner of the Winnebagoes, who killed him with a view to prepare the entertainment. It was not done for want of provisions, for at that time the camp was plentifully supplied; neither does it appear that, in this case, it was fondness for the taste of human flesh, but, doubtless, a desire to vent their rage and spleen upon their prisoner, which induced them to prepare and partake of this disgusting repast. The Dacotas have always spoken of such deeds in terms of the highest reprobation; and we heard of one case only as having happened among them; it occurred in the year 1811: during a very general famine, three women partook of the flesh of a man who had previously died of hunger; but even in this case, where they were urged by a necessity which probably no white man could have resisted, their conduct was generally blamed; and two of them having died a short time afterwards, their death was supposed to have been brought on by this food. The third still lives; she is regarded with horror by the rest of the nation, who also consider her present state of corpulence as produced by that fatal food; they state it, as their opinion, that she will die choked with the fat of the man of whom she ate.

We have heard some cases of cannibalism related of them by their neighbours, but none appeared so well substantiated as to be entitled to belief, especially as the opinion which we have adopted is supported by the uniform testimony of all the travellers who have visited them, from Hennepin to the present day.*

* It appears that Tommo (the Dacota who guided Major Long's party from Prairie du Chien) told Mr Colhoun that he had eaten of a Chippewa, called Hahatong; he spoke of it without any repugnance, pointed to his breast, saying that he had found that part to be the most delicate. This appears to be a solitary instance, and we only mention it because we wish to avoid the charge of concealing any fact that may affect our general position, that the Dacotas do not imitate their neighbours in this gratification of

The treatment of their prisoners, by the Dacotas, has generally been considered as kind; and we find that even as far back as the visit of that traveller, they deserved that character. Hennepin, who certainly was much addicted to exaggeration, and who might have been alarmed at innocent gestures, the intention of which he might mistake, has given such an account of the treatment which he received from them, as fully confirms our statement. Their enemies seem to place great confidence in this virtue of theirs, as is manifest from the following transaction, which happened about thirty years ago. A battle had been fought on Knife Lake between the Chippewas and Dacotas; two hundred warriors of the latter had surprised and cut up about fifteen of the former, killed their wives and children amounting to about forty, and taken eight or ten prisoners. They then withdrew to the village of Tetankatane on the St. Peter, which at that time consisted of about three hundred lodges. They were engaged in celebrating their victory and dancing the scalp dance; on looking round, one of the party was surprised to behold a warrior painted all over with black, and marked with ten streaks of vermillion which covered fresh wounds. He was immediately recognised to be a distinguished Chippewa chief, called, in his own language, Keche Wabesches, by the Sioux, Natapa Hecha, both which terms signify the Big Martin; it was the same chief who commanded the small party, the defeat of

a depraved appetite. Otherwise, we should have taken no notice of the fact, as the only interpreter at that time was George Wade, a youth whose qualifications in that capacity, both as to the knowledge of the language and integrity, we strongly suspect.

which they were then celebrating. Under cover of a blanket he had approached, thus near undiscovered, passed through the village, and it was only when he found himself in the presence of the warriors, that he dropped his mantle. In his left hand he held a calumet of peace, his right was raised to the heavens, as if calling for mercy. But his attitude was firm, his manner imposing and undismayed. He was immediately seized, and made to sit down; the warriors formed a circle to protect him against the insults of the women and children, the weak and the coward, who are generally prone to triumph over the unprotected. The intrusion of any enemy, while they were engaged at their sacred rites, was by many considered a mortal offence; those disposed to spare him sent word to Renville's father and some other French traders, who were encamped on the opposite side of the river; by the influence of the traders he was permitted to go over to their camp until his fate should be decided. After some deliberation, they determined upon sparing him; they formed a large ring of warriors convened in council, and, having summoned the chief, they asked him what had induced him to venture among them; he replied that, having searched the field of battle after their departure, he had not discovered the body of his young daughter, who was but five or six years of age, and concluded that she was a prisoner, he had resolved to come and claim her from them; the black colour, with which he was painted, was a symbol of his mortification; his wounds were still fresh. The Dacotas having agreed to release her, the prisoners were all brought up; he immediately recognized his daughter, wept over her, and embraced her. He remained two days among them, and was much feasted, the Dacotas expressing the greatest admiration of his valour. On his departure, they loaded his canoe with presents, and one hundred of them accompanied him, as a protection, as far as Rum river. During his stay he observed the scalps of his wife, brother, and other relations, and pointed each out. When asked by the warriors why he had not fought with the same desperate courage to resist their attacks, which he had manifested when he surprised them on the St. Croix river, he replied, it was not his courage, but his strength which had failed; he had fought until he fell senseless, being wounded in many places, both by arrows and fire-arms.

Instances have occurred, however, in which the Dacotas have killed their prisoners of war, and, in some cases, long after they had been taken. Thus, for example's sake, it is related of the mother of Takopepeshene, that she once killed a young Chippewa girl whom she had adopted as her daughter four or five years before. This she did to avenge the death of her nephews, who had been killed by the Chippewas; this occurrence took place in 1807: and some of the circumstances attending the eng*gement between the two nations, exhibit the great animosity which prevails between the Chippewas and Dacotas. The latter had, it is said, ascended Chippewa river on a hunting excursion, under the command of Shakea, the Redwing chief, when their leader informed them that he had dreamed of the near approach of their enemy. This prediction was unheeded; but the subsequent night, at about two o'clock, the camp was assaulted by the Chippewas, who gained some advantage over the Dacotas; finding them, however, more numerous than they had anticipated, the Chippewas withdrew, leaving the field to them. The Dacotas pursued and overtook them on an island covered with aspen: they fired the woods; the conflagration spreading over the island, many of the Chippewas perished. It is stated, that the Sioux boys afterwards amused themselves in cutting off the lower joint of the fingers of the slain, as well as strips of skin from their arms; and of these they made necklaces, &c.

The difficulties, misfortunes, and ill-treatment which attend prisoners among Indian nations, as well as the equanimity and perseverance which they manifest in order to effect their escape, appear almost incredible to those who are unacquainted with the Indian character; yet there can be no doubt in the minds of those who have made a study of it. The following narrative of the perils and adventures of a Yankton woman, whom we saw near Lake Travers, has been related to us under circumstances, which have almost banished scepticism, although it at first appears miraculous.

Her name was Shenanska,* or the White Buffalo Robe. When we saw her, she was about seventy years of age. She relates that, in her youth, while yet under twenty, she was taken captive by a party of Chippewas; the man to whose lot she fell was cruel and relentless; among other hardships, he obliged her to walk naked, for three days, before the whole party; and whenever, from fatigue, she slackened her pace, she was scourged by her captors. At last, on the third day, they reached a stream, where, fancying themselves secure from all pursuit, they prepared to sojourn some time; and that evening she was doomed to undergo a still more barbarous treatment, when a Chippewa warrior came in,

* Shĕnânskâ.

whose mind was more generous than that of the others; he declared himself her protector, and said he would adopt her as his daughter. Whether from his influence as a brave man, or from his decisive manner, or from some other motive she knows not, but she was relinquished, though reluctantly, by her former master; and her adopted father conveyed her to his family, which was far to the north. In the autumn they returned towards the Dacota lands, in pursuit of buffalo. Although the treatment which Shenanska had received from her adopted father was mild, yet her life was rendered unpleasant by his wife, who used her in an unfeeling manner. Considering the infant child of the Chippewa mother to be, in part at least, the cause of her troubles, Shenanska determined to destroy it; and on one occasion, while both parents were away, she stabbed it in the side with a moccassin awl. The infant immediately expired; she replaced it in its cradle. When, on her return to the lodge, the mother saw her child in the cradle, she inquired if it had been long sleeping: Shenanska replied in the affirmative. Having gone nearer to the infant, and discovered that it was dead, although she did not observe the wound, the mother instantly seized an axe, and struck a blow on Shenanska's head, who fell into a swoon. The blow was not a mortal one; she soon recovered from the effects of it, and having determined to make her escape, succeeded in leaving the lodge unobserved. She travelled towards the lands of her countrymen; and, after eleven days of a fatiguing march, during which she at one time suffered so much from hunger that she was forced to feed upon bits of skin and leather, collected at a deserted encampment, she found herself in sight of her native coteau, and was flattering herself with the hope of soon meeting with a party of her friends, when she fell in with a band of Assiniboins, mortal enemies to her tribe. From these she would have met with instant death, had not their chief interfered in her favour. By him she was treated kindly; but, after remaining a day in his camp, he advised her to make her escape, as otherwise she must fall a victim to the resentment of the party. He supplied her with provisions, a horse, and every thing she might require for the route. Again she started on a solitary journey, which lasted forty days, before she met her friends. On approaching their camp, her appearance was so much altered, that they knew her not. Her own father hesitated in recognizing her as his daughter; at last, when she spoke and mentioned her name, her friends all collected around her, while she related to them her adventures. After she had finished her narrative, her father seized his knife and stabbed himself, in testimony of the grief he experienced at all she had suffered; a mode of expressing sympathy for past troubles which, however, is not common among the Indians.

The Dacotas appear to take but little pains in the education of their children; they follow no regular system. What the children learn, on the subject of their religious opinions and traditions, is collected gradually, and altogether in the course of unpremeditated conversations. The only attention which they receive is towards the development of those qualifications, both of mind and body, which shall enable them to make active hunters and dauntless warriors. To rise early, to be inured to fatigue, to hunt skilfully, to undergo hunger without repining, are the only points to which the Dacota thinks it important to attend to in the education of his children. Corrections are never resorted to; they are never flogged; indeed, with the exception of occasionally throwing cold water upon them, to make them rise in a morning, they never resort to any authoritative measures, all which they consider as cruel and unnatural. Their fondness for their children is extreme, especially that of mothers for their daughters. It is not an uncommon thing to see a mother carry water, hew wood, and undergo much fatigue, to spare it to her daughters. This is especially the case with the mothers of those young Indian females, whom the traders take as their companions. It does not appear that the daughters feel the least compunction at the trouble which their parents undergo; they consider it all as a matter of course, being doubtless prepared to go through the same drudgery for their children when they shall require it.

No event appears of more importance to a Dacota parent than the bestowing of a name upon his offspring; it is attended with much ceremony; a large feast or sacrifice is prepared; the relations and friends are invited. The name which is given is generally one derived from some visible object in the heavens or earth. The infant is made to support a pipe, the stem of which is directed towards the object from which the name is taken; a sacrifice is offered to the spirit which is supposed to reside in that object. These sacrifices are extensive and costly; they consist of dogs and other animals, of skins, of scarlet cloth, tobacco, &c. It appears to us well established that this was originally an Indian institution, and not, as we at first apprehended, a mere imitation of the rejoicings which, among some Christian sects, attend the ceremony of naming a child. We are told of some Indian nations endeavouring to stimulate their youths into dreams, visions, &c.* but this has not appeared to us to be the case with the Dacotas: when dreams do occur, they are held to be favours, and much importance is attached to them, but no attempt is made to give rise to them.

Polygamy is allowed, and no regulations whatever exist upon this subject; it appears to be rather tolerated than encouraged; every man follows his inclination upon that point, and is esteemed neither more nor less on account of the number of his wives or children. It is probable that most men have more than one, though few have many wives. The Dacotas destroy neither their children nor their old relations; to the latter their conduct is perhaps not as kind and attentive as it ought to be; but they make up for it by their attachment to their children, who receive care and kind treatment in proportion to their wants. The practice of shaping the heads of infants is unknown to them.

The Dacotas have prophets among them, but none that are so distinguished as those of the Shawanese. They are always prepared to oppose the incredulous with several stories, or anecdotes, to which they assert that they were in most cases witnesses. It would be vain to attempt to convince them of their error on this point, probably because they are pleased with it, and are in no manner desirous of being convinced that it is but a delusion. Even the half-breed interpreters share in this belief; at least they profess themselves unable to account otherwise for the success that attends those prophecies. In relating two or three of these stories,

---

* Transactions of the Historical and Literary Committee of the American Philosophical Society. Philadelphia, 1819, vol. i. p. 238.

we deem it unnecessary for us to premise them, by stating that we are not believers in them, as Carver appears to have been in the prophecies of his friend, the chief Priest of the Killistinoes, but that we merely recite them in order to show how far credulity will extend.

About twenty years ago, a large party of Indians, collected near Lake Travers, were quite destitute of tobacco; not knowing how to procure any, they applied to Tatankanaje (Standing Buffalo), a prophet of some distinction, and the uncle of the present chief of the Kahras. This man usually carried about him a little stone idol, carved into a human shape; this he called his little man, and to it he always applied when consulted in the way of his profession. Tatankanaje being requested to advise the best means of obtaining tobacco, made answer to them, that if they would go to a certain place, which he pointed out to them, they would find his idol, and, by examining it, they would observe in its hand a piece of tobacco. They did as he bade them, and found in the little fellow's hand a piece about four inches long; this was brought to the camp, and was thought to redound much to the credit both of the prophet and the idol; but Tatankanaje then observed, that he would consult the little man, and ascertain where he had found the tobacco, and how he came by it. This he did by putting interrogatories to him, to which he pretended that audible answers were returned, though of the many present not one heard them beside himself. The purport of these answers, however, as he subsequently informed them, was, that at a spot on the St. Peter, near to Redwood river, there was a boat, loaded with goods; that her commander, a French trader, having been murdered by the Sioux, the crew had been alarmed, and had run away, leaving the boat unguarded, together with her cargo, consisting principally of tobacco; that the little man had seen her, and finding a piece of tobacco on a keg, had brought it up. The prophet having invited them to seek for it, they repaired to the spot, found the boat, took the tobacco, and returned the rest of the goods to the first French traders that passed up the river. This event happened, as we were informed, in the presence of Renville and Freniers, two French traders of reputation, both considered as intelligent and enlightened men; they were the fathers of the two half-breed traders with whom we were acquainted. The story is given with all the particulars that might be wished for; the name of the owner of the boat was Benjamin La Goterie, a name well known in that country. The story has been current ever since. The traders, who appear to credit it, state that it was impossible for the prophet to have visited the spot and returned without his absence being known, as the distance exceeds one hundred miles; from whom he received his intelligence they never knew. As to the Dacotas themselves, they never considered it possible that it might be a knavery of the prophet's, but attributed it altogether to his " mystic lore."

On another occasion, Tatankanaje acquired great reputation, in consequence of a prediction that he would lead a war party; that on the day which he appointed, and at a particular spot which he described, he would fall in with a camp of fifteen Assiniboin lodges, that he would attack and defeat them, kill a certain number of the enemy, and make a stated amount of prisoners: he predicted, in like manner, the loss of lives which would attend this victory. The event justified, as it is said the prediction; not only as to the general results, but even as to the circumstances of time, place, number of killed and wounded on both sides, and amount of prisoners taken from the enemy. Of course, so valuable a prophet was constantly resorted to for the recovery of stolen property, or of goods that were lost—for a knowledge of the fate of persons that were travelling—for the cure of diseases—and for all such other important points, upon which the credulity both of civilized and savage man induces them to lend a willing ear to the impositions of knaves. Of his talent in recovering property, we regret that we can only mention a circumstance in which the object at stake was very trifling. Some one had ventured to steal away the prophet's bridle; it was concealed in a lodge that formed one in a camp of one hundred lodges. The prophet took a mirror in his hand, and walked round the village, until, as he said, he saw the lost bridle reflected in his mirror: he entered the adjoining lodge, and recovered his property.

Not only do they prophecy, but they perform tricks of legerdemain, all which they ascribe to the success of their incantations. We are indebted to Mr. Charles Hess, a French trader, with whom Mr. Say had several conferences at Fort St. Anthony, for the account of a trick performed by an Assiniboin. The magician asserted, in Mr. Hess's presence, as well as in that of many Indians, that he could cause water to flow into an empty keg, though he might at that time be upon a dry prairie, and at a distance from any spring or stream. Mr. Hess having told him that he did not believe him, but that, if he succeeded, he would give him a keg of whiskey, the Indian offered to repeat the trick. He exhibited to them his keg, which they examined, and all judged to be empty. The bung was removed, the cask turned over, and no liquid issued from it. The Indian then commenced his incantations, raising his keg towards the heavens, dancing, and performing many unmeaning gestures; after which he presented it to the Indian chief that was present, bidding him to drink of the water which it contained; the latter drank of it, found it very good, and passed it to his neighbour; the cask was circulated, to the great satisfaction of all the Indians, who drank of its contents, and even Mr. Hess was convinced that the keg really held pure water. He was, however, unable to detect the deception, but supposed that a bladder filled with water had been fastened within the keg, and that, owing to the agitation communicated to it, the bladder had been burst by means of spikes, driven into the ends of the keg for that purpose; and that, in this manner, the water had been diffused throughout the keg. The magician claimed and obtained his reward; but, when alone with him, Mr. Hess charged him with being an impostor, and told him the manner in which he suspected that the trick had been performed. The magician confessed the truth of Mr. Hess's statement, but begged that he would not disclose it to the Indians.

The person who communicated this fact to us, is one of the most respectable traders whom we have seen; at the time that we met with him he was in great distress, owing to the recent loss of part of his family, aggravated by a very painful calculous disease under which he was then labouring, and which had induced him to visit the fort in hopes of obtaining relief from the surgeon of the garrison.

Having always traded with the Chippewas, married among them, and been considered as connected with them, he had entertained great apprehensions of the Dacotas; for the Indians generally extend to those that trade with their enemies the same animosity which they bear to those nations. About a year before the time when we saw him he was residing at Pembina, on Red river. Provisions became so scarce at that place, that the settlers were reduced to live upon lettuce seasoned with salt; about one hundred and fifty of them had gone out to hunt buffalo; and he at last resolved to go and join them, with four of the settlers and his family, consisting of two daughters. They had travelled five days across the prairie, killing game enough for a bare subsistence, and keeping a constant guard for fear of being surprised by the Yanktons, who rove over those prairies. The extent to which he carried his precautions shows the deep presentiment which oppressed him at the time; often, as he informed us himself, after his party had passed over the top of a gentle swell or little elevation in the prairie, he would cause them to halt, while he would turn back, and crawl along the ground to the top of the hill, then, raising his head above the surface, concealing it at the same time behind a little grass which he had cut for the purpose, observe whether there were Indians to be seen in any direction. His friends ridiculed his fears, and two of them separated from him: but the event proved how well-founded his apprehensions were. On the sixth day, his horse having broken the halter by which he was fastened, Mr. Hess left the camp in search of him, and soon caught him; his companions, at that moment, observed two buffaloes on the prairie, and as his horse was the fleetest, they called out to him to chase them; he did so, and was for awhile separated from his party. In leaving the encampment, the anxious parent advised them to be watchful, and it was with the utmost reluctance that he separated from them. While he was killing the buffalo, a dog came up to him; this excited his suspicions; he followed the dog back, and, after a long ride across the prairie, came to a small valley where he observed his cart, and flattered himself with meeting with his family. On approaching, his consternation was extreme, when he saw one of his companions feathered with arrows, scalped, and his feet separated from his legs. A little further lay his daughter, murdered, and with a knife still lodged in her breast; with streaming eyes he withdrew it; but it was too late—she was lifeless. He in vain rode three times round the place, in search of his other daughter; he could find no trace of her. At some distance he discovered the corpse of his other companion, likewise pierced with arrows.

The distracted parent remained for a while unable to resolve in his mind what course he ought to pursue: he attempted to dig a grave for the unfortunate victims; but, being only provided with a knife, he soon gave up this attempt as a vain one; he then determined to leave his dog to watch the corpses, and to return to Pembina for assistance. We cannot dwell upon the sad particulars of the feelings and sufferings of the agonized father as he left the body of one of his daughters, swearing that he would follow, even into the camp of his enemies, his other child, who, he still hoped, might have survived this calamity. After three days and nights spent in travelling on foot, without either rest or food, he at last reached Pembina. On hearing his sad tale, the inhabitants were so much panic-struck, that none at the settlement would venture with him into the prairie to inter his friends, and remove his cart and other property. Hearing, however, that his surviving daughter was in one of the Yankton villages, he set out with the desperate resolution of recovering her, or perishing in the attempt. At the termination of another arduous journey across the prairie, he reached the camp and was met by many Yanktons, one of whom, a tall athletic man, inquired of him whether he was a friend or foe. " You know me," said Charles Hess, "as your foe; you know me by the name of the Standing Bull; you know you have killed one of my daughters, and taken the other prisoner." The Indian stepped backwards and pointed his arrow at him; Mr. Hess levelled his gun at his opponent. The Dacota seeing this, relaxed his bow, and extended his hand to him. The Indians all complimented him upon his valour; they invited him to feast at most of the lodges. He saw his daughter; she informed him that she had been kindly treated, and that her master was unwilling to part with her. Two horses were offered for her release by some Indians of a neighbouring nation, who were passing that way, and who were friendly to Hess; these were refused: four horses were, in like manner, offered and refused. At last her master consented to release her for the following ransom, *viz.* two fathoms of scarlet cloth, two white blankets, two fathoms of blue *strouding*, a chief's coat, a tin kettle, two guns, one pair of fine pistols, a framed looking-glass and a paper one, two knives, six double handfuls of gunpowder, two hundred bullets, and a quantity of blue beads.

So high a ransom fell heavy upon this poor man, who had lost his little all at the same time that his daughter was taken prisoner : he had to resort to the other traders for assistance; and they bestowed it upon him with that generous sympathy which is more easily found among rude and uncivilized men than among the more refined. They supplied him with goods on a long credit; with these he returned to the camp, and ransomed his daughter, who, while he was relating this said tale to us, was sitting by, engaged in decorating a piece of leather with porcupine quills, a work in which the Chippewas excel. A circumstance which, we believe, added to the distress of the parent, was that he found some difficulty in prevailing upon his daughter to leave the Yanktons ; she had been so kindly treated that she cared but little about returning to her own father. We have not learned in what light she was considered, whether as a prisoner, or as an adopted daughter.

The uniform but laborious life, which these Indians lead, protects them against many of the diseases incident upon civilization, though it at the same time exposes them to some direful complaints, which their total ignorance of the healing art, and their superstitious confidence in their magicians, prevent them from curing. Among the diseases which are said to be unknown to the Dacotas, may be ranked the following, *viz.* intermittent fevers in the prairies which are distant from the Mississippi, and probably even in those which border upon that river above the Falls of St. Anthony, Plica Polonica, baldness, (?) nymphomania, spina bifida, and St. Vitus's dance, scurvy, coup de soleil, chlorosis, and leucorrhœa. Among those which are known, but which are of very rare occurrence, we will mention jaundice, decayed teeth, and tooth-ache; in dentition children suffer much; in such cases the gum is never cut, but the children are allowed smooth stones and other hard substances to rub against their gums. As a palliative for tooth-ache the root of the Gerardria is not unfrequently applied. Hydrophobia is prevented by cutting out the wounded part. Dysentery is not common; it is cured by the free use of sassafras. Deafness is rare, and deaf and dumb cases are exceedingly scarce. Their most prevalent disease is hepatitis, which is hereditary and very frequent. They use for its cure the oil of rattlesnakes and of other serpents, they say with some benefit; but Renville informed us that he had never seen a person affected with it, that was cured. Frozen limbs are common, and are sometimes lost. They have been cured by the use of a plant known by the traders under the name of the Vinaigrier, or Vinegar Plant. The Dacotas resist cold much better than white men. Hypochondriasis is very common; it affects them as it does white men; they attempt no other remedy but songs and dances. A woman, that was once affected with it, imagined that nothing would relieve her but cold water; she jumped into a stream where the water was only two feet deep, and she was drowned. Hernia is known, but not cured. Hysteria is also known. For dropsy they have no remedy. Diseases of the breast are very common, and are attributed to their constant smoking. Rickets occur in children, in which case they receive a great deal of nursing. Syphilis appears to have been communicated to the Dacotas by white men, and through the women who had intercourse with them; this disease was totally unknown to those residing on the St. Peter, previous to the establishment of the garrison at Fort St. Anthony; and it is generally believed, that the first case among them was that of Tommo (our guide), who was infected with it at Prairie du Chien. The small-pox was, in like manner, originally unknown to them; but it has proved very destructive, at different times, since their intercourse with white men; it exerted its influence very fatally about fifteen years ago; among the many instances of its baneful extension, it is related that, at that time, of forty or fifty individuals who resided in five lodges, only one survived this plague. The Dacotas appear to entertain no prejudice against the use of the vaccine matter: they have, in many cases, applied it when offered to them; the absence of the surgeon from his post at St. Anthony, at the time we passed through, prevented our ascertaining the success which he had met with among them; all the surgeons of our frontier posts ought to be abundantly supplied with the virus, and their stock of it occasionally renewed, until its increased consumption by the Indian will enable them to obtain from them fresh virus, as often as they may require it. The Dacotas have no mode of curing the small-pox, and almost every person affected with this disease falls a victim to it.

Venesection is resorted to by the Sioux in cases of contusions, head aches, and pains in the breast. To a wooden handle they fix a small blade of flint, which is covered with sinew except at its point; they apply it to the vein, which is then cut open by a slight fillip of the finger. They also draw blood by scarifying, and by suction. Poisoned weapons are used by them in their wars: Mr. Cameron, a trader, was poisoned by an Indian, who administered to him some of the plant used for that purpose.

The steam bath is prepared by them as by other Indians; but is not so usually practised as a remedy; it being resorted to for the purpose of obtaining good luck, and as a religious ceremony, in the manner which Dr. Richardson describes as having seen practised by a Cree (Killistino), at Carlton-House.* It is, however, sometimes used to cure rheumatism, which disease is not a very common one among them. To cure swellings they rub the skin with roots and plants; and sometimes use aromatic herbs, to impart to their bodies a pleasant odour. When the pain is internal, they very frequently make incisions in the skin and suck up the blood, accompanying the operation with songs. It is probable, from the relief which they derive from this operation in certain cases, that they have been led to expect the same abatement to their grief, or disease of the mind, by resorting to a similar remedy, and hence the practice of lacerating their arms, thighs, legs, breast, &c. after the death of a friend. They generally, however, accompany this with lamentations, which they consider as affording great relief. In such cases they also resort to liquor when they can get it, in order to drown all care. Col. Snelling mentioned to us, that when a Dacota in the vicinity of his garrison loses any of his relations, he generally repairs to him with a note from the Indian agent, desiring that he may receive a bottle of whiskey. When asked by the Colonel what is the use of the liquor on so melancholy an occasion, the Indians uniformly answer, that it is to produce a flow of tears, for indeed, without it, they are unable to cry.

Sterility among women is by no means uncommon, neither is it disreputable. It frequently happens that a woman, reputed barren, will bear children if she change her husband. Menstruation commences later among the

* Franklin's Narrative of a Journey to the Shores of the Polar Sea. Philadelphia, 1824, p. 67.

Dacotas than among the Potawatomis, for with the former it seldom comes on before the age of fifteen or sixteen, while the latter menstruate at fourteen; this difference is easily accounted for by the more severe climate which the Dacotas inhabit, and by their greater exposure to privations of every kind; they have various emmenagogues. Women are frequently liable, during pregnancy, to lethargy and sick stomach, and we are informed that the Dacota women have their faces covered with spots, in the same manner as white women. Being hardened to exercise, they attend to their usual occupations, even in the last stages of gestation. This has frequently been brought up as a proof that the delicacy of white women, in that situation, was rather the result than the cause of the great care which they take of themselves; but it appears to us very probable that the proportion of accidents which occur to Indian women during the period of pregnancy, is greater than among white women; and that this would be much diminished if they were permitted to take the same care to avoid the causes of accidents, as is common among civilized nations. The process of parturition is generally easy, though in some instances the labour has lasted from two to four days. They administer medicines in such cases, and among these the rattle of the rattlesnake, in doses of one segment at a time. Inflammation and abscess of the breast are known, but are not of very common occurrence; for these the only remedies are singing and sucking. A custom, which has been improperly ascribed to all Indian women, is that of bathing in cold water immediately after parturition; we have already stated that it does not exist among the Potawatomis; but the Dacotas adhere to it very pertinaciously. We have heard of an instance of a very delicate female who resides at Prairie du Chien. Her mother is a Dacota, but her father being a white man, she was educated among civilized women, and has acquired their habits. She married a respectable inhabitant of the place, and having been delivered of a child, she was confined to her room with the precautions usual among white women; her mother, who was absent at the time, hearing of her situation, came to see her, and finding her in bed, chided her severely, asked her if she was going to imitate all the nonsensical tricks and fashions of white women, and then dragged her out of bed, to the astonishment of her husband and of all the by standers, and ducked her in the Mississippi, according to the manners of her nation. We have not heard that any accident resulted from this harsh treatment; nor that any evil arises from the practice which prevails among them of breaking the ice in winter, in order that both mother and child may bathe immediately after parturition.

Among the Dacotas there are professed midwives, but the women are sometimes delivered by their husbands, brothers, sisters, &c.; the medicine man is generally present, but never operates: his only business is to sing, and to assist by his prayers and incantations. They never bleed during labour. Children are suckled for a long while, from two to five years generally, until a new pregnancy interrupts the secretion of milk. When the mother's milk fails, the child is suckled by another.

We have said that there exists among the Sioux no marriage ceremony, properly speaking. When a white man wishes a wife, as it is usual for all the traders to take Indian women, he has only to express his wish to the parents and relations, who always consent to it, stipulating the amount of the presents which he shall make to them. One of the gentlemen of the Columbia Fur Company informed us, that he had given for his wife, to her brother a keg of rum, and to her mother a complete dress; but he calculated that the presents which he was obliged to make to the relations amounted annually to sixty or seventy dollars in goods, worth about thirty dollars in cash. To an Indian it does not of course cost so much, as less is expected from him than from a trader. Our informant added that it was always better to make these presents, because otherwise the wife would make greater ones, as it would be impossible for her to resist the importunities of her friends, and particularly of her mother.

According to the best information which we have obtained, the number of cinædi is very small among the Dacotas. We heard of but two, one in the village of Keoxa, the other among the Miakechakesa; there are probably a few others, but the number is certainly very small, and they are held in the utmost contempt.

What struck Lewis and Clarke most, among the Sioux, " was an institution, peculiar to them and to the Kite Indians, from whom it is said to have been copied. It is an association of the most active and brave young men, who are bound to each other by attachment, secured by a vow, never to retreat before any danger, or give way to their enemies."* Of this interesting institution we have collected the following features. It constitutes what is called the " Dance of the Brave;" or more properly, perhaps, " those who perform the Dance of the Brave."

* Vol. i. p. 60.

There exists in some of the bands of the Dacotas, and probably also among some of the other Missouri Indians, an association called the Nanpashene,* those who never fly or retreat. A society of this kind originates in an union of two friends, who, when a warlike expedition is projected, propose to form an association. They send for a third warrior, and these three appoint the whole number, which seldom exceeds thirty or forty. When they are all collected, the two founders state to them that the object of the meeting is to form a company of " the Dauntless," and they advise them to prepare their dresses, which generally requires about a fortnight. In the meanwhile, the two founders prepare the lodge of the association, which none but its members are suffered to enter.

When all the members are collected together, they commence their songs and dances and their fasts, which last three days, during which time they reside in the lodge, but occasionally sally out to sing and dance in the camp. This fast is of the most strict nature, as they dare take neither food nor drink during the three days. One of the most striking features of the association is, that it is limited in its duration, and that its activity is suspended by the death of any one of its members. The duty which it enjoins is not destruction to its enemies, but the rushing into danger with songs and dances. It matters not whether they inflict any injury upon the enemy at the time. Indeed, as long as the association is in activity, they cannot kill one, for it is one of their obligations to go out unarmed. A society of this kind sometimes continues actively employed for a whole year,

* Nänpàshènc̀.

during which time its members cannot provide themselves with food or drink, but they must wait until it is offered to them by their friends. When a person once enters into the Nanpashene, he is bound to it for life; for although its duration is limited, yet it may be renewed at the call of any of its members, in which case all are bound to join in; but, during the term of its suspension, each may act for himself as he pleases. It is not always that an Indian is willing to enter into this society, for though it is held in high honour, yet it requires a more than usual courage to expose one's self passively to the greatest dangers, under a strict obligation, which none dare violate, never to retreat from it. In the commencement of the association, the two founders having selected a third, and this one nominated a fourth member, these meet in the lodge appropriated to their purpose, and as soon as they have entered it, and smoked the pipe of war, they cannot retract. These four assume the appropriate dress, and issue out of the lodge singing and dancing; they select such of the warriors as they think will be good members of the band, and convey them, whether willing or not, to their lodge. If the warrior enter it, even but for a moment, he is bound to the association and cannot withdraw; but if he succeed in effecting his escape before he enters the lodge, he is free. Vacancies in their body are never filled; the association continues until it is annihilated by the death of all its members, when a new one may be formed. They have occasional meetings for feasts and sacrifices. Their fasts are both frequent and rigid. It is difficult to determine, with precision, what the object of the institution is, but it seems to be to convince the enemy, that there are in their band a number of men so heedless of danger, that they will rush into it under a solemn pledge never to retreat, and also without the usual motive of selling their lives at a high price, by the number of the enemy whom they will have previously destroyed. It must be admitted that the passive courage, which this association requires of its members, presents perhaps the highest degree which man has ever manifested: for they are not even animated by a religious or a superstitious feeling; they do not believe that this self-devotion will ensure success to their party. They, it is true, entertain the opinion that it is more difficult to kill them than other warriors; yet this does not detract in the least from their merit, as they know they must, sooner or later, fall victims to the dangers to which they expose themselves. The great divinity to which this association looks up for support, is the thunder, to which frequent sacrifices are offered, especially by the two founders who are its leaders. The sacrifices are made at the door of the lodge, and consist of pieces of meat stuck upon a wooden fork, and inclined to the west. The members of this association have a costly and splendid dress, made of antelopes' skin; they wear feathers upon their heads. Every band of the Sioux has not an association of this kind; some have two or three societies, one of which has alone the title of the brave; the others being called the soldiers, the buffalo, &c. The object of these appears to be different, as they are not bound to that passive exposure to danger, which characterizes the Nanpashene.

The Dacotas that reside along the Mississippi and St. Peter raise maize in tolerable abundance; they also cultivate beans, pumpkins, and other vegetables; some of them, such as Wapasha, appear to be aware of the advantages which attend agriculture, but all are not equally so; and the occasional supplies of these articles which they receive from the Indian agents and officers of our government, whenever they are in want of food, no doubt tend to encourage their lazy habits. Col. Snelling once offered a chief the use of a plough, and of a person to teach him the manner of working it, in order that his band might raise potatoes. The chief made no answer for some time, but continued to smoke his pipe with great deliberation; when this was exhausted, and he had carefully laid it aside, he rose, advanced towards the colonel, shook his hand, and observed that he had taken the offer into consideration, and had concluded that he would be a great fool were he to accept of it, when he recollected that his father always supplied him with provisions, as often as he was in need of them. The Dacotas do not profess, as the Potawatomis do, to have been acquainted with the preparation of sugar from the sap of the maple tree, previous to their intercourse with white traders. Their food is usually prepared by boiling it in iron pots, which they procure from the traders, and, as far as we have observed, they appear to prefer their meat well done. In their degree of cleanliness they vary much, some being far more particular than others. The Dacotas may upon the whole be considered as not very uncleanly; and as far as relates to their persons, they attend much to this particular. They had no substitute for ardent spirits, and were completely unacquainted with intoxication previous to their intercourse with Europeans.

Of their divisions of time it is difficult to obtain correct information. The interpreters, even the most intelligent, are so prone to connect their own opinions with those of the Indians, that they can scarcely be trusted in this particular. We have not been able, however, to trace among them any idea of the lost moon, ascribed to them by Carver. The following division of the year was furnished by Renville, and is added, though we place but little confidence in its accuracy, at least as having been in use among the Indians previous to their intercourse with white men. They are said to divide the year into twelve moons, commencing with the September one, and distinguishing them as follows:—

September, Wajopi we,* *Commencement of wild rice.*
October, Siushtaupi we, *End of wild rice.*
November, Takehuha we, *Rutting deer.*
December, Tahechapshon we, *Deer shedding its horn.*
January, We tarhe, *Hard moon.*
February, Wechata we, *Raccoon.*
March, Wishta wasa we, *Sore-eye.*
April, Mahahahandi we, *Hunting.*
May, Mahahakanda we, *Oviparous game.*
June, Wajustechasha we, *Strawberries.*
July, Tschanpasha we, *Cherries.*
August, Tatanka kehowa we, *Rutting buffalo.*

Among the Indians whom we saw at Fort St. Anthony, there was one who was called the fool. His countenance had a great appearance of simplicity, being totally devoid of expression; his face was long, his eyes downcast and vacant; his person was much ornamented; the upper part of his face was painted with bright vermilion; the lower part was black, leaving but a narrow strip along the upper lip, which was of the natural colour; his ornaments were more childish and toyish than those

"* Wè" signifies moon.

which the Indians usually wear. This man was formerly gifted with a common share of intellect: but he has, through the wantonness of some Indians, been reduced to his present state of idiocy. He was a long time since taken prisoner by his enemies, who, with a view to amuse themselves with his fears, tied him to a stake, and threatened to burn him alive; a little fire was kindled, so as merely to scorch him; but when he was loosened, his intellect was disordered, and has continued so ever since. In some instances, however, he still displays his natural sagacity. He is a good hunter; being at one time very poor, he made a sort of pike, with which he went out to hunt, and was very successful, particularly in killing raccoons; the skins which he sold on his return enabled him to purchase a gun, blanket, &c. He is much trusted by the officers of the garrison, and had just returned from Prairie du Chien with despatches, having travelled the distance on foot in four days.

Like all the Indian nations with whom the white man has come into contact, the Dacota presents to us at this day but a noble ruin. No longer united for purposes of common defence, they have long since ceased to meet at the same council fire; their alliances with other nations are now mere mockeries; their wars have dwindled into petty conflicts. Instead of marching, as they formerly did, by hundreds, they now issue forth in small detachments, presenting rather the character of a band of marauders than of an expedition of warriors. When they lighted the common calumet at the General Council Fire, it was always among the Mende Wahkantoan, who then resided near Spirit Lake, and who were considered as the oldest band of the nation, their chiefs being of longer standing than those of the other tribes; among themselves they use the appellation of brothers. They are related with the Shiennes, and with the Arricaras, and by marriages they are connected with the Pawnees, Osages, &c.; but to these nations they only apply the term of friend. With the Omawhaws they wage a deadly warfare. We were told that the Iawas were formerly a 'band of the Dacotas, and that they were distinguished by the term of the Titatons, but that they separated long since, and that their language had been so much altered as to be unintelligible to the Dacotas. But this information is probably incorrect, for Governor Clarke, during his late visit to the seat of government, with a deputation of Indians from many nations, informed Mr. Colhoun, that the Iawas, Winnebagoes, and Otoes appeared to him to be of common descent, and to speak dialects of the same language; and he expressed his opinion, that an inquiry into the matter would result in determining them to be of that nation, which, as we learn from Mr. Jefferson's "Notes," emigrated from Ocoquan. Mr. Joseph Snelling, who accompanied that deputation, likewise informed Mr. Colhoun, that in a speech made by the Iawa chief while in the city of Washington, the former union of the Winnebagoes and Otoes with his nation, was distinctly asserted. This confirms the information obtained by Mr. Say, on the former expedition, (Vide Account of an Expedition to the Rocky Mountains, vol. i. p. 338, 339, and 342,) and disproves the assertion that the Iawas were ever connected with the Dacotas. It may likewise be questioned, whether the Omawhaws, whom Carver connects, as well as the Shiennes and Arricaras, with the Naudowessies of the plains, were not descended from a different stock.

Of the history of the Dacotas very little is known;

they have been engaged from time immemorial in a destructive war against the Chippewas. All the efforts of our government have tended to produce but temporary suspensions of arms, which have been in all cases violated within a short time after they had been made. Lahontan informs us that they defeated a party of Iroquois, on an island of the Mississippi, prior to the year 1688. In 1697,* they destroyed a party of Miamis, on the southern coast of Lake Michigan, between St. Joseph and Kikalemazo rivers; and Charlevoix states that in 1701,† the Sauks, Winnebagoes, Menomonies, Foxes, Potawatomis, and Kickapoos, assembled at Green Bay to go to war with them, but that they were dissuaded from it by a French emissary. The Chippewas informed Carver, in 1767, that a war had continued without any interruption between them and the Dacotas for upwards of forty winters. They appear to have no tradition or knowledge of the Lenni-Lenape, Aligawi, or other nations that were found east of the Alleghany Mountains. In speaking of the early impression made by the Dacotas on Europeans, Charlevoix observed, that they were considered to have a better conception than any other Indians of the attributes of the Supreme Being.

Our visit to Lake Travers having been announced to the gentlemen of the Columbia Fur Company, by a messenger sent to them from Big Stone Lake, the party were received on their arrival with a national salute; and other demonstrations of friendly hospitality were manifested, not only at that time, but also during the few days which they spent there.

---

* Charlevoix's Hist. de la Nouv. France, tom. iii. p. 310.
† Ibid. p. 405.

The Columbia Fur Company was created in 1822; it consists of but few individuals, who being all practically acquainted with the Indian trade, in which they had previously been engaged in the service of the Hudson's Bay or North-West Company, resolved, after the consolidation of these two companies into one, to establish themselves on the United States' territory, and to trade with the Indians south of the boundary line, under licenses granted by the Indian agent at the mouth of the St. Peter. Their capital is not very large, but being all active, intelligent, and experienced, they will, we doubt not, succeed. Their principal establishment is at Lake Travers; its situation is judiciously selected, as it is at the head of the navigation of the St. Peter and Red Rivers, in the midst of a country which abounds in buffalo, so that they can lay in ample stores of provisions for their wintering parties. By extending their excursions to the head waters of the Mississippi, and as far on the Missouri as the Indians will permit, they will be able to obtain large supplies of beaver and other valuable skins, and as their object appears to be merely to trade with the Indians, and not to hunt upon their lands, they will, it is to be hoped, continue on amicable terms with them.

The following statement of the amount of furs formerly packed up by the British companies, and produced altogether by the trade on Red River and its tributaries, has been communicated to us by the gentlemen of the Columbia Fur Company. As this statement is restricted to the value of the fur trade on the *South* side of the boundary line, we think there can be no impropriety in publishing it. All that relates to the British territories, and that we have been able to collect from our own observations, or which has been kindly communicated to us in the course of conversations with the officers of the Hudson's Bay Company, we have no wish to publish, and we should consider it highly censurable so to do; but as this relates to a trade in which they can have no further interest, no objection can, we trust, be taken to it.

Names.	No. of packs.	No. of skins, or wt. of each pack.	Value of pack. Sp. dol.	Total. Sp. dol.
Beaver	10	100 lbs. wt.	400	4,000
Bear	20	12 skins	75*	1,500
Buffalo	400	10 skins	40	16,000
Martin	10	100 lbs.	300	3,000
Otter	10	100 lbs.	600	6,000
Fisher	25	—	450	11,250
Elk	40	16 skins	80	3,200
Mynx	10	—	200	2,000
Muskrat	40	500 skins	200	8,000
Lynx	20	—	280	5,600
Swan	2	60 skins	60	120
Rabbit	4	400 skins	8	32
Wolverine	1	400 skins	—	75
Cowskins (dressed)	20	16 skins	80	1,600
Wolves	10	—	40	400
Moose	10	—	80	800
Fox	5	—	260	1,300
	637			Sp. dol. 64,877

* This item we find stated in our notes at Spa. dol. 450 per pack, but we apprehend that the statement is very much overrated, although it is said to refer to the finest quality. Six dollars per skin is probably a fair price.

The above prices are, we believe, those of the Montreal market. This statement establishes the average value of the packs at about one hundred dollars; and if we exclude the buffalo robes, which are sold at forty dollars a pack, the other furs will average upwards of two hundred dollars. The amount of the less valuable furs, such as those of wolves, wolverines, rabbits, &c. might be increased, if there were a market for them.

In addition to these, the country supplies annually one thousand bags of pounded buffalo meat (Pemmican),* valued at four thousand dollars. The Columbia Fur Company can, if it be active, share this trade with the American Fur Company; these are the only associations that trade at present with the Indians in that part of the United States. Independent of this the trade of the Missouri and its tributaries may probably prove very valuable. It will be the interest of both the companies to keep on amicable terms. The practice which has too often prevailed among Indian traders, to endeavour to increase their business by

* Pemmican is the meat of the buffalo, prepared for preservation in the following manner: the flesh is cut into thin slices, which are jerked in the sun or smoke, the latter being preferable; it is then dried before the fire until it becomes crisp, after which it is laid upon one stone, and pounded with another fixed into a wooden handle; after it has been reduced into as fine a powder as possible, which is, however, far from being very minute, it is mixed up with an equal weight of buffalo grease, or marrow fat poured on when hot and liquid. Before the mixture cools, it is introduced into skin bags, and well shaken, so that it may settle into a compact mass. Sometimes, in order to give it a pleasant taste, it is mixed with a sort of wild cherry, which is pounded and introduced, stone and all. The Pemmican forms a wholesome and strong food, which, when prepared with care, and from good materials, is very palatable. It has the advantage that it may be eaten without any preparatory cooking. Sometimes it is heated in a pan, and is equal to the best hashed meat.

injuring the interests or the reputation of their competitors, is as injudicious as the means which they adopted were frequently criminal; they lower the character of the white man in the opinion of the Indians, and excite them to deeds at which they would otherwise revolt.

The principal interest which we experienced in the neighbourhood of Lake Travers, was from an acquaintance with Wanotan* (the Charger), the most distinguished chief of the Yanktoanan tribe, which, as we were informed, is subdivided into six bands. He is one of the greatest men of the Dacota nation, and although but twenty-eight years of age, he has already acquired great renown as a warrior. At the early age of eighteen he exhibited much valour, in the war against the Americans, and was wounded several times. He was then inexperienced, and served under his father, who was the chief of his tribe, and who bore a mortal enmity to the Americans. Wanotan has since learned to form a better estimate of our nation. He is aware that it is the interest of his people to remain at peace with us, and would probably, in case of another war between the United States and England, take part with the former. Those who know him well, commend his sagacity and judgment, as well as his valour. He is a tall man, being upwards of six feet high; his countenance would be esteemed handsome in any country, his features being regular and well-shaped. There is an intelligence that beams through his eye, which is not the usual concomitant of Indian features. His manners are dignified and reserved; his attitudes are graceful and easy, though

* Wånótån.

they appear to be somewhat studied. When speaking of the Dacotas, we purposely postponed mentioning the frequent vows which they make, and their strict adherence to them, because one of the best evidences which we have collected on this point connects itself with the character of Wanotan, and may give a favourable idea of his extreme fortitude in enduring pain. In the summer of 1822 he undertook a journey, from which, apprehending much danger on the part of the Chippewas, he made a vow to the Sun, that, if he returned safe, he would abstain from all food or drink for the space of four successive days and nights, and that he would distribute among his people all the property which he possessed, including all his lodges, horses, dogs, &c. On his return, which happened without accident, he celebrated the dance of the sun; this consisted in making three cuts through his skin, one on his breast, and one on each of his arms. The skin was cut in the manner of a loop, so as to permit a rope to pass between the flesh and the strip of skin which was thus divided from the body. The ropes being passed through, their ends were secured to a tall vertical pole, planted at about forty yards from his lodge. He then began to dance round this pole, at the commencement of this fast, frequently swinging himself in the air, so as to be supported merely by the cords which were secured to the strips of skin separated from his arms and breast. He continued this exercise with few intermissions during the whole of his fast, until the fourth day about ten o'clock, A.M., when the strip of skin from his breast gave way; notwithstanding which he interrupted not the dance, although supported merely by his arms. At noon the strip from his left arm snapped off: his uncle then thought that he had suffered enough; he drew his knife and cut off the skin from the right arm, upon which Wanotan fell to the ground and swooned. The heat at the time was extreme. He was left exposed in that state to the sun until night, when his friends brought him some provisions. After the ceremony was over, he distributed to them the whole of his property, among which were five fine horses, and he and his two squaws left his lodge, abandoning every article of their furniture.

As we appeared upon the brow of the hill which commands the company's fort, a salute was fired from a number of Indian tents which were pitched in the vicinity, from the largest of which the American colours were flying; and as soon as we had dismounted from our horses, we received an invitation to a feast which Wanotan had prepared for us. The gentlemen of the company informed us, that as soon as the Indians had heard of our contemplated visit, they had commenced their preparations for a festival, and that they had killed three of their dogs. We repaired to a sort of pavilion which they had erected by the union of several large skin-lodges. Fine buffalo-robes were spread all around, and the air was perfumed by the odour of sweet scenting grass which had been burned in it. On entering the lodge we saw the chief seated near the further end of it, and one of his principal men pointed out to us the place which was destined for our accommodation; it was at the upper end of the lodge, the Indians who were in it taking no further notice of us. These consisted of the chief, his son, a lad about eight years old, and eight or ten of the principal warriors. The chief's dress presented a mixture of the European and aboriginal costume; he wore moccassins and leggings of splendid scarlet cloth, a blue breech-cloth, a fine shirt of printed muslin, over this a frock coat of fine blue cloth with scarlet facings, somewhat similar to the undress uniform coat of a Prussian officer; this was buttoned and secured round his waist by a belt. Upon his head he wore a blue cloth cap, made like a German fatigue cap. A very handsome Mackinaw blanket, slightly ornamented with paint, was thrown over his person. His son, whose features strongly favoured those of his father, wore a dress somewhat similar, except that his coat was party-coloured, one half being made of blue, and the other half of scarlet cloth. He wore a round hat with a plated silver band and a large cockade. From his neck were suspended several silver medals, doubtless presents to his father. This lad appeared to be a great favourite of Wanotan's, who seems to indulge him more than is customary with Indians to do. As soon as we had taken our seats, the chief passed his pipe round, and while we were engaged in smoking, two of the Indians arose and uncovered the large kettles which were standing over the fire: they emptied their contents into a dozen of wooden dishes which were placed all round the lodge; these consisted of buffalo meat boiled with tepsin, also the same vegetable boiled without the meat, in buffalo grease, and finally, the much esteemed dog meat, all which were dressed without salt. In compliance with the established usage of travellers to taste of every thing, we all partook of the latter with a mixed feeling of curiosity and reluctance. Could we have divested ourselves entirely of the prejudices of education, we should doubtless have unhesitatingly acknowledged this to be one of the best dishes that we had ever tasted: it was remarkably fat, was sweet and palatable: it had none of that dry stringy character which we had expected to find in it, and it was entirely destitute of the strong taste which we had apprehended that it possessed. It was not an unusual appetite, or the want of good meat to compare with it, which led us to form this favourable opinion of the dog, for we had, on the same dish, the best meat which our prairies afford; but so strongly rooted are the prejudices of education, that, though we all unaffectedly admitted the excellence of this food, yet few of us could be induced to eat much of it. We were warned by our trading friends that the bones of this animal are treated with great respect by the Dacotas; we, therefore, took great care to replace them in the dishes; and we are informed, that after such a feast is concluded, the bones are carefully collected, the flesh scraped off from them, and that after being washed, they are buried in the ground, partly, as it is said, to testify to the dog-species, that in feasting upon one of their number no disrepect was meant to the species itself, and partly also from a belief, that the bones of the animal will rise and reproduce another. The meat of this animal, as we saw it, was thought to resemble that of the finest Welch mutton, except that it was of a much darker colour. Having so far overcome our repugnance as to taste it, we no longer wonder that the dog should be considered a dainty dish by those in whom education has not created a prejudice against this flesh. In China it is said, that fattened pups are frequently sold in the market-place; and it appears that the invitation to a feast of dog meat is the greatest distinction that can be offered to a stranger by any of the Indian nations east of the Rocky Mountains. That this is not the case among some of the nations west of those mountains, appears from the fact that Lewis and Clarke were called, in derision, by the Indians of the Columbia, Dog Eaters.

In the Dacota's treatment of his dogs, during life and after death, we observe one of those strange inconsistencies which so frequently prevail in the character of man, whether civilized or savage. While living, the dog is a beast of burden, and as such exposed to undergo much fatigue and ill-treatment; it is at the same time a most valuable animal. The traders, who have imitated the Indians in their use of the dog, speak of it as almost indispensable to them. Mr. Jeffries, one of the partners of the Columbia Fur Company, informed us, that he had the preceding winter transported in a log-cart one thousand pounds weight of goods, with the assistance of six and rarely eight dogs; and that he travelled from Lake Travers to the Mandan villages in eleven days. On a long journey, the allowance of load is one hundred pounds per dog. For winter travelling, in a country so frequently covered with snow, the dog is the most convenient beast of burden, as it may be fed either on dried meat, or on the fresh meat which is occasionally procured. In travelling on the snow with dog trains, it is usual for a man to walk a-head of the dogs, with snowshoes, in order to trample down the snow, in which otherwise they would sink. We learn from Mr. Back's notes,* that the feet of the dogs are sometimes very much injured, and that in one instance, where they were perfectly raw, he attempted to tie shoes on them, which did not succeed. Whether it be usual for the Dacotas to do so, we very much question; though it would appear from Purchas' Pilgrim, that these have been used by

---

* Franklin's Journey to the Shores of the Polar Sea, ut sup. p. 251.

some nations; and we are told by Olaus Magnus, that in the north of Europe, a somewhat similar practice existed as regards horses' feet,* and probably at the time that he visited the country, which was in 1518. The dogs are a great assistance to the squaws, who would otherwise be compelled to carry all their baggage and provisions themselves, but who frequently beat and abuse them. After death, the dog forms one of the best articles of food for the Indian, and is reserved for great occasions, as it is, in their opinion, invested with a sacred character, which makes it a fit offering in sacrifices and in feasts to strangers. The respect paid to the bones of the dog contrasts strongly with the ill usage which the animal meets with during life.

The feast which Wanotan had prepared seemed to be destined rather for one hundred than for ten persons; as soon as we had finished eating, the Indians requested that our soldiers might be allowed to come and partake of it, a request which was of course granted. When the soldiers appeared, the dishes were placed before them, and the Indians, who had probably been fasting all day, made a violent inroad upon the meal, evidently preferring the dog to the buffalo meat. According to the Indian usage, it would have been proper for us to have waited until they had finished their repast, when probably some speeches would have been made; but the feast appeared likely to be prolonged to a late hour, and the heat was so oppressive in the lodge, owing to the season, and to the number collected therein, as also

---

* " Transeunt homines et equi quasi super clypeos militares. * * * Crates seu arcus levi ac lato subere, seu cortice tiliano contextos, pedibus propriis ac equorum alligant."—Olai Magni Gentium Septentrionalium Historiæ Breviarium. Amstelodami, 1669. L. iv. c. 13.

undoubtedly to the immense quantities of hot meat exposed in the dishes, that we were compelled to apologize to Wanotan for our sudden departure.

Upon the whole, we were much gratified by this feast; it was worthy of the powerful chief who gave it; it was offered with an open hand and a free heart; it was served up with the usual ceremonies, and it included abundance of their best and most highly prized food.

The next day Wanotan came to pay us a formal visit; he was dressed in the full habit of an Indian chief; we have never seen a more dignified looking person, or a more becoming dress. The most prominent part of his apparel was a splendid cloak or mantle of buffalo skins, dressed so as to be of a fine white colour; it was decorated with small tufts of owls' feathers, and others of various hues, and is probably a remnant of a dress once in general use among the aborigines of our territory, and still worn in the north-east and north-west parts of this continent, as well as in the South Sea Islands; it is what was called by the first European visitors of North America, the feather-mantle and feather-blanket, which was by them much admired. A splendid necklace, formed of about sixty claws of the grizzly bear, imparted a manly character to his whole appearance. His leggings, jacket, and moccassins, were in the real Dacota fashion, being made of white skins, profusely decorated with human hair; his moccassins were variegated with the plumage of several birds. In his hair he wore nine sticks neatly cut and smoothed, and painted with vermilion; these designated the number of gunshot wounds which he had received; they were secured by a strip of red cloth; two plaited tresses of his hair were allowed to hang forward: his face was tastefully painted with vermilion: in his hand he wore a large fan of feathers of the turkey, which he frequently used.

We have never seen a nobler face, or a more impressive character, than that of the Dacota chief, as he stood that afternoon, in this manly and characteristic dress, contemplating a dance performed by the men of his own nation. It was a study worthy of the pencil of Vandyke, and of the graver of Berwick. It would require the utmost talent of the artist to convey a fair idea of this chief, to display his manly and regular features, strongly stamped, it is true, with the Indian character, but admirably blended with an expression of mildness and modesty; and it would require no less talent to represent the graceful and unstudied folds of his mantle. However difficult the task of executing such a portrait, Mr. Seymour undertook it; and a plate engraved from his design, has been introduced as a frontispiece to this volume: it will impart, however, but a faint idea of the features and dress of this distinguished chief.

Having requested that the warriors should favour us with a dance, Wanotan had one performed for us in the afternoon; he apologized for the imperfection of the dancers, the best being then absent from the place. The dresses which they wore were more carefully arranged than usual, and indicated that some pains had been taken for the occasion. Among the fantastic ornaments which they had assumed, a paper of pins opened and hanging from the head-dress of one of the warriors was conspicuous. In his hand he held a wand about ten feet long, to which was attached a piece of red cloth of the same length, and about six inches wide; one of the edges of this band was fastened to the staff, the other was furnished with black and white feathers, closely secured to it by their quills, and forming a sort of fringe. This was one of the two insignia or wands of the Association of the Nanpashene : but the most singular dress was that of Wanotan's son, who, for the first time in his life, wore the distinguished national garb in which he is represented in the frontispiece plate to this volume. The dresses were evidently made for his father, and too large for him, so that they gave to his figure a stiff and clumsy appearance, which strongly reminded us of the awkward gait of those children who, among civilized nations, are allowed at too early an age to assume the dress of riper years, by which they lose their infantine grace and ease. This is one of the many features in which we delight in tracing an analogy between the propensities of man in his natural state, and in his more refined condition. This lad wore a very large head-dress, consisting of feathers made of the war-eagle, and which in form was precisely similar to that of the King of the Friendly Islands, as represented in Cook's Voyages. His dress was made of many ermine-skins, variously disposed upon a white leather cloak. The performers stood in a ring, each with the wing of a bird in his hand, with which he beat time on his gun, arrow, or something that would emit a sound. They commenced their singing in a low tone, gradually raising it for a few minutes, then closing it suddenly with a shrill yell; after a slight interruption, they recommenced the same air, which they sang without any variation for near three-quarters of an hour. Major Long reduced it to notes, and an idea of this low and melancholy, but not unpleasant air, may be formed from the first tune in the plate. This was accompanied by a few unmeaning words. Occasionally one of the performers would advance into the centre of the ring, and relate his warlike adventures. Among those who did this was a slender and active warrior, not tall, but distinguished by his very thin lips and nose; he was pointed out to us as the man who had assaulted Mr. Hess's party in the manner which we have already related. Among the many feats which this warrior enumerated he took care to omit his murders of white men. The dance which had accompanied this had nothing particular; they frequently laughed aloud, and appeared to go through the exercise with much spirit. After the dance had continued some time, a few presents were divided among them: upon receiving them they hastily ran away, apparently as much satisfied as we were.

END OF VOL. I.

VOLUME II

CONTENTS TO VOLUME II.

CHAP. I.
Page

The party leave Lake Travers.—They fall in with large herds of buffalo.—Observations upon the rovings of this animal.—Meeting with a war party of the Wahkpakotas who manifest hostile dispositions.—Arrival at Pembina 1

CHAP. II.
Fort Douglas and Lord Selkirk's colony.—Bark canoes.—Lake Winnepeek.—Fort Alexander.—River Winnepeek.—Rapids.—Portages.—Fine falls.—Lake of the Woods.—North-westernmost point of the boundary line.—Rainy Lake river and lake.—Fort.—Series of rapids and lakes.—Dividing ridge.—Falls of Kamanatekwoya.—Arrival at Fort William 54

CHAP. III.
Account of the Chippewa Indians.—Their usages, manners, and customs 147

CHAP. IV.
Departure from Fort William.—Trap formations on Lake Superior.—Michipicotton house.—Arrival at the Sault de Ste. Marie.—Conclusion of the Journey 170

CHAP. V.
General description of the Country traversed by the Expedition, designed as a topographical report to the War Department, by S. H. Long, Major United States' Topographical Engineers........................... 202
I. Of the Country between Philadelphia and the Ohio River 203
II. Of the Country between the Ohio River and Lake Michigan...................................... 205

a

	Page
III. Of the Country and navigable communications between Lake Michigan and the Mississippi River	208
IV. Of the St. Peter River and adjacent country. Also of the Coteau des Prairies	216
V. Of Red River and the adjacent Country	221
VI. Of the Country between Lakes Winnepeek and Superior	227
VII. Remarks on a variety of subjects connected with the topography of the Country	237
1st. Of the natural features of the Country in a military point of view	ibid.
2d. Of the Indians inhabiting the Country traversed by the Expedition	240
3d. Statements relative to the elevation of different parts of the Country	243
4th. Of the accompanying Map	246

APPENDIX.

Part I.—Natural History. §. 1. Zoology, by Thomas Say.

A. Class Polypi—Order Vaginati	3
B. Class Pisces	4
C. Class Mollusca	5
D. Class Vermes—Order Cryptobranchia	14
E. Class Insecta—Genus Cicindela	16
Order Orthoptera	39
Hemiptera	ibid.
Neuroptera	44
Hymenoptera	50
Diptera	86
§. 2. Botany. A Catalogue of Plants collected in the North-western territory, by Mr. Thomas Say, in the year 1823. By Lewis D. de Schweinitz	105
Part II.—Astronomy	124
Part III.—Meteorology	140
Part IV.—Indian Vocabularies	145

NARRATIVE OF AN EXPEDITION

TO THE

SOURCE OF ST. PETER'S RIVER,

&c. &c. &c.

CHAPTER I.

The party leave Lake Travers. They fall in with large herds of Buffalo. Observations upon the rovings of this animal. Meeting with a war party of the Wahkpakotas who manifest hostile dispositions. Arrival at Pembina.

THE fort of the Columbia Fur Company has been determined, by Mr. Colhoun, to be in latitude 45° 39′ 52″ north, and in longitude 96° 34′ 30″ west; the magnetic variation at this place amounts to 12° 28′ 50″ east. The lake upon which it stands is about fifteen miles long; in breadth it scarcely exceeds one mile. It is the handsomest of the three lakes which we saw near the head of the St. Peter. It is incased more than one hundred feet below the adjoining prairies, but the valley in which it lies is about double the breadth of the lake itself, and is filled with large fragments of primitive rocks. A view of this lake has been given in the Frontispiece to volume second, it includes the Company's fort, the Indian lodges near it, and also a scaffold, upon which the remains of a Sioux had been deposited. The horizon is bounded by a distant view of the Coteau des Prairies. The lake has received its present appellation, from the circumstance that it is in a direction nearly transverse to that of the Big Stone and Qui Parle Lakes, these being directly to the north-west, while Lake Travers points to the north-east. By the Indians it is called Otter-tail Lake, from its form. On the 26th of July, we left the fort, and, as we ascended the bluff in the rear of the establishment, we fired a salute in return for that which we had received on our arrival. Having ascended the St. Peter up to its head in Big Stone Lake, our next object was to proceed " to the intersection between Red River and the 49th degree of north latitude ;" and as we were informed that that stream runs nearly north and south, we determined to travel the usual route to Pembina and Fort Douglas, two of the posts of the Hudson's Bay Company, between which the 49th parallel was reported to strike the river.

On leaving Lake Travers, our party was strengthened by the addition of Mr. Jeffries, one of the Company, who agreed to guide us to Pembina, and by four Frenchmen, who were returning to that place, with six carts which had been employed to convey the families and baggage of several Swiss emigrants, from the British settlements to the St. Peter. Of these carts, we chartered four to convey our baggage and provisions. As it was expected that, after having travelled forty miles, we should meet with no Dacotas, it was agreed that when Renville should have accompanied us that distance, he should be at liberty to return to the fort where business required his presence. Vague reports of large parties of Dacotas had been circulated for some days past, and a rumour that five hundred lodges of the Yanktoanan were collected on Shienne River, made us desirous of being accompanied by Wanotan, which he readily agreed to do; finding, however, that these reports were groundless, and that this excursion would be inconvenient to him, as it would deprive him of the opportunity of laying in a store of buffalo meat for winter, we reluctantly acquiesced in his wish to be released from his promise.

The first day of our journey was unpleasant; it was across dry prairies. We stopped to dine upon the banks of what is termed Mushtincha (Mŭshtĭnchâ) Watapan, (Hare River). At the time that we crossed it, the stream had disappeared; a little stagnant water, collected in hollows, offered but an unpleasant drink for ourselves and our horses. This valley is a mere trench in the prairie, into which the waters collect after heavy rains; it affords them a passage to the more permanent streams. Its bed is about fifteen yards wide. The woods became very scarce as we advanced, only a few points being seen at a distance; the plain upon which we were travelling was apparently boundless; it was covered with a short grass of a pale or yellowish-green hue. The eye of the mineralogist could not detect a single stone within a mile's travel, and the few that were observed during the day, were rolled and uninteresting. In some places pebbles were as abundant as if we had been travelling upon the bed of some former river or lake; the mind endeavours in vain to establish limits to the vast expanse of water, which certainly at some former day overflowed the whole of that country.

On the bluff which encloses the lake we saw a few small tumuli, the last that were observed by our party; we have not been able to hear of the existence of any to the northwest of this place. We have, therefore, during this expedition, traced these ancient Indian works from Irville in Ohio to the head of Red River, upon a distance of upwards of eight hundred miles in a direct line, and nearly double that amount according to our devious route. We have occasionally met with them very abundant, bearing evident signs of the most consummate design, and yet we are as unable to form a correct estimate of the authors of these extensive works, of the period at which they were executed, and of the objects for which they were erected, as any of the travellers who have preceded us. If for the purpose of commemorating the names and heroic deeds of warriors or statesmen, how inadequate the means to the object proposed! How inferior in this respect to the splendid and permanent pyramids of Cheops, of Cholula, of Teotihuacan; yet the labour which has been wasted upon these tumuli would, if concentrated, have more than sufficed to erect any one or perhaps all those pyramids. In looking back to the numerous tumuli which we have seen, we cannot help admitting in the words of one of our fellow-travellers, that " the splendid antiquities of the East ministered to the pride of man; they are glorious trophies of victory, gained by human genius and power over time. History tells us the interesting circumstances connected with them; they, in turn, confirm her story. But here ferocious conquerors have torn her pages, or they remain unfilled by a posterity forgetful that it is a duty to cherish her, not only for instruction's sake, but also that the benefactors of mankind may receive their merited share of fame, and that the censure of after ages may light upon those who have proved the tyrants of their species. Here we find nothing to rescue ' ab injuria oblivionis." So rude and concise are the epitaphs, so faint and time-worn the characters on these tombs, that we strain our eyes in vain, we can read no further than the ' Hic jacet—'*"

* Mr. Colhoun's MS.

The dullness of our morning ride was dissipated by the distant view of the buffalo grazing upon the prairie. We shall not attempt to depict the joy, which the first cry of " buffaloes in sight," created in the whole company; all were in activity. The practised hunters immediately gave chase to the buffaloes, and before sunset, three of these noble animals had been slain. We encamped early to enjoy what, to many of our party, was an entirely new scene. The spot which we were obliged to select, was utterly destitute of wood, and the only fuel which we could procure was the buffalo dung, which lay profusely scattered over the prairie. This made a fine warm fire, giving out no smell. The meat was cooked, and eaten with great delight. The party never were, perhaps, in greater spirits than during that evening. They considered themselves on their way home; for the first time they saw abundance of game before them, and a prospect of its continuance for a few days, whence they anticipated ample supplies of stores in the camp.

The spot of our encampment is called, both by Indians and traders, Buffalo Lake; it is only an extension of Lake Travers, being separated but by a marsh overgrown with high grass, through which a canoe can navigate at all times. It is immediately below this place that the lake assumes the characters of a stream, and receives the name of Sioux or Swan River. Mr. Colhoun endeavoured to determine the situation of this place, but a high southerly wind impeded his observations. Previous to encamping, we passed a party of squaws engaged in conveying to their camp some slices of fresh meat to jerk; their fellow-labourers were dogs. Each of the dogs had the ends of two poles crossed and fastened over the shoulders, with a piece of hide underneath to prevent chafing. The other extremities dragged on the ground. This sort of vehicle was secured to the animal by a string passing round the breast, and another under the abdomen; transverse sticks, the ends of which were fastened in the poles, kept these at a proper distance, and supported the meat. This seems to be the only mode of harnessing dogs, practised among the Sioux; we believe they never use them in teams, as is customary with the traders. Some of the gentlemen of the party went to the Indian camp, and were rewarded for their pains by eating of the swan's meat, which we had not yet had an opportunity of tasting; they found it very indifferent.

The next morning, as we proceeded, the buffaloes began to thicken before us; in every direction numbers of them were seen. They generally collected in herds of thousands together, keeping at a distance from us, though sometimes suffering us to approach very near to them, and, in some cases, indeed, running through our line of march. We stopped in the morning at a few Indian lodges, which we were pleased to find were those of our acquaintance Wanotan, the Yanktoanan chief. He invited us to partake of some fresh buffalo meat, which, being obtained from a fat cow, far exceeded in quality that which we had tasted the preceding evening. Wanotan assured us, that, from the information he had obtained, he thought we should not meet with any Dacotas after passing the Bois des Sioux, a small grove at a distance, and beyond which we expected to encamp that night. Some of the gentlemen having expressed a desire to see the chief hunt the buffalo with his bow and arrow, he complied with their request. In the mean while, the body of the party continued their route, crossed the dry bed of Sioux River, and proceeded as far as the Boix des Sioux, where they formed their encampment at an early hour, owing to a very heavy and continued rain; at this place, they were overtaken by the gentlemen who had gone out with Wanotan, and were much interested by the recital of his address and success in hunting. These gentlemen had likewise killed a couple of calves, which gave us an opportunity of tasting the buffalo veal; we found it good, but not to be compared to the beef of that animal. The Indians, we believe, never kill the calves when they can help it. We saw one of these little creatures that had been brought to Lake Travers, and which they intended to domesticate; it was a male calf, about two or three months old, of a uniform dun colour; the hump had not yet begun to form; it almost continually made a grunting noise, not unlike that of a hog. A domestic cow nourished it without discovering any thing more than occasional uneasiness at its hard sucking, though at first she submitted only through force.

The squaws at Wanotan's lodge were engaged in jerking the meat and dressing the skins which he had obtained. We had some curiosity to observe their mode of operating. The meat was cut up in thin and broad slices and exposed on poles, all round the lodge. Two days of exposure to a hot sun are sufficient to dry the meat so that it will keep. The skins are dressed in a very simple manner; the green skin is stretched on the ground by means of stakes driven through its edges; then with a piece of bone, sharpened to a cutting edge, about an inch wide, and similar to a chisel, the softer portions on the flesh side are scraped off, and with an instrument of iron similar to the bit of a carpenter's plane, the hair is removed from the outside. If the operation be interrupted here, the product is a sort of parchment; but if the skin be intended for mocassins or clothing, it is then worked with the hands in the brain of animals, which gives it the requisite degree of softness. In order to qualify it for exposure to moisture, the skin is sometimes smoked, but this deprives it of its natural white appearance. When the skin has been prepared with care, but not smoked, the shirt and leggings made from it, with broad edges, left without the seam and cut into fringe, form a very handsome dress. Instead of the brains of animals, strong soap-suds could be used in the dressing of the skin, and we have it upon the authority of Lawson, that " young Indian corn, beaten to a pulp, will effect the same as the brains *."

We observed that Wanotan used the common Sioux bow, not exceeding four feet in length; the arrows were proportional. At Wapasha's some of the party observed a bow of from five to six feet, which he was engaged in rasping; but perhaps it was intended to be cut off to the usual size.

Our route that day led us near to Sioux River; for some distance we had on our right a ridge of about thirty or forty feet in height, which as we advanced inclined to the northeast and soon disappeared. By the Dacotas, Sioux River is called Kantoko (Kǎntǒkǒ,) from a thicket of plum bushes near its head. A few insulated patches of wood seen scattered over the prairie form the "Isles des Bois" of the voyagers. We were shown, at a distance, on the west bank of the river, an elevation, called by the Indians the Thunder's Nest; at its base there are a number of salt ponds.

As we were travelling along the prairie that morning, we were delighted to see our former companion, Lieut. Scott, from whom we had been separated for upwards of three weeks By the most active exertions, Mr. Scott had been enabled to descend the Mississippi to Prairie du Chien and return to Fort St. Anthony, then to ascend along the St.

---

* Lawson's New Voyage to North Carolina, ut supra, p. 209.

Peter a certain distance, when his horse failing, he was obliged to retrace his steps to the fort. After which he re-ascended the river, and finally overtook us, having travelled upwards of eight hundred miles, part of which was performed alone, and without any other subsistence than that obtained by hunting. His anxiety to overtake the party had led him to neglect his health and comfort during that journey. On his arrival, he took the direction of the escort which, until then, Mr. Denny had commanded. Our numbers remained, however, the same, as Renville parted from us that morning.

The Bois des Sioux is supposed to be the northernmost limit of the undisputed property of the Sioux on Red River. Beyond this they never hunt without being prepared for war, as the prairies between this place and the Wild Rice River to the east, and Turtle River to the west of Red River, form a sort of debatable land, which both Chippewas and Dacotas claim, and upon which both frequently hunt, but always in a state of preparation for hostilities.

After travelling nine miles beyond the Bois des Sioux, the party came to a stream, called Red River. This stream branches out, at about four miles above the place where we struck it; one of its branches rises, as we have mentioned, in Lake Travers, but is dried up during some parts of the year. The other rises in Otter-tail Lake, which is in the neighbourhood of the head of the Riviere de Corbeau. By the Indians this branch is called Otter-tail River, and the stream continues, after the junction of the two, to be called by them Sioux or Swan River, until it receives the Red Fork that rises in Red Lake; they then apply to the stream the name of Red River; while the traders have bestowed this appellation upon the branch that rises in Otter-tail Lake.

That lake is, as we were informed by one of our carters,

situated about one hundred and fifty miles in a north-easterly course from the head of Lake Travers; it is, according to his statement, about twenty-four miles long, and from four and a half to five miles wide. From the point at which we crossed Red River, Otter-tail Lake bears north-east, and is distant about seventy or eighty miles. Near to the head of the river are high lands, which were visible at various times during the day, they are called the "Montagnes des Feuilles," or Leaf Mountains. Mr. Jeffries described the country in that direction as being full of small lakes and "islands of wood." We forded Red River, it was about twenty-five yards wide, and two and a half feet deep. Its current was very rapid; the colour of its waters was white, owing to the muddy nature of its banks. As we were crossing it one of the carts was by the carelessness of the driver upset, just as it descended the bank, so that its contents became wet; as these consisted principally of the jerked meat, we were obliged to stop on the opposite bank to dry it, lest it should spoil. This detained us a long while, and afforded to some of the party an opportunity of shooting buffalo. The harassed state of our horses had obliged Major Long, that morning, to issue an order to prevent the "running of the buffalo," as it is called here, or the chasing of them on horseback. Such a chace frequently extends over four or five miles, and the excitement, which the horses themselves derive from it, is sometimes sufficient to impel them to run until their strength is completely exhausted. This measure, prescribed by a prudent care of our horses, was likewise in accordance with the dictates of humanity; for all who are not hunters, callous to the sight of a tortured animal, must regret the very indiscriminate slaughter which is usually made of the buffalo; yet it must be acknowledged that the sport has something dignified and highly interesting, and that it requires no small share of self-controul to remain a passive observer of it. Notwithstanding the general orders issued to that effect, about fifteen buffaloes were killed in one day.

After having dried our meat, we continued our journey, and soon discovered, at a distance, a herd of elk, (Cervus major,) to which three of the gentlemen immediately gave chase. This herd consisted of about fifty or sixty elks. After having approached on horseback as near as they could, without alarming them, the gentlemen dismounted, and crept for about a quarter of a mile on their hands and knees, leading their horses, until they came within eighty yards, when they all fired, and one of the herd fell. Mr. Colhoun, who was one of the party, then mounted his horse and pursued the herd for more than a mile. His horse being the best in the company, he got up with them in half that distance, but the horse was so much alarmed by the appearance of the elks, having probably never seen the animal before, that no spurring on the part of the rider, could urge him on near enough to give effect to the pistol shots which he fired. While Mr. Colhoun was chasing them, he observed that the elks in the rear would frequently stop to look at him. When in herds, elks are easily overtaken, but when they are alone it is much more difficult. This animal is however represented as being short-winded. The elk are generally approached in a creeping posture; this mode is also used in hunting buffaloes, by those whose horses are not very fleet. In order to protect their guns from the moisture of the grass, as well as to prevent them from being accidentally cocked, it is usual for the hunters to carry them in leather cases. The animal which our companions killed proved to be a female; they were engaged until near sunset in skinning and cutting it up, so that it was late in the evening when they reached the camp; this they found in a state of activity, owing to the adventures which the party had experienced in the afternoon.

While riding quietly across the prairie, with the eye intent upon the beautiful prospect of the buffaloes that were grazing, our attention was suddenly aroused by the discharge of a gun in the vicinity of the river, which flowed about half a mile west of the course that we were then travelling. While we were reckoning up our party, to know if any had straggled to a distance, we saw two Indians running across the prairie; their number increased very soon to twelve or fifteen, who hastened towards us, but as soon as they came near our party, stopped and examined us with minuteness; after which they presented their hands to us; we gave them ours. It was immediately observed that they were in a complete state of preparation for war, being perfectly naked, with the exception of a breech-cloth. They had even laid their blankets by. All of them were armed with guns, apparently in very good order, or with bows and arrows, and some with both. Their appearance though at first friendly soon became insulting. Their party had, in the mean while, increased to thirty or forty, so that they outnumbered ours. We found that they belonged to the Wahkpakota or Leaf Indians, whose character, even among their own countrymen, is very bad. Mr. Jefferies, who was to act as interpreter, being away, we availed ourselves of Mr. Snelling's knowledge of the language to communicate to them, in the course of conversation, our objects and intentions, as well as the friendly reception which we had met with on the part of Wanotan and the other Indians whom we had seen. In a tone more imperative than courteous, they expressed their wish that we should go to their camp and speak to their old chief. This we declined doing, informing them that some of our party had separated from us, and that we had a long journey to travel. They pointed to the sun, which was then low in the horizon, and added that we had no time to proceed further, and that we had better encamp with them that night. As an inducement, they added that we should be provided with squaws, whose beauty they commended much. This offer was alone sufficient to stamp them as worthless members of their nation, for the Dacotas agree in this respect with the Sauks, considering, as Wennebea expressed himself, that "men were not made like dogs for promiscuous intercourse." In this particular as well as in many others, the Dacotas differ materially from the Indians of the Missouri, whose manners Mr. Say described in the "Account of the Expedition to the Rocky Mountains." Major Long declined their invitation, whereupon they insisted that our party should encamp at a neighbouring grove, which they pointed out to us, as they observed that this would be a convenient place for their chief to come and smoke with us in the evening. While this conversation was going on, Mr. Say remarked that, either through design or accident, the Indians had intermixed themselves so much with our party, that every one of our number was placed between two or more of theirs. Mr. Snelling overheard them talking of our horses, admiring them, and examining the points of each; one of their band had even ventured so far as to ask him which horse was considered the best of the party. Finding that all further conversation was a waste of time, and having given them as much tobacco as our small stock of Indian presents allowed us to spare, Major Long mounted his horse, and gave his men orders to march. The Indians attempted no opposition at the time; but after we had travelled about a quarter of a mile, they following in our rear, a gun was fired at some distance on the prairie, to the right of our line, and a number of mounted Indians were seen in that direction, coming towards us. Those who had followed us, then made a signal to them that we were white men; and ran up to us to desire that, as their chief was then coming up, we would stop and shake hands with him; the party halted, until the mounted Indians had come up and greeted us in the usual manner. Observing that their chief was not among them, Major Long again set his men in motion, but before we had proceeded far, several of them ran up to the head of the line, fired their guns across our path, reloaded them immediately, and formed a crescent in front of the leader, to prevent him from proceeding. At that time the number of the Indians must have been about seventy or eighty, while ours amounted only to twenty-five. Their intentions could not be misunderstood. It was probable that they did not care much to harm our persons, but they were anxious to pilfer our baggage, and especially to secure our horses; and as we were resolved not to part with them without a struggle, it was evident that the first gun fired would be the signal for an attack, which must end in the total destruction of our party; for the number of the Indians, and their mode of dispersing upon the prairie, and continually changing their situation during a skirmish, would have given them a very great advantage over us, as, in order to protect our horses and baggage, we would have remained collected in a body, and exposed to their arrows and balls. But even in such a case, they must have lost some of their number, and this consideration, all-powerful with Indians, probably induced them to defer their attack until night, when their advantages would be still greater; and hence their anxiety that we should encamp in their vicinity. Had Major Long been perfectly free to act as he pleased, he would have avoided all further conversation, and have proceeded the whole night without stopping at all that evening; but this he could not do as long as some of the gentlemen were separated, for in such a case they would have been easily cut off by the Indians. It was with a view to give them a chance to overtake us, that he had continued the conference so long, and that he finally decided upon encamping at a point of wood then in sight, but farther than that which had been proposed by the Indians. With this view, the Major ordered the men to march; when one of the Indians advanced up to the head of the line, stopped the horse of the leader, and cocked his gun. The soldier who was there, and whose name was George Bunker, immediately imitated this action, determined to be prepared for a shot as soon as his antagonist; at this moment Major Long marched up to the head of the line, and led off the party. There can be no doubt that the resolution thus manifested had a great influence in preventing the Indians from making an immediate attack. It was night before we reached the place where we intended to halt. The tents were not pitched. The position was selected at a distance from the river, as the banks of the stream are skirted with woods in which a number of Indians were distinctly seen. Our horses were staked with very short ropes, the arms were all examined and loaded afresh, six centinels placed on duty, and the rest of the party remained up ready to resist any attack; a large fire was kindled in order to apprize our companions of our situation; and in this unpleasant uncertainty about their fate we remained until they made their appearance. They had fortunately seen no Indians. The supply of provisions which they brought was tasted, but found inferior to the buffalo. The fat of the elk partakes of the nature of tallow, and is much less fusible than that of other animals, so that unless eaten very hot it consolidates and adheres to the mouth. The best part of the animal is the udder, which, being fixed upon a forked stick, was roasted before the fire. As soon as our meal was finished the fire was extinguished. A few Indians had accompanied us to our camp, but all withdrew after a while except an old worthless man, who was recognized by several of the party, as his character was notorious at Fort St. Anthony. This fellow was one of the most impudent of the band, ceaselessly begging for tobacco, whiskey, &c. When he was told that the party had no whiskey with them, and that they had given as much tobacco as they could spare, he observed, with the greatest effrontery, " what then can you give me?" Observing that Mr. Keating was drinking out of his canteen, one of these Indians came up to him, and extended his hand, asking for whiskey; being told that it contained water and not whiskey, he attempted to take the canteen, which was, however, resisted.

The party being again safely united, Major Long considering that if an attack was intended, it would be made a short time before daylight, determined to allow the horses to rest until midnight, when the moon, rising, would make it pleasant and safe to travel. Accordingly at that hour we resumed our line of march. Our preparations for departure were made with the greatest expedition and silence, so as not to be observed by the Indians at a distance, and to avoid disturbing the old man that was sleeping or affecting to sleep under one of our carts; in the latter purpose, however, we failed; the old man awoke, and seeing what we were about, he left us immediately, notwithstanding the attempt made to amuse him with conversation until we should be ready to start; but we could not detain him; we saw him walk over the prairie, and by the light of the moon traced his figure until he got near to the river, when he disappeared in the woods. This was the last Dacota whom we saw.

Our march was continued without interruption for six hours; we have reason to believe that it is to this sudden departure that we owe our having escaped an attack from that band.

It may be interesting to mention, that the Dacotas have means of communicating information to those of their party that are at a distance. We had an opportunity of observing these telegraphic communications in more than one instance. In this case, in order to inform the mounted Indians that were seen at a distance on the prairie that we were white men, and that they might approach without fear, a few of them separated from the group, and ran round a circle several times, a signal which was immediately understood by their friends.

Had not our attention been seriously occupied by the hostile dispositions manifested by these Indians, we should have taken much interest in witnessing one of their great diversions. Some time before we met them, we observed a fine buffalo bull, who seemed to challenge a combat with our party; he travelled for about two miles abreast of us, and almost within gunshot; his eyes were intently bent upon us. Though occasionally driven off by our dog, he would constantly return, and continue in a parallel line, as though he were watching our motions. This fearless character, so unlike that of buffaloes in general, excited our surprize and admiration; and accordingly we determined to spare him, and see how long he would continue to travel with us. But the noble animal offered too strong a temptation to the Indians; seeing him stop at the same place where we had halted, a few of them, especially the youngest of the party, ran up to him, and in a few moments several balls, and perhaps a dozen of arrows, had reduced the animal to the last gasp. They then approached on all sides, and while he was engaged in keeping off those on his left, the youths on his right would come so near to him as to draw his attention to them; the animal appeared galled, his rage was extreme, but his weakness was equally so. At length some of them came very near to him, and caught hold of his tail; at that moment he was observed to be tottering; they all drew off, the animal fell, and after two or three convulsive throes he expired; a shout from the Indians announced the death of their victim. This seemed to be a schooling for the youngest of their party, a few of whom were mere boys. Mr. Seymour took a sketch of this singular diversion, which is represented in **Plate 7**; it is taken at the moment when the animal is tottering, but it does not express all the fire and rage which he manifested to the last.

When we stopped for breakfast the next morning, we heard some guns fired in the woods, which convinced us that some of the marauders were still in our vicinity; we continued our journey, however, without any impediment, avoiding the firing of guns, the separation of any of the party, or any other measure which might warn the Indians of our situation. We encamped at an early hour. Our journey across the prairies was extremely unpleasant; there was nothing to relieve the monotony of the scene; the buffaloes were fast diminishing in numbers, besides which, the regret, which those who were fond of hunting experienced at the fine chances which they were necessarily losing, abated the interest which we should otherwise have felt in beholding this imposing monarch of our prairies.

The calm repose of these prairies seemed to be more disturbed during the night, as the lowings of the buffalo on the west bank of Red River were then frequent and distinct; they contrasted strongly with the barkings of the wolf. During the first few nights that followed our adventure with the Indians, it was deemed advisable to increase the number of our sentinels, and with a view to stimulate them to vigilance, the officers and gentlemen of the party undertook the duty of watching in turn. These nights made a more lively impression upon several of the party, than any of those that had preceded them. The beautiful and boundless expanse of the prairies, as seen by the bright moonlight which we enjoyed during that period, the freshness of the night air, the stillness of the scenery, interrupted only by the melancholy howlings of the wolf, and the prolonged lowing of the buffalo, the recollection of the dangers which had lately threatened us, and against the recurrence of which we were then watching, all these were likely to suggest to the mind melancholy yet not unpleasant reflections.

In such a state the mind is apt to magnify and to form an incorrect opinion of the various objects which present themselves to the eye. It was, while watching on the night of the 29th, that Mr. Say's attention was suddenly directed to an object in the prairie. He saw it approaching with caution, and immediately the idea that it was probably an enemy, induced him to creep in the direction from which the object approached; it had the aspect of a wolf, but this he immediately conceived to be a stratagem of the wily Indian, who, to conceal his approach, had assumed a false garb. So intent was he upon this idea, that he scarcely considered it possible that it should in reality be but a wolf. He felt a strong temptation to fire upon it, but the fear of alarming the whole camp induced him to desist, and he was only satisfied of the true nature of the object of his attention, when the latter, alarmed at the rustling made by Mr. Say's creeping through the grass, scampered off on his four legs, with a rapidity and agility that satisfied him that this was its natural posture.

At this encampment Mr. Colhoun estimated Red River to be twenty yards wide, and its current about half a knot per hour. Its banks are boggy, and the water is thickened with particles of the rich light-blue clay through which it flows.

On the morning of the 30th we resumed our march at a very early hour, proceeding by moonlight. We crossed before breakfast a stream called Buffalo River, which, from the muddiness of the banks, offered some difficulty. It is about eight yards wide. In the afternoon we reached Menomone or Wild-rice River, the wading of which was more difficult; it was, however, effected without accident; but a very heavy shower, which fell immediately after we had crossed the river, detained us a long while; after which our tents, baggage, &c. were found so wet, that it was deemed expedient to take advantage of the returning sunshine to dry them; our situation in the valley being a very exposed one, we removed our tents to an eminence in the neighbourhood, where we found a position favourable for defence in case of need. Wild-rice River is twelve yards wide, where we crossed it, which was nine miles above its mouth; it was about three feet deep at the time. On that day we saw but one buffalo, it was at a late hour in the afternoon. This animal was killed by one of the party, and was the last that we saw. Mr. Colhoun has endeavoured to trace the extent of country over which the buffalo is known to rove at present, or to have formerly inhabited. Every thing that connects itself with the history of this strange and interesting animal, which by an old author is described as resembling " in some respect a Lion, in other the Camels, Horses, Oxen, Sheep, or Goats *," must be important to collect, for its numbers have diminished so rapidly within a century, its rovings have been so much restricted, that there is reason to apprehend that it will soon disappear from the face of the land.

The buffalo was formerly found throughout the whole territory of the United States, with the exception of that part which lies east of Hudson's River and Lake Champlain, and of narrow strips of coast on the Atlantic and the Gulf of Mexico, that were swampy, and had low thick woods. That it did not exist within eighty or one hundred miles of the Atlantic coast is rendered probable from the circumstance that all the early writers whom Mr. Colhoun has consulted on the subject, and they are numerous, do not mention them as existing there, but further back. Thomas Morton, one of the first settlers of New England, says, that the Indians " have also made description of great heards of well growne beasts, that live about the parts of this lake," Erocoise, now Lake Ontario, " such as the Christian world, (until this discovery,) hath not bin made acquainted with. These Beasts are of the bignesse of a Cowe, their flesh being very good foode, their hides good lether, their fleeces very useful being a kind of wolle, as fine almost as the wolle of the Beaver, and the Salvages do make garments thereof." He adds, " It is tenne yeares since first the relation of these things came to the eares of the English †." We have introduced this quotation, partly with a view to show that the fineness of the buffalo wool,

---

* Purchas his Pilgrimage, London, 1614, p. 778.
† New English Canaan, by Thomas Morton. Amsterdam, 1637. p. 98.

which has caused it within a few years to become an object of commerce, was known as far back as Morton's time. He compares it to that of the beaver, and with some truth; we were shown lower down on Red River, hats that appeared to be of a very good quality. They had been made in London with the wool of the buffalo. An acquaintance on the part of Europeans with the animal itself, can be referred to nearly a century before that; for in 1532, Guzman met with buffalo in the province of Cinaloa *. De Laet says, upon the authority of Gomara, when speaking of the buffalo in Quivira, that they are almost black, and seldom diversified with white spots †. In his History, written subsequently to 1684, Hubbard does not enumerate this animal among those of New England. Purchas informs us that in 1613, the adventurers discovered in Virginia, " a slow kinde of cattell as bigge as kine, which were good meate ‡." From Lawson we find that great plenty of buffaloes, elks, &c. existed near Cape Fear River and its tributaries §. And we know that some of those who first settled the Abbeville district, in South Carolina, in 1756, found the buffalo there. De Soto's party, who traversed East Florida, Georgia, Alabama, Mississippi, Arkansa Territory, and Louisiana, from 1539 to 1543, saw no buffalo; they were told that the animal was north of them; however they frequently met with buffalo hides, particularly when west of the Mississippi; and Du Pratz, who published in 1758, informs us that at that time the animal did not exist in lower Louisiana. We know, however, of one author, Bernard Romans, who wrote in 1774, and who speaks of the buffalo as a benefit of nature be-

* De Laet Americæ Utriusque Descriptio.   Lugd. Batav. Anno. 1633. Lib. 6. Cap. 6.
† Idem, Lib. 6. Cap. 17.   ‡ Purchas, ut supra, p. 759.
§ Lawson, ut supra, p. 48. 115, &c.

stowed upon Florida. There can be no doubt that the animal approached the Gulf of Mexico near the Bay of St. Bernard, for Alvar Nunez about the year 1535, saw them not far from the coast, and Joutel, one hundred and fifty years afterwards, saw them at the Bay of St. Bernard. It is probable that this bay is the lowest point of latitude at which this animal has been found east of the Rocky Mountains. There can be no doubt of their existence west of those mountains, though Father Venegas does not include them among the animals of California, and although they were not seen west of the mountains by Lewis and Clarke, nor mentioned by Harmon or Mackenzie as existing in New Caledonia, a country of indefinite extent, which is included between the Pacific Ocean, the Rocky Mountains, the territory of the United States, and the Russian possessions on the north-west coast of America. Yet its existence at present on the Columbia appears to be well ascertained, and we are told that there is a tradition among the natives, that, shortly before the visit of our enterprising explorers, destructive fires had raged over the prairies, and driven the buffalo east of the mountains. Mr. Dougherty, the very able and intelligent sub-agent who accompanied the expedition to the Rocky Mountains, and who communicated so much valuable matter to Mr. Say, asserted that he had seen a few of them in the mountains, but not west of them. It is highly probable that the buffalo ranged on the western side of the Rocky Mountains, to as low a latitude as on the eastern side. De Laet says, on the authority of Herrera, that they grazed as far south as the banks of the River Yaquimi*. In the same chapter this author states, that Martin Perez had, in 1591, estimated the province of

---

* " Juxta Yaquimi fluminis ripas, tauri vaccæque et prægrandes cervi pascuntur."—Ut supra, Lib. 6. Cap. 6.

Cinaloa, in which this river runs, to be three hundred leagues from the city of Mexico. This river is supposed to be the same which, on Mr. Tanner's map of North America, (Philadelphia, 1822,) is named Hiaqui, and situated between the 27th and 28th degrees of north latitude. Perhaps, however, it may be the Rio Gila which empties itself in latitude 32°. Although we may not be able to determine with precision the southern limit of the roamings of the buffalo, west of the mountains, the fact of their existence there in great abundance, is amply settled on the authority of Gomara, by the testimony of De Laet, L. 6, C. 17, and of Purchas, p. 778. Its limits to the north are not easier to determine. In Hakluyt's collection we have an extract of a letter from Mr. Anthonie Parkhurst, in 1578, in which he uses these words; in the island of Newfoundland there " are mightie beastes, like to camels in greatnesse, and their feete cloven. I did see them farre off, not able to discerne them perfectly, but their steps shewed that their feete were cloven and bigger than the feete of Camels. I suppose them to be a kind of Buffes which I read to bee in the countreys adjacent and very many in the firme land*." In the same collection, p. 689, we find in the account of Sir Humfrey Gilbert's voyages, which commenced in 1583, that there are said to be in Newfoundland, " buttolfes, or a beast it seemeth by the tract and foote very large in maner of an oxe." It may, however, be questioned, whether these were not musk oxen, instead of the common buffalo or bison of our prairies. We have no authority whatever which warrants us in admitting that the buffalo existed north of Lakes Ontario, Erie, &c. and east of Lake Winnepeek. From what we know of the country between Nelson's River,

* The principall navigations, voyages, and discoveries of the English nation, &c. by Richard Hakluyt. London, 1589. p. 676.

Hudson's Bay, and the lower lakes, including New South Wales and Upper Canada, we are inclined to believe that the buffalo never abounded there, if indeed any were ever found north of the lakes. But to the west of Lake Winnepeek we know that they are found as far north as the 62d degree of north latitude. Captain Franklin's party killed one on Salt River, about the 60th degree. Probably they are found all over the prairies, which are bounded on the north by a line commencing at the point at which the 62° meets the base of the Rocky Mountains, and running in a south-easterly direction to the southern extremity of Lake Winnepeek, which is but very little north of the 50th degree. On the Saskatchawan, buffaloes are very abundant. It may be proper to mention here, that the small white buffalo, of which Mackenzie makes frequent mention on the authority of the Indians, who told them that they lived in the mountains, is probably not the bison; for Lewis and Clarke inform us that the Indians designated by that name the mountain sheep*. It is probable that, west of the Rocky Mountains, the buffalo does not extend north of the Columbia.

At present it is scarcely seen east of the Mississippi, and south of the St. Lawrence. Governor Cass' party found, in 1819, buffaloes on the east side of the Mississippi, above the falls of St. Anthony. Every year this animal's rovings are restricted. In 1822, the limit of its wanderings down the St. Peter was Great Swan Lake, near Camp Crescent. In 1823, the gentlemen of the Columbia Fur Company were obliged to travel five days, in a north-west direction from Lake Travers, before they fell in with the game, but they then soon succeeded in killing sixty animals; the herds after-

---

* Vol. ii. p. 325.

wards advanced very near to Lake Travers, and perhaps even extended somewhat down the St. Peter. There can be no doubt but this constant subtraction from the buffalo's roamings must affect his numbers; certainly more than the practice of killing only the cows and leaving the bulls; a custom which has probably prevailed among the Indians for a long while, and which we cannot therefore consider as the source of the great modern diminution in their numbers. Civilization in its steady march destroys the larger gregarious animals, and even drives back the hunting man, unless he change his mode of life. If the deer were more social in its habits, that interesting tenant of our forests would have been long since driven to the asylum of the buffalo, the elk, and the beaver.

All the buffaloes which our party saw, were of an uniform dun colour. We were informed that they had been sometimes seen white or spotted. The age of the animal is said to be indicated by the number of rugæ or transverse lines on the horns. Mr. Colhoun killed a bull, that by this process of reckoning, was supposed to be twenty-six years old; in this calculation the first four rugæ are allowed for the first year. If this mode of calculation be correct, as is generally supposed, the buffalo probably attains a greater age than the tame ox. The frame of the buffalo is much larger than that of domestic cattle, and though its fore parts are uncouth, the hind parts are handsomely formed. Cows are considered more delicate eating than bulls, especially during the rutting season, when the latter assume a rank and strong flavour. This was the case about the time that our party saw them. We had no opportunity of killing cows, and as the bulls were lean, we ate principally the tongue and liver of those that we killed. These, together with the hump, hump ribs, marrow bones, heart, tender loin, and hunter's roast, (fillet near the shoulder blade,) constitute the choice pieces, and when buffaloes are plenty, are the only parts that are eaten. At Lake Travers, it is estimated that cows generally yield from two hundred and fifty to three hundred pounds of good meat. This is exclusive of the head and other parts. There are eight bones, (viz. those from the four legs and thighs,) which are enumerated as marrow bones. It is difficult to conjecture the quantity of marrow which they afford, either singly or collectively, but the marrow of one bone is frequently sufficient for a meal. To obtain it, the flesh is scraped off from the bones, and they are thrown into the fire; after remaining a few minutes, they are withdrawn, the bones broken, and the marrow, taken out with a stick splintered at one end, is eaten without any accompaniment. It is a very rich delicate food, resembling when roasted in colour and consistence a custard. It is by some persons preferred raw, but did not appear to us in that state to be so palatable.

In pursuing a herd of buffalo, particularly if it consist of bulls, a strong odour of musk is emitted, and is left in their wake, and their feet make the grass crackle as if it were on fire. We mentioned that the buffalo bulls frequently approached very near to our line, which, by some of our fellow-travellers, was attributed to the imperfect vision of the animal, whose eyes are obscured by the great quantity of hair which covers its face; this is probably, however, incorrect; it either arises from the greater fearlessness of the bulls during the rutting season, or perhaps from the circumstance that though they distinguish men very well, they are not aware of their nature by sight alone. It is the odour of man which is principally required to drive them off. We have seen bulls approach to windward of our line with the greatest composure, pass near us, but the moment they fell to leeward, the smell would set them galloping with the greatest speed. The quickness of their olfactory nerves is well known; sometimes when the wind is strong, they will be made aware of the presence of men, at two or more miles to windward of them. Buffaloes and elks are seen on the same prairies, and do not appear to be affected by each other's presence, they do not however herd together; each associates only with the animals of its own kind. We saw on the prairies with the buffalo, besides the elk, only the common prairie wolf, which appears to be the common attendant on the buffalo. Among the birds which we remarked were the bald eagle, (Falco leucocephalus,) and the hooping crane. The buffalo is often seen wallowing and throwing up the dust, which at a great distance resembles the spouting of a whale.

The difficulty of killing this animal is very great, and may be judged of by the fact that Mr. Peale fired fourteen balls into the chest of a buffalo before he killed him, and Mr. Scott, with a view to ascertain whether a ball fired at the head would break the frontal bone, discharged his rifle at a dead bull within ten paces; the ball did not penetrate, but merely entangled itself in the hair where it was found. It had, however, struck the forehead, and left a mark before it rebounded. This agreed with the general impression which Mr. Scott had formed on the subject, having been stationed more or less for the last ten years in a buffalo country, and having had frequent opportunities of firing at them in every direction. His skill and address in shooting, are proverbial on the Mississippi and Missouri. We had many occasions of witnessing them ourselves, though the great scarcity of game of any kind observed during the whole of the expedition, except on the prairies at the head of Red River, limited his opportunities of displaying his rare talent.

When we consider the great force, size, agility, and speed of the buffalo, we must regret that no successful experiment has as yet been made to domesticate this noble animal, and appropriate it to the wants of man. Instead of endeavouring to turn to use the many valuable animals which formerly roved over our country, the settlers seem to have been satisfied with importing those from Europe. There can, we think, be but little doubt that the buffalo might, by proper management, be domesticated, and made to replace with great advantage the European Ox. We have seen it, in one instance, used with apparent facility. Another experiment, which would certainly be very interesting, would be to ascertain whether the breeds might not be crossed, and what would be the result. We have, it is true, heard it asserted, and the impression appears to be general in that country, that a domestic bull had in certain cases impregnated a buffalo cow, and that the produce had partaken of the characters of both parents; but that a favourable issue could not be expected in the case of impregnation of the domestic cow, by the buffalo bull, because the pelvis of the former being too small for the issue of the calf, both the cow and her progeny would die before parturition. Mr. Say has endeavoured, but in vain, to trace the report to its source; having always found those who related it to speak on conjecture, he is inclined to doubt whether the experiment has ever been tried; indeed we were told, on Lake Winnepeek, where we saw a pair of buffaloes that were kept with domestic cattle, that during the rutting season the buffalo bull would not suffer the common cow to approach him. Perhaps, however, this natural antipathy might be made to wear away. The experiment is certainly worth trying.

While in the vicinity of the buffalo we were entirely free from the torment of mosquitoes, from what reason we know not; we can scarcely believe that the animal attracts them all to itself. It is probable that as we were at some distance we should have had a few of them were there not some other cause for their disappearance which we have not been able to discover; we at first attributed their absence to the cold nights which we experienced, but after leaving the buffalo we encountered still colder nights, and although all the other circumstances seemed the same, yet the insect reappeared.

On the 31st, the party continued its route, without any observation except for latitude, which was found at meridian to be 47° 26′ 41″ north. In the morning a female elk was killed by one of the Frenchmen that accompanied us. Our marches had, since we met with the Indians, been commenced at an early hour in the morning, but a very dense fog which covered the prairies until past sunrise detained us late on that day. Our apprehensions of being followed were, however, completely quieted on observing a large column of smoke behind us, which proved that the Indians had fired the prairies. The beds of two small streams, Plum and Sand-hill Rivers, were crossed this day. In the former there was no water, and we were obliged to satisfy our thirst with the stagnant fluid found in a pool, the quality of which was not improved by its having been resorted to by buffaloes. Having travelled eight miles on the morning of the first of August, and being within a short distance of the Grand or Red Fork of Red River, Mr. Colhoun took an observation for longitude on the bank of that river. The result was that we were in longitude 96° 53′ 45″ west, and our latitude a few miles beyond this, at the fording of the Red Fork, was 47° 47′ 25″. This branch was forty yards wide where we forded it; from the steepness of the banks we experienced some difficulty in getting our carts over. Its bed is sandy, and its current very rapid. On the 2d of August we suffered much from cold. The thermometer, which had stood at 83° the preceding day at noon in the shade, had sunk to 43° at sunrise. This variation was greater than any we had as yet observed, but for a number of days previous, the variation from sunrise to noon averaged 30°. The transition from great heat during the day to very cold nights was extremely unpleasant; it produced very copious dews, much heavier than any we had ever experienced. We were upon prairies, unsheltered by any tree, and from our mode of travelling very much exposed; frequently our clothes were as wet as if they had been soaked in water; this was one of the circumstances that made the mounting guard at night so arduous a duty both to the soldiers and gentlemen.

We had an opportunity of observing while travelling upon these prairies the long twilight nights which characterize high latitudes. We had scarcely more than five hours of night, and as the moon was at that time pretty full, we seldom experienced any darkness during the whole of our journey to Pembina.

There were numerous ponds of stagnant water upon these prairies, in one of which a beaver was seen, but at too great a distance to be shot at; in the vicinity Mr. Scott killed a line-tailed squirrel* which Mr. Say prepared; it appears therefore that this little animal inhabits prairies as well as woods. While pursuing pigeons, Mr. Scott shot a

* Sciurus grammurus, (Say,) Account of an Expedition to the Rocky Mountains, vol. ii. p. 72.

Falco Columbarius. The country was extremely dry, there were no streams of running water. The prairies were covered in a number of places with saline efflorescences, but no salt springs were observed. On the 2d of August the latitude of our noon encampment was 48° 2′ 39″, and on the 4th, it was 48° 39′ 45″.

On the 5th, we travelled fifteen miles before breakfast, and reached Red River, which we crossed in a barge, opposite to the settlement called Pembina, where we remained four days.

This completed a journey of two hundred and fifty-six miles, performed in eleven days, averaging therefore about twenty three miles per day. Had it not been for our meeting with the buffalo, and with the party of Indians, we should scarcely have experienced on that part of our journey any thing to which we could look back with interest. The dull monotony of a journey upon prairie land never appeared to us so fatiguing. No trees were to be seen except those that fringed the water courses, these consisted principally of several varieties of oak, of the white, and some red elm, linden, gray-ash, red-maple, cottonwood, aspen, hackberry, ironwood, hop-horn-beam, and white and red pine. On Red Lake we were told that the trees consist of fir, sugar-maple, and birch. The country is very flat, and remarkably deficient in water. There are no vallies, and but few brooks, streams, or even springs.

The streams that enter Red River from its source to the 49th degree of north latitude are, on its right bank, Buffalo, Wild-rice, Plum, Sand-hill, Red Fork, Swamp, and the "Two Rivers;" on its left bank, Pse, Shienne, Elm, Goose, Turtle, Saline, Park, and Pembina. Of these it may be observed, that some confusion exists as to the names of the streams, from the circumstance that different appellations are applied to them, by the Dacotas, the Chippewas, and the traders. A concordance between these different synonimies is difficult to establish; thus the term Pse, applied by the Sioux to one of the western tributaries, has the same meaning as the word Menomone, used by the Chippewa to designate one of the rivers that fall in on the east bank, and both are by the traders called Wild-rice, or Folle Avoine. We have used those names that were least likely to create a confusion, and as that of Menomone was preoccupied, we have kept the name of Pse for the western, and Wild-rice for the eastern tributary. However bad the names may be, we have preferred retaining them than increasing the confusion by substituting new terms. It is to be regretted that the practice of retaining the Indian appellations has not been more generally adopted by travellers; they have rejected the melodious and original names, to substitute others less pleasant to the ear, and worn out by frequent use, not only on this, but also on the other side of the Atlantic.

Buffalo River rises in a chain of small lakes, surrounded by a large forest, (Bois Grand), which is said to extend to the Mississippi. Its course from its source is about northwest, its length sixty miles, its breadth where we crossed it eight yards; its bottom muddy.

Wild-rice River is about one hundred and twenty miles long; its name is derived from the abundance of wild rice which grows in a circular lake, about eighteen miles diameter, in which it takes its rise. It is said that the supply of grain which this lake yields is inexhaustible. The course of the river is about parallel to that of Buffalo River; its breadth, nine miles above its mouth, was twelve yards.

The bed of Plum rivulet was five yards wide, that of Sand-hill ten, but both were dry.

The Red Fork, which, by the Indians, is considered as the main branch, takes its name from the Red Lake, in which it rises. Both are said to be translations of the term *bloody*, used by the Indians, and which is doubtless derived from some slaughter committed in that vicinity; not, as is the case with many other rivers which have the same appellation, from the colour of their bed.

In times of flood the Red Fork is navigable for barges throughout its length to Red Lake, a distance of one hundred and twenty miles; in ordinary stages of water, canoes can ascend to its source. This is the most important tributary of Red River, containing probably an equal quantity of water with the main stream itself. Mr. Jeffries informed us that Red Lake had the form of a crescent, with its back to the south-west, that its dimensions were sixty miles by twenty-four. Carver says, p. 72, that " Red Lake is a comparatively small lake, at the head of a branch of the Bourbon River, which is called by some Red River. Its form is nearly round, and about sixty miles in circumference." Carver had not visited the lake. The general course of the Red Fork from this lake is north-west; it receives a few small tributaries, the most important of which are Clear River, entering about thirty miles from its mouth on the south-west side, and Thief River, entering it from the north-east. The woods along Red Fork are very thick, and extend to about half a mile on either side. Hazlenuts were very abundant, and nearly ripe at that time. Below the junction of Red Fork with the main stream, Red River was observed to be about forty yards wide, and its current was about one knot per hour. The bed of Swamp River was dry. At the place where we crossed the " Two Rivers," each was about ten yards wide; they unite two miles below, and fall into Red River about ten miles beyond their junction. At the confluence of the two branches there is a considerable salt spring.

As we travelled on the east bank of Red River, we saw none of the tributaries that come in from the west, but Mr. Jeffries, who is well acquainted with the country, has described them to us as follows:—

The Pse River rises near the Coteau des Prairies, at the distance of about forty miles from Lake Travers.

The Shienne or Shåhiådå, (river of the Shiĕn, a nation driven by the Sioux to the Upper Missouri,) is a considerable stream, being as wide as Red River itself, above their junction; it has a fine clear water. Its general course is north-east.

Turtle River is formed by the junction of two branches, about forty miles above its mouth; it is of the size of Wild-rice River; it takes its source in Devil Lake; its course is north of west.

Big Salt River is a considerable stream, which rises in a lake of the same name, which is about a mile and a half in circumference.

Park River is of the same size as Big Salt River, and is formed by the union of several insignificant streams.

About one mile above the village of Pembina, the river of the same name falls into Red River; this is probably, next to the Red Fork, the largest tributary south of the 49th degree; about three miles above its mouth it receives the Tongue River, which is a large brook.

There are doubtless in this country a great many salt springs, especially below the Red Fork; we saw none, but we were informed that fine springs exist on Big and Little Saline Rivers, on the "Two Rivers," &c. where the salt is found in white efflorescences, so as to be annually collected there by the colonists of Pembina; notwithstanding which, at that settlement, the price of this article is from four to six dollars per barrel, weighing eighty lbs. One of the residents on this river cleared five hundred dollars in one winter by the salt which he collected. Probably by boring to a small depth abundant springs would be obtained. We had no opportunity of ascertaining the geological features of the country, having seen on the whole route no rock in place, and but few rolled stones, none of which had attained to any size. The soil of the prairies is occasionally sandy, though this does not appear to be its prevailing character; it is rather a dry argillaceous ground, which, within a few miles of the river and its tributaries, yields good grass, but at a distance from it presents but a scanty growth. We do not profess to be judges of prairie land; but we observed that where trees do grow, the soil appears extremely fertile. It is probable, that the fires, which annually overrun these prairies, destroy all the vegetable matter, and tend to keep the ground in an impoverished state. We observed a very great difference in the soil of those parts of the prairie from which the grass had not been burnt off the preceding year.

The causes of these conflagrations are numerous. The Indian frequently sets the prairies on fire in order to distract the pursuit of his enemies by the smoke, or to destroy all trace of his passage; to keep the country open, and thus invite the buffalo to it; to be able to see and chace his game with more facility; as a means of communicating intelligence to a distance with a view to give notice to his friends of his approach, or to warn them of the presence of an enemy. The traders often burn the prairies with the same view. Independent of these, the fires of encampments frequently spread in dry weather, and burn away the grass to a great distance. We may therefore consider fire as the cause of the continuance, if not of the original existence, of prairies, at least over much of our country; but there are some parts, and in this class we would be induced to include the country on Red River, where the great drought, the want of streams to moisten the soil, and perhaps some other causes, unite in preventing the growth of trees.

The settlement of Pembina is situated on Red River, about one hundred and seventy miles above its mouth. The river is here only fifty yards wide, but its depth is very considerable, in the middle of the stream not less than from ten to twenty feet; it is deeply incased, which prevents the water from overflowing the country, though its swells are considerable. An old trader, who has resided there for upwards of forty years, informed us, that he had once witnessed a flood which covered the banks; the water having risen sixty-six feet, but this report appeared to us very doubtful. The usual rises are from fifteen to twenty feet.

The principal inhabitant of the place, Mr. Nolen, being apprized of our arrival, furnished us the means of crossing the river, and entertained us several times at his house during our stay in his vicinity. We are indebted to him for much polite attention.

Pembina constituted the upper settlement made on the tract of land granted to the late Lord Selkirk by the Hudson's Bay Company. It may be well to observe, that by virtue of a charter from Charles the Second, granted in 1670, to Prince Rupert and others, constituting the "honourable Hudson's Bay Company," the whole of the British dominions lying contiguous to Hudson's Bay or its tributaries, has been claimed by that company, not only as regards the monopoly of the fur trade, but also as respects the right to the soil, and to the jurisdiction of the country. About the year 1812, Lord Selkirk, who was one of the principal partners, obtained from the company a grant of a considerable tract of land, including both banks of Red River up to the Red or Grand Fork. To this he extinguished the Indian title by the payment of a certain amount, and the promise of an annuity to the Indians. He then opened the lands for settlement, inviting a number of British subjects to go and reside upon them, and with a view to strengthen his infant colony, he engaged recruits from Switzerland and other countries, and especially increased it by a number of soldiers belonging to the de Meuron and de Watteville regiments, two foreign corps that were in the pay of England during the late war, and that were disbanded in Canada in the year 1815. Two principal settlements were formed, one at Fort Douglas, which is at the confluence of the Assiniboin and Red Rivers, and the other one hundred and twenty miles by water above that, and near the mouth of a small stream named by the Chippewas Anepeminan sipi, from a small red berry termed by them anepeminan, which name has been shortened and corrupted into Pembina *, (Viburnum oxycoccos.)

The Hudson's Bay Company had a fort here, until the spring of 1823, when observations, made by their own astronomers, led them to suspect that it was south of the boundary line, and they therefore abandoned it, removing all that could be sent down the river with advantage. The Catholic clergyman, who had been supported at this place, was at the same time removed to Fort Douglas, and a large and neat chapel built by the settlers for their accommoda-

* The *b* has been introduced by Europeans; the theme of the word is Nepin, summer, and Minan, berry.

tion is now fast going to decay. The settlement consists of about three hundred and fifty souls, residing in sixty log houses or cabins; they do not appear to possess the qualifications for good settlers; few of them are farmers; most of them are half-breeds, who having been educated by their Indian mothers, have imbibed the roving, unsettled, and indolent habits of Indians. Accustomed from their early infancy to the arts of the fur trade, which may be considered as one of the worst schools for morals, they have acquired no small share of cunning and artifice. These form at least two-thirds of the male inhabitants. The rest consist of Swiss and Scotch settlers, most of the former are old soldiers, as unfit for agricultural pursuits as the half-breeds themselves. The only good colonists are the Scotch, who have brought over with them, as usual, their steady habits, and their indefatigable perseverance. Although the soil about Pembina is very good, and will, when well cultivated, yield a plentiful return, yet, from the character of the population, as well as from the infant state of the colony, it does not at present yield sufficient produce to support the settlers, who therefore devote much of their time to hunting; this, which perhaps in the origin was the effect of an imperfect state of agriculture, soon acted as a cause; for experience shows, that men addicted to hunting never can make good farmers. At the time when we arrived at the colony, most of the settlers had gone from home, taking with them their families, horses, &c. They were then chasing the buffalo in the prairies, and had been absent forty-five days without being heard from. The settlement was in the greatest need of provisions; fortunately for us, who were likewise destitute, they arrived the next day. Their return afforded us a spectacle that was really novel and interesting; their march was a triumphant one, and presented a much greater concourse of men, women and children than we had expected to meet in those distant prairies. The procession consisted of one hundred and fifteen carts, each loaded with about eight hundred pounds of the finest buffalo meat; there were three hundred persons, including the women. The number of their horses, some of which were very good, was not under two hundred. Twenty hunters, mounted on their best steeds, rode in abreast; having heard of our arrival, they fired a salute as they passed our camp. These men receive here the name of *Gens libres* or Freemen, to distinguish them from the servants of the Hudson's Bay Company, who are called *Engagés*. Those that are partly of Indian extraction, are nick-named *Bois brulé*, (Burnt Wood,) from their dark complexion.

A swift horse is held by them to be the most valuable property; they are good judges of horses, particularly of racers, with which they may chace the buffalo. Their horses are procured from our southern prairies, or from the internal provinces of New Spain, whence they are stolen by the Indians, and traded or re-stolen throughout the whole distance, until they get into the possession of these men. Their dress is singular, but not deficient in beauty; it is a mixture of the European and Indian habits. All of them have a blue capote with a hood, which they use only in bad weather; the capote is secured round their waist by a military sash; they wear a shirt of calico or painted muslin, mocassins and leather leggings fastened round the leg by garters ornamented with beads, &c. The Bois brulés often dispense with a hat; when they have one, it is generally variegated in the Indian manner, with feathers, gilt lace, and other tawdry ornaments.

The character of the Bois brulé countenance is peculiar.

Their eyes are small, black, and piercing; their hair generally long, not unfrequently curled, and of the deepest black; their nose is short and turned up; their mouth wide; their teeth good; their complexion of a deep olive, which varies according to the quantity of Indian blood which they have in them. They are smart, active, excellent runners. One of them, we were told, often chased the buffalo on foot; we did not, however, see him do it. This man had a handsome, well-proportioned figure, of which Mr. Seymour took a sketch. He was very strong, and was known to have three times discharged, from his bow, an arrow, which, after perforating one buffalo, had killed a second; an achievement which is sometimes performed by Indians, though it is rare, as it requires great muscular strength. Their countenance is full of expression, which partakes of cunning and malice. When angry, it assumes all the force of the Indian features, and denotes perhaps more of the demoniac spirit than is generally met with, even in the countenance of the aborigines.

The great mixture of nations, which consist of English, Scotch, French, Italians, Germans, Swiss, united with Indians of different tribes, viz. Chippewas, Crees, Dacotas, &c. has been unfavourable to the state of their morals; for, as is generally the case, they have been more prone to imitate the vices than the virtues of each stock; we can therefore ascribe to this combination of heterogeneous ingredients, but a very low rank in the scale of civilization. They are but little superior to the Indians themselves. Their cabins are built, however, with a little more art; they cultivate small fields of wheat, maize, barley, potatoes, turnips, tobacco, &c. A few of the more respectable inhabitants keep cows and attend to agriculture, but we saw neither a plough nor a yoke of oxen in use, in the whole of the upper settlement. Considering the high latitude of Pembina, the above-mentioned plants thrive well. Maize yields tolerable crops; so does tobacco, which even yields seed. The wheat which is in greatest repute here is the bearded wheat. The price of agricultural produce is apparently very high. Wheat sells for two dollars per bushel; Indian corn for three dollars; barley, which is much used by the colonists in soup, yields three dollars; potatoes from fifty cents to one dollar; and the other vegetables in proportion. It may be well, however, to add, that these are mere nominal prices, there is no specie currency, every thing is traded for in the way of exchange for some other commodity, at the rates affixed to them by the Hudson's Bay Company, of which the following may give an idea. Gun powder at one dollar and a quarter per lb. Buck and small shot at seventy-five cents per lb. Tobacco two dollars per lb.

The main object of the party in visiting this place being the determination of the 49th degree of latitude, Mr. Colhoun lost no time in taking observations. The first one which he made was near Mr. Nolen's house, and although not very satisfactory, yet it showed that we were near to the boundary line, as it indicated 48° 59′ 27″. We then pitched our camp a little further down on the bank of the river, and as near as we could judge to the boundary line. A large skin lodge, which was lent to us, sheltered the gentlemen of the party during our stay there; our flies were pitched around it for the use of the soldiers. In honour of the President of the United States, this place received the name of Camp Monroe. A flag-staff was planted, which, after a series of observations, made during four days, was determined to be in latitude 48° 59′ 57$\frac{1}{3}$″ north. The magnetic variation having been ascertained to be 13° 17′ 25″ east, the distance to the boundary line was measured off, and an oak post fixed on it, bearing on the north side the letters G. B. and on the south side those U. S. On the 8th of August, at noon, the flag was hoisted on the staff, which bore south $44_o\ 25'$ west of the post, at a distance of $207\frac{1}{2}$ feet. A national salute was fired at the time, and a proclamation made by Major Long, that " by virtue of the authority vested in him by the President of the United States, the country situated upon Red River, above that point, was declared to be comprehended within the territory of the United States." This declaration was made in the presence of all the inhabitants collected for that purpose. They appeared well satisfied on hearing that the whole of the settlement of Pembina, with the exception of a single loghouse, standing near the left bank of the river, would be included in the territory of the United States. While fixing the posts, the colonists requested that they might be shown how the line would run; when this was done, the first observation they made was, that all the buffalo would be on our side of the line; this remark shows the great interest they take in this animal, to which all their thoughts recur. We might almost apply to them the observation made by Gomara of the natives of the province of Quivira, and which is strictly true of the Dacotas. " The people have no other riches, (than the buffalo); they are unto them meat, drink, apparel; their hides also yield them houses and ropes; their sinews and hair, thread; their horns, mawes, and bladders, vessels; their dung, fire; the calves skins budgets wherewith they draw and keep water *."

* " Præter hæc animalia, nullas præterea divitias noverunt barbari ; hæc ipsis cibum potumque subministrant, (caro autem optimi est saporis,) tergoribus illorum corpora sua pariter atque casulas muniunt; e laciniis eorum funes contorquent; ossa illis stilos; nervi villique funes; cornua buccinas; vesicæ utres; fimus denique siccus fomites præbet." Vide De Laet, ut supra, L. 6, C. 17. and Purchas p. 778.

The spot upon which we were encamped was a fine level prairie on the edge of the woods that skirt the river; two or three lodges were built in our vicinity; these Mr. Seymour sketched, and they are represented in plate 8, which shows the two different kinds of lodges used by the northwest Indians; those who reside on the prairies, and who hunt the buffalo, use the skin lodge, which is formed by a number of buffalo skins, united into one, and wound round a number of light sticks or poles, so as to form a conical tent. Of this nature are all the lodges used by the Dacotas. On the other hand the Chippewas, who for the most part live to the north-east of the buffalo regions, and who have no more of these skins than they require for their personal use, construct their lodges of large pieces of the birch-bark, which they fix upon a frame, made of the young branches of trees, bent so as to form an oblong lodge. These are covered with bark, which, when they travel, is rolled up and carried by the women. The plate gives a good idea of the dress, appearance, and attitudes of the Indians and half-breeds that surrounded us. It likewise exhibits two dogs, carrying burdens in the manner of pack-horses. We have ascertained that a good dog will sell here for twenty dollars, payable in goods. This animal generally consumes from six to ten pounds of fresh meat, or four pounds of dry meat per day; it is never fed but at night, otherwise it is indolent all day. We were not a little amused at examining the house of a man that takes dogs to board and lodge for the summer, receiving about three dollars a head for the season. He returns them in the autumn to their masters, who use them during the winter season. He feeds them in summer altogether upon fish, chiefly the *hyodon*. In a short time he caught enough to support during the day thirty or forty dogs, which he then had under his care; sometimes the number of his boarders is far greater. It is said that hydrophobia never occurs among dogs in these climates.

Although the weather was not as favourable as might have been wished for the astronomical observations, yet the point at which the boundary line passes is probably determined with as much accuracy as the nature of our instruments permitted; and we are happy to state, that it coincides very well with approximate observations taken by Mr. Fidler, who was employed as surveyor to the Hudson's Bay Company.

The fur trade of Pembina, which results from animals killed on the south side of the boundary line, has been estimated as follows:

	Packs.	No. of skins in each pack.	Price per pack.	Amount. Dollars.
Beaver	4	400	400	1600
Martin	$\frac{1}{2}$ or	300		300
Otter, a few skins				
Fisher		200 skins		300
Bear, (finest),		150 do.		900
Elk, (dressed),		300 do.		1200
Minx		200 do.		100
Muskrat		4500 do.		1800
Wolverine		250 do.		500
Fox		200 do.		400
			Dollars	7100

This constitutes the amount of furs annually made up for the use of the company, and which is probably rated at the nominal value of the country. They might in addition to these collect a large quantity of buffalo, grizzly bear, wolf, hare, rabbit, swan, and prairie wolf. But the company having found but little advantage in trading in these furs, they are not sought after. By comparing this amount with that yielded by the fur trade on the St. Peter alone, we shall be able to judge of the small importance to be attached to the trade of Pembina. Twelve trading houses on the St. Peter made up the year before we visited the country about two hundred and thirty six packs, which consisted of

	No. of packs.	Weight and No. of skins in each.
Buffalo	168	10
Muskrat	40	600
Raccoon	6	100 lbs. .. 80
Beaver	4	100 lbs. .. 80
Otter	4	100 lbs. .. 60 (prime).
Fisher	3	100 lbs. ..120
Minx	4	100 lbs. ..450
Bear	6	100 lbs. .. 14
Red Fox	1	100 lbs. ..120

Martins, very few; they inhabit in preference evergreen woods.

Ermine abundant, but not traded.

Lynx, less than one pack.

Antelope, none.

Thus the trade of the St. Peter, reduced as it is at present, is still far more important than that of Pembina. But whatever this trade may be, it will diminish as the population increases; hence it is only to the agricultural resources of this settlement that we must look with a view to the future improvement of the country. And no doubt can exist that, in this respect, Pembina will equal, if not surpass, all other settlements on Red River. The most important question, however, which suggests itself to us is, not what can be raised, but what market can be obtained for the produce of the country; and here it must be acknowledged, that there are but few facilities for a foreign market. The communication with Hudson's Bay is too long and too difficult to offer any well grounded hope of its being ever resorted to for an export trade. That with Lake Superior may be carried on by two routes, either by Lakes Winnepeek, and of the Woods, or by Red Lake; but both of these present great difficulties; the easiest navigation to the sea is undoubtedly up Red River to Otter-tail Lake, and thence by the Riviere de Corbeau and the Mississippi to New Orleans. We do not consider the route by Lake Travers and the St. Peter as offering any prospect of being ever adopted. The only foreign market which appears to us therefore as open to Pembina, is that obtained through the port of New Orleans; but the distance of upwards of three thousand miles must for ever render this route an unprofitable one; the intermediate country, far from presenting any hopes of a market, will likewise have a surplus agricultural product to send down to the mouth of the Mississippi, where it will arrive less encumbered with expenses of transportation. The produce raised at Pembina never can be sufficiently valuable to compensate these disadvantages; and we very much question, whether the country be adapted to the raising of hemp, as was anticipated by the founder of the colony; to the west and northwest we see no prospect of a market. It has been said, that the support of the persons engaged in the fur trade would be an object for the agriculturist; but if it be borne in mind, that in the days of the greatest prosperity of the British fur trade, and at a time when the two rival companies had a much larger number of Engagés than they probably will ever have in future, the aggregate of the servants of both companies did not exceed five thousand men; we shall remain convinced that the supply of so small a population offers no brilliant prospects to the colony. Whatever may be the amount of the population of Pembina at a future period, it will, we think, have to depend much upon the internal resources of the country; it can look to no foreign trade. Great hopes appear to have been entertained, by some of the colonists, of the discovery of valuable mines; and they have already had among them some who have announced the existence of silver ore, and have even asserted that they had obtained the metal out of it. We saw no ore of this kind; the prairies do not present any character that would lead us to anticipate the discovery of mines in their neighbourhood. There is a mountain on Pembina River, about thirty leagues from the settlement, in which these mines are supposed to exist; we saw a specimen from it, but it was the common iron pyrites. Coal has been represented as being found there; whether there be any foundation for the report we know not.

Of the plants observed in this neigbourhood, besides the Pembina, we can only mention the common hop; and the raspberry-bush, which yields fruit in great abundance and of a very superior quality; also a large kind of whortleberry, the fruit of which is double the size of ours, and more oval. The forest-trees are the same which we had previously seen on Red River. The zoology of the country is not very diversified. Among the birds seen by Mr. Say, during our stay at Pembina, were the turkey-buzzard [*], red-headed woodpecker, flicker, hemp-bird [†], king-bird [‡], sparrow-hawk [§], house-wren, robin [||], chimey-bird [¶], barn-swallow [**],

[*] Cathartes aura.   [†] Fringilla tristis.   [‡] Tyrannus pipiri, Vieil.
[§] Tinnunculus sparverius.   [||] Turdus migratorius,   [¶] Hirundo pelasgia.
[**] Hirundo Americana.

night-hawk *, whip-poor-will †, bald-eagle, hairy woodpecker, great heron ‡, grakle §, kildeer ‖, blue-winged teal, ruddy duck ¶, rose-breasted grosbeak **, crow, raven, and pigeon ††, the last of which is very abundant in the woods.

Among the quadrupeds were the pouched rat ‡‡, flying squirrel §§, Hudson's Bay squirrel ‖‖. Wolves are very numerous and bold. Some came up to our lodge during the night, and bit very severely one of our horses that was staked near it.

We may conclude this imperfect statement of the present situation and future prospects of this colony, with a tabular view of the distance from Pembina to some of the most important places; premising, however, that estimates made upon such an immense extent of territory, and in countries as yet very little explored, must of course be liable to errors; it is only upon loose calculations that these estimates are founded.

1. *Distance from Pembina to York Factory, on Hudson's Bay.*

	Miles.
From Pembina to the mouth of Red River	163
Along the east side of Lake Winnepeek	300
Play Green Lake	14
Saskatchewina River and Portage	35
Carried over	512

* Caprimulgus popetue, Vieil.   † Caprimulgus Virginianus.
‡ Ardea Herodias.   § Icterus quiscala.   ‖ Charadrius vociferus.
¶ Anas rubidus, Wilson.   ** Loxia Ludoviciana.
†† Columba migratoria.
‡‡ Pseudostoma bursaria, (Say.) See Account of an Expedition to the Rocky Mountains, vol. i. p. 406.
§§ Pteromys volucella.   ‖‖ Sciurus Hudsonius.

	Miles.
Brought over	512
Hare Lake	7
Each-away-man's brook, in dry seasons no water; ten beaver dams kept in repair	28
Rivulets and small lakes, 5 portages	50
Holy Lake	30
Trout River, many rapids, 2 portages	13
Knee Lake	47
Jack-tent River, many rapids, 5 portages	10
Swampy Lake	7
Hill River, series of shoals, strong rapids, innumerable sunken rocks, 12 portages, and many discharges	62
Main river, comes from South or Nipegon, Steel River, must be towed up	27
Hayes River	52
	845

The above admeasurements were made by David Thompson, Esq. one of the best geographers in the British dominions of North America, and at present employed on the boundary line commission. They are extracted from "A Narrative of Occurrences in the Indian Countries of North America, London and Montreal, 1818."

2. *Distance from Pembina by the St. Peter to New Orleans.*

	Miles.
From Pembina to the mouth of the Grand Fork of Red River	130
Thence to the mouth of the River de Sioux	180
Carried over	310

SOURCE OF ST. PETER'S RIVER.   51

	Miles.
Brought over	310
Length of the River des Sioux	35
Length of Lake Travers	15
Portage to the St. Peter	1
Length of the St. Peter	500
From the mouth of the St. Peter to New Orleans upwards of	2000
	2861

3. *Distance from Pembina to New Orleans, by Otter-tail Lake and the Riviere de Corbeau.*

	Miles.
From Pembina to the mouth of Sioux River	310
To the head of Otter-tail River	75
Two small lakes and portages	4
Thence to the Mississippi by Leaf and de Corbeau Rivers, a distance, as stated by Pike, (App. Part I. p. 53,) of	360
Distance to the Falls of St. Anthony	300
Thence to New Orleans, say	2000
	3049

The distance from the Mississippi to Otter-tail Lake, by this route, appears to us very much overrated.

4. *Distance from Pembina to Buffalo by Lakes Winnepeek and of the Woods*

	Miles.
From Pembina down Red River to Lake Winnepeek	165
Across the lake to the mouth of Winnepeek River	65
Up Winnepeek River to the Lake of the Woods	175
Carried over	405

	Miles.
Brought forward	405
Across the Lake of the Woods	75
To Fort William on Lake Superior	453
Along the northern coast of the lake to the Sault de Ste. Marie	316
To Mackinaw	84
To Detroit	300
To Buffalo	270
	1903

On this route there are seventy-two portages.

5. *Distance from Pembina to Buffalo by Red Lake.*

	Miles.
To the mouth of Grand Fork	130
Up Grand Fork to Red Lake Portage	200
Thence by a series of lakes and portages to Cassina Lake	70
Through Cassina Lake	7
To Sandy Lake	271
Through Sandy Lake	3
Up West Savannah River	18
Savannah Portage	6
Down East Savannah River	24
Down river St. Louis to Fond du Lac	75
Along the southern coast of Lake Superior to Sault de Ste. Marie	505
Thence to Buffalo	654
	1963

The distances from Cassina Lake to the Sault de Ste. Marie by this route, are those given by Mr. Schoolcraft

SOURCE OF ST. PETER'S RIVER.   53

in his Narrative Journal of Travels, &c. ut supra, p. 169, 204, 236, and 253. We might add several other routes; but the data which we have are not sufficient for us to establish even estimates of the distances. The shortest route from Lake Superior to tide water is not through the St. Lawrence, but through Michipicotton Bay, Brunswick and Moose Rivers, &c. to Moose Factory on James' Bay; loaded canoes pass through in sixteen days; the distance cannot exceed eight hundred and fifty miles. It will soon be used by the Hudson's Bay Company to the exclusion of that at present travelled between Fort William and York Factory.

Several of the routes which we have enumerated can be travelled at much shorter distances by wheels in summer, or by sledges in winter. The object which we have had in view is not to give exact distances, which, in the present state of the country, is as unnecessary, as it would prove impossible, but to show that direct water communications exist by various routes between the waters of the Gulf of Mexico, the Gulf of St. Lawrence, and Hudson's Bay; and that, in this respect, North America presents perhaps an unparalleled instance of direct water communications for thousands of miles. Some of these routes are, it is true, very much obstructed by rapids and falls, which occasion portages and lightening places. Still there can be no doubt that, at a future period, new routes will be discovered, or the old ones will be so much improved as to admit of a comparatively easy communication with the elevated plains which furnish the sources of Nelson's River, the St. Lawrence, and the Mississippi.

CHAPTER II.

Fort Douglas, and Lord Selkirk's colony. Bark canoes. Lake Winnepeek. Fort Alexander. River Winnepeek. Rapids. Portages. Fine falls. Lake of the Woods. North-westernmost point of the boundary line. Rainy Lake river and lake. Fort. Series of rapids and lakes. Dividing ridge. Falls of the Kamanetekwoya. Arrival at Fort William.

WITH a view to comply with his instructions, Major Long proposed to travel along the northern boundary of the United States to Lake Superior; but he was informed at Pembina that such an undertaking would be impracticable; the whole of the country from Red Lake to Lake Winnepeek, Lake of the Woods, and Lake Superior, being covered with small lagoons and marshes, which rendered it impenetrable for horses. The only practicable mode was to follow the principal streams in bark canoes, which being very light could be carried whenever the navigation was obstructed by shoals, rapids, &c. Several routes were suggested; that by Lake Winnepeek appeared the best, and was adopted. It is the same which was formerly travelled by the partners and clerks of the North-west Company, and which is still occasionally used by the Hudson's Bay Company. Our horses becoming useless, we had to dispose of them, and in this transaction we were more fortunate than we could have expected. Horses from the United

States are in great repute, and notwithstanding the hardships which ours had undergone they were sold, without much difficulty, at a rate which varied from forty to one hundred dollars, averaging about sixty-six dollars. This was, however, payable in services, stores, and such goods as we required. Our mode of travelling in bark canoes obliged us to obtain an additional supply of men accustomed to this kind of navigation. Of these we hired several at Pembina; and it being thought that the rest of them, as well as the canoes, &c. could be had on more advantageous terms at Fort Douglas, Major Long proceeded by land to that place, while the other gentlemen availed themselves of Mr. Nolen's polite offer to take a passage in a barge which he was sending down the river with a load of provisions.

Mr. Snelling and Mr. Jeffries having volunteered their services to this place only, and considering that, as we had left the Dacota territory, we had no further necessity for Sioux interpreters, resumed their march homewards, the former gentleman to his father's garrison on the Mississippi, the latter to his residence on Lake Travers. As an escort they took with them corporal M'Phail, and privates Newman and Irvine, three men whose services were no longer required, and who behaved themselves well while with us. We are happy to add that this party reached its destination without accident.

On the 9th of August, Major Long left Pembina, and reached Fort Douglas the second day after. He estimated the distance by land at sixty-one miles. It had generally been rated at seventy-five miles, which is undoubtedly too much, as it has often been travelled in one day on horseback, and even in a light carriage, on the snow. After travelling about fifty miles on the west side, he crossed over to the east bank, which he followed until he came to the confluence of the Assiniboin and Red Rivers, when he again crossed the river and arrived at the Hudson's Bay Company's fort, where he was hospitably received by Donald Mackenzie, Esquire, chief factor, and one of the counsellors of the company. As soon as Major Long had explained to this gentleman the nature and objects of his party, and the circumstances which had induced him to proceed through the Company's territory, Mr. Mackenzie made a free and liberal offer of his services and assistance in any thing that depended upon him. This he did even before he had seen the recommendatory letter which Major Long had received from His Excellency, the Right Honourable Stratford Canning, Envoy Extraordinary and Minister Plenipotentiary from his Britannic Majesty; a letter, which, as it was very obligingly given by Mr. Canning, and as it no doubt contributed much to ensure to the party the very hospitable reception which we experienced while in his Britannic Majesty's dominions, we have great pleasure in inserting here [*]. It is impossible for us to convey in adequate terms, the very warm gratitude which we feel for Mr. Mackenzie's kind attentions. Independent of that assistance which his official situation enabled him to afford,

---

[*] *Washington City, May 1st,* 1823.

SIR,

This letter will be exhibited to you by Major Stephen H. Long, of the United States' Topographical Engineers, who, for objects purely scientific, has been ordered to conduct an exploring expedition up the St. Peter's River, thence to proceed to the 49th degree of north latitude, and thence to the lakes on his return home. The American government, conceiving it possible that Major Long may have occasion to pass on his way through some of the British posts or settlements along the frontiers, have requested me to state the nature of the expedition, and to recommend that officer and his party, to the civilities of his Majesty's officers and subjects in the North-west Territory. It is on this account that I furnish Major Long with the present letter, not doubting that it will afford you pleasure to treat both him and the party which he conducts, in case of their

he contributed to all the comforts which we experienced in the subsequent part of our journey, by liberal additions to our stores from his own private stock. One instance will suffice to show how extensive and how particular was his attention. Observing that some of the gentlemen were fond of reading, and knowing from experience that a voyage in bark canoes is very tedious, unless it be relieved by books, he immediately offered, and insisted upon their accepting, some of the most interesting works in his library. Those who are fond of literature, and who reflect upon the distance at which Mr. Mackenzie was from all repositories of books, will fully appreciate the liberality which could induce him to part with the works of Milton, Hume, Cowper, &c. &c. and unless they be aware of the pressing manner in which he insisted upon the acceptance of these books, they will scarcely excuse the gentlemen of the party for thus robbing him of treasures very difficult to replace. The gentlemen of the party left Pembina on the 10th of August, in a barge belonging to Mr. Nolen, and which had been built in London; the soldiers were divided in three wooden canoes. The journey to the lower settlement required three days. The distance by water has been variously stated. Mr. Thompson, the able surveyor to whom we previously alluded, estimated it at ninety miles; we have seen it laid

---

approaching your station, with attention and good offices suitable to the friendly relations subsisting between the two countries.

I am, sir, with truth and regard,
Your most obedient humble servant,
STRATFORD CANNING.

To any officer of his Majesty or other person having authority in the posts or settlements situated within his Majesty's North-western American Territories.

down at one hundred and eighty; our guide allowed it to be forty leagues. While descending, Mr. Colhoun admitted it to be one hundred and seventeen miles, but as he considered his estimate to be a low one, we may safely assume it to be at least one hundred and twenty miles. The general course of the river is north, but the stream is extremely winding; we never had before us a reach or view of more than one mile, and this only on one occasion. The breadth of the river, after leaving Pembina, is very uniform, and is about seventy yards. Its depth is not great. In many points its navigation was obstructed by shoals, and in one or two spots by primitive rocks apparently out of place; but the river was at that time unusually low. In an ordinary stage of water, it must afford a pleasant and safe navigation; its bed as well as the banks are muddy; they rise from eight to twenty-two feet. We saw along the bank trees, which, from the bark being rubbed by ice, seemed to indicate that the river at times rises at least fifteen feet. Our guide told us, but we are induced to doubt the accuracy of his statement, that sometimes it rises forty feet and inundates the prairies between Fort Douglas and Pembina, so that canoes are paddled over the prairies. Without admitting this, we may believe that in many seasons the river would afford ample scope for a steamboat navigation. There are no rapids, properly speaking, in the river; the current averages about one mile per hour. Sometimes the prairies approach to the edge of the water, but generally there is a line of woods which extends along the banks, on a breadth of from fifty yards to half a mile. This consists, near the margin of the river, of a thick growth of willow, next to which comes cotton-wood, and higher on the bank, aspen, bass, elm, oak, &c.

At about seventy miles from Pembina, while we stopped

for breakfast, we were informed that there was a salt spring in the vicinity; to this we immediately repaired; we found it to be in the bed of a brook, called Saline River; the brook was dry at the time; there was a stagnant pool of water, which contained probably about five per cent. of salt; the spring which supplies this pool must be a very large one. We were informed that this spring, which was worked during one season, had been abandoned, being considered the weakest in the country. We observed, with some surprise, the Salicornia herbacea growing very abundantly around it. We brought home specimens of it. Mr. Schweinitz states, on the authority of Mr. Nuttall, that this is the only inland locality of this plant, besides the Onondago salt springs in the State of New York, (vide Appendix 1, Botany.) At this place Lieut. Scott saw an antelope, (Antilocapra Americana, Ord,) but did not succeed in killing it. A singular fact respecting this antelope was that it approached very near to Mr. Say, without evincing the least apprehension; unfortunately he was at that time so intent upon the collecting of insects, that he was not even aware of its presence. This animal is not abundant here; we occasionally saw tracks of it, as well as of the elk and bear, on the soft mud near the river bank, but the most frequent tracks were those of the wolf. Mr. Say killed here a Muscicapa ruticilla and Totanus flavipes. But the most abundant game we saw were ducks and pigeons, of which we might have killed many, had we been able to spare the time; our sportsmen, however, occasionally fired at them and were generally very successful. In the evening the soldiers caught a great many fish of the genus Hyodon, called there Doré.

Along the bank there is an abundance of bushes, bearing

a small wild cherry; the Pembina, and several other berries, some of which are very pleasant to the taste.

Two observations for latitude were taken on the river; one about one mile below the mouth of the Wăsŭshkwătăpĕ, or Muskrat River, at noon on the 12th of August, gave for result, 49° 35′ 55″ north. The other made at the same hour on the 13th, and within three miles of the confluence of the Assiniboin with Red River, gave 49° 51′ 3″.

The first house of the lower settlement is situated about twenty miles by water above the fort, but the country is thickly settled only within three miles of the mouth of the Assiniboin. At the lower settlement there are two forts, one called Fort Gerry belonging to the Hudson's Bay Company; the other, called Fort Douglas, is the property of the colony; there are also two houses of worship, one of them of the Protestant Episcopal Church, erected and supported at the expense of the London Bible Society, who likewise supply the funds for a free school. The clergyman, who attended both to the church and school, had left there a short time before our arrival, on a visit to England. The other church is the cathedral of a Roman Catholic Bishop established there. His diocese extends north of the United States' boundary line, from the Rocky Mountains to Upper Canada. He is styled Bishop, *(in partibus,)* of Julianopolis. A Catholic school, instituted at this place by the Missionaries, and conducted upon the same plan as Mr. M'Coy's on the St. Joseph, appears to have been attended with the same success. The whole of the expenses of this Catholic ecclesiastical establishment is, we believe, defrayed by the Bishop of Quebec.

The population of the settlement amounts to about six hundred. There is an appearance of neatness, and even of comfort, in many of the cabins belonging to the Swiss and Scotch settlers. The agricultural improvements are daily becoming more respectable, and adding to the prosperity of the colony. The soil is not so good as at Pembina, yet large crops of grain have been obtained. It appears well adapted to the growth of wheat, barley, oats, and potatoes. Maize has not yet had a fair trial. Of wheat they have repeatedly obtained from twenty to forty and even more bushels to the acre. Perhaps the greatest desideratum at Fort Douglas is wood, which, growing only upon the banks of the rivers, is becoming scarce. They have a few tradesmen and manufacturers among them. A tanner, who appears to understand his business well, has been brought over, and makes very good leather from buffalo hides, so that they are not all at present reduced to the necessity of wearing mocassins. An attempt has also been made to convert the wool of the buffalo to some useful purpose. An association has been formed for this object, which has contracted with the Hudson's Bay Company for the requisite supply of skins; they pluck out the hair that covers the wool; and then separate the latter by an ingenious process into the different qualities, which are said to be no less than eight or nine. The coarse wool is manufactured into a good substantial cloth; the fine qualities are sent to England, where, it is said, they find a ready market. Mr. Pritchard, who superintends this important establishment, kindly showed it to us, and communicated some interesting facts relating to it. It was in his possession that we saw a hat, manufactured by his brother in London, in which the beaver had been replaced by buffalo wool.

A number of gentlemen, formerly officers in the colony, have remained and settled here; some of them are represented as wealthy; several of them expect their families over. These, with the family of the governor, whose arrival was daily looked to, will form a small society, calculated to refine the manners of the colonists. It must be admitted that the choice of the settlers was in some respects unfortunate; instead of good agriculturists, a number of tradesmen and mechanics were brought over from Switzerland; some of them were watchmakers, unacquainted with the culture of the soil. We could not help pitying a poor man, who had been an apothecary in Switzerland; he was possessed of that pharmaceutical and chemical knowledge which the Swiss apothecaries generally have, and hearing of a settlement about to be formed on a large scale, imagined that one of his profession would be much wanted. He accordingly joined the party, stocked with aniseed, Palma Christi seed, &c. all which he soon found would be of no use to the colony or to himself. The place was healthy, but destitute of grain; his hopes of a botanical garden dwindled away at the necessity of handling a plough, and attending to the more important cultivation of wheat, potatoes, &c.

The history of Red River would, if correctly and impartially written, offer many useful lessons. The place was first visited by the French, and their arrival there is referred to the visit of the Chevalier de la Veranderie, who is said to have been the first French officer that travelled to the Rocky mountains. He built a fort at the mouth of the Assiniboin, called it the Fort de la Reine, and garrisoned it with soldiers. The French continued to trade there alone for many years, but about the year 1767, the first English traders visited it; and, it appears, that about fifty years since, it was a place of great resort both for English and French traders. At that time, or soon after, there were six opposition companies, which after a while dwindled into the famous North-west Company, one of the most active and enterprising trading associations that was ever created. The trade was then extremely profitable; in one season, a trader might almost realize a fortune. As an instance of what it was even eighteen years ago, we may mention, that Desmarais, the man who guided our canoes from Fort Douglas to Lake Superior, purchased at one time from an Indian, two packs of beaver skins, containing about one hundred and twenty skins, and weighing about one hundred and eighty pounds, for which he gave two (three point,) blankets, eight quarts of his best rum, and a pocket looking-glass. These goods were rated by the company at thirty dollars, but had probably not cost fifteen. The beavers sold in Montreal for upwards of four hundred dollars; this was considered fair dealing with the Indians.

The first colony was planted in the year 1812, when Miles Macdonell, who was appointed its governor, built a fort on Red River. The colony throve indifferently well, but quarrels broke out between the colonists and the North-west Company's servants. We have no wish to enter into particulars on the subject of this unfortunate division; suffice it to say, that a disunion, founded upon commercial rivalry, had for a long time previous existed between the Hudson's Bay and the North-west Companies; the colony was considered by the latter as planted for the purpose of strengthening the interest of the former. Fears were expressed that the establishment of the colony would prove ruinous to their commercial transactions, as agriculture and a fur trade cannot flourish in the same country. Apprehensions were likewise entertained that the colony would civilize the Indians, and divert them from hunting. From these and other causes, the new settlers became involved in the quarrel. There were probably provocations and wrongs on both sides; finally the colony was assaulted by a party of Bois Brulés, supposed to be connected with the North-west Company; and in 1815, the inhabitants were all dispersed; they returned, however, to their homes, and were again assaulted in 1816, and again driven from their settlements, after the murder of their governor, and of about twenty of the colonists. From this moment a real civil war may be said to have been carried on between the servants of the two companies. Both appealed to the government of Canada, and to the British Ministers. For a while these complaints were unheeded, but finally the evil became so great that a remedy was sought for, and found in a combination of the two companies on terms which were not made public. A general amnesty ensued. The evil which has been done to this country, twenty years will not obliterate. The immense sums of money incurred in prosecutions, recriminations, &c. may be forgotten, but the lawless spirit inculcated on the Bois Brulés, who were engaged on either side, will require years to tame it. Even at this day the traveller feels that he treads upon dangerous ground if he alludes to it; for the spirit of party is not eradicated. We may, however, hope that the instructive lesson, that commercial rivalry must be kept within bounds, will not be forgotten, and that by the wise and conciliatory steps which the company has taken, the seeds of discord will be completely removed, and that the country will rise to that prosperity, to which its fine soil and good climate entitle it.

The terms upon which the colonists were brought hither, varied probably in almost every case, according to the talents and abilities of the individual. It is probable that to all, great advantages in the way of land were offered, and even assistance in cattle, tools, &c. Within a few years, the great difficulties being removed, and the apprehensions of hostilities having ceased, the land has been offered for sale. The price was at first two dollars per acre; but this having been thought too high in the present state of the colony, it was reduced in 1823 to one dollar per acre. We cannot fail in wishing this colony success, because it will not, we think, vitally affect the interests of the fur trade, which is chiefly carried on to the north-west of the settlement, and because, even if it did, the benefits and advantages, which would result from it, would be much greater than those arising out of the fur trade. When we take into consideration that the whole of that trade is limited to two ships of three hundred tons each, which sail annually from Hudson's Bay to England, and whose return cargoes of British goods are amply sufficient to purchase the furs, and supply the wants of traders, we shall be convinced that the prosperity of England, either in a commercial or a manufacturing point of view cannot be materially affected by the rise or decline of this trade. The evil which it has done to Canada has been frequently and justly deplored; it has allured many of her youths from the steady occupations of agriculture, to attend the wandering pursuits of the traders; it has instilled into their minds a taste for extravagance and dissipation; it has accustomed them to the lawless habits, which have been, for a century back, a subject of regret to the missionaries and to the philanthropists. No doubt can exist that the young men who have been annually sent out from Canada, and who were formerly termed the "Coureurs de Bois," have had more influence in demoralizing the Indians of North America, than any other cause whatever. They have distributed liquor more freely, and more extensively, than any other traders; they have accustomed the Indians to that promiscuous intercourse, which destroys every rational as well as every virtuous feeling; they have made them parties in their quarrels, thereby exciting them to acts of hostility against white men.

One of the greatest evils, which the colonists have experienced, was the abundance of grasshoppers, that almost ruined the crops for one or two years. This was only, however, at the lower settlement; none were seen at Pembina. Cattle appear to be very much wanted, and supplies are anxiously expected; some were brought over, at first, from England, they throve very well; after which they procured some from Mackinaw, and in 1822, a drove was brought by Mr. Dickson from Clarksville, but he lost many on the way. Another drove was daily expected at the time our party was there. Lord Selkirk had a fine farm, which he intended to stock with Merino sheep; but all, that were brought over, were destroyed during the dissensions. Hogs have not succeeded so well. Norwegians were brought over with a view to domesticate the indigenous Reindeer, and substitute them for dogs; and an establishment, called Norway house, was formed at the northern extremity of Lake Winnepeek, but it does not appear to have met with great success. Dogs are the most numerous of the domestic animals. Some care seems to be taken at present, to prevent their roving at large as they formerly did, proving a great hindrance to the agricultural pursuits of the colonists.

Our camp was situated on a high bluff, about seventy or eighty feet above the level of Red River, near Fort Gerry, which is at the junction of the two streams. Fort Douglas lies about one mile below this on the river. The Assiniboin is a beautiful romantic stream, whose breadth, at its mouth, does not exceed fifty yards, yet it is an important river on account of its length. We were informed that it was at least five hundred miles long; and it was given in evidence, during one of the numerous law suits arising out of the discussion between the two companies, that the Hudson's Bay Company's fort on the Riviere qui appelle, (a tributary of the Assiniboin) was distant four hundred miles from Fort Douglas. A little above the fort, the river is said to expand considerably. The name of this stream has of late been written Ossiniboin, but we believe the old spelling agrees better with the Chippewa etymology of the term, Assin, *stone*. As the district of land, ceded to the late Lord Selkirk by the Hudson's Bay company, has received the official name of Ossiniboia, it is probable that this new orthography will prevail. The extent of this territory, as stated in Governor Macdonnell's proclamation, will be seen in Major Long's topographical report. (Chapter 13.) The United States' boundary line will, of course, cut off much of this province; still it will leave it nearly as large as the State of Georgia.

The prospectus of this colony, as published by the late Lord Selkirk, has been censured very harshly by many, who have taxed him with wilful misrepresentations, intended to mislead those whom he wished to enlist as colonists. This charge does not appear to us to be just. His prospectus presents the description of a really fine country, expressed in those terms of warm commendation which we should naturally expect from a mind of a sanguine and generous disposition such as the whole course of his public and private life indicates that of the distinguished founder of this colony to have been. The great exertions and sacrifices, which he made in behalf of the settlers, prove that he was sincere and ardent in the wishes which he manifested for their success; he expended a large fortune, and, what is a better test of his sincerity, he underwent many personal hardships and dangers, to protect his settlers against those whom he considered as the persecutors of the colony. Whatever opinion may therefore be entertained of the expediency of his measures or of the policy of his colonial system, all must acquit him of any selfish or interested motives, or of any abandonment of those whom he had induced to settle on Red River. It is not from the success or failure of a measure, that the motives of its promoters are to be deduced; and in this case it appears to us by no means improbable, that if the colonists had not been involved in the quarrel with the North-west Company, the Red River settlement might have realized the hopes and wishes of its founder.

One of the principal hardships which the colony had to undergo was from the severity of the winters. The maximum of cold, or lowest point to which the thermometer descended in the winter of 1822-23, was -52° (F.) But this is amply compensated by the warmth of the summer; and the rapidity of the vegetation makes up for the shortness of the season. From the quantity of wild fruit about here, we are led to believe, that with a little care, good orchards might be obtained. The fruit consists of apples, plumbs, pembina, and several varieties of raspberries, one of which is deeper coloured, smaller, and more oval than the domestic raspberry of our gardens; it partakes of the flavour of the strawberry.

We were detained several days at the settlement, by the preparations required for our navigation; but the time spent there was rendered very interesting, by the singular association of features which the country presented, as we observed it while seated on the elevated bank upon which Fort Gerry stands. The beautiful confluence of the Assiniboin and Red Rivers washed the base of the bluff.

Extensive prairies, upon which a number of domestic cows were grazing, lay before us, while a young buffalo bull, which had been presented to the bishop, was seen on the opposite bank, employed at labour. Both the banks of the river displayed occasional groups of Indian lodges and European tents, belonging to the Indians, half-breeds, or to our party. On the stream, a number of canoes, constructed either from logs or birch bark, were seen occasionally gliding before us, under the quick and dexterous management of the paddlers; while some, filled with Indian boys, engaged in successfully angling for beautiful little silver fishes, the hyodon of the naturalist, were moored immmediately in front of us. Canadian carters were frequently passing by, urging on their spare and lazy horses, by the often and angrily repeated words, "marche donc." Several Indians with their squaws, and children without number, of every possible shade of colour between the red and white, idled away their time upon the bank; numerous dogs played, barked, or snarled, at the gateway of the fort. These and many other features, which were peculiar to this spot, offered us food for pleasant contemplation. But an object, which once observed rivetted our attention, was the sight of a crazed woman standing alone in a canoe, which she was steering with apparent ease. She had a tall commanding figure; a soft expression of melancholy beauty, such as is often seen in the women of mixed European and Indian blood. Her dark eyes had, from the disordered state of her mind, received a wild and peculiarly interesting expression. She struck the water at irregular intervals with a long paddle which she held by the middle, singing at the same time a melancholy air, that struck our ear melodiously and sweetly, as we heard it from a distance. Perhaps, however, it was but the effect of an association of ideas, which lent a melancholy interest to her voice. We made some inquiries about her, and were told that she was the wife of one of the settlers. She was a half-breed, whose insanity was supposed to have sprung from a religious melancholy. Being one of those whom the missionaries had converted, she had become very pious, but her intellect was too frail for the doctrines which had been taught to her; in endeavouring to become familiar with them, she had been gradually affected with a malady, which at that time seemed incurable. While we were listening to this story, the wind heightened, the evening approached; all the canoes had disappeared from the river except her's, which she still kept on the stream, notwithstanding the high breeze which roughened its surface. We expressed our apprehensions lest her canoe would be upset, but we were told that she understood the management of it as well as if possessed of reason; her only pleasure and occupation seemed to be to move about alone in this frail bark; and her friends, believing that there was but little danger in it, indulged her in this her only diversion. Meanwhile the canoe was swiftly impelled from us towards the opposite bank; the loose wrapper which she wore, acted as a sail that received the wind and wafted her across. We saw her land in safety, and felt easier when we observed the poor maniac descend from her canoe. The next day she crossed the river, came towards us, and with much modesty presented to us a small parcel of papers, neatly folded up and secured by a thread; she desired that it might be given to her mother in Montreal. There was no superscription. We opened it, it contained but a printed sheet of a religious tract. Having performed her errand, she made a slight inclination and passed away.

The time of the party was likewise occupied in hearing

Mr. Mackenzie relate some of the interesting adventures of his life. This gentleman, who is of the family of Sir Alexander Mackenzie, has spent twenty-four years in the Indian trade, and has travelled over the greater part of North America. He wintered as far north as the sixty-second degree of latitude, on the river which bears the name of his distinguished kinsman. He was one of the party consisting of Messrs. Hunt, Crooks, Stewart, Mathews, &c. who in the employ of Mr. John J. Astor, of New York, crossed the Rocky Mountains, and penetrated to the mouth of the Columbia, where they made the first settlement for the American Fur Company. Mr. Mackenzie spent ten years on that side of the mountains. In the course of his travels he followed for upwards of six hundred miles the stream usually called, in Lewis and Clarke's travels, the Multnomah, but the true name of which, according to Mr. Mackenzie, is the Wallamut*. Of all these he communicated many interesting particulars, as well as of the animals found in that part of the country.

We had an interview with an old Chippewa chief, the leader of a party that resides near Red Lake. Although he dwells in the territory of the United States, yet as we met with him on British soil, we confined our conversation to general topics, avoiding all political subjects. This man had a peculiar expression in his face, which induced Mr. Seymour to take a likeness of him; it is the left hand figure in the plate containing the three Indian heads. We

---

* Mr. Henry, a trader, whom we met at Fort William, and who likewise imparted to us some valuable information concerning that part of the country, did not consider the Wallamut to be the name of the stream itself, but of a fall of about forty feet, situated in the river, a short distance above its confluence with the Columbia. The river itself has a distinct name, which Mr. Henry could not recollect at the time.

have omitted to record his name; by the French traders he is called the "Blackman," *homme noir*.

The position of Fort Gerry was determined from a series of observations to be in latitude 49° 53′ 35″ north, and in longitude 97° 00′ 50″ west.

On Sunday, the 17th of August, our preparations being finished, we left this place, at which we had experienced much kindness, not only on the part of Mr. Mackenzie, but also of Mr. Kemp, the acting governor*, and of a number of the inhabitants.

We embarked in our canoes at noon, and proceeded down the river. Our party, which had been reduced at Pembina by the departure of six of our fellow-travellers, was reinforced here by the addition of a Chippewa interpreter, a pilot, and nine canoe men, of whom five were Canadians, and four Bois Brulés. Our numbers therefore amounted to twenty-nine. We were divided into three bark canoes, known by the name of "canots du nord." Although these are made nearly on the same model, yet there is great difference in their speed, burden, soundness, &c. according to the skill manifested in their construction. A canoe of this kind is generally constructed of ribs of cedar bent so as to impart to it its proper form, the ends being secured to a band that forms the superior edge of the vessel, and acts as a gunwale; over these ribs the birch bark is laid in as large pieces as possible, generally so that there shall be but two longitudinal seams, and two or three transverse; between the bark and the ribs very thin splints of cedar are placed so as to prevent the bark from splitting; all the joints are sewed with long threads obtained by splitting the roots of a

* Mr. Bulger, the late governor, left Fort Douglas a few days before our arrival. A new governor was daily expected; in the interim the colony was governed by Mr. Mackenzie, as chief factor, and Mr. Kemp as acting governor.

tree called by the voyagers *epinette*, and which is probably a spruce *. To this thread the term watap (w'átá'p,) used by the Chippewas, is applied by the Canadians; the seams as well as the cracks are covered with pitch, (called by the Chippewas Péké,) made of the gum of the epinette; this is applied hot, and renders the canoe water tight. In this manner a little vessel is obtained, very well calculated for travelling on these waters, as it will carry a burden of upwards of three thousand pounds; and when any obstruction in the navigation is encountered, the cargo may be discharged, and the canoe easily carried by two men. Those which we used were thirty feet long, by about four feet wide in the middle, and perhaps thirty inches deep. A number of transverse bars serve to keep the canoe in its proper shape. The seats of the paddlers are suspended to the gunwale. The bow and stern are sharp and turned upwards. The great objection that attends the use of bark canoes is the difficulty of keeping them water-tight. It requires the greatest attention to prevent them from touching a rock, or even the shore, as they would otherwise break; hence they are never brought near to the bank; two men keep the canoe afloat at a distance, while the rest of the crew load or unload her; the canoe is unloaded every night, raised out of the water, and left on the beach, bottom upwards; this is also occasionally done when they stop during the day; it affords an opportunity of allowing the canoe to dry, otherwise the bark absorbs much water, and becomes very heavy. All motion on the part of those on board is to be avoided, as it causes the pitch to crack, and renders the canoe leaky. This mode of conveyance is the only one in use in the country, and answers very well; it requires, however, skil-

---

* Abies alba.

ful men to manage the canoes. Much art is particularly displayed by the bowsmen and sternsmen to steer them; the middle-men have only to paddle fast or slow, forward or backward, as they are directed. In steering through rapids the bowsman has the most difficult post; he is, therefore, always considered to be the captain of the boat; his wages, as well as those of the man in the stern, are higher than those of the middle-men. When several canoes go together, they constitute what is termed on those waters a brigade, and to these a pilot or guide is appointed, who is generally an experienced man, responsible for the loss of the canoes, and to whom all are subordinate; he is not obliged to paddle himself. We had engaged the services of one Baptiste Desmarais, who proved a faithful and active guide, well skilled in his business; he conducted our brigade with dexterity and success. When they carry passengers, the guides are sometimes apt to assume too much authority and consequence. The responsibility which attaches to their station, in case of the loss or detention of the canoes under their guidance, requires that they should direct the march, and fix upon the proper places and times to encamp; this gives them an opportunity of displaying their brief authority in a manner that is oftentimes unpleasant to those not accustomed to it, but in this respect we had but little cause to complain of Desmarais, for we found him obliging and respectful in his demeanor to the party.

Our soldiers, who at first were unacquainted with this kind of navigation, soon became expert paddlers, and answered well in that capacity; but it requires the long experience of the voyagers to render them as cautious and handy in the management of these canoes as their frailty requires. In this respect we found the Bois Brulés far superior to the Canadians.

Our journey down Red River was performed in a day and a half; we encamped the first night on a small island, about thirty-five miles below the settlement; and the next morning at an early hour we reached the mouth of Red River, which is situated forty-three miles below that of the Assiniboin. The stream retains much the same characters as above Fort Douglas. There are several rapids, more remarkable for the shallowness and rocky nature of the bed than for the swiftness of the water. At the first rapid, which is about twelve miles below the fort, the banks cease to be muddy; they become gravelly, the soil is thin and of a pale hue; the growth was principally small aspen. At twenty-eight miles, we saw limestone *in situ*; it is a horizontal secondary rock, such as probably lies under these prairies. It was the first rock which we saw in place after we had left the primitive islands in the valley of the St. Peter, unless indeed the rapids in Red River be occasioned by ledges of primitive rocks in place, which is not impossible, but which we could not ascertain at the time that we passed over them. We observed in the limestone no organic remains, although it probably contains some. This is the only place where limestone has been found, by the settlers, at the surface; it is therefore resorted to for the lime used in building at the fort, as well as for the tan yard, and for the other wants of the colony, &c. At the island upon which we encamped on the 17th of August, the river was much wider; the eastern channel was small, but the western was about two hundred yards wide. This was the second island which we had observed on Red River from its head to this place; the first island was but a short distance above. Below this place there are several other islands; they are for the most part small and thickly overgrown with aspen. Among the remarkable features of Red River may be enumerated its total want of islands, excepting near its mouth, and the circumstance that it has no bottom or valley properly speaking; it runs in a mere trench in the prairie. Towards the mouth of the river the country becomes an impenetrable swamp.

Having already enumerated the tributaries of Red River south of the 49th degree, we shall briefly note those which occur between Pembina and the mouth of the river. These consist, on the right bank, of the Reed-grass and Muskrat Rivers; on the left, of Swampy, Plumb, Gratiats, Saline, Muddy, Assiniboin and Death Rivers.

Reed-grass River is by the Chippewas termed Pekwionusk (Pĕkwiŏnŭsk); at its mouth it is twenty yards wide; it rises near the Lake of the woods, and, as we were told, within two leagues of it. The interval which divides its source from the lake being marshy, the canoes are dragged through it. Desmarais informed us that he would return by that route, and that he could walk in three days from its source to its mouth.

The Wasushkwatape (Wăsŭshkwătăpĕ) or Muskrat River is twelve yards wide at its mouth.

Swampy or Petopek (Pĕtŏpĕk) River is a mere brook; so is the Pekasun (Pĕkăsŭn), or Plumb River, both of which were dry at the time we saw them. Below these a small rivulet receives the name of Kaomenakashe (Kăŏmĕnăkăshĕ,) Gratiats of the French.

Saline we have already stated was a dry brook. The Wenagomo (Wĕnăgŏmŏ,) or Muddy River, is also inconsiderable. The Assiniboin has been described. It receives, as we were told, several tributaries designated by the names of Cypress, la Souris, Mushroom, Au Milieu, Qui Appelle, &c.

The last of the tributaries of Red River is Death River, or Onepowe Sepe (Ŏnĕpŏwĕ Sĕpĕ), a small stream which has received this gloomy name from the circumstance that two hundred and fifty lodges of Chippewas are said to have been destroyed there, about forty-five years since, by the Dacotas.

Red River discharges itself into Lake Winnepeek by four channels.

Lake Winnepeek receives its name from the muddy or sallow appearance of its waters; We (Wĕ) signifies muddy, and Nepe (Nĕpĕ́) water, in Chippewa. It is a large sheet of water with low marshy banks to the south and south-west. To the north-east the shore swells into broad hills, of no great elevation, which are covered with a thin growth of pine*, spruce †, juniper ‡, tamarack or tacca-mahac §, red cedar ‖, white birch ¶, and a sort of poplar similar to the balm of Gilead **. Among the shrubs there are rose bushes, pembina, and a bush yielding a small dark blue berry, resembling in form and colour the huckleberry, but sweeter and higher flavoured; by the French traders it is called *poire;* it has received the English name of service-berry; the Chippewas call it Osakwakko minan (O'sàk-wàkkó mìnàn ††.) Lake Winnepeek is about two hundred and seventy miles long, by eighty broad in its widest, and fifteen in its narrowest part. Its general direction is about north north-west. Its shore is much indented. We coasted it for about thirty-five miles, very near to its south-eastern extremity; proceeding from one projecting point to another, our course, which was at first a little east of north, soon became due north, (by the compass,) and continued so until we came near to the entrance of

---

* Pinus alba, nigra, &c. † Abies Canadensis, Mich.
‡ Juniperus communis. § Laryx Americana, Mich.
‖ Juniperus Virginiana, Mich. ¶ Betula papyracea.
** Populus balsamifera. †† Mespilus arborea, Mich.

Winnepeek bay. As we travelled near to the eastern shore, we always kept land in sight on our right, but on the left, the eye met with nothing but an uniform sheet of water, limited by no land, diversified by no island. The wind blew somewhat fresh when we first reached the lake, so that a long swell upon its surface gave us an opportunity of admiring the buoyancy of our canoes. After travelling eighteen miles on the lake, we landed on a fine pebbly beach, which we were told was encompassed in the rear by a deep swamp called the " Grand Marais." This beach was covered with pebbles and boulders of sienitic and calcareous rocks, which, from their aspect, showed that we were near the junction of the primitive and secondary formations. After having dined and repaired one of our canoes, which was leaky, we proceeded on our journey.

Lake Winnepeek appears to have been the same as was formerly called by travellers, Lake of the Assinipoils. It is mentioned under this name by Lahontan and Charlevoix; Carver gives it its modern appellation. The situation of this lake, in the centre of the continent of North America, is singular and interesting. Few lakes receive so many and such large streams; by many of these, and of the rivers that flow from it, a direct communication is kept up, not only with several distant points of the Eastern and Atlantic Ocean, but also with the Pacific or Western. An observation for latitude taken on the shores of this lake, gave 50° 41' 3" north. Previous to entering the lake, we passed two small Indian villages, one situated at Death River takes its name from that stream, the other receives an appellation indicative of its situation at the mouth of Red River.

On the 19th of August we reached the peninsula, which lies at the mouth of the bay into which Winnepeek River discharges its waters. This peninsula was then under water, so as to leave exposed merely an island of about four miles long and three broad, usually called Elk Island. In order to avoid passing all round it, it is usual to unload and carry the canoes and their cargo over this peninsula, which forms two small portages of about thirty yards long. Our canoes passed, however, without difficulty, owing to a high wind, which sweeping the surface of the lake from the north-west, had raised the water upon this bar. At this place our canoes were steered nearly east. This was considered the most distant part of our journey. We reached it in one hundred and twelve days, having travelled over upwards of two thousand and one hundred miles, without any accident, and with but little difficulty. At this place we left the track usually travelled by the Hudson's Bay Company's canoes, to take that formerly followed by those of the North-west Company. The brigade that carries the furs from Fort Douglas to York Factory, the ancient Fort Bourbon of the French, passes to the west of Elk Island. It performs its voyage in about fifteen or twenty days. On its return, the voyage requires from thirty to thirty-five days, on account of the length of time consumed in ascending the streams. It is usual for the Company's ships to leave England together, with supplies of goods; they generally sail about the last of June, arrive at York Factory about the middle of August, and return to England with the furs brought down in the spring. The brigade does not wait their arrival, but carries and distributes at all the posts, the goods imported the preceding year, so that there is always one year's supply in advance at York Factory.

On reaching the outlet of Winnepeek River, we observed a great change in the aspect of the water, which was clear and transparent; this was soon accounted for by meeting with sienitic rocks in place, and we were informed by our guides that similar rocks extend all the way up the river. About a mile beyond this we reached Fort Alexander. The junction of the primitive and secondary rocks is therefore about 50° 45′ of north latitude and about 96° 30′ of west longitude. It appears probable, from all the information which we have collected, that the whole of the eastern shore of Lake Winnepeek, is occupied by a primitive formation, while the western is composed of secondary, and these probably limestone, rocks. This accounts for the fact that the prairies are limited to the east by that lake, while they extend as far north as the Saskatchawan and to a considerable distance up that stream. It appears to us by no means improbable that the excavation of this lake was occasioned by the easier decomposition of the strata at the junction of the two formations. No where, perhaps, upon the surface of the earth, is a difference in the geological characters of the country attended by a more striking diversity in the superficial or topographical aspect. We observe here, that wherever the primitive rocks prevail, the country abounds in lakes, swamps, short streams filled with falls and rapids, as is the case with the whole country which extends from Lake Winnepeek to Lake Superior, and which reaches nearly to the Falls of St. Anthony on the Mississippi, while the secondary formation is covered with fine high and dry prairies. The track which our party followed must have been very near to the eastern limit of the secondary or prairie country, as all the eastern tributaries of Red River or the St. Peter, are represented as rising in those small lakes and lagoons. It would be curious to ascertain whether the small group of lakes called Devil Lake, &c. situated between the two Coteaux des Prairies, may not be occasioned by a reappearance of primitive formations at that place.

Fort Alexander, usually called "Fort du Bas de la Riviere," was one of the most important posts of the Northwest Company, being a distributing one, whither all the goods and furs were sent. Its position was in this respect well chosen, but it has now lost all its importance. One of our canoes being very leaky, we determined to make it undergo a complete repair, and with this view remained there a day. The situation of Fort Alexander, surrounded with marshes, restricted our walks and confined us to the immediate vicinity of the establishment. Its position was ascertained, by observations, to be in latitude 50° 36' 30" north. It was at this place that we saw a buffalo bull and cow, with their calf, associating with domestic cattle. They were young, but had been so far tamed as to come and lick salt on the hand, even of strangers. Their size appeared very great compared with that of the European bull. Although but three years old, the buffalo bull measured within half an inch of sixteen hands; this was inclusive of the hump. We were told, that before the cow calved she ran several miles into the woods, and remained there some time. When the calf was found, it was very wild, but at the time we saw it, it had become at least as tame as a domestic calf.

A question, which has been much discussed by travellers, is that of the supposed periodical rises in the lakes; we do not propose to take part in this discussion at present, but we may state that we observed at Fort Alexander an appearance, such as has probably more than once been mistaken for an effect of tide. On our arrival, we pitched our tents upon a sort of wharf projecting into the river, and elevated about two feet above the level of the water. In the afternoon a high wind blew from the lake, and accumulated the waters into the bay, so as to cause them to overflow the wharf and oblige us to remove our tents. The next morning, the waters had subsided to their former level. Had we not been aware of the accidental cause which produced this local rise, we might probably have mistaken it for the effect of a regular or periodical tide, which it resembled very much.

During our stay at Fort Alexander, we were politely treated by the superintendant, Mr. Bell, at whose table we ate of a fish new to us, called in those parts a sturgeon, but very unlike the sturgeon of our waters. It was well tasted, with a good firm flesh, and tolerably rich; it is the principal subsistence of the residents upon those waters. Mr. Bell likewise offered us some Buffalo meat, (the tongue and hump,) that had been salted; it was very good, and in our opinion far superior to the jerked meat. We enquired why the salting was not usually resorted to instead of the jerking of the meat. Salt is so abundant on the prairies, that the expense or trouble would probably be but little greater. We were informed, however, that the prairie salt did not preserve flesh as well as that which was brought from England, with which the buffalo of which we had eaten had been cured. It is probable that in the salt of the prairie there are impurities, perhaps deliquescent salts, which render it unfit for the preservation of meat unless purified.

In the afternoon of the 20th, we resumed our journey, and ascended the bay about six miles, with a fine fair wind, which allowed us to spread a sail. We afterwards entered Winnepeek River, and found it to be a most majestic and impressive stream; its width is considerable, but is very variable, as it runs through a primitive formation in which it has excavated basins of irregular dimensions connected by narrow channels, through which the whole volume of waters, which is very considerable, proceeds with an inconceivable rapidity. The rocks through which it passes are decidedly primitive, but assume that chaotic appearance, (if we may be permitted to apply the term,) which we had already observed in the primitive rocks of the valley of the St. Peter. We can only account for the features which they present by supposing that they were formed under the influence of a very great crystallizing force, which was disturbed by some extraneous causes. Hence we observe within a small compass a number of different centres of crystallization at which different rocks were probably forming at the same time; within a few feet of each other there was a tendency to form gneiss, or sienite, granite, or micaschist, &c.; the consequence of which is that, at those centres, we observe distinct and well characterized rocks, while the intermediate space is filled by an irregular and rapid transition from the one into the other. We observed no distinct signs of stratification. At first we were inclined to refer this mode of formation, though on a much more gigantic scale, to that of the Schnecken-stein or topaz rock of Saxony. But we soon observed that the difference was immense, for while this exhibits an union of masses of homogeneous composition, differing only in position; the rocks of the Winnepeek do not present the "platten und grosmassigen absonderung" of the Wernerian school; they display no such homogeneous composition, and no division into masses; they on the contrary exhibit a connexion between all the parts, a fusion of the one into the other.

At one spot, (Portage de l'Islet,) we observed a granite with an excess of felspar throughout the mass, which occasions in it a fine lamellar structure; this is however interrupted in numberless places by veins of coarse-grained granite. In some cases we see in these veins *apparently* fragments of other rocks imbedded in them. These fragments, however, are always composed of one or more of the four simple minerals which constitute the whole mass, viz. quartz, mica, felspar, and amphibole. Although they present the appearance of fragments, still we see no reason to doubt their being of contemporaneous origin; indeeed, when examined with the microscope, we have frequently traced a gradual passage of the felspar of the vein into that of the imbedded fragment; it was not a mere impregnation of the rock by the felspar, as is often observable in the vicinity of metallic veins, where the rock has received a portion of the metal of the vein; but we could trace an uninterrupted union in the crystallization of the felspar of the vein with that of the imbedded mass. In some cases also, veins posterior in formation to the mass of the rock were distinctly observed. They were frequently seen intersecting older ones in a gneiss rock, and exhibiting very beautiful and diversified instances of a shift or slide of the older vein at its intersection by the more recent one.

In the afternoon, we passed in the river several rapids and falls, which occasion what are called by the voyagers the " Décharges" and the " Portages." The former term is applied whenever the obstruction is but a partial one, in which case the canoe is lightened, and either paddled or towed over the rapid. In such cases the passengers always leave the canoe, and as much of the baggage or load is taken out as the shallowness of the water requires. The portages are those places where the obstruction being greater, the whole of the cargo, as well as the canoe itself has to be carried over; these vary much in length. We met with seventy-two between Lake Winnepeek and Lake Superior; the shortest was but about five yards, while the longest was nearly four miles long. Many places are considered as décharges or lightening places, when descending the stream, which by ascending canoes are enumerated as portages. This occasions some confusion in the terms. The remarkable points in this navigation are so numerous that it is difficult for the Indians or the voyagers to find names for them; hence the terms which they apply are at best insignificant. They are frequently repeated, and oftentimes quite inapplicable. One of the characteristic traits of the Chippewas is to give names directly the reverse of the property which the objects presents, as a grove was by the Romans called *lucus, (à non lucendo.)* We observe this practice to prevail with our Bois brulés canoe men, who had no sooner seen our black man, Andrew, than they immediately agreed among themselves to apply to him the the term Wapishka, (Wăpĭshkă) which means white. This nickname was not given to him, however, in derision, as that of snowball is frequently applied to those of his colour among civilized men; neither was it with a view to wound his feelings, for he was never, as we believe, made acquainted with the signification of this term.

As soon as a canoe reaches a portage, a scene of bustle and activity takes place, which none can picture to themselves but such as have seen it. The goods are unloaded, and conveyed across, while the canoe is carried by the stern and bowsmen. As soon as they have reached the end of the portage, it is launched and reloaded without any loss of time. An obstruction of one hundred yards does not detain them more than twenty minutes. We had occasion, however, more than once, to regret their speed, which caused them to toss our baggage very unceremoniously, using it as they would packs of furs, which are so made up as not to be injured by this rough treatment. The whole care and attention of a voyager seems to centre in his canoe, which he handles with an astonishing degree of dexterity and caution.

Voyagers compute distances on the water by *pipes*, which are the intervals between the times when they cease to paddle in order to smoke their pipe. We cannot determine, however, the length of a *pipe*, having found it to vary according to the hurry of the voyagers, the peculiar disposition of the guide, the nature of the weather, &c. &c. When a portage exceeds half a mile in length, it is generally divided into what are termed *pauses* or distances travelled without stopping to rest. These also vary much in length according to the greater or less difficulty of the portage, its length, &c. A pause averages about a third of a mile.

On the 20th of August, we passed three lightening places and three portages, none of which were long. We encamped immediately above the Portage des Chenes, having travelled fourteen miles. The evening being very favourable for observations, Mr. Colhoun determined the position of this portage to be in latitude 50° 31′ 30″, and in longitude 95° 55′ 5″.

It was at our evening's encampment that the splendid scenery of the Winnepeek first displayed itself to our view, realizing all that the mind could have fancied of wild and sublime beauty, and far surpassing any that we had ever seen. The characters which we admire in the scenery of the Winnepeek, are the immense volume of waters, the extreme rapidity of the current, the great variety of form which the cascades and falls present, and the incomparable wildness of the rocky scenery which produces these falls, and which contrasts by its gloom, its immoveable and unchangeable features, with the bright dazzling effect of the silvery sheet of water, passing from a smooth and unruffled expanse, to a broken and foaming cataract. It is in the effect of the rocky bed of the Winnepeek, that its numerous falls surpass all others which we have seen; the cataract of Niagara, which far exceeds them in volume, is uniform and monotonous in comparison; the horizontal ledges of secondary rocks of the latter are as far inferior in picturesque effect to the dark water-worn granite and sienite of the former, as the height of the bluffs at Niagara exceeds that of the rocky banks of the Winnepeek.

The falls on this river have another advantage, which is, that the whole country has a picturesque appearance, which prepares the mind, and keeps it in a proper disposition, to appreciate the splendour of its cataracts, while the country around Niagara is flat, uniform, and uninteresting.

On the Winnepeek we have constantly in view changes in the rocks, which contribute to those of the surface; they present at times the schistose appearance of a gneiss and mica-slate, which disappears at the recurrence of the dark-coloured granite or reddish sienite; these being filled with veins of felspar, display on a gigantic scale the beautiful striped appearance, which has given to some of the marbles of Italy their well-deserved celebrity.

The place of our encampment was characterized by one of those peculiar effects of water, which, once seen, leave an indelible impression upon the mind. After having passed over numerous rocks, which form diversified cascades, (the whole height of which is about thirty feet), the water is suddenly received into a basin enclosed by high rocks, where it is forced to sojourn awhile, by the small size of the aperture through which it issues; here the waters present the characters of a troubled ocean, whose waves rise high and beat against the adjoining shores, and against the few rocky islands which are seen in the midst of this basin; it is to this character that the spot owes the name which it receives from the natives, " the fall of the moving waters." They may be called the lower falls of Winnepeek River. We reached them in time to watch the beautiful effect of the setting sun, whose beams reflected by the stream imparted to it the appearance of a sea on fire. This was soon replaced by the moon, which cast a more placid light upon the waves, and heightened the charm of the scenery by the melancholy mantle which it spread over it. One of the most imposing characters of these falls is the tremendous noise which they produce, and which, in comparison to their size, is thought to exceed that of Niagara, Montmorency, Schaffhousen, St. Anthony, the Cohoes, or other falls which any of our party have ever seen. A scarcity of vegetation covers these rocks and contributes to the picturesque effect of the spot. Instead of the heavy forests which formerly sheltered Niagara, we have here a spare growth of aspen, birch, spruce, and other evergreens, whose size, generally small, adds to the wild and barren appearance of the rocks. The night which we spent near these falls, was one of the most interesting in the expedition; our tents were pitched so that we had a view of the splendid effect arising from the play of the moonbeams upon the surface of this ocean-like basin, and our eyes were constantly bent upon it until the noise of the cataract lulled us to sleep.

The artist could not behold, without rapture, a scene so worthy of being painted, and accordingly Mr. Seymour employed all that remained of daylight in sketching its principal beauties. In this he was well favoured, as a long projecting rock in the bed of the stream, affords a satisfactory and comprehensive view of all its features. As these were the finest falls on Winnepeek River, we should have wished to represent them in this work, but it was found impossible to retain their effect when reduced to the required size. We found near this a fragment of a mineral resembling the phonolite or klingstein shieffer. It contained small cubic crystals of iron pyrites. It was angular, and probably broken from a neighbouring rock, but we could not discover it in its original site.

The next day, being the 21st of August, we reached an expansion in the river, that forms a small lake called Lac du Bonnet, at the upper end of which we encamped. This lake is about fifteen miles long, and from six hundred yards to four miles in breadth; it presents a fine glassy and smooth surface, free from any current; this afforded to our paddlers a relaxation from the hard task of working up stream. Previously we had passed one *décharge* and three portages; of these, only one was fatiguing; it was about one mile long. At these portages, the rapids, though very fine, are not to be compared to the lower falls. The general features of this country still continued the same; the rocks at times attained a greater height, though they never rose into hills. At one of the portages we observed small black crystals, probably of tourmaline, shooting through the mass. A little beyond this, at the upper " Portage du Rocher du Bonnet," a fine white clay was seen, in which small fragments of lamellar felspar were observed. This was evidently a kaolin, or decomposed felspar; it appeared to be very abundant; at the surface where we saw it, it was much intermixed with the soil which appeared somewhat deeper and better than usual, but, we doubt not, that with a little exertion the clay might be obtained perfectly pure, and well suited to the manufacture of porcelain. A number of blocks of blue limestone, which we saw at some of these portages, led us to believe that we were then at no great distance from the secondary formations. Our evening encampment was, however, upon a very fine mass of granite, projecting into Bonnet Lake. The rock likewise appeared in insulated masses in the middle of the lake. These are, for the most part, destitute of vegetation. As we proceeded, we observed that the trees of deciduous foliage had almost disappeared, and that their place was supplied by a greater abundance of evergreens, such as tamarack, juniper, spruce, white pine, pitch pine, &c. Among the bushes we chiefly remarked the huckleberry, raspberry, black currant, and a wild cherry, which was then ripe, and which, notwithstanding its slightly astringent taste, was palatable. Among the birds Mr. Say saw the cedar-bird *, fish-hawk †, kingfisher ‡, kildeer, the black-headed tern, and numberless ducks. The notes of the whip-poor-will had been heard while on Lake Winnepeek. At the evening encampment, we observed on the shore myriads of dead bodies of a new species of ephemera, Baëtes alba, (Vide Appendix I. Entomology,) cast on it by the waves, and after sunset a very numerous swarm of the same insect collected over the surface of the water, where they did not, however, remain long; they totally disappeared before we retired to rest. We saw several families of Indians that came up to us in small and very neat bark canoes. The master of one of these was very desirous of exchanging with us a handsome wooden bowl for some pemmican, but as we had none to

---

* Bombycivora Carolinensis. † Falco haliætus.
‡ Alcedo alcyon.

spare, we declined his offer. Another canoe came up soon after to exchange dried moose meat for powder and balls; this we agreed too, and anxiously waited for our next meal in order to taste of this new food. Whether it was owing to a bad choice of pieces, or to the nature of the meat itself, we know not, but certain it is, that it was found very inferior to the jerked buffalo meat; we found it dry, tough, and tasteless.

On the 22d, we proceeded through the upper part of Bonnet Lake, and soon reached the rapids. The current was so swift, and the obstructions so great, that paddling was found unavailing, and the voyagers preferred *setting* the canoes with poles; in order to diminish the load the soldiers were landed; they walked along the shore. Although the bed of Winnepeek River displays in many places larger falls, and bolder features than at this spot, yet there was no part of the stream which pleased us more than that which lies immediately above the lake. The river presents so many and such varied appearances, produced by the rush of waters over the rocky barriers which extend across its bed, that it was impossible for any of us to remain uninterested spectators of its wonderful scenery. Although the rocks rise but to a moderate height, their outline is very bold; the current at all times swift, often partakes of the nature of a torrent, and occasionally gives rise to beautiful cascades. The corroding effect of the stream upon the rock has produced many basins or coves in which the water forms eddies, and, not unfrequently, presents a smooth expanse, contrasting with the rough billows of the adjoining torrent. The red colour of the sienite is relieved by streaks of black mica which intersect its surface, and give it the appearance of designs executed on a gigantic scale. The trees which cover this rock offer to the eye a pleasing aspect; the aspen, distinguished by the silvery white of its bark, and by its leaves lightly quivering at every breath of air, is intermixed with birch, and occasionally with spruce trees; a dense and almost impenetrable undergrowth of firs forms a sort of curtain along the banks of the river, and is interspersed with bushes loaded with plumbs, haws, pembina, &c. One of the objects which contributed most to enliven the scene was the great abundance of fish in the river; they were frequently observed leaping out of the water; for few streams are so well stocked with fish as this is; they are principally the sturgeon, salmon, pike, &c. Over these falls eagles and hawks soared high in the air, watching for the easy prey, which they derive from the numbers of fish, that are wounded or killed by being hurried against the rocks by the irresistible force of the current. Several canoes of Indians were also seen on the stream engaged in fishing; Chippewa lodges, constructed of bark, and bleached by long exposure to the air, formed small white specks which reflected the rays of the sun, and were visible at a great distance. As we proceeded along these rapids our canoe-men entertained us with songs more remarkable for the wildness and originality of their notes than for the skill and method with which they were sung. It is one of the delights of these men to sing in unison as they proceed, and the effect is very fine, though, perhaps, to those tutored in music " the sounds that thrilled rocks along" might have appeared somewhat harsh. Such were the features which we admired that morning, and which received an additional lustre from a bright sun and cloudless sky. But when in the afternoon the wind blew high, and the heavens were darkened with clouds, the scene became almost terrific; the waves arose, and it required the fullest confidence in the skill and experience of our guide to hush all apprehension, as we observed him make for a projecting point where a small eddy, barely thirty feet in length, presented the only landing place for the canoes. Our paddlers strained every nerve, and it was evident that all were convinced that nothing short of the utmost exertion on their part could urge the light canoe onwards against the force of the stream; at last, having, by strong and quickly repeated strokes of the paddle, reached the eddy, one of the men immediately jumped into the stream to stop the frail bark, and prevent it from being dashed against the shore; two men were scarcely able to keep the canoe in its place, as its bow touched the rocks while the stern was still in the rapid. She was quickly unloaded, and raised from the waters, and while the men were engaged in transporting the baggage across, we stopped on the rock to watch the progress of the other canoes, which were conducted with equal skill to the landing place. In contemplating this scene the interest was heightened by the recollection that perhaps no other country presents such splendid and wild features as those that we were then beholding.

In the evening we were visited by a few Chippewas, who came to exchange wild rice for ammunition. They had heard of our visit to Pembina, and had prepared themselves to welcome us. In the course of the day we observed hung up, near the door of a cabin, a bear's snout, which, we were told, was put up, according to the Chippewa custom, as a sort of trophy. We stopped to procure some of the meat, but were informed, that although the animal had been killed only on the preceding day, still it had been all consumed, fresh meat being a rare treat to those that inhabit the banks of this river. Indeed, their game appears to be restricted almost exclusively to a few bears; moose are seldom found so far south; beaver has become scarce; the country is too wet for deer; and the absence of prairies restricts the buffalo from roving in that direction. The principal subsistence of these Indians, and perhaps of the greater part of the Chippewa nation, is fish and wild rice, of which they collect a great quantity in their numerous marshes, lakes, &c. In the course of this day we observed signs of an igneous action upon some of the rocks; we had already remarked the phenomenon on one or more occasion, but the characters were indistinct; whereas, at one of the portages passed on the 22d of August, the semi-vitrification at the surface of the fragment of a rock found there, appeared more distinct. The general character of the country was still, however, a gneiss and granite, which offered many instructive views of veins of the latter rock shooting through the gneiss; they were judged to be, for the most part, of contemporaneous formation.

The river, as we proceeded, lost altogether the usual characters of a stream; it appeared to be a series of lakes of from one hundred yards to three or four miles in diameter, which were united by rapids. These lakes were encompassed by an iron-bound coast, which the current had indented into bays. A difference of level of several feet, separated these lakes, and gave rise to the rapids; in one case where the portage did not exceed fifteen yards in length, there was a fall of six feet. In these small lakes numerous islands are seen, all resting upon a rocky foundation. On the 23d, after proceeding eight miles, we arrived at the falls, called by the Chippewas, Awakane Pawetik (Awåk'ån'e[1] Påw'etîk), which has been translated "Slave Fall." It is related that a slave of the Chippewas, having escaped from his master, was travelling down the river with all possible speed in a canoe, and that being very closely pursued, he, either accidentally or intentionally, it is not known which, suffered his canoe to approach so close to the fall, that it was carried down by the torrent, and never afterwards seen. The river at this place is about eighty yards wide, and the fall, in the course of one hundred yards, is computed at twenty feet. At the upper part of it there is a fine cascade, below which the rapids continue for a short distance, presenting a beautiful landscape; this was sketched by Mr. Seymour. Notwithstanding the real beauty of this spot, we experienced some disappointment. It had been represented to us as the finest on the river, and finding it inferior in wildness and effect to that of " the moving waters," the pleasure which it would otherwise have afforded was checked.

The navigation of this stream is frequently attended with fatal accidents, and the number of wooden crosses which we observed at some of the rapids, are the brief mementos erected by the survivors, to the memory of the shipwrecked voyagers; they form, as it were, beacons which point out the dangers of the stream. These accidents are generally occasioned by the breaking of the tow-line. The only chance of escape which the canoe-men have, in such cases, if they be not too close to the rapid, is to throw themselves into the stream, and endeavour to swim to one of the eddies, which fortunately are very numerous. We were told of a canoe that was lost at Slave falls by the breaking of the tow-line; the men who were in it had sufficient presence of mind to abandon the canoe; they were saved, while the bark was shattered in its way down the stream, and lost in the rapid; its cargo was picked up at some distance below. This fall is about eighty miles above Fort Alexander. It is probable that this, as well as the other rapids of the river, is at times much finer than it was when we saw it, for the stream was considered low. Its depth varied much; in the lakes it was sometimes eight, ten, or twenty feet deep, while at the rapids the rock was scarcely covered. From the water-marks observed on the banks, it appears that, in times of flood, the surface is elevated from five to nine feet, (according to the breadth of the river), above the level at which we saw it.

Two and a half miles above this fall we reached another, which, for beauty, is second only to the lower falls. It is formed by two chains of rocks stretching across the stream; the upper one occasions a cascade of about ten feet, and the lower one of fifteen; the length of the falls, including all the rapids, is about two hundred yards; the breadth of the stream about one hundred and fifty. The lower sheet of water is divided into three parts by two islands, and the effect is quite picturesque; the foam produced by these two falls, exceeds that observed at any other, and imparts to the river, for a certain distance, a white, milky aspect. Mr. Seymour's view of this fall, which we have called the Upper Falls of the Winnepeek, was not taken at a favourable spot, as the rocky nature of the bank prevented him from landing at a place from which an advantageous view of both the falls could be obtained. The Bois brulés call this the fall of the "petite pointe de Bois." A short distance above this, another, called Jack's fall, was seen, which was also very fine. On the 23d we passed six portages and one towing-place. The distance travelled was thirty-two miles, and on the first twenty, the fall in the river could not have been less than one hundred and fifty feet.

After passing Jack's falls, a great change in the appearance of the river was observed, and was distinctly traced to a difference in the nature of the rock. The granite and sienite were replaced by a slate, which appeared to vary from a mica to a clay-slate, presenting chiefly the characters of the latter. It is very distinctly stratified. The strata are nearly vertical. Its junction with the granite was observed in many places; the slate was superposed. The hills which we had observed above Bonnet Lake, did not continue after the slate had made its appearance. A corresponding change in the features of the stream is observed. The river expands considerably, being in some places several miles wide; it includes a great number of islands, all of which have a solid, rocky foundation. The colour of the rock is of a deep blue or black, imparting the same hue to the water. The river is not deep; its current is swift, especially near the islands, but it is free from ripples; we observed none of the foaming rapids which characterize the lower part of the stream. The islands, which in some places are countless, are generally small and of a form nearly square; from the vertical stratification of the rock their banks are perpendicular; they generally rise from ten to twenty feet above the level of the water. Their surface is covered with a thick growth of trees, which are, for the most part however, small. They consist of a dwarf species of pitch-pine, called by the Canadians, cypress; of the spruce, juniper, tamarack, &c.; the white birch becomes more abundant; the undergrowth is very luxuriant. The soil appears much better than that on the granite. In some parts the rock appears covered with a ferruginous incrustation, produced probably by the decomposition of iron pyrites which abounds in it.

A large loon flew by in the afternoon; its screamings

which had of late been frequent are, by many, considered as sure indications of the approach of stormy weather; we heard them frequently, but had no opportunity of forming a conclusive opinion as to the degree of importance to be attached to this prognostic. As far as one instance of successful prediction proves the truth of this sign, the rain, which fell during the night, confirmed the preconceived opinion of those who had asserted its universality. The difference in the rocks did not continue long, for, after having travelled about fifteen miles on the 24th of August, the slate ceased and was replaced by granite, which soon passed into a decided sienite, producing a wilder and more uninhabitable country than any we had as yet seen; the sienite rises, apparently in great confusion, in steep masses which are rounded at their summit; they are covered with moss, and support but a very thin growth of scrubby pines on their surface. The country cannot be called beautiful, though it is certainly picturesque; the broad sheet of water, with its rapid current, is the only fine feature which it presents. This place affords no means of sustenance either to brutes or men. We accordingly observed few, if any, signs of animals. On the whole of Winnepeek River we saw but three trophies indicating the capture of large game; one of these consisted of the horns of a reindeer, they were not of full size, the animal having been killed while they were in the velvet. We have made no mention of the tributaries which Winnepeek River receives, because we consider them as the mere outlets of small lakes situated near our route; from the information which we have received from those experienced in the characters of this region, and which our own observation fully confirms, as far as we have had an opportunity of judging, the whole of the country may be considered as an immense lake, interspersed with innumerable barren and rocky islands, which were, probably, at some epocha of comparatively recent date, covered with water. This, which was kept up to a level far superior to that to which it now attains, by barriers which we shall not attempt to trace, has broken its bounds, and the country has been very extensively drained. Whether this operation is still continued can be but a matter of conjecture; we see, however, nothing that makes it either impossible or even improbable. That at one time the Mississippi was one of the great outlets, appears to us equally probable; and that the innumerable boulders which cover its valley, and which are analogous in character to the rocks which we have observed *in situ* on the Winnepeek and elewhere, have been derived from the great convulsions to which we allude, appears to us equally apparent. We are not prepared to enter into any discussion as to the manner in which these bouldders have been dispersed; we profess ourselves as little satisfied as any geologists can be, with the various theories which have been suggested in Europe to account for the boulders of the Jura, or for those which cover the north of Germany, and which are probably analogous to the rocks observed, in place, in the Scandinavian peninsula. We are not prepared to admit that the boulders of the state of Ohio have been projected by a subterraneous explosion, or have been washed by the mere force of the stream, or floated down upon masses of ice, &c. &c.; but we cannot resist the conclusion of our senses, that they have not always lain where we now find them, that they have been removed from their original site, that every thing makes it probable that they were formerly connected with the primitive formations of the St. Peter, the Winnepeek, the Lake of the Woods, &c. Thus far we think ourselves warranted to proceed from observations. The rest must be a matter of speculation, and we are not disposed to indulge in it. We shall therefore restrict ourselves to the following conclusions. 1. That the whole of the country between Lake Superior and Lake Winnepeek was formerly covered with water to a much greater height than it is at present. 2. That this inland sea was bounded by barriers which were broken, at a time probably posterior to the deposition of the secondary limestone of Ohio; wherefore the fragments, which result from this great convulsion of nature, are found resting upon those secondary formations. 3. That this process of draining was carried on at first, partly, at least, through the valley of the Mississippi. 4. That it is not improbable that this draining is still continued. 5. That if this be the case, it is partially through the valley of the Mississippi, but chiefly through Nelson's River.

Most of the streams which are mentioned by the guides as rivers emptying into the Winnepeek, are upon closer inquiry found to be mere branches of the same river that divide off at distances of twenty or thirty miles, and which again unite with the main stream, or, as we should deem it more probable, they are parts of the general system of lakes which cover the whole country. One of these branches is termed the English River, because it has been ascended by the Hudson's Bay Company's traders to its sources, which interlock with those of Albany River; it offers a direct communication between Lake Winnepeek and Albany Factory, of James' Bay.

On the 24th we passed two portages and three lightening places. Our canoe-men experienced great satisfaction at the sight of a canoe, which passed us in the middle of the day, from Montreal. There was on board a gentleman, bearer of despatches, who had left London on the 23d of May, having passed in the space of three months from the extreme of civilization and population to one of the wildest and most deserted spots on the surface of the earth. The accidental meeting in such a solitude with one who belongs to a civilized country, and who speaks the same language, is delightful; we forget that we meet with a stranger, with one of a different nation; we are in such cases almost inclined to greet an utter stranger as though he were a friend from whom we had been long separated. The hurry with which both parties were travelling prevented us, however, from delaying any time; and with a sincere welcome, and mutual good wishes for the success of our respective journeys, we passed, and soon lost sight of each other's canoes.

On the 25th of August we proceeded and reached the head of Winnepeek River. Our paddlers had a comparatively easy task all day except at one place, where they attempted to paddle up the stream instead of resorting to the towing line as is usual. This place, called the " Grandes Dalles," presents the most rapid current against which we have ever seen a canoe paddled. It is a narrow strait, not exceeding forty yards in breadth; it is bounded on both sides by perpendicular precipices of granite; great exertions are required on the part of the canoe-men in order to ascend this, and one of the canoes, after two unavailing attempts to stem the current with paddles, was towed up with a line. A short distance above this we passed a cross at a place called the " Petites Dalles." This spot has acquired a melancholy celebrity as having been the scene of the murder of one Owen Keveney, one of the men employed by the Hudson's Bay Company or the colony. His death was almost the only crime committed in the

Indian territories that was punished. After a protracted trial, his murderer, de Reinhard, was convicted and executed. We heard all the particulars of the transaction with some interest, from the circumstance that Desmarais had acted as guide to the canoe in which the unfortunate Keveny was travelling, and that he was one of the principal witnesses, and had even been indicted as a party to the crime. Much stress was laid in the course of the trial upon the question whether this spot was included in the province of Upper Canada, and it became necessary to examine this point; after very full testimony had been received from the best geographers in the country, it was decided that the limits of Canada did not extend that far.

While we were resting upon one of the islands, an Indian came up in his canoe with his family and supplied us with fresh sturgeon and with dried huckleberries. These are said to be cured in a manner which will preserve them for two or three years; they are first dried in the sun, then smoked by placing them upon a net over a slow fire until the skin bursts, and the juice begins to flow; after which they are again exposed to the sun, until they become dry. The smoky taste which they acquire improves their flavour.

After passing through a small lake, rendered very rough by a stormy wind, we reached Rat portage, which is about one hundred yards long, we crossed it and encamped on the shore of the Lake of the Woods. We are informed that there is a communication by a fine fall from the lake into the river, and that it is to avoid this fall that the portage is made across an island. We did not see the fall. We had scarcely reached the eastern end of the portage when a heavy rain commenced, to which we remained exposed during the greater part of the afternoon.

Rat portage has become a point of some importance, as

it appears probable that the north-westernmost point of the boundary line of the United States will be at or near its extremity, according to the tenor of the seventh article of the treaty of Ghent, which provides that the commissioners appointed to regulate the boundary line shall fix and determine that part of the line which extends from the water communication between Lake Huron and Lake Superior to the most north-western point of the Lake of the Woods; and which further enjoins that they shall particularize the latitude and longitude of that point.

The determination of the north-westernmost point of a lake which presents a great number of bays and indentations, will be an object of difficult accomplishment; we had heard from the Indians that the boundary line had been run to Rat portage, and were therefore anxious to find it out. We saw evidences of the commissioners having been there but a short time previously, but no land marks could be discovered. We subsequently, however, met John Bigsby, M.D., surgeon in his Britannic Majesty's service, a gentleman who is attached to the boundary line commission, and who has taken advantage of the situation which he fills, to investigate very fully and extensively the geology of British North America. We have had frequent communications with Dr. Bigsby concerning the geology of that part of the country which lies between the Lake of the Woods and the Sault de Ste. Marie; and are pleased to find that our observations correspond well with his. Our specimens were likewise very concordant; with this exception, however, that Dr. Bigsby's stay in the country having been much longer than ours, he was enabled to visit many more places than we were. His investigations were therefore more full and more minute, and his specimens selected with more care. In travelling so rapidly as we did, we were obliged to confine ourselves to the observation of the general features of the country, without having time to search for localities, of minerals. In this respect Dr. Bigsby was more fortunate; he has kindly communicated several to us, and in mentioning them we shall always state to whom we are indebted for them. With this acknowledgment we beg leave to offer to that gentleman our thanks for the liberal access he afforded us to his valuable collections, as well as for the information which he freely and kindly imparted.

From Dr. Bigsby we heard that the line had not yet been run; the commissioners having hitherto been engaged in making separate surveys west of Lake Superior.

It appears that Rat portage is about nine or ten miles from the northernmost extremity of the Lake. The lake is elevated about ten or twelve feet above Winnepeek River, at the point where we left it. Its latitude, according to M'Kenzie is 49° 37' and its longitude $94\frac{1}{4}$° west. Dr. Bigsby set it in latitude 49° 44' 22'' probably from an observation of Mr. Thompson's. Previous to our arrival at Rat portage, we observed that the rocks had again changed to a slate, of which the stratification was very distinctly directed from east-north-east to west-south-west. The inclination was nearly a vertical one; the colour of the slate is a dark green; it is very decidedly a micaceous slate, at least on Rat portage. This produces the same feature which we had observed in Winnepeek River, above Jack's Fall, but which becomes more distinct in the Lake of the Woods. The stream expands and includes an immense number of islands. It is to this circumstance that the lake owes its picturesque appearance and its name, as every one of these islands is covered with trees. The aspect of the lake differs essentially from any other that we had previously seen. At Rat portage our view was limited by an island which nearly closes the bay at which the portage terminates; but after we had passed that island we found ourselves upon a smooth sheet of water, interspersed with numberless islands, which break the uniformity of the water scenery. Few of these islands are large; all rest upon solid rock, and are covered with small trees, chiefly pine, spruce, hazel, willow, cherry, &c. besides vast quantities of bushes, bearing berries. The prickly pear abounds in these islands. The rocky shores are partly concealed by the moss and lichen which cover their surface, and by the grass and bushes which grow out from their deep crevices. In this respect the rocks in the lake differ from those in the river, as the latter are always bare, to a certain elevation, which indicates that of the floods that occasionally swell it; the dark lines, which are seen running horizontally along the shore, point out the height of the various floods which have at different times occurred.

The weather was so unfavourable during our stay at the portage, as to prevent us from taking any observation. It having cleared up at night, we proceeded at two A.M. with a fine moonlight. At one of the islands, (Cosse's), while we stopped for breakfast, Mr. Seymour sketched the scenery of the lake.

The Lake of the Woods has been described to us as being about three hundred miles in circumference. Its shores are very much indented by bays, in which an immense quantity of wild rice is annually collected. Our passage through the lake, which was nearly in a diagonal direction, was effected in a time very little exceeding two days. The number of islands which we saw was immense; at one time, looking merely before us, we could count upwards of fifty in sight. All are on solid rock, except one, near the mouth of Rainy-lake River, which is a sand-bar, probably formed by an accumulation of sand carried down by the river. This was the more remarkable, as it was the first sand-bar observed since we entered Winnepeek River. The Indians had, with their usual attention to the features of the country, remarked this bar, and they called the lake Pekwaonga Osagaagan (Pĕkwȧ̊ongȧ̊ Ȯsȧ̊gȧ̊lgȧn,) which means " the lake of the island of sand-mounds," owing to the mounds formed on this bar by the accumulation of the sand by the winds. It is true that the lake is also sometimes called Metekoka (Mĕtĕkȯkȧ̊) Osagaagan, which signifies Lake of the Woods, but this is supposed to be a modern appellation, translated from the name which the French traders gave it when they first saw it. The distance which we travelled in the lake was about eighty miles, which probably was its longest diameter. Observations were made to determine its position; they gave for the situation of Cosse's Island, distant sixteen miles from Rat portage, 49° 36′ 42″ north; for that of Red-rock Island, passed on the 27th of August, 49° 11′ 33″; for Sandy Island, 48° 56′ 4″ north; and finally, the entrance of Rainy-lake River was determined to be in latitude 48° 53′ 40″ north, and longitude 94° 21′ 15″ west. The variation of the compass in the lake was 11° 1′ 25″ east.

With a view to avoid a circuitous navigation round a projecting peninsula, it is usual for voyagers to make a small portage over this point. It did not exceed one hundred yards at the time we crossed it. Our guide says that it is often under water, so that the canoes pass without difficulty. This requires a rise of about five or six feet above the level of the waters at that time. We found in great abundance the plant which bears the wild-rice; it was quite ripe at that season. The Indians collect the grain in great plenty, considering it as one of their best articles of food, and that upon which they can place the greatest reliance. We have been led to make some enquiry as to the extent of the region in which wild-rice grows, and we find it to be very great. Mackenzie says, that wild-rice is hardly seen, or does not come to maturity, north of the fiftieth degree of latitude, and, we believe that it does not grow west of the Mississippi below the mouth of the Missouri, or on any part of this river. Its western extremities are probably about the sources of the St. Peter; it ranges in latitude from the 31st to the 50th degree, and in longitude from the Atlantic to the 97th degree; for we were informed, by Gen. Brown, that it had been observed on Black River in the state of New York; we know that it exists on the Delaware above and below Philadelphia; and it appears that it is also found in the south-east corner of South Carolina, at a place called from this circumstance, the "Wild-oats Marsh." Gen. Macomb, who has seen this marsh, states the wild-oats to be the same as the wild-rice of our N. W. territory. Doubtless it is to this plant that Hakluyt alludes when he states that in "Virginia there is a kind of reed which beareth a seed almost like unto our rice or wheat, and being boiled is good meal." This grain, which probably resembles oats more than rice in its appearance, was fit for harvest when we were in the Lake of the Woods, and we were told that the Indians were dispersed in all the small bays collecting it; we ate of it frequently on the journey, and found it palatable, though inferior to domestic rice; it is probable that the grain which we had was not well separated from the hull, and from this circumstance was not as good as that which is prepared with more care.

Although most of the islands in the lake are formed of

slaty rock, yet some, as for instance, the Red-rock Island, on which observations were made on the 27th of August, are composed of granite; in this case the felspar is of a reddish appearance, and imparts to the granite the colour from which the name of the island was derived. We have frequently observed in the islands which we visited that the north-eastern extremity was bounded with boulders, the average diameter of which might be about two feet. Though these sometimes extend all round the island, still it is more usual to observe them only at the north-eastern point, seeming to indicate that they were carried down from that quarter. The direction of the strata of mica-slate appears to vary from north 60° to north 80° east. The angle with the horizon varies from 65° or 70° to the perpendicular. The rock is penetrated in some places with iron pyrites; veins of quartz also appear occasionally through the mass. We saw no limestone, but Dr. Bigsby informed us that he had observed some on the shore of the lake. It is probable that we had in sight during our course through the lake, at least 200 islands, whence an idea may be formed of the immense number which it contains. Towards the south-eastern part of the lake there is a space without islands, and this gives rise to what is termed the " Grand traverse," which is, however, only ten miles long. From the number of islands, when a slight wind blows upon the lake, it soon raises a high but short wave, which is very dangerous to bark canoes; hence the least wind will sometimes occasion a considerable delay in the journey. Desmarais was once encamped eleven days without being able to cross these ten miles; and he has heard of canoes being detained on the adjoining islands for twenty-two days. We were fortunate, as the wind which had blown the preceding day had fallen, and we passed the *traverse* without difficulty.

We met in it a canoe with three men who were coming from Rainy lake; they had been detained twenty-four hours by the wind.

As we approached the south-east extremity of the lake, an arm of considerable extent, running in a southerly direction, appeared on our right; it is through this that the connection with Red River, by means of Reed-grass River, is made.

From the observations made on Red-rock and the Sand-bar islands, it appears that the 49th parallel of latitude passes through this traverse. Among the animals seen by Mr. Say, were two kinds of gulls, one of which was probably the Herring-gull, Larus argenteus, young; also a number of pelicans, and a few ducks; swans, it is said, do not exist on this lake; the Testudo geographica was also seen, as well as a soft-shelled turtle, of which the species could not be determined, the lower shell alone being visible. Catesby's spotted frog was found to be abundant as far as we travelled.

We saw on the Lake of the Woods but few Indians, probably not more than twenty altogether, this being the season when they are dispersed. On one of the islands we observed a recent grave, over which a pole was supported by means of stones; it was stripped of its bark, and rings of red paint had been described upon it; its top was bushy and a wooden spoon was suspended from it.

We entered Rainy-lake River on the morning of the 28th of August, and reached its head early on the 31st. The length of this stream is about one hundred miles. Its breadth at its mouth is about four hundred yards; it becomes narrower above; its average breadth is three hundred yards; its current is rapid and uniform; there are very few obstructions to the navigation, there being but two places at which canoes are lightened and towed up. The longest of these is about one mile.

At its mouth the banks of this stream are low and marshy; beyond this they rise somewhat, but present few hills; the river runs in many places over a pebbly bed. The country assumes a more smiling appearance, which led us to anticipate the meeting with limestone rocks; we saw none along the river, but some precipices, seen at a distance, were supposed from their horizontal stratification to be composed of limestone. On the river the rocks seldom appear in place; where we saw them they were principally mica-slate, sometimes, however, sienite. Dr. Bigsby found staurotide in the slate of this river.

The country is much drier; there are fine pieces of meadow land; the grass is of a pleasanter, livelier green; the vegetation more luxuriant; the white maple is seen; the birch attains a larger size. We observed here, however, as we had for a long time past, a total absence of walnut, hickory, and beech. The poplar is very abundant on Rainy River.

Among the animals which are occasionally seen here, are the bear, otter, wolverine, carcajou, moose, squirrel, wolf, weasel, beaver, muskrat, fox, &c. The martin, and fisher are very abundant. The principal fish in the river is the sturgeon.

Among the objects which chiefly attracted our notice, were the interesting ephemera which we had seen on Winnepeek River. They became so abundant on Rainy River towards sunset, that they presented the appearance of a snow shower. They continued for some time, until they were driven by the wind into a small tributary valley where they formed white clouds, beautifully relieved against the dark green of the forest, deepened in its shade by the approach of night. The ensuing morning their dead bodies were seen floating on the stream, and drifted by the wind into small coves near the shore. From their great abundance, Mr. Say was led to believe that this short-lived insect never witnesses a rising sun, but that after performing, in a short time, all the duties assigned to it in its perfect state, it deposits its eggs and expires in the night, a few hours after it has been evolved from the chrysalis. The next evening the ephemera were again seen very abundantly, but it was evident that this was a new swarm, and not part of that previously observed.

The mosquetoes, which had not been seen for some time past, again made their appearance while we were on Rainy River; the weather, which was warm and moist, contributed to increase their numbers. Although we experienced much rain while on this river, and on the lake from which it flows, we have not been able to discover that the climate is more damp there than elsewhere; the name which they bear may have been, therefore, derived from an accidental fall of rain experienced there by the first white visitors, or it may be derived from the colour of their waters, which have much of the appearance of rain water, and which differ greatly from the limpid character of that of Winnepeek River.

Rainy-lake River receives but few tributaries. We shall mention only the River of Rapids, Pine River, Black River, and the Grand and Little Fork.

The first of these is so called from the fine rapids which it presents immediately above its mouth; it is said to take its rise in lakes and swamps; its course is about eighty miles long; it enters from the left bank.

Pine River, which flows from the north, is about thirty yards wide at its mouth.

Black River is a small tributary from the south-east.

The Grand Fork, which enters from the left bank, is the largest tributary of the river, and probably contains as much water as the main stream above their confluence. It rises near a small lake called by the name of Lake Winnepeek, and which we have distinguished from that previously mentioned, by the designation of *Little* Winnepeek Lake; it is in the vicinity of Red Lake. Mr. Davenport, one of the agents of the American Fur Company, represented this fork as being one hundred leagues long, very rapid, and not well supplied with water; it has two short portages; it passes through a small lake called *Sachawgan* Lake; from this there is a long portage, (ten *pauses*), to Little Lake, which has an outlet half a mile long into Little Winnepeek Lake. The whole distance may be ascended in eight or nine days by loaded canoes. A trade has been carried on by the American Fur Company, between Rainy Lake and Fond du Lac, by means of the Grand Fork of Rainy River, Little Lake Winnepeek, the Mississippi, Sandy Lake, Savannah River, and the River St. Louis.

The Little Fork which enters above the Grand Fork, is a wide stream, but it is unimportant, as it does not extend far into the country, and as it furnishes no medium of communication with other lakes or streams.

We saw but few islands in Rainy River, and these were generally small. We occasionally observed stakes which had been used by the boundary line commissioners, to determine the breadth of the river in several places.

During this part of our journey our provisions were not so good as they had previously been. Until we reached Lake Travers, we had depended chiefly upon the salt pork, &c. which we carried along with us, and upon the biscuit which was prepared for our party at Fort St. Anthony. From Lake Travers to Pembina, we had much fresh buffalo and some dried meat. But after leaving Fort Douglas, we lived altogether upon the jerked buffalo and pemmican which we had purchased. These had not been well prepared, and a large portion was found to be in a very bad condition. This, and the immense quantity eaten by our Engagés, whose appetite far exceeded any thing that we had ever witnessed, soon reduced our stock. The private stores of the officers' and gentlemen's mess, such as tea, sugar, &c. were so nearly expended as to require that they should be used in a sparing manner. We therefore resorted to a number of wild plants, of which infusions were made and tried as substitutes for the imported tea; and although to some of the party these appeared good, yet by the greater part the change was not relished. Among the plants which we used were the Ledum latifolium of Pursh, the Stachys anisatus, and the Gaultheria procumbens of Nuttall.

Being informed that at the head of Rainy River there were two settlements, one on the north shore, belonging to the Hudson's Bay Company, and the other on the south, kept up by the American Fur Company, we stopped at the latter, but found it destitute of provisions, and of the articles required for the repair of our canoes. Notwithstanding, therefore, the polite reception of the superintendant, Mr. Davenport, we crossed over to the north shore, where Mr. M'Gillivray gave us the same hospitable treatment which we had received at the other trading posts of the Hudson's Bay Company. We remained at this place two days, to repair our canoes, which had suffered from the rapids in Winnepeek River. One of them being very heavy, and in bad order, was broken up, and its materials used to repair the others.

At Rainy Lake we met with a man, whose interesting adventures deserve to be made known to the public; of these we regret that it is not in our power to give more than a very brief and imperfect outline. We had heard at various places of a citizen of the United States, who had been at an early age taken prisoner by a party of Indians, and who, having been educated among them, had acquired their language, habits, and manners, to the exclusion of those of his country. While at the Red River settlement, we were informed that he had been assaulted by an Indian and severely, some added mortally, wounded. On our arrival at Rainy Lake Fort, Mr. M'Gillivray requested Mr. Say to visit this man and examine his wound; Mr. Say found John Tanner, for such was his name, in a neat European tent, resting on a good comfortable bed, with his two daughters beside him. On inspecting the wound it was found that the ball had passed through the right arm above the elbow, and thence through the breast. The assault having been made about forty days previous, the breast had healed, and the bones of the arm had united perfectly and properly; but the wound in the arm was still open, though apparently in an improving condition; the patient was able to walk about.

At the time that the shot was fired, Tanner was on his way to the United States with his family; this had interrupted his voyage. Feeling himself better, but still unable to travel alone, he applied to Major Long for a passage in our canoes for himself and his daughters; this request was granted. He removed his tent from the enclosure within the British pickets to our camp; all his preparations were made, and the poor man's heart was light and happy at the idea of resuming his journey in such company as secured him against apprehensions of an attack, when his happiness met with a terrible and unexpected check. We had appointed to depart on the morning of the 3d of September;

the preceding evening, his daughters asked and obtained his consent to go to the fort to see an old half-breed Indian woman from whom they had experienced much kindness. They were seen going into the fort, but did not return; the father becoming uneasy went in search of them, but could obtain no information concerning their fate; he applied to Major Long, who visited Mr. M'Gillivray with Mr. Say, and stated to him the circumstance, desiring that he would use his influence and authority to cause the children to be restored to their parent. The efforts of this gentleman were, however, unavailing. The children were not found; and at the time that we left the fort, it was not known what had become of them. Tanner was placed in a most distressing dilemma; he had re-entered the Indian country but a short time before for the mere purpose of taking his daughters to Mackinaw; if he returned without them, the object of his voyage would be frustrated, and the hopes of ever again seeing his children would be rendered very faint. On the other hand, if he remained in the country without any one to attend him in his wounded and infirm condition, his situation would be very difficult. The Indian who had assaulted him was supposed to be lurking in the neighbourhood, and would probably renew his attempt; at any rate, he could scarcely hope to find an opportunity of returning to the United States for a long while. Under all these circumstances he determined to persist in his former intention; and in this he was strongly encouraged by the assurances given to him by Dr. M'Laughlin [*], a gentleman who had

---

[*] Dr. John M'Laughlin was formerly a partner in the North-west Company, and after the consolidation of the two societies he obtained a share in the Hudson's Bay Company. His usual residence was at Rainy Lake; on our arrival there he was absent, having gone to the annual meeting of the partners at York Factory. He returned on the 1st of September. His attentions to us during

proved himself a warm friend of his, and who had just resumed the superintendance of the fort. This gentleman assured him that all his efforts should be used to discover the place where his daughters were, and that he would rescue and protect them until the ensuing spring, when Tanner expected to return to Rainy Lake in search of them. After having travelled with us a few miles on the 3d of September, his pain was so much aggravated, and his arm swollen, by the motion of the canoe, that he found himself unable to proceed; we landed him, and placed him under the care of a dependant on the fort whom we saw engaged in fishing. It was evident that Tanner's grief at being obliged to stop was much mitigated by the hope of being able personally to renew his search after his daughters. Those who appeared unfriendly to Tanner at the fort, endeavoured to impress upon his mind the belief that the girls had eloped from him with a view to return to their mother who was on the Lake of the Woods; but the father replied that the uniform attachment which they had always manifested to him, as well as their ready compliance with his wish that they should proceed with us, must ever prevent his harbouring such an idea; he thought, and probably with good cause, that his daughters had been concealed by some of the half-breeds or dependants on the fort; their age, which was about fourteen or fifteen, their comely appearance and engaging manners, were such as to warrant the apprehensions of their anxious parent. If this was the case, we doubt not that Dr. M'Laughlin's exertions will have led to their discovery.

the short time that we saw him were of the most flattering kind, and evinced a generous disposition; they could be compared only to those of Mr. Mackenzie. We have met with no persons who have in a short time acquired so great a claim to our respect and gratitude as these two gentlemen.

The hope which we had entertaiued of having Tanner for a fellow-traveller during the rest of the journey, as well as the fear of increasing his pain by too much conversation, prevented Mr. Say from securing a complete history of his life, but the following is believed to be accurate :—

John Tanner was the son of a clergyman, who removed with his family to the banks of the Ohio, near the mouth of the Miami River, some time previous to the year 1790. He had been settled there but about ten days when apprehensions were entertained of an attack from a party of Indians. The unsettled state of that part of the country, at the time, exposed its scattered inhabitants to frequent incursions from their savage neighbours. Tanner was then about nine years of age; notwithstanding the prohibition of his father, he had wandered to a short distance from the house, and had just filled his hat with walnuts, picked from a neighbouring tree, when he was seized upon by a party of Indians, who by their threats forced him to silence, and carried him off. This party was commanded, it is said, by an Indian who resided near Saganaw, and whose wife had lately lost her son. Bereft of her only child, the mother appeared inconsolable, and finally begged that her husband would make a prisoner of one, about the same age, to whom she might transfer all the affection which she had borne to her own offspring. With this view the Indian had armed a party of his friends, proceeded down towards the settlements, found this child, carried him off, and returned with him to his wife, who was delighted on beholding a boy so nearly of the age of that which she had lost.

By these Indians young Tanner was treated with kindness; he rose to manhood, became distinguished as a brave man and a hunter. From circumstances which we have not ascertained, his adopted parents, who belonged to the

Saganaw tribe of the Ottawa nation, removed to a more western country; the man died; his wife became the leader of a small party that resided occasionally on the Lake of the Woods, or on Red River, or the Assiniboin. Tanner was offered the situation of chief, which he wisely declined, judging that his white origin would make him an object of suspicion. He appeared satisfied with his success as a hunter, and had no further ambition. We were told by those who had long known him, that although he had acquired many of the characteristics of Indians, still he had some peculiarities which marked him as one of a different origin. He had never been seen to taste of ardent spirits, or to smoak a pipe. Instead of purchasing trifles and gewgaws as is customary with Indians, he devoted the produce of his hunts, which were always successful, to the acquisition of articles of clothing useful to himself, to his adopted mother, or to her relations. In this state he appears to have lived perfectly happy, respected and esteemed by all his fellow-hunters. In the year 1816, he rendered an important service to Lord Selkirk's settlement, by guiding a party of new settlers, who were under the direction of Governor M'Donnell and Captain D'Orsonnen from Rainy Lake to Fort Douglas; this reinforcement arrived at so timely a moment as to make Tanner a great favourite at the settlement. He was pointed out to Lord Selkirk during that nobleman's visit to his colony. His Lordship took great interest in his situation, and by his exertions, Tanner's family was discovered. His recollections of the scenes of his early youth, though faint at first, gradually brightened. He had forgotten his father's name, or rather it had become confused in his recollection with that of a friend of his family called Taylor, so that this was at first thought to be his name.

Tanner placed in our hands a letter which was written by Lord Selkirk, and which is dated Lexington, Nov. 25, 1817. It was written after a personal interview with Mrs. Taylor, whose account of the family corroborated Tanner's statement in the most important particulars. There were some slight discrepancies, but these were no other than might have been expected from the imperfect recollections of a child of nine years of age, after twenty-six years of estrangement from his country and friends. It is perhaps somewhat singular that he should have totally forgotten a language which he must have undoubtedly spoken with considerable fluency at the time that he was taken prisoner. The following extract from Lord Selkirk's letter, at present in our possession, shows how far his recollections extended.

" The circumstances that Mrs. Taylor mentioned of his family coincide with those which he told me in the north, particularly that he had a brother called *Ned,* and two sisters married previously to his being carried off. Also that his father was a big lusty man, as the young man described him. The only point of difference is, that Mrs. Taylor said that Ned Tanner was older than the boy John, who was carried away, whereas I had understood him to be younger; but as I could converse with John only through an interpreter, such a mistake might easily arise. Mrs. T. also said that old John Tanner had been settled in Kentucky several years before 1790, but that possibly he might have removed at that date, by the river, from some other part of the state. The young man told me that his father had changed his residence a very short time before he was carried off, and had been settled on the banks of the Ohio only about ten days, when the attack of the Indians took place. He mentioned particularly his having come down the river in a large boat or flat with horses or cattle. He also mentioned, that, at the place where his father lived previous to his removal, there was a brook running in a cavern under ground, where they used to go with a candle to take water," &c.

Through the benevolent and active interference of Lord Selkirk, Tanner was restored to his family, who recognized him and received him well. He had already brought several of his children into the United States, and had three of them at Mackinaw, when, in 1823, he determined to return to the Lake of the Woods for the others. The Indians, it appears, manifested great unwillingness to allow the two young girls to be taken out of the country, and they opposed his endeavours, until finally, with the assistance of Dr. M'Laughlin, he succeeded in removing the children. He appears to have felt but little affection for the mother of his daughters, and wished her to remain in the country; but she, finding her efforts to keep her daughters unavailing, resolved to go with them. They had passed Rainy Lake and were at the Portage de l'Isle, in Bad, (Maligne), River, when the wife induced an Indian, who was travelling with them, to shoot Tanner. She, it appears, bribed him with the promise of her elder daughter.

The poor man was near falling a victim to the plot; his wife ran away with the Indian, took her daughters with her, and left him alone and wounded; fortunately he was picked up by a canoe going to Rainy Lake; they conveyed him there; his daughters joined him, and as he said, treated him with the utmost kindness. His wife proceeded down the river with her accomplice, who was said to have had a bad name, even among the Indians, previous to this circumstance.

We have endeavoured to acquire some knowledge of the character and principles of a man, whose early impressions must have been completely extirpated by those of the men among whom he spent the greater part of his life. He vowed to be revenged on the Indian who had shot him; heedless of the personal danger which he must incur from another visit to the country, he resolved upon returning to Rainy Lake as soon as he should have regained his strength, in order to pursue and punish his enemy. Any observations which were made to him, on the impropriety of his feelings, only drew from him this answer; "Why did he shoot me? If he wished to kill me, it is my duty to kill him, for he is a bad man." This was uttered in a cold, decisive manner; it was not the result of passion, but of a conviction, founded upon a process of reasoning, to which he had been long accustomed. In his intercourse with traders he appears to have been honourable, and this reflects the more credit upon him, as it was at a time, when an active competition between rival traders frequently induced them to stimulate the Indians to frauds which affected their opponents. One instance appears well attested. In a letter, dated Montreal, Nov. 1818, and which was written by Mr. John Allan, it is stated, that " Tanner did not choose to traffic exclusively with any trader, but used to take goods on credit, at the same time, from parties trading in opposition to one another, and on one occasion, brought two parcels of furs to a post of the North-west Company, at the fork of Red River; he employed the contents of one parcel to pay a debt which he had contracted there, and, having done so, was about to go with his other parcel of furs, to discharge, in like manner, a debt which he had contracted with a neighbouring trader of the Hudson's Bay Company; some opposition to the taking away of his furs was made, by the person in charge of the North-west Company's fort, who endeavoured to prevail on Tanner to sell the whole to him. When persuasion failed, threats were resorted to by the trader, and as Tanner still persisted in doing as he pleased with his own property, a pistol was presented to his breast; on which, pointing to his bare bosom, he undauntedly told the trader to fire, declaring that, although but a stranger and a slave in that country, he would not be so much of a woman as to raise a weapon against any man, and afterwards, through fear, desist from killing him. By this bold conduct he maintained his right to the disposal of his furs, which he immediately applied to the payment of a just debt."

Of his attachment to his children, he gave a strong proof by the long and perilous journey which he undertook to visit his daughters; and the distress which he felt, when they had disappeared, was among the most heart-rending scenes which we have ever witnessed. His language was the natural expression of grief deeply felt. If the abandonment, which he had meditated of his wife, presents him to our consideration in a less deserving light as a husband, it must be borne in mind, in extenuation, that the woman who could, under any circumstances, be induced to plan and instigate another person to so atrocious a crime as that in which she afterwards shared, could not be an amiable companion, and could probably have no claim upon his affections.

What will be the future destiny of Tanner appears to us very uncertain. We much question whether he can ever be satisfied with sharing in the occupations and comforts of civilized life. We think it more probable that the wandering and irregular habits which he seems to have imbibed from the Indians will soon drive him back from the settlements to his usual haunts in the woods. He was at one time considered, by zealous persons, as a fit instrument for the conversion of Indians to Christianity, but we doubt whether he can ever be brought to feel that deep conviction in the truths of Revelation, which is required to make fit ministers of the gospel. While his strong mind appears to have rejected the superstitions of Indians, it has imbibed a sort of philosophic incredulity, which would make him but a slow and unwilling convert to the purest of faiths.

Tanner was of a disposition naturally stern, which his mode of life and the sentiments of his companions have but increased. He was said, by many, never to have been seen to shed a tear; when he was bereft of his daughters, he wept not; his grief was of too stern a character. But it was evident that the conflict of emotions in his mind, at the time that he was compelled to land from our canoes, overpowered him, and his eyes glistened with a tear which he attempted in vain to shake off.

There is a feature in his character which we have not alluded to, and, as it is honourable to him, we should be loath to omit it. We allude to his warm gratitude for all those who have at various times manifested kindness to him. His affection for his Indian mother, and for her family, was great. Of the late Lord Selkirk he always spoke with much feeling. To Dr. M'Laughlin he appeared sincerely attached. He frequently mentioned the kind sympathy manifested to him by Major Delafield, of the boundary line commission, who would have taken him in his canoe, but that at that time his wounds did not admit of his removal.

Such is the sketch of the life and character of this interesting man, as far as we have been able to collect them from personal interviews with him, from the account of Dr. M'Laughlin and others, who had known him for many years, and especially from the perusal of the documents which he had in his possession, and which fully establish him to be the son of the Rev. John Tanner, late of the neighbourhood of Frankfort, in Kentucky. These documents consist of letters from Lord Selkirk, from Mr. Edward Tanner, and from other persons who interested themselves in his behalf. Tanner had promised to supply us with the particulars of his life and adventures, and with a full account of the manners and habits of the Ottawas and Chippewas, among whom he had resided. His well-established character for candour make it an object of much regret that the state of his wounds prevented him from continuing with us. His language, though broken, was intelligible; he had in his intercourse with white men, since 1817, acquired enough of the English language to converse in it, though always with much difficulty.

At Rainy Lake fort there is a very fine water-fall, surpassed by two or three only of those on Winnepeek River. The whole of the waters of the lake discharge themselves into the river by these falls, the height of which is about twenty-five feet. The beauty of the spot depends much upon the wildness of the rocky scenery, occasioning a foaming or dashing of waves that is very striking. The rock is chiefly sienite, in which we thought we could distinguish a tendency to a stratification directed about north-east, and inclining about 65 degrees to the south-east. This, however, may have been a local feature. The principal growth about the lake is the pitch pine, white pine, and spruce. The soil is rather light, but in the immediate vicinity of the fort it is excellent; potatoes and wheat are cultivated, together with maize, pease, beans, pumpkins, water and musk melons, &c. &c. The wild strawberry seemed to be more abundant there than elsewhere. Our soldiers were kept busy, while encamped at the fort, in fishing for the pike and fresh-water salmon, which are found in great abundance and excellence at the falls. The Testudo geographica is found there. Among the birds Mr. Say killed the ruby-throated humming bird, black-headed titmouse *, and pileated wood-pecker †. There are remains of beaver dams near to the fort; and it is probable that this was formerly a favourite haunt of this animal, which has been entirely hunted out by the residents on the lake.

We proceeded through Rainy Lake, for a distance of about fifty miles, on a general easterly course. We found it to resemble in its characters the Lake of the Woods; it contains many islands, all resting upon a rock which for the most part is a mica-slate, whose strata are directed north 70 degrees east, and nearly vertical; we have in a few places seen granite, sienite, &c. The islands betray a rapid and constant decomposition by the crumbling of the vertical strata, so that we doubt not that the physical characters of the lake, as well as the size and form of the islands, must undergo very striking changes in the lapse of ages. From Rainy Lake the voyagers pass into a number of small rivers or narrow channels, separated by portages. Among these rivers they distinguish that of the "New Portage," de la Croix, Maligne or Bad River, &c. Among the lakes are Vermilion, Namakan (Nămăkăn), or Sturgeon Lake, and de la Croix. There can be no doubt that the level of the water changes much, even at this elevated sum-

* Parus atricapillus.   † Picus pileatus.

mit, for we find that the routes followed by canoes vary frequently. We are informed that that which we pursued is often so dry as to admit of an easy portage of a mile in the bed of a river which at that time contained sufficient water to float our canoes, even with their heavy loads. As these routes are not all equally long, the shortest and easiest are selected whenever the level of the water admits of their being travelled. In determining the boundary line the commissioners will doubtless take this point into consideration, so as to establish it along those streams which afford an uninterrupted navigation at all seasons. We observed as we advanced that the country became more broken, the hills were higher, the islands rose to a greater height, and the region assumed characters indicating a dividing ridge. A journey of a few days more brought us to the " Portage de la Prairie," one end of which communicates with the waters of Lake Winnepeek, while the stream at the other end flows towards Lake Superior. This was the point to which we had been long anxiously looking, and we experienced much real satisfaction on reaching it. The difficulties which we had experienced within the last few days were increased by the badness of the weather. The features of the country became more dreary than ever, and were in no manner relieved by the picturesque effect of the rocks. One afternoon, that of the 6th, we had, it is true, enjoyed great delight from the stillness and soft beauties of Deep River. This stream has a narrow and smooth channel which winds through an alluvial region. Its course is so meandring that our compass frequently ranged through upwards of two-thirds of its circumference in the space of half a mile. The scene was such as a painter might have selected to depict a perfect calm of nature; the great depth of the stream, as well as its narrow bed and crooked channel, contribute to impart to it a darker hue than is usually observed in water; and its reflection of the trees and other objects on its banks exceeded in intensity all that we had as yet seen; the beautiful pembina bushes, loaded with their neat little crimson berry, were reflected as though by a mirror; it was about sunset when we ascended this short but highly romantic stream. With the exception of the few individuals that composed our party, not an animated being was in sight; it really seemed as if we had passed beyond the limits of the inhabited world.

Beyond this, we found a small lake, at the upper end of which we encamped; the air was perfumed by the sweet-scented grass, (Holcus odoratus), which we found here in greater abundance than elsewhere, it had already grown into seed, of which we collected some. At this place, the cold, which had been gradually increasing, became very unpleasant; the dews were still heavy, and on the morning of the 7th we found ice about our encampment. The Portage des Français which we then passed, was a very difficult one; it was about two miles and a quarter long, and was so swampy that it offered great difficulties. Towards the summit level, the portages become longer and more difficult. At the time when the North-west Company carried on an extensive trade by this route, the portages were kept in good repair; the bushes being cut off, the paths well traced, and causeways erected wherever the ground was swampy. The case is otherwise at present; the little travelling along this route has occasioned them to be neglected, and they are in a worse state than if they had never been attended to, for the decayed timber, arising from the broken causeways which were formerly removed, now produces many dangerous holes. Many accidents occur in the portages, especially to such as carry heavy loads. Not unfrequently one of those that carry the canoes slips, in which case the whole weight falls upon him, and crushes him. An accident of this kind gave rise to the name of Deadman's Lake and portage which we passed on the 6th. Next to this was a lake, called Doré, which we have named Hyodon, from the beautiful fish of that genus, (Hyodon tergissus, Lesuer), which abounds in it. Beyond this we entered the Thousand lakes, so called from the apparent division of a sheet of water into numberless small lakes, by thousands of small rocky islands. A more gloomy name is that of Cannibal or Wandigo (Wȧndĭgȯ) Lake, which is derived from the unnatural deed which was perpetrated in its vicinity. It is said that a party of Indians, belonging to the Oschekkamega Wenenewak, (Ȯschĕkkȧ́megȧ Wĕnĕnĕwȧk) or band of the cross-ridge, were once encamped near this lake in the year 1811, and were quite destitute of provisions; they amounted to about forty; their numbers gradually diminished through famine, the survivors feeding upon the bodies of their deceased relations; finally there remained but one woman, who had subsisted upon the corpses of her own husband and children, whom she had killed for this purpose. She was afterwards met by another party of Indians, who, sharing in the common belief, that those who have once fed upon this flesh, always hunger for it, put an end to her existence. The Ochekkamega band, inhabiting a very barren country, are often reduced to cannibalism from necessity, and the frequent recurrence of it has almost deprived them of the abhorrence which men naturally feel for anthropophagy. It was not therefore from horror, but rather from a feeling of self-preservation, that this woman's life was taken away.

While ascending Bad River, Mr. Say observed on the bank a beautiful little animal, which was soon made out to be a fox, probably of the rare and valuable species called the Cross Fox. The animal was shot at, and wounded, but unfortunately he succeeded in making his escape. From the trace of blood which was left on the rocks, it was judged that he could not have run far, but as the woods were very thick, our hunters failed in discovering him.

Among the plants, none appeared to call for particular notice from Lake de la Croix to the height of land, except the raspberry, which yielded fruit in the greatest abundance and of a very superior quality. The minerals presented but little diversity; in one place, the rock, which is a mica-slate, contains many small nodules of quartz, and probably of garnet, which impart to it a rough appearance, and have caused it to be noted by the voyagers under the name of the " Rocher Grenuilleux." But the crystals of garnet were so small and ill-defined, that it was with difficulty they could be made out. The only good crystals which we saw were of tourmaline, in a granitic rock which forms the Island of the Straits, in Little Sturgeon Lake. These were beautiful, about an inch long, and terminated at both ends, but they could not be detached except by blasting, which we had neither the time nor the means to execute. They were of an intense black, the more remarkable, as most of the rocks which we observed in the portages, as we advanced in our journey, were almost free from colouring matter. We frequently found granite, whose mica was of a silvery white, the quartz transparent and colourless, and the felspar resembling the adularia or moonstone. Near the dividing ridge many of the portages were extremely swampy.

Although the country is hilly near the summit level, yet the highest ground, between the waters of the Winnepeek and St. Lawrence, is not more than one hundred and fifty feet above the level of the two lakes in which these waters are supposed to have their source. We are induced to consider the country as inclining towards Lake Superior, from which circumstance the water at the north-east extremity of the portage, is less elevated than at its south-west end. The length of the portage is but very little more than two and a half miles. We had been told that there is a water communication at this place between the two streams, but we believe that this is not the case. The highest water of the St. Lawrence, which we saw, was in a small pool called Cold Water Lake. This is a basin which is only one hundred and fifty yards long and about twenty wide. Its name is very appropriate, the temperature of its water being much lower than that of the surrounding lakes and streams. It is supplied by a spring issuing from the side of the hill, and which is not more than two hundred yards from the lake. This is one of the finest springs we have ever seen; its temperature, which was only 41° of Fahrenheit's thermometer, is lower than that of any spring which we have examined. The temperature of the lake is about 42°. That of the atmosphere at the time we made the observation was 63°. We saw no rocks in place about the spring, but entertain no doubt that the whole country is granitic.

We reached Cold Water Lake on the morning of the 10th of September, and commenced our journey down the streams which fall into Lake Superior, near Fort William, which place we reached on the 13th. Our course from the height of land to Lake Superior was through Cold Water, Muddy, and White-fish Lakes, Cats-tail River, Dog River and Lake, and the Kamanatekwoya River. There were along this part of the route many portages, and these were both long and difficult. The first day we passed through the several lakes, descended Cats-tail River, and proceeded about fifteen miles down Dog's River, where we with difficulty found an encamping ground. Cats-tail River has a very circuitous course through a valley about three miles wide, which is embanked by hills rising to at least one hundred and fifty feet. The valley partakes of an alluvial character, and consists principally of sand. The stream runs through it, being incased but a small depth below its level. The hills which bound the valley are chiefly granitic; at one place where we passed near their base, we saw a beautiful pink granite, which extended for about half a mile. It was divided into large masses, showing no signs of stratification. There are no material obstructions to the navigation of the two rivers, so that we proceeded with much speed, until we reached on the 11th the Dog portage, which divides Dog Lake from the Kamanatekwoya or River of Fort William. In the lake, which may perhaps be considered as a mere expansion of the same stream, which receives two different names above and below that place, we observed a recurrence of granitic islands, similar to those west of the height of land. We were shown, in this lake, an arm of it which extends to the south-west, and which, as we were informed, connects the lake by an uninterrupted water communication with the Thousand Lakes, west of the Prairie portage. This route is shorter than that which we travelled, but is filled with rapids. If this be really the case, and we have reason to believe that it is so, we draw from it three very interesting conclusions. 1st. That there is an interlockage between the waters of Lakes Superior and Winnepeek. 2d. That the waters at the west end of the Prairie portage are much more elevated than those at the east end, since there is all the difference of level between Dog Lake and the

Thousand Lakes, which is represented as considerable, and also all that observed in the western waters, from the Thousand Lakes up to the west end of the Prairie portage. There being but an inconsiderable rapid between Cold Water Lake and Dog Lake, we may assume the level of the water in both these lakes to be very nearly the same. The third conclusion is drawn from the fact, that a height of land or dividing hill was observed on the route which we travelled, and that it is known to exist on the Grand Portage route, which connects the De la Croix Lake with Lake Superior, some distance south of Fort William; while in the intermediate route between Dog Lake and the Thousand Lakes, no such dividing hill occurs; whence we observe that this does not constitute a dividing ridge, properly speaking, but merely separated and disconnected hills, between which there are probably water communications. We find a confirmation of this opinion in the fact that an uninterrupted water communication exists likewise between Dog Lake and the English River which we have previously noted as entering Winnepeek River above the Slave Falls. A connection also exists between Dog Lake and Nipegon Lake at the head of Nipegon River. From all these facts we are led to the belief, that at the place where a dividing ridge is generally indicated upon maps, there are many uninterrupted water communications between the waters of Lakes Superior and Winnepeek, and James' Bay.

Dog portage receives its name from the figure of a dog carved upon the hill over which it passes. This figure is nearly obliterated, but from the description probably resembles representations of otters, &c. near Lake Travers; it is supposed to have been executed by a party of Sioux, who had advanced thus far on a warlike excursion; this shows how far they sometimes carry their inroads into their enemies' territory.

On descending Dog portage we found mica-slate *in situ* on the east side of the hill, and this we observed still more distinctly at the next portage, where the sharp lamina of the slate, resembling the blades of cutting instruments, have caused it to receive the name of Knife or Devil portage. Although it was late when our party reached this place, yet we had occasion to observe a junction of the slaty and greenstone rocks. The greenstone is under the slate, whose strata are directed north fifty degrees west, and incline to the north-east about seventy degrees. There does not appear to be a passage from the one into the other; but a tendency to the formation of both rocks probably existed at one time, whence the mica-slate was deposited immediately after the greenstone, no interval of time occurring between the formation of the two, as appears from the fact that we find patches of the latter enclosed in the inferior strata of the former, and also some portions of mica-slate in the superior part of the greenstone mass; as the latter is not stratified, we could not determine whether the slate lay in parallel superposition, though we have reason to believe that it does. We observed that the masses of greenstone enclosed in the mica-slate lay in a direction parallel to the stratification.

The descent on the east side of the height of land is very rapid, as can easily be observed in passing the portages. On the 12th of September, we travelled thirty-five miles, and the difference of level which we observed in the water during that day exceeded two hundred and seventy feet. The splendid water-falls which we observed we will not attempt to describe. One of them, however, we cannot pass over without particular mention, as it may probably rank among the finest that are known; from the Indians it has received the beautiful appellation of Falls of Kakabikka (Kåkåbĭkkå,) and as no attempt has as yet been made to give it an European name, we hope that its original appellation will be retained as that of Niagara has been. In the Chippewa language Kakabikka signifies the "cleft rock." This fall is remarkable on account of the volume of water which it presents, the great height from which it falls, the picturesque appearance of the rocks which surround it, the wildness of the vegetation that accompanies it, and finally, on account of the very great noise which it produces, and which we believe to be far greater than that of Niagara. It yields to the latter in one respect, however, which is in point of breadth, but in this perhaps it acquires an additional beauty; for the immense breadth of Niagara certainly takes away from the effect which its great height would otherwise produce; while the falls of Kakabikka, restricted by the rocks to a breadth of fifty yards, present a height apparently more imposing. The rock was measured by Lieutenants Scott and Denny, who found the perpendicular pitch to be about one hundred and thirty feet. The edge of the rock is placed obliquely to the bed of the river; its surface is entirely covered, but is probably rough, so that the water is broken before it leaves the rock, and forms an uniformly white and nearly vertical sheet of water descending into the abyss below, where it meets with a rocky bed which produces a considerable spray; the stream continues foaming for a long distance. The hand of art has as yet done nothing to modify the appearance of this beautiful spot, so that we saw it in all its wild beauties; no ladders have been erected to facilitate the descent; no trees felled to clear the prospect; we were therefore obliged to satisfy ourselves with that view of it which the rock naturally presents. The finest prospect is one taken at a short distance below, but nearly on the same level with the upper channel of the river. Mr. Seymour's view, is taken from that spot; it presents but a small portion of the fall. The observer, if standing at the branches on the left side of the plate, can at one glance catch the whole sheet of water; but in order to convey such a view on paper, it would require that the painter should place himself on the lower level of the river, having the whole fall before him. Mr. Seymour could not obtain such a view, as the vertical nature of the cleft in the rock prevents a descent to the bed of the river. We were informed that canoes had sometimes ascended the stream to a small rocky island, situated about two hundred and fifty yards below the fall, but this attempt was not made, as it would have been attended with danger to our canoes, which in our situation were too valuable to be hazarded. The chasm, into which the water falls, is bounded for several miles by bluffs of rocks which rise to a height of upwards of one hundred and fifty feet. They are of a dark colour, that contrasts strongly with the white foam of the waters.

Directly opposite to the place from which we contemplated the fall, there is in the rock a cavity, which, in the superstitious legends of the Indians, is regarded as the residence of the evil spirit. The entrance to this cavity is scarcely large enough to admit a man. About a quarter of a mile below the fall there is a sort of a cove in the right bank; it is about three hundred yards in diameter, and bounded by the steep bluffs on all sides, except in front, where the river passes. The portage road, which is about three quarters of a mile long, terminates at this place; a descent to the level of the water having been made by the North-west Company. After having visited the falls, we stopped in this cove for dinner; we attempted to walk along the edge of the river up to the foot of the fall, but our progress was obstructed by the bluff, whose base is washed by the stream. We were not a little gratified, on being informed by our guides that we had passed all the difficult spots. The portages were all over except a short one. The navigation of the river below this spot, is easy for boats going down stream; the current being very rapid, in many places as much as eight miles per hour.

We observed, on the 12th, a very important change in the geological features of the country. In the morning, the rock was a very decided mica-slate, which gradually passed into a clay-slate, whose primitive characters were inferred from a vertical stratification observed in several places, and especially at a portage called the "Portage du Raccourci," or of the *short cut;* in one place the rock abounds in iron pyrites. At the Mountain Portage, or that made at the Falls of Kakabikka, the rock was found to be in very distinct horizontal stratification. The connexion of this with the former rocks could not be observed, but we are induced to believe that there is a distinct passage of the one into the other. At the descent of this portage we could study the characters of the rock. We observed that the whole mountain is composed of an alternation of strata; some are formed of a clay-slate, and others of a grauwacke or sandstone, formed by the union of grains of quartz and felspar united together by an argillo-calcareous cement. There are a number of small specks of calcareous spar. The rock contains nodules of silex of a colour which varies from an ash-gray to a light black; it is pellucid. In some cases it assumes the characters of a Lydian stone. We observed throughout the mountain many points of iron pyrites; in some cases also, a little copper pyrites was seen. The sandstone is formed of rounded grains of felspar and quartz. We incline to the opinion that this is a transition rock, from the absence or great scarcity of organic remains; we sought in vain for them; it is probable that a more minute search would disclose some. We saw small nodules which, at first sight, were considered as probably of an organic nature, but upon closer investigation they did not justify this belief. The seams of the slate are lined with calcareous and ferruginous incrustations; the latter appear to be in great measure derived from the decomposition of the iron pyrites. While descending the river in our canoes, near *Bad* Portage, we observed the compass vary much; the north pole pointed to the southeast; this continued for a few moments, and induced us to believe that we were then near to a bed of iron ore, which influenced our instruments.

The great mist which arises about the falls, and probably also the nature of the rock, produce a fertile soil, supporting a fine forest of large hazel, spruce, tamarack, red or pitch pine, white pine, larch, &c. The cottonwood was observed on the 12th, for the first time on our return. The aspen had been seen on the 7th, while crossing Frenchman's Portage. The bushes consisted of pembina, raspberry, black and red cherry, &c. besides which there was an abundance of whortleberries, &c. The scented grass grew very thickly near the place, and its perfume added to the pleasure we experienced while contemplating the falls. As we passed the portage we could feel in many places the earth quaking under us from the great concussion produced by the fall of water.

Proceeding down the river, about ten miles below the falls of Kakabikka, we encamped at a portage, occasioned by a considerable bed of flint or silex in every respect similar to that observed at the Mountain portage. It is probable that this flint was in like manner enclosed in the slaty rock, and that being of a more durable nature it has resisted decomposition, while all the surrounding slate was washed away. At this place we found large plums, apparently of a good quality, but they were not yet ripe. The next day, we proceeded on our journey, and were overtaken by a canoe in which one of the partners of the Hudson's Bay Company, Mr. Henry, was travelling. We had the pleasure of witnessing a spirited competition between his canoe-men and ours, in which the former had the advantage. The country improved as we advanced; the banks of the river were generally low, and covered with a fine vegetation, indicating a strong soil. We passed at the foot of a hill called Thunder Mountain; it is supposed to be about five hundred feet high. We passed the ruins of the old fort de Meuron, erected by Lord Selkirk. We were likewise shown the remains of a winter road opened by him from this river to the Grand Portage; it extends in a southerly direction, and is about thirty-six miles long. As we descended the river, divided into three channels, we took the northernmost, and at about ten o'clock on the morning of the 13th, we reached Fort William, having performed a journey of about eight hundred and twenty miles in twenty-seven days, and without accident. The usual passage is about twenty days, and in some cases the distance has been travelled in fifteen, yet considering the nature of our party and our mode of travelling, this was sufficiently expeditious, as we were detained three days by rainy weather, &c. Instead of an experienced crew, one half of them had never been in a bark canoe before; and the time necessarily consumed by the gentlemen of the party in making observations, delayed the canoes a considerable while. On reaching the termination of our voyage in canoes, we could not help feeling some interest in the fate of our Engagés, for although their irregular habits, and their wild pursuits, render them at times disagreeable companions, yet their independant disposition, their endurance of all hardships and fatigues with the greatest equanimity, and their light and buoyant spirits, excited our astonishment, and won our admiration. Leading a laborious and hazardous life, in a country destitute of game, they generally subsist upon maize boiled with fat. The maize is first cleared of its husk and then boiled in water. One quart of prepared grain, and two ounces of melted suet, form the usual ration of an Engagé, unless pemmican can be procured. We were likewise obliged to live for a long while upon this unpalatable food; the only variety we had was a sort of hasty pudding, made with meal and buffalo grease, and seasoned with service berry. We have not dwelt much upon the details of a canoe life, although they are extremely interesting to those who share in them for a short time, because this subject has been ably handled by other travellers, and by none better than by Sir Alexander Mackenzie, whose account of the fur trade presents a lively and correct delineation of this mode of travelling. On reference to that work, it will be observed that we followed from Lake Winnepeek to Lake de la Croix, the same course which he had travelled. At this place we had the option of continuing by the course which we pursued, or of following the boundary line to the Grand Portage, which is about forty miles south-west of the mouth of the Kamanatekwoya. We preferred the former route as it appeared to be the shortest and in best repair, and as the Grand Portage route had been fully explored by the boundary line commission; another motive was, the apprehension that our canoes might, at that season of the year, be detained some time on Lake Superior, in coasting from the Grand Portage to Fort William. In the annexed note, will be found an estimate of the distances from Fort Douglas to Lake Superior, as well as a recapitulation of the Portages and *Decharges* on that route, together with the length of several of the Portages*.

---

* *Estimate of distances from Fort Douglas to Fort William.*

	Miles.
From Fort Douglas to the mouth of Red River	43
Through Lake Winnepeek	64
Up Winnepeek River	175
Through the Lake of the Woods	80
Up Rainy Lake River	104
Through Rainy Lake	45
Up small streams and lakes to the height of land	194
Through small lakes, Dog and Kamanatekwoya Rivers, to Fort William	118
	823

These distances agree tolerably well with those given by Mackenzie.

LIST OF PORTAGES AND DECHARGES.
Winnepeek and Rainy Rivers, &c.

1. No name.   Length.
2. Portage des Eaux mouvantes.
3. Decharge de l'Illet.
4. Decharge du défunt Minet.
5. Portage des Grandes Eaux qui remuent.
6. Portage des Chênes.
7. Portage de la Terre blanche.
8. Portage du Rocher du Bonnet.   Yards
9. Portage du Bonnet 1760
10.
11. } Portage du Rocher du Bonnet d'en haut.
12. Decharge de la Riviere blanche.
13. Portage (1er,) de la Riviere blanche.

SOURCE OF ST. PETER'S RIVER.

We heard, while on our journey, that the water of Muddy Lake, near the height of land, was so viscid, that

		Yards
14.	Portage (2de,) de la Riviere blanche,	
15.	Decharge de la Chute à Bas rond.	
16.	Portage de l'Agacé.	
17.	Portage du Grand Galet.	
18.	Decharge du Grand Galet.	
19.	Portage du Cantara.	
20.	Portage, dernier, de la Riviere blanche.	
21.	Decharge des Petites Dalles.	
22.	Decharge de la Batture des petites Dalles.	
23.	Portage du Grand rapide, this is the shortest on the route	15
24.	Portage de la Barriere.	
25.	Portage de la Chute de l'Esclave	400
26.	Portage du Bois brulé.	
27.	Portage de la Petite Pointe de Bois	100
28.	Portage de la Grande Pointe de Bois	350
29.	Decharge de Jacob.	
30.	Portage de Jacob.	
31.	Portage de l'Isle.	
32.	Decharge de la Cave.	
33.	Portage de la Terre blanche	100
34.	Decharge du Petit rocher de Charette.	
35.	Portage de la Terre Jaune	80
36.	Grande Decharge.	
37.	Portage du Rat	100
38.	Portage du lac des Bois	100
39.	Decharge du long Sault.	
40.	Decharge du Manito.	
41.	Portage du lac de la Pluie	320
42.	Decharge du petit Rapide du lac de la Pluie.	
43. 44.	Portage Neuf	320 180

De la Croix River.

45. Portage, (1er,) de la Riviere de la Croix.
46. Portage, (2de,) de la Riviere de la Croix.
47. Portage, (3me,) de la Riviere de la Croix.

Bad River.

48. Portage de l'Isle.

it was with the greatest difficulty that the canoes could be paddled through it. We observed no such character

49. Portage du Rocher Grenuilleux.
50. Decharge de l'Islette.
51. Decharge du Defunt Courchin.
52. Portage du Petit rocher.

Lakes, &c. near the height of land. Yards
53. Portage des Grosses Roches 500
54. Portage des Deux Rivieres 1320
55. Portage des Morts 550
56. Portage des Français 3960
57. Portage de la Pente... 550
58. Portage du Baril 550
59. Portage de la Savanne...................................... 3960
60. Portage du Milieu 3080
61. Portage de la Prairie 4620
62. Portage du petit lac de l'Eau froide.
63. Portage de Jourdain.

Dog River.
64. Decharge de la Riviere des Chiens.
65. Portage du Chien... 3168

On the Kamanatekwoya.
66. Portage des Couteaux ou du Diable.
67. Decharge des Roses.†
68. Decharges des Grandes Dalles.†
69. Decharge des Epinettes.†
70. Decharge des Fossilles.†
71. Decharge des Bouleaux.†
72. Decharge Mauvaise.
73. Decharge du Défunt Bellanger.†
74. ⎫
75. ⎬ Decharge du Plainchant.
76. ⎭
77. Portage de Plainchant.
78. Decharge du Raccourci.
79. Portage du Raccourci.
80. Portage de l'Isle.
81. Decharge du Recollect.

SOURCE OF ST. PETER'S RIVER. 143

in this lake; it appeared to us that the canoes moved as freely there as elsewhere. Mackenzie mentions having himself seen a lake of this kind near the height of land on the Grand Portage route. He states that " it has a peculiar suction or attractive power, so that it is difficult to paddle a canoe over it," and further, that he himself "found it very difficult to get away from this attractive power, with six men and great exertion*." We observed no such attractive power.

From Rainy Lake to Lake Superior we did not meet with a single quadruped. The only animals we saw were about thirty or forty birds, chiefly ducks. Among the birds observed were the Canada jay*, blue jay†, hairy woodpecker, Indian hen, golden plover‡, and woodcock. We killed five pheasants§ on the 7th of September; on the 4th, we heard, near Rainy Lake, the notes of the whip-poor-will. A rail was also seen, but it disappeared too soon to enable Mr. Say to determine the species.

The mosquitoes, which troubled us but little after we left Red River, were replaced near the height of land, by some

	Yards
82. Portage Ecarté	880
83. Portage de la Montagne	1408
84. Decharge du Paresseux:	

Bad as these names are, we have preferred retaining them, than attempting a new nomenclature. We have not even attempted a translation, which, in most cases, would be unnecessary.

Those rapids marked with a † were passed over by our canoes without unloading. When ascending the stream the canoes are always lightened and towed up.

* Voyages through the Continent of North America, by Sir Alexander Mackenzie. Philadelphia, 1802, vol. i. p. xlviii.

† Garrulus Canadensis.   † Garrulus cristatus.

‡ Vanellus Helveticus of authors, according to Ord's reprint of Wilson's Ornihology.   § Tetrao umbellus.

dipterous insects belonging to two distinct species of the genus Simulium*. Their punctures were equally severe with those of the mosquitoes, but they were not so numerous; they principally attacked the face and neck, sometimes, however, they crept under our clothes; they seemed to prefer warm and dry weather, differing in this respect from the mosquitoes, which prefer a humid atmosphere.

A number of aquatic plants were observed in Cats-tail River; among these was one resembling our splatterdock†, but smaller; its leaf always floats, but never projects above the water; its flower and seed-vessel are smaller than those which we have generally seen. Besides these there is a small plant, the leaf-stalks of which are elongated; its leaf, which is small, floats upon the water. We saw another plant with small yellow flowers, and leaves very much divided; its stalk projected six or eight inches above the surface of the water‡.

The Kamanatekwoya receives no tributary of any importance. There is a communication between it and the Thousand lakes, similar to that which we noted as existing between those lakes and Dog Lake. That from the Kamanatekwoya passes more to the south, and confirms the conclusions which we had drawn from the existence of the former; it is said to offer a more easy navigation. The White-fish River, which unites with the Kamanatekwoya below the Great Falls, affords, as it is said, a communication with the waters of the Grand Portage route.

From Rainy Lake to Fort William we saw no Indians except one Chippewa and his wife, whom we met on Dog

---

* One of these is the S. venustum, Say, Jour. Acad. Nat. Sci. vol. iii. p. 28.
† Nuphar lutea. ‡ Ranunculus delphinefolius, Torrey.

River; they were near an otter's hole, and were in hopes of a successful hunt. We are informed that the otters found on these streams are very good; indeed, the quality of the furs generally improves as the animals are obtained in more northern latitudes. While on the Missouri in 1820, Mr. Say was told by Manuel Lisa, one of the most extensive fur-traders in Louisiana, that the otters of the St. Peter were preferable to those of the Missouri. Lisa was impressed with the belief that he could distinguish the one from the other, even when obtained from interlocking streams. He had made up at one time a pack of otter weighing one hundred lbs. although it contained but forty-five skins; they were all, however, from a tributary of the St. Peter. The Missouri skins are inferior both in size and in intensity of colour. When the otter is pursued in winter, it attempts to escape by alternately springing and sliding upon the ice. It subsists upon fish, and meat of almost any kind; it eats frogs, muscles, muskrats, &c. The otters sometimes emigrate in numbers; they seem to be well acquainted with the neighbouring lakes and water-courses. We were told by Mr. Jeffries that they had been known to winter with the beaver, as had been ascertained by opening beaver lodges, in which sometimes, but not often, one or two otters were found. Hunters usually catch them by means of steel traps, or dead falls, sometimes they smoke them out of their holes; at other times they shoot them.

The fisher inhabits thick woods, holes in trees, and fissures in rocks. It resorts to the shores of lakes, and banks of rivers, in pursuit of mice, frogs, and other animal food. It crosses rivers, but can no more be considered as a water animal than the fox. It is taken in steel and wooden traps;

sometimes it is shot by means of spring guns, sometimes also it is chased and fired at.

Mr. Say observed in the small lakes a number of leeches, among which four new species have been established.—Vide Appendix I. D.

CHAPTER III.

Account of the Chippewa Indians. Their usages, manners, and customs.

HAVING described with some detail the manners and habits of the Potawatomis and Sauks, we shall curtail our observations and notes upon the Chippewas, because they have derived, from their common Algonquin origin, customs and usages, in many respects very similar. The languages of these nations will, on reference to the vocabularies, (see Appendix,) be found to have a great analogy, while all will be observed to differ much from that of the Dacotas.

The term Chippewa, which is generally applied to this nation, is derived from that of O'chĕpĕ'wăg, which they restrict to the Indians who reside near Fond du Lac, it signifies plaited shoes, from the fashion among those Indians of puckering their mocassins. The whole nation are by themselves styled Neenawesik (Nĕĕnăwĕ'sĭk), which signifies *natural language,* implying that they speak an original tongue, and that other nations have an acquired one. The term Neenawesik includes, however, all those that speak the same language, and that are usually designated under the names of Algonquin, Nypsins, (living near Montreal,) Ottawak, Meskigouk, Menomones, and even the Sauks. At least such was the statement of Charles Bruce, a man who was considered as well acquainted with the Indian manners and habits, and who was recommended to Major

Long, as one on whose assertions implicit reliance might be placed. He accompanied the party as interpreter, from Fort Douglas to Fort William. Much of the information contained in this chapter was obtained from him. We are induced to believe that he never wilfully misrepresented a fact; but we did not find him to be as intelligent as he had been stated to be, and we have therefore omitted such parts of his narrative as savoured of ignorance or credulity. He is a half-breed Chippewa, and his information chiefly relates to the Chippewas, properly speaking, who may be included within the following limits: from the Sault de Ste. Marie by a slightly curved line running somewhat south of west, to the Chippewa River of Lake Pepin; thence, in a direction west of north, to Spirit Lake, and thence to the head of the river Aile de Corbeau; thence to Red River near the Red Fork; thence to the confluence of Mouse, (or la Souris,) and Assiniboin Rivers; thence to a point on the Saskatchawan, about one hundred and twenty miles above its mouth; thence to the Riviere des Brochets; thence to the Riviere de Sang; and thence to the Sault de Ste. Marie. This immense tract of land includes a vast proportion of water, since it embraces the whole of Lake Superior, Winnepeek, of the Woods, &c. From this circumstance, the population of this nation certainly bears no comparison to the extent of country which they claim. They are reported by old travellers to have been very numerous. Mackenzie attributes the diminution of their numbers to the inroads of the Dacotas, and to the ravages of the small pox; he considered their population as being on the increase, at the time that he passed through their country. From what we have seen and heard on the subject, we are induced to believe that it has diminished since that time, and that it is probably rapidly wasting away. The country which they inhabit is almost destitute of large game; it was, at one time, well stocked with beaver, otter, and other small animals, which, when sparingly used, may have supported a tolerably large population, but which having been almost hunted out of the country, in consequence of the improvident destruction growing out of the fur trade, have left the land totally destitute, and must have caused a corresponding diminution in the number of inhabitants. We doubt whether the population ever was large; but if so, it has certainly diminished very considerably. The Chippewas are divided into small bands, designated by local appellations, which indicate the spots near which they rove. These bands consist of but few families each. Those near whose residence we passed, are as follows:—

1. Mĭskwȧk-kȧ́ Mḗwḗ Sȧ̊gȧ̊́gȧn Wḗnḗnḗwȧk, or the people that inhabit the lake of Red Waters.

2. Ȯnḗpȯ́wḗ Sḗpḗ́ Wenenewak, people of Death River.

3. Sȧ̊gḗ́ Wenenewak, the people at the entrance or mouth of Red River.

4. Wȧ̊bȧ̊sḗmȯ́ Wenenewak, or White Dog Tribe. They reside near a white rock, which is an object of great superstition.

5. Wȧnȧ̊mȧ̊kḗ́ Wȧ̊jḗnḗnȋk, or the people that eat of meat out of skin bags, (pemmican.) These inhabit near the Lake of the Woods, but hunt the buffalo annually on the prairies to the south-west of the lake.

6. Kȯ́chḗchḗ́ Wenenewak, those that live at the mouth of Rainy River.

7. Oschekkamega Wenenewak, or those of the cross or transverse ridge.

8. Kḗchḗkȧ̊mḗ́ Wenenewak, those near the great waters; they reside in the vicinity of Fort William.

9. Ȯmȧ̊schkȧ̊sḗ́ Wenenewak, those of the white firestone

rock; they reside on the north shore of Lake Superior, near a rock from which they supply themselves with flint.

10. Påwĕtĕkŏ Wenenewak, or people of the rapid; these inhabit near the Sault de Ste. Marie.

We can form no idea of the population of each of these bands, or of that of the whole nation; but, although we travelled over about fourteen hundred miles of country claimed by the Chippewas, from the main fork of Red River to the Sault de Ste. Marie, the whole amount of Indians whom we fell in with did not exceed one hundred.

We heard of no traditions respecting their origin upon which any confidence might be placed. The tales we heard were so much intermixed with childish details, and contained so many coincidences with the Mosaic doctrines, evidently derived from their intercourse with white men, that they do not deserve to be noted. The Chippewas appear at present to be in the lowest stage of advancement. They have no national councils; their dispersed condition and their excessive indulgence in spirituous liquors have destroyed their national character.

They entertain, as all the Indians whom we saw did, a belief in a Supreme Being, author of all good; and in a subordinate one, who has both the power and the inclination to do all mischief. They also people the sun, moon, stars, &c. with spirits. Their form of sacrifices differs from that of the Sioux in this, that he who offers the sacrifice frequently partakes of it. It is usual that he who makes the sacrifice should appoint one of the magicians or speakers of the nation, to manage the feast. This man disposes of all, invites the guests; among whom he may include, if he pleases, the person who provides the feast, in which case alone the latter is allowed to eat of the meats prepared; their sacrifices are unaccompanied by dances. Human sacrifices do not exist at present, but there seems to be a tradition that they formerly existed, and were not confined to enemies; but the subject is obscure.

In fasts they place their principal reliance, considering them as instrumental in producing dreams, which they value above all things; these are supposed to lose their efficacy if they be divulged.

Polygamy is held to be agreeable in the eyes of the Great Spirit, as he that has most children is held in highest estimation; one of their chiefs had nine wives.

In the assigning of a name to a child, much interest is taken. The father applies to one whom he considers as well gifted or favoured by the spirits above, and entreats him to bestow a name upon his offspring. A day is fixed for the ceremony; the friend settles what objects will be required on the occasion, and whatever they may be, the parent never fails in providing them; if not from his own hunt, he obtains them from others. Guests are invited; as soon as the manager appears, the whole of the provisions are placed before him; he takes for himself the head, heart, and other choice parts. The residue he divides among the guests. The tobacco being laid before him, he fills a pipe, offers the stem to the spirits, smokes of it himself, and then proceeds to relate his own adventures, his experience in religious matters, his intercourse with spirits, &c. He generally premises by observing, that when young, he dreamt of a certain object, and valuing his dream much had never divulged the subject of it, but that, in consideration of his great regard for his friend, he will mention the object of his dream, and name his young friend after it. He then relates the circumstances attending it, and bestows the name upon the child. It is immediately repeated by all present. The feasting then commences, and is continued until all the provisions are eaten up; if there be more prepared than the guests can eat, other invitations are sent out, for none can leave the feast until all is consumed. The manager becomes a second parent to the child, who is held to be under great obligations to him. The duty never devolves upon women.

A feast to which still greater importance is attached is that which is given by a parent on the occasion of the first animal killed by his child. This ceremony is alluded to by Harmon [*], but he does not mention that this extends, as we were told, to the very smallest animal, and is not restricted to the first success in the chase. We are informed that if an infant should kill a bird, mosquitoe, or even a flea, this is hoarded with care by the parent; it is dried, and as soon as he has killed game enough to give a feast, he invites his friends to share in the repast, in which his son's first trophy is included. The most distinguished friend is, as usual, invited to preside, and it is his exclusive privilege to eat the whole of the animal killed by the child. The future success of the individual is considered to depend upon the age at which this feast was given; the younger the child is, the greater the promise which he gives of future distinction.

The number of children, which a man has, varies much; the average is four; they seldom have as many as seven, unless they have many wives. The pride and honour of parents depend upon the extent of their family. This causes them to attach a high price to them. In some cases this affection is displayed in a barbarous and unfeeling manner, as in an instance which Bruce wit-

---

[*] Ut supra, p. 346.

nessed. A Chippewa having ill-treated his wife during pregnancy, she abandoned him, withdrew to her father's, and was delivered of a child. She soon after returned to the vicinity of her former residence; the father claimed the infant; she refused to deliver it; he seized upon it and attempted to take it, while she strongly opposed his effort; in this conflict the poor infant's arm was broken and lacerated. Such instances of extreme barbarity are probably very rare. Generally speaking, the Chippewas become attached to their wives and seldom repudiate them. But in their manners they are rough, even when they do not wish to produce serious injury. Thus, in punishing their children, they frequently strike them so rudely as to stun them. Frequently, likewise, their brutal conduct to their wives produces abortions.

The Chippewas have no marriage ceremony. The business of promoting unions rests principally with the female relations, and originates with those either of the man or woman. In such cases the preliminaries are settled between the mothers without consulting their children. When the terms are agreed upon, and the customary presents exchanged, the property of the girl is removed to the lodge of the man, whom the mother has selected. The disappearance of her property is the first intimation which she receives of the contemplated change in her condition. She is then accompanied to the man's cabin; this is generally done during his absence. On his return he finds a female at his usual resting-place, and her baggage placed near his; the purport of this change he cannot misunderstand. If the parties give consent, they are from that moment considered as man and wife. If, as is often the case, one or both of them be unwilling, they remain as strangers to each other, avoiding all conversation; but the parents who have a great influence, and considerable perseverance, generally succeed in bringing them to second their views. Sometimes, however, when the antipathy is great, one or the other elopes from the lodge. An union is sometimes brought on by an inclination between the parties themselves, in which case they apply to their parents to induce them to promote the match; if these object, and the inclination be a strong one, the parental opposition is overlooked, and the union takes place. We are not disposed to believe that there is frequently among the Chippewas an inclination entirely destitute of sensual considerations, and partaking of the nature of a sentiment; such may exist in a few instances, but in their state of society it appears almost impossible that it should be a common occurrence.

The Chippewas believe that there is in man an essence, entirely distinct from the body; they call it Ochechag, (Ŏ′chĕchȧg), and appear to apply to it the qualities which we refer to the soul. They believe that it quits the body at the time of death, and repairs to what they term Cheke Chekchekame (Chĕkĕ Chĕkchĕkȧmĕ). This region is supposed to be situated to the south, and on the shores of the Great Ocean. Previous to arriving there they meet with a stream, which they are obliged to cross upon a large snake that answers the purpose of a bridge. Those who die from drowning never succeed in crossing the stream; they are thrown into it, and remain there for ever. Some souls come to the edge of the stream, but are prevented from passing by the snake that threatens to devour them; these are the souls of persons in a lethargy or trance. Being refused a passage, these souls return to their bodies and reanimate them. They believe that animals have souls, and even that inorganic substances, such as kettles, &c.

have in them a similar essence. In this land of souls all are treated according to their merits. Those who have been good men are free from pain; they have no duties to perform; their time is spent in dancing and singing, and they feed upon mushrooms which are very abundant. The souls of bad men are haunted by the phantoms of the persons or things that they have injured; thus, if a man has destroyed much property, the phantoms of the wrecks of this property obstruct his passage wherever he goes; if he has been cruel to his dogs or horses, they also torment him after death; the ghosts of those, whom during his life-time he wronged, are there permitted to avenge their injuries. They think that when a soul has crossed the stream it cannot return to its body, yet they believe in apparitions, and entertain the opinion that the spirits of the departed will frequently revisit the abodes of their friends, in order to invite them to the other world, and to forewarn them of their approaching dissolution.

The usual mode of disposing of their dead consists in interring them. It has been observed that the Chippewa graves are always dug very deep, at least six or eight feet; whereas the Dacotas make but shallow graves. Great respect is paid by the Chippewas to the corpses of their distinguished men; they are wrapped up in cloths, blankets, or bark, and raised on scaffolds. We heard of a very distinguished chief of theirs, who died upwards of forty years since, and was deposited on a scaffold near Fort Charlotte, the former grand depôt of the North-west Company. When the company were induced to remove their depôt to the mouth of the Kamanatekwoya, and construct Fort William, the Indians imagined that it would be unbecoming the dignity of their friend to rest any where but near a fort; they therefore conveyed his remains to Fort William, erected a scaffold near it, and upon it they placed the body of their revered chief; whenever there is occasion for it they renew its shroud. As a mark of respect to the deceased, who was very friendly to white men, the company have planted a British flag over his remains, which attention was extremely gratifying to the Indians.

The Chippewas obtain the wild rice, upon which they chiefly subsist, by going in canoes, (two men in each canoe) into the rivers or lakes in which it grows. Both men are provided with long poles. When they have reached a field of rice, one of the men with his pole turns down into the canoe the plant from one side, and the other thrashes it until all the grain is separated from the stem. The same operation is performed with that on the other side; after which they move their canoe to another place, and continue until they have obtained a sufficient supply. They can, in this manner, often collect with ease from twenty to thirty bushels per day. The grain is subsequently dried over a small fire by placing it in a fine sieve made of reeds, secured in a square frame. It is then collected into a small hole, and trampled under foot in order to separate the hull without crushing the grain, which is afterwards separated from the chaff by stirring it in wooden platters, exposed to a gentle wind.

Although the fields of this plant appear to be inexhaustible, yet from improvidence, or otherwise, the inhabitants are frequently in great want. We have already illustrated, by one instance, the cruel necessity to which they are frequently reduced. We might have obtained a number of well-authenticated stories on this subject. Bruce knew a man, who in a journey with his wife and two children, aged six and eight years, from the Manitoba Lake to Fort Douglas, had been induced by famine to kill his children;

both he and his wife supported themselves upon this food. But there are instances in which the excuse of famine cannot be pleaded. Frequently after a battle, a warrior will fall upon the body of an enemy, cut off his head, which is accounted the choicest piece, and invite his friends to follow his example, which they are always prone to do; thus, prompted by no necessity or scarcity, they feast upon human flesh. In such cases they are actuated by no superstition; it is not the hope of becoming braver or stouter, but it is merely the desire to satiate their rage upon their enemy which leads them to perpetrate this unnatural deed. But instances are even known, when neither the heat of a battle, nor the desire of venting their revenge on the spot, can be adduced in extenuation; when this meat has been jerked, laid aside, and kept for years, and afterwards taken out and cooked up with other meat in order to make a festival to which guests were invited, and in which none could have refrained from sharing, without being liable to the charge of faintheartedness. It is from these circumstances that we are led to ascribe to the Chippewas the revolting practice of cannibalism, not founded upon scarcity of provisions alone; not stimulated by superstitious notions; not perpetrated merely in the heat of passion; but springing from the worst of motives, a concentrated and lasting revenge, motives which, far from offering any palliation, only add to the abhorrence which we must feel for the perpetrators of this abominable practice.

Among the Chippewas the institution of the *Totem* exists as among the Sauks, and serves as an important distinguishing feature between these two nations and the Dacotas.

The principal disease to which the Chippewas are liable is a consumption of the lungs, induced by the great fatigues and exposures which they undergo; it generally affects them between the ages of thirty and forty; they linger under its influence for a year or two, but always fall victims to it. Having no remedy of any efficacy against it, they resort to a number of plants, in which, however, they place but little reliance, unless accompanied by charms and incantations. Many of them die of a bowel complaint, which prevails every year, and which is produced by an excessive use of berries and unripe vegetables. This disease does not partake, however, of the nature of a dysentery.

It is about thirty or forty years since the small-pox overran the country, and the terror which it inspired is still to be traced among them.

All the Chippewas attend more or less to medicine, and are acquainted with some plants which afford salutary remedies; but there are some men who make a particular study of the subject, and who are supposed to excel in it; they are consulted in all dangerous cases, and are paid for their attendance: the fees are very high. Harmon informs us that among the Carriers, the physicians receive high fees, but that it is usual for them to return the amount paid when the patient dies. The Chippewa physician more resembles that of civilized nations in this point, for whenever the patient dies, his death is ascribed, not to the impotency of the physician's prescription, but to the fault of nature, so the fee is kept. Their mode of treatment depends more upon the adoption of proper spells than the prescription of suitable remedies. Every dose which is administered, is accompanied by certain songs, in which the efficacy of the remedy is supposed to reside. The medicines are always pulverized and compounded, to prevent their nature from being detected. Those who are skilled in medicine, will instruct others in their secrets, whenever a sufficiently large fee is offered them. Diseases are generally considered as having been cast by some person who was ill-disposed towards the patient, either on account of an offence offered, or a civility withheld. When the sorcerer or physician comes, the patient begs that he will transfer the disease to some other person, to whom he may chance to bear a grudge. To effect this, the sorcerer frames to himself a small wooden image of his patient's enemy; he pierces this image in the heart and introduces into it small powders, red, black, &c. which, being accompanied by the proper incantation, are supposed to achieve the desired object. Great reliance is placed in the virtue of these compositions, and there are but few young men or women among the Chippewas, who have not compositions of this kind, to promote love in those in whom they feel an interest. These are generally powders of different colours; sometimes they insert them into punctures made in the heart of the little images which they procure for this purpose. They address the images by the names of those whom they suppose them to represent, bidding them to requite their affection. Married women are likewise provided with powders, which they rub over the heart of their husbands while asleep, in order to secure themselves against any infidelity.

Soothsayers exist among them, both male and female, but the great medicines or charms are only practised by men. Their jugglers appear to be well skilled in the art of imposition. Bruce witnessed their powers frequently, but never could discover their secrets. Thus he has frequently seen the trick alluded to by Carver, of the Killisteno who threw off all the ropes with which he had been fastened, though he was bound hand and foot. It is well known that Dr. Richardson witnessed the failure of the experiment in one instance; and probably the result would be the same with all, who would use the same precautions which were adopted in that case.

Bruce states that a magician once chewed certain roots in his presence, and that his breath appeared to be on fire; it seemed as if he exhaled flames. Another one smoked through a pipe, the stem of which was made luminous every time he drew his breath, and instead of smoke, it was flame which issued from his mouth. Others take up red hot stones with their hands, apparently without any injury; they introduce ignited coals into their mouth, likewise without any pain; in such cases they protect their mouth and hands with certain compositions, which they keep secret. As we witnessed no exhibition of this kind, we shall attempt no explanation of their tricks, but merely add, that the number of persons whom we met with, some of whom were well informed, and who all attest having seen these tricks, prove that the Chippewas have, among them, some men well skilled in jugglery.

Poisons are frequently administered by Chippewas to those whom they consider as enemies; these are all of a vegetable nature, and are introduced into their meat or drink.

Insanity is not common among them; it is sometimes affected with a view to succeed in obtaining objects which are at first refused. We heard of two instances, which may serve to show how far an Indian will maintain a deception, if he thinks he may carry his point by it. A Chippewa, named Ogemans, (Ŏgĕmáns), who resided near Dog Lake, was married to a woman called Demoya, (Dĕmŏyă̇,) but had conceived an affection for her sister named Okoj (Ŏ'kŏj,) who lived in the same cabin; the latter having refused his offer to take her as a second wife, he affected insanity. His ravings were terrible; nothing could appease him but her presence; the moment he touched her hand or came near her, he was as gentle as they could wish. At one time in the middle of a winter's night, he sprang from his couch, broke through the frail bark which formed his cabin, and escaped into the woods, howling and screaming in the wildest manner; his wife and her sister followed him, endeavouring to calm him and bring him home, but he seemed to have set all their powers at defiance. At last Okoj came near him, and the moment she laid her hand upon him, he became quite tractable. In this manner he continued for a long while, convincing all the Indians who saw him that he was possessed by a spirit, which nothing but the approach of Okoj could reduce. So deep was their conviction and her's that she at last consented to become his wife, and never after was he troubled by a return of madness. Bruce lived in his cabin for part of that time, and although he suspected that his insanity was feigned, yet he never could detect him.

Another instance, of a somewhat similar nature, happened in the presence of the same interpreter; a young Canadian had secured the affections of an Indian girl called Nisette, whose mother was a squaw that had been converted by the missionaries; being very pious, the mother insisted that the young folks should be united by a clergyman. None being in the country at the time, they travelled to an Algonquin village, situated on the Lake of the Two Mountains, where there was a missionary. Meanwhile the Canadian's love cooled away, and by the time they reached the village he cared no more for the poor girl. Disappointed in her affections, she was observed to sicken, she became subject to fits, her intellect appeared disordered, and she was finally considered as quite insane. The only lucid intervals which she had were in the presence of her inconstant lover. Whenever he came near her, her reason would return, and she would appear the same as before. Flattered by what he deemed so strong an evidence of his influence over her, the Canadian felt a return of kindness towards her, and was finally induced to renew his attentions, which being well received, they were soon united by the clergyman. Her reason appeared to be restored, and her improving health showed that her happiness was complete. Although she never was charged with having resorted to a stratagem, our guide who had been with her a long while, and who represented her as a modest, virtuous, and interesting girl, had always considered her insanity as assumed, with a view to work upon the feelings of her inconstant friend. This woman, though a half-breed, had been educated altogether among the Indians, spoke but the Chippewa language, and might be considered as being, in point of manners, thoughts, and principles, altogether an Indian. We were informed that her father had given her the French name of Lisette, which was, by the Chippewas, called Nisette, as the L appears to be wanting in their language. Among the several hundreds of Chippewa words with which we have become acquainted, not one presents an L. This is the more curious, as we believe this letter occurs in other languages of Algonquin origin.

The Chippewas are not naturally very strong, but they are active; they will walk, swim, paddle, &c. for a length of time without any apparent fatigue; they are inured to exercise and heedless of exposures of all kinds; they make good hunters and skilful fishers. They are generally tall and thin, and are easily distinguished from the Missouri Indians by the absence of the aquiline nose, which may be considered characteristic of the latter; their bodies and shoulders are well set and well proportioned; their legs are not very good, generally destitute of calf, with thick knees and ancles; their feet are large; their arms and hands small and well-shaped; they possess great strength in the wrist; their voice is strong and harmonious, many of them sing, and their ear appears good. Of their musical talent we cannot, however, form a high estimation. We heard one of their songs, which accompanies the scalp-dance. The words of it as furnished by one of our half-bred canoe-men were Wagonan nandawandank otagame keoshemot, (Wȧgȯn'ȧn n'ȧndȧw'ȧndȧnk ȯtȧgȧmĕ kĕŏshĕmŏt), which was translated, "What does he, the Sauk, mean, that he runs off thus?" The song is said to have been composed on the occasion of a Sauk having joined the Dacotas, and guided a party of their warriors against the Chippewas; on being discovered the Sauk made his escape.

Their sight is keen, but it becomes weak at an early age; they are frequently afflicted with sore eyes, which is supposed to be caused by their constant exposure to the reflection of the sun by the water during the summer, and by the snow in the winter season. Blindness is not common. Many of them become deaf at an early age; their stomach is naturally very strong, but is impaired by the inordinate excesses in which they indulge when provided with food. They appear to be deficient in mechanical ingenuity, and do not cultivate the few natural talents with which they are gifted. Their ornaments consist of beads, paints, and other trifles, which they obtain from traders at very high prices. Their cabins are constructed of birch bark, secured to a slight frame by means of heavy poles placed upon it to prevent the wind from blowing it away.

Hospitality is one of their chief virtues. Their disposition though cheerful is taciturn; the women are more loquacious; in conversation the Chippewas use but little action; their features seldom indicate the emotions which agitate their breasts; but their eyes are very expressive. Smoaking is their favourite pursuit, and the pipe is the first object offered to a stranger. The Chippewas are considered to be very ambitlous of the situation of chiefs; the intrigues in which they will engage to obtain this post are sometimes very unjustifiable. Their envy of each other's acquisitions is very great, and would probably rise into party spirit if they were not so much dispersed. A few of them are addicted to lying and thieving; these are, however, held in disrepute. The Chippewas cannot be considered as of a very irascible temperament; but when once injured they never forget or neglect to avenge the insult offered them. They are great boasters, and have a high opinion of themselves. Some Indians are represented as supposing themselves to hold a rank in creation inferior to that of the white man, but this is certainly not the case with the Chippewas, who have a common expression which they use when any thing awkard or foolish is done, Wametegogin * gegakepatese, (Wămĕtĕgŏgĭn gĕgăkĕpătĕsĕ), which signifies " as stupid as a white man." They consider themselves as created for the noblest purposes. The great Spirit made them that they should live, hunt, and prepare medicines and charms, in which they fancy that they excel. White men, on the other hand, were doomed to the drudgeries of manufacturing cloths, guns, &c. for the use of the Indians.

We found much difficulty in ascertaining the division of time among the Chippewas. Our interpreter at first asserted that there were thirteen moons, then made out but

* Wametegogin does not properly mean a white man, but one who elevates logs in the air, probably from the beams or eaves used in the construction of white men's cabins.

twelve. We are induced to doubt the accuracy of his statement. It is probable, that disconnected as the Chippewas are, and scattered as we find them over an immense tract of country, the terms by which they designate their moons vary much among themselves. It may be questioned whether they have any well defined ideas on that subject. The following are the designations which Bruce communicated.

Kisis signifies *Moon* in Chippewa.

Names of Moons.	Signification.	Concordance.
1. Mĕkĭssăwĕ kĭsĭs,	Eagle,	} March.
Nămăpĭnnĕ kisis,	Carp,	
2. Nĕpĕnĕsă kisis,	Summer birds,	
Ŏnăpămŏ kisis,	Freezing,	} April.
Nĕkĕg kisis,	Wild goose,	
3. Săgĭpăkăwĕ kisis,	Opening leaves,	May.
4. Ŏtăĕmĕnĕ kisis,	Ripe Strawberries,	June.
5. Mĕnĭnĕ kisis,	Huckleberry,	July.
6. Ăpĭttănĕnĕpĕnĕ kisis,	Midsummer,	August.
7. Ămănŏsŏ kisis,	Rutting,	September.
8. Pĕnăkwĕ kisis,	Falling leaves,	October.
9. Ŏshĕkĕpĭppŏn kisis,	Approach of Winter,	} November.
Tăkwăhkĕ kisis,	Hardening earth,	
10. Pĭppŏn kisis,	Winter,	December.
11. Nănăbŭshĕ kisis,	Name of a Man *,	January.
12. Kăchă kisis,	Great moon,	} February.
Kănŏsĭs kisis,	Long moon,	

Chastity is a virtue in high repute among the Chippe-

---

* Nanabush is the name of a fabulous character, whose story appears to be a very long and perplexed one, which we regret that we could not unravel. In the account which we obtained, it appeared that the histories of Adam, Noah, &c. had all been referred to one man, and blended with the original Chippewa traditions.

was, and without which no woman could expect to be taken as a wife by a warrior. Many of the young females are, however, seduced into intrigues which they are obliged to keep secret, if they have any respect for their character; to conceal their crime they do not hesitate to have recourse to abortions. It is not true of the Chippewas that men visit the cabins of those whom they wish to marry, and commence their intercourse by nocturnal assignations; the young men will frequently resort to this, but never when they wish to take a woman as a wife; they know that such a step would injure her reputation. When a mere passing intrigue is their object, they usually carry it on at night. Incest is not unknown to them, but it is held in great abhorrence. Barrenness is held disreputable in women, as it is considered as being brought on by incontinence or wilful abortions. Chippewa women do not bathe in cold water after parturition; in this they differ from the Dacotas, and we are induced to believe that bathing in that situation has never been practised by any of the Algonquin nations. The character of a good woman rests merely in the observance of chastity, of obedience to her husband, and of affection to her children. In case she becomes a widow she ought to exhibit her grief by remaining unmarried for the space of a year, abstaining from all intercourse with men during that time, partaking in no pleasures, wearing no ornaments or bright colours, but clothing herself in a ragged dress. It is considered an essential duty of a good man to supply his wife with the best dresses that he can afford. The respect for father and mother is greater than that entertained for grandfathers, &c.; in this particular the opinion of the Chippewas differs from that of the Sauks. The relation of fraternity is strongly marked; a man is held to be bound to marry the widow of his deceased brother, yet he ought not to do it until after a year of widowhood. He is likewise considered as obliged to provide for his brother's offspring, but this care not unfrequently devolves upon the grandfather. Cousins german are considered in the same light as brothers and held to be bound by the same rules; relationship is not felt beyond this degree. Persons are often adopted as relations; thus, when a man has conceived a strong friendship for another, he informs him of the fact; stating, at the same time, that he considers him as resembling a brother, father, or other relation whom he may have lost, and requesting him to assume that character; if the proposition be agreeable to the other, it is accepted, and they ever after stand bound to each other in the same manner as if their relationship was one of blood instead of adoption. They are then required to aid, assist, defend, and avenge each other. If the relationship which they have assumed as existing between them be not of a nature that precludes the marrying of the widow, the survivor is obliged to take her for his wife, as well as to provide for the maintenance of her children. The Chippewas seldom attain to an old age; the average length of men's lives varies from thirty to forty, that of women from twenty to thirty years. Those who live to an advanced age are found to experience the same impairment of their faculties which attend a protracted life among white men. One of the faculties which they retain longest is that of memory, the excellency of which appears to be one of the distinguishing traits of the Chippewas.

Suicide is not of common occurrence among them; some men are impelled to it by disappointments; sometimes also by a high sense of shame. An Indian who had been created a chief by the Hudson's Bay Company, and who had received presents from them, subsequently traded with the North-west Company. Having returned some time after to the Hudson's Bay Company's fort, he was upbraided by the superintendant as a faithless and ungrateful man; he immediately went out of the fort and hung himself. Among women suicide is far more frequent, and is the result of jealousy, or of disappointments in love; sometimes extreme grief at the loss of a child will lead to it. The Chippewas hold it to be a foolish, not a reprehensible action. They do not consider it as entailing any punishment in the other world. The souls of those who perish in this manner meet, as they think, with a treatment corresponding with the general tenour of their lives, and are not affected by this last act of theirs.

Duelling is not practised among them; we heard of but one instance of a combat between two individuals, which, from the attending circumstances, approaches to the nature of the duels of civilized men. Two warriors of distinction, who had been noted for their mutual attachment, ceased to be friends; the cause of their disunion remained a secret; no apparent motive could be ascribed to it; it did not spring from any quarrel about their mistresses, or from gambling. After the coldness had subsisted for some time, they were again seen together, and hopes were entertained that the breach had been made up. One evening both were known to be in search of each other; they met, and welcomed with their left hands, uttering an expression corresponding to our word *well;* one of them then passed his right hand behind him and drew his knife; the other immediately did the same, and before the byestanders were aware of their object, each had plunged his knife twice in the bosom of his adversary. Both fell severely wounded; one died, the other survived his wounds. He was observed ever after to be melancholy; but he never could be induced to explain the motives of the quarrel, or the circumstances of the meeting. There were not a few among them who considered the encounter as premeditated. The man died some time after, and his secret was buried with him.

When warriors return from a successful excursion, they are met and welcomed by such as staid at home; these take away from them every article of property which they have, giving them others of at least equal value in exchange; the articles thus taken from the warriors are held in high estimation, being considered as relics; this extends to their horses, guns, &c. The women dance the scalp-dance; those, whose husbands have brought home scalps, use them exultingly, and relate the adventures which led to their capture. Warriors are never made slaves; if any be taken prisoners they are soon killed, so are the old women; the marriageable women are reduced to servitude, and are treated with great cruelty by the squaws; the children are generally spared and incorporated into families, where they frequently meet with tolerably good treatment.

CHAPTER IV.

Departure from Fort William. Trap formations on Lake Superior. Michipicotton house. Arrival at the Sault de Ste. Marie. Conclusion of the Journey.

THE route which we travelled from Lake de la Croix to Lake Superior was first explored and laid out by Messrs. M'Gillivray, M'Leod, and M'Kay, and is very creditable to them; it being probably one of the best and most eligible means of communication between these two points. Fort William was erected in 1803, on a scale commensurate with the importance, which was justly attached to the principal depôt of a company remarkable for its active and ambitious views. It covers an area of two hundred yards square, enclosed by a strong picketting, fortified by three block-houses. The accommodations which it affords were sufficient, in the days of the prosperity of the North-west Company, to receive forty partners, and at least as many clerks, who, being all attended by their families, were provided with separate quarters. In the large mess-room, where we were handsomely and kindly entertained by the superintendant, Roderick Mackenzie, Esq. much mirth and hilarity formerly prevailed, but from the immense size and deserted appearance of this elegant apartment it had acquired a gloomy character. We regretted to find that this establishment, which had cost a great deal of money, and which had been embellished with many of the luxuries of civilized countries, is about to be suffered to fall to ruin;

the change in the direction of the trade having made this a place of but very little importance.

The residents of the fort chiefly support themselves upon the produce of their fisheries, which yield abundance of choice food. We were present at the hauling in of the net, which contained upwards of three hundred fish, consisting principally of white-fish, trout, the salmon of the Ohio, sturgeon, suckers, perch, &c. Of these the white-fish deservedly ranks first; it is, we think, the best fish we have ever eaten, and is remarkable for the whiteness and firmness of its flesh, as well as for the total absence of the strong or fishy taste, which characterizes almost every kind of fish. Its weight varies from three to six pounds. The largest known are said to be caught in the Athabasca, and to weigh twenty-two pounds.

The garden near the fort is in good order, and yields very large potatoes, turnips, &c. but maize and wheat do not come to maturity, so that the tilling of the ground is not attended to.

The fort is situated, according to Mr. Colhoun's observations, in latitude 48° 23' 33" north. It stands on the river, at about a mile from its discharge into Lake Superior; the country around it, to a considerable distance, is level, rising gradually from the lake-shore till it mingles with the highlands, at a distance from four to five miles from the lake. The situation is very cold, and the quantity of snow which falls annually is considerable. The winters are long; they last about seven months.

The proceeding through the lake in canoes being judged unadvisable, we refitted an old boat which had been left by the Boundary-line Commissioners; it was the only craft of the kind which we could obtain, and although it was very old and crazy, yet our soldiers, who were better accustomed to rowing than paddling, hailed with pleasure a change in our mode of travelling. This boat was about thirty feet long, and barely sufficient for the accommodation of our party, which was then reduced to twenty-two persons, of whom four were Engagés.

Our provisions, which were nearly exhausted, were replaced by a supply of a few bags of maize prepared in the usual manner for voyagers. As no meat could be procured, we were obliged to satisfy ourselves with the maize and suet allowed to Engagés.

On the afternoon of the 15th of September, we took leave of Messrs. Mackenzie and Henry, and commenced our voyage along the north coast of Lake Superior. The weather was fair, the wind favourable and not too strong; we hoisted a sail, descended the river, entered the lake, and soon lost sight of the fort. The river discharges its waters into a bay which is separated from the lake by a barrier of small islands, one of which has received the name of Paté, or pye, from its form. This is a high turreted rock, elevated several hundred feet. We passed at a distance from it, but it appeared to be formed of nearly vertical cliffs, and the upper part presented the appearance of a columnar division, while the lower seemed as though it were formed of the same horizontally stratified slate, which we had seen at the Falls of Kakabikka. Our course gave us an opportunity of observing about three-fourths of its circumference, on all which sides it appeared to be inaccessible. We were told, however, that it had been ascended, and that there is, on its summit, a small lake, stocked with excellent fish. As we entered this bay, Isle Royal could be distinguished as a faint blue streak, pencilled along the horizon; and after we had cleared the cluster of small islands which enclose the bay, it was seen stretching out far before us, its extremity bearing south-east of our course.

Having crossed the bay, which is about fifteen miles wide, we passed a promontory called Thunder Point, the elevation of which was estimated at eight hundred feet. This, as well as the rest of the shores, has a bold and fine outline. It is doubtless formed of the same rock as the islands; its dark red colour, deepened by the effects of the weather, is picturesquely relieved by an orange-coloured lichen which in many places conceals the rock. The weather being very fair, and the wind having subsided, we determined to continue our route in order to pass a part of the lake, which, being unsheltered by islands, is very rough when the least wind raises a swell. Having merely stopped for supper, we resumed our voyage by moonlight. The effect of that evening scene was beautiful beyond description; tall cliffs filled with caverns, and curiously indented by numerous little coves, rose abruptly from the smooth and undisturbed surface of the lake, whose unbounded expanse lay then open to view. In the midst of such scenery, where both the rock and the lake had an appearance of immensity, and where nought else could be detected by the eye, our small boat seemed a mere speck upon the surface of the waters. At about midnight, we had again reached a cluster of islands, which were very numerous and small; we continued along them until two o'clock, when the moon setting left us in total darkness; as it became both difficult and dangerous to continue our course, we sought for a landing-place, which we had some difficulty in finding. There we spent the rest of the night; the next morning we observed that the place where we had landed was covered with an immense number of small waterworn stones, which were found to consist of an amygdaloidal rock. There were a number of cavities and druses in these, which were lined with minerals of the zeolite family. These stones, which had been seen at the evening encampment near Thunder Point, had given the first intimation of our approach to a formation of a different nature from those which we had previously seen; subsequent observations fully confirmed the fact. On the 16th we continued our voyage, but under the disadvantages arising from a high and adverse wind, which prevented us from making much headway; as long as we could keep under the lee of the islands our progress was satisfactory, but the moment we were exposed to the lake wind our boat moved but slowly. After many arduous exertions on the part of our soldiers to cross one of the short channels that separate some of the islands, we were obliged to retrace our course, and seek a night's shelter on the last island which we had passed. The geologist met here with a very interesting rock; it was the amygdaloid in place. This appeared to be a reddish wacke filled with geodes of quartz, hyaline, agate, cornelian, jasper, onyx, &c. besides mesotype and stilbite. The latter mineral is found very generally disseminated; it lines small fissures or cracks in the rock which are generally not more than from one-sixteenth to one-twelfth of an inch in thickness. It is of a fine red colour. In the geodes we observed all those varieties of quartz, which have given so much celebrity to the rocks of Oberstein on the Rhine. It is impossible on beholding this spot on Lake Superior, not to admit it to be a secondary trap formation, similar to those of Germany, Scotland, &c. We find here also, probably, the original site from which have been derived all the specimens of jasper, cornelian, &c. previously mentioned as existing on the banks of the Mississippi, and for which Lake Pepin has long been celebrated. When we consider the easy decomposition of the wacke in which these geodes are imbedded, we cannot be surprised that the latter are always found loose and separated from the imbedding rock. The amygdaloid was not observed to be stratified, but in some places, it presented a columnar division. We are therefore induced to attribute the columnar appearance, which we thought we had seen in the Paté island, to the presence of trap rocks at its surface, it appears to us probable that all the islands which we saw are more or less covered with this interesting formation, which was probably deposited at a period subsequent to that at which the horizontal slate was formed. The examination of the geological structure of the north coast of Lake Superior will probably renew the discussion of the aqueous or igneous formation of the trap rocks. Upon this point we will not dwell, because we have no new facts to offer. Our visit to this coast was of too transient and hasty a nature to permit us to extend our observations. We, however, confess ourselves unable to discover in secondary trap rocks in general any signs of a Neptunian origin. If we were disposed to launch into theory, we might connect the existence of these trap rocks with the evident signs of the action of heat observed upon some of the rocks which we met in Winnepeek River. We might perhaps also attempt to refer to volcanic phenomena on a great scale, the changes to which we have already hinted as having taken place in that country. The rupture of the great barrier which confined the waters of the immense lake might be shown to have been probably produced by such causes. This opinion is not quite original, for Mackenzie has stated that he thought he could discover along the north coast of Lake Superior evidences of volcanic action.

The physical revolutions, of which this part of our continent was the theatre, were too great to attempt to assign to them any but an immense cause. By those, who object to the igneous or volcanic theory of the formation of trap rocks, it will perhaps be argued, that the immense extent of country, on the shores of Lake Superior, which is covered with these rocks, opposes the hypothesis of their being the product of volcanoes; but the same has been said of the secondary trap formation of Bohemia, Auvergne, &c. While the igneous origin of these is supported by the respectable names of Desmarest, Humboldt, Von Buch, D'Aubuisson, &c. we may, arguing from the sound principle, that like effects may in both hemispheres be traced to similar causes, be permitted to consider the trap rocks, which we observed, as being probably of a volcanic origin.

We are not aware that the spot which we visited has ever been examined by any geologists, except by Dr. Bigsby and Major Delafield. The former of these gentlemen we met at the Sault de Ste. Marie, after our observations on these rocks had been completed; if he has published his views on the subject we have not yet seen them. We have not seen Major Delafield, nor do we know of any publication of his upon this subject, so that the above observations are offered rather with a view to call the attention of future travellers to this interesting question, than from any wish on our part to express a decided opinion upon a subject which, in the present state of our acquaintance with that country, we freely confess to be beyond our reach.

These amygdaloidal rocks, interspersed with other varieties of trap rocks, were frequently seen on the coast of the lake. We, however, often saw also sienite, but never had an opportunity of examining the junction of the two rocks. On the morning of the 17th, we observed a beautiful red porphyry, which on inspection we found to be formed by fine crystals of felspar, united by a cement of the same mineral in the compact state; there was also some hyaline quartz throughout the mass, but whether in regular crystals or not we could not determine. This porphyry is not stratified; it very readily decomposes and crumbles into dust, forming a fine gravel of a brick-red colour, affording good beaches for the landing of boats. This rock evinces a disposition to break in vertical and probably columnar fragments, which are, however, soon destroyed by the easy decomposition of the mass. Beyond the place where we saw the porphyry, the amygdaloid recurred under the same appearance, except that its colour was of a bluish cast. It contains a considerable quantity of carbonate of lime, presenting a fine lamellar structure; the carbonate of lime lines fissures in which it has sometimes formed small but distinct crystals. At the evening encampment of the 17th, there were no rocks in place; the beach was strewed with numerous water-worn boulders, among which we observed many fragments of an impure green carbonate of copper, which could not have proceeded from a great distance, as its softness would have soon caused it to break.

The next morning we passed two barges, which we learned were attached to a schooner that is employed under the command of Lieut. Bayfield, of the British navy, in making a survey of the coast; this is a task of some difficulty, but of considerable interest. This part of the coast is termed the flat countries, and is marked so upon several maps; to prevent the mistakes which might arise from this name, it may be well to state that the term is a translation of the Chippewa word Payagua schinkg (Páyáguá schínkg,) which, according to the antithesis frequently introduced in the names given to particular objects, is here used in opposition to the mountainous and rugged features of the country.

We passed on the 18th a river called Rapid River, from a fine fall which interrupts its course very near to its mouth. We did not see the fall, but the spray rising in a white cloud was very visible, and indicated a considerable cascade. The wind increased so much towards night, that we were highly pleased on reaching a fine bay, in which a sandy beach offered us a safe harbour for our boat; this place is called Bottle Bay. The breeze heightened into a storm, which was accompanied by a heavy rain, that continued all night; the weather was very cold, and our tent-flies had become so thin as to offer no protection against either rainy or cold weather. We had fortunately a plentiful supply of wood near us, and we endeavoured to make ourselves as comfortable as our situation admitted of. The waves in the lake were so high that we were prevented from proceeding the next day. The bay in which we had landed was surrounded by projecting points of land on all sides but one, and this was sheltered by an island which stretched across its entrance. In order to enjoy the splendid spectacle of the lake during a storm, several of the party crossed the point of land which separated our harbour from the main body of water. The large waves which were impelled against the shore were of a more delicate green than those of the sea. It was a noble sight to observe each wave as it approached the high and rugged rock upon which we stood, and as it broke at the base of the cliff, throwing up a foaming spray to a height of at least twenty-five feet. The trees that grow in the vicinity of this bay consist of two kinds of spruce, of the tamarack, larch, white cedar, blister balsam*, white and yellow

* Abies balsamifera.

birch, and mountain-ash. Some of the party amused themselves at our encampments with setting fire to the evergreen trees; the long and thick moss, which hangs from one bough to another, communicated the fire instantaneously to the top of the tree, and the brisk blaze which it occasioned produced a fine but awful spectacle. The gum was seen exuding plentifully through every pore of the tree.

There was a heavy fall of snow on the morning of the 20th, but the wind having fallen, we resumed our journey, and continued all day with a fine sailing breeze; we passed a bay, into which a small river discharges itself, and saw at a distance a trading house of the Hudson's Bay Company; but as it would have detained us much to go thither, we proceeded on our journey without stopping. This establishment is called the Peek, which is an abbreviation of the term Pekatek, (Pĕkătĕk) used by the Indians. We encamped beyond this bay on a rock, which appeared to be formed of a talcose-slate, subordinate to the great sienitic formation. As we advanced, the evergreens became more rare, and were replaced by large birch, both yellow and white, and by the aspen.

On the morning of the 21st, as we were preparing to start, one of the men was reported to be missing. His name was Daniel Brown; he was at first supposed to have strayed a little from camp, and a few guns were fired to bring him back; these failing in their object, some uneasiness was felt on his account, as he had expressed himself unwell the evening before, and had been seen up before day-light; but on loading the canoes a few of the articles were observed to be missing; a closer inspection proved that a number of things had been removed; not only the public stores had been pilfered, but even the baggage of some of the gentlemen, and the knapsacks of the soldiers had been opened and robbed. The disappearance of all this property at one time placed the point of Brown's desertion beyond a doubt; yet if ever a man had cause to adhere strictly to his engagement, it was he; for his term of service was nearly completed, and on his starting with the expedition he had been promised his discharge on reaching Mackinaw; a considerable sum was due to him as arrears of pay and ration; he knew that we were fast approaching the settlements. Another motive to restrain him might have been the improbability, not to say impossibility, of his being able to subsist in the country; the only settlement within one hundred miles was the Peek house, which was then closed. The country where he remained has been described to us as covered with such impenetrable swamps, that we very much question whether he ever made his way out of it. Brown had engaged voluntarily in our service, had shown himself active and well disposed. We therefore regretted his desertion, more however on his account than on our own.

After waiting a suitable time for him, we proceeded onwards with a head wind and high sea, which retarded our progress so much as to induce us to stop in a small cove, which received the name of Sunday Harbour. In the evening we proceeded some distance, and made our encampment in a small and dangerous bay, where, for want of better accommodation, we spread our blankets upon a beach covered with large boulders.

On the monring of the 22d we resumed our journey with a high south-easterly wind. We observed, as we advanced, that the country being all sienitic, presented a wilder and more barren appearance than where the trap rocks prevailed; it did not rise to such a height, the shores probably seldom exceeding two hundred feet; but good harbours became more scarce, owing doubtless to the greater resistance which the sienite offers than the trap rocks, to the destructive action of the waves. The rocks are likewise less ragged; they are steep and rounded at their surface. The divisions which they present are very irregular; we question much whether the rock be stratified, though in some places it assumes that appearance, especially when seen from a distance; for on approaching, the divisions are found to be irregular, at least in all places where we had an opportunity of studying them closely. Mr. Seymour made a very correct delineation of the appearance of the coast, at a point somewhat west of the " Otter's head." From a distance, we had almost been induced to consider the rock at that place as divided by vertical fissures, but on drawing closer, the features were found to be different. At a distance inland, the mountains appear higher, and it is by no means improbable, that they equal, if they do not exceed, in elevation, the height of the coast west of the Peek. The mass which constitutes these rocks, we have called a sienite, though it differs materially from the common sienite by the presence of quartz, which in some places forms at least one-third of the mass; perhaps the term of amphibolic granite would be more correct; we think a new name ought to be introduced into science, to designate a rock which constitutes such extensive formations. We have applied the term sienite instead of greenstone, which we believe Dr. Bigsby generally uses, because the proportion of felspar has appeared to us to predominate over that of amphibole. It bears to granite the same analogy that the *protogine* of Jurine does; for in it, the mica is replaced by amphibole, while in the protogine its place is supplied by talc. In some spots the protogine is also found, as well as a more compound rock, formed of quartz, felspar, amphibole, and talc; but these cannot be said to constitute important features; they are, at best, formations subordinate to the general sienitic mass. The colour of the rock is influenced by that of the felspar which is in great excess, and is of a flesh colour; the amphibole is green. The quartz sometimes penetrates the rock in the manner of veins, but this accident is considered of contemporaneous origin with the formation of the mass itself, because, in detached fragments of the same, the quartz of the vein, and that in the body of the rock itself, were found to run one into the other.

We were detained in this harbour forty-eight hours by the prevalence of the storm. At midnight we were awakened by one of the party, with the unpleasant information, that the boat was in danger of being dashed to pieces against the large stones or small rocks on the shore. The wind was blowing a gale from the south-south-west. A heavy swell was rolling into the harbour, breaking, with a loud noise and high spray, against the immoveable rock on each side, and expending its violence in a dangerous surf upon the stony shore on which our boat was fastened. All our force was immediately summoned, and with much difficulty we succeeded in raising the boat upon logs. Being old and very leaky, it required great care. Had it been unfortunately broken, our situation on that deserted coast would have been very precarious. Few persons have ever attempted to travel by land along the lake shore, and this only in winter, when the swamps, rivers, and small lakes are frozen up. But at other times of the year, it is thought that all travelling, except in boats or canoes, would be impracticable. What rendered our situation more distressing was the state of our provisions, at all times very scanty, but which had lately been much reduced by the pilfering of the deserter. The small store of maize obtained at Fort William was nearly exhausted; no game of any consequence could be seen; the only animals we obtained were a small hare, a pheasant, and half a dozen of red squirrels. With a view to accustom ourselves to the food which must probably soon become our sole dependance, as well as to spare our provisions, we collected some of the lichen which grows upon the rocks, and which is designated by the name of " tripe de roche;" when absolutely destitute of provisions, the Indians sometimes resort to this for food, and the voyagers are also compelled to use it in some cases. One of the clerks at Rainy Lake Fort, Mr. Weeks, informed us that he had seen Captain Franklin, on his return from the Polar Sea, when that enterprising officer and his party, very much reduced in number by privations of all kinds, had been obliged to support themselves for thirty-one days, without meat, merely upon the *tripe de roche*, and the bones and pieces of leather which they could pick up at old camps. Although we were not quite so destitute as Captain Franklin, yet we made two meals upon the rock tripe, and they stand recorded in our recollections as the most unpalatable of which we have ever partaken. The moss is collected, and boiled in water, when, if young and tender, it resolves itself into a thin jelly; we were not well skilled in the selection of the moss, so that, instead of taking the tender and delicate, we took large pieces which, having probably undergone a change in their properties occasioned by age, did not resolve themselves completely in jelly, but left a black matter floating in the liquid, and imparting to it as unsightly an appearance as its taste was disagreeable; we endeavoured by red and black pepper to render it tolerable, but all in vain. When all travellers, in those northern regions, have been exposed to the most severe privations, we should find but little grace in complaining of a couple of meals made upon this food. We will therefore merely add, that we have never tasted a more nauseating food; and that our short experience of it has enabled us to sympathize sincerely in the sufferings which Captain Franklin's party underwent.

A heavy rain, which fell in the evening of the 23d, abated the force of the wind, and the next morning we again ventured in our boat; the waves were high and retarded our progress, but our anxiety to proceed impelled us on. We doubled a high promontory called the Otter's-head, from a fancied resemblance between that object and a large block of stone which appears to be formed in the shape of a truncated pyramid, and to be at least ten feet square, and thirty feet high. It forms a distinct landmark, which, being very elevated, can be seen from a distance. It is considered half way from Fort William to the Sault de Ste. Marie. In the afternoon we saw a very fine water-fall, at least thirty feet high; the stream which gives rise to it is considerable, and the fall is close to the lake shore. This was so picturesque that we stopped awhile, to allow Mr. Seymour to take a sketch of it. Proceeding onwards we reached in the evening the western extremity of an island, known by the name of Michipicotton island; opposite to this the rock becomes a talcose-slate, directed north and south, and inclined about sixty degrees to the west. On the 25th, our course was in the strait between the island and main land; this channel is about fifteen miles wide, and the recurrence of the sienitic rock convinced us that the talcose-slate was only a subordinate formation. We entered on that day the deeply indented bay of Michipicotton, which is so wide that voyagers never dare trust themselves across it in open boats, but always coast it. In this case we were particularly anxious to enter it, as our party had been on very short allowance for some time past, and as a fishing establishment exists at the head of the bay. With this view we continued our journey late, and stopped at a very ineligible situation on the shore, where, there being no means of pitching our flies, we lay exposed all night in a snow storm. The weather, which had become very cold, afforded Mr. Colhoun an opportunity of making a curious observation, which he has noted in the following words:

"I carry my pocket compass in a fob. When it is taken out, one end of the needle is found adhering to the face of the instrument, which is enamelled like that of a watch. The adhesion is not overcome by the approach of steel, but it yields to the weight of the needle, for if it be sufficiently inclined the other end adheres in turn. The duration of this phenomenon varies according to the temperature of the atmosphere; at the lowest temperature, which we have experienced, the needle was unable to traverse for the space of fifteen minutes, as if the cold rendered the operating principle slow to retire. During the warm weather, I frequently remarked a disturbance, but it so quickly subsided, that I was content to attribute it to an accidental agitation of the compass. Electricity, evolved from the body, will be at once looked to, as the cause of this phenomenon, from the connexion long known to exist between it and magnetism. Whether the needle be operated upon immediately, or through the substance of which the face is composed, future observation must determine. Perhaps the Chinese would say that the magnetic virtue is not suspended, but only beneficially modified by some property or concomitant of vital heat, and there appears to be sufficient ground to establish for them a claim to the discovery of its influence, in the last sentence of the following quotation :

"' It has been related on the authority of some Chinese books, that these needles do not receive their virtue from the loadstone, though the Chinese possess that mineral in abundance, but from a curious mixture of orpiment, cinnabar, sandrak, and filings of steel, which, being reduced into a fine powder, are made into a kind of paste by a sufficient quantity of blood drawn from the comb of a white cock. In this paste the needles were said to be put, being previously rolled in paper, and there kept seven days and seven nights, over a clear charcoal fire. After this operation, being taken out, and *worn three days longer next to the skin of a man,* they are found fit for use, pointing directly to the north, and *unliable to the frequent variations which affect those that are touched by the loadstone.*'—History of Marine Architecture, by John Charnock, London, 1802, vol. iii, p. 299 *."

Sleep being out of the question during this war of the elements, we resumed our journey long before day-light, and proceeded until about nine o'clock, when we reached the head of the bay. The preceding evening we had stopped at the mouth of a river called "la Chienne" which is renowned for the excellent white-fish caught near it. We met there a few Chippewas who had arrived the preceding day, but who had not yet succeeded in obtaining a supply of fish.

We saw a boat adrift in the bay, and would have approached it, if the waves had not been so high. At the mouth of Michipicotton River there is an extensive sandbar; on the opposite side of which we observed a person in a

* Mr. Colhoun's MS.

canoe, who, after having made signs to us which we did not understand, disappeared among the rocks. We entered the river with considerable difficulty, and landed in safety at Michipicotton house, which we found under the care of Mr. Mac Intosh, the son of the superintendant, and Mr. Robinson, a clerk of the Company's. It was the latter gentleman who had seen us from his canoe, and made signs to us to follow him through an easier pass. The superintendant was absent, having left that place a few days previous on his way to the Sault de Ste. Marie. At this house we saw the fishery followed on a scale far superior to any we had as yet witnessed. The abundance of fine white-fish, trout, &c. which we saw on the shores, was a great source of delight to such as like us were nearly famished. The trouts which we ate there appeared to us distinct from any other fish, and we regret that they had all been cut up before Mr. Say was enabled to obtain specimens for study and preservation. This trout is of a dusky colour, with light spots irregularly scattered upon its surface; it is a richer and more substantial food than the white-fish, but not so delicate; its flesh is of a reddish tinge which approaches that of the European salmon. The season for catching the trout had nearly expired, while that of the white-fish was just commencing; at that time the latter fish ascends the river from the lake in order to cast its spawn; the time of its migration is perhaps more regular than the analogous one of the shad and herring on the Atlantic coast. This fish is caught in small seines or nets; the number of individuals hauled up at one time varies from fifty to five hundred, and, in some cases, even twelve hundred have been caught at one time. For two seasons previous to our arrival, it was observed that the migrations up Michipicotton River had been much less considerable than usual, but this diminution is probably the result of accidental circumstances which will not, it is believed, affect the general produce of the river. The white-fish usually returns to the lake about the middle of November. The residents at this post cure a large quantity of the white-fish for winter; this is, however, an expensive preparation, as their salt costs them about two dollars per bushel; they formerly obtained English salt at Montreal at one dollar per barrel. They object to the salt made in the United States; the impurities which it contains render it unfit for the preservation of the white-fish, at least such is the opinion of those with whom we conversed. We mentioned to them the successful experiments made in England on the substitution of sugar for salt in the preservation of fish, and they promised to repeat them; if the maple sugar should answer as well as the cane sugar, there would probably be economy in using it in place of salt. A circumstance which was ascertained here, and which may interest the agriculturist, is that cattle will feed upon fish. We saw cows that have little if any other food, and that thrive well, yielding abundance of good milk, the taste of which is not in the least affected by that of the fish. This is another instance of the carnivorous disposition of cows in certain cases; it may be added to those already published, one of which is as old as the days of Herodotus.

In the immediate vicinity of the post we saw nothing but sand; and there is an extent of at least one mile square which appears to be formed entirely by the sand brought down by Michipicotton River. This stream is there about one hundred and forty yards wide; it affords an easy communication with Moose River. We were told that the country north of this bay resembles that near Winnepeek River, being entirely formed of small lakes, rivers, rapids, and enclosing large rocky islands. The country is quite impassable during the summer season except with a bark canoe, which the traveller carries over the portages, and which he again launches after arriving at a navigable stream or lake. In winter the whole country being frozen and covered with snow affords an easy mode of travelling to those who are accustomed to the use of snow-shoes. On these, travellers have frequently walked from Michipicotton to Hudson's Bay in twenty-one days; they usually drag after them a small train or sledge, in which their provisions are packed; they travel in this manner from forty to fifty miles per day; it is said, that they have even walked seventy-five miles, but as these are estimated, and not measured, miles, it is probable that the distances were over-rated. The degree of cold experienced at Michipicotton is very great; the winter before our visit to the fort, an alcoholic thermometer fell to —35° (F.) It has been often known to descend to —37°, and it was not ascertained that this was the maximum of cold. From these circumstances potatoes and turnips are the only produce raised near the fort.

This place is acquiring more importance, being much resorted to by canoes going to Moose Factory. The dividing ridge between the waters of Hudson's Bay and those of Lake Superior, if indeed the term dividing ridge can be applied to such a country, is said to be about thirty miles north of the lake. Every river in this part of the country presents more or less beautiful cascades. There is a very handsome one about two miles above the fort on a small branch of the Michipicotton; and one at a greater distance is represented as being very beautiful; we saw the cloud arising above it, and from its size suppose the cataract to be very great. Mr. Mac Intosh showed us very fine foliated and transparent gypsum which came from Moose River, where he represents it as being very abundant. From his description it would appear that the country on Moose River is of a different nature from that on Lake Superior; he did not represent it, however, as being a prairie country. A walk up the river offered us the largest whortle-berries which we have ever seen; they were highly flavoured and very abundant, even more so than those in the vicinity of the Falls of Kakabikka. Other berries also grew abundantly.

Notwithstanding our desire to get under weigh, we were compelled by stress of weather to remain at Michipicotton one day, during which time we experienced a heavy southwesterly gale accompanied by rain, hail, snow, and sleet. The next morning, the wind having apparently abated a little, we resumed our journey, but as soon as we left the river and entered the lake, we found ourselves exposed to a storm so violent that we were obliged again to return to the land. We had advanced but about five miles during near three hours of hard rowing. With considerable difficulty we got our boat round a promontory, and hauled it up, on the shore, in a small cove which appeared tolerably safe. On looking back to the various difficulties which we have experienced on the route, we are induced to believe that we were at no period of the journey exposed to so imminent a danger as on that morning when we were sailing in a crazy boat, on a very rough sea, near an iron-bound coast, in which there were but few harbours. We landed, however, in safety, and lay by till the next morning. With a view to keep ourselves as warm as possible, we used our flies and sail in the manner that the Sioux construct their skin lodges, winding them round, in a conical form, upon a frame of light poles, which had been left there by some

Indians. In this manner we sheltered ourselves partially against the effects of the snow and wind.

We had on the west coast of Michipicotton bay observed a slaty rock, of a dark colour, sometimes almost black; it was well stratified; the direction of the strata was north 40° west, their inclination was vertical. It is found in some parts to contain much quartz and iron pyrites. This rock rises higher than the coast usually does; it forms a vertical cliff, which appears to be undergoing a very rapid destruction; but the fragments, instead of collecting at the base and forming an inclined plane, are washed away, so that the waters of the lake come up to this vertical bank, which rises like a wall, enclosing the lake. It is probable that, at the junction of this rock with the sienite, the river has forced its way into the lake, and that the wide bay of Michipicotton has been opened, for on the east side we again saw the sienitic rocks predominating. At the bay in which we stopped, five miles east of the trading house, we observed the sienite to be intermixed with other rocks, one of which contains a greater abundance of hornblende, and forms a real greenstone; another portion is mixed with talc, and a third portion contains hard nodules of quartz, which would at first convey the idea of a conglomerate, but which, being examined more closely, appear to present no characters but such as are entirely compatible with a primitive and highly crystalline formation; these nodules of quartz are connected by a talcose cement. All these varieties are found together, and belong to the same general mass, of which they form but local or partial features. They are all penetrated by iron pyrites, in great abundance, which in some points were evidently mixed with copper pyrites; all these were examined with care, in hopes of meeting with the native copper, and with other ores of the same metal besides the pyrites; our search was, however, unsuccessful. The great interest which generally prevails on the subject of the copper mines of Lake Superior, as they are called, will perhaps justify us in offering, on this subject, a few observations, which we hazard with some diffidence. We have seen native copper strewed in many directions, over the great valley drained by the Mississippi and its tributaries, and we know from the reports of all travellers that it exists in many places. It has also been found in several spots on Lake Superior, where it was long since looked to as an object of great promise. The largest mass of it that is known exists on the Ontonagon River, and for a correct account of the characters of this interesting block we are indebted to Mr. Schoolcraft. Our journey having been conducted on the north shore of the lake, we of course had no opportunity of seeing this interesting mass; but all that we know of the native copper of that country leads us to the belief that it has not yet been found *in situ*, and that therefore these loose masses ought not to be looked to as indicative of mines in their immediate vicinity. The great weight and size of the mass on the Ontonagon might, it is true, induce us to believe that it has not been transported from a great distance, if the much greater size and weight of the boulders which are dispersed along the vallies of the Mississippi did not attest, that, whatever may have been the cause which produced these revolutions, the force with which it operated must have been immense. It is not, therefore, to these masses of native copper, but to the ores of this metal found in rocks *in situ* that our attention ought principally to be directed with a view to discover copper mines. We have ourselves seen a number of localities of copper pyrites throughout the primitive rocks of the north coast of Lake Superior, but these were always in small specks. A more minute examination might probably lead to more successful results. We believe that there is a site of copper mines somewhere near this lake, and we think it in no manner improbable that the masses of native copper which occur, from the south shore of Lake Superior down the valley of the Mississippi, have been scattered by the same cause which dispersed the boulders of sienitic rock. Whether the native copper found to the north-west on Copper Mine River comes from the same place, is a subject upon which we have no data, and therefore can form no opinion. Perhaps, as Mr. Schoolcraft suggests, the Porcupine Mountains, if well explored, would be found to contain copper ores. We do not at present recollect any places where the pyrites or any other ore of copper has been found in any quantity on Lake Superior. Mr. Schoolcraft, it is true, handed to one of our party some fragments of ores of copper, brought to him in 1823 by an Indian, who said he had found them on Keweena or Kewewenon point, on the south shore of the lake. Upon the vague reports of an Indian we shall build no theory; the question which appears to us of far greater importance is not where the copper lies, but what shall we do with it if it should be found. We are very doubtful whether any other advantage would result from it, at least for a century to come, than the mere addition in books of science of a new locality of this metal. It does not appear to us, that in the present state of that section of our country, and with the unpromising prospects which it now offers, these mines could be worked for a great length of time. Copper, we know, exists in many other parts of our extensive country, and much nearer to the centres of civilization and population. Instead, therefore, of wasting our endeavours and resources, in a futile attempt to discover mines in so remote and dreary a country, let us apply them to the investigation of those sections, where mines could, if found, be turned to immediate advantage. Had the French, who first overran our country, considered this point, and instead of wasting their resources in idle searches, instead of fitting out an expedition to ascend the Mississippi two thousand miles, for the sole purpose of collecting green earth on the St. Peter, had they spent the same amount in France, in working the mines that have since been opened there, they would have rendered an essential service to their country and benefited their fortunes. Whereas, by the course which they were led to pursue, they added but little to science, at the same time that they ruined themselves.

These observations are offered with the more hesitation, as they are not founded on an extensive acquaintance with the localities of native copper, &c. but rather upon a general, perhaps some may think a hasty and superficial, inspection of the features and resources of that section of country, which many have considered as destined to become the seat of future mining operations on a great scale.

After remaining twenty-four hours encamped, we resumed our voyage, though with the disadvantage of a high sea, and cold and snowy weather; but the wind being favourable we proceeded with facility, coasting along the eastern shore of Michipicotton Bay; after travelling twenty-seven miles, we reached Cape Gargantua which we doubled, and which may be considered as the entrance of the bay. We stopped for a meal at what appeared to be a very safe harbour near to the point. The name of this place is supposed to be derived from a high rock, which rises in a disconnected manner at the entrance of the harbour. To a fanciful imagination it might appear a Colossus. The spot has in truth a very beautiful and characteristic appearance; the rock, which is an amygdaloid, having but little solidity, appears to be fast wasting away under the destructive influence of the waves, producing a number of picturesque and irregularly shaped masses, projecting to a small height above the level of the lake. In one of these there is a cavity, which by some might be taken for the crater of a volcano, though it probably owes its present appearance merely to the action of the waves upon the rock. This spot is held in great veneration by the Indians, who, whenever they pass it, deposit near it presents of tobacco and other valuable articles, which, in their simple faith, they expect will propitiate the spirit that dwells there.

This place offers one of the best localities for zeolites, and will probably, when better explored, yield specimens of great beauty. We collected some fragments, rather with a view to mark the locality than on account of the merit of the specimens; but Dr. Bigsby, who was there several times, has obtained some very good pieces, for one of which we are indebted to his liberality.

Proceeding onwards we passed several islands, known by the name of Fox and Montreal Islands, and after a long and swift sail, at a distance from the shore, to avoid all its indentations, we reached the place of our evening encampment. While on the trap rocks, we observed that the soil was not deep, but that what there was of it was good, and that it supported a fine growth of cedar. The Montreal Islands were observed to present sandy beaches; the country became lower and less dreary. In the evening we however found no suitable place to pitch our tents, but spread our blankets on the stony beach, having no means of sheltering ourselves from a heavy fall of snow which occurred during the night. At this place we observed two rocks in immediate contact, one of which was a granite formed by a fine pink-coloured felspar, intermixed with a very small proportion of quartz and mica. Near it was a mica-slate, which we judged to constitute a subordinate formation.

On the 29th we reached at an early hour a projecting point, called the Point de Memens, a corruption of the Indian word Marmoaze, which signifies an assemblage of rocks. We there met with a trap rock in place, but the beach is strewed with water-worn fragments of conglomerates or sand-stone; these were the first conglomerates which we observed on the lake shore. After leaving this point we proceeded on a long stretch, thirty-one miles long, to what is termed the Grand Cape, which we reached late at night. Our course led us near to a group of small islands, called Maple Islands, and there we first observed the sugar tree in abundance. Being during part of this day at a considerable distance from the north shore, we with great satisfaction discovered the south coast of the lake to be in sight; this afforded us a sure indication of the approaching close of our navigation on this lake. The part of the south shore which first disclosed itself to our view is termed White-fish Point. The land appeared to be very low, and nearly overflowed by the waters of the lake. The next point of land which is disclosed on the south shore is Iroquois Point, differing but little from the former in its general character.

We had reached the Grand Point at too late an hour to judge of its real situation; it was only, therefore, on the next morning, that we became aware that we had arrived at the eastern extremity of the lake, and that on doubling that cape we should enter a bay from which the river St. Mary issues. We left the Grand Point on the morning of the 30th of September, the weather was fair and pleasant;

after travelling a short distance, the rocks were observed to recede gradually from the lake, the shores of which were lined with sandy beaches; but the hills at a distance decreased rapidly in height, and from the change in their vegetation, appeared to indicate a difference in their geological character.

The Pointe aux Chênes, or Oak Point, may be considered as the commencement of St. Mary's River, which at the Pointe aux Pins, one mile lower down, is about three miles wide, and has a rapid current and a devious bed. The wind being fair, we spread a sail, and in two hours' time reached the head of the rapid which is termed the Sault de Ste. Marie. We landed, left our boat, and walked along the Portage road, on the south bank of the river, to the " Cantonment Brady," which is the highest military post occupied by the United States' troops on the chain of lakes. A mill-race has been dug from the head of the rapid to the fort; it is somewhat less than a mile long; it discloses the nature of the rocks, which consist of red sandstone horizontally stratified. This was the first spot at which we observed this rock in place, but Dr. Bigsby has informed us that he found it in many of the spots at which he occasionally encamped on the north shore of the lake. In Mr. Schoolcraft's narrative we are informed that this rock extends to a very considerable distance along the south shore of Lake Superior. The canal or mill-race, which the garrison has opened at the Sault, has been made with much less difficulty and expense than would at first have been expected from the apparent magnitude of the undertaking; at a very slight additional expense the canal might be enlarged so as to render it navigable for bark canoes of the largest size.

Our party travelled the distance from Fort William to

the Sault de Ste. Marie in fifteen days; this passage was considered very short considering the season. An idea can be formed of our success in this respect from the circumstance that the superintendant of Michipicotton house, Mr. Mac Intosh, who left his post eight days before we did, arrived at the Sault three hours after we had landed; yet this gentleman was travelling with a crew of experienced voyagers, but being in a canoe he was frequently obliged to lie by. Our boat, though flat-bottomed and in a bad condition, answered our purpose very well. The north coast of the lake, along which we travelled, is considered somewhat safer at that time of the year than the southern; it is said to afford many good harbours, the entrances to most of these are, however, concealed; hence none but experienced pilots can find them out. Our Engagés not being well acquainted with the coast, we were frequently at a loss for harbours when we needed them most. The route which we travelled on the lake was estimated by Major Long at three hundred and eighty-three miles; no doubt a considerable saving in the distance could be effected in fine weather by keeping further off from the coast, and by cutting across Michipicotton bay. The season during which we travelled on the lake was unusually boisterous and severe; we had snow, hail, or rain, for nearly the whole of the time.

The country along the lake is one of the most dreary imaginable, considering its latitude, and the facility with which it may be approached. Its surface is every where rocky, broken, and unproductive, even in the natural growth of trees common to rugged regions; its climate is cold and inhospitable; the means of subsistence are so circumscribed that man finds no possibility of residing on it in a savage state. Game is extremely scarce. Few, if any esculent plants grow spontaneously. Fish, it is true, abound in its waters, but only such as can be plentifully caught by means of nets; the total absence of sandy beaches on the greater part of its extent prevents the use of nets, and of course precludes even this last mode of subsistence. Accordingly all the Chippewas that we saw on the lake did not exceed half a dozen families. If a few fertile valleys should ever be found in the country they will be so closely surrounded by rocky hills and dangerous swamps as to render them no desirable abode for civilized men. Indeed to estimate the future population of this section of country from its present aspect, it would be a highly exaggerated allowance to admit a single inhabitant for every thousand acres of land. But from its very wildness and dreariness this coast draws a charm which we should vainly hope to find in more favoured regions. The high hills, the rugged precipices, the rocky shores, with their spare vegetation, are relieved by the transparency and purity of the waters that wash their base; these are often so great that the pebbles can be distinctly seen at a depth of more than twenty feet. The canoe frequently appears as if suspended in air, so transparent is the liquid upon which it floats; the spectator, who remains too long intently gazing at the bottom, feels his head grow giddy, as if he were looking down into a deep abyss.

At Cantonment Brady, the party were kindly and hospitably received by the officers of the garrison, which was at that time under the command of Major Cutler of the 2d. regt. United States' Infantry. The gentlemen of the party enjoyed a few interviews with Mr. H. R. Schoolcraft, who was stationed there as Indian agent; they found this gentleman very obliging in communicating to them his observations on the topography and mineralogy of the country, as also upon the character and dispositions of the Indians within his agency. Mr. Schoolcraft has devoted much time to this latter subject, and has collected much valuable information, which he kindly offered to impart to our gentlemen; they however declined this kind offer, having ascertained that Mr. Schoolcraft had previously intended the information for Governor Cass, who, as they were pleased to hear, is collecting materials towards a general account of the Indians within the district of Michigan. From the industry with which these materials are collected, no doubt can be entertained that whenever Governor Cass will publish his account of these interesting nations, it will contribute much towards the history of the aboriginal tribes of America. Indeed the certainty that this work will offer a much more complete and satisfactory account of the Chippewas than we could have done, was one of the motives which induced us to curtail our observations on this subject.

Having brought the history of our voyage to the Sault de Ste. Marie, we deem it proper to conclude it there, being persuaded that the observations which we made after that time, having been of a hasty and superficial nature, could contribute but little to the history of a country which has been so long known, upon which so much has been written, and which, by becoming the seat of military operations, during the war of 1812, has acquired so great a degree of celebrity.

It will be sufficient for us to state that the party left the Sault in their open boat, on the 3d of October, and reached the island of Mackinaw on the next day. There they divided. Lieuts. Scott and Denny proceeded with the ten soldiers to Green Bay, thence to ascend the Fox River to the portage, and descended the Wisconsan to the Mississippi.

SOURCE OF ST. PETER'S RIVER. 201

We have heard with satisfaction, by a letter from Lieut. Scott, that he with the men under his command reached Fort St. Anthony without any accident, though they suffered much from cold weather. At Mackinaw Major Long embarked with Messrs. Say, Keating, Colhoun, and Seymour, on board the revenue cutter, the Dallas, which carried them as far as Detroit. On this voyage across Lake Huron and St. Clair, they were three days, during which they received the kindest attentions from the commander of the cutter, Captain Knapp, who very politely gave up to them the use of his cabin. After remaining three days at Detroit they proceeded to Buffalo, on board of the steam boat that plies upon Lake Erie. They then visited Niagara, and travelled by land to Rochester, where they struck the Erie canal; they proceeded down the canal to Albany, a distance of two hundred and fifty eight miles. On the 26th of October they reached Philadelphia, having been absent about six months, during which time they travelled over upwards of four thousand five hundred miles, the whole party being blessed with health, meeting with no accident of any account, and undergoing hardships and privations, far less considerable than those which they had expected to undergo, and which have tried the perseverance and courage of other explorers.

CHAPTER V.

General description of the country traversed by the Expedition, designed as a topographical report to the War Department, by S. H. LONG, Major United States' Topographical Engineers.

THE region, whose description is intended in the present essay, as embracing the route of the Expedition, is limited on the N. W. by the intersection of the 51st degree of N. latitude with the 97th of W. longitude, and, on the S. E. by that of the 40th degree of latitude with the 74th degree of longitude west of Greenwich. Its figure is rhomboidal, about thirteen hundred miles long, from E. S. E. to W. N. W. and has an average width of between four and five hundred miles. Its boundaries may be traced on the accompanying map, being coincident with the route of the Expedition.

The researches of the Expedition were more immediately limited to the region above specified, but our attention has been nevertheless directed to the attainment of new information relative to other parts of the country, whenever a favourable opportunity presented. The substance of the whole is briefly embodied in the following remarks, with the view of giving a geographical outline as complete and satisfactory as circumstances will permit.

In order to render the description as plain and perspicuous as practicable, we shall arrange our remarks under separate heads, corresponding to particular divisions of the route of the Expedition, and conclude with a few observations of a more general nature and application. The following division of the subject may therefore be regarded as applicable, viz.

1st. Of the country between Philadelphia and the Ohio River.

2d. Of the country between the Ohio River and Lake Michigan.

3d. Of the country and navigable communications between Lake Michigan and the Mississippi.

4th. Of St. Peter's River and the adjacent country. Also of the Coteau des Prairies.

5th. Of Red River and the adjacent country.

6th. Of the country between Lakes Winnepeek and Superior.

7th. Remarks on the variety of subjects connected with the topography of the country.

I. *Of the Country between Philadelphia and the Ohio River.*

After all that has been written in description of this part of the country, a very few remarks relative to its general aspect and character will suffice, on this occasion. Eastward of the Alleghany Mountains, the country is most agreeably diversified with hills and valleys, and is prolific in all the vegetable products common to a temperate climate, and suited to the convenience and welfare of man and beast. On approaching the range of mountains just mentioned, the elevation above tide water gradually increases, and the irregularities of the surface become more apparent. Connected with these appearances some slight change of climate is perceptible, and is evinced by a more frequent occurrence and longer continuance of frosts and snows upon the surface. On entering upon the mountainous range, a difference both of aspect and character is readily perceived. A multiplicity of ridges, stretching in a north-easterly and south-westerly direction, alternating with valleys of various widths and depths, is here presented; the ridges rise to the height of from twelve hundred to three thousand feet above tide water. A change of climate, corresponding to the difference of altitude, is also observable; and it is remarked that frosts occur on some of the ridges, more or less frequently in every month of the year. Such is the change of climate occasioned by a difference of elevation in these ridges, that maize, which grows in great perfection in the valleys, cannot be raised upon the mountains, where the altitude is greater than about fifteen hundred feet. It is remarkable also that wheat grown upon the mountains, at a considerable elevation above their base, is heavier by a few pounds in the bushel, and is said to be of a better quality in other respects, than that of the valleys and other adjacent grounds.

The surface of the ridges is often broken and rugged, and generally covered with a profusion of rocks and stones, of the older sandstone formation. The mountain growth consists principally of pitch pines, scrub oaks, chesnut, hemlock, aspen, laurel, bramble, &c.

North-westwardly of the Alleghany Mountains, the country presents a surface exceedingly diversified with hills and valleys, yet more generally susceptible of cultivation, and not less fertile than to the eastward. Its general elevation above tide water may be estimated at about one thousand feet, and its climate in most respects is very similar to that of the country adjacent to the mountains, on the other side, in the same latitudes. In this respect, however, as also in its productiveness, some slight difference may be occasioned by the natural condition of the two tracts, in a geological point of view, the country eastward of the range being of a primitive, and that westward of a secondary character, limestone being common to both.

II. *Of the Country between the Ohio River and Lake Michigan.*

On this part of the route are presented two varieties of country, distinctly marked; the one exceedingly hilly, like that between the Alleghanies and Ohio, before noticed, and the other of a waving aspect, presenting extensive flats, with occasional hills and swells of moderate height and declivity. The line of division between these two tracts commences on the Mississippi, near Cape Girardeau, and runs north-eastwardly to the Miami River, thence eastwardly to the Muskingum, which it crosses near Zanesville, and thence north-eastwardly, passing along the sources of Big-Beaver River, and terminating near the eastern extremity of Lake Erie. (See Account of the Expedition from Pittsburgh to the Rocky Mountains, vol. ii. p. 333). The region situated between this line and the Ohio River exhibits, as before hinted, a surface exceedingly diversified with hills and valleys; the hills uniformly present rounded summits; rocks are seldom abundant upon the surface, though secondary lime and sandstones prevail at a moderate depth below; precipices no where occur except as boundaries to the numerous water-courses. The general elevation of this region may be estimated at between six hundred and one thousand feet above tide water, gradually increasing from the mouth of the Ohio upwards. The inequalities of surface do not render it unfit for cultivation. The valleys, especially of the principal streams, are exceedingly fertile, and the hills, though less productive, afford the means of subsistence in abundance. The soil of both is almost uniformly an argillaceous loam; that of the former is deep, and contains much lime and vegetable mould, that of the latter is less prolific, though deeper than is usually to be met with in hilly regions, and much more easily cultivated, owing to its being light and free from stone.

North-westwardly of the limit above mentioned, the country wears a very different aspect, palpably manifest in travelling in the direction of the assumed line. The river valleys are broader and more regularly defined, being separated from the high lands by parallel ranges of bluffs or mural banks. No hills of any considerable height or magnitude, if we except numerous swells, some of which are broad and extensive, are here to be seen. Extensive tracts of flat country, with scarcely an undulation upon their surface are presented; also many large swamps and morasses, some of which are deep and miry. The country on the Sandusky and St. Mary's Rivers, as also upon many other streams in this quarter, abounds in blemishes of the nature last mentioned, for which remedies no doubt will be provided, as soon as the population and wealth of the country are sufficiently advanced to admit of the various improvements that are practicable.

In the northerly parts of Illinois and Indiana, as also in the west corner of the state of Ohio, are extensive champaigns, flat and marshy, of a soil apparently very rich, but too wet for cultivation. A large proportion of the flat lands of Ohio and Indiana, however, is heavily wooded, and is for the most part denominated the Beech lands, the red beech being the prevailing growth upon it. The soil of these lands is thin, but remarkably black, resting upon a bed of sand, gravel, or pebbles. In addition to the tree just mentioned, the woodlands comprise the oak, ash, elm, hiccory, sugar-tree, wild cherry, black walnut, liriodendron, poplar, hop-horn-beam, and in some places cotton-wood and sycamore, most of which attain a gigantic size.

The general elevation of this portion of the country may be estimated, as before, at about one thousand feet above tide water. It is remarkable, that the strip or zone of country in which numerous tributaries of the Ohio interlock with those of Lake Erie, should decrease in altitude as we proceed from the Miami River, eastward; also, that a hilly region should intervene between the Ohio River and the zone above mentioned, or the country in which its tributaries, from the north, have their origin, of greater elevation than that of the zone itself. Yet however repugnant to the doctrines of the geologist, and however discordant to the general principles of hydrography, such is nevertheless the case, as has been satisfactorily ascertained by the surveys recently made in Ohio, on the several canal routes that have been explored. From the Miami northwestward to Lake Michigan, a very gradual declension of the surface takes place, insomuch, that in the vicinity of the lake, the general level is about seven hundred feet above tide water.

In regard to the facilities for artificial water communications, between the lakes and the Mississippi, through this district of country, no doubts can exist, but in relation to the supply of water on the several summits in a dry season. Of the routes across the state of Ohio, notice has already been taken in a former part of this work. The route through the Maumee and Wabash, and that through the two St. Joseph's and Kankakee Rivers, remain to be explored. Of the practicability of these routes there can be no question, except as to the quantity of water that can be brought to their summits, as before intimated.

A water communication connecting the west end of Lake Erie with the southern extremity of Lake Michigan will ere long become a subject of great interest, inasmuch as it must be regarded as an important link in the grand chain of internal navigation connecting New York with the country of the Mississippi. The route by which this is to be effected remains also to be explored, but the abundance and size of the water-courses intervening between these two places leave but little room to doubt of its practicability.

III. *Of the Country and navigable Communications between Lake Michigan and the Mississippi River.*

No part of the region traversed by the Expedition can be considered more interesting than that now under consideration. The surface, which is generally prairie, is agreeably diversified by gentle swells and valleys, and checkered with skirts of woodland fringing its numerous water-courses. The soil in many places is exuberant in a high degree, and is no where infested with rocks or stones. The bottoms especially exhibit proofs of the greatest fecundity, in the rankness of their vegetable products; to these valuable traits must be added the abundance of lead ore, which prevails in many places; all of which conspire to render this country quite as valuable as any other tract of equal extent within the basin of the Mississippi. In this brief recital of the natural advantages and resources of the country, it should not be forgotten, that the facilities for water communications between the lake and the Mississippi are numerous; there being no less than three different routes through which loaded canoes have passed from one to the other in times of inundation, without the intervention of portages.

The foregoing remarks are intended as applicable more particularly to the tract bounded, north by the Wisconsan and Fox Rivers, south by the Illinois, east by Lake Michigan, and west by the Mississippi River, than which few countries of equal extent can boast of a finer aspect. The rivers included within the limits just assigned, are the Chicago, Milwacke, Manitowacke, and several others of less note, tributary to Lake Michigan, the Des Plaines, De Page, Fox, Mequin, &c. tributary to the Illinois, the Rock and Makabea or Small Fox River, and several others of smaller size that mingle their waters with the Mississippi. Rock River has many tributaries, among which are the Kishwake, Pektannon, Little Pektannon, and Wassemon Rivers, all respectable streams, never before recognised in the geography of the country. The valleys of the water-courses generally, and particularly of those just mentioned, are bounded by parallel ranges of hills, of moderate height and gentle declivity.

The country embracing the southern extremity of Lake Michigan, and extending inland many miles from the lake, presents no hills except the elevated sand-drifts that bound that extremity of the lake. On the contrary, an extensive flat embracing woodlands and meadows alternating with each other, spreads from the St. Joseph to the Des Plaines, and from the lake to the Kankakee. Its soil is apparently good, but the chilling northerly winds, which blow from the lake, charged with vapour, seem to carry with them blast and mildew, and render its prolific energies abortive. At Chicago, which is situate within this tract, attempts have been made to cultivate maize, wheat, oats, and other products, but they have often proved fruitless.

In the vicinity of the Mississippi, the high lands on both sides of the river are intersected by numerous deep ravines and water-courses, which, together with the bluffs and precipices by which the river valley is bounded, give to that part of the country a hilly and broken aspect. At the mouth of the Illinois the high lands are elevated from one hundred to one hundred and fifty feet above the river. At Prairie du Chien their elevation is four or five hundred feet. About one hundred miles above this place, the high lands are said to be more elevated than on any other part of the Mississippi, rising to seven or eight hundred feet. At the mouth of the St. Peter, their height varies from one hundred to one hundred and fifty feet.

On the Wisconsan River, at the distance of fifty or sixty miles eastward of the Mississippi, commences a region of hilly country, which extends northwardly to Lake Superior, and embraces the head waters of the Wisconsan, Fox, Menomone, Ontonagon, Bois Brulé, St. Croix, Chippewa, Black, and Prairie de la Croix Rivers. To this region the name of the Wisconsan Hills has been given, which are terminated on the south by the Ocooch and Smoky Mountains, whose altitude is about twelve hundred feet above the common level, or two thousand feet above tide water. Its aspect is exceedingly diversified by hills and valleys, the former of which are high and rugged, supporting a heavy growth of pine, &c. while the latter often present extensive flats, abounding in lakes, swamps, and ponds, yielding wild rice in great abundance and perfection. The rocks of the southern portion of this region may be regarded as of a secondary character, while those of the northern, according to Mr. Schoolcraft, are primitive. In the former of these localities lead has been found, and no doubt exists in great abundance, and in the latter it is believed that rich and extensive beds of copper ore are of frequent occurrence. To the westward of the Wisconsan Hills, the country assumes an aspect somewhat similar to that mentioned in the former part of this article, though it does not deserve so high a rank in an agricultural point of view. The soil is more sandy and bibulous, the surface more broken, the forest trees are less stately, and vegetation less luxuriant.

On the west of the Mississippi above Prairie du Chien, upland forests of considerable magnitude present themselves at the distance of six or eight miles from the river, and continue in view for the distance of nearly one hundred miles above that place. Their extent westward, however, cannot be very great, for the prairie region, in which the De Moyen has its sources, commences at the distance of above one hundred miles from the Mississippi, and excludes all appearance of woodlands except in insulated groves and narrow skirts bordering upon the water-courses.

The growth of this section of the country comprises the following trees, viz. the white, black, red and post oak, hiccory, walnut, sugar-tree, maple, linden, cotton-wood, white, blue, and black ash, elm, hop-horn-beam, red cedar, sassafras, willow, aspen, &c. in addition to which sycamore, coffee-tree, mulberry, pêcan, Spanish and willow oak, persimmon, honey-locusts, black and red haw, crab-apple, plum, pawpaw, dog-wood, spice-wood, &c. are found in the country below Rock River. Gum, cherry, red birch, butter-nut, or white walnut, red hickory, and slippery elm, are occasionally to be met with. Yellow, pitch and white pine of an excellent quality abound upon the Wisconsan Hills. White birch, white cedar, spruce, juniper, &c. sometimes appear in the woodlands above Prairie du Chien. The undergrowth of the country consists principally of hazle, sumac, elder, prickly ash, alder, thorn, bramble bush, laurel, gooseberry, black currant, chokeberry, sand cherry, grape-vine, hop-vine, bitter-sweet, night-shade, honeysuckle, wild gourd, poison-vine, spikenard, sarsaparilla, grasses, ferns, and a variety of other herbage, conspicuous in many instances for the beauty of its flowers. The islands, which are exceedingly numerous in this part of the Mississippi and its principal tributaries, sustain a dense growth of cotton-wood and willows, surmounting thickets of shrubbery and vines, rendered almost impenetrable by the luxuriance of their growth.

Under this division of our subject, we shall particularly notice a portion of the Upper Mississippi, (by which is meant that portion of this noble river, situated above the confluence of the Missouri,) the Illinois and the Wisconsan Rivers, referring to the accompanying map for the names and localities of the rest.

The valley of the Upper Mississippi, below the Falls of St. Anthony, varies from three to ten or twelve miles in width, except at the De Moyen and Rock Island rapids, where its breadth is so contracted that it affords sufficient room only for the bed of the river, which at the former place is about twelve hundred yards wide, and at the latter from eight hundred to one thousand. It is uniformly bounded by high bluffs, which are generally abrupt, and often precipitous. Within the valley, especially in the vicinity of Lake Pepin, insulated knobs and hills of considerable magnitude, based upon horizontal strata of rocks, and towering to various heights, from one hundred to five hundred feet, are frequently to be met with. These must be regarded as the remains of the high country, through which the river in process of time has scooped out its broad and deep valley. They serve not only to beautify the landscape, but to remind the traveller of the great changes wrought upon the surface of the globe by the agency of water.

The upper Mississippi is also remarkable for the great width of its bed, and the multiplicity of islands it embosoms. It spreads in many places to the width of five or six miles, and seems to lose itself among countless islands through which it flows in numberless small channels. Between the mouth of the Missouri and Lake Pepin, no less than six hundred and forty islands of considerable size have been enumerated. Lake Pepin is a very beautiful enlargement of the river, twenty-two miles long and from one to three broad, destitute of islands, and affording a great depth of water. Above the lake the river becomes narrower, and the islands smaller and less numerous.

The valley country is made up of prairies and woodlands alternating with each other; the former of which are usually elevated above the reach of floods, and are richly carpeted with herbage and flowers, while the latter sustain a dense and heavy growth of trees, intermixed with vines and shrubbery, and are, for the most part, subject to inundation in flood time.

During the spring floods, which usually prevail during the months of April, May, and June, this part of the Mississippi is navigable to the mouth of the St. Peter for boats of great burden. In a low stage of water the rapids above mentioned oppose serious obstructions to the navigation, which is also rendered still more precarious by the numerous shoals and bars with which the bed of the river is infested. The rapidity of the current decreases as we ascend, being about three miles per hour at the mouth of the Illinois, and one mile and a half near that of the St. Peter. At the De Moyen rapids, the river is hurried down a descent of about thirty feet in the distance of eleven miles, and at the rapids of Rock Island, which are about fifteen miles long, the aggregate descent is about forty-five feet.

A description of the Falls of St. Anthony has been already given in the preceding narrative. For a description of the Mississippi above this point, we beg leave to refer to the "Account of Pike's Expedition to the Source" of that river, as also to the narrative published by Mr. Schoolcraft, and to that which Captain Douglas is preparing for the press.

The Illinois River is to be ranked among the most important of the western rivers, inasmuch as it affords greater facilities as a water communication between the lakes and the Mississippi than any other stream. Its length from its mouth to its source, at the junction of the Kankakee and Des Plaines, is three hundred miles. For a distance of fifty miles on the upper part of the river shoals abound, which are serious impediments to its navigation in a low stage of water. The most formidable obstructions of this nature are the rapids situated at the confluence of Vermilion River, which are utterly impassable for boats except in times of flood. Below this, the navigation is exceedingly easy, for boats of moderate draft and burden, to the mouth of the river, a distance of two hundred and fifty miles. The current throughout the distance last mentioned is exceedingly gentle, often quite imperceptible; indeed, this part of the river may with much propriety be denominated an extended pool of stagnant water. Its valley is broad and bounded by parallel ranges of bluffs, presenting, in most places along the margin of the river, low bottoms covered with a dense growth of timber trees, surmounting thickets of weeds, vines, and bushes almost impenetrable. The woodlands thus situated are subject to inundations, during the prevalence of a moderate freshet, but in their rear, at a considerable distance from the river, are extensive prairies of a rolling aspect, and richly adorned with herbage. The ascent to the highlands across the bluffs, is generally gradual, but in some instances abrupt.

The navigable communication above mentioned is continued from the head of the Illinois by two different routes, viz. to Chicago fifty miles through the River Des Plaines and a small water-course connecting the stream just mentioned with Chicago River; and to the St. Joseph of the Lake about one hundred and twenty miles, through the Kankakee, and a small tributary of the St. Joseph interlocking with that river in a tract of marshy country. Through both of these routes loaded boats have passed from the lakes to the Illinois during the vernal floods. The route first mentioned is very direct, and is now frequently traversed with boats of burden; the other is extremely tortuous along the windings of the Kankakee, and is seldom practicable.

The Wisconsan, from its magnitude and importance, deserves a high rank among the tributaries of the Mississippi. When swollen by a freshet it affords an easy navigation for boats of considerable burden through a distance of more than one hundred and eighty miles. Its current is rapid, and, like the Mississippi, it embosoms innumerable islands. In a low stage of water its navigation is obstructed by numerous shoals and sand-banks. At the distance from its mouth above mentioned, there is a portage of one mile and a half, across a flat meadow, which is occasionally subject to inundation, to a branch of Fox River of Green Bay, thus affording another navigable communication between the lakes and the Mississippi, through which boats have been known to pass. The valley of the Wisconsan is somewhat narrower than those of most other rivers of this region, but in other respects it is very similar to them. The high country here assumes a more hilly and broken aspect, and the soil becomes more sandy and meagre.

While on the subject of water communications it is proper to remark, that a third route, viz. by way of the Rock and Milwacke Rivers, has been found practicable for canoes.

IV. *Of the St. Peter River and adjacent Country. Also of the Coteau des Prairies.*

The St. Peter, called in the Sioux language Menesota Watapan, or River of turbid water, receives most of its waters from a remarkable ridge distinguished by the name of Coteau des Prairies, hereafter to be noticed. Its most remote source is a small lake, called Pole-cat Lake, about three miles in circumference, situated at the base of the ridge just mentioned, in latitude about 45° 40′ N. and longitude 96° 36′ W. It enters the Mississippi nine miles below the Falls of St. Anthony, in N. latitude 44° 53′ 49″ and W. longitude 93° 8′ 7″. Its length, following its meanders, is about five hundred miles, but in the direction of its immediate valley, does not exceed two hundred and seventy-five miles. Its course is exceedingly serpentine, varying from side to side of its valley, and is interrupted by several rocky ridges extending across the bed of the River, and occasioning falls of considerable descent. About fifteen miles from its source it passes into Big Stone Lake, which is about twenty-five miles long, and from four hundred yards to one mile and a half wide, lying in a direction corresponding with the course of the river. Near the lower extremity of the lake is an island of considerable size, inhabited by a pretty numerous band of the Sioux. Twenty-five miles lower down it enters Lac qui Parle, which is a handsome little lake seven and a half miles in length, and whose breadth does not exceed one mile. It receives from the west several small tributaries, the most considerable of which are the Blue Earth, the Liard, or Cotton-wood, the Yellow Medicine Rivers, and the Spirit Mountain Rivulet, all of which take their rise in the Coteau des Prairies. Its proximity to the Mississippi precludes any room for tributaries of any considerable size from the eastward, for a distance of more than two hundred miles from its mouth, above which it receives two streams of respectable size, viz. the Epervier and the Medicine Bark, the latter of which rises near Otter-tail Lake and the River de Corbeau, and enters about sixteen miles below the Lac qui Parle.

During the spring freshets, and at other times when floods prevail, the St. Peter is navigable for Mackinaw boats and pirogues, from its mouth to the head of Big Stone Lake, there being but two obstructions that are impassable on such occasions, viz. at Patterson's Fall and the Grand Portage, at which are carrying places or portages of moderate length. For a distance of about forty miles on the lower part of the river it is from sixty to eighty yards wide only, and navigable for pirogues and canoes, in all stages of the water; higher up, its navigation is obstructed in low water by numerous shoals and rapids.

The only tributaries worthy of notice are the Blue Earth, the Liard, improperly called White-wood, the Red-wood, or more properly Red-tree, the Yellow Medicine, the Beaver, and the Spirit Mountain Rivers, all rising in the Coteau des Prairies, and entering from the west, also the Epervier and Miawahkan or Medicine Bark, from the north-east; the latter of which rises in the vicinity of Otter-tail Lake, to which it is said to be navigable for canoes in a wet season, and is the same that has often been denominated Chippewa River. Of these streams the Blue Earth is the most considerable, its sources interlocking with waters tributary to the Missouri, in a district of country, where the Coteau des Prairies is said to have its southerly termination. The others are all of inconsiderable magnitude, as may be readily inferred from the description already given of the principal.

The country of the St. Peter possesses many features highly interesting both in a geological and agricultural point of view. Its physical character and structure, as also those of the other regions treated of in this paper, have been discussed in the course of the preceding narrative. In regard to its soil and aspect, much may be said in its praise. The immediate valley of the river has an average width of about one mile and a half, and is connected by bluffs or parallel ranges of hills, which attain an elevation of about one hundred feet. The lower portion of the valley, embracing nearly one-half the length of the river, is low and marshy, subject to inundation, and abounding in lakes, swamps, and lagoons. Nevertheless, it sustains in many places a dense and heavy growth of trees, consisting principally of oak, elm, white maple, ash, linden, white-walnut, wild cherry, &c. together with a luxuriant undergrowth of shrubbery, vines, grasses, and weeds. The neighbouring highlands present numerous copses and groves of considerable magnitude, containing several of the trees before enumerated. Prairies are frequent, and some of them spacious, on this part of the river, both in the valley and upon the adjacent highlands, so that forests of any considerable extent are entirely excluded.

On the upper part of the river the valley assumes a different character, expanding in some cases to the width of two or three miles, and embracing extensive tracts of rolling or level prairies. The bottoms are more elevated, and seldom give place to swamps or ponds. The woodlands become less frequent and the prairies more extensive till at length all that appears of the former are mere skirts fringing the water-courses.

The uplands on both sides of the valley are of a rolling aspect, in some instances inclining to hilly; rocks occasionally appear upon the surface, but are no where abundant. The stratifications, on which the country is based, consist of secondary sand and limestone, perforated in several places, towards the head of the river, by peaks and ridges of primitive rock, which rise twenty or thirty feet above the water-table of the country. The aggregate descent of the St. Peter may be estimated at about one hundred and fifty feet*, the general level of the country at its source having an elevation of about eighty feet above the river.

On retiring from the river in either direction the country becomes undulatory, but no hills remarkable for their magnitude occur, till we arrive at the Coteau des Prairies, on the west, and at the Pine ridges, &c. which are represented as the birth place of the waters of the Mississippi,

---

* In vol. i. p. 364, the descent of the St. Peter was from general considerations estimated at sixty feet, but Major Long is of opinion that one hundred and fifty feet accords better with known facts in relation to the descent of water-courses.

on the east. The height to which these last attain is said to be inconsiderable; they do not probably rise more than a few feet above the general level above mentioned.

The Coteau des Prairies is a very remarkable feature in the aspect of this region, situated between the waters of the Mississippi and those of the Missouri. It may be regarded as the dividing ridge between those waters, and is doubtless the grand dike which has obstructed the latter in its progress eastward, and caused it to flow southwardly through a distance of many hundred miles, before it could again resume a direct course to the former. This huge swell has an elevation of about one thousand feet above the common level of the country just described, and extends from the 44th degree of latitude, in a direction north-north-west to the sources of Pembina river, in latitude 49° north. It presents a rounded summit, with but few irregularities of surface, and is for the most part destitute of a woody growth. Its easterly slope exhibits a gradual declivity, intersected at intervals by ravines which serve as channels to numerous streams, that pay tribute to the St. Peter and Red Rivers. The distance from Lake Travers to the base of the Coteau, is about twenty-five miles in a westerly direction, while that to its summit is said to be more than double that distance. Its width, character of its western slope, &c. could not be satisfactorily ascertained. It is said, however, that this ridge is succeeded by another, parallel to it and of a similar appearance, at the distance of thirty or forty miles, between which and the first is a river of moderate size, probably Jacque or James River of the Missouri. It is further stated also, that the western declivity of these ridges is considerably less than the eastern, which is in accordance with the deductions to which the hydrography of the country gives rise. At both extremities the

Coteau loses itself in a multiplicity of hills and swells, which give to the country an aspect highly varied.

V. *Of Red River and the adjacent Country.*

This stream is tributary to Lake Winnepeek, whose waters have their estuary in Hudson's Bay. Its immediate source is Lake Travers, situated northwardly, and within three miles of Big Stone Lake, and in flood time, communicating at its upper extremity with the St. Peter's River, which is here a mere brook, and passes the lake at the distance of a few hundred yards only. This lake is about fifteen miles long and between one and two wide, stretching from south-west to north-east. By observations taken at the establishment of the Columbia Fur Company, situated two miles from the head of the lake, its latitude was found to be 45° 39′ 52″ and its longitude 96° 34′ 30″. At the north-eastern extremity of Lake Travers, is situated a pool of considerable size called Buffalo Lake, communicating with the former. The channel through which these are drained is denominated Riviere des Sioux, or more correctly Swan Rivulet, and is about thirty miles long. At the time of our passing it, (Aug. 1823,) it contained no water except in stagnant pools. At the distance above mentioned it unites with a considerable stream from the north-east, called Grand or Otter-tail River, which has its source in a lake of the same name. The lake is about twenty-four miles long and five broad, and is situated near the head waters of the Mississippi, at the distance of about one hundred and fifty miles north-eastwardly from Lake Travers. These two streams may be regarded as the constituents of Red River. The general course of the river is northward, inclining a little to the west; it is exceedingly tortuous; its length, following its meanders, being more than five hundred miles, while in the direction of its valley it does not exceed three hundred and sixty. It receives numerous tributaries, of which the following are the principal, and enter it in the order here mentioned, commencing with the uppermost, viz.

The Pse or Rice River, the Shienne, the Buffalo, Elm, Wild-rice, the Plum and Sandhill Rivulets. The Goose River, the Red Fork, the Turtle, Big Saline and Park Rivers, the Swamp Brook, the "Two Rivers," and Pembina River, all within the territory of the United States. The Reed Grass, Scotchman, Rat, Muddy, Assiniboin, and Death Rivers, entering northwardly of the 49th degree of north latitude. The localities of their heads, their connexion with other waters, their relative extents and consequently their magnitudes, will be more readily understood by a reference to our narrative.

Red River is navigable for canoes, and even pirogues of two tons burden, from its mouth to its source, as also to the sources of several of its tributaries when swollen by freshets. On such occasions canoes have been known to pass from Lake Travers, its source, into the St. Peter, and back again, without inconvenience. The voyage down the river is now seldom performed, owing to the limited nature of the trade in this direction. Formerly the Hudson's Bay Company had a trading establishment on Lake Travers, (the same that is now occupied by the Columbia Fur Company,) between which and their establishments lower down the river considerable intercourse existed. It abounds in rapids, which, together with its numerous and extensive windings, render the passage by water very tedious.

The aggregate descent from Lake Travers to Lake Winnepeek, or from the source to the *debouchure* of Red River, a distance of about six hundred miles, following the meanders of that stream, amounts probably to two hundred feet.

Otter-tail River is navigable as above to its source, through which a water communication is continued forming a connexion with the Riviere de Corbeau of the Mississippi, and the Medicine-Bark of the St. Peter. The Wild-rice River and the Red Fork are connected in the same manner with other sources of the Mississippi, affording navigable communications between the subsidiary lakes at their respective heads, and others tributary to that great river. Reed Grass River has a two-fold connexion with other waters, serving as a channel of intercourse between Red River and the source of the Mississippi, as also that of one of the tributaries of Rainy River. Rat River also affords a communication between Red River and the Lake of the Woods. These several communications are only practicable in very wet seasons, and the transition from their summits into other waters, is interrupted by portages of greater or less extent, but in no instances by ridges of any considerable height.

The Goose and Turtle Rivers, both of which take their rise in Devil Lake, are navigable to that place, and the lake itself, which is said to be made up of a multiplicity of small pools, connected by navigable channels, affords an extent of navigation of about one hundred miles.

The Assiniboin River is the largest of all the tributaries of Red River, and in point of magnitude and extent, vies even with the principal, Their point of junction is in north latitude 49° 53′ 35″ and west longitude 97° 00′ 50″. Its sources mingle with the waters of the Saskatchawan, north-westwardly from the point just mentioned. In its progress downward, it forms an extensive curve with a convexity to the south-west, and receives numerous subsidiaries, among which is a stream of respectable size, called Mouse River, that is said to receive some of its waters from a point within one mile of the Missouri River. The Assiniboin is navigable at all stages of the water to a great distance, and is the channel of continual intercourse between several British trading establishments located on its waters, and one of their principal depôts situated at the mouth of the river.

The immediate valley of Red River is not bounded by parallel ranges of bluffs or banks like that of the St. Peter and other tributaries of the Mississippi, but expands to a great width, terminated on the west by highlands connected with the Coteau des Prairies, and on the east by the ridges and swamps in which the waters of the Mississippi, St. Lawrence, and Nelson's Rivers find a common origin. A broad expanse of verdant prairie, spreading beyond the utmost extent of vision, is here presented to the view. If we except the margin of the river and those of its tributary streams, which are fringed with trees and shrubbery, there is very little to interrupt the simplicity and uniformity of the scenery; scarcely is there an undulation to variegate the prospect, save what is afforded by an optical illusion that makes the traveller fancy himself in the centre of a basin, and surrounded by an amphitheatre of rising ground at no great distance, which constantly eludes his approach.

The soil is generally thin, of a light complexion, and argillaceous structure. The dwarfish appearance of the herbage which it supports, especially on the upper portion of the valley, indicates either a want of fecundity or the admixture of salts or other ingredients not congenial to vegetation. In many places, however, the soil appears rich, supporting a dense and luxuriant growth of grass.

weeds, &c. As we descend along the river, the indications of fertility multiply, the soil becomes deeper and the vegetation more thrifty, woodlands become more frequent, and the trees attain a larger size.

The flatness of surface that almost uniformly prevails throughout the valley of Red River, may be regarded as a defect in its natural character that cannot easily be remedied.

The colony planted by the Earl of Selkirk occupies two positions on the banks of this river, one at the confluence of the Assiniboin, usually called Fort Douglas, and the other about sixty miles above, called Pembina. The amount of population at both places, exclusive of those in the immediate employ of the Hudson's Bay Company, does not exceed one thousand souls, about three hundred of whom, principally *metifs* of French and Indian extraction, reside at Pembina, within the limits of the United States. This village is situated on both sides of the river, at the distance of about two miles below the mouth of Pembina River. The settlements at the confluence of the two rivers above mentioned, are scattered through a considerable tract of country embracing an extent of about twenty miles along the bank of Red River; here are two stockade works, viz. Forts Gerry and Douglas; the former called the Hudson's Bay Company's fort, and the latter the Colony's; also the remains of two others of a similar character, one Catholic Chapel, and one church for Protestant Episcopalians; a more particular account of which has been given in the preceding narrative.

Agriculture has been commenced at both these places, and is attended with success. Wheat, barley, millet, pulse, together with potatoes and other culinary roots, have been cultivated to great advantage. Maize is cultivated in small quantities, but, at best, it is of a very stinted growth, and affords a very scanty and uncertain crop. Black cattle have been lately introduced, and succeed well. As yet they have no sheep, and but few swine; of the success of the latter there can be little doubt, however the climate may counteract that of the former. Their horses are hardy, which is almost the only excellence they possess; the services of this animal in the sledge are superseded by the use of dogs, which are here among the most useful of domestic animals.

The region granted to the late Lord Selkirk, and called Ossiniboia, has the following limits, viz. " Beginning on the western shore of the Lake Winipie, at a point in 52° 30′ N. latitude, and thence running due west to the Lake Winipigashish, otherwise called Little Winipie, thence in a southerly direction through the said lake, so as to strike its western shore, in latitude 52°, thence due west to the place where the parallel 52° intersects the western branch of Red River, otherwise called Assiniboin River, thence due south from that point of intersection to the height of land which separates the waters running into Hudson's Bay from those of the Missouri and Mississippi Rivers, thence in an easterly direction along the height of land to the source of the river Winipie, (meaning by such last-named river the principal branch of the waters which unite in the lake Saginagas,) thence along the main stream of those waters and the middle of the several lakes through which they pass to the mouth of the Winipie River, and thence in a northerly direction through the middle of the Lake Winipie to the place of beginning, which territory is called Ossiniboia," or Assiniboia.

The 49th parallel of north latitude, which is the northern boundary of the United States, crosses Red River at a point so far down, as to include within the limits of our territory all the village of Pembina, with the exception of two or three cabins. The boundary is designated at this place by an oaken post, erected by the exploring party, which stands on the west upland bank of the river within a few paces of the brow of the bank, with the letters U. S. inscribed on the south, and G. B. on the north sides of the post.

VI. *Of the Country between Lakes Winnepeek and Superior.*

The hydrography of this region is as yet very defective, and although it may be traversed in a thousand directions, must for ever remain so, if the shape, magnitude, and position of innumerable lakes embosoming myriads of islands, and the courses, sinuosities, and declivities of countless channels by which they are united, are deemed essential as rudiments of that science. The country is literally a wilderness of lakes, islands, and peninsulas; a mazy waste, so inhospitable and irreclaimable, as to mock the art and enterprize of man, and bid defiance to his industry.

The water route most frequented between the Lake of the Woods and Lake Winnepeek, is denominated Winnepeek River, which enters the lake last mentioned in latitude 50° 36′ 30″, and has an extent of about one hundred and seventy miles. It is composed of a series of deep and broad basins rising one above another, and serving as the channel of a huge volume of water, which is precipitated from one basin to another in tumultuous cataracts of the most romantic character. Of these water falls, there are no less than thirty-one in the route above mentioned, which interrupt the passage of canoes, and at all of which are carrying places. The aggregate descent of water in Winnepeek River may be estimated at four hundred and ten feet, which may be considered as the elevation of the Lake of the Woods above Lake Winnepeek. The route by Covert and Sturgeon Dam Rivers is probably the most direct, (the lower portion of which is the same with that above mentioned,) but the obstructions are said to be more numerous and formidable, especially in a low stage of water. Besides these there are numerous other deviations from the main route, some of which have been traversed, but the number that remains to be explored is doubtless far greater.

At the distance of about sixty miles below the Lake of the Woods, Winnepeek River receives a large tributary from the north, called English River, which is of a character similar to that of the principal, and nearly as large as the latter above their junction. Its head waters interlock with those of Albany River, which empties into James' Bay, and is the principal channel of intercourse between Lake Winnepeek and the trading establishments on that river.

The Lake of the Woods is about seventy-five miles long, and of irregular widths, from ten to thirty-five or forty miles Compared with other lakes, it deserves a high rank on the scale of beauty. The scenery is wild and romantic in a high degree, its shores being faced with precipices and crowned with hills and knobs of variable heights, clad with a dense foliage of shrubbery and evergreens. Its surface is beautifully studded with countless islands of various sizes and forms, disclosing between them the continued sheet of its wide-spreading waters, the extent of which enlarges upon the vision as the traveller advances upon the lake, till the main land is shut out from the view by the islands that multiply around him.

The 49th parallel of north latitude crosses the lake within the distance of about twelve miles from its southerly extremity.

The region bordering upon the waters above described,

is one of the most dreary imaginable. Its climate is rigorous, its surface exceedingly rugged and broken, and its products so limited and meagre, that it seems never to have been claimed as a residence either by man or beast. A solitary moose, caraboo, or bear, is occasionally to be found; and a half-starved family of savages sometimes fix a temporary residence upon some of the water-courses, and subsist miserably upon fish, but it seems as if comfort and competency were denied to both.

The prevailing rocks are primitive, and are almost exclusively the ingredients of which the hills are composed, while the earthy portions of the valley are made up of the coarse and unproductive detritus afforded by their disintegration. The soil is uniformly thin, and in many places totally wanting. The stinted growth of the woodlands, and the dwarfish character of vegetation which prevail generally throughout this region, are attributable to these causes. The islands of the lakes and river are similar to the circumjacent highlands, being uniformly based upon rock and presenting rugged and broken surfaces.

The growth found on the lower part of the river, comprises only the aspen, white birch, spruce, tamarack, and scrub-oak, none of which attain any considerable magnitude. As we approach the Lake of the Woods, the following trees make their appearance, viz. two species of pine, called the white and red epinette, the former of which is more commonly called the larch. From the latter is extracted the gum employed for pitching canoes, which usually have their ribs and lining constructed of its timber; a small species of pitch pine called by the Canadians cypress, which also furnishes a gum inferior to that above mentioned; and the liard, a variety of the poplar, more commonly called the Balm of Gilead.

The undergrowth is dense in many places, and consists of stinted oak, chokecherry, hazle, pembina or bush cranberry, service-berry, arrow-wood, wild plum, raspberry, briar-bush, whortleberry, sumac, wild rose, sweet briar; sand cherry, red and black cherry, pea-vine, gooseberry, currant, bear-berry, &c. &c.

Above the Lake of the Woods, Rainy River becomes the channel of communication, and extends one hundred miles to the lake of the same name. It has an average breadth of about three hundred yards, is deep and gentle, and has no obstructions to its navigation, within forty-eight miles of its mouth; at this distance are situated the rapids of Rainy River, which are about one mile long, and have an aggregate descent of about ten feet. About ten miles further up is another inconsiderable rapid, with a fall of three feet. At the outlet of Rainy Lake is a rapid of about five feet descent, and two miles and a half below are the Falls of Rainy River, down which the torrent pours with terrific grandeur through an aggregate descent of twenty-five feet in the distance of but a few yards. At this place are situated an establishment of the Hudson's Bay Company on the north side of the river, and one belonging to the American Fur Company on the south. Twenty miles below the falls is the entrance of a considerable tributary from the southwest called the Grand Fork, which affords a channel of communication between the principal and Little Winnepeek Lake of the Mississippi, navigable in wet seasons. It receives several other streams of less note. Between the Lake of the Woods and Rainy Lake there is another water route which is sometimes travelled; it is delineated on the map as the back route.

The contrast between the country of Rainy River and that before described is no less striking than that between the two water-courses themselves. Here bottoms and table lands of considerable extent are often to be met with, wearing the aspect of a secondary region; these are, however, generally terminated, at no great distance, by tracts of a rugged and broken character. Rocks are seldom to be found in the immediate valley or bed of the river. The forests are more dense and heavy, and contain several trees not enumerated in the foregoing list, viz. white-oak, ash, hickory, water-maple, white-walnut, linden, elm, &c. The pine and white-birch become more abundant, and attain a more stately size.

From the estimates above given, making some allowance for the general descent of the river, it will appear that the surface of Rainy Lake is elevated about sixty feet above that of the Lake of the Woods, or four hundred and seventy feet above that of Lake Winnepeek.

Pursuing our course upwards we passed through Rainy, Sturgeon, La Croix, Upper Sturgeon, Doré, Cannibal, and Thousand Lakes, besides numerous others of less note and size, and also the channels by which they are connected, which, in the language of the voyagers, are denominated rivers, and known by various names, before we reach the dividing ridge between the waters of Lakes Winnepeek and Superior. Several routes are practicable through this part of the country, but the one we pursued is said to be the most frequented. The route connected with the Grand Portage, which was the only route frequented till within a few years, is united to the new route by two channels, one branching off at Lac de la Croix, and the other at Upper Sturgeon Lake, both of which unite in Lake Saganaga, and enter Lake Superior at Pigeon River.

The country along these routes is very similar to that on Winnepeek River, though of an aspect somewhat more inviting. Patches of ground susceptible of cultivation, here and there present themselves. The trees of the forest exhibit a greater variety, and attain a larger size; as we approach the dividing ridge between the waters of Lake Superior and those of Hudson's Bay, tracts of flat and marshy lands become more numerous and extensive, and in the immediate vicinity of that limit the country appears to be formed almost exclusively of swamps, quagmires, and stagnant pools. The swamps sustain a growth of spruce, epinette, or larch, and some pine, exceedingly dense, and in many places rendered almost impenetrable by a profusion of furze and bushes.

The lakes of this region are of all possible shapes, exceedingly numerous, and thronged with islands. As on the route before described, the lakes here rise one above another in continual gradations, but less abruptly, giving an altitude to the uppermost on the route at least equal to one hundred and thirty feet, making the entire elevation above Winnepeek about six hundred feet.

The altitude of the dividing ridge, above the water-table of the adjacent country, is no where greater than about one hundred and fifty feet, the head waters of the streams tributary to Hudson's Bay being somewhat more elevated than those of Lake Superior.

The channel of communication thence to Lake Superior, is through Dog River, the lower portion of which is more commonly called the Kamanatekwoya. This river is exceedingly serpentine in its course, has a regular bed, and a rapid current. About forty miles below the point where we entered it, is a lake of the same name, about twelve miles long and from one to five broad. The river receives several tributaries, the most considerable of which is the Cypress, entering from the west above Dog Lake. Two

SOURCE OF ST. PETER'S RIVER.

others, (names unknown,) one of which enters Dog Lake from the north-east, and is said to communicate with the English River before noticed, and the other into the south-west part of the same lake, affording a commuication with the Thousand Lakes, which is sometimes travelled; besides these there are two others of considerable size from the west, one called Mataway sha-boon-da-wan or Long-lodge River, connecting, like the last mentioned, with the same lake; and the other White-fish River, through which there is a route for canoes, communicating with the Grand Portage Route, it is however seldom travelled.

On this route the portages are equally as numerous, and more extensive than on the other, nor are its other impediments less formidable. Rapids and cataracts abound; among the latter is one of the most magnificent cascades to be witnessed in any country, it is denominated by the Indians, the Falls of Kakabikka or Cleft Rock, and is situated about thirty miles upward from the mouth of the river, which is here contracted to the width of about fifty yards, and supplied with a volume of water unusually large for that width. Thus confined, the whole body of the river is precipitated, in a dense sheet, down a perpendicular precipice more than one hundred and thirty feet into a deep chasm, bounded by perpendicular cliffs of the height just mentioned; the banks of the river, for a distance of nearly one-half of a mile below, are completely insurmountable, rising perpendicularly, and in many places overhanging their bases. The chasm throughout this distance, is no wider than is necessary to give free passage to the water, which is mantled with foam and hurried down with great rapidity. This scenery, although it is less extensive, yet vies in grandeur and sublimity with that of the Falls of Niagara. In beholding it, the spectator is inspired with equal awe, the principal features are equally terrific, while the deep intonation, which is not only heard but felt at the distance of four or five hundred yards, is more sensible than that of its rival, and has a nearer resemblance to the roar of distant thunder and the rumblings of an earthquake. Below the Falls of Kakabikka, the river presents a continued rapid for the distance of about twenty miles, below which it quietly passes through serpentine folds to its mouth, which is in an arm of the lake called Kamana Bay. The whole descent of the water from Coldwater Lake, (the first water eastward of the dividing ridge on our route), to Lake Superior, may be estimated at about six hundred feet.

The country on this part of the route is somewhat more inviting than any other part of the region now under consideration. Bottoms of considerable extent frequently occur, but in the upper portion of the river they are low and subject to inundation. The high lands are less broken, rising to the height of one hundred and fifty or two hundred feet. As we descend, the country becomes still more interesting, exhibiting many indications of an exuberant soil. The growth is similar to that before mentioned, with the addition of the fur and white pine, which occasionally present themselves. The liard becomes more stately and plentiful, and the trees generally attain a much larger size. A dense undergrowth of shrubbery, vines, and bramble, prevails. These, together with other indications which might be enumerated, seem to distinguish the valley of this river as the future residence of civilized man.

Near the mouth of Dog River is situated Fort William, formerly the principal depôt of the North-west Company. This site was selected as being more eligible on some accounts, than that of Fort Charlotte at the mouth of Pigeon

River on the Grand Portage Route, which was consequently abandoned. The circumstance of the latter site being contiguous to the line of demarcation between the territories of Great Britain and the United States, no doubt had considerable influence in bringing about this measure.

The country on the north of Lake Superior, both in regard to aspect and character, bears a strong similitude to that of Winnepeek River. The growth is generally stinted, and consists principally of cedar, spruce, white and yellow birch, liard, aspin, scrub oaks, alder, &c. The lake coast is indented with numerous bays and inlets, and presents an uninterrupted succession of hills, based upon rocks, and faced with precipices. The hills are generally from one hundred and fifty to four hundred feet high; there are several, however, in the vicinity of Fort William, considerably higher, among the largest of which are Fort William Mountain and Thunder Point, rising five or six hundred feet above the lake. These appear to be the remains of a slaty formation which once covered the neighbouring country, and which still appears at the Falls of Kakabikka, forming the precipices of that interesting spot, and at various other places.

Isle Royale, which is the largest island of Lake Superior, is about fifty miles long and from two to six broad, and is surrounded by a multiplicity of small grassy islands. It is situated off Kamana Bay, between which and the island is a cluster of small islands, called the Paté or Pie Islands, based upon rock, of a turreted form, flat upon their summits, and elevated between two and three hundred feet. Between Kamana and Michipicotton Bays, the margin of the laké is thickly studded with islands and peninsulas, the shores of which are invariably rocky-bound and precipitous. Michipicotton Island, situated at the entrance of the bay of the same name, is second in magnitude to Isle Royale. The other islands of the lake are inconsiderable in point of size. Eastward of Michipicotton Bay, sandbars occasionally present themselves, connected with small islands and tracts of flat land, interposed between the hills and margin of the lake. Westward of the same point no sand banks are to be met with, except occasionally at the *debouchures* of the larger streams. Small parcels of tillable ground are occasionally to be found along the coast, but they occupy but a very inconsiderable portion of the surface. Agreeably to the best intelligence that could be had, the country back of the lake, to the distance of fifty or sixty miles, is very similar in aspect and character to that in the vicinity of the lake.

On the southerly coast, we have no information more authentic than that furnished by Mr. Schoolcraft in his narrative of Governor Cass' expedition, from which we should infer, that a region equally as unproductive and inhospitable is there presented.

In concluding our observations relative to this part of our route, we would remark generally, that no part of the country can ever admit of a dense population, if we except perhaps the valley of Rainy River, which is of no very considerable extent. The most favourable estimate of its future population, founded upon present appearances, would not admit of more than a single soul to every thousand acres of country. Yet, notwithstanding the rudeness of its aspect, the severity of its climate, and the sterility of its surface, it is possessed of some features grateful and interesting in a high degree. No country can boast of a greater variety, beauty, and grandeur of water scenery. In the few places where agriculture has been attempted and found practicable, wheat succeeds well. Potatoes grow to great perfection.

Turnips, beets, and other culinary roots are raised to great advantage, and onions, notwithstanding the shortness of the summer, attain their full size in a single season.

It may be thought that this chapter ought to contain some general account of the great northern lakes, but we are constrained to evade this subject, on account of the limited nature of our intelligence in relation thereto, and more especially, because a description far more complete and satisfactory may shortly be expected, as the result of the labours and researches of the Commissioners employed in determining the boundary line between the United States, and the territory of Great Britain. We shall therefore merely remark on the present occasion, that throughout the Lakes Erie, Huron, St. Clair, Michigan, and Green Bay, and the several straits by which they are connected, there exist no impediments to steam-boat and sloop navigation, unless the want of safe and commodious harbours, which generally prevails, be considered as such. The passage into Lake Superior is effectually obstructed by a rapid, denominated the Sault of St. Mary, down which there is a descent of nearly twenty feet, in the distance of four or five hundred yards. But the facility with which a canal or side-cut of any appropriate dimensions can be formed, seems to divest this strait of every formidable character, and place it completely under the controul of art. The surface of the ground through which a canal may be cut rises no more than five or six feet above Lake Superior, and the distance does not exceed thirteen hundred yards.

VII. *Remarks on a variety of subjects connected with the topography of the country.*

1st. Of the natural features of the country in a military point of view.

In this view it is proper to comprehend not only the extreme northerly frontier of the United States, but to consider it in connexion with the boundary which nature seems to have fixed as the western limit of our population, viz. the Great American Desert. From what has been stated in relation to the country surrounding Lake Superior and extending north-westwardly to Lake Winnepeek, it may be inferred that we shall always remain secure from the inroads of any regular hostile force in that direction. Indeed the nature of the country is such as affords a more formidable barrier to the invasions of an enemy than any *cordon* of posts that art could devise. This barrier is intercepted by a space of considerable extent, including the valley of Red River, and extending westward to the Great Desert, through which there are two considerable passes, the one by way of the Red and St. Peter Rivers, and the other by that of the Assiniboin and Missouri, through which an enemy from the north might gain access to the heart of the western country. But when we consider that the policy of the Hudson's Bay Company, in whom is vested the right of soil to all that part of the British possessions drained by the tributaries of Hudson's Bay, is opposed to the colonization of their territory, their interest prompting them to foster the fur trade, the products of which must diminish in proportion to the increase of population, we have very little to apprehend from the attack of a powerful enemy in that quarter. Added to this the utter impracticability of transporting by ordinary means heavy ordnance, and other munitions of war, up Nelson's River, or by any other route, to the valley of Red River, must for a long time to come place an enterprize of this nature beyond the reach of any hostile power. Accordingly, under present prospects, no hostilities are to be apprehended in that part of our frontier, except such as may be inflicted through the medium of the savages. A large portion of the Great American Desert, a sterile dreary waste, three or four hundred miles in width, stretching along the eastern verge of the Rocky Mountains, from Red River of the South to Athabasca in the north, a distance of more than fourteen hundred miles, may be added as a continuation of the line of our natural defence. Thus a portion of our frontier, embracing an extent of nearly two thousand miles, is so well fortified by nature as to require no artificial structures but such as are appropriate in Indian warfare. No regular military works will of course be required on that extent of frontier, except such as may be required to protect the American fur trade, and counteract the hostile purposes of the Indians.

Before we dismiss this subject, we would remark, that the strait of Mackinaw, (Michilimachinack), presents itself as one of the most important passes to an extensive interior coast, and indirectly to the very vitals of the western country that is any where to be found westward of the Alleghany Mountains. By means of this channel the whole coast of Lake Michigan, embracing an extent of more than six hundred miles, is open to the attack and depredations of any regular force that might be disposed to wage hostilities in that direction. Whereas if the entrance into Lake Michigan through this pass, were effectually guarded by a chain of military works stretching across the straits, at or near the Island of Mackinaw, any future danger to be apprehended in that quarter, would be effectually obviated, and it would no longer be necessary to maintain garrisons at Green Bay, Chicago, and other points on the lake, except for the purpose of restraining the Indians and securing the frontier against their attacks. The practicability of establishing a line of works that would effectually command the passage of the straits, has not yet been proved; no doubts are entertained, however, that such an object is attainable.

The importance of this pass appears the more striking, when viewed in connexion with the easterly arm of Lake Huron, which extends far into the interior of Upper Canada, and to which munitions of war and naval stores of every description may be easily conveyed fron the depôts of both Canadas. An enemy designing to attack the western country might here prepare an armament in complete security, and operate to great advantage through the straits. Not only the practicability, but the efficacy of an attack in this direction, has been fully demonstrated in some of the events of the late war.

2d. Of the Indians inhabiting the country traversed by the Expedition.

A few remarks on this subject, in addition to those heretofore made in the narrative, will here suffice.

The march of civilization, which has been carried triumphantly nearly to the sources of the Scioto, Miami, and Wabash, has been almost uniformly attended by the retreat of the nations formerly inhabiting in that quarter. The Shawnees, Delawares, Miamis, Potawatomis, and Kickapoos, who once overran the extensive region that now embraces the states of Ohio, Indiana, and Illinois, are now nearly extirpated; small remnants of these once powerful nations are scattered through the northerly and westerly parts of this region, all of whom begin to be convinced, that the lapse of a few years more must bring about their utter extermination, unless they resort to agriculture as a means of prolonging their existence.

A similar destiny awaits the Otawas, Menomones, Winnebagoes, Sauks, Foxes, and Iawas, who now inhabit the countries of the Mississippi and Lake Michigan, northwardly of the 42nd parallel of north latitude. The numerous bands of the Dacota or Sioux nation, together with those of their irreconcileable enemies the Chippewas, are daily becoming less numerous and powerful, in consequence of an incessant warfare which has for a long time existed between those nations, and of the frequent hostilities that take place between them and other neighbouring Indians; and although they have at present but little occasion to be alarmed at the prospect of having their country wrested from them by a white population, yet their final extirpation cannot be viewed as an event very remote.

There can exist but little doubt, that most if not all of these Indians would, in any emergency decidedly favourable to their views, take up arms against the people of the United States. They have no calamity to dread so fatal to their repose, as that of the inroads of our population upon their territory, and no evil so much to be deprecated, and so pernicious to their welfare, as that of a free intercourse between them and a semi-barbarian race, often resident among them, and always ready to occupy the ground from which they have retreated. There is, however, no new occasion to enlarge upon this part of the subject, and we shall conclude with briefly stating, that the intercourse, between the citizens of the United States and the Indians, is of a nature calculated to vitiate and deprave the former, while it engenders distrust, malevolence, and hatred in the minds of the latter. In fine, the language held forth by the Indian in relation to the Americans is, that they have claim to no other feeling but that of abhorrence; and that it is from principles of policy, and not of esteem and reverence, that he treats them with deference, professes friendship for them, and allows them to share in his confidence.

It may here be remarked, that the Indians westward of the Mississippi are, for the most part, addicted to an erratic life, migrating from place to place in quest of game on which they principally subsist. They are divided into numerous bands, each of which has its appropriate leader, and in all their movements they are prepared for any event whether of the chase or warfare.

The Chippewas, from the nature of the country they inhabit, are distributed into families rather than tribes, the general scarcity of game, and other necessaries of life, rendering it impracticable for them to dwell in large numbers at any one point. In the event of a war, several families unite in forming a martial force suitable for the occasion. They subsist principally upon fish and wild rice, the latter of which is very abundant in the region they inhabit, and would afford them a competent supply of food, were they sufficiently industrious in collecting it, and frugal in its expenditure.

However gloomy the prospect of the Indians, as it relates to the means in their own power of ameliorating their condition, we cannot forbear to entertain the hope, that the humane exertions made in their behalf by our government, and especially by charitable missionary institutions, will prove efficacious in promoting their welfare. The efforts of the Baptist Missionary Society, which have been particularly noticed in the preceding narrative, have been bestowed in a manner that promises great advantage to the unfortunate savage, and nothing seems wanting to secure unbounded success, but perseverance in the same benevolent course. In witnessing the striking change that has been effected in the character and habits of Indian youths, during a short period of instruction in agriculture and the rudiments of an English education, we are irresistibly led to the belief that a brighter day may dawn upon our savage brethren, and that the shades of barbarism in which they have been so long enveloped will, ere long, give place to the cheering light and benign influence of civilization.

3*d*. Statements relative to the elevation of different parts of the country.

With the exception of those items of intelligence drawn immediately from the canal-surveys in New York and Ohio, all that can be said on this subject is of a speculative nature, and may be styled conjectures rather than statements. Under the article Mississippi, in the Edinburgh Encyclopedia, American edition, it is stated by the writer of that article, that the Ohio, at Pittsburg, has a greater elevation than Lake Erie by two hundred and sixty-five feet, which no doubt exceeds the true elevation by at least one hundred, if not one hundred and fifty feet, and we would rather assume the difference, viz. one hundred and fifteen feet, as a nearer approximation to the truth. From the surveys recently made in the state of Ohio, it would appear that the point at which the Ohio passes the plane coincident with the surface of Lake Erie, which has an elevation of five hundred and sixty-five feet above tide-water, is situated at no great distance below Wheeling in Virginia. Hence we must infer, that the descent of the Ohio, between Pittsburg and the point alluded to, is one hundred and fifteen feet, which is as great a descent as can fairly be attributed to that portion of the river, especially when we are assured by the documents relative to the surveys in Ohio, that the descent between the mouth of the Muskingum and Cincinnati, a distance nearly double that of the portion just mentioned, is no more than one hundred and twenty-seven feet. Hence also we may assume six hundred and eighty feet as the elevation of the Ohio, at Pittsburg, above tide-water; and that the aggregate fall of the Ohio, below that place, is about three hundred and eighty feet, while that of the Mississippi, below the mouth of the former, is about three hundred feet. If we suppose the plane of Lake Erie extended westwardly, its coincidence with the bed of the Illinois or rather of the Des Plaines, will probably take place at a point about twenty miles above the entrance of the Kankakee*. The same plane extended would intersect the Mississippi in or near the De Moyen rapids, probably at their head. The surfaces of Lakes Huron and Michigan may be regarded as having an elevation of six feet, and that of Lake Superior of thirty feet, above the plane above mentioned.

The writer above alluded to advances a doctrine, to the correctness of which we feel considerable reluctance in yielding our assent, viz. that the surface of the Gulf of Mexico is elevated one hundred and twenty-five feet above that of Chesapeake Bay, or in other words, that the gulf stream is occasioned in a great measure, if not exclu-

---

* In Vol. II. page 382, of the Account of an Expedition from Pittsburg to the Rocky Mountains, a mistake has been committed, which we here take occasion to rectify. Instead of four hundred and fifty feet, which is there stated as the altitude of the head of the Illinois above tide-water, it should have been five hundred and fifty feet.

sively, by a declivity in the Atlantic Ocean, corresponding to the velocity and direction of its current. Until the truth of this proposition be satisfactorily established, we shall content ourselves with the assumption that the level of mean tide is the same at the respective estuaries of the Mississippi, Hudson, and St. Lawrence Rivers.

Agreeably to the authority above cited, the source of the Mississippi has an elevation of thirteen hundred and thirty feet, which may not greatly exceed the truth, yet we are inclined to think that twelve hundred would be a nearer approximation.

In order to simplify our ideas upon this subject, and exhibit them in a manner less prolix, we shall embody the several statements, made in this and the preceding articles of this paper, in a tabular form, with the view of introducing at the same time, the probable altitudes of other points relative to which no remarks have herein been made.

A Table, shewing the probable Altitudes, in Feet, of the Water level, at a variety of Points therein specified, above Tide-Water.

Points indicated.	Elevation.
Mouth of the Ohio River	300
Ohio River, at Cincinnati *	414
Do. at the Mouth of Scioto River *	464
Do. at the Mouth of Muskingum River *	541
Surface of Lake Erie *, River des Plaines, 20 miles above its mouth; Mississippi, at the head of the rapids De Moyen; and the Ohio a few miles below Wheeling, Virginia	565

Points indicated.	Elevation.
Lakes Huron and Michigan	571
Lake Superior	595
The Ohio at Pittsburg; the Mississippi at the mouth of the St. Peter; and the Missouri at the mouth of the River Platte	680
Sources of the St. Peter and Red Rivers	830
Source of the Muskingum *	902
Source of Big Beaver *	907
Source of the Scioto *	919
Source of the Miami *	964
Lake of the Woods	1040
Rainy Lake	1100
Sources of the streams on the route of the Expedition, tributary to Lakes Winnepeek and Superior, and head waters of the Mississippi	1200
Dog Lake	1000
Lake Winnepeek	630

4*th*. Of the accompanying Map.

This document has been compiled principally from elements obtained during the progress of the Expedition. The astronomical observations and calculations, fixing the latitude and longitude of the several points, were made by Mr. Colhoun, astronomer, &c. for the Expedition, as recorded in the Appendix.

To the gentlemen of the Hudson's Bay Company we feel much indebted for the geographical information they

---

* The altitudes annexed to the several plans distinguished by an asterisk, are deduced from the measurements actually made in connection with the canal-surveys of New York and Ohio.

gave us, as well as for the generosity and hospitality we uniformly experienced at their hands. The kind letter of the Right Hon. Stratford Canning, Plenipotentiary of his Britannic Majesty, at Washington, ensured us a most friendly and cordial reception among the officers and gentlemen of that company.

It will be perceived that the locality assigned to the southern extremity of Green Bay, and the direction of Fox River, one of its tributaries, also the shape of Lake Michigan, are different from the representations usually given of them in other maps, which uniformly make the difference of latitude between Mackinaw and Fort Howard much too great; the actual difference, agreeably to the best information we could obtain in relation to the subject, being only about one degree. The alteration is to be attributed principally to this circumstance.

The delineations of that part of the Mississippi, situated above the Falls of St. Anthony, are copied from Pike's map of that river; those of the western part of Lake Superior, and the eastern part of Lake Huron, from Bouchett's Map of Upper and Lower Canada.

For a sketch of the surveys made in Michigan territory, from which we have made our delineations of the country along the west side of the straits between Lakes Erie and Huron, we are indebted to the politeness of Mr. H. S. Tanner, whose excellent maps of New York, Pennsylvania, Ohio, Indiana, and Illinois, we have consulted for information relative to the older parts of the country traversed by the Expedition.

To Dr. Bigsby, an English gentleman attached to the British commission for determining the boundary between the United States and the British possessions, we are much indebted for various items of geographical intelligence relative to Lake Superior, Lake of the Woods, and the intervening country.

The southern coast of Lake Superior, together with the rivers, lakes, &c. situated between that lake and the Mississippi, has been delineated almost entirely from information kindly imparted by H. R. Schoolcraft, Esq.

The route of the Expedition is designated on the map by dotted lines and asterisks, the latter of which represent our places of encampment, and have the date annexed.

APPENDIX.

[A]

PART IV.

VOCABULARY OF INDIAN LANGUAGES.

OF the following Vocabulary, Mr. SAY obtained that of the Killisteno language; the others were taken down by me. In order to enable the philologists to establish a comparison between the languages spoken by the Indians whom we saw, and those visited by the party that travelled to the Rocky mountains, Major Long desired that the same system should be adopted, viz. that accompanied by Walker's Pronouncing Key. Had it not been for this circumstance, I would have adopted the German vowels, as they appear to me more simple and satisfactory. In the vocabularies which I obtained, I found the nasal sounds to be very frequent, and to be exactly the same as those in the French language. In order to distinguish these, I have used the sign ñ. It appeared likewise necessary to designate the long and short vowels, in order fully to convey the Indian sounds; this I have attempted to do by the introduction of the accents; the grave being used to distinguish the long, and the acute the short syllables. This has rendered our present system still more complicated, and has increased my regret that the valuable suggestions of Mr. Du Ponceau and Mr. Pickering* could

---

* See Mr. Du Ponceau's " Dissertation on English Phonology," in the Trans. of the Amer. Philos. Soc. N. S. Vol. I. and Mr. Pickering's " Essay on the Orthography of the Indian Languages," in the 4th vol. of the Memoirs of the Amer. Academy of Arts and Sciences.

APPENDIX.

not be adopted. The system which was proposed by the latter gentleman might probably be rendered more simple; it may, doubtless, be made the foundation of an easy and satisfactory method of noting vocabularies.

The great analogy which exists between the Sauk, Chippewa, and Cree languages, will be readily remarked, especially by those who will attempt to pronounce the words according to the key. The difference which they present to the eye will then vanish; thus the syllable *kwa*, used by me, has the same sound as that of *qua*, used by Mr. Say. The Sauk vocabulary was taken from Wennebea, through an interpreter; the Dacota from Renville; the Chippewa from Bruce; and the Killisteno from a half-breed of that nation.

WILLIAM H. KEATING.

VOCABULARY OF INDIAN LANGUAGES.

⁎ ñ indicates a nasal sound. Fāte, fär, fǎll, făt;—mē, mĕt;—nō, mŏve, nŏr, nŏt;—pīne, pĭn;—tūbe, tŭb, bŭll;—ŏil;—pȯṳnd. The sign ' indicates a long, and ˘ a short syllable.

	SAKEWI, or SAUK.	DACOTA, or SIOUX.	OCHIPPEWAG, or CHIPPEWA.	KILLISTENO, or CREE.
Head	wĕshi	phá	ó'schtĕkwăn	ŏstickqwăn
Hair	nĕn'ŏssŏnĕ	nássōtä	mĕnĕsis	wăshtăkáyăh
Face	ĕ'skishĕkŏkĕ'	ĕtä	ŏ'schkiñjik	
Forehead	nĕ'kĕshi	ĕtäi	ŏ'skăttik	ŏskătĕk
Eye	n'ĕshishĕkwi	ĕshtä, or wĭshtä	ŏ'schkiñjik	(same as the Sauk)
Ear	nĕktŏwăkáyĕ	nŏhĕ	tăwăk	ŏtŏwăhkiyăh
Nose	n'ĕkkiw'ănĕ	pŏhĕ	schăñgwĕn	ŏskĕnŭn
Nostrils	·	ʻ	tănăcŭm	·
Lip	ʻ	ishtĕ	·	··
Mouth	n'ĕktŏnĕ	ĕ̇	ŏtŏn	·
Chin	nĕktămăkănĕ	ikŏ	ŏ'tămĕkăn, or ŏ'kwăkŏn	quăscŏnăvĕ
Tooth	nĕpitañ	hĕ	wĕbit	wĕpetăh
Tongue	nĕnănĕ'wĕ	chĕjĕ	tănnănnĕ	wŏlăănĕ
Skin	n'ĕwăssămä	hă	ŏ'shăki	wăhsăkki

VOCABULARY OF INDIAN LANGUAGES.

	SAKEWI, or SAUK.	DACOTA, or SIOUX.	OCHIPPEWAG, or CHIPPEWA.	KILLISTENO, or CREE.
Beard	mésétónäkänän	pŏtahi	mésăkótónán, or méshétónán	méástoänäh
Neck	nékw'ákäné	táhŏ	kw'ăgán	méquŏĭoh
Throat	ŏkótóäkän	dŏtä		mékótägún
Arm	n'äpónén'ĕk	ĭstŏ	ŏn'ĭk	mispétún
Hand	nép'ákwĭnétché	năpé	nénintchĭn	métĭsché
Finger	ékwénénänésĭkänétché, or the place where the hand divides	näpsŭkázŏ	népénähkkwännénintchän	änscŏŭcänänäh
Thumb	nékétchénétché (large finger)	näpsŭhŏnkä		
Fore finger	nétá'ŏnékänétché (pointing finger)			
Little finger	nétéschkwänétché (last finger)	áshté		
Nail	néskäshä	shäké		
Leg	nénäná	hŏ	ŏ'schkĭngĭn	ŏskát
Thigh	néb'ŏäm	chéchä	ŏ'kát	ŏpwŏĭm
Foot	nék'äché	séh'ä	ŏ'pwäm	ŏsétäh
Toes	nänésékänésétäkän	séhŭkäsä, or sésŭkässä	ŏ'sĭt	
Copulation	ém'äkwé	täwéch'ékétä	népénähkkwännésittän	mŭshäwä
Penis	nénäkäyé	ché	ŏmännän	átäki
Testicles	m'énéchŏäké	ĭtká	wĭnnák	
Vulva	mé'kéténäké	shŏn	áhkkétĭn	áki
Meat	huy'äsé	tändŏ	wéyäs	wĭäs

VOCABULARY OF INDIAN LANGUAGES.

	SAKEWI, or SAUK.	DACOTA, or SIOUX.	OCHIPEWAG, or CHIPPEWA.	KILLISTENO, or CREE.
Blood	mèskwè	wá	mìshkw'à	mèkŏ
Heart	ŏt'à	chántá	ŏta'è	mètá
Bone	ŏ'k'ánè	cohŏ	ŏkán	ŏskánŭh
Horn	wèwènè'k	hà	èshkán	áskŭn
Chief	kèmàchkè'	-	ŏkèmáñ	-
Man	nènèŏ	-	ènnènnè	nàhpaŏ
Old man	pàshètŏ	wèchàchè'tà	àshkèwinzè	-
Soldier	kèshkètwŏàkè	w'èchàhènchà	shèmàgànish	-
Woman	kwiŏkè, or kwiŏkè	àkèchètá	èhkkwà	squáoù
Old woman	Mètámŏàn	wènŏhènchà	mindèmáyà	-
Boy	kwèèssà	wàhkàncàtàn	kwèwèsiñs	nàhpàsis
Friend	nàhkàmà	ŏkè'chètŏ	nìtsdèkèwin	nèwìchàwàgŏn
Girl	skwèssà	kèchu	ishkwàsiñs	squàsès
Magician	mànètòŏsichè'kè'	wèkŏschkà	màmàndàwis	-
Father	nŏssà	wàhkán	ŏs	nŏhtàkwè
Mother	kèkènàn	àtà	ningà (my mother)	nècàhwè
Son	nèkwèssà	èmàñ	ŏ'kwìs	nècŏsis
Daughter	Tànès	mèchènckchè	ŏ'tàhmnìss	-
Pretty	wèw'ènmèss'èŏ	mèchŏnckchè	ŏ'nèjish	kàtòwàssèsin
Ugly	mèànèssèŏ	wàshtà	mànàtìs	miàtsis

VOCABULARY OF INDIAN LANGUAGES.

	SAKEWI, or SAUK.	DACOTA, or SIOUX.	OCHIPPEWAG, or CHIPPEWA.	KILLISTENO, or CREE.
Child	àpènòn	òkè'shèòpà	à'pènòchè	
Brother	lèssèmà	mèsònkà	sàngnà	òsèmùh
Sister	nètèkwèmà	tànkàchè	missiñ	òmèstih
God	tèpènèmènòk	wàhkàntànkà	kàchàmànètò	kshàmànnitò
Devil	màtchè mànètò	wàhkànshèchà	màchàmànètò	màtchàmànnitò
Heaven	àpèmèkè	màhkpèà	wàhkwà, or tèjik	kèsik
Heal	wèshòtin	dèndità	kèzhittà	kèsàpàyyò
Cold	kè'seàn	snè	kissè'nà	kèsin
Rain	kèmè'àn	màhàju	kèmèwàn	kèmèwùn
Snow	àkòn	wà	kh'òn	kònùn
Ice	mè'kwàmè'à	chàhà		miskwàmè
Hail	màssickònàn	wàssù	sàsàgàn	
Summer	nepènwè	mèdòkètò	nèpin	nèpin
Winter	pàpòwè	wànjètò	pipp'òn	pèpùn
Spring	mè'nòkkòmù	wètò	sèkwàn	
Autumn	tàkwàhkè	tànyètò	tàkwàkin	
Morning	kèkshèàp.	hàhànà	kèkeshàp	kèkèp
Evening	pàk'òtè	tàssètò	ònàgùsh	tàkòsin
Dawn of day	wàsàpànwè		wàssàyà	
Day	kèshèkè	àmpà	kèjik	kèsekàhò

VOCABULARY OF INDIAN LANGUAGES.

	SAKEWI, or SAUK.	DACOTA, or SIOUX.	OCHIPEWAG, or CHIPPEWA.	KILLISTENO, or CREE.
Night	tăpăkkè	hiyĕtŏ	tĕpĭk	tĕbĕskăhŏ
Sun	kèjĕssŏă	wĕ	kiŭs	pĕshim
Moon	tăpăkĕpĕjĕs	hiyĕtŏ wĕ	tĕpĭkkĕsis	tĕbĕskăhpĕshim
Star	ănăkwăkĕ	wĕchăkĕpĕ	ănăng	ăttăh
Earth	hăkĕ	măkă	ăhkĕ	ăshkĕ
Water	nĕpĕ	mĕnĕ	nĕpĕ	nĕpĕ
Whiskey	ĕ'skwătăwăbŏ	{ mĕnĕwăhkău mĕnĕpĕtă by the Aseneboins }	skŏtăwăpĕ	
Steam-boat	ĕ'skwătăhĕpămŏhŏnmikŏi			
Medicine	nătăiwănŏn	pĕjĕătă	măshkăpĕ	
Mysterious medicine		wăhkăn	nĕmăshkwă	
Fire	ĕ'skwătă'	pĕtă	skŏtă	skŏtăŏ
Wood	mĕtĕkwĕ	chăn	mĕtĭk	mĕshtĭk
Tree	nămătă			mĕshtĭk
Bean	ănăchĕmĕ	wămănĕchă	ărrĕshĕmin	
Leaf	tătăpăcŏăn	wăhkpă	ărrĕpish	nĕpĕăh
Maize	tămin	wămĕnăhĕsă	măndăhmĭn	
Pumpkin	wăpĭkŭhnĕ'	wămĕnŏn	ăkŏssĕmăn	
Bark	ănăkăkwă'	chănhă	wĕkwăs	kĕskŭtĕnŏ
Tobacco	săimăn	chănd'ĕ	ăssămăn	

VOCABULARY OF INDIAN LANGUAGES.

	SAKEWI, or SAUK.	DACOTA, or SIOUX.	OCHIPPEWAG, or CHIPPEWA.	KILLISTENO, or CREE.
Hazle-nuts	kikéàtahn	òmañ	påkåhn	shåkàtènàh
Hill	påkwåkkèwè'	hrà	wàchèò	òshàtènòù
Valley	tàtòàkè'	kàksèzà	påssàtènañ	sèpè
River	sèpòà	wàtàpañ	sèpè	
Brook	sèpòhå'kè'n			
Spring	tàhkèppà	mènèhòndàkà (running water)	mòkèchèwànèpèk	mòpìchèwànèpà
Gelding	à'nkàtòskàshà'	shùktànkàsùsùwànèchà	àyàkwà pàjàkòkàngè	
Horse	kèchènèshòà	shùktànkà orshònkàwàhkàn	pàjàkòkàngè	mèshtàtìm
Mare	èckwàhàhèmà	shùktànkà wèyèdè	nòñjàpàjàkòkàngè	kìshàhshìs
Colt	màkk'òsàsà'	shùktànkà chènchà	àyàpàpàjàkòkàngès	
Dog	àlèmòñ	skònkhà	ànnèmòsh	àhtìm
Wolf, prairie	nànàmòhà	shùktòkèchà	màngàn	màhhèkàn
——, large	kèchèmòhà			
Fox	wak'òà'	sòhèdà	wàkòsh	
Bird	wìshkàñòn	zìtkà	pènàshè	pèàshès
Turkey	pènàòn	zìchàtànkà	mèzìssà	
War-eagle	kèttèwà	wàmèndè	mèkìssà	
Buck elk	kèchèmà	hàhàkà	àyàpà mòschkòs	
Doe	mòschàw'à	pòpàn	nòñjà òmòsckòs	
Egg	wàwàn	wèntèkà		wàhwè

VOCABULARY OF INDIAN LANGUAGES.

	SAKEWI, or SAUK.	DACOTA, or SIOUX.	OCHIPPEWAG, or CHIPPEWA.	KILLISTENO, or CREE.
Buck deer	é'yäpä	täméndäkä	äyäpi wäwäshkösh	"
Doe	ó'kówä	täweenä	nónjä wäwäshkósh	"
Fawn	kätäkänän	tämendechenchä	wäwäshkäshins	"
Fish	mémäs	hóhän	kék'ön	képösiö
Squirrel	änekwä	zechä	chétämön	"
Prairie dog		pishinzä		"
Snake	mänétö	wämenduskä	kénäpik	shéshekwáö
Bison	mä'n'éssöä	tätänkä	péjikkä	éähpicömöshtüsh
Black-tailed deer		tähenchä	mäkätä wänäösh	
Bear	mökkwä	wähankshechä and mätö	mäckwä	müshquäh
Raccoon	ässépänän	wechä	éssäpän	
Louse	wäpikkwäké	héhä	ikkwä	éhkwä, or éhquäh
Antelope		tätöká		"
Skunk	shékäkwä	mäkhä	shekähk	"
Flea	pépekwä	hä	päpik	pépek
Musk-rat	äsóskwä	sintöpä	wäshäshk	"
Rabbit	mäshöwä	müstinchä		wähpös
Bow	mäctää	étäsipä	métikwäp	ätchäpé
Arrow	ämin	wähintäpä	métikwänwá	áttös
Knife	mätés	isän, or minä	mökkömmän	mökömän

VOCABULARY OF INDIAN LANGUAGES.

	SAKEWI, or SAUK.	DACOTA, or SIOUX.	OCHIPPEWAG, or CHIPPEWA.	KILLISTENO, or CREE.
Pipe	pwàkàn	chàndòpà	pwàgàn	mùspwàhkon
Canoe	chémàn	wàtà	thèmàn	òsè
House	wèkèàb	tèbè	wèkèwàm	wùsquàèkòn
Copper	mòskwàpèkwè'	mànzàze	òsàwàbik	—
Stone	àsènnè	èàn	àssin	èsinè
Body	wèyàwè	—	—	—
Iron	pèyàpèkkwè	màzà	pèwàpik	pèwàpishk
Yes	hìhà	hàn	hàwin	hàlèh
No	hàkowà	hèhà	kàwin	nèhmàh
None	hàkwàyà	tòàshènè? or wànèchà?	kàwinàwèyà	nèhmàtoquòù
White	wàpèskàyà	skà	wàpishkà	wàpishkàwò
Red	mòskwà	shà, or dùtà	miskwà	mèhquàò
Black	màkàtàwà	sàpà	màkàtà	kùskètàwàò
Blue	è'skèpàkèà	tò	òshàwòhkwà	shèpàtòkwà (green)
Yellow	è'ssàwà	zè	sàwà	shàwàhò
Light	kàchèmèsàkwàtè	òjanjan	kèjik	kèsègòstàgì
Darkness	pèkkwàtàyàwè	pàsà	tèpik	èquòsquòù
I (ego)	—	mèà, or mish	nìn	nèyàh
Me	nènà	do. do	—	—
One	nèkòtè	wàjèdàn	pàjik	pàayùk

VOCABULARY OF INDIAN LANGUAGES.

	SAKEWI, or SAUK.	DACOTA, or SIOUX.	OCHIPPEWAG, or CHIPPEWA.	KILLISTENO, or CREE.
Two	nish	nòpá	nij	nèshùh
Three	néssóá	yámé'ná	nèssòi	nèshtò
Four	néàwá	tòpá	nèwin	niàwò
Five	néànanon	zápátán	nánán	néànún
Six	kotòàshèc	shákpè	gotòàssú	nègòtòàsèk
Seven	nòwèc	shákò	ninjòàssòà	tipácoh
Eight	shòàshèc	sháhéndoà	nishwàssò	áánánèò
Nine	shác	náptùánki	shángássòà	tákáts
Ten	kwèchá	wèkáchémé'ná	métàssòá	mètátá
Eleven	nèkòtènèssúà	ákèwáje	áshè pájik métàssòà (ten with one)	páágòsáp
Twelve	nèshènèssòi	áhènòpá	áshè nij métàssòà (ten with two)	nèsòsáp
Soul	nénùnkán⁴n	náhè		
Beaver		chápá	ámikk	
Otter			nèkik	
Hell			kàkèkàmáchishkòtá	
Clouds		mákpèáshòtè'		
Great Bear (star)		wèchákèhòhápá		
North		wàsèátá		
South		ètòkáhá		
East		wèháhèápátá (rising sun)		

VOCABULARY OF INDIAN LANGUAGES.

	SAKEWI, or SAUK.	DACOTA, or SIOUX.	OCHIPPEWAG, or CHIPPEWA.	KILLISTENO, or CREE.
West		wèhóhpèàtà (setting sun)		
Hundred		òpàuwàhrì		
Thousand		kòkòtòpàwàhrì		
Bank (of a river)		màyà		
Meat of fish			òskòù	
Fog			àwàn	
Hollow			wàhnàkkà	
Moose			mŏns	
Brass			òsàwàbèkkàsìn (yellow stone)	
Wild rice		Psè	mànòmìnàn	
Peas			ànèchèmìnàn	
Service berry			òsàkwàkkòmìnàn	
Berry (of any kind)			mìnàn	
Nobody			kàwìnàwìyà	
You				kèyùh
Him				wèyùh
Us				nèyìn

LONDON:

PRINTED BY R. GILBERT, ST. JOHN'S SQUARE.